Wonderful Town:
New York Stories from *The New Yorker* (with Susan Choi)

Life Stories:
Profiles from *The New Yorker*

THE NEW GILDED AGE

THE NEW

GILDED AGE

THE NEW YORKER
LOOKS AT THE CULTURE OF AFFLUENCE

EDITED BY

DAVID REMNICK

RANDOM HOUSE | NEW YORK

All of the pieces in this collection were originally published in *The New Yorker*.
The publication date of each piece is given at the end of the piece.

Library of Congress Cataloging-in-Publication Data

The new gilded age: The New Yorker looks at the culture of affluence /
edited by David Remnick.
p.   cm.
ISBN 0-375-50541-5 (alk. paper)
1. United States—Civilization—1970–   2. Popular culture—United States. 3. United States—
Economic conditions—1981–   4. United States—Social conditions—1980–
I. Remnick, David.   II. New Yorker (New York, N.Y. : 1925)

E169.12 .N445   2000
973.92—dc21
00-059095

Random House website address: www.atrandom.com

Printed in the United States of America on acid-free paper

24689753

First Edition

Book design by JoAnne Metsch

ACKNOWLEDGMENTS

I am grateful to all the *New Yorker* staffers—editors, assistants, librarians, fact checkers—who work with such care and attention. Thanks to Henry Finder, who edited so many of the pieces here and helped with every detail; to Dorothy Wickenden, whose judgment was also crucial; and to Pamela Maffei McCarthy and Ed Klaris, who made this book happen, from idea to publication. Thanks to Dana Goodyear and Brenda Phipps, who were of great help to me in this project. Above all, my gratitude to the writers.

CONTENTS

INTRODUCTION

DAVID REMNICK

Not long ago, Bill Gates built himself a mansion on Lake Washington. The house is a short drive from the Microsoft corporate headquarters, in the city of Redmond, Washington. It is most famous for its electronic gadgetry, for screens that show near-exact replicas of great works of art—Cézanne's *Mont Sainte-Victoire* one moment, Matisse's bathers the next. The rooms are "programmed" to suit a guest's taste in music, cuisine, temperature. And yet in this house of so much modern technology there is one relic of the pre-E-book age. In Gates's library, a sentence from *The Great Gatsby* unspools around the dome: "He had come a long way to this blue lawn and his dream must have seemed so close that he could hardly fail to grasp it." A fascinating sentence, considering Jay Gatsby's fate as a contradictory symbol of aspiration, self-creation, wealth, and hollowness.

The New Gilded Age, this American moment of prosperity, satisfaction, and self-satisfaction, is rife with such contradictions. The first, and most basic, has to do with the nature and the extent of its gildedness. The American record of economic growth is unprecedented and, since March 1991, uninterrupted, and has inscribed itself on the landscape—the McMansions of suburbia, the princely constructions along the oceans, the real-estate manias from Manhattan to Palo Alto. And yet its origins remain a subject of debate. Reaganites ascribe the boom to the tax cuts and other fiscal policies of the eighties; Clintonites give credit to an administration that slashed deficits and made accommodations to the bond markets in 1993 and later. To Silicon Valley dwellers, the answer seems equally obvious: a technological revolution has not merely accelerated growth but created an entirely new economy, a new world, one with its own rules and without economic or imaginative limits. Yet how many will be invited to join this new

world? There is the population that has prospered (though to wildly varying degrees), and then there are those who have fallen further behind; no one remains
untouched.

The New Yorker has tried in the past few years to capture something of this
age—its leading figures, its manners, its mechanisms, its politics, its ironies.
This book collects the articles resulting from that effort. Over the decades, *The
New Yorker* has published a variety of anthologies. Many of them are retrospective; they look back on a theme and the way it has been expressed (as in a book
of love stories, edited by Roger Angell), or they look back on the development of
a form, on the evolution of the short story or the Profile. This collection is quite
different, for it represents attention paid to a historical moment while we are still
living it. And the pieces here, while they stand on their own, are also tiles in a
larger mosaic.

At first glance, ours seems an utterly blithe and lucky time, lacking the tu-
mult and trauma of, say, the war years or the sixties. But it is not so easily understood as either its boosters or its bashers would have it. Some of the pieces in
this collection, like Mark Singer's Profile of Donald Trump and Michael
Specter's Profile of the humble shoemaker Manolo Blahnik, record an era of excess and self-absorption. Others, however, strike different notes. John Cassidy's
Profile of Alan Greenspan explores the peculiar history of a man who is the wiz-
ard of this American Oz, a Wall Street banker steeped in the objectivist principles of Ayn Rand, who now fiddles mysteriously with the gears of the American
prosperity. Joan Didion, in her sly appreciation of Martha Stewart, David Denby,
in his fevered diary of stock speculation, Susan Orlean, in her walks with a New
York City real-estate broker, and David Brooks, in his surveys of the new class
structures, are among the writers here who look at the ways that American ambitions, anxieties, and manners have shifted in recent years. Larissa MacFar-
quhar and Malcolm Gladwell go beyond the stock portraits of the New Economy
(the young men in backpacks with a hundred million dollars in the bank and a
quart of milk in the fridge) to the subterranean rules of the new world, the new
networks of business life, the way human—and commercial—connections are
now achieved. And John Updike, Daphne Merkin, Arthur Krystal, and Adam
Gopnik are among the writers who react personally to the age. A century ago,
at the height of the first Gilded Age, Henry James came home from Europe and
described his fascination with the density of American decoration: the lobby of
the Waldorf-Astoria, the hall of mirrors in Peacock Alley. There was, as Gopnik
points out in his piece "Metamoney," a solidity to the age and to the gold itself.
In the late 1990s, as the New Gilded Age took hold, the government issued re-
designed bills with a stripped-down aesthetic. "The New Money looks like our
Gilded Age," Gopnik writes. "In its combination of overkill and emptiness, the
New Money evokes the new midtown hotels, with their black-and-white 'Deco'
marble lobbies, wedged into tiny lots, and then the cold sealed rooms immediately above—the luxury falling off as soon as you've checked in."

Invariably, Manhattan and Silicon Valley are central precincts here, but they are hardly the only precincts of the New Gilded Age, and celebration and irony are hardly its only moods. Adrian Nicole LeBlanc, a young scholar and writer, spent years hanging out in the South Bronx to produce her remarkable narrative, "Landing from the Sky." Just as Jacob Riis's portraits of the Lower East Side were part of the literature of the Gilded Age, LeBlanc's work is part of ours. Nicholas Lemann reports from Philadelphia on the way the structures of old eastern cities and old money have disintegrated. Bill Buford reports from the sweatshops of Lower Manhattan and the Garment District. And William Finnegan, in "After Seattle," goes on the road with a young woman who is helping to lead the passionate, if often inchoate, political fights against the World Bank, the International Monetary Fund, the World Trade Organization, and, generally, the New Economy's rosiest assumptions.

The New Yorker, which recently celebrated its seventy-fifth anniversary, began publishing the same year that *The Great Gatsby* appeared. Both the fledgling magazine and Fitzgerald's novel set a gimlet eye on an age of money: its attractions and its costs. We cannot know when this age, the New Gilded Age, will end and what will signal the end. Here and there the market plunges, forcing us, if only for a moment, to consider its impermanence. It was Gatsby who used to dream each night of the "universe of ineffable gaudiness," and to him those dreams were a "satisfactory hint of the unreality of reality, a promise that the rock of the world was founded securely on a fairy's wing."

THE

BARONS

THE CONNECTOR

C ERTAIN people are so uncannily familiar that they seem less individuals than manifestations of a type. Jason McCabe Calacanis—twenty-eight years old, part Greek, part Irish, a native of Bay Ridge, Brooklyn—is one such person. He's the buoyant carnival barker with big ideas about vaudeville, the teen-age huckster in the trainer mustache and the cheap suit, filibustering his way into a fat cat's office with plans for a railroad. In his current incarnation, Calacanis is the founder of a miniature media empire that began, three years ago, with the *Silicon Alley Reporter*, a monthly magazine covering New York's Internet industry—which is known as Silicon Alley—and has since added a daily E-mail version, a Los Angeles version (the *Digital Coast Reporter*), and a series of conferences. He has a refined sense of the mechanics of status and display, and has not only climbed nearly to the top of Silicon Alley's social ladder but crafted many of its rungs. He knows what he wants, and he expresses it with a disarming absence of guile or doubt. "I don't see why I can't be the next Michael Eisner or Barry Diller," he says cheerfully. "Someone has to be."

Calacanis descended upon Silicon Alley in 1996 like Warhol upon a Brillo factory. Where the world saw twenty-five-year-olds in T-shirts fiddling unprofitably with monotonous graphic effects, Calacanis saw twenty-eight-year-old C.E.O.s with initial public offerings and Palm Pilots. He saw a time when New York content companies would make Silicon Valley technology look dull— "just plumbing." He saw glamour and money. But it wasn't money that drew him, or the Internet per se, so much as the scent of something big. These twenty-five-year-olds, he was convinced, were going to change the world, and he wanted to be one of them. Or, rather, he wanted to be their consigliere. He wanted to be the insider's insider: the one who knew everyone, who dropped hints and joined hands, who sensed what was happening before anyone else. He wanted to tell Silicon Alley what to make of itself, and to tell the world what to make of Silicon Alley. He wanted to be first on the bus to the future.

As one after another of the erstwhile twenty-five-year-olds takes his company public and becomes a multimillionaire, Calacanis likes to remark on the way in which Silicon Alley is taken seriously by Wall Street and ponder the small but noticeable role that he—his magazines, his conferences, the dinner parties he held and the introductions he arranged—has played in bringing it all about. He has discovered, too, to his delight, that his boat has risen with the tide, and the world is looking at him differently. What used to sound like callow cheerleading now sounds like daring realism. "Last winter, I spoke to the Harvard Business School," Calacanis recalls. "Now, I would never get admitted to that school, except maybe to work in the cafeteria—I got 1150 on my S.A.T.s. But I got to speak to the whole class here in New York, and I told them, 'I have one piece of advice for you: quit. Leave school tomorrow, take whatever money you have left that you would have spent on tuition, and start an Internet company. Because if you stay in school for the next two years—if, when everybody else is dreaming and innovating, you spend time on the bench, watching the game go by—you'll miss the greatest land grab, the greatest gold rush of all time, and you'll regret it for the rest of your life.' You should have seen the look on their faces: they were terrified. And you know why? Because they knew I was right."

Calacanis is muscular and compact, and this, along with the tight fit of his clothing and the vivid pinks of his face, gives the impression that he has been shrunk. Perhaps because of his long training in martial arts (he is a fourth-degree black belt in Tae Kwon Do), his movements are curiously orthodox, like those of an action figure. He is not one to lounge or flail about. When he is holding forth on some recent triumph or on the future, his face shines with the manic glee of the last uncaptured child in a game of tag.

One recent morning, Calacanis had scheduled an editorial meeting for nine o'clock. At nine-forty-five, he erupted from the elevator and strode into the *Reporter*'s offices, on Union Square, leading Toro, his corpulent bulldog, by a leash. Although spiritually Calacanis is committed to staying two steps ahead of the curve, in his daily activities he is invariably late. He had an interview scheduled later that day with Fernando Espuelas, the C.E.O. of StarMedia—the most prominent Spanish-and-Portuguese-language Internet media company—and he had dressed up for the occasion: tight black trousers, thin black dress shoes, a gray jacket that might have been part of a suit. Next to Calacanis's desk is Toro's cage, surrounded by the detritus of canine ennui—a shredded tennis ball, a soggy artificial bone. Behind his chair, two larger-than-human cardboard figures from "Star Wars" stand at attention: Darth Vader and an obscure galactic bounty hunter named Boba Fett. Boba Fett has only four lines in all the "Star Wars" movies, but he is the insider's "Star Wars" character.

The editorial staff of the *Silicon Alley Reporter* consists of eight people, seven of whom were present that morning. With the exception of Karol Martesko, the magazine's publisher, no one appeared to be over twenty-five; two interns— one large, one very small—looked as though they had yet to enter high school. Still, the *Reporter* had come a long way since its inauguration, in the fall of 1996, having expanded from a sixteen-page photocopy to a two-hundred-page glossy magazine. (Calacanis claims that he has had "many offers" to buy the magazine. Asked about rumors that one such offer, worth several million dollars, was made by Jann Wenner, he confirmed that he had met with Wenner, but he declined to say more. "These relationships are like dating," he says. "It's not classy to talk about the details.") Calacanis called the meeting to order. First on the agenda was the next issue's cover, which was turning out to be something of a problem. People kept backing out, and the current option was not entirely satisfactory. "She doesn't have a job," Calacanis said. "It would be kind of weird to put an unemployed person on the cover."

"Let's stick with our original mission," Martesko suggested, with an evil smile. "Let's make her a star." In its early days, the *Reporter* endeared itself to its constituency by according celebrity treatment to Silicon Alley's would-be entrepreneurs, putting them on the cover as though they were movie stars and publishing photographs of them posing at parties in a back-page feature entitled "Digital Dim Sum." But those days were over. Calacanis looked at Martesko reprovingly. "Let's get someone with a job," he said.

Next on the agenda was the magazine's annual "Silicon Alley 100" issue, which lists, in order of importance, the people who matter in the Internet business in New York. Calacanis wanted to expand last year's passport-size snapshots to more glamorous full-page portraits with a small amount of text.

"Whole body or only the head?" Steve Morris, the art director, wanted to know. It was not an idle question. Something had gone wrong with the previous cover's closeup, and Glenn Meyers, the C.E.O. of the Internet consulting company Rare Medium, had come out looking as though he had been heavily seasoned with paprika.

"They're ordering a ton of copies," Calacanis protested when he was reminded of this.

"Yeah, to get them out of circulation."

Calacanis paused to take this in. The large intern whispered to the small one that he had discovered a Web site named Doodie.com. "It's the best Web site ever," he said. "There's a new poop cartoon every day."

Next, Calacanis announced with a flourish a plan to publish a coffee-table book of the Silicon Alley crème de la crème—bringing together the top hundred from the "100" lists of the past two years. This idea was greeted with tentative giggling.

"Umm, who exactly is going to buy this book?" one of the editors inquired, after a moment, when it became clear from Calacanis's face that the idea was not a joke.

"Jeff Dachis, at Razorfish," Calacanis said. "How many copies do you think he's going to buy? A thousand!"

More giggling, louder this time. Calacanis raised his arms in self-defense. "I'm serious! He'll buy a thousand copies and send them to his clients with a Post-it stuck on his page." But he confessed to his staff that he was anxious about the "100" group photograph. Last year, more than eighty people had assembled in his loft for the picture, but he wondered whether this year the project was feasible. "Some of those guys are billionaires now," he mused. "I don't know if they'll show up."

IT is generally agreed that it was the "100" list, inaugurated late in 1997, that put Calacanis on the map. No matter what anybody thought of him and his magazine, there was something about a published ranking that carried a potency all its own. Everybody wanted to be on the list, and everybody who made it cared who ranked above and below him. Better still, those who made it tended to note that fact in their publicity material, and this had the effect of bolstering the list's (and the magazine's) reputation. There had been new-media awards ceremonies before the list came out, but they tended to focus on the doomed technology of CD-ROMS, and they rewarded artistic achievement. Calacanis's list rewarded importance, and, for the most part, that meant business. It was not just a matter of money, however. If the list had simply tabulated corporate wealth, it would have been nothing more than an accounting exercise. By measuring importance, it preserved that crucial dimension of mystery and subjectivity which made it productively controversial. "The '100' list creates tremendous resentment," one Alley figure who's made it on both times says. "Behind Jason's back, most people say nasty things about him, but to his face they are nice as nice can be, because to be on the map of New York cyberbusiness they've got to be in his '100.' "

Calacanis knows this, of course, and welcomes it as a sign of clout. "People who don't get on it probably think I'm a little full of myself, a little drunk with the power of the magazine," he says, and shrugs. "They feel spurned because I don't love them, and they think—wrongly—that if I loved them my love would make them successful. God forbid someone should look at himself in the mirror and think, I had a bad idea."

But the list served a second function, too: it signalled that on lower Broadway, where a minute ago there had been nothing, there were now a hundred new-media people worth writing about. As such, it is a key element of Calacanis's campaign to convince the world that Silicon Alley is the place in which the new-media business will come gloriously into its own. His argument, which he repeats frequently, is that now, as in the early days of any medium, it is the technology people who make the money and attract the attention, but later on only the creative types, in New York and Los Angeles, will have a hope of inventing the new genres of entertainment and advertising required to arrest the evanescent attentions of the Internet consumer. Calacanis has had limited success in promoting this view. "There are thousands of little guys in New York," Henry Blodget, an Internet analyst at Merrill Lynch, says. "And they're little for a reason, which is that content isn't big business."

In the early afternoon, Calacanis rode a taxi uptown to the Sheraton on Seventh Avenue, to drop in on a trade show sponsored by Jupiter, an Internet market-research company. He strolled past the exhibits, sampling the atmosphere. "Look how empty this place is," he said, sotto voce. "My show? Packed." He wandered over to the beverage stand, poured himself a cup of coffee, looked about in vain for milk, and shook his head genially as though docking points in a game. "My show will be classy," he pronounced. "We serve wine and mimosas at lunch, and we have sushi. It's a more mature environment."

Calacanis's conferences, like his "100" list, are masterpieces of social engineering. He creates a complex and ingenious caste system involving concentric layers of hierarchy, of dinners within parties and interviews within panels, of exclusivity both real and apparent: there are events you pay to get into, events you have to be important to get into, and events you pay to get into in order to meet those who are important, who get in free. He compensates his speakers with flattery (for most, he doesn't even cover expenses), knowing that few C.E.O.s can resist being presented to their colleagues as thinkers. He adds glamour by throwing in modish cultural figures—an actor from *Star Trek*, a rapper, a producer of *The Blair Witch Project*, the Belgian anarchist responsible for the Bill Gates pie-throwing incident. For entertainment, he invents games, such as Ready, Set, Pitch!, in which, before a live audience, would-be entrepreneurs try to talk a panel of venture capitalists and financiers into giving them seed money.

Having sized up the booths and found them wanting, Calacanis rode the escalator down to the first floor and sauntered over to chat with James Healy, of IN2.com. Healy's company had recently been acquired, and Calacanis wanted to congratulate him. (Healy had consulted him on the wisdom of the move, and Calacanis had put him in touch with a few people.) A skinny young man approached, wearing a turquoise polo shirt with his company's logo embroidered on it in yellow. "I want to go big," the young man confided to Calacanis, holding his hands apart to show he wasn't kidding around. "Really big. You've heard of convergence? Well, I want to do all media. I'd like to sit down with you sometime." A smiling young blond woman with noticeable cleavage and a badge identifying her as a representative of Excite@Home wandered over to chat and pitch. A large young man carrying a heavy bag lingered awkwardly during their conversation, then moved in to offer his card. He represented a company named @Philly, and had been very happy to learn that Calacanis was planning a trip to Philadelphia. Calacanis listened to each, cocking his ear for the punch line, nodding rapidly and shifting from foot to foot. He tries to avoid pitches, but he realizes that, as he puts it, "if I only hang out with billionaires, I'll miss the next wave."

• • •

ONE Monday morning, Calacanis showed up at Coffee Shop, on Union Square, for breakfast with a cousin. He wore a close-fitting T-shirt—black, with a white *Silicon Alley Reporter* logo—and his face was a bouquet of happy pinks. He had exciting news to relate. The last three phone calls he had received at the office on Friday evening were from a contact of his who suggested that Francis Ford Coppola might want to speak at his L.A. conference in September; from someone at Microsoft, who advised him that Steve Ballmer, the president of Microsoft, wanted to be interviewed by the *Silicon Alley Reporter* the Friday following; and from the office of the mayor of Los Angeles, which indicated that the mayor would like to write a proclamation for the conference. Calacanis related these facts with breathless exhilaration, as though he had just put down the receiver. The cousin was used to this exuberance—Calacanis visited him in New Jersey in the summers when they were children. But the cousin has followed a more conventional path, taking a job in a well-respected, elderly firm that affords him a great deal of security.

Calacanis's relationship to his background is two-sided but without conflict. On the one hand, he describes himself as a working-class guy from Brooklyn who waited tables late nights in his father's restaurant and watched wise guys beat each other up with tire irons outside on the street. He likes to tell his own up-by-the-bootstraps story: how he almost got kicked out of high school for drinking and failing his classes but was saved by the discipline of Tae Kwon Do (he has also run in the New York City Marathon for the past eleven years); how his father's second restaurant went out of business just before his freshman year of college, at Fordham, obliging him to put himself through school by repairing computers; how he used to haul the first few issues of the *Reporter* around town in a luggage cart and leave piles of them, free, in bookshops, cafés, and Silicon Alley offices. "Coming from Brooklyn," he says, "I didn't know the characteristics of the Upper East Side versus the Upper West Side, or what going to Dalton meant. It was like in the movie *Moonstruck,* when Cher leaves Brooklyn to go to the Met: for her, it's like going to Europe." Douglas Rushkoff, the author of *Media Virus* and *Coercion,* who writes a column in the *Silicon Alley Reporter* and attends Knicks games with Calacanis, tells the story of a trip he and Calacanis took to a conference in Austin last spring. "Jason upgraded to first class to sit with me," Rushkoff says, "and it was the first time he'd flown anything but coach. So we're sitting together, and when they came along with the nuts I said, 'Watch with these nuts, they're going to be warm,' and he said, 'No, they're not.' But then they gave him his nuts and he said, 'Wow, they are warm, they warm the nuts!' And for the next week or two he was telling people how he'd gone in first class and they'd warmed the nuts."

At the same time, Calacanis is clearly engaged in an ongoing project of self-improvement. He wears an expensive brand of cologne: Égoïste, by Chanel. He likes to order types of sushi that do not appear on the menu, in order to let the chef know that he is dealing with a serious person. He lives in a loft (he never refers to it as an apartment) in Chelsea that hews strictly to an early-nineties downtown-industrial aesthetic, which is to say that, except for a kitchen area in one corner, there is nothing in it but a half-empty clothing rack, a phlegmatic potted palm, and, in another corner, a television and two middle-aged sofas.

Calacanis's aspirations are not intellectual. His favorite author is Michael Crichton; his heroes are Bob Dylan, Lenny Bruce, and Howard Stern. "I have no fear at this point," he maintains. "In the beginning, I felt like such an outsider I just sat on the sidelines, but now when people drop some name I'll ask, 'Who's that?' And they'll say, 'You don't know who that is?' And I'll say, 'No.' And they'll tell me, 'He's a poet from the eighteenth century,' and I'll say, 'O.K., now I know.' " Those members of the cyber world who hail from more cosmopolitan backgrounds regard Calacanis either angrily, as a buffoonish nouveau ("Jason's smug and self-aggrandizing," one person raged over the phone. "He thinks he's the mayor of Silicon Alley, but he's more like the court jester"), or with a distanced curiosity. "There's something untempered and unmodulated about him," Stefanie Syman, the co-founder and executive editor of the on-line magazine *Feed,* says. "Most of us grew up with some degree of privilege, which taught us to have a complicated relationship to pitching and selling and to our desire to get what we want in the world. Jason's relationship to all that is very uncomplicated." Rushkoff often finds himself defending Calacanis against a range of charges. He says, "Of all the people that I've met in this cyberbusiness, Jason's the one who would risk his neck to rescue me if I were getting mugged. The others would call the cops on their cell phones."

EVER since Calacanis started publishing his second, L.A.-oriented magazine, the *Digital Coast Reporter,* in the spring of 1998, he has been spending a lot of time in Los Angeles, and he has found networking out there to be a very different business from networking in New York. In New York, he explains, to introduce one contact to another is to risk diminishing your credit with both, so you don't usually gather people together unless you have in mind a particular purpose with a fair chance of success. In L.A., on the other hand, a person's social worth is measured by the sheer quantity of connections he generates. There is much less of a sense, in California, that introducing an insignificant person to a famous person might cause the famous person to become irritated with you. Calacanis recently met with a Hollywood agent turned Internet venture capitalist and was charmed when the venture capitalist asked him if he knew Danny DeVito, as though he perfectly well might. "There's a frantic pollination going on out there," Calacanis says. "Someone will say, 'Oh, I was just on the phone with Francis Ford Coppola talking about you, and he's really into what you're doing and wants to meet up.' Everybody's rushing to network, and there's no thought of why we're networking. It's just, like, Hey, let's hang out."

Calacanis conducted his initial entry into the L.A. Internet world with a characteristic combination of naïve tactlessness and calculated belligerence.

Two years ago, somebody gave Mayor Richard Riordan a copy of the *Silicon Alley Reporter*, and the Mayor, perceiving its value as a tool for civic boosterism, held it up in a meeting and declared that Los Angeles needed a publication just like it. Shortly afterward, Calacanis received a phone call. "The guy who ran the hip new-media association out there called me up and told me, 'I'll have a cocktail party for you, because I know everybody—I'll invite fifty people to this bar, Rix,' " Calacanis relates. "So I said, 'Great,' and I pulled out my two-thousand-person E-mail list from the *Daily* and sent out a one-liner saying, 'I'm going to be in L.A. and I'm having drinks at Rix.' Now, Rix is a small place: one bartender, and the bar can fit maybe twenty people from one end to the other. Conservative estimate: three hundred people showed up to see me. I was backed into a corner, everyone was trying to get face time, trying to get me to write about his company. I had a stack of cards like this at the end of the night, and I could tell by the look in his eye that the other guy was very nervous about me coming into the market. A few days later, he told me his group wanted to be partners with me, and I said, 'That's generous, but I do my own thing.' So he said, as a threat, 'You know, you could be very easily taken as an outsider. We're the home-town brand.' But I said, 'Thanks, anyway.' And now nobody knows who they are anymore. They're gone."

People keep telling Calacanis that he will end up in L.A., and the thought is not displeasing to him; in fact, he recently bought an apartment in Santa Monica. He can see himself getting into the TV or movie business someday. Producing, maybe, or writing. For a time, his E-mails carried the name Jason "Hollywood" McCabe Calacanis. He already has a toe in television, hosting a Net-TV talk show on Pseudo.com. He is beginning to think that his acclimatization to the West Coast will require a change of wardrobe as well. Clothing is a topic that Calacanis started considering seriously only a short time ago, and he approaches it as a question of packaging. He used to shop mostly at the Gap, and for his work in offices he bought himself a couple of snappy hundred-and-forty-nine-dollar double-breasted suits. Then a girlfriend told him that if he wanted to succeed in the media business he needed to start dressing better, which meant wearing black. He saw the wisdom of this advice, and has since dressed exclusively in black, with a few notable exceptions, such as an orange shirt from Agnès B. Lately, though, he has perceived that his all-black wardrobe is wrong for L.A.—that people don't wear black in L.A., and, anyhow, you can get pretty sweaty wearing black while driving a convertible—so he's considering buying a second wardrobe, which he will keep in his apartment there, consisting entirely of white.

OF all the roles that Calacanis has written for himself, the one in which he seems most confident—in which his salesman's tenor broadens to a patriarchal bass—is as host at a restaurant. No doubt, this is partly because of his years working as a waiter in his father's place in Brooklyn, but perhaps, too, in the world of Silicon Alley the distribution of a good as tangible as food has regained some sort of ritual significance. One balmy evening in the West Village, in the back room of Ithaka, a viny Greek restaurant on Barrow Street, Calacanis gathered together fifteen C.E.O.s, presidents, and other Silicon Alley figures. Among them were Kevin O'Connor, the C.E.O. of DoubleClick, an on-line advertising company that is worth more than four billion dollars; Theresa Duncan, a digital filmmaker; and Chan Suh, the C.E.O. of Agency.com, an Internet consulting company whose 1998 revenues were sixty-five million dollars. Calacanis likes to hold soirées for the Old Guard: the ones who've been around since the beginning, in 1994. Back then, most people who were involved in the Internet in New York cherished artistic aspirations of some sort—everyone had started a zine, or dabbled in video. When Kyle Shannon, now the chief creative officer of Agency.com, founded one of the first Silicon Alley industry groups, he called it the World Wide Web Artists' Consortium. These days, the Alley scene is mostly split along traditional lines—the business types, many of whom are now very rich, in one corner, and the artistic and intellectual types, who aren't, in another—and small dinners like these are one of the few circumstances in which the two still encounter one another.

"There's this surreal thing going on that nobody talks about," Calacanis said, "which is that some of us can look across this table and think, We both started in the same place, we knew each other when, and now you're worth a hundred million and I'm worth nothing." Back then, Silicon Alley was a much more sociable place than it is now: someone was always throwing a party to launch a company or promote a new product. In 1996, Pseudo.com sponsored a fête at Roseland in which dozens of naked people were lifted to the crest of a thirty-foot-high plastic bubble by a cherry picker. In those lighthearted days, Calacanis worked as a gossip writer for the magazine *Paper*, covering the new-media world in a column entitled "Cybersurfer's Sillycon Alley." He proclaimed the scene's winners and losers ("cheesy@best.com"), and became notorious for publicizing the conjoining and dissolution of new-media couples. He is, as he will hasten to assert, no longer a gossip columnist, but the bold-type sensibility lingers in his writing style, which is characterized by enthusiastic punctuation. Advertisements for the *Silicon Alley Reporter* ask, "Don't you get it?!?"

Calacanis rose to greet each guest as he arrived, and proffered introductions. Those who had appeared on the cover of his magazine he introduced as such: June '98, meet November '97. One C.E.O., apologizing for his lateness, explained that he'd been very busy recently. "You guys are like sharks," Calacanis demurred, raising his hands to show that he understood perfectly. "If you stop, you die." The C.E.O.s were dressed conventionally, in suits or sports jackets and button-down shirts. Many carried themselves with an air of eerie serenity, as though already, in their thirties, they had decided what they wanted out of life and achieved it. Only Calacanis, with eight thousand dollars in his bank account, still emitted, beneath his hostly bonhomie, an anxious, flickering energy. The movie *Analyze This* was mentioned, and Calacanis jumped in to quote a whole scene from memory. Later, in dealmaking mode, he called one of the guests over and gestured to him to lean in close. "You want to be head of Playboy.com?" he asked under his breath. "You need to speak to Christie Hefner."

The equivalent crowd in Silicon Valley, I was told, would get together at Chi-Chi's, dressed in jeans and rock-concert T-shirts. "The whole thing in the Valley is, who can be worth the most and not have his life change," Henry Blodget observes. "You know—'I've made five billion dollars but I still live in my trailer.' In New York, there's more of an I'm-creative attitude, and a hangover from the eighties which means you've got to show it. A.O.L.'s last party was so New York. There were security guards wearing wireless headsets, they got the best sushi chef in the world to fly in from Tokyo, Donald Trump was there, the place was filled with models, and I was thinking, Oh boy, this is not the A.O.L. I used to know."

At Ithaka, the C.E.O.s talked of Woodstock and Giuliani, and Calacanis took charge of the appetizers. He is a deft hand with a spoon and fork. Grape-leaf packets, fried cheese (a specialty of the house), feta, tomatoes, olives—he plucked each, one-handed, from its serving platter and placed it gently on a plate, while, with the other hand, directing plates around the table until everyone was served. Calacanis does not drink, but he knows how wine can warm up an evening, so he made sure that the glasses stayed full, and, later, when the ouzo appeared, that everyone downed a shot. For a few minutes, he sat back to observe his handiwork, chewing rapidly and forcefully, his eyes darting about the table, ear cocked for the hum of profitable conversation. He had one foot propped up on the chair next to him, the white cotton lining of his trouser pocket protruding like a mute reminder of financial reality. He took out his cell phone and quickly checked his messages.

Calacanis is the sort of person who is frequently described as a character out of a movie, but he does not belong in one of the great old films about journalism. In *Network,* and *Citizen Kane,* and *Sweet Smell of Success,* the journalist schemes and stabs in a world in which rewards are scarce and must be ruthlessly fought over: the good are beaten down and weak, the strong go bad, and the bad are diabolical. Calacanis, by merit of having stumbled upon an underpopulated world in its infancy, has found himself in an unusual position: his own celebrity depends upon the celebrity of Silicon Alley, and thus the prosperity of those around him can only bolster his enterprise. It is a world for which he is perfectly suited, seeming, as he does, to be shielded from the more corrosive effects of envy by delight in his own victories and an unbounded ability to see glory in the future. He declares, "People always say, 'I wish I was around in the fifties so I could have been there for the revolution of TV, or the twenties for the revolution in film, or the sixties so I could have been a radical.' But this is it: you're in it. I tell people, Dare to be great. This is the time."

OCTOBER 18, 1999

EVERYWOMAN.COM

ACCORDING to "The Web Guide to Martha Stewart—The UNOFFICIAL Site!," which was created by a former graduate student named Kerry Ogata as "a thesis procrastination technique" and then passed on to those who now maintain it, the fifty-eight-year-old chairman and C.E.O. of Martha Stewart Living Omnimedia L.L.C. ("MSO" on the New York Stock Exchange) needs only four hours of sleep a night, utilizes the saved hours by grooming her six cats and gardening by flashlight, prefers Macs in the office and a PowerBook for herself, commutes between her house in Westport and her two houses in East Hampton and her Manhattan apartment in a G.M.C. Suburban ("with chauffeur") or a Jaguar XJ6 ("she drives herself"), was raised the second-oldest of six children in a Polish-American family in Nutley, New Jersey, has one daughter, Alexis, and survived "a non-amicable divorce" from her husband of twenty-six years, Andrew Stewart ("Andy" on the site), who then "married Martha's former assistant who is 21 years younger than he is."

Contributors to the site's "Opinions" page, like good friends everywhere, have mixed feelings about Andy's defection, which occurred in 1987, while Martha was on the road promoting *Martha Stewart Weddings*, the preface to which offered a possibly prescient view of her own 1961 wedding. "I was a naïve nineteen-year-old, still a student at Barnard, and Andy was beginning Yale Law School, so it seemed appropriate to be married in St. Paul's Chapel at Columbia in an Episcopalian service, mainly because we didn't have anyplace else to go," she wrote, and included a photograph showing the wedding dress she and her mother had made of embroidered Swiss organdy bought on West Thirty-eighth Street. On-line, the relative cases of "Martha" and of "Andy" and even of "Alexis," who originally took her mother's side in the divorce, get debated with startling familiarity. "BTW, I don't blame Andy," one contributor offers. "I think he took all he could. I think it's too bad that Alexis felt she had to choose." Another contributor, another view: "I work fifty hours a week and admit sometimes I don't have time to 'be all that I can be' but when Martha started out she was doing this part-time and raising Alexis and making a home for that schmuck Andy (I bet he is sorry he ever left her)."

Although "The UNOFFICIAL Site!" is just that, unofficial, "not affiliated with Martha Stewart, her agents, Martha Stewart Living Omnimedia, LLC or any other Martha Stewart Enterprises," its fairly lighthearted approach to its subject's protean competence ("What can't Martha do? According to Martha herself, 'Hang-gliding, and I hate shopping for clothes' ") should in no way be construed as disloyalty to Martha's objectives, which are, as the prospectus prepared for Martha Stewart Living Omnimedia's initial public offering last October explained, "to provide our original 'how-to' content and information to as many consumers as possible" and "to turn our consumers into 'doers' by offering them the information and products they need for do-it-yourself ingenuity 'the Martha Stewart way.' " The creators and users of "The UNOFFICIAL Site!" clearly maintain a special relationship with the subject at hand, as do the creators and users of other unofficial or self-invented sites crafted in the same spirit: "My Martha Stewart Page," say, or "Gothic Martha Stewart," which advises teen-agers living at home on how they can "goth up" their rooms without freaking their parents ("First of all, don't paint everything black") by taking their cues from Martha.

"Martha adores finding old linens and gently worn furniture at flea markets," users of "Gothic Martha Stewart" are reminded. "She sews a lot of her own household dressings. She paints and experiments with unusual painting techniques on objects small and large. She loves flowers, live and dried . . . and even though her surroundings look very rich, many of her ideas are created from rather simple and inexpensive materials, like fabric scraps and second-hand dishes." For the creator of "My Martha Stewart Page," even the "extremely anal" quality of Martha's expressed preoccupation with the appearance of her liquid-detergent dispenser can be a learning experience, a source of concern that becomes a source of illumination: "It makes me worry about her. . . . Of course it is just this strangeness that makes me love her. She helps me know I'm OK—everyone's OK. . . . She seems perfect, but she's not. She's obsessed. She's frantic. She's a control freak beyond my wildest dreams. And that shows me two things: A) no one is perfect and B) there's a price for everything."

There is an unusual bonding here, a proprietary intimacy that eludes conventional precepts of merchandising to go to the very heart of the enterprise, the brand, what Martha prefers to call the "presence": the two magazines (*Martha Stewart Living* and *Martha Stewart Weddings*) that between them reach ten million readers, the twenty-seven books that have sold eight and a half mil-

lion copies, the weekday radio show carried on two hundred and seventy stations, the syndicated "AskMartha" column that appears in two hundred and
thirty-three newspapers, the televised show six days a week on CBS, the weekly
slot on the CBS morning show, the cable-TV show (*From Martha's Kitchen*,
the Food Network's top-rated weekly show among women aged twenty-five to
fifty-four), the Web site (www.marthastewart.com) with more than one million registered users and six hundred and twenty-seven thousand hits a
month, the merchandising tie-ins with Kmart and Sears and Sherwin-
Williams (Kmart alone last year sold more than a billion dollars' worth of
Martha Stewart merchandise), the catalogue operation (Martha by Mail) from
which some twenty-eight hundred products (Valentine Garlands, Valentine
Treat Bags, Ready-to-Decorate Cookies, Sweetheart Cake Rings, Heart Dessert
Scoops, Heart Rosette Sets, Heart-Shaped Pancake Molds, and Lace-Paper
Valentine Kits, to name a few from the on-line "Valentine's Day" pages) can be
ordered either from the catalogues themselves (eleven annual editions, fifteen
million copies) or from Web pages with exceptionally inviting layouts and se-
ductively logical links.

These products are not inexpensive. The Lace-Paper Valentine Kit contains
enough card stock and paper lace to make "about forty" valentines, which
could be viewed as something less than a buy at forty-two dollars plus time and
labor. On the "Cakes and Cake Stands" page, the Holiday Cake-Stencil Set,
which consists of eight nine-inch plastic stencils for the decorative dusting of
cakes with confectioners' sugar or cocoa, sells for twenty-eight dollars. On the
"marthasflowers" pages, twenty-five tea roses, which are available for eighteen dollars a dozen at Roses Only in New York, cost fifty-two dollars, and the
larger of the two "suggested vases" to put them in (an example of the site's link-
ing logic) another seventy-eight dollars. A set of fifty Scalloped Tulle Rounds,
eight-and-three-quarter-inch circles of tulle in which to tie up wedding favors,
costs eighteen dollars, and the seam binding used to tie them ("sold separately," another natural link) costs, in the six-color Seam-Binding Ribbon Collection, fifty-six dollars. Seam binding sells retail for pennies, and, at Paron on
West Fifty-seventh Street in New York, not the least expensive source, one-
hundred-and-eight-inch-wide tulle sells for four dollars a yard. Since the
amount of one-hundred-and-eight-inch tulle required to make fifty Scalloped
Tulle Rounds would be slightly over a yard, the on-line buyer can be paying
only for the imprimatur of "Martha," whose genius it was to take the once familiar notion of doing-it-yourself to previously uncharted territory: somewhere east of actually doing it yourself, somewhere west of paying Robert
Isabell to do it.

THIS is a billion-dollar company the only real product of which, in other
words, is Martha Stewart herself, an unusual business condition acknowl-

edged in the prospectus prepared for Martha Stewart Living Omnimedia's strikingly successful October I.P.O. "Our business would be adversely affected if Martha Stewart's public image or reputation were to be tarnished," the "Risk Factors" section of the prospectus read in part. "Martha Stewart, as well as her name, her image, and the trademarks and other intellectual property rights relating to these, are integral to our marketing efforts and form the core of our brand name. Our continued success and the value of our brand name therefore depends, to a large degree, on the reputation of Martha Stewart."

The perils of totally identifying a brand with a single living and therefore vulnerable human being were much discussed around the time of the I.P.O., and the question of what would happen to Martha Stewart Living Omnimedia if Martha Stewart were to become ill or die ("the diminution or loss of the services of Martha Stewart," in the words of the prospectus) remained open. "That was always an issue for us," Don Logan, the president of Time Inc., told the Los Angeles *Times* in 1997, a few months after Stewart managed to raise enough of what she called "internally generated capital," $53.3 million, to buy herself out of Time Warner, which had been resisting expansion of a business built entirely around a single personality. "I think we are now spread very nicely over an area where our information can be trusted," Stewart herself maintained, and it did seem clear that the very expansion and repetition of the name that had made Time Warner nervous—every "Martha Stewart" item sold, every "Martha Stewart Everyday" commercial aired—was paradoxically serving to insulate the brand from the possible loss of the personality behind it.

The related question, of what would happen if "Martha Stewart's public image or reputation were to be tarnished," seemed less worrisome, since in any practical way the question of whether it was possible to tarnish Martha Stewart's public image or reputation had already been answered, with the 1997 publication and ascension to the New York *Times* best-seller list of *Just Desserts*, an unauthorized biography of Martha Stewart by Jerry Oppenheimer, whose previous books were unauthorized biographies of Rock Hudson, Barbara Walters, and Ethel Kennedy. "My investigative juices began to flow," Oppenheimer wrote in the preface to *Just Desserts*. "If her stories were true, I foresaw a book about a perfect woman who had brought perfection to the masses. If her stories were not true, I foresaw a book that would shatter myths."

Investigative juices flowing, Oppenheimer discovered that Martha was "driven." Martha, moreover, sometimes "didn't tell the whole story." Martha could be "a real screamer" when situations did not go as planned, although the case Oppenheimer makes on this point suggests, at worst, merit on both sides. Martha was said to have "started to shriek," for example, when a catering partner backed a car over the "picture-perfect" Shaker picnic basket she had just finished packing with her own blueberry pies. Similarly, Martha was said to have been "just totally freaked" when a smokehouse fire interrupted the shooting of a holiday special and she found that the hose she had personally dragged to the smokehouse ("followed by various blasé crew people, faux-concerned family members, smirking kitchen assistants, and a macho Brazilian groundskeeper") was too short to reach the flames. After running back to the house, getting an extension for the hose, and putting out the fire, Martha, many would think understandably, exchanged words with the groundskeeper, "whom she fired on the spot in front of everyone after he talked back to her."

Other divined faults include idealizing her early family life (p. 34), embellishing "everything" (p. 42), omitting a key ingredient when a rival preteen caterer asked for her chocolate-cake recipe (p. 43), telling readers of *Martha Stewart Living* that she had as a young girl "sought to discover the key to good literature" even though "a close friend" reported that she had "passionately devoured" the Nancy Drew and Cherry Ames novels (p. 48), misspelling "villainous" in a review of William Makepeace Thackeray's *Vanity Fair* for the Nutley High School literary magazine (p. 51), having to ask what Kwanza was during a 1995 appearance on *Larry King Live* (p. 71), and not only wanting a larger engagement diamond than the one Andy had picked out for her at Harry Winston but obtaining it, at a better price, in the diamond district (p. 101). "That should have set off an alarm," a "lifelong friend" told Oppenheimer. "How many women would do something like that? It was a bad omen."

This lumping together of insignificant immaturities and economies for conversion into character flaws (a former assistant in the catering business Martha ran in Westport during the nineteen-seventies presents the damning charge "Nothing went to waste. . . . Martha's philosophy was like someone at a restaurant who had eaten half his steak and tells the waiter 'Oh, wrap it up, and I'll take it home' ") continues for four hundred and fourteen pages, at which point Oppenheimer, in full myth-shattering mode, reveals his trump card, "an eerie corporate manifesto" that "somehow slipped out of Martha's offices and made its way from one Time Inc. executive's desk to another and eventually from a Xerox machine to the outside world. . . . The white paper, replete with what was described as an incomprehensible flow chart, declared, in part":

In Martha's vision, the shared value of the MSL enterprises are highly personal—reflecting her individual goals, beliefs, values and aspirations. . . . "Martha's Way" can be obtained because she puts us in direct touch with everything we need to know, and tells/shows us exactly what we have to do. . . . MSL enterprises are founded on the proposition that Martha herself is both leader and teacher. . . . While the ranks of "teaching disciples" within MSL may grow and extend, their authority rests on their direct association with Martha; their work emanates from her approach and philosophies; and their techniques, and products and results meet her test. . . . The magazine, books, television series, and other distribution sources are only vehicles to enable personal communication with Martha. . . . She is not, and won't allow herself to be, an institutional image and fiction like Betty Crocker. . . . She is the creative and driving center. . . . By listening to Martha and following her lead, we can achieve real results in our homes too—ourselves—just like she has. . . . It is easy to do. Martha has already "figured it out." She will personally take us by the hand and show us how to do it.

Oppenheimer construes this purloined memo or mission statement as sinister, of a piece with the Guyana Kool-Aid massacre ("From its wording, some wondered whether Martha's world was more gentrified Jonestown than happy homemaker"), but in fact it remains an unexceptionable, and quite accurate, assessment of what makes the enterprise go. Martha Stewart Living Omnimedia L.L.C. connects on a level that transcends the absurdly labor-intensive and in many cases prohibitively expensive table settings and decorating touches (the "poinsettia wreath made entirely of ribbon" featured on one December show would require of even a diligent maker, Martha herself allowed, "a couple of hours" and, "if you use the very best ribbon, two or three hundred dollars") over which its chairman toils six mornings a week on CBS. Nor is the connection about her recipes, which are the recipes of Sunbelt Junior League cookbooks (Grapefruit Mimosas, Apple Cheddar Turnovers, and Southwestern Style S'Mores are a few from the most recent issue of *Martha Stewart Entertaining*), reflecting American middle-class home cooking as it has existed pretty much through the postwar years. There is in a Martha Stewart recipe none of, say, Elizabeth David's transforming logic and assurance, none of Julia Child's mastery of technique.

What there is instead is "Martha," full focus, establishing "personal communication" with the viewer or reader, showing, telling, leading, teaching, "loving it" when the simplest possible shaken-in-a-jar vinaigrette emulsifies right there onscreen. She presents herself not as an authority but as the friend who has "figured it out," the enterprising if occasionally manic neighbor who will waste no opportunity to share an educational footnote. "True," or "Ceylon," cinnamon, the reader of *Martha Stewart Living* will learn, "originally came from the island now called Sri Lanka," and "by the time of the Roman Empire . . . was valued at fifteen times its weight in silver." In a television segment about how to serve champagne, Martha will advise her viewers that the largest champagne bottle, the Balthazar, was named after the king of Babylon, "555 to 539 B.C." While explaining how to decorate the house for the holidays around the theme "The Twelve Days of Christmas," Martha will slip in this doubtful but nonetheless useful gloss, a way for the decorator to perceive herself as doing something more significant than painting pressed-paper eggs with two or three coats of white semi-gloss acrylic paint, followed by another two or three coats of yellow-tinted acrylic varnish, and finishing the result with ribbon and beads: "With the egg so clearly associated with new life, it is not surprising that the six geese a-laying represented the six days of Creation in the carol."

THE message Martha is actually sending, the reason large numbers of American women count watching her a comforting and obscurely inspirational experience, seems not very well understood. There has been a flurry of academic work done on the cultural meaning of her success (in the summer of 1998, the New York *Times* reported that "about two dozen scholars across the United States and Canada" were producing such studies as "A Look at Linen Closets: Liminality, Structure and Anti-Structure in Martha Stewart Living" and locating "the fear of transgression" in the magazine's "recurrent images of fences, hedges and garden walls"), but there remains, both in the bond she makes and in the outrage she provokes, something unaddressed, something pitched, like a dog whistle, too high for traditional textual analysis. The outrage, which reaches sometimes startling levels, centers on the misconception that she has somehow tricked her admirers into not noticing the ambition that brought her to their attention. To her critics, she seems to represent a fraud to be exposed, a wrong to be righted. "She's a shark," one declares in *Salon*. "However much she's got, Martha wants more. And she wants it her way and in her world, not in the balls-out boys' club realms of real estate or technology, but in the delicate land of doily hearts and wedding cakes."

"I can't believe people don't see the irony in the fact that this 'ultimate homemaker' has made a multi-million dollar empire out of baking cookies and selling bed sheets," a posting reads in *Salon*'s "ongoing discussion" of Martha. "I read an interview in *Wired* where she said she gets home at 11 P.M. most days, which means she's obviously too busy to be the perfect mom/wife/homemaker—a role which many women feel like they have to live up to because of the image MS projects." Another reader cuts to the chase: "Wasn't there some buzz a while back about Martha stealing her daughter's BF?" The answer: "I thought that was Erica Kane. You know, when she stole Kendra's BF. I think you're getting them confused. Actually, why would any man want to date MS? She is so frigid looking that my television actually gets cold when she's on." "The trouble is that Stewart is about as genuine as Hollywood," a writer in *The Scotsman* charges. "Hers may seem to be a nostalgic siren call for a return to Fifties-style homemaking with an updated elegance, but is she in fact sending out a fraudulent message—putting pressure on American women to achieve impossible perfection in yet another sphere, one in which, unlike ordinary women, Stewart herself has legions of helpers?"

This entire notion of "the perfect mom/wife/homemaker," of the "nostalgic siren call for a return to Fifties-style homemaking," is a considerable misunderstanding of what Martha Stewart actually transmits, the promise she makes her readers and viewers, which is that know-how in the house will translate to can-do outside it. What she offers, and what more strictly professional shelter and food magazines and shows do not, is the promise of transferred manna, transferred luck. She projects a level of taste that transforms the often pointlessly ornamented details of what she is actually doing. The possibility of moving out of the perfected house and into the headier ether of executive action, of doing as Martha does, is clearly presented: "Now I, as a single human being, have six personal fax numbers, fourteen personal phone numbers, seven car-phone numbers, and two cell-phone numbers," as she told readers of *Martha Stewart Living.* On October 19th, the evening of her triumphant I.P.O., she explained, on *The Charlie Rose Show,* the genesis of the enterprise. "I was serving a desire—not only mine, but every homemaker's desire, to elevate that job of homemaker," she said. "It was floundering, I think. And we all wanted to escape it, to get out of the house, get that high-paying job and pay somebody else to do everything that we didn't think was really worthy of our attention. And all of a sudden I realized: it was terribly worthy of our attention."

THINK about this. Here was a woman who had elevated "that job of homemaker" to a level where even her G.M.C. Suburban came equipped with a Sony MZ-B3 MiniDisc Recorder for dictation and a Sony ICD-50 Recorder for short messages and a Watchman FDL-PT22 TV set, plus phones, plus PowerBook. Here was a woman whose idea of how to dress for "that job of homemaker" involved Jil Sander. "Jil's responded to the needs of people like me," she is quoted as having said on "The UNOFFICIAL Site!" "I'm busy; I travel a lot; I want to look great in a picture." Here was a woman who had that very October morning been driven down to the big board to dispense brioches and fresh-squeezed orange juice from a striped tent while Morgan Stanley Dean Witter and Merrill Lynch and Bear, Stearns and Donaldson, Lufkin & Jenrette and Banc of America Securities increased the value of her personal stock in the company she personally invented to $614 million. This does not play into any "nostalgic siren call" for a return to the kind of "homemaking" that seized America during those postwar years when the conversion of industry to peacetime production mandated the creation of a market for Kelvinators, yet Martha was the first to share the moment with her readers.

"The mood was festive, the business community receptive, and the stock began trading with the new symbol MSO," she confided in her "Letter from Martha" in the December *Martha Stewart Living,* and there between the lines was the promise from the mission statement: *It is easy to do. Martha has already "figured it out." She will personally take us by the hand and show us how to do it.* What she will show us how to do, it turns out, is a little more invigorating than your average poinsettia-wreath project: "The process was extremely interesting, from deciding exactly what the company was (an 'integrated multimedia company' with promising internet capabilities) to creating a complicated and lengthy prospectus that was vetted and revetted (only to be vetted again by the Securities and Exchange Commission) to selling the company with a road show that took us to more than twenty cities in fourteen days (as far off as Europe)." This is getting out of the house with a vengeance, and on your own terms, the secret dream of any woman who has ever made a success of a PTA cake sale. "You could bottle that chili sauce," neighbors say to home cooks all over America. "You could make a fortune on those date bars." You could bottle it, you could sell it, you can survive when all else fails: I myself believed for most of my adult life that I could support myself and my family, in the catastrophic absence of all other income sources, by catering.

The "cultural meaning" of Martha Stewart's success, in other words, lies deep in the success itself, which is why even her troubles and strivings are part of the message, not detrimental but integral to the brand. She has branded herself not as Superwoman but as Everywoman, a distinction that seems to remain unclear to her critics. Martha herself gets it, and talks about herself in print as if catching up her oldest friend. "I sacrificed family, husband," she said in a 1996 *Fortune* conversation with Charlotte Beers, the former C.E.O. of Ogilvy & Mather and a member of Martha Stewart Living Omnimedia's board of directors, and Darla Moore, the president of Richard Rainwater's investment firm and the inventor of "debtor in possession" financing for companies in bankruptcy. The tone of this conversation was odd, considerably more confessional than the average dialogue among senior executives who know they are being taped by *Fortune*. "Not my choice," Martha confided about her divorce. "His choice. Now, I'm so happy that it happened. It took a long time for me to realize that it freed me to do more things. I don't think I would have accomplished what I have if I had stayed married. No way. And it allowed me to make friends that I know I never would have had."

MARTHA'S readers understand her divorce, both its pain and its upside. They saw her through it, just as they saw her through her dealings with the S.E.C., her twenty-city road show, her triumph on Wall Street. This relationship between Martha and her readers is a good deal more complicated than the many parodies of and jokes about it would allow. "While fans don't grow on fruit trees (well, some do), they can be found all over America: in malls, and Kmarts, in tract houses and trailer parks, in raised ranches, Tudor condos and Winnebagos," the parody Martha is made to say in HarperCollins' *Martha Stuart's Better Than You at Entertaining.* "Wherever there are women dissatisfied with how they live, with who they are and who they are not, that is where you'll find potential fans of mine." These parodies are themselves interesting: too broad, misogynistic in a cartoon way (stripping Martha to her underwear has been a reliable motif of countless online parodies), curiously nervous ("Keeping Razors Circumcision-Sharp" is one feature in *Martha Stuart's Better Than You at Entertaining*), oddly uncomfortable, a little too intent on marginalizing a rather considerable number of women by making light of their situations and their aspirations.

Something here is perceived as threatening, and a glance at "The UNOFFICIAL Site!," the subliminal focus of which is somewhere other than on homemaking skills, suggests what it is. What makes Martha "a good role model in many ways," one contributor writes, is that "she's a strong woman who's in charge, and she has indeed changed the way our country, if not the world, views what used to be called 'women's work.' " From an eleven-year-old: "Being successful is important in life. . . . It is fun to say 'When I become Martha Stewart I'm going to have all the things Martha has.' " Even a contributor who admits to an "essentially anti-Martha persona" admires her "intelligence" and "drive," the way in which this "supreme chef, baker, gardener, decorator, artist, and entrepreneur" showed what it took "to get where she is, where most men aren't and can't. . . . She owns her own corporation in her own name, her own magazine, her own show."

A keen interest in and admiration for business acumen pervades the site. "I know people are threatened by Martha and Time Warner Inc. is going to blow a very 'good thing' if they let Martha and her empire walk in the near future," a contributor to "The UNOFFICIAL Site!" wrote at the time Stewart was trying to buy herself out of Time Warner. "I support Martha in everything she does and I would bet if a man wanted to attach his name to all he did . . . this wouldn't be a question." Their own words tell the story these readers and viewers take from Martha: Martha is *in charge,* Martha is *where most men aren't and can't,* Martha has *her own magazine,* Martha has *her own show,* Martha not only has *her own corporation* but has it *in her own name.*

This is not a story about a woman who made the best of traditional skills. This is a story about a woman who did her own I.P.O. This is the "woman's pluck" story, the dust-bowl story, the burying-your-child-on-the-trail story, the I-will-never-go-hungry-again story, the Mildred Pierce story, the story about how the sheer nerve of even professionally unskilled women can prevail, show the men; the story that has historically encouraged women in this country, even as it has threatened men. The dreams and the fears into which Martha Stewart taps are not of "feminine" domesticity but of female power, of the woman who sits down at the table with the men and, still in her apron, walks away with the chips.

FEBRUARY 21, 2000

THE FOUNTAINHEAD

A T five to ten on a brisk morning a couple of months ago, Alan Greenspan, the chairman of the Federal Reserve System, walked into Room 216 of the Hart Office Building, on Capitol Hill, holding a bunch of news-papers under one arm, the pink *Financial Times* visible on the outside. He was dressed much as he usually is: black shoes, dark socks, a gray suit with a faint-pink chalk stripe running through it, a light-blue button-down shirt, and a dark-red tie. At the age of seventy-four, Greenspan has a face that resembles that of a mountain rescue dog. Lines on his forehead are not mere wrinkles but waves etched into his skull. He has sad brown eyes, a big, bulbous nose, and a long, narrow mouth, the corners of which are often turned down, giving him a mournful cast. He walked to the front of the room, sat at the witness's table, opened a bottle of water, and poured himself a glass. The manufacturer's label had been removed from the bottle so that he wouldn't appear to be endorsing a brand. He looked as nervous as Tiger Woods on the practice tee.

Greenspan was on Capitol Hill to deliver a twice-yearly report on monetary policy to the Senate Committee on Banking—one of the few concessions to ac-countability in a role that was designed to be above electoral politics. In recent years, however, Greenspan's appearances on Capitol Hill have often been less like congressional hearings than like regal audiences. This one started out along the same lines. At ten o'clock, Senator Phil Gramm, the Texas Republi-can who chairs the committee, got things going by reviewing the Fed's policy of raising interest rates, which began last June and has resulted in five succes-sive hikes, each of a quarter point, the most recent of them occurring last month. "I'm not going to get into the business of trying to second-guess the monetary policy of the most successful central banker in the history of the

United States," Gramm declared in his exaggerated Texas drawl. Greenspan explained why the Fed had felt compelled to increase interest rates. The economy, partly fuelled by the stock market's remarkable rise—the so-called "wealth effect"—was growing too rapidly. Although there were few signs of rising prices at the moment, the pool of available workers was dwindling, and the level of imports was growing strongly. Neither trend could continue indefinitely without sparking inflation. The Fed needed to restrain the economy, and this could be done only by raising the cost of borrowing.

The senators listened in respectful silence, but then something surprising happened. Jim Bunning, a Republican from Kentucky, started it, by labelling Greenspan's policy "misguided" and saying it could easily "become more of a threat to our economy than inflation will ever be." Paul Sarbanes, of Maryland, the senior Democrat on the committee, followed up, describing a recent visit to a job-training program in Baltimore, where he had met a troubled youth who had just found his first job. "This young fellow, he's far removed from the wealth effect," Sarbanes said. "He's barely struggling to get into a job situation. Now, what's going to happen here?" Other senators began to grumble, too, and even Gramm ended up sounding a semi-critical note. "I think people hear what you are saying and conclude that you believe that equities are overvalued," he told Greenspan. "I would guess that equity values are not only not overvalued but may still be undervalued." The Fed chairman stared through thick spectacles, his hands clasped in front of him. Occasionally, he appeared to gulp for air, like a goldfish. At one point, he tried to engage Bunning, but he was quickly interrupted. "If we get prime interest rates at double digits, we are going to stop this economy in its tracks," the Kentucky Republican snapped. "I don't want to see that happen on your watch, and I surely don't want to see it happen on my watch." Greenspan realized it was hopeless. "I appreciate that, Senator," he said quietly. "I have the same view."

In the weeks following the hearing, as the stock markets shot up and down like a stunt plane with a drunken pilot in the cockpit, criticism of Greenspan spread to the media. The editorial pages of the *Times* and the *Wall Street Journal*, which usually agree on little, both questioned the Fed's logic in raising interest rates; John Crudele, whose financial column in the New York *Post* is widely read on Wall Street, went so far as to suggest that the Fed chairman should resign while the going was good. The attacks on Greenspan, who has been in his job since August, 1987, didn't go unnoticed. A couple of weeks ago, I ran into a senior Fed official with more than twenty years' experience and asked him to compare Greenspan's current situation with that of October, 1987, when the stock market crashed. "I think he is facing his greatest challenge now," the official said. "We are suggesting, as an institution, that the stock market is too high, and that we are going to rein in inflation that's not there yet. What he did in 1987 was important, but it was what you would expect a central banker to do—try to calm the markets and assure financial stability. This is much less straightforward." While I was considering that statement, the official added another variable to the equation: "We've lost Bob Rubin as Treasury Secretary, and Larry Summers"—Robert Rubin's replacement—"able man that he is, doesn't have the same credibility or experience. That leaves Alan with his hands on the wheel. He is really exposed."

Greenspan may be exposed, but he is also a survivor, perhaps the greatest survivor in all Washington. This past January, President Clinton nominated him for a fourth four-year term as Fed chairman. In length of service, Greenspan has now surpassed all his predecessors save two. Assuming he remains healthy—and he has never had a major illness—he will complete his fourth term at the start of 2004, when he will be seventy-seven. "He strikes me as being completely unfazed by critical editorials," Roger Ferguson, the Fed's vice-chairman, who has served alongside Greenspan for two and a half years, told me recently. "He is clearly a man who understands that he has been put in place by the President and Congress to execute a mission. Sometimes it will make him a cover boy and sometimes performing the role will get people saying things that aren't so positive." The veteran NBC News correspondent Andrea Mitchell, who has been married to Greenspan for three years, made a similar point when I spoke with her on the telephone a few weeks ago. "When he made the decision to accept renomination, which was a great honor, he knew that at that moment things were as good as one could imagine them being," Mitchell told me. Far from becoming disheartened by the criticism, Mitchell said, Greenspan thrives on it. "Other people would be daunted by the ups and downs, by the fact that you are only as good or bad as your last decision, that you can't ever rest on your track record. I would find that more than a little frightening. He finds it exhilarating."

"EXHILARATING" is not a word many people associate with Greenspan, but there is more to him than the lugubrious figure who appears on C-SPAN and CNBC. He was born on March 6, 1926, in New York City. His parents were both Jewish: Herbert Greenspan, a self-educated financier, and Rose Goldsmith, a fun-loving girl of seventeen who liked to sing and dance. Three years after Greenspan was born, Herbert and Rose divorced. Rose moved back in with her parents, in Washington Heights, and took a job in a furniture store across the Harlem River, in the Bronx. Greenspan was brought up as the only child of a single mother, to whom he remained devoted. (He called her practically every day at seven in the morning until her death, in 1995.) His cousin Wesley Halpert lived nearby, and the two boys would spend hours imitating Laurel and Hardy and playing ball. A few weeks ago, I visited Halpert, who, at seventy-six, is a busy dentist on the East Side. He turned out to be a tall, broad-shouldered man, with a full head of white hair, and the same calm presence and measured way of speaking as his famous cousin. After doing his last fillings

of the day, Halpert sat down and talked about Washington Heights before the
Second World War. Then, as now, it was a neighborhood of working-class immigrants and their children. Most of the immigrants had come from Europe,
rather than the Caribbean and Latin America, as is the case today, but the ethnic lines were just as sharp. "We were all afraid of the Irish kids," Halpert told
me. "One day, we were invaded by a bunch of them. Alan and I were playing
ball against a wall. They were all bigger and older than we were, and there
were a lot of them. They started tormenting us, and Alan sailed right into
them, his fists going like this"—the old man pumped his fists up and down like
a young Mike Tyson—"and we chased them away."

A photograph of Greenspan from his days at George Washington High
School, on West 192nd Street, shows a tall, loose-limbed youth, with dark
wavy hair, in an old-fashioned swimsuit. He didn't display much interest in his
studies except for arithmetic. "He knew all the baseball averages," Halpert recalled. "He loved numbers." Most kids in Washington Heights supported the
New York Giants, but Greenspan was a Brooklyn Dodgers fan. Music was another passion, which he inherited from his mother. At family gatherings,
Greenspan was a star attraction. His uncle, Halpert's father, would give him a
dime to sing the Depression song "Brother, Can You Spare a Dime?" "He'd sing
it in a lovely boy's voice," Halpert said. When Greenspan finished high school,
he applied to Juilliard and spent two years there, studying the saxophone and
the clarinet. In 1944, at the end of his sophomore year, he dropped out and decided to try to make some money by playing professionally.

It was the beginning of the bebop era. Jazz orchestras, featuring virtuosos
like Dizzy Gillespie, were starting to emerge; and some of the old swing bands
were forced to update themselves. One such outfit was the Henry Jerome Band,
which played regularly at the Childs restaurant in the Paramount Theatre
building, in Times Square. The band's manager, who also played in its horn
section, was a young law student named Leonard Garment—the same
Leonard Garment who went on to become President Nixon's counsel during
Watergate. Garment still recalls the day when Alan Greenspan showed up
at the Paramount. "He had exactly the same face, a slightly ironic, self-
measuring smile, very interior-oriented," Garment told me a few weeks ago. "I
played jazz tenor saxophone. Alan came into the band and played the other
tenor saxophone, and he also played the clarinet and the flute. He was very
good, very solid." Greenspan stayed with the band a year, during which time it
alternated between touring and playing in New York. Even on the road, he was
quiet and reserved. He put his interest in numbers to good use, assisting Henry
Jerome, the bandleader, with the bookkeeping, and aiding some of his fellow-
players with their income taxes, always a problem for itinerant musicians. In
other areas, too, he helped to keep his colleagues in line. Above the Childs
restaurant was a Walgreen drugstore that had a row of phone booths. Some of
the musicians used the booths to smoke marijuana, and the drugstore man-

ager would complain to Garment. When Garment didn't have time to retrieve the miscreants himself, he would dispatch his fellow tenor sax to do the job. "I'd say, 'Alan, could you get some of those guys down here? Tell them it's time to play and to stop smoking,' " Garment recalled.

Greenspan enjoyed the show-business life, but soon realized it wasn't a viable career. "I was a pretty good amateur musician, but I was average as a professional, and I was aware of that because you learn pretty quickly how good some professional musicians are," he told Steven Beckner, a journalist who wrote a book about Greenspan. "I realized it's innate. You either have it or you don't." During his time in the band, Greenspan had started reading books about business and finance, and he found them fascinating. In 1945, he quit and started taking classes at New York University's business school, which was then called the School of Commerce.

Back in the forties, N.Y.U. was not the vibrant, cosmopolitan institution it is now. The economics department, in particular, was known as a citadel of conservatism. Ludwig Von Mises, the Austrian scourge of socialism, taught there, as did Walter Spahr, the head of the National Committee to Return to the Gold Standard. Robert Kavesh, who went on to become a professor of economics at N.Y.U., was in the year behind Greenspan. "We met when I got out of the Navy, in 1946," Kavesh told me recently. "We spent a lot of time together at lunchtime. We would walk around Washington Square. Picture multitudes of former servicemen standing in the sunshine, and just a few women. That's how it was. Alan was always painfully shy, and I think it hurt him with the girls. Let's just say he wasn't too successful. He was a very quiet person. He was interested in most of the things people in their early twenties are interested in: he was interested in baseball; he was interested in girls; and he was also interested in economics, which was a very exciting subject in those days."

It was during one of Walter Spahr's antediluvian lectures that Kavesh noticed Greenspan ignoring the professor and reading "The Economics of John Maynard Keynes," by Dudley Dillard, one of the first books about the legendary British economist to be published in America. Keynes, whose theories were designed to justify active management of the economy by the government, was then anathema at N.Y.U., and at most other American universities, but Kavesh was not surprised to see his friend reading about him. "He was trying to absorb everything and every point of view," Kavesh told me. "He loved economics, and he loved those simple diagrams of savings and investment that really were the Keynesian contribution. We would talk, and he would get truly animated. He was not a from-birth conservative, not at all. In fact, it was presumed that everyone in our circle was a Democrat, because the role of government in economic life had been well established by the war, the financing of the war, and the ending of the Depression. We were truly all Keynesians." In 1948, Greenspan graduated summa cum laude, and although he received his master's from N.Y.U. two years later and also enrolled in night classes at Columbia, he showed little interest in pursuing an academic career. (He finally obtained his Ph.D., from N.Y.U., in 1977, after submitting a thesis on the stock market and investment which he had started working on more than twenty years previously.) "It was presumed if you studied economics seriously in those days that you would go on to be a teacher," Kavesh said. "There was a hierarchy. The highest level was to teach; second, to work for government; third, sully your hands in the business world. Alan chose the last approach."

GREENSPAN likes to remind people that he has been observing the United States economy on a daily basis for more than half a century. In 1948, he took a job with the National Industrial Conference Board, a New York research group financed by big corporations. One of the businessmen who called for advice about the economy was William Townsend, a veteran Wall Street bond trader. Townsend was impressed by Greenspan, and in 1953 he asked him to join his firm as a partner. The offer came with an annual salary of around six thousand dollars, not much money even then, but it was a partnership, and Greenspan accepted. The decision made his career. During the next two decades, he built Townsend-Greenspan & Company into a thriving economics consultancy, with a roster of corporate clients that included Alcoa, U.S. Steel, and J. P. Morgan. (Townsend died in 1958, but his young partner left his name on the door.)

From the beginning, Greenspan's approach to the economy was heavily empirical. Townsend-Greenspan analyzed the various economic statistics that emerged on a daily basis from the Commerce Department and other government agencies, then provided its clients with a judgment about what they implied for the future growth of the economy. Greenspan became an expert on the national income accounts, the complicated statistical framework that the government uses to calculate the gross domestic product, but he also studied the individual sectors that his clients operated in, such as steel and banking. "I was at various times a specialist in virtually every major industry and generally knowledgeable about the remainder," he told Lawrence B. Lindsey, who was a Fed governor from 1991 to 1997. "When you go through every industry over your lifetime, you should know how the system works."

In many ways, Greenspan's job hasn't changed much since the fifties. He is still paid to analyze economic trends and predict future developments. The difference is that, along with other members of the Federal Open Market Committee, which is the policymaking arm of the Federal Reserve System, he now gets to set interest rates, not merely analyze them. Every morning, Greenspan is picked up at his home, in Northwest Washington, by his official car, a black Mercury Grand Marquis, and driven to the Fed's headquarters, in Foggy Bottom. When he's not in meetings, Greenspan spends much of his time alone in a big, bright office overlooking Constitution Avenue, doing what he likes best:

studying and thinking. On average, he spends two or three hours each day doing his own economic research, and at least another two or three hours reading reports prepared by the Fed staff and others. A visitor to his office earlier this year discovered Greenspan knee-deep in economic statistics dating back to the nineteen-fifties. He explained that he was trying to revamp a forty-year-old mathematical model that Townsend-Greenspan had used to estimate the total realized capital gains on sales of existing homes. (The figure is significant to economists because people can use money they make from home sales to finance extra consumption.) Home sales aren't Greenspan's only research interest. Last year, he and Darrel Cohen, a staff economist at the Fed, published a paper in *The Review of Economics and Statistics* which detailed a new way to predict the total number of motor vehicles sold each year in the United States—surely the first time a Fed chairman has published a refereed academic paper while in office.

Greenspan's knowledge of the economy regularly surprises his colleagues. "I remember one instance when spring floods were making many of the bridges on the Mississippi River unusable," Lindsey wrote in a recent book, *Economic Puppetmasters*. "At the time of the weekly Board of Governors meeting, the U.S. economy was literally linked together by a single bridge. Greenspan not only knew the location of the bridge, but also the various reroutings that could be used to get merchandise there." Greenspan isn't just a fact gerbil. (Data by itself is vacuous, he often says.) Like all good economists, he looks at a wide range of numbers and then tries to find a conceptual structure that will explain them. "He's not a monetarist, he's not a Keynesian—he's himself," William McDonough, the president of the Federal Reserve Bank of New York, told me when I visited his office on Liberty Street a few weeks ago. "It's not just a tremendous interest in the data for its own sake but, rather, he draws conclusions from the data which are insightful and unique." Many economists rely on complex computer models to predict the future, but Greenspan has long been suspicious of such methods. Back in the sixties, Townsend-Greenspan acquired a new computer with a memory of sixteen kilobytes, which was then considered enormous, to use for economic forecasting. "We thought we could really pin down the business cycle," Greenspan told a meeting of business economists a few years back. Unfortunately, the economy didn't coöperate. "It moved. . . . It wigged when it should have wagged." Greenspan drew an unequivocal lesson from this experience. "That crazy economy out there doesn't stand still long enough for us to get a fix on it. . . . Our computer models are running at an accelerating pace, but the economy manages to keep that much ahead of us."

AS 1952 began, Greenspan had a good job, a duplex apartment in Forest Hills, which he shared with his mother, and a promising future. By the end of the year, his mother had moved out and been replaced by a wife, a pretty young painter named Joan Mitchell. Last month, I visited Joan Mitchell Blumenthal, as she is now called, at the East Side apartment she shares with her second husband, Allan Blumenthal, a psychiatrist. At the age of seventy, she is still strikingly attractive, with blond hair, blue eyes, and a reserved manner. She sat down in a leather armchair, quieted her toy poodle, pulled her knees up beneath her, and recounted meeting Greenspan, on a blind date organized by a friend, shortly after she moved to New York after graduating from U.C.L.A.: "The first date was lovely because during our first telephone conversation he laid out three things we could do. One of them was a sporting event, another was a Broadway show, and the third was a concert at Carnegie Hall involving some Bach. I said, 'Without a doubt, the concert at Carnegie Hall. I've been dying to go there all my life.' We went, and it was very enjoyable. We talked a great deal about music. He told me about the Henry Jerome Band and all that, and later, in fact, we went to the hotel where the band was playing, and I met the band members. They told me they knew Alan wouldn't stay with them forever because he was just too good at doing their taxes."

Mitchell Blumenthal found Greenspan smart, sweet, and charming. Following an eight-month courtship, they got married in a small ceremony at the Pierre Hotel; but after the wedding things didn't turn out as planned. "I can only tell you that it had nothing to do with respect for each other, or even fondness for each other, but a real difference over what we wanted out of life," Mitchell Blumenthal said. "I found life a little dull. I wanted to have fun; he wanted to play golf. I didn't want to live in Forest Hills; he did want to live in Forest Hills. It was like that." After living together for ten months, the couple separated amicably, and they still talk now and again. In the early fifties, the only ground for divorce in New York State was infidelity, and neither Greenspan nor Mitchell Blumenthal wanted that. "We found out that you could get an annulment much quicker and more cheaply than a divorce," Mitchell Blumenthal explained. "Which is why, I think, for a long time after he became famous people didn't know that he'd been married before."

The failure of the marriage left a lasting mark on Greenspan—it would be more than forty years before he remarried—but it was through Mitchell Blumenthal that he met a woman who became his close friend and intellectual mentor: Ayn Rand, the Russian-born novelist, libertarian, and libertine. A couple that Mitchell Blumenthal knew, Barbara and Nathaniel Branden, were friends of Rand in California. Shortly after Mitchell Blumenthal moved to New York, the Brandens and Rand did likewise. Rand, already famous for her 1943 novel, *The Fountainhead*, took an apartment on East Thirty-sixth Street, and continued work on *Atlas Shrugged*. Later, she moved to a larger apartment a couple of blocks south. Every Saturday night, she would invite a group of friends to her apartment to read and discuss her latest writings. (As ironic as ever, Rand later dubbed the right-wing reading group the Collective.) Mitchell

Blumenthal tried to interest Greenspan in the gatherings, but he didn't start attending regularly until after the two of them had split up. In *My Years with Ayn Rand*, a memoir published last year, Nathaniel Branden gives a memorable portrait of Greenspan as he appeared to Rand and her acolytes: "He was tall and solidly built, with black hair, dark horn-rim glasses, and a propensity for dark, funereal suits. At age twenty-six, he was somberness incarnate, looking chronically weary, resigned, and unhappy. Barbara, Ayn, Frank"—O'Connor, Rand's long-suffering husband—"and I once encountered him as he and Joan were coming out of an elevator. 'He looks like an undertaker,' Ayn commented."

Greenspan has never been shy about acknowledging his intellectual debt to Rand. "What she did—through long discussions and lots of arguments into the night—was to make me think why capitalism is not only efficient and practical, but also moral," he told a reporter from the *Times* in 1974. When Greenspan met Rand, he saw himself as a logical positivist, believing that all moral codes were arbitrary human constructs that cannot be verified. Rand regarded logical positivism as a dead end. In her controversial philosophy of objectivism, she argued that capitalism was innately superior to other socioeconomic systems, such as feudalism and socialism, because it was based on voluntary exchange on the part of rational, self-interested individuals. The laudatory descriptions of capitalism contained in the drafts of *Atlas Shrugged* struck the young Greenspan as inspired. "Ayn, this is *incredible*," he blurted out at one meeting described by Branden. "No one has ever dramatized what industrial achievement actually means as you have."

Rand, for her part, initially acted coolly towards the newest member of her coterie. "The trouble with A.G. is, he thinks Henry Luce is important," she said on one occasion. "Do you think Alan might basically be a social climber?" she inquired on another. Eventually, Rand was won over by the clarity of Greenspan's mind and the breadth of his knowledge. "It took a long time to impress that lady, but he did it, and in fact she once told me, some years later, that he was perhaps the most sensitive reader from a literary point of view that she'd ever had," Mitchell Blumenthal said. Rand and Greenspan became close, though, contrary to speculation, they never had a sexual relationship. (Rand did have young lovers, Nathaniel Branden among them.) As the years went by, many members of Rand's circle split from her in rancorous circumstances, but Greenspan continued to see her regularly until her death, in 1982. Even today, he speaks highly of Rand. "She did things in her personal life which I would not approve of, but ideas stand on their own," he said to one recent visitor. "What was a syllogism back then is a syllogism today."

When Robert Kavesh, Greenspan's college friend, returned to New York, in 1956, after getting his Ph.D. and teaching at Dartmouth, he was surprised to find Greenspan's "whole approach to economics changed" almost beyond recognition. "We were fast friends once again, but he was trying to sell me that

Ayn Rand philosophy with no success—not my stuff," Kavesh told me. "He had become a markets, markets, markets person: what you need is pure, unadulterated laissez-faire." In the early sixties, Greenspan contributed some economics articles to *The Objectivist Newsletter,* which to this day, make provocative reading. In one piece Greenspan attacked efforts by the government to restrain corporate monopolies, arguing that "the entire antitrust system must be opened for review"; in another he said that the welfare state, "stripped of its academic jargon . . . is nothing more than a mechanism by which governments confiscate the wealth of productive members of a society to support a wide variety of welfare schemes"; and in a third article, lambasting the very idea of government regulation, he maintained that capitalism "holds integrity and trustworthiness as cardinal virtues and makes them pay off in the marketplace, thus demanding that men survive by means of virtues, not of vices. It is this superlatively moral system that the welfare statists propose to improve upon by means of preventive law, snooping bureaucrats, and the chronic goad of fear."

QUOTES like these are hard to square with contemporary descriptions of Greenspan from his colleagues and friends. (Alice Rivlin, a Fed governor from June, 1996, to July, 1999: "He's not very ideological." Andrea Mitchell: "He is not doctrinaire." William McDonough: "Broad-gauged. He would have been the perfect P.P.E."—politics, philosophy, and economics—"candidate at Oxbridge.") One possible explanation for the difference between Greenspan circa 1960 and Greenspan circa 2000 is that his views have changed. "I think what's happened is that he has come to see that life is a little more complicated than Ayn Rand had pictured," Robert Kavesh said to me. "If you've ever read her stuff, there's black and white, there's good and evil, there's absolutism and relativism. Relativism is the worst thing you could be convicted of. I think Alan has come to realize that life is sort of gray in many respects." The problem with Kavesh's argument is that its subject doesn't agree with it. During a recent conversation with a fellow-economist, Greenspan insisted that his general view of how the world works has not changed much at all since the nineteen-fifties. He also warned his interlocutor to distinguish carefully between what he believes personally and how he acts as chairman of the Fed.

That was sound advice. In an idealized free market, of the type Rand rhapsodized about, there would be no need for a central bank, let alone active economic management of the type associated with Keynes and his followers. But Greenspan has not survived as long as he has in Washington by being perceived as a right-wing ideologue. On the contrary, he has cultivated an image as a pragmatic policymaker who is willing (and able) to work with people of all political stripes. A good example of this was his reaction to the Mexican financial crisis, which erupted in early 1995. With the Mexican government struggling to pay its debts, and billions of dollars of Wall Street money at risk, many of Greenspan's fellow-Republicans argued against a bailout, because it would only encourage investors to act equally rashly in the future—a problem known to economists as "moral hazard." Greenspan privately supported some of these arguments, but he nonetheless agreed, along with Treasury Secretary Robert Rubin and Lawrence Summers, who was then a Treasury under-secretary, to a rescue package for the Mexican government that included some nineteen billion dollars guaranteed by the United States. (All the money was later repaid, with interest.) "His view, which I think was right, was that what we did in Mexico had a moral-hazard aspect to it that was unattractive," Rubin told me recently when I visited his office at Citigroup, where he is now a senior executive. "On the other hand, life is very often a choice between unattractive alternatives, and the question is which is the least unattractive. His view there, and it was also Larry's view and my view, was that the moral-hazard aspect was a by-product of doing something else so important—avoiding Mexico going into default, with possible contagion effects—that you simply had to ac-cept the negative effect in order to get the greater good." Rubin tossed a small glass globe from hand to hand. "That's a mode of thinking that, unfortunately, is very hard for some people in Washington to relate to."

When the financial crisis spread to Asia, in the summer of 1997, Greenspan again rejected arguments that the United States government should do noth-ing. Together with Rubin and Summers, he encouraged Western and Japanese banks to roll over Korea's debts and helped persuade a reluctant Congress to approve a big increase in United States contributions to the International Mon-etary Fund; emergency loans worth tens of billions of dollars were extended to the stricken Asian countries, most of which are now enjoying economic recov-eries. According to Rubin, Greenspan's ability to work effectively with him and Summers depended on the willingness of all three to set ideology aside and focus on practicalities. "Larry and Alan are both very strong personalities, smart as hell, and they both have views. I have views, too," Rubin said. "Yet it worked out remarkably well, and it was very important. People don't realize how close we came to disaster. The whole system almost came off the rails."

The most striking example of Greenspan's intellectual flexibility was his will-ingness to keep interest rates low in the second half of the last decade. Until a few years ago, most economists, Greenspan included, believed the maximum rate at which the economy could expand without sparking an upturn in infla-tion was about two and a half percent a year. Between the fourth quarter of 1995 and the fourth quarter of 1999, the economy grew at an annual rate of more than four percent, but it was not until last June that the Fed raised inter-est rates, and even then it acted gradually. As a result of this permissiveness, all sorts of good things happened: wages of nonsupervisory workers jumped sig-nificantly, thereby spreading some of the spoils of prosperity; unemployment fell to levels not seen since 1970, and among blacks and Hispanics the jobless rate fell to all-time lows; and inflation, far from rising, as the old theories pre-dicted it should, fell. This upsurge in noninflationary growth was facilitated by economic troubles abroad and falling commodity prices, but the key factor at home was a doubling in the growth rate of productivity—the amount of out-put produced by each worker—to three and a half percent a year. Greenspan didn't engineer this transformation, but he was one of the first economists to recognize it as more than a temporary blip. As long ago as 1997, he had sug-gested that what was happening in the economy, with the proliferation of in-formation technology, and the Internet in particular, may turn out to be a "once or twice a century" occurrence. Under his leadership, the Fed allowed the productivity resurgence to take place, and did not interrupt it out of a fear that rapid economic growth would spark inflation, which a more hidebound central bank would have done. "I think that's his greatest achievement," William McDonough, the New York Fed president, who has been vice-chairman of the Federal Open Market Committee since August, 1993, told me. "Now, one can argue that it's been the F.O.M.C.'s greatest achievement, but the fact is Alan's been not only the chairman but the intellectual leader."

The Fed's policy of watchful inaction helped to sustain a virtuous circle in the economy. With interest rates low and consumers optimistic, American firms invested at record rates, especially in information technology. All this new investment paid off in higher productivity growth, which, in turn, led to increased profits, thereby encouraging firms to invest even more. This self-reinforcing process produced the longest economic expansion on record, but eventually it also presented Greenspan with an acute dilemma: Had it gone too far, producing an economy that was performing, in some ways, too well?

ONE day in 1966, Greenspan was walking along Broad Street, near his office, when he ran into Leonard Garment, whom he hadn't seen since the two of them played tenor sax in the Henry Jerome Band. Garment was now a success-ful Wall Street lawyer, and one of his legal partners was Richard Nixon, who had moved to New York from Los Angeles after losing the California governor's race in 1962. Garment saw himself as a Democrat, but he had become in-volved in the effort to launch a "new Nixon." Greenspan and he agreed to have lunch at the Bankers Club. There, Greenspan explained to Garment the finer points of financial futures, and Garment asked Greenspan if he would like to meet Nixon. "They met, and I sat with them for an hour or so, over lunch," Garment recalled. "Nixon was very interested. He made it clear to me that he wanted Greenspan to become involved." It wasn't the first occasion on which Greenspan had flirted with Presidential politics. Back in the early fifties, Arthur Burns, who had been Greenspan's mentor at Columbia, had offered him a job on the Council of Economic Advisers, which Burns headed during the first Eisenhower Administration. Greenspan decided against taking it. But now he agreed to join Nixon's policy team, which was based in New York, in a building on Park Avenue. For the following twenty years, he was to spend his time moving back and forth between Wall Street finance and Washington politics.

Greenspan's province extended well beyond economics, to areas such as housing, crime, and welfare. He even cranked up his office computer and developed a mathematical model of the electoral college, which was used for political strategizing. When Nixon defeated Hubert Humphrey, in 1968, he put Greenspan in charge of budget negotiations during the transition. Many observers thought Greenspan would end up as White House budget director, but he returned to Wall Street instead. "Nixon wanted Alan to come in—he could have had a substantial appointment," Martin Anderson, a fellow Ayn Rand enthusiast who was also a member of the policy team, told me last month from his office at the Hoover Institution, where he is a fellow. "He said no. He wanted to stay with his company." I asked Anderson about Greenspan's politics in those days. "His views were exactly the same as they are now. They haven't changed at all," he replied. "He's a Greenspan conservative, which means that on most issues he would be called a conservative Republican, but on some issues he wouldn't." A little-known example of the latter, Anderson went on, was Greenspan's role in the ending of the draft. After Nixon was elected, he set up a commission, under former Secretary of Defense Thomas Gates, Jr., to study the issue. Greenspan was appointed to the commission, and he argued for radical reform. When the commission's report was published, in 1970, it recommended an all-volunteer military, giving Nixon the political cover he needed to eventually end the draft.

In July, 1974, Herbert Stein, the chairman of the Council of Economic Advisers, resigned, and Greenspan was nominated to replace him. But Watergate was in full swing, and the nomination languished. By late summer, it seemed likely that Vice-President Gerald Ford would soon replace Nixon. Ford asked William Seidman, one of his senior aides, whether he should proceed with Greenspan's nomination. Seidman, who later headed the Federal Deposit Insurance Corporation and is now a commentator for CNBC, met Greenspan, and approved him. "I thought he was a good economist and a Republican economist, which there weren't a lot of in those days," Seidman said to me last month. "He assured me that he was pure economist and not politician. It turned out that he was a better politician than any of us thought." A couple of weeks before Nixon resigned, Greenspan went to see Ford. "We spent about an hour together, and, to be honest with you, I was very impressed with him," the former President told me when I called him at his office in Rancho Mirage, California, a couple of weeks ago. "I could tell he was very thoughtful. I just took an instant liking to him. It turned out to be a good judgment."

The Ford Administration soon found itself faced with the deepest recession since the thirties: inflation was high and unemployment was rising sharply. Some people in the White House were calling for big tax cuts to get the economy moving, but Greenspan opposed such a policy, on the ground that it would increase the budget deficit, which was already at a record level. The White House budget office put together two possible fiscal packages. Ford recalled for me the debates that followed: "Alan analyzed them and said, 'Look here, if you take the conservative one, you will be accused of being too tight-fisted, but in the long run, if you are reëlected, you will have good economic times in 1977, '78. On the other hand, if you take the more expansive choice you may get some good times in 1976, but if you are reëlected you will pay a penalty, because you will go through another economic downturn in 1977, '78.' I said to him, 'Well, what do you recommend?' He said, 'I think it would be wise to take the more conservative one, even though you'll probably get some politically unattractive statistical data in September or October, just before the election.' We took the conservative approach, and, sure enough, in October unemployment had a little upshot and things didn't look so encouraging." There was a pause on the line, then Ford continued. "I happen to think that was the major reason we lost the election. In November, if you go back and look at the records, the situation turned very optimistic." I asked Ford, who lost to Jimmy Carter by just two percent of the vote, whether he regretted following Greenspan's advice. "I have no regrets," he replied, his voice firm. "My conscience has always been clear. It was one of those gambles. It didn't turn out politically, but it was good for the country."

A quarter of a century after Greenspan's advice may have cost Ford his reëlection, the two are firm friends, and occasional golf partners. Ford, a keen player, told me that Greenspan, who swings left-handed, "isn't a bad golfer for a person who doesn't play very much." Greenspan has always respected Ford's honesty and integrity. He has told friends that, of the five Presidents he has dealt with, Ford was the one he felt closest to.

AFTER the 1976 election, Greenspan returned to Wall Street, but he continued to dabble in Republican politics. When Ronald Reagan became President, in 1981, he appointed Greenspan to his Economic Policy Advisory Board, a body of outside experts which also included Arthur Burns, Milton Friedman, George Shultz, William Simon, and Paul McCracken. As Martin Anderson, who at the time was Assistant to the President for Policy Development, tells it, Greenspan and the others played an important role in persuading Reagan to stick with his controversial policy of tax cuts despite the enormous budget deficits they produced. "After a few months went by, Don Regan"—the Treasury Secretary—"and David Stockman"—the budget director—"became very concerned about the growing deficit," Anderson told me. "They wanted to slow down the tax cut, delay it, stop it. So I would go out and call George Shultz, and he'd call a meeting, and all these guys would come in. They'd gather in the Roosevelt Room. The President would come in and wink at

Arthur Burns, tap Friedman on the shoulder, laugh with Alan Greenspan, and talk a bit. They were his old friends. They all sat there and told him two things: one, he was a terrific President; two, to continue what he was doing. It was the right thing to do. It was the only way to get out of the recession. Then they'd all leave, and we'd go back and start over again." Greenspan and his colleagues believed they were advocating big tax cuts matched by equally big spending cuts, but that was never a realistic possibility. The tax cuts went ahead, Congress refused to cut spending significantly, and the budget deficit exploded; by the time Greenspan became Fed chairman, in August of 1987, it was running at more than two hundred billion dollars a year.

Greenspan was nominated to the Fed post by President Reagan, who acted on the advice of his then Treasury Secretary, James Baker. Baker was yet another political heavyweight whom Greenspan had cultivated. His ability to impress influential people, although rarely remarked upon, is, in many ways, the key to his success. Anderson, who watched Greenspan work with two Presidents, puts it down to a combination of brains, common sense, and trustworthiness. "In Washington, that's golden," Anderson told me. "If you get someone who's smart, who recommends things that work, and who can be trusted, he'll stay forever. I don't care what party he's in." William Seidman, who worked with Greenspan during the Ford and Bush Administrations, offered a tarter explanation. "He has the best bedside manner I've ever seen," Seidman said. "He's very nonconfrontational, but also very good at persuading people. Part of his mystique, I think, is that he's hard to understand, but that also gives him a certain genius aspect."

It was Greenspan's cozy links with the rich and powerful which caused the most embarrassing incident of his career. In 1984, the New York law firm of Paul Weiss, Rifkind, Wharton & Garrison hired him to conduct a financial study of one of its clients, the fast-growing Lincoln Savings & Loan Association, of Irvine, California. Lincoln, which was owned by Charles Keating, Jr., an Arizona entrepreneur, wanted federal banking regulators to exempt it from a rule that limited the percentage of depositors' money it could channel into real-estate development and other direct investments. In February, 1985, Greenspan wrote a letter to the regulators in which he described Lincoln's management as "seasoned and expert in selecting and making direct investments," and praised it for having "restored the association to a vibrant and healthy state, with a strong net worth position." Lincoln didn't receive the exemption it wanted, but it continued to grow rapidly and to invest in risky areas. In April, 1989, it was taken over by the government at a cost to taxpayers of two billion dollars. "Of course I'm embarrassed by my failure to foresee what eventually transpired," Greenspan told the *Times* a few months after Lincoln went belly-up. "I was wrong about Lincoln. I was wrong about what they would ultimately do and the problems they would ultimately create."

Greenspan's links to Charles Keating were raised at his confirmation hearings in 1987, but more was made of his history as a Republican adviser. The men who created the Fed, in the years before the First World War, knew that capitalism and democracy were a combustible combination, one that could, all too easily, lead to inflationary spirals, speculative manias, and terrifying busts. The only way to remedy these problems, they believed, was to create an independent custodian of American capitalism, a prestigious individual who could be part umpire, part policeman, and part preacher.

The opportunity for Greenspan to prove his independence arrived quickly. Between March, 1988, and March, 1989, the Fed raised short-term interest rates from six and a half percent to almost ten percent, to head off inflation. The resultant recession didn't start until August 1990, and lasted less than a year, but as 1992 approached President Bush's economic advisers grew increasingly concerned that the Fed was not cutting interest rates quickly enough to insure a vigorous recovery. Nicholas Brady, the Treasury Secretary, was an old pal of Greenspan's from Wall Street, but that didn't prevent Brady from repeatedly calling for more interest-rate cuts. The friendship between Brady and Greenspan turned increasingly sour. At one point, Brady even cancelled his weekly lunches with the Fed chairman. After Bush's defeat, some Republicans blamed Greenspan for losing them the election. (Arguably, it was the second time he had cost the G.O.P. the White House.)

With Bill Clinton's arrival in the Oval Office, in 1993, relations between the Fed and the White House improved sharply. Part of it was personal chemistry: Greenspan was impressed by the new President's agile mind, which could pick up complicated economic concepts quickly, and by his willingness to adopt conservative financial policies. (Greenspan has told colleagues that he regards Clinton and Nixon as the two smartest Presidents he has dealt with.) Part of it was politics: the Clinton Administration, unlike its predecessor, made little attempt to bully the Fed. This was not accidental, as Robert Rubin, who headed the National Economic Council for the first two years of the Clinton Presidency, explained to me: "What happened in the past was that Presidents tended to get upset when whatever the Fed chairman was doing wasn't consistent with their purposes. This President had the good sense to recognize from the very beginning that by not trying, even verbally or rhetorically, to interfere with the activities of the Fed, he himself could gain credibility with respect to economic issues. And he was right." The Fed chairman resumed his weekly lunches with the Treasury Secretary, who was now Lloyd Bentsen. These meetings continued when Bentsen was succeeded, in 1994, by Rubin, and when Rubin was replaced, last year, by Larry Summers.

The entente cordiale between the White House and the Fed has been one of the distinguishing features of the Clinton Administration. Bob Woodward, in his 1994 book, *The Agenda,* suggested that Greenspan reached an agreement with the Clinton Administration, in which the Fed chairman promised to keep interest rates steady if the White House delivered a credible budget-reduction package. "Not true," Rubin said to me. What actually happened, Rubin went on, was that the President assumed that a substantial budget package would give the Fed more leeway to keep interest rates low, and this helped persuade him to adopt a strict fiscal policy. "But it was an assumption as opposed to a deal," Rubin insisted.

THE Marriner S. Eccles Federal Reserve Board Building, built in 1936, is an austere white marble box extending for an entire city block along Constitution Avenue between Twentieth Street and Twenty-first Street. Visitors pass through security on the C Street side and find themselves in a large open area dominated by Doric columns and a grand marble staircase. At the top of the staircase and through a hallway is the Fed's inner sanctum: a long corridor lined by the governors' offices and a large, ornate boardroom that was used during the Second World War for the Arcadia Conference, at which Roosevelt and Churchill mapped out the Allied campaign against Hitler.

Eight times a year, the boardroom houses a meeting of the Federal Open Market Committee. (The committee has twelve seats: seven are taken up by Fed governors appointed by the President; the five others rotate among the presidents of the twelve regional Reserve Banks. At the moment, two of the governors' seats are vacant.) The meetings begin with charts and a presentation by Michael Prell and Karen Johnson, the Fed's top staff economists. It is one of the Fed's many peculiarities that these officials are paid substantially more than the Fed chairman. (Prell earns about a hundred and seventy-five thousand dollars a year, Greenspan just over a hundred and forty-one thousand.) After Prell and Johnson, Greenspan goes around the table and asks each committee member for his or her opinion before stating his own. This process is not just ceremonial. There are seventeen people currently eligible to serve on the F.O.M.C., and thirteen have doctorates in economics. Greenspan is the undisputed leader all the same, and the other members are reluctant to vote against him. "He produces consensus in the same way other good leaders do: by listening extremely closely to what others have to say, by synthesizing that very well, and by sensing the broad middle," Roger Ferguson, the Fed's vice-chairman, told me. "Also, he clearly has a point of view about the economy. He presents it in speeches. He presents it privately as well."

The current debate within the F.O.M.C. is not whether to raise interest rates further but by how much. Greenspan, after playing the Randian hero, liberating the forces of Internet capitalism, has now reverted to the more traditional central banker's role of restraining a rampaging economy. Complicating his thinking is the stock market. In a now famous December, 1996, speech, he posed the question "How do we know when irrational exuberance has unduly escalated asset values?" The query wasn't purely rhetorical. For the next year or so, Greenspan and his staff studied the question, before concluding that it couldn't be answered sensibly. With no signposts to guide him, Greenspan decided that the Fed should stand aside and let the stock market find its own level. Whether or not the decision was soundly based—some observers, including me, have argued it wasn't—it proved unsustainable. Eventually, the rising stock market revved up the economy to such an extent that Greenspan could sit on his hands no longer.

He is now in the awkward position of arguing, simultaneously, that the Fed needs to restrain the economy; that the economy is zooming mainly because of the rising stock market; and that the Fed is not targeting stock prices. In principle, the three statements might be reconciled—although not easily. In practice, if Greenspan is determined to slow down the economy he will almost certainly have to keep raising interest rates until the stock market cracks (not merely shakes). He still believes it is impossible to determine with certainty when a healthy bull market turns into a speculative bubble, but he has also told colleagues that he now suspects that what is happening on Wall Street has elements of a bubble. He is particularly alarmed by the spread of computer day-trading, which he compares to casino gambling. In lighthearted moments, he has been heard to suggest that all day traders should be forced, before they start trading, to take an examination in which they are asked to identify the products of the companies that they intend to buy and sell.

With the Fed raising interest rates, the big question is whether the bubble will deflate gradually. History doesn't teach any simple lessons. In 1929 and 1987, Fed interest-rate hikes were followed, at some distance, by stock-market collapses. In Japan a decade ago, the central bank raised interest rates explicitly to burst a speculative bubble. There was no collapse, but a slow, inexorable decline in stock prices ensued. Greenspan is well aware that another stock-market crash is a real possibility, but that threat probably won't deter him from raising interest rates further if he believes it is necessary. To him, the Fed's primary duty is to keep the economy on a sustainable course of growth. He also believes that a Wall Street crash would not necessarily be such a bad thing for the economy, as long as the Fed acted wisely in its wake. "Remember the big one-day decline we had back in October 1987?" he asked Lawrence Lindsey. "Its impact on the economy was not all that great. Then, there was the severe decline in stock prices in Japan early in this decade. True, it took growth out of the system, but most of what they have experienced since is the result of an increasingly corrosive nonperforming loan problem. There's no guarantee that even if you get a 1929, you'll end up with a 1932."

GREENSPAN and Mitchell live in a renovated three-bedroom farmhouse, which Mitchell bought when she moved to the capital in 1976. Every day, Greenspan gets up around five-thirty and spends an hour or two sitting in the bath, reading and writing. These early-morning soaks have acquired near-mythical status, but they are real enough. Greenspan started taking them in the early seventies, after he injured his back. He discovered that the water helped his brain as well as his disks—he often says his I.Q. is fifteen points higher at five-thirty in the morning than it is at five-thirty in the afternoon—and many of his important speeches are conceived or reworked in the tub. "Things do get wet," Mitchell said to me. "I'm amazed that his staff is able to read his chicken scratches, one word bleeding into the next."

When Mitchell isn't out of town on assignment, she and Greenspan like to spend their evenings at home, often eating food prepared for them by their longtime housekeeper. Mitchell is something of a gourmet, but Greenspan likes plain food, such as grilled fish and vegetables. Occasionally, he drinks a glass of wine, but not often. The night before I spoke to Mitchell, they had eaten at home and Greenspan had watched the Baltimore Orioles in their first televised spring-training game. The couple had their first date in 1984, but Greenspan didn't get around to proposing until Christmas Day of 1996. Mitchell says the long courtship didn't bother her. "I knew he was committed to me, and that we planned to spend the rest of our lives together," she told me. Mitchell is fifty-three, twenty-one years younger than her husband, but she said that the age difference has never been a factor. "He's very boyish, he's athletic, and Alan's curiosity is such an important part of his makeup," she said. "He's wide open to possibilities."

Greenspan and Mitchell are regulars on the Washington social circuit, where their friends include Jim Lehrer, of *NewsHour,* and his wife, Kate, a novelist; the CNN anchor Judy Woodruff, and her husband, Al Hunt, of the *Wall Street Journal;* Katharine Graham, of the Washington *Post;* the former C.I.A. chief William Webster, and his wife, Lynda; and James Wolfensohn, the head of the World Bank, and his wife, Elaine. Webster is Greenspan's regular tennis partner at Chevy Chase Country Club. Last year, they made the semifinals in the seniors section but lost in a tiebreaker. The Wolfensohns own a house in Wyoming, which Greenspan and Mitchell visit every August when the Fed chairman has to go West for the Kansas City Reserve Bank's annual policy conference, in Jackson Hole. For Greenspan and Mitchell, as for many of their friends, work and play are usually intertwined. Their honeymoon was a weekend in Venice tacked on to a bankers' meeting in Basel, Switzerland, which Greenspan had to attend. When I asked Mitchell if she thought her husband had ever considered retirement, she laughed and said, "This is not a man who will ever retire. He is too alive and too interested. For an economist, he's got the best job imaginable."

A few weeks ago, I got an idea of what Mitchell meant when I went to a conference at Boston College, where Greenspan was a keynote speaker. As far as I could tell, practically every Massachusetts resident over forty with an annual salary of more than two hundred thousand dollars was in the audience. Edward Markey, a Massachusetts congressman, introduced Greenspan as the

"Babe Ruth of our economic policy." It happened to be the Fed chairman's seventy-fourth birthday, and before he started to speak a chocolate cake with six lighted candles was carried onto the stage. As Greenspan bowed his head to blow out the candles, Markey led the audience in a rousing chorus of "Happy Birthday, Mr. Chairman." When the singing was over, Greenspan ambled to a microphone and said, in his best Woody Allen manner, "If I'd known all of this was about to happen, I would have been on my way to San Francisco." After the laughter subsided, he reiterated his suspicion that "we are now living through a pivotal period in American economic history," in which the growing use of information technology was bringing about "dramatic changes in the way goods and services are produced and in the way they are distributed to final users."

The crowd gave Greenspan a standing ovation. But pivots can swing both ways. In 1929, the revered Fed chairman Roy A. Young saw his good name destroyed overnight by the Great Crash; in the early nineteen-seventies, Greenspan's old mentor Arthur Burns was similarly tarnished by the onset of stagflation. If Greenspan succeeds in slowing down the economy without provoking a recession, he will, surely, go down as one of the great Fed chairmen. If the speculative boom turns to bust, Greenspan will be held responsible for allowing it to get going in the first place. His current reputation will seem as overvalued as an Internet stock, and he will have to fend off angry investors— many of whom bought into his vision of a New Economy—just as he fought off those Irish toughs long ago on the streets of Washington Heights. Whatever happens, Greenspan will be remembered as the public face of American capitalism as it entered the Information Age, with all the world before it, and all challengers seemingly vanquished. For a true Randian, there could be no better fate.

APRIL 24, 2000

TRUMP SOLO

ONE morning last week, Donald Trump, who under routine circum-stances tolerates publicity no more grudgingly than an infant toler-ates a few daily feedings, sat in his office on the twenty-sixth floor of Trump Tower, his mood rather subdued. As could be expected, given the fact that his three-and-a-half-year-old marriage to Marla Maples was ending, paparazzi were staking out the exits of Trump Tower, while all weekend helicopters had been hovering over Mar-a-Lago, his private club in Palm Beach. And what would come of it? "I think the thing I'm worst at is managing the press," he said. "The thing I'm best at is business and conceiving. The press portrays me as a wild flamethrower. In actuality, I think I'm much different from that. I think I'm totally inaccurately portrayed."

So, though he'd agreed to a conversation at this decisive moment, it called for wariness, the usual quota of prefatory "off-the-record"s and then some. He wore a navy-blue suit, white shirt, black-onyx-and-gold links, and a crimson print necktie. Every strand of his interesting hair—its gravity-defying ducktails and dry pompadour, its telltale absence of gray—was where he wanted it to be. He was working his way through his daily gallon of Diet Coke and trying out a few diversionary maneuvers. Yes, it was true, the end of a marriage was a sad thing. Meanwhile, was I aware of what a success he'd had with the Nation's Parade, the Veterans Day celebration he'd been very supportive of back in 1995? Well, here was a little something he wanted to show me, a nice certifi-cate signed by both Joseph Orlando, president, and Harry Feinberg, secretary-treasurer, of the New York chapter of the 4th Armored Division Association, acknowledging Trump's participation as an associate grand marshal. A mil-lion four hundred thousand people had turned out for the celebration, he said, handing me some press clippings. "O.K., I see this story says a half million spectators. But, trust me, I heard a million four." Here was another clipping, from the *Times*, just the other day, confirming that rents on Fifth Avenue were the highest in the world. "And who owns more of Fifth Avenue than I do?" Or how about the new building across from the United Nations Secretariat, where he planned a "very luxurious hotel-condominium project, a major project." Who would finance it? "Any one of twenty-five different groups. They all want to finance it."

Months earlier, I'd asked Trump whom he customarily confided in during moments of tribulation. "Nobody," he said. "It's just not my thing"—a reply that didn't surprise me a bit. Salesmen, and Trump is nothing if not a brilliant salesman, specialize in simulated intimacy rather than the real thing. His modus operandi had a sharp focus: fly the flag, never budge from the premise that the universe revolves around you, and, above all, stay in character. The Trump tour de force—his evolution from rough-edged rich kid with Brooklyn and Queens political-clubhouse connections to an international name-brand commodity—remains, unmistakably, the most rewarding accomplishment of his ingenious career. The patented Trump palaver, a gaseous blather of "fantastic"s and "amazing"s and "terrific"s and "incredible"s and various synonyms for "biggest," is an indispensable ingredient of the name brand. In addition to connoting a certain quality of construction, service, and security—perhaps only Trump can explicate the meaningful distinctions between "super luxury" and "super super luxury"—his eponym subliminally suggests that a building *belongs* to him even after it's been sold off as condominiums.

Everywhere inside the Trump Organization headquarters, the walls were lined with framed magazine covers, each a shot of Trump or someone who looked an awful lot like him. The profusion of these images—of a man who possessed unusual skills, though not, evidently, a gene for irony—seemed the sum of his appetite for self-reflection. His unique talent—being "Trump" or, as he often referred to himself, "the Trumpster," looming ubiquitous by reducing himself to a persona—exempted him from introspection.

If the gossips hinted that he'd been cuckolded, they had it all wrong; untying the marital knot was based upon straightforward economics. He had a prenuptial agreement, because "if you're a person of wealth you have to have one." In the words of his attorney, Jay Goldberg, the agreement was "as solid as concrete." It would reportedly pay Marla a million dollars, plus some form of child support and alimony, and the time to do a deal was sooner rather than later. A year from now, she would become entitled to a percentage of his net worth. And, as a source *very close* to Trump made plain, "If it goes from a fixed amount to what could be a very enormous amount—even a small percentage of two and a half billion dollars or whatever is a lot of money—we're talking about very huge things. The numbers are much bigger than people understand."

The long-term matrimonial odds had never been terrifically auspicious.

What was Marla Maples, after all, but a tabloid cartoon of the Other Woman, an alliteration you could throw the cliché manual at: a leggy, curvaceous blond-bombshell beauty-pageant-winning actress-model-whatever? After a couple of years of deftly choreographed love spats, Donald and Marla produced a love child, whom they could not resist naming Tiffany. A few months before they went legit, Marla told a television interviewer that the contemplation of marriage tended to induce in Donald the occasional "little freak-out" or visit from the "fear monster." Her role, she explained, was "to work with him and help him get over that fear monster." Whenever they travelled, she said, she took along her wedding dress. ("Might as well. You've got to be prepared.") The ceremony, at the Plaza Hotel, right before Christmas, 1993, drew an audience of a thousand but, judging by the heavy turnout of Atlantic City high rollers, one not deemed A-list. The Trump Taj Mahal casino commemorated the occasion by issuing a Donald-and-Marla five-dollar gambling chip.

The last time around, splitting with Ivana, he'd lost the P.R. battle from the git-go. After falling an entire news cycle behind Ivana's spinmeisters, he never managed to catch up. In one ill-advised eruption, he told Liz Smith that his wife reminded him of his bête noire Leona Helmsley, and the columnist chided, "Shame on you, Donald! How dare you say that about the mother of your children?" His only moment of unadulterated, so to speak, gratification occurred when an acquaintance of Marla's blabbed about his swordsmanship. The screamer "BEST SEX I'VE EVER HAD"—an instant classic—is widely regarded as the most libel-proof headline ever published by the *Post*. On the surface, the coincidence of his first marital breakup with the fact that he owed a few billion he couldn't exactly pay back seemed extraordinarily unpropitious. In retrospect, his timing was *excellent*. Ivana had hoped to nullify a postnuptial agreement whose provenance could be traced to Donald's late friend and preceptor the lawyer-fixer and humanitarian Roy Cohn. Though the agreement entitled her to fourteen million dollars plus a forty-six-room house in Connecticut, she and her counsel decided to ask for half of everything Trump owned; extrapolating from Donald's blustery pronouncements over the years, they pegged her share at two and a half billion. In the end, she was forced to settle for the terms stipulated in the agreement because Donald, at that juncture, conveniently appeared to be broke.

Now, of course, according to Trump, things were much different. Business was stronger than ever. And, of course, he wanted to be fair to Marla. Only a million bucks? Hey, a deal was a deal. He meant "fair" in a larger sense: "I think it's very unfair to Marla, or, for that matter, anyone—while there are many positive things, like life style, which is at the highest level—I think it's unfair to Marla always to be subjected to somebody who enjoys his business and does it at a very high level and does it on a big scale. There are lots of compensating balances. You live in the Mar-a-Lagos of the world, you live in the best apartment. But, I think you understand, I don't have very much time. I just don't have very much time. There's nothing I can do about what I do other than stopping. And I just don't want to stop."

A SECURITIES analyst who has studied Trump's peregrinations for many years believes, "Deep down, he wants to be Madonna." In other words, to ask how the gods could have permitted Trump's resurrection is to mistake profound superficiality for profundity, performance art for serious drama. A prime example of superficiality at its most rewarding: the Trump International Hotel & Tower, a fifty-two-story hotel-condominium conversion of the former Gulf & Western Building, on Columbus Circle, which opened last January. The Trump name on the skyscraper belies the fact that his ownership is limited to his penthouse apartment and a stake in the hotel's restaurant and garage, which he received as part of his development fee. During the grand-opening ceremonies, however, such details seemed not to matter as he gave this assessment: "One of the great buildings anywhere in New York, anywhere in the world."

The festivities that day included a feng-shui ritual in the lobby, a gesture of respect to the building's high proportion of Asian buyers, who regard a Trump property as a good place to sink flight capital. An efficient schmoozer, Trump worked the room quickly—a backslap and a wink, a finger on the lapels, no more than a minute with anyone who wasn't a police commissioner, a district attorney, or a mayoral candidate—and then he was ready to go. His executive assistant, Norma Foerderer, and two other Trump Organization executives were waiting in a car to return to the office. Before it pulled away, he experienced a tug of noblesse oblige. "Hold on, just lemme say hello to these Kinney guys," he said, jumping out to greet a group of parking attendants. "Good job, fellas. You're gonna be working here for years to come." It was a quintessential Trumpian gesture, of the sort that explains his popularity among people who barely dare to dream of living in one of his creations.

Back at the office, a *Times* reporter, Michael Gordon, was on the line, calling from Moscow. Gordon had just interviewed a Russian artist named Zurab Tsereteli, a man with a sense of grandiosity familiar to Trump. Was it true, Gordon asked, that Tsereteli and Trump had discussed erecting on the Hudson River a statue of Christopher Columbus that was six feet taller than the Statue of Liberty?

"Yes, it's already been made, from what I understand," said Trump, who had met Tsereteli a couple of months earlier, in Moscow. "It's got forty million dollars' worth of bronze in it, and Zurab would like it to be at my West Side Yards development"—a seventy-five-acre tract called Riverside South—"and we are working toward that end."

According to Trump, the head had arrived in America, the rest of the body was still in Moscow, and the whole thing was being donated by the Russian government. "The mayor of Moscow has written a letter to Rudy Giuliani stating that they would like to make a gift of this great work by Zurab. It would be my honor if we could work it out with the City of New York. I am absolutely favorably disposed toward it. Zurab is a very unusual guy. This man is major and legit."

Trump hung up and said to me, "See what I do? All this bullshit. Know what? After shaking five thousand hands, I think I'll go wash mine."

Norma Foerderer, however, had some pressing business. A lecture agency in Canada was offering Trump a chance to give three speeches over three consecutive days, for seventy-five thousand dollars a pop. "Plus," she said, "they provide a private jet, secretarial services, and a weekend at a ski resort."

How did Trump feel about it?

"My attitude is if somebody's willing to pay me two hundred and twenty-five thousand dollars to make a speech, it seems stupid not to show up. You know why I'll do it? Because I don't think anyone's ever been paid that much."

Would it be fresh material?

"It'll be fresh to them."

Next item: Norma had drafted a letter to Mar-a-Lago members, inviting them to a dinner featuring a speech by George Pataki and entertainment by Marvin Hamlisch. "Oh, and speaking of the Governor, I just got a call. They're shooting a new 'I Love New York' video and they'd like Libby Pataki to go up and down our escalator. I said fine."

A Mar-a-Lago entertainment booker named Jim Grau called about a Carly Simon concert. Trump switched on his speakerphone: "Is she gonna do it?"

"Well, two things have to be done, Donald. No. 1, she'd like to hear from you. And, No. 2, she'd like to turn it in some degree into a benefit for Christopher Reeve."

"That's not a bad idea," said Trump. "Is Christopher Reeve gonna come? He can come down on my plane. So what do I have to do, call her?"

"I want to tell you how we got Carly on this because some of your friends are involved."

"Jim, I don't give a shit. Who the hell cares?"

"Please, Donald. Remember when you had your yacht up there? You had Rose Styron aboard. And her husband wrote *Sophie's Choice*. And it's through her good offices—"

"O.K. Good. So thank 'em and maybe invite 'em."

Click.

"Part of my problem," Trump said to me, "is that I have to do a lot of things myself. It takes so much time. Julio Iglesias is coming to Mar-a-Lago, but I have to *call* Julio, I have to have *lunch* with Julio. I have Pavarotti coming. Pavarotti doesn't perform for anybody. He's the highest-paid performer in the world. A million dollars a performance. The hardest guy to get. If I call him, he'll do it—for a *huge* amount less. Why? Because they like me, they respect me, I don't know."

• • •

DURING Trump's ascendancy, in the nineteen-eighties, the essence of his performance art—an opera-buffa parody of wealth—accounted for his populist appeal as well as for the opprobrium of those who regard with distaste the spectacle of an unbridled id. Delineating his commercial aesthetic, he once told an interviewer, "I have glitzy casinos because people expect it. . . . Glitz works in Atlantic City. . . . And in my residential buildings I sometimes use flash, which is a level below glitz." His first monument to himself, Trump Tower, on Fifth Avenue at Fifty-sixth Street, which opened its doors in 1984, possessed many genuinely impressive elements—a sixty-eight-story sawtoothed silhouette, a salmon-colored Italian-marble atrium equipped with an eighty-foot waterfall—and became an instant tourist attraction. In Atlantic City, the idea was to slather on as much ornamentation as possible, the goal being (a) to titillate with the fantasy that a Trump-like life was a lifelike life and (b) to distract from the fact that he'd lured you inside to pick your pocket.

At times, neither glitz nor flash could disguise financial reality. A story in the *Times* three months ago contained a reference to his past "brush with bankruptcy," and Trump, though gratified that the *Times* gave him play on the front page, took umbrage at that phrase. He "never went bankrupt," he wrote in a letter to the editor, nor did he "ever, at any time, come close." Having triumphed over adversity, Trump assumes the prerogative to write history.

In fact, by 1990, he was not only at risk, he was, by any rational standard, hugely in the red. Excessively friendly bankers infected with the promiscuous optimism that made the eighties so memorable and so forgettable had financed Trump's acquisitive impulses to the tune of three billion seven hundred and fifty million dollars. The personally guaranteed portion—almost a billion—represented the value of Trump's goodwill, putative creditworthiness, and capacity for shame. A debt restructuring began in the spring of 1990 and continued for several years. In the process, six hundred or seven hundred or perhaps eight hundred million of his creditors' dollars vaporized and drifted wherever lost money goes. In America, there is no such thing as a debtors' prison, nor is there a tidy moral to this story.

Several of Trump's trophies—the Plaza Hotel and all three Atlantic City casinos—were subjected to "prepackaged bankruptcy," an efficiency maneuver that is less costly than the full-blown thing. Because the New Jersey Casino Control Act requires "financial stability" for a gaming license, it seems hard to avoid the inference that Trump's Atlantic City holdings were in serious jeopardy. Nevertheless, "blip" is the alternative "b" word he prefers, as in "So the market, as you know, turns lousy and I have this blip."

Trump began plotting his comeback before the rest of the world—or, perhaps, even he—fully grasped the direness of his situation. In April of 1990, he announced to the *Wall Street Journal* a plan to sell certain assets and become the "king of cash," a stratagem that would supposedly set the stage for a shrewd campaign of bargain hunting. That same month, he drew down the final twenty-five million dollars of an unsecured hundred-million-dollar personal line of credit from Bankers Trust. Within seven weeks, he failed to deliver a forty-three-million-dollar payment due to bondholders of the Trump Castle Casino, and he also missed a thirty-million-dollar interest payment to one of the estimated hundred and fifty banks that were concerned about his well-being. An army of bankruptcy lawyers began camping out in various boardrooms.

Making the blip go away entailed, among other sacrifices, forfeiting management control of the Plaza and handing over the titles to the Trump Shuttle (the old Eastern Airlines Boston–New York–Washington route) and a twin-towered thirty-two-story condominium building near West Palm Beach, Florida. He also said goodbye to his two-hundred-and-eighty-two-foot yacht, the *Trump Princess,* and to his Boeing 727. Appraisers inventoried the contents of his Trump Tower homestead. Liens were attached to just about everything but his Brioni suits. Perhaps the ultimate indignity was having to agree to a personal spending cap of four hundred and fifty thousand dollars a month.

IT would have been tactically wise, to say nothing of tactful, if, as Trump's creditors wrote off large chunks of their portfolios, he could have curbed his breathtaking propensity for self-aggrandizement. The bravado diminished somewhat for a couple of years—largely because the press stopped paying attention—but by 1993 he was proclaiming, "This year has been the most successful year I've had in business." Every year since, he's issued the same news flash. A spate of Trump-comeback articles appeared in 1996, including several timed to coincide with his fiftieth birthday.

Then, last October, Trump came into possession of what a normal person would regard as real money. For a hundred and forty-two million dollars, he sold his half interest in the Grand Hyatt Hotel, on Forty-second Street, to the Pritzker family, of Chicago, his longtime, and long-estranged, partners in the property. Most of the proceeds weren't his to keep, but he walked away with more than twenty-five million dollars. The chief significance of the Grand Hyatt sale was that it enabled Trump to extinguish the remnants of his once monstrous personally guaranteed debt. When *Forbes* published its annual list of the four hundred richest Americans, he sneaked on (three hundred and seventy-third position) with an estimated net worth of four hundred and fifty million. Trump, meanwhile, had compiled his own unaudited appraisal, one he was willing to share along with the amusing caveat "I've never shown this to a reporter before." According to his calculations, he was actually worth two and a quarter billion dollars—*Forbes* had lowballed him by eighty percent. Still, he had officially rejoined the plutocracy, his first appearance since the blip.

Jay Goldberg, who in addition to handling Trump's matrimonial legal matters also represented him in the Grand Hyatt deal, told me that, after it closed, his client confessed that the novelty of being unencumbered had him lying awake nights. When I asked Trump about this, he said, "Leverage is an amazing phenomenon. I love leverage. Plus, I've never been a huge sleeper." Trump doesn't drink or smoke, claims he's never even had a cup of coffee. He functions, evidently, according to inverse logic and metabolism. What most people would find unpleasantly stimulating—owing vastly more than you should to lenders who, figuratively, at least, can carve you into small pieces—somehow engenders in him a soothing narcotic effect. That, in any event, is the impression Trump seeks to convey, though the point is now moot. Bankers, typically not the most perspicacious species on earth, from time to time get religion, and there aren't many who will soon be lining up to thrust fresh bazillions at him.

WHEN I met with Trump for the first time, several months ago, he set out to acquaint me with facts that, to his consternation, had remained stubbornly hidden from the public. Several times, he uttered the phrase "off the record, but you can use it." I understood the implication—I was his tool—but failed to see the purpose. "If you have me saying these things, even though they're true, I sound like a schmuck," he explained. How to account, then, for the bombast of the previous two decades? Alair Townsend, a former deputy mayor in the Koch administration, once quipped, "I wouldn't believe Donald Trump if his tongue were notarized." In time, this bon mot became misattributed to Leona Helmsley, who was only too happy to claim authorship. Last fall, after Evander Holyfield upset Mike Tyson in a heavyweight title fight, Trump snookered the *News* into reporting that he'd collected twenty million bucks by betting a million on the underdog. This prompted the *Post* to make calls to some Las Vegas bookies, who confirmed—shockingly!—that nobody had been handling that kind of action or laying odds close to 20–1. Trump never blinked, just moved on to the next bright idea.

"I don't think people know how big my business is," Trump told me. "Somehow, they know Trump the celebrity. But I'm the biggest developer in New York. And I'm the biggest there is in the casino business. And that's pretty good to be the biggest in both. So that's a lot of stuff." He talked about 40 Wall Street—"truly one of the most beautiful buildings in New York"—a seventy-two-story landmark that he was renovating. He said he owned the new Niketown store, tucked under Trump Tower; there was a deal to convert the Mayfair Hotel, at Sixty-fifth and Park, into "super-super-luxury apartments . . . but that's like a small one." He owned the land under the Ritz-Carlton, on Central Park South. ("That's a little thing. Nobody knows that I own that. In that way, I'm not really understood.") With CBS, he now owned the Miss U.S.A., Miss Teen U.S.A., and Miss Universe beauty pageants. He pointed to a stack of papers on his desk, closing documents for the Trump International Hotel & Tower. "Look at these contracts. I get these to sign every day. I've signed hundreds of these. Here's a contract for two-point-two million dollars. It's a building that isn't even opened yet. It's eighty-three percent sold, and nobody even knows it's there. For each contract, I need to sign twenty-two times, and if you think that's easy . . . You know, all the buyers want my signature. I had someone else who works for me signing, and at the closings the buyers got angry. I told myself, 'You know, these people are paying a million eight, a million seven, two million nine, four million one—for those kinds of numbers, I'll sign the fucking contract.' I understand. Fuck it. It's just more work."

As a real-estate impresario, Trump certainly has no peer. His assertion that he is the biggest real-estate *developer* in New York, however, presumes an elastic definition of that term. Several active developers—among them the Rudins, the Roses, the Milsteins—have added more residential and commercial space to the Manhattan market and have historically held on to what they built. When the outer boroughs figure in the tally—and if Donald isn't allowed to claim credit for the middle-income high-rise rental projects that generated the fortune amassed by his ninety-one-year-old father, Fred—he slips further in the rankings. But if one's standard of comparison is simply the number of buildings that bear the developer's name, Donald dominates the field. Trump's vaunted art of the deal has given way to the art of "image ownership." By appearing to exert control over assets that aren't necessarily his—at least not in ways that his pronouncements suggest—he exercises his real talent: using his name as a form of leverage. "It's German in derivation," he has said. "Nobody really knows where it came from. It's very unusual, but it just is a good name to have."

In the Trump International Hotel & Tower makeover, his role is, in effect, that of broker-promoter rather than risktaker. In 1993, the General Electric Pension Trust, which took over the building in a foreclosure, hired the Galbreath Company, an international real-estate management firm, to recommend how to salvage its mortgage on a nearly empty skyscraper that had an annoying tendency to sway in the wind. Along came Trump, proposing a three-way joint venture. G.E. would put up all the money—two hundred and seventy-five million dollars—and Trump and Galbreath would provide expertise. The market timing proved remarkably favorable. When Trump totted up the profits and calculated that his share came to more than forty million bucks, self-restraint eluded him, and he took out advertisements announcing "The Most Successful Condominium Tower Ever Built in the United States."

A minor specimen of his image ownership is his ballyhooed "half interest" in the Empire State Building, which he acquired in 1994. Trump's initial investment—not a dime—matches his apparent return thus far. His partners, the illegitimate daughter and disreputable son-in-law of an even more disreputable Japanese billionaire named Hideki Yokoi, seem to have paid forty million dollars for the building, though their title, even on a sunny day, is somewhat clouded. Under the terms of leases executed in 1961, the building is operated by a partnership controlled by Peter Malkin and the estate of the late Harry Helmsley. The lessees receive almost ninety million dollars a year from the building's tenants but are required to pay the lessors (Trump's partners) only about a million nine hundred thousand. Trump himself doesn't share in these proceeds, and the leases don't expire until 2076. Only if he can devise a way to break the leases will his "ownership" acquire any value. His strategy—suing the Malkin-Helmsley group for a hundred million dollars, alleging, among other things, that they've violated the leases by allowing the building to become a "rodent infested" commercial slum—has proved fruitless. In February, when an armed madman on the eighty-sixth-floor observation deck killed a sightseer and wounded six others before shooting himself, it seemed a foregone conclusion that Trump, ever vigilant, would exploit the tragedy, and he did not disappoint. "Leona Helmsley should be ashamed of herself," he told the *Post.*

One day, when I was in Trump's office, he took a phone call from an investment banker, an opaque conversation that, after he hung up, I asked him to elucidate.

"Whatever complicates the world more I do," he said.

Come again?

"It's always good to do things nice and complicated so that nobody can figure it out."

Case in point: The widely held perception is that Trump is the sole visionary and master builder of Riverside South, the mega-development planned for the former Penn Central Yards, on the West Side. Trump began pawing at the property in 1974, obtained a formal option in 1977, allowed it to lapse in 1979, and reëntered the picture in 1984, when Chase Manhattan lent him eighty-four million dollars for land-purchase and development expenses. In the years that followed, he trotted out several elephantine proposals, diverse and invariably overly dense residential and commercial mixtures. "Zoning for me is a life process," Trump told me. "Zoning is something I have done and ultimately always get because people appreciate what I'm asking for and they know it's going to be the highest quality." In fact, the consensus among the West Side neighbors who studied Trump's designs was that they did not appreciate what he was asking for. An exotically banal hundred-and-fifty-story phallus—"The World's Tallest Building"—provided the centerpiece of his most vilified scheme.

The oddest passage in this byzantine history began in the late eighties, when an assortment of high-minded civic groups united to oppose Trump, enlisted their own architects, and drafted a greatly scaled-back alternative plan. The civic groups hoped to persuade Chase Manhattan, which held Trump's mortgage, to help them entice a developer who could wrest the property from their nemesis. To their dismay, and sheepish amazement, they discovered that one developer was willing to pursue their design: Trump. Over time, the so-called "civic alternative" has become, in the public mind, thanks to Trump's drumbeating, *his* proposal; he has appropriated conceptual ownership.

Three years ago, a syndicate of Asian investors, led by Henry Cheng, of Hong

Kong's New World Development Company, assumed the task of arranging construction financing. This transaction altered Trump's involvement to a glorified form of sweat equity; for a fee paid by the investment syndicate, Trump Organization staff people would collaborate with a team from New World, monitoring the construction already under way and working on designs, zoning, and planning for the phases to come. Only when New World has recovered its investment, plus interest, will Trump begin to see any real profit—twenty-five years, at least, after he first cast his covetous eye at the Penn Central rail yards. According to Trump's unaudited net-worth statement, which identifies Riverside South as "Trump Boulevard," he "owns 30–50% of the project, depending on performance." This "ownership," however, is a potential profit share rather than actual equity. Six hundred million dollars is the value Trump imputes to this highly provisional asset.

OF course, the "comeback" Trump is much the same as the Trump of the eighties; there is no "new" Trump, just as there was never a "new" Nixon. Rather, all along there have been several Trumps: the hyperbole addict who prevaricates for fun and profit; the knowledgeable builder whose associates profess awe at his attention to detail; the narcissist whose self-absorption doesn't account for his dead-on ability to exploit other people's weaknesses; the perpetual seventeen-year-old who lives in a zero-sum world of winners and "total losers," loyal friends and "complete scumbags"; the insatiable publicity hound who courts the press on a daily basis and, when he doesn't like what he reads, attacks the messengers as "human garbage"; the chairman and largest stockholder of a billion-dollar public corporation who seems unable to resist heralding overly optimistic earnings projections, which then fail to materialize, thereby eroding the value of his investment—in sum, a fellow both slippery and naïve, artfully calculating and recklessly heedless of consequences.

Trump's most caustic detractors in New York real-estate circles disparage him as "a casino operator in New Jersey," as if to say, "He's not really even one of us." Such derision is rooted in resentment that his rescue from oblivion—his strategy for remaining the marketable real-estate commodity "Trump"— hinged upon his ability to pump cash out of Atlantic City. The Trump image is nowhere more concentrated than in Atlantic City, and it is there, of late, that the Trump alchemy—transforming other people's money into his own wealth—has been most strenuously tested.

To bail himself out with the banks, Trump converted his casinos to public ownership, despite the fact that the constraints inherent in answering to shareholders do not come to him naturally. Inside the Trump Organization, for instance, there is talk of "the Donald factor," the three to five dollars per share that Wall Street presumably discounts Trump Hotels & Casino Resorts by allowing for his braggadocio and unpredictability. The initial public offering, in

June, 1995, raised a hundred and forty million dollars, at fourteen dollars a share. Less than a year later, a secondary offering, at thirty-one dollars per share, brought in an additional three hundred and eighty million dollars. Trump's personal stake in the company now stands at close to forty percent. As chairman, Donald had an excellent year in 1996, drawing a million-dollar salary, another million for miscellaneous "services," and a bonus of five million. As a shareholder, however, he did considerably less well. A year ago, the stock traded at thirty-five dollars; it now sells for around ten.

Notwithstanding Trump's insistence that things have never been better, Trump Hotels & Casino Resorts has to cope with several thorny liabilities, starting with a junk-bond debt load of a billion seven hundred million dollars. In 1996, the company's losses amounted to three dollars and twenty-seven cents per share—attributable, in part, to extraordinary expenses but also to the fact that the Atlantic City gaming industry has all but stopped growing. And, most glaringly, there was the burden of the Trump Castle, which experienced a ten-per-cent revenue decline, the worst of any casino in Atlantic City.

Last October, the Castle, a heavily leveraged consistent money loser that had been wholly owned by Trump, was bought into Trump Hotels, a transaction that gave him five million eight hundred and thirty-seven thousand shares of stock. Within two weeks—helped along by a reduced earnings estimate from a leading analyst—the stock price, which had been eroding since the spring, began to slide more precipitously, triggering a shareholder lawsuit that accused Trump of self-dealing and a "gross breach of his fiduciary duties." At which point he began looking for a partner. The deal Trump came up with called for Colony Capital, a sharp real-estate outfit from Los Angeles, to buy fifty-one percent of the Castle for a price that seemed to vindicate the terms under which he'd unloaded it on the public company. Closer inspection revealed, however, that Colony's capital injection would give it high-yield preferred, rather than common, stock—in other words, less an investment than a loan. Trump-l'oeil: Instead of trying to persuade the world that he owned something that wasn't his, he was trying to convey the impression that he would part with an onerous asset that, as a practical matter, he would still be stuck with. In any event, in March the entire deal fell apart. Trump, in character, claimed that he, not Colony, had called it off.

The short-term attempt to solve the Castle's problems is a four-million-dollar cosmetic overhaul. This so-called "re-theming" will culminate in June, when the casino acquires a new name: Trump Marina. One day this winter, I accompanied Trump when he buzzed into Atlantic City for a re-theming meeting with Nicholas Ribis, the president and chief executive officer of Trump Hotels, and several Castle executives. The discussion ranged from the size of the lettering on the outside of the building to the sparkling gray granite in the lobby to potential future renderings, including a version with an as yet unbuilt hotel tower and a permanently docked yacht to be called *Miss Universe.* Why the boat? "It's just an attraction," Trump said. "You understand, this would be part of a phase-two or phase-three expansion. It's going to be the largest yacht in the world."

From the re-theming meeting, we headed for the casino, and along the way Trump received warm salutations. A white-haired woman wearing a pink warmup suit and carrying a bucket of quarters said, "Mr. Trump, I just love you, darling." He replied, "Thank you. I love you, too," then turned to me and said, "You see, they're good people. And I like people. You've gotta be nice. They're like friends."

The Castle had two thousand two hundred and thirty-nine slot machines, including, in a far corner, thirteen brand-new and slightly terrifying *Wheel of Fortune*–theme contraptions, which were about to be officially unveiled. On hand were representatives of International Game Technology (the machines' manufacturer), a press entourage worthy of a military briefing in the wake of a Grenada-calibre invasion, and a couple of hundred onlookers—all drawn by the prospect of a personal appearance by Vanna White, the doyenne of *Wheel of Fortune*. Trump's arrival generated satisfying expressions of awe from the rubberneckers, though not the spontaneous burst of applause that greeted Vanna, who had been conscripted for what was described as "the ceremonial first pull."

When Trump spoke, he told the gathering, "This is the beginning of a new generation of machine." Vanna pulled the crank, but the crush of reporters made it impossible to tell what was going on or even what denomination of currency had been sacrificed. The demographics of the crowd suggested that the most efficient machine would be one that permitted direct deposit of a Social Security check. After a delay that featured a digital musical cacophony, the machine spat back a few coins. Trump said, "Ladies and gentlemen, it took a little while. We hope it doesn't take you as long. And we just want to thank you for being our friends." And then we were out of there. "This is what we do. What can I tell you?" Trump said, as we made our way through the casino.

Vanna White was scheduled to join us for the helicopter flight back to New York, and later, as we swung over Long Island City, heading for a heliport on the East Side, Trump gave Vanna a little hug and, not for the first time, praised her star turn at the Castle. "For the opening of thirteen slot machines, I'd say we did all right today," he said, and then they slapped high fives.

IN a 1990 *Playboy* interview, Trump said that the yacht, the glitzy casinos, the gleaming bronze of Trump Tower were all "props for the show," adding that "the show is 'Trump' and it is sold-out performances everywhere." In 1985, the show moved to Palm Beach. For ten million dollars, Trump bought Mar-a-Lago, a hundred-and-eighteen-room Hispano-Moorish-Venetian castle built in the twenties by Marjorie Merriweather Post and E. F. Hutton, set on seventeen and a half acres extending from the ocean to Lake Worth. Ever since, his meticulous restoration and literal regilding of the property have been a work in progress. The winter of 1995–96 was Mar-a-Lago's first full season as a commercial venture, a private club with a twenty-five-thousand-dollar initiation fee (which later rose to fifty thousand and is now quoted at seventy-five thousand). The combination of the Post-Hutton pedigree and Trump's stewardship offered a paradigm of how an aggressively enterprising devotion to Good Taste inevitably transmutes to Bad Taste—but might nevertheless pay for itself.

Only Trump and certain of his minions know who among Mar-a-Lago's more than three hundred listed members has actually forked over initiation fees and who's paid how much for the privilege. Across the years, there have been routine leaks by a mysterious unnamed spokesman within the Trump Organization to the effect that this or that member of the British Royal Family was planning to buy a pied-à-terre in Trump Tower. It therefore came as no surprise when, during early recruiting efforts at Mar-a-Lago, Trump announced that the Prince and Princess of Wales, their mutual antipathy notwithstanding, had signed up. Was there any documentation? Well, um, Chuck and Di were *honorary* members. Among the honorary members who have yet to pass through Mar-a-Lago's portals are Henry Kissinger and Elizabeth Taylor.

The most direct but not exactly most serene way to travel to Mar-a-Lago, I discovered one weekend not long ago, is aboard Trump's 727, the same aircraft he gave up during the blip and, after an almost decent interval, bought back. My fellow-passengers included Eric Javits, a lawyer and nephew of the late Senator Jacob Javits, bumming a ride; Ghislaine Maxwell, the daughter of the late publishing tycoon and inadequate swimmer Robert Maxwell, also bumming a ride; Matthew Calamari, a telephone-booth-size bodyguard who is the head of security for the entire Trump Organization; and Eric Trump, Donald's thirteen-year-old son.

The solid-gold fixtures and hardware (sinks, seat-belt clasps, door hinges, screws), well-stocked bar and larder, queen-size bed, and bidet (easily outfitted with a leather-cushioned cover in case of sudden turbulence) implied hedonistic possibilities—the plane often ferried high rollers to Atlantic City—but I witnessed only good clean fun. We hadn't been airborne long when Trump decided to watch a movie. He'd brought along *Michael,* a recent release, but twenty minutes after popping it into the VCR he got bored and switched to an old favorite, a Jean Claude Van Damme slugfest called *Bloodsport,* which he pronounced "an incredible, fantastic movie." By assigning to his son the task of fast-forwarding through all the plot exposition—Trump's goal being "to get this two-hour movie down to forty-five minutes"—he eliminated any lulls between the nose hammering, kidney tenderizing, and shin whacking. When a beefy bad guy who was about to squish a normal-sized good guy received a crippling blow to the scrotum, I laughed. "Admit it, you're laughing!" Trump shouted. "You want to write that Donald Trump was loving this ridiculous

Jean Claude Van Damme movie, but are you willing to put in there that you were loving it, too?"

A small convoy of limousines greeted us on the runway in Palm Beach, and during the ten-minute drive to Mar-a-Lago Trump waxed enthusiastic about a "spectacular, world-class" golf course he was planning to build on county-owned land directly opposite the airport. Trump, by the way, is a skilled golfer. A source extremely close to him—by which I mean off the record, but I can use it—told me that Claude Harmon, a former winner of the Masters tournament and for thirty-three years the club pro at Winged Foot, in Mamaroneck, New York, once described Donald as "the best weekend player" he'd ever seen.

The only formal event on Trump's agenda had already got under way. Annually, the publisher of *Forbes* invites eleven corporate potentates to Florida, where they spend a couple of nights aboard the company yacht, the *Highlander*, and, during the day, adroitly palpate each other's brains and size up each other's short games. A supplementary group of capital-gains-tax skeptics had been invited to a Friday-night banquet in the Mar-a-Lago ballroom. Trump arrived between the roast-duck appetizer and the roasted-portabello-mushroom salad and took his seat next to Malcolm S. (Steve) Forbes, Jr., the erstwhile Presidential candidate and the chief executive of *Forbes*, at a table that also included *les grands fromages* of Hertz, Merrill Lynch, the C.I.T. Group, and Countrywide Credit Industries. At an adjacent table, Marla Maples Trump, who had just returned from Shreveport, Louisiana, where she was rehearsing her role as co-host of the Miss U.S.A. pageant, discussed global politics and the sleeping habits of three-year-old Tiffany with the corporate chiefs and chief spouses of A.T. & T., Sprint, and Office Depot. During coffee, Donald assured everyone present that they were "very special" to him, that he wanted them to think of Mar-a-Lago as home, and that they were all welcome to drop by the spa the next day for a freebie.

Tony Senecal, a former mayor of Martinsburg, West Virginia, who now doubles as Trump's butler and Mar-a-Lago's resident historian, told me, "Some of the restoration work that's being done here is so subtle it's almost not Trump-like." Subtlety, however, is not the dominant motif. Weary from handling Trump's legal work, Jay Goldberg used to retreat with his wife to Mar-a-Lago for a week each year. Never mind the tapestries, murals, frescoes, winged statuary, life-size portrait of Trump (titled "The Visionary"), bathtub-size flower-filled samovars, vaulted Corinthian colonnade, thirty-four-foot ceilings, blinding chandeliers, marquetry, overstuffed and gold-leaf-stamped everything else, Goldberg told me; what nudged him around the bend was a small piece of fruit.

"We were surrounded by a staff of twenty people," he said, "including a footman. I didn't even know what that was. I thought maybe a chiropodist. Anyway, wherever I turned there was always a bowl of fresh fruit. So there I am, in our room, and I decide to step into the bathroom to take a leak. And on the way

I grab a kumquat and eat it. Well, by the time I come out of the bathroom the *kumquat has been replaced.*"

As for the Mar-a-Lago spa, aerobic exercise is an activity Trump indulges in "as little as possible," and he's therefore chosen not to micromanage its daily affairs. Instead, he brought in a Texas outfit called the Greenhouse Spa, proven specialists in mud wraps, manual lymphatic drainage, reflexology, shiatsu and Hawaiian hot-rock massage, loofah polishes, sea-salt rubs, aromatherapy, acupuncture, peat baths, and Japanese steeping-tub protocol. Evidently, Trump's philosophy of wellness is rooted in a belief that prolonged exposure to exceptionally attractive young female spa attendants will instill in the male clientele a will to live. Accordingly, he limits his role to a pocket veto of key hiring decisions. While giving me a tour of the main exercise room, where Tony Bennett, who does a couple of gigs at Mar-a-Lago each season and has been designated an "artist-in-residence," was taking a brisk walk on a treadmill, Trump introduced me to "our resident physician, Dr. Ginger Lea Southall"—a recent chiropractic-college graduate. As Dr. Ginger, out of earshot, manipulated the sore back of a grateful member, I asked Trump where she had done her training. "I'm not sure," he said. "Baywatch Medical School? Does that sound right? I'll tell you the truth. Once I saw Dr. Ginger's photograph, I didn't really need to look at her résumé or anyone else's. Are you asking, 'Did we hire her because she'd trained at Mount Sinai for fifteen years?' The answer is no. And I'll tell you why: because by the time she's spent fifteen years at Mount Sinai, we don't want to look at her."

MY visit happened to coincide with the coldest weather of the winter, and this gave me a convenient excuse, at frequent intervals, to retreat to my thousand-dollar-a-night suite and huddle under the bedcovers in fetal position. Which is where I was around ten-thirty Saturday night, when I got a call from Tony Senecal, summoning me to the ballroom. The furnishings had been altered since the *Forbes* banquet the previous evening. Now there was just a row of armchairs in the center of the room and a couple of low tables, an arrangement that meant Donald and Marla were getting ready for a late dinner in front of the TV. They'd already been out to a movie with Eric and Tiffany and some friends and bodyguards, and now a theatre-size screen had descended from the ceiling so that they could watch a pay-per-view telecast of a junior-welterweight-championship boxing match between Oscar de la Hoya and Miguel Angel Gonzalez.

Marla was eating something green, while Donald had ordered his favorite, meat loaf and mashed potatoes. "We have a chef who makes the greatest meat loaf in the world," he said. "It's so great I told him to put it on the menu. So whenever we have it, half the people order it. But then afterward, if you ask them what they ate, they always deny it."

Trump is not only a boxing fan but an occasional promoter, and big bouts are regularly staged at his hotels in Atlantic City. Whenever he shows up in person, he drops by to wish the fighters luck beforehand and is always accorded a warm welcome, with the exception of a chilly reception not long ago from the idiosyncratic Polish head-butter and rabbit-puncher Andrew Golota. This was just before Golota went out and pounded Riddick Bowe into retirement, only to get himself disqualified for a series of low blows that would've been perfectly legal in *Bloodsport*.

"Golota's a killer," Trump said admiringly. "A stone-cold killer."

When I asked Marla how she felt about boxing, she said, "I enjoy it a lot, just as long as nobody gets hurt."

WHEN a call came a while back from Aleksandr Ivanovich Lebed, the retired general, amateur boxer, and restless pretender to the Presidency of Russia, explaining that he was headed to New York and wanted to arrange a meeting, Trump was pleased but not surprised. The list of superpower leaders and geopolitical strategists with whom Trump has engaged in frank and fruitful exchanges of viewpoints includes Mikhail Gorbachev, Richard Nixon, Jimmy Carter, Ronald Reagan, George Bush, former Secretary of Defense William Perry, and the entire Joint Chiefs of Staff. (He's also pals with Sylvester Stallone and Clint Eastwood, men's men who enjoy international reputations for racking up massive body counts.) In 1987, fresh from his grandest public-relations coup—repairing in three and a half months, under budget and for no fee, the Wollman skating rink, in Central Park, a job that the city of New York had spent six years and twelve million dollars bungling—Trump contemplated how, in a larger sphere, he could advertise himself as a doer and dealmaker. One stunt involved orchestrating an "invitation" from the federal government to examine the Williamsburg Bridge, which was falling apart. Trump had no real interest in the job, but by putting on a hard hat and taking a stroll on the bridge for the cameras he stoked the fantasy that he could rebuild the city's entire infrastructure. From there it was only a short leap to saving the planet. What if, say, a troublemaker like Muammar Qaddafi got his hands on a nuclear arsenal? Well, Trump declared, he stood ready to work with the leaders of the then Soviet Union to coördinate a formula for coping with Armageddon-minded lunatics.

The clear purpose of Lebed's trip to America, an unofficial visit that coincided with the second Clinton Inaugural, was to add some reassuring human texture to his image as a plainspoken tough guy. Simultaneously, his domestic political prospects could be enhanced if voters back home got the message that Western capitalists felt comfortable with him. Somewhere in Lebed's calculations was the understanding that, to the nouveau entrepreneurs of the freebooter's paradise that is now Russia, Trump looked and smelled like very old money.

Their rendezvous was scheduled for midmorning. Having enlisted as an interpreter Inga Bogutska, a receptionist whose father, by coincidence, was a Russian general, Trump decided to greet his visitor in the lobby. When it turned out that Lebed, en route from an audience with a group of *Times* editors and reporters, was running late, Trump occupied himself by practicing his golf swing and surveying the female pedestrians in the atrium. Finally, Lebed arrived, a middle-aged but ageless fellow with a weathered, fleshy face and hooded eyes, wearing a gray business suit and an impassive expression. After posing for a *Times* photographer, they rode an elevator to the twenty-sixth floor, and along the way Trump asked, "So, how is everything in New York?"

"Well, it's hard to give an assessment, but I think it is brilliant," Lebed replied. He had a deep, bullfroggy voice, and his entourage of a half-dozen men included an interpreter, who rendered Inga Bogutska superfluous.

"Yes, it's been doing very well," Trump agreed. "New York is on a very strong up. And we've been reading a lot of great things about this gentleman and his country."

Inside his office, Trump immediately began sharing with Lebed some of his treasured possessions. "This is a shoe that was given to me by Shaquille O'Neal," he said. "Basketball. *Shaquille O'Neal.* Seven feet three inches, I guess. This is his sneaker, the actual sneaker. In fact, he gave this to me after a game."

"I've always said," Lebed sagely observed, "that after size 45, which I wear, then you start wearing trunks on your feet."

"That's true," said Trump. He moved on to a replica of a Mike Tyson heavyweight-championship belt, followed by an Evander Holyfield glove. "He gave me this on my fiftieth birthday. And then he beat Tyson. I didn't know who to root for. And then, again, here is Shaquille O'Neal's shirt. Here, you might want to see this. This was part of an advertisement for Versace, the fashion designer. These are photographs of Madonna on the stairs at Mar-a-Lago, my house in Florida. And this photograph shows something that we just finished and are very proud of. It's a big hotel called Trump International. And it's been very successful. So we've had a lot of fun."

Trump introduced Lebed to Howard Lorber, who had accompanied him a few months earlier on his journey to Moscow, where they looked at properties to which the Trump moniker might be appended. "Howard has major investments in Russia," he told Lebed, but when Lorber itemized various ventures none seemed to ring a bell.

"See, they don't know you," Trump told Lorber. "With all that investment, they don't know you. Trump they know."

Some "poisonous people" at the *Times,* Lebed informed Trump, were "spreading some funny rumors that you are going to cram Moscow with casinos."

Laughing, Trump said, "Is that right?"

"I told them that I know you build skyscrapers in New York. High-quality skyscrapers."

"We are actually looking at something in Moscow right now, and it would be skyscrapers and hotels, not casinos. Only quality stuff. But thank you for defending me. I'll soon be going again to Moscow. We're looking at the Moskva Hotel. We're also looking at the Rossiya. That's a very big project; I think it's the largest hotel in the world. And we're working with the local government, the mayor of Moscow and the mayor's people. So far, they've been very responsive."

Lebed: "You must be a very confident person. You are building straight into the center."

Trump: "I always go into the center."

Lebed: "I hope I'm not offending by saying this, but I think you are a litmus testing paper. You are at the end of the edge. If Trump goes to Moscow, I think America will follow. So I consider these projects of yours to be very important. And I'd like to help you as best I can in putting your projects into life. I want to create a canal or riverbed for capital flow. I want to minimize the risks and get rid of situations where the entrepreneur has to try to hide his head between his shoulders. I told the New York *Times* I was talking to you because you are a professional—a high-level professional—and if you invest, you invest in real stuff. Serious, high-quality projects. And you deal with serious people. And I deem you to be a very serious person. That's why I'm meeting you."

Trump: "Well, that's very nice. Thank you very much. I have something for you. This is a little token of my respect. I hope you like it. This is a book called *The Art of the Deal,* which a lot of people have read. And if you read this book you'll know the art of the deal better than I do."

The conversation turned to Lebed's lunch arrangements and travel logistics—"It's very tiring to meet so many people," he confessed—and the dialogue began to feel stilted, as if Trump's limitations as a Kremlinologist had exhausted the potential topics. There was, however, one more subject he wanted to cover.

"Now, you were a boxer, right?" he said. "We have a lot of big matches at my hotels. We just had a match between Riddick Bowe and Andrew Golota, from Poland, who won the fight but was disqualified. He's actually a great fighter if he can ever get through a match without being disqualified. And, to me, you look tougher than Andrew Golota."

In response, Lebed pressed an index finger to his nose, or what was left of it, and flattened it against his face.

"You do look seriously tough," Trump continued. "Were you an Olympic boxer?"

"No, I had a rather modest career."

"Really? The newspapers said you had a great career."

"At a certain point, my company leader put the question straight: either you do the sports or you do the military service. And I selected the military."

"You made the right decision," Trump agreed, as if putting to rest any notion he might have entertained about promoting a Lebed exhibition bout in Atlantic City.

Norma Foerderer came in with a camera to snap a few shots for the Trump archives and to congratulate the general for his fancy footwork in Chechnya. Phone numbers were exchanged, and Lebed, before departing, offered Trump a benediction: "You leave on the earth a very good trace for centuries. We're all mortal, but the things you build will stay forever. You've already proven wrong the assertion that the higher the attic, the more trash there is."

When Trump returned from escorting Lebed to the elevator, I asked him his impressions.

"First of all, you wouldn't want to play nuclear weapons with this fucker," he said. "Does he look as tough and cold as you've ever seen? This is not like your average real-estate guy who's rough and mean. This guy's beyond that. You see it in the eyes. This guy is a killer. How about when I asked, 'Were you a boxer?' Whoa—that nose is a piece of rubber. But me he liked. When we went out to the elevator, he was grabbing me, holding me, he felt very good. And he liked what I do. You know what? I think I did a good job for the country today."

The phone rang—Jesse Jackson calling about some office space Trump had promised to help the Rainbow Coalition lease at 40 Wall Street. ("Hello, Jesse. How ya doin'? You were on Rosie's show? She's terrific, right? Yeah, I think she is. . . . Okay-y-y, how are *you*?") Trump hung up, sat forward, his eyebrows arched, smiling a smile that contained equal measures of surprise and self-satisfaction. "You gotta say, I cover the gamut. Does the kid cover the gamut? Boy, it never ends. I mean, people have no idea. Cool life. You know, it's sort of a cool life."

ONE Saturday this winter, Trump and I had an appointment at Trump Tower. After I'd waited ten minutes, the concierge directed me to the penthouse. When I emerged from the elevator, there Donald stood, wearing a black cashmere topcoat, navy suit, blue-and-white pin-striped shirt, and maroon necktie. "I thought you might like to see my apartment," he said, and as I squinted against the glare of gilt and mirrors in the entrance corridor he added, "I don't really do this." That we both knew this to be a transparent fib—photo spreads of the fifty-three-room triplex and its rooftop park had appeared in several magazines, and it had been featured on *Lifestyles of the Rich and Famous*— in no way undermined my enjoyment of the visual and aural assault that followed: the twenty-nine-foot-high living room with its erupting fountain and vaulted ceiling decorated with neo-Romantic frescoes; the two-story dining room with its carved ivory frieze ("I admit that the ivory's kind of a no-no"); the onyx columns with marble capitals that had come from "a castle in Italy"; the chandelier that originally hung in "a castle in Austria"; the African blue-onyx lavatory. As we admired the view of Central Park, to the north, he said, "This is the greatest apartment ever built. There's never been anything like it. There's no apartment like this anywhere. It was harder to build this apartment than the rest of the building. A lot of it I did just to see if it could be done. All the very wealthy people who think they know great apartments come here and they say, 'Donald, forget it. This is the greatest.' " Very few touches suggested that real people actually lived there—where was it, exactly, that Trump sat around in his boxers, eating roast-beef sandwiches, channel surfing, and scratching where it itched? Where was it that Marla threw her jogging clothes?—but no matter. "Come here, I'll show you how life works," he said, and we turned a couple of corners and wound up in a sitting room that had a Renoir on one wall and a view that extended beyond the Statue of Liberty. "My apartments that face the Park go for twice as much as the apartments that face south. But I consider *this* view to be more beautiful than *that* view, especially at night. As a cityscape, it can't be beat."

We then drove down to 40 Wall Street, where members of a German television crew were waiting for Trump to show them around. ("This will be the finest office building anywhere in New York. Not just downtown—anywhere in New York.") Along the way, we stopped for a light at Forty-second Street and First Avenue. The driver of a panel truck in the next lane began waving, then rolled down his window and burbled, "I never see you in person!" He was fortyish, wore a blue watch cap, and spoke with a Hispanic inflection. "But I see you a lot on TV."

"Good," said Trump. "Thank you. I think."

"Where's Marla?"

"She's in Louisiana, getting ready to host the Miss U.S.A. pageant. You better watch it. O.K.?"

"O.K., I promise," said the man in the truck. "Have a nice day, Mr. Trump. And have a *profitable* day."

"Always."

Later, Trump said to me, "You want to know what total recognition is? I'll tell you how you know you've got it. When the Nigerians on the street corners who don't speak a word of English, who have no clue, who're selling watches for some guy in New Jersey—when you walk by and those guys say, 'Trump! Trump!' That's total recognition."

Next, we headed north, to Mount Kisco, in Westchester County—specifically to Seven Springs, a fifty-five-room limestone-and-granite Georgian splendor completed in 1917 by Eugene Meyer, the father of Katharine Graham. If things proceeded according to plan, within a year and a half the house would become the centerpiece of the Trump Mansion at Seven Springs, a golf club where anyone willing to part with two hundred and fifty thousand dollars could tee up. As we approached, Trump made certain I paid attention to the walls lining the driveway. "Look at the quality of this granite. Because I'm like, you know, into quality. Look at the quality of that wall. Hand-carved granite, and the same with the house." Entering a room where two men were replastering a ceiling, Trump exulted, "We've got the pros here! You don't see too many plasterers anymore. I take a union plasterer from New York and bring him up here. You know why? Because he's the best." We canvassed the upper floors and then the basement, where Trump sized up the bowling alley as a potential spa. "This is very much Mar-a-Lago all over again," he said. "A great building, great land, great location. Then the question is what to do with it."

From the rear terrace, Trump mapped out some holes of the golf course: an elevated tee above a par three, across a ravine filled with laurel and dogwood; a couple of parallel par fours above the slope that led to a reservoir. Then he turned to me and said, "I bought this whole thing for seven and a half million dollars. People ask, 'How'd you do that?' I said, 'I don't know.' Does that make sense?" Not really, nor did his next utterance: "You know, nobody's ever seen a granite house before."

Granite? Nobody? Never? In the history of humankind? Impressive.

A few months ago, Marla Maples Trump, with a straight face, told an interviewer about life with hubby: "He really has the desire to have me be more of the traditional wife. He definitely wants his dinner promptly served at seven. And if he's home at six-thirty it should be ready by six-thirty." Oh well, so much for that.

In Trump's office the other morning, I asked whether, in light of his domestic shuffle, he planned to change his living arrangements. He smiled for the first time that day and said, "Where am I going to live? That might be the most difficult question you've asked so far. I want to finish the work on my apartment at Trump International. That should take a few months, maybe two, maybe six. And then I think I'll live there for maybe six months. Let's just say, for a period of time. The buildings always work better when I'm living there."

What about the Trump Tower apartment? Would that sit empty?

"Well, I wouldn't sell that. And, of course, there's no one who would ever build an apartment like that. The penthouse at Trump International isn't nearly as big. It's maybe seven thousand square feet. But it's got a living room that is the most spectacular residential room in New York. A twenty-five-foot ceiling. I'm telling you, the best room anywhere. Do you understand?"

I think I did: the only apartment with a better view than the best apartment in the world was the same apartment. Except for the one across the Park, which had the most spectacular living room in the world. No one had ever seen a granite house before. And, most important, every square inch belonged to Trump, who had aspired to and achieved the ultimate luxury, an existence unmolested by the rumbling of a soul. "Trump"—a fellow with universal recognition but with a suspicion that an interior life was an intolerable inconvenience, a creature everywhere and nowhere, uniquely capable of inhabiting it all at once, all alone.

MAY 19, 1997

HARD CORE

THE more Bill Gates dwelled on his problems with the government, the more agitated he became and the more one could sense his anger in public appearances and in private conversation. The government had pursued his company, Microsoft, since 1990, beginning with what at first seemed a routine Federal Trade Commission investigation, but that pursuit escalated in 1997, when the Department of Justice began one of the largest antitrust actions in United States history. It was, Gates told me recently, as if the government were announcing, "O.K., we'll show that we can take some blood out of these boys!"

Gates had little comfort in knowing that Microsoft, which he co-founded in 1975, had bested the competition, including such giants as I.B.M.; or that its software served as the essential code controlling more than three-quarters of all personal computers; or that his company, unlike such stock-market favorites as Amazon.com, enjoyed astonishing profit margins of nearly forty cents on each revenue dollar and its stock price had made it the world's most valued corporation. Despite being the richest man on the planet—last month, his net worth was estimated at a hundred billion dollars—Gates nevertheless believed that he was a victim. The United States government had become a menace unlike any he had encountered in the business world.

Gates felt that the government was trying to dictate to him how to run his company—telling him that he had to alter contracts with computer manufacturers and Internet companies, and asserting that for Microsoft to include its own Internet browser, Internet Explorer, in its Windows software was an illegal use of monopoly power. Gates's response was: Didn't the package make computing simpler? Didn't consumers benefit because the extra features were free? How dare anyone demand that Microsoft either untie this package or include a rival browser, like Netscape. Would the government tell Coca-Cola to include a can of Pepsi in every six-pack?

Within the company, Gates and most of his senior staff were implacable. They invoked a phrase, "hard core," to describe both their stance and their corporate culture. To be hard core was to be a believer, a gladiator who preferred combat to compromise. They might wear T-shirts and baggy shorts to work, and play soccer on the grass of their two-hundred-and-ninety-five-acre corporate campus, in Redmond, Washington, but Microsoft executives were tough. They would hold rallies in Redmond at which Steve Ballmer, now the company president, pumped up the troops by leading them in a war whoop, screaming for victory.

For a time, peace between Microsoft and the government seemed possible. In 1994, both sides signed a consent decree that placed a few curbs on the company. But in 1995 the Justice Department challenged Microsoft's proposed acquisition of Intuit, the dominant financial-software company, and in October of 1997 Justice filed a petition claiming that Microsoft had deliberately violated the consent decree. This started the legal machinery that led, in 1998, to the extraordinary antitrust suit against Microsoft.

Nevertheless, Gates's legal staff often assured him that Microsoft would overcome this obstacle. William H. Neukom, his longtime general counsel at Microsoft, told him that the law was its shield; and Gates, who is the son of an attorney, embraced the belief that the law, like science, relied upon pristine facts. Yet Gates also knew that politics could sway the law. So he fretted; and he became apoplectic when federal judge Thomas Penfield Jackson, in December of 1997, issued an order to stop Microsoft from "bundling," or including its Internet Explorer with its Windows operating system—a decision that Microsoft immediately appealed, saying that removing the browser would cripple the operating system. "He just ordered it!" Gates told me months later, still incredulous.

BY the time Gates appeared as a speaker at the annual gathering of the World Economic Forum, in Davos, Switzerland, in late January of 1998, his public-relations handlers were surrounding him as if he were a heavyweight champion making his way to the ring. At a media lunch, I found myself seated next to Gates at a table for ten that included his wife, Melinda French Gates; several editors; and the chairman and C.E.O. of Coca-Cola, M. Douglas Ivester. Gates has never liked small talk. He turned to me and complained about a panel I'd moderated a few days before. He said I had allowed enemies of Microsoft to bully his chief technology officer, Nathan Myhrvold. (Myhrvold had more than held his own in the exchange.) Gates sat huddled over, his arms folded across his chest; his brown hair was unparted, unwashed, and combed straight down and into bangs, like a little boy's. He rocked gently back and forth in his chair, his eyes fixed on the floor. His manner was gruff, and he seemed unwilling (or unable) to camouflage his rage. Melinda Gates tried discreetly to get his attention, but he would not look up. Then he suddenly declared, "Neither Nathan nor anyone else from Microsoft will ever appear again on such a panel!"

When Gates was introduced, as the luncheon speaker, a moment later, he refastened his C.E.O. mask and spoke calmly for about twenty minutes, offering a compelling exegesis on the future of computing and the alarming speed of change. He responded easily to questions from reporters about Microsoft's legal woes. I asked Gates what he had to say to those who believe that Microsoft has behaved arrogantly, as if the government had no right to ask questions.

Gates plunged into a five-minute tirade, which was memorable less for what he said than for the raw hurt he betrayed. Reporters whispered, "What's bugging him?" After taking several more questions, he returned to the table and, hovering above me, bellowed, "What do you mean, 'arrogant'?" Ivester's eyes bulged, as if to say, This is not how Fortune 500 C.E.O.s behave! Melinda Gates looked stricken.

"Remember when you said neither Nathan nor anyone else from Microsoft would appear on a panel again?" I said. "That was arrogant."

"What do you expect me to do? Order Nathan to appear?" Gates asked.

"No. But if he won't appear, you appear. This is a democracy, and people have a right to ask questions."

Just as suddenly, the belligerent Gates was transformed into a vulnerable adolescent. "What should I do?" he asked plaintively. Everyone at the table fell silent.

OVER the next several months, stories about Microsoft's alleged tactics appeared in the press. It was said that several years earlier senior Microsoft executives had offered an alliance with Netscape and also an infusion of capital to the company if it would abandon most of the browser market to Microsoft, and that one Microsoft executive reportedly had threatened to cut off its "air supply" if it refused. It was said that Microsoft had forbidden Compaq Computer to drop the Internet Explorer icon that appeared on computer screens—the desktop—when the machine was turned on; otherwise, Gates & Company would refuse to sell its Windows 95 operating system to the P.C. maker. In March of 1998, Gates was summoned to testify before the Senate Judiciary Committee, and there he reluctantly admitted that Microsoft's contracts with certain Internet service or content providers precluded them from promoting Netscape. Such behavior might qualify as the "restraint of trade" forbidden by antitrust laws.

When it began to seem likely that the government would launch an antitrust suit, a Microsoft team, led by Bill Neukom, met in April and May with the Justice Department in an attempt to head it off. Gates himself had an audience with Assistant Attorney General Joel I. Klein, who was the chief of the Antitrust Division, to explain Microsoft's position. The two met in the late afternoon of May 5th, at the Washington office of Sullivan & Cromwell, the

Wall Street law firm that has done much of Microsoft's outside legal work for the past decade. Gates was "very passionate, very forceful," alternately informative and irate, a government official who was there recalls. "He began with a presentation of his plans for Windows. . . . It was reasonably civil. When questions were raised, however, he grew angry, condescending, snide, and petulant."

Justice officials argued that Microsoft's power was impregnable because consumers were so dependent on Windows. Gates exclaimed, "You give me any seat at the table"—he mentioned Linux, an upstart operating system, and Java, a computer language created by Sun Microsystems, a Microsoft foe—"and I can blow away Microsoft!" If his competitors had half a brain, he was suggesting, Microsoft would be toast. Gates told me later that he was also trying to say something else: "Where did this 'monopoly' come from? Do I own all the diskettes in the country? . . . It's such a silly proposition to think that in an intellectual-property area you don't have massive competition. There is nothing that Microsoft has that guarantees its position."

Most of the government officials were surprised. Normally, when a target of a lawsuit asks for a meeting the target is solicitous. They saw in Gates a swagger that announced, in the words of one Justice official, "I'm the toughest kid on the block." Neukom told me that Gates was trying to seek common ground, but that he "was frustrated that the government seemed to have such a vague understanding of our technology." Government officials, Neukom recalled, kept asking why Microsoft needed certain features included in the operating system, and Gates kept warning that the government should not be in the software-design business.

This meeting was followed by a great many telephone calls and by ten days of negotiations, all aimed at a possible settlement. "They put on the table Thursday morning"—May 14th—"something that could have been, for the first time, significant," Klein recalled. Klein thought that he heard Microsoft signal a willingness to include a Netscape icon on every copy of the desktop. Perhaps, both Klein and Neukom hoped, the gap between them had narrowed. Gates recalled, "We said, 'O.K., we'll at least sit and listen.' "

Gates later told me that the Justice Department had been so vague, so "open-ended" in its demands, that "anybody could be part of Windows"; it was as if Microsoft were to be the mule for the entire software industry. Neukom kept recalling what had happened to Sears after 1977, when it signed a consent order stipulating that it would encourage competition by not opening stores in malls; then malls redefined shopping. By late Saturday morning, May 16th, they had reached an impasse.

THE following Monday, Klein, accompanied by Attorney General Janet Reno, announced that, on behalf of the United States government and joined by attorneys general representing twenty states and the District of Columbia, he was charging Microsoft with breaking the law in two essential ways. First, it had employed illegal tactics to crush or coerce competitors and sometimes allies, thus harming consumers—a key test of antitrust law. And, second, the government claimed that it had violated antitrust laws in an attempt to preserve its Windows monopoly and use it to dominate new markets.

Competitors applauded, although more than a few were torn between a fear of Microsoft and a distaste for government meddling. "I don't think there's much doubt as to the facts," said Eric Schmidt, the chairman and C.E.O. of Novell, a software competitor and a sometime Microsoft partner. "There is a very large question about what to do about it. I don't think anyone's in favor of a Department of Microsoft Management." Scott McNealy, the C.E.O. of Sun Microsystems, welcomed the government's lawsuit, because, he told me, he feared that, if left unchecked, Microsoft could use its dominance over operating systems to "leverage into other businesses." McNealy speaks of Gates as an unstoppable force who will ruthlessly smash all competitors, yet then declares that new technology has "the shelf life of a banana."

Gates was heartened in June of 1998 when the federal Court of Appeals overturned Judge Jackson's December order for Microsoft to separate its browser from Windows. Jackson, the higher court ruled, had "erred procedurally" by issuing an injunction before Microsoft was allowed to challenge it, and had erred "substantively" by acting as if judges should try to "oversee product design." Instead of being harmed, the court said, consumers benefitted from a free, easy-to-use browser that was integrated. Nevertheless, Gates himself remained distraught. He did not, he told me in an E-mail exchange, "expect competitors to try and use the government to help them get an advantage over us." He went on, "You are welcome to say I was naïve about this." He was shocked that his government had sued and that it kept broadening the charges. He saw himself as demonized, a point he emphasized both publicly and privately. Friends compared him to Joseph K. in Kafka's novel *The Trial*—a man charged with vague crimes he does not comprehend. On the eve of his own trial, Gates moaned to friends, "This isn't justice!"

II–"A GREAT TRIAL"

AN antitrust trial is rarely a courtroom drama, with climactic moments when witnesses suddenly shrivel and break down. It depends on the accretion of relevant fact piled on irrelevant fact. "I don't think you generally get a smoking gun in antitrust cases," said Judge Thomas Hogan, who was appointed to the district court in 1982. In most of the cases he has presided over, including his 1997 ruling that a merger between Staples and Office Depot would harm consumers, "you have to weigh all the facts," but it comes down to "certain key facts" from among all the competing claims. Inevitably, the credibility of the witnesses helps a judge sort out what to believe.

The Microsoft trial, which began last October and, barring settlement, may not yield a definitive ruling for several years, is of historic import. George L. Priest, the John M. Olin Professor of Law and Economics at the Yale Law School, cited only two other trials "that have been of this calibre": the 1911 Standard Oil case, and the Socony-Vacuum Oil case, in 1940. "There have been very few where the imagination of the country is caught up in the outcome of the trial," Priest said. "This ranks with one of the great antitrust cases in the history of the Sherman Act."

The roots of antitrust law go back almost four centuries, to English common-law cases aimed at curbing monopolies. In this country, just after the Civil War, state governments began to sue companies that rigged prices and choked competition. Then, in 1888, Presidential platforms of both political parties attacked wicked corporate "trusts," and over the next several decades two pieces of national legislation were enacted that remain the cornerstones of antitrust law. The first was the Sherman Act, of 1890, whose words, such as these in Section 1, appear deceptively simple:

Every contract, combination in the form of trust or otherwise, or conspiracy, in restraint of trade or commerce among the several States, or with foreign nations, is declared to be illegal.

Section 2 says:

Every person who shall monopolize, or attempt to monopolize, or combine or conspire with any other person or persons, to monopolize any part of the trade or commerce among the several States . . . shall be deemed guilty of a felony.

The Clayton Antitrust Act, of 1914, allows injured citizens or corporations to file lawsuits against antitrust violators, and a later amendment, the Robinson-Patman Act, bans price discrimination where the effect "may be substantially to lessen competition or tend to create a monopoly."

The complex task of proving that Microsoft and Gates violated these laws fell to the government's chief trial counsel, David Boies, a man who does not use a P.C. Except for a few years in the late seventies, when he was chief counsel to Edward Kennedy's Senate Judiciary Committee, Boies had been in private practice his entire professional life. In some thirty years at Cravath, Swaine & Moore, he has appeared in court on behalf of clients such as I.B.M., in its successful thirteen-year battle to block a government claim that it was an illegal monopoly, and the Federal Deposit Insurance Corporation, in its case against Michael Milken, winning a $1.1-billion judgment.

Boies, whose father taught high-school history in the northern Illinois farm community of Marengo, studied law at Northwestern, then at Yale, and once earned extra money by playing in bridge tournaments, where his uncanny memory gave him an advantage. After Yale, where he ranked second in his class, he was recruited by Cravath, which he left in 1997 to establish a boutique law practice with an old friend, Jonathan Schiller.

JOEL KLEIN recruited Boies to the Justice Department in December of 1997. "He's been through the I.B.M. wars," Klein told me. "I didn't want to get stuck in some quagmire. You need someone who knows how to move a case." Boies's usual fee exceeds six hundred dollars an hour, but the government was paying less than a tenth of that. (At Cravath, Boies's annual pay package amounted to two million dollars.) Nevertheless, Boies is not terribly righteous about his public service; indeed, he concedes that he might have represented Microsoft if it had asked first. "I certainly didn't think Microsoft was an evil empire," he said. "Nor do I think so now." Boies was interested in taking the case not least because he was in the arena and might help define whether static antitrust laws should apply to fast-changing technology companies. "I had a view that the antitrust laws applied to the software industry. I did not have a view as to whether Microsoft's conduct was or was not a violation of the antitrust laws. I did have the view that it was not entitled to a blanket pass."

One of the ironies of the case, said William Kovacic, a law professor at George Washington University Law School, who was a member of the Federal Trade Commission's Bureau of Competition during the Carter and Reagan Administrations, "is that the very litigation success that David Boies and his colleagues at Cravath had in the seventies and early eighties with I.B.M. now became the obstacle to their prevailing in this matter. One of the big challenges for the government brief-writers is to sidestep lots of the decisions from that period that embrace the idea that the dominant firms ought to be encouraged to compete and to compete hard."

In court, Boies had come to be feared for his mastery of detail, his timing, and his charm. In a 1992 action brought by the government of the Philippines against Westinghouse, after the plaintiff's lawyer had finished a brilliant opening statement, the judge announced that the court would adjourn for the day. Boies, at the defense table, shot out of his seat and, insisting that he was so outraged by the falsehoods his opponent had uttered that he couldn't bear the thought of jurors' spending the night burdened by them, pleaded with the judge to allow him fifteen or twenty minutes to start his opening statement. The judge relented, and Boies reversed the momentum. "If I had let the jury walk out of there without challenging the integrity of what they had heard, it would have been an uphill battle," he recalls.

In the thirty-three years that Boies has been practicing law, he said, he has never had a trial victory reversed on appeal. The First Amendment attorney Floyd Abrams said of Boies, "In a very soft-spoken way, he's able to lure people who testify for his opponent into utterly indefensible positions. Precisely because he doesn't scream at them, they feel more secure to state as fact matters that under cross-examination become highly dubious. The remarkable thing is that it happens over and over again."

BOIES, who has thin brown hair and protruding ears, gives an impression of studied casualness. In court, he always wears a navy suit with pants that drape over black sneakers; a blue-and-white pin-striped button-down shirt; a square-bottomed dark-blue knit tie, which dangles above his beltless waist; and a black Timex strapped over his left cuff, so he can easily read the time. The suits, shirts, and ties are purchased in batches from Lands' End. During the trial, Boies stayed in a modest apartment that the Justice Department rented for him. Despite his casual demeanor, his intensity is such that he routinely walks past associates without noticing them. He has become a celebrity in Washington restaurants, where he picks up thick lamb chops in his hands and chews the bones clean. Sometimes he takes a quick nap in a booth at the Capitol Grill. Playing tennis or Ping-Pong with any of his children—he has six, and has been married three times—he plays to win, as he does at craps or card tables in Las Vegas, which he visits several times each year. "When he plays craps," Mary Boies, herself an attorney, says of her husband, "he remembers every roll, every sequence."

Just before ten o'clock on October 19, 1998, the first day of the Microsoft trial, Boies entered the block-long, eight-story E. Barrett Prettyman United States Courthouse, in Washington, rode the elevator to the second floor, then walked past a line of reporters parked against a mauve marble wall who were vying for the forty daily press seats, past an even longer line of spectators on the opposite wall, and entered Courtroom No. 2, where Judge John J. Sirica had tried the Watergate defendants. The room has no windows, and there is no street noise.

Then the door to the Judge's private corridor opened and Deputy Marshal R. Kirkland Bowden, who has worked in this court since 1962, called out "All rise!" Judge Thomas Penfield Jackson entered and ascended his platform. Although Jackson, who is now sixty-two, was the first judge appointed by President Reagan to this district court and therefore might be assumed to oppose intrusive government, Microsoft executives have learned to be wary of him. He was the judge who ordered Microsoft to separate Internet Explorer from Windows, and since then he had made a number of preliminary decisions that angered the company, such as allowing unwanted excerpts from Gates's twenty-hour-long videotaped pretrial deposition to be played in court. Before the trial began, Jackson had announced that it was his intention to speed it along by limiting to twelve the number of witnesses each side could call and by stipulating that all testimony be submitted in written form, so that all cross-examinations could occur without delay.

After a flurry of procedural maneuvers and a brief opening by a representative of the states involved, Boies rose and stepped to the microphone on the podium in front of the Judge, ready to make the government's opening argument. Mary Boies looked on from the spectator section. Joel Klein, the bald top of his head bobbing, shifted in the aisle seat of the bench behind the counsel table. The Microsoft counsel, Bill Neukom, sitting at the head of the Microsoft table, stared straight ahead, his pen and pad poised. Judge Jackson, who has white hair and gold-framed half-glasses, nodded with a welcoming smile to each table of attorneys.

For nearly three hours, glancing occasionally at a few notes he had written on a manila folder, Boies described, first in summary form and then in chronological order, how, in his view, Microsoft had violated the antitrust laws—in particular, by "restraint of trade or commerce"—and so became a predatory monopoly. Coercion, he claimed, was standard operating procedure at Bill Gates's Microsoft. Boies then gave a signal and played the first of many excerpts from Gates's videotaped deposition—an excerpt that gave a portrait of Gates at odds with the decisive, fearless straight shooter of common lore. Shown slouched in a leather chair, and compulsively sipping from a can of Diet Coke, Gates appeared on several court screens:

BOIES: Are you aware of any instances in which representatives of Microsoft have met with competitors in an attempt to allocate markets?

GATES: I am not aware of any such thing, and I know it's very much against the way we operate. . . .

BOIES: Now, have you ever read the complaint in this case?

GATES: No. . . .

BOIES: Do you know whether in the complaint there are allegations concerning a 1995 meeting between Netscape and Microsoft representatives relating to alleged market-division discussions?

GATES: I haven't read the complaint, so I don't know for sure. But I think somebody said that that is in there.

More than a few spectators laughed at Gates's professed ignorance. Boies now paced in front of the bench, a pointer in his hand, and asked an aide to roll the second video. Gates again filled the screen, and, in response to a question from Boies about his understanding of Netscape's strategy back in mid-1995, Gates said that at the time "I had no sense of what Netscape was doing."

Using his pointer, Boies displayed on the screens various Gates documents, including a May 26, 1995, memo titled "The Internet Tidal Wave," which showed that Gates quite clearly saw the importance of Netscape. In it he wrote to his managers, "A new competitor 'born' on the Internet is Netscape. Their browser is dominant, with 70 percent usage share, allowing them to determine which network extensions will catch on." With control over how software worked on-line, Gates noted, Netscape could cheapen Windows and "commoditize the underlying operating system," by which he meant that people using any number of programs, for browsers, for word processing, for spreadsheets, for printers—for all sorts of applications—might begin to move away from Windows.

With a nod from Boies, an E-mail written by Gates five days later and sent to his senior executives appeared on the screens. It said, "I think there is a very powerful deal of some kind we can do with Netscape"—a deal that would reduce competition. "We could even pay them money as part of the deal, buying some piece of them or something." Then, just a few weeks before the meeting with Netscape—the meeting that Gates said he was not involved in—he wrote, "I would really like to see something like this happen!!"

A division of markets was proposed at the June 21st meeting, Boies argued, producing E-mails from both Netscape and Microsoft. "What you have here is, in and of itself, an attempt at monopolization," he went on, a "restraint of trade" effort prohibited by law. Why would Netscape feel compelled to coöperate? Because, Boies claimed, Microsoft's leverage stemmed from Windows, which controlled ninety percent of the P.C. operating-system market (a somewhat inflated number, since it excluded the Macintosh and all other machines not running on Intel-type chips). Any computer manufacturer, or any maker of printers or software-application programs, from spreadsheets to browsers, needed to know Microsoft's Application Program Interfaces, or A.P.I.s, in order to be able to connect to Windows, Boies said. He charged that Microsoft was predatory because it threatened to crush Netscape if it did not comply. There would be testimony, Boies promised, that one of Gates's "top lieutenants" threatened to "choke Netscape's air supply."

For three critical months, Boies said, Microsoft had withheld A.P.I.s that Netscape required to be compatible with Windows 95, the latest version of Microsoft's operating system. Unlike Netscape, which tried to sell its browser, Microsoft adopted what Boies called "a predatory pricing campaign" and gave its browser away, bundling it with Windows. "Our business model works even if all Internet software is free," Gates told a reporter in an article that Boies cited. Microsoft imposed contracts on computer manufacturers, Boies said—on A.O.L. and on software companies like Intuit—restricting their ability to do business with Netscape.

IN his narrative, Boies sometimes seemed to be speaking less about a software company than about the Mob. He told the court how Gates had alternately coerced and seduced A.O.L. into abandoning Netscape's browser and promoting Internet Explorer. As evidence, Boies produced a January 21, 1996, E-mail in which an A.O.L. executive described an encounter with Gates: "Gates delivered a characteristically blunt query: How much do we need to pay you to screw Netscape? ('this is your lucky day')."

Boies went on to tell of Microsoft's desire to boost its browser share, and its fury at learning that some P.C. manufacturers and Internet service providers were reconfiguring the boot-up screen displaying the Windows 95 logo. He then produced an E-mail from one Microsoft executive asking, "Do you think we should look at making this harder?" Difficult to do in Windows 95, came a reply, but it added, "We'll do something to make this hard" in Windows 98. In other words, Boies told the Judge, Microsoft was saying, "We're going to manipulate the technology, not for innovation, not for consumer benefit, not for technological advances, but to hurt competitors." Boies produced a March, 1997, memo from a Hewlett-Packard executive to Microsoft, which began, "We were very disappointed," and then referred to Microsoft's refusal to let Hewlett-Packard customize the startup sequence. This had "resulted in significant and costly problems," the memo went on to say. "From a consumer perspective, we are hurting our industry. . . . If we had a choice of another supplier, based on your actions, I assure you that you would not be our supplier of choice."

Microsoft, Boies continued, offered inducements to Intuit to spurn Netscape (Intuit turned them down), and it also threatened to terminate the vital software applications it had been providing for the Apple Macintosh if Apple didn't limit its ties to Netscape. Even Microsoft's close allies, Boies said, were bullied. He told of how irate Gates had been in the summer of 1995 when he met with Intel, the dominant chip maker, about software research it was doing, and said to a group of Intel executives, including the Intel chairman, Andrew S. Grove, that he wanted them to abandon that quest. "Again, what you have is Microsoft trying to tell another company what products it can and cannot ship," said Boies.

Boies said that by mid-1998 Netscape's share of the browser market had dropped from more than seventy-five percent to about fifty percent, while Microsoft's browser share climbed from twenty percent at the beginning of 1997 to fifty percent. By one estimate, Microsoft was now capturing seventy-six percent of new browser users, Boies said.

The courtroom's own air supply was hot, and the heat seemed to make Judge Jackson and more than a few other people in the courtroom drowsy; Jackson rubbed his eyes and sometimes closed them, then jolted upright, straining to stay awake by chewing on ice cubes. Boies took this as a cue, and summed up. Without "some kind of intervention," he said, Microsoft would soon succeed in murdering Netscape. Boies promised to prove his case by using the very technology that Microsoft depended on—E-mail. Microsoft's E-mails and the more than three million pages of documents that the government had collected from them were the equivalent, Boies implied, of the kinds of wiretaps the government used to snare criminals.

Boies had finished by two-thirty, an hour and twenty-five minutes earlier than the time Judge Jackson had set for adjournment. Looking down from the bench, Jackson asked Microsoft's chief trial counsel, "Do you want to start now, or would you prefer to defer until tomorrow morning?"

"Tomorrow morning would be fine, Your Honor," was the reply.

Boies was secretly thrilled, for it meant that the government's opening charge would dominate the evening news. "If it had been left to me," Boies whispered later, "I would have jumped to speak and declare, 'I cannot let a moment go by without rising to protest.' "

The courtroom began to empty, and a ritual began: Reporters clustered just outside the courtroom, checking quotes (since no recording equipment was allowed inside), and, more subtly, checking what their colleagues planned to use as the lead of their stories. Then the reporters raced down a flight of stairs and out onto the granite courthouse steps, facing Constitution Avenue, where cameras waited. There David Boies, accompanied by the government team, gave his version of what had happened in court, answered questions, and then ceded his space to the Microsoft team, who offered their own spin. On this first day, Bill Neukom, the lead Microsoft counsel, squinted into the sun and accused the government of using "snippets taken out of context" and material "based entirely on loose and unreliable rhetoric." E-mail, he said, is written in haste, is often full of bluster, and is not necessarily an accurate reflection of what people think and do. "None of these snippets, none of this rhetoric, even approaches proof of anti-competitive conduct," he declared. Still, late that night, after monitoring the TV, the radio, the Web, and the print news accounts, a former newspaperman named Greg Shaw, who was the second-in-command of Microsoft's public-relations department, wrote a memorandum and E-mailed it to the company's senior executives, including Gates. It began, "Opening day of the trial today was as tough for Microsoft's image as we all expected. It was very bad."

III—MICROSOFT STRIKES BACK

COURTROOM NO. 2 was packed on the next day, with reporters and spectators eager to hear Microsoft's opening arguments. Boies sat at the head of the government table, facing the Judge; and the same seat at the Microsoft table was filled by Neukom.

Bill Neukom is fifty-seven, and like Boies he has been married three times and has a brood of children—four, in his case. But if Boies were to be portrayed by Tom Hanks in a movie version of this trial, Neukom would be played by

James Mason. He is six feet four and has wavy silver hair that does not flutter in breezes. He never wears the same suit twice in a week. His shirts are starched, his cuffs are fastened by gold or silver cufflinks, and his assortment of vivid bow ties seems inexhaustible. A man of elaborate courtesies, he always holds the gate for an opposing lawyer and never appears rushed as he glides through the courtroom.

Neukom's father co-founded and ran the San Francisco office of McKinsey & Company, and he and two brothers and a sister were reared in nearby San Mateo. After graduating from Dartmouth, and from Stanford Law, he moved to Seattle. He eventually joined the firm of Shidler, McBroom, Gates & Lucas, where he worked mostly on real-estate and contract law and a few criminal cases. A fateful moment in his career came in 1978, when a senior partner in the firm, the elder William H. Gates, strolled into his office and said, "My kid's bringing his little business up here to Seattle, and would you take a shot at looking out for him?" Neukom recalled, "To this day, I don't know why he stopped by my door."

Bill Gates's father remembers why. "The company was becoming more and more important to the law firm," he explained. "We needed someone to work with it—someone with good judgment, with very good people skills." Then the company got so big that Neukom suggested it form its own legal department. In 1985, a year before Microsoft first sold its stock, the department consisted of Neukom and two other employees. Fourteen years later, it consisted of more than four hundred employees, of whom about a hundred and fifty were lawyers.

Over the years, Neukom became a Seattle civic leader, and was active in the American Bar Association, where he served as one of five national officers. He is now a tireless promoter of Microsoft's philanthropic endeavors and the founder of the Neukom Family Foundation, whose purpose is to invest in education and health-care projects for the poor. Among his gifts to the foundation was a transfer, in June of 1998, of ninety-six thousand five hundred shares of Microsoft stock valued at nearly five and a half million dollars. (S.E.C. filings reveal that he owns Microsoft stock worth more than a hundred million dollars.) Some at Microsoft dismiss Neukom as a legal nerd or a slick bureaucrat, but he has long been close to Gates. Throughout this trial, Neukom E-mailed regular reports to Gates on developments in the courtroom. He is often described as patient. When Apple and Microsoft were locked in a patent dispute, Neukom told Gates to ignore the bad press and pay attention to the law. Five years later, in 1993, when the courts ruled as Neukom had calmly predicted, he became a source of reassurance within Microsoft.

IF Boies was the quarterback of his team, Neukom was the coach of his. In court, Neukom silently presided at the table, his tortoiseshell half-glasses sliding down his long Roman nose while he carefully scribbled notes, left-handed, on yellow legal pads, neatly folding each page. He described his role: "I've got to put the right team on the field." His designated quarterback was John L. Warden, a partner in Sullivan & Cromwell. By contrast with the thin, slightly dishevelled Boies, Warden, who is portly, fairly announces himself. He wears dark-framed round glasses, carries a thick, expensive leather case in one hand and, often, a bowler in the other, and marches down the courthouse corridor with his arms pumping and his wing-tip shoes slapping the carpet.

Warden is formal in court. On this occasion, his hands clasped firmly on the sides of the podium, he introduced himself, Neukom, and then seven other members of the legal team. He read his prepared celebratory remarks in defense of Gates: "The antitrust laws are not a code of civility in business, and a personal attack on a man whose vision and innovation have been at the core of the vast benefits that people are reaping from the Information Age is no substitute for proof of anti-competitive conduct and anti-competitive effects."

The evidence, Warden went on to say, "will confirm what Microsoft has been saying all along; namely, that Internet Explorer technologies are an integral part of the operating system and cannot be removed from Windows 98 without seriously degrading it." The two are dependent on each other to perform tasks like "the shutter in a camera." The consumer benefits of this bundled product are readily apparent, Warden pointed out; after all, "ordinary consumers who buy computers at Wal-Mart have no interest in piecing together an operating system from a grab bag of separately marketed components. They want their new machine to come out of the box . . . and just work." Consumers chose Microsoft only after Microsoft had produced a technically better browser, he said, and not because of Microsoft's muscle.

Rarely gesturing, Warden read on, turning now to the coercion charges. The government contends, he said, that Microsoft's contracts with P.C. makers and others were examples of exclusionary contracts, prohibited by the antitrust laws. Not so; they were "pro-competitive," because they helped to "reduce Netscape's overwhelming dominance and gave consumers a choice," he declared, and went on to say that this sort of contract is common. As for Internet service providers, to whom customers pay a monthly fee to gain access to the Internet, Warden said, Microsoft had contracts with only eleven out of more than three thousand, and these did not prohibit them from doing business with Netscape. Besides, since these contracts "became a lightning rod for criticism of Microsoft," he went on, the company had already suspended many of their provisions. Nor would Microsoft enter into any more contracts of this kind, "so this issue is truly moot."

The contracts that Microsoft had with computer manufacturers, Warden claimed, would show that Microsoft didn't interfere with P.C. makers who chose to install software on top of Windows 98: "If they think it adds value, that is their business." The important point for the court to register, Warden said, is that Netscape has not been foreclosed in its ability to distribute its product. Nor have customers been hindered in their ability to download Netscape on their P.C.s; sixteen million copies were downloaded in June, July, and August alone. He said that the claims made about an alleged "air supply" threat were bogus. The discussions with Netscape, like those with Apple or Intel, were normal in an industry where companies both compete and coöperate, always "urging your prospective partner not to ally with your principal competitors."

Warden, who was raised in southern Illinois, read his statement in a drawl so pronounced that his words were sometimes slurred. Microsoft did not have monopoly power under any legal definition, he said, because in the software business competitors faced "no structural barriers to entry." In the software business, he added, there are "no factories to build, no mineral deposits to locate, and no distribution infrastructure to develop." There were also no constraints on how many copies could be produced—just brains, and the capital to support them, were required, and both were plentiful. He pointed out, "Any competitive position can be lost overnight if someone else creates a technically superior or more user-friendly product."

There is a theory advanced by some economists, and embraced by the government, that superior products will not always win—that in certain industries, like high-tech, products with a large market share will tend to lock in customers. Warden argued that "if such lock-in effects existed, it would have been impossible for Microsoft to make a dent in Netscape's commanding lead in Web-browsing software, a point the government's economic experts ignore." P.C. makers have alternatives, he said, but "they install Windows because that's what their customers want."

Concluding his presentation, Warden said he hoped the court would decide "that this is not really an antitrust case but a return of the Luddites," and he went on, "The government's case is a fundamentally misconceived attack on the creation of innovative new products by operation of the free market."

IV—MAN FROM NETSCAPE

BOIES and Warden both made compelling points, but sometimes they sounded like academics. Boies still had not proved consumer harm, which is one crucial test for antitrust law, and, with computer prices plunging and Microsoft giving its browser away, this would not be an easy case to make. No doubt, Microsoft had contracts limiting the business A.O.L. and others could undertake with Netscape, but doesn't that resemble what Coca-Cola does when it demands that McDonald's not serve Pepsi-Cola? And, yes, Microsoft did give its browser away to lure customers from Netscape. But many companies offer products at a loss in order to build market share.

Warden's opening argument had at least as many vulnerabilities. Anyone

who covered Microsoft between 1995 and 1997 knows that the company believed it was in a struggle with Netscape, and invoked Netscape as a spur, a
way to keep Microsoft hard core. The company fought hard—gave its browser
away, delayed software upgrades, threatened retaliation, and wrote restrictive
contracts. Bundling the browser in with Windows was a weapon to beat
Netscape, not just a means to better serve consumers.

In the eyes of the law, the Sherman Act's crucial questions, as the Supreme
Court has ruled, are: Did the company possess monopoly power? And was that
power achieved or preserved through improper means? Other companies may
exert leverage, using muscle to convince others to do it their way, but when a
monopoly acts in that manner we graduate from hard core to restraint of
trade. Coca-Cola muscles McDonald's, but Coca-Cola doesn't dominate the
soft-drink market the way Microsoft dominates P.C. operating systems.

In the end, the Microsoft trial may determine whether antitrust laws can
fairly be applied to technology companies and the Internet, where classic monopoly characteristics—rising prices, control of finite resources, distribution
barriers to entry, and choke holds on innovation—are not as apparent, even if
the allegations of coercive tactics are familiar.

The center of gravity among economists has shifted away from the populism
that previously animated antitrust legislation. Throughout its century-old history, the law has undergone as many twists and turns as an Albanian road. For
every legal precedent cited by the government, Microsoft can cite its own. The
government touts the 1912 *United States v. Terminal Railroad Association of
St. Louis* case, in which the court ruled that a company that controlled every
rail route into the city could not restrict access so as to disadvantage its competitors. The government believes that Windows is just such an "essential facility." Microsoft touts the 1979 *Berkey Photo v. Eastman Kodak* decision,
which held that "any firm, even a monopolist, may generally bring its products
to market whenever and however it chooses," and be given freedom to innovate. (It was John Warden who won the case on appeal.) One influential decision in recent antitrust law was written in 1984 by Supreme Court Justice
Stephen Breyer when he served on the First Circuit Court of Appeals. In *Kartell
v. Blue Shield* he wrote that the Sherman Act was originally seen "as a way of
protecting consumers against prices that were too *high*, not too low. . . . Courts
at least should be cautious—reluctant to condemn too speedily—an arrangement that, on its face, appears to bring low price benefits to the consumers." Increasingly, the courts are also aware that, by the time government acts, often
the problem has abated, as happened with I.B.M.

THROUGHOUT the trial, it was as if two different companies were being described. Each government witness would paint a grim picture of Bill Gates and
Microsoft and its rapacious culture, and each Microsoft witness would offer a

pious portrait of a model entrepreneurial company. At the heart of the government's foreclosure-and-coercion case, however, was Netscape, and for this reason the government called as the first of its twelve witnesses James Barksdale, the C.E.O. of the company. His written testimony, which, like the testimony of all others, had been distributed to reporters in advance, ran to a hundred and twenty-six double-spaced pages. Barksdale claimed that Microsoft had crossed a legal line by using the "bullying and tough tactics" of a "monopolist" to "squelch competition in the browser market."

Before Barksdale was sworn in, on the second day of the trial, John Warden rose and moved that parts of Barksdale's written testimony be stricken because it contained "multiple layers of hearsay," which in some cases was "fourth-hand hearsay." Judge Jackson immediately ruled that if this were a jury trial "it might be dealt with somewhat differently," but that he would "admit the testimony in toto." However, he added, he would recognize hearsay evidence as such and give Warden every opportunity to rebut it. Warden thanked the Judge, and Neukom registered no emotion as he sat at the Microsoft table scribbling notes. But this ruling, and one that Jackson made that afternoon, denying Microsoft's motion to disallow the playing of Gates's video as if he were a witness, angered Microsoft. Weeks later, when I saw Gates at a New York dinner in his honor, he was still furious, cursing and sputtering that the Judge had permitted hearsay to masquerade as fact at the trial.

Barksdale was a formidable-looking witness—a handsome man with wavy gray hair and the courtly manners and slow drawl of a youth spent in Jackson, Mississippi. He had an unusual résumé for Silicon Valley. He was neither a young inventor with more hubris than experience nor an entrepreneur who disdained management. Barksdale, who was fifty-five, wore as many management ribbons as any executive in the Valley, starting with his first eight years—from 1965 to 1972—spent at I.B.M., where he began as a salesman, and continuing to his most recent role, as president and chief operating officer of McCaw Cellular Communications, the cellular giant that had been acquired by A.T. & T. in 1994. In January, 1995, he became the president and C.E.O. of the startup Netscape, a company whose key product, Netscape Navigator, helped propel the Internet revolution. There were two million users of its pioneering Web browser when Barksdale joined the company. A year later, there were fifteen million.

From the beginning, Neukom and his legal team believed that their mission was to refute nearly every fact submitted by a government witness, so Warden, in his cross-examination, chose to follow scrupulously Barksdale's written testimony. He asked Barksdale a stupefying number of questions, including a request that he explain "the improvements" Netscape had made to its software, which is not the best request to make of a former salesman. Barksdale obligingly enumerated its many new features, ending with "I could get you a long list."

"That will do, thanks," Warden said.

"I hope you buy the product," said Barksdale, with a sly smile.

Theatrically, Barksdale won, but Warden had also driven home a point: ever since the advent of the P.C., when customers were required to pay extra for options like spreadsheets and disk drives, computer companies have tried to combine features. At times Warden's approach seemed to perplex the Judge, however. Warden, trying to get Barksdale to define what he meant by "monopoly product," pressed him to distinguish between a diamond monopoly and a soup monopoly.

"What's your question?" asked the Judge.

"My question is he's used the term 'monopoly power,' and I want to know what it means."

"I thought he defined it once."

After a while, Warden brought up the "air supply" quote and asked when Barksdale had first heard it. Barksdale pleasantly surprised Warden by saying he had heard that Larry Ellison, the chairman and C.E.O. of Oracle, used it to mean to "disadvantage a competitor." The idea was thus planted that Microsoft executives were not the only ones who talked like cowboys. Warden burrowed in, asking whether Barksdale had actually heard it from Paul Maritz, a Microsoft executive who was said to have used that phrase. Barksdale admitted that he had not actually witnessed this. Warden moved on to ask Barksdale whether Netscape's ambition was to destroy Microsoft by using its browser as a substitute for Microsoft's operating system. Barksdale maintained that he had never said that, but admitted that the inventor of his browser, who was his chief technologist, the twenty-six-year-old Marc Andreessen, had made such a claim; in fact, Andreessen had once said that Netscape would "reduce Windows to a set of poorly debugged device drivers." This was the joke of "a young man," Barksdale said, and not for a minute did he believe that Netscape could fully replace Microsoft's Windows platform as the jumping-off point for other applications. By the end of the witness's first day, Warden had got through only the first thirteen pages of Barksdale's written testimony.

IN many ways, the first few days in the courtroom established a story line for the trial: David—Boies, that is—slays a bumbling Goliath. In his arsenal was a mordant wit. While questioning Barksdale, for example, Boies, the non-P.C. user, asked about the "log in" to an Internet service provider.

"No, it's 'log on,' " corrected Barksdale.

Boies smiled, and said, "I knew that! I was just testing to see whether you were paying attention."

Boies produced E-mails that Netscape executives sent after the June 21st meeting complaining that Microsoft had not given them parts of the A.P.I. code they needed to make use of certain features in Windows 95, which was released in August, 1995. Microsoft did not deliver that code until October,

1995, claimed one E-mail, "which caused us to miss most of the holiday selling season." (Microsoft denied this.)

At the end of Barksdale's second day on the stand, Warden, trailed by Neukom, marched out of the courtroom. He quickly passed Boies, who was standing just outside the courtroom, surrounded by reporters. The reporters thought Microsoft's legal team was rigid; Microsoft's lawyers thought they were obeying court rules, which said that journalists were not supposed to interview lawyers in the courthouse. This was a rule that would bend as the trial went on. But Microsoft's aloof behavior in the courtroom and on the steps reinforced an impression that the company was being guided by legal pedants who were ignoring the larger public trial at their peril.

Still, Warden's cross-examination did score a few points over Barksdale and over the government. Seeking to demonstrate that Netscape, not Microsoft, had taken the initiative, Warden submitted as evidence a December 29, 1994, E-mail sent at 3 A.M. by the Netscape co-founder, chairman, and then C.E.O., James Clark, to Brad Silverberg, a senior Microsoft executive, saying abjectly that his company "never planned to compete" with Microsoft and offering to sell Microsoft a chunk of Netscape. The E-mail was sent at a moment when Netscape's revenues were slim and its capital was shrinking. Barksdale read, "We want to make this company a success, but not at Microsoft's expense. We'd like to work with you. Working together could be in your self-interest as well as ours. Depending on the interest level, you might take an equity position in Netscape." Barksdale appeared to be flabbergasted, and told Warden that this was the first time he had seen the E-mail. Then Warden, in perhaps the most dramatic moment of his cross-examination, asked Barksdale if he considered Clark "a truthful man." Barksdale did not immediately respond, and when he did he hardly gave Clark a ringing endorsement: "I regard him as a salesman." Barksdale said he thought Clark was freelancing. Warden, however, had introduced an element of doubt: Maybe the June, 1995, meeting was Netscape's idea. Maybe Netscape was the aggressor, and not Microsoft.

Barksdale was followed by the senior vice-president of business affairs at A.O.L., David M. Colburn, who wore a stubbly beard, cowboy boots, and a perpetual smirk. Colburn's testimony, like Barksdale's, offered still more evidence of what Microsoft considered hardball tactics and the government considered thuggery. Concerned that Microsoft had too much power, A.O.L., on March 11, 1996, had signed an agreement with Netscape to license its browser. Microsoft then offered to feature A.O.L. in Windows 95—if A.O.L. agreed to limit the distribution and promotion of Netscape. On March 12, 1996, A.O.L. acceded to Microsoft's terms, despite the deal it had made a day earlier with Netscape.

Warden, in his cross-examination, produced internal A.O.L. documents that said that by 1996 Microsoft's browser was technically superior—in other words, that A.O.L. had chosen Internet Explorer on the merits. He also produced a draft memo from the chief executive of A.O.L., Steve Case, in which Case agreed with Andreessen's description of Microsoft as "the Beast From Redmond" and called for a "grand alliance" among A.O.L., Netscape, and other companies to defeat this corporate monster.

"In your various dealings with the Department of Justice, stirring them up against the 'Beast From Redmond,' did you disclose that you made a market-division proposal to Netscape?" Warden asked.

No, Colburn said. It wasn't a market division. It was a common search for a "strategic relationship."

However, Microsoft was establishing a theme it would return to throughout the trial: Every company does what Microsoft has been accused of doing. In turn, the argument received this government retort: Not every company is a monopoly, and the law prohibits a monopoly from doing what other companies are allowed to do.

A FEW days later, Boies announced that he would play more of Gates's video deposition. Microsoft objected to releasing any of the tape to the press, whereupon Judge Jackson beckoned both sides to the bench. The Microsoft team's sullen faces conveyed a palpable sense that they felt surrounded by a hostile government in a hostile city with hostile reporters waiting to pounce. Boies told the Judge it was the government's understanding that once the excerpt of Gates's video deposition was played in the courtroom, both the transcript of the exchange and the taped part of the exchange could be released. With Neukom standing stoically behind him, Warden said he had no objection to releasing the transcript but did object to releasing copies of the tape, which could be broadcast on television and thus, in effect, allow cameras to invade the courtroom.

"If it were open to me, Mr. Warden, I probably would adopt your position in toto," Jackson said. But the rule he had followed all along, he explained, was "that anything which is presented in open court is available to the press."

After the lunch break, Gates again appeared on the courtroom's various screens. Still sipping from a can of Diet Coke, he rarely looked up at his off-camera interlocutor, and alternately rocked slowly back and forth or slouched forward as he was quizzed by Boies or by a New York State Assistant Attorney General named Stephen Houck. In a long portion of the deposition, Boies asked Gates whether he had ever threatened to cancel Macintosh Office, a suite of business applications. After Gates said no, Boies stopped the tape and told the court that he would like to introduce some new exhibits. One of these was a June 27, 1997, E-mail from a Microsoft employee named Ben Waldman to Gates asking him to agree to complete the upgrade of Macintosh Office and "detach this issue from the current Apple discussions." Waldman, who oversees relations with Apple Computer, continued, "The threat to cancel Mac Office 97 is certainly the strongest bargaining point we have, as doing so will do a great deal of harm to Apple immediately." Gates said that he didn't recall receiving the E-mail, and that in any case it concerned nothing more than an "internal debate" about a single upgrade.

In August, 1997, Apple and Microsoft finally made a "deal" about their "relationship," and Apple endorsed Microsoft's browser. Now Boies asked, "Does the deal prohibit them from shipping Netscape's browser without also shipping Internet Explorer?"

Gates said he wasn't sure.

"It's your testimony, sitting here today under oath, that you simply don't know, one way or the other, whether Apple is today free to ship Netscape's browser without also shipping Internet Explorer?"

"That's right."

Gates was a terrible witness. But, even if he sometimes skirted the truth, this didn't mean he was guilty of creating a monopoly. Disagreeable behavior may not be criminal. Over breakfast one morning, Neukom expressed his disdain. The government's case, he said, evades the central conclusion of the Court of Appeals decision that permitted Microsoft to tie a browser into its operating system. "The law is designed to encourage companies to innovate and enhance services for consumers."

V–INSIDE THE BEAST

A FEW months into the trial, I visited Microsoft's headquarters, in Redmond, just outside Seattle. Here the employees refer to the place where they work as a campus, far removed from regulators in Washington, D.C., and from competitors in Silicon Valley. They live on a self-contained planet, where phones rarely ring, where E-mail communication is said to total three and a half million exchanges per day, where espresso and focaccia are served in the cafeterias, where organized sports help keep the employees on campus, and where most waking hours are spent in front of a P.C. screen. The average age of the more than thirty-one thousand employees is thirty-four.

In Redmond, one encounters a sense of embattlement. James Allchin, a senior Microsoft executive, whose testimony at the trial would make headlines, told me, "I feel we're on the brink of disaster every day. If you're reading newspapers and watching what's happening—new devices, new operating systems, attacks that claim intellectual property means nothing—it's like a massive attack all the time." On another day, I talked to Yusuf Mehdi, who is thirty-two and directs marketing for Windows, and he said, "I don't think I've ever been more worried. . . . The threat is obsolescence. How do we respond to people who say, 'My TV doesn't crash'? How do we respond to people who say, as Netscape does, 'Why do you need Windows? You can just use the Web.' We need to figure out how to make it in this new Internet world. I look around and see tens of companies that might have better ideas."

To come up with better ideas, Microsoft spends an extraordinary three billion dollars each year on research and development. A portion of this budget is earmarked for pure research—for recruiting and funding the best scientists and engineers. In an era when such theoretical research is usually sacrificed as impractical, and companies strive to cut costs and boost their stock price, Microsoft is a rare oasis. But it is also a place seeking to dominate the realm of new products: browsers for wireless devices, software that permits P.C.s to boot up instantly, laptop batteries that last for twelve hours, P.C.s that accept voice commands and translate handwriting into type, interactive toys and dolls, auto P.C.s that function as radios and CD players as well as navigation devices that map a driver's destination and then offer voice instruction to turn right or left at the next corner.

Among the development projects that Gates is now most excited about is a product called ClearType, which seeks to improve the resolution on P.C. screens. Bill Hill, who was born in Scotland fifty years ago and joined Microsoft in 1995, comes to work each day wearing Bermuda shorts and with his hair in a ponytail. His mission has been to increase the resolution on an L.C.D. computer screen from eighty-eight pixel dots per inch to three hundred per inch. Words on the screen will therefore look the way words do on paper, spurring advances in electronic books and maybe in on-line reading. "Trying to portray type with a pixel is like trying to paint the *Mona Lisa* with a paint roller," Hill told me. "We've changed the size of the paint roller." Microsoft plans to make ClearType available later this year. Eventually, ClearType and many of the new technologies like voice and handwriting recognition that Microsoft is developing may, like its browser, be included in Windows. Microsoft claims such developments serve consumers; the Justice Department claims they serve to solidify Microsoft's monopoly.

IN obvious ways, the Microsoft culture is egalitarian; almost all the people there have the same modest offices, the same kind of computer equipment, and the same relatively modest salaries. (Gates's base salary is three hundred and sixty-nine thousand dollars.) Almost everyone has access to Microsoft's generous stock-option grants. In other ways, though, Microsoft is a meritocracy, where people are pitted against each other and the ablest survive. Rob Glaser, the C.E.O. of RealNetworks, a maker of multimedia Internet applications, who worked alongside Gates for ten years but is now sometimes considered an adversary, says that the people at Microsoft think of the world as a "very Darwinian place." He went on to explain that the peer pressure is to push, to boast of being hard core; so a Gates negotiation is more a head-on competition than an opportunity for both sides to win. "I once said to Bill, in 1992, 'Shouldn't we worry about the court of public opinion?' I was trying to ask a meaningful question, even if this term was not mathematically well-defined. When you're in the lead, you can play a statesmanlike role of not winning every concession. While still maintaining leadership, you don't have to leverage every advantage that you have. Bill thought it was a vague, inarticulate idea."

Gates dominates not with charisma or with charm but with his brains and his passion. "Bill can be a bad sport at games," a friend told me, recalling a game of charades. On this occasion, Gates was losing, the friend said. Suddenly, his voice rising, "he accused his friends of cheating: 'You're not allowed to do that! Wait a minute! This is an infraction!' If he couldn't win, he'd find an infraction. It was absurd. But when you think about it, it all fits. 'The government is wrong! They're just wrong!' "

Nevertheless, it is almost impossible to imagine Microsoft without Bill Gates. Rick Rashid, the vice-president of research at Microsoft, said to me, "Most company or university people tend to have a cynical attitude concerning the people they work for. They complain that their company doesn't understand them. That just doesn't happen here."

TO many people who had been sitting in court during the first several weeks of this trial, it seemed that Gates and his adjutants had seen too many "Godfather" movies. I came to think that Microsoft's behavior seemed more childlike than Mob-like, recalling the sort of self-centeredness one finds in a teen-ager. The lingering question in court was: How could such a smart man give such a wobbly deposition? Christine Varney, a former Federal Trade Commissioner, who represented Netscape at the trial, said of Gates, "He's got really good lawyers. I suspect he didn't listen to them. . . . Microsoft's lawyers are treated like gardeners." A variation on this Gates-is-to-blame theme was expressed by a Gates friend: he said he saw Gates's behavior as argumentative—failing to concede the obvious. The friend went on, "It sets him up to be untruthful, because he contradicts things he need not have contradicted. It stems from a belief that he can out-debate, out-micro-language Boies. I get that impression because I know the guy. If I didn't, I'd be stunned. It's like in a gangland trial where the gangster says, 'No, I'm in the olive-oil business.' It seems disingenuous."

Others blame Gates's lawyers. "He couldn't have been briefed," Boies said. If Gates went off on tangents or was unresponsive, he continued, it was the lawyers' task to rein in their client: "If I were his attorney and in the room, I would have stopped the deposition." Neukom shrugs off these theories. "He was advised to be precise," he said, defending both Gates and himself. "He was asked questions. It was not possible to remember every E-mail, every contract or conversation."

When I talked to Gates in the late spring, I asked him how he would explain the gap between the omniscient C.E.O. described by employees and the senescent Gates on the videotape. He leaned forward and said, "I'd love to have you pick any part of the deposition and let me answer."

What about the part, I suggested, when he refused to say he was "concerned" about Netscape?

Gates replied, referring to Boies, "He was trying to make it as though we only had one competitor, which was Netscape. Look at that sequence of questions. . . . Take market share. There are so many ways of measuring browser market share. . . . Whose job is it to ask precise questions? That's the lawyer's job." He continued, "Are you saying that you wish that when he asked 'Are you concerned?' I had just said, 'Yes, that's the only thing I was concerned about,' and under any definition of the word 'concerned' the answer absolutely has to be 'yes'? That is, totally, a misportrayal of those years. . . . I don't know what it means for a company to be 'concerned.' Honestly, I don't. I mean, am I concerned about Squiggle Corporation right now? I've never heard of Squiggle Corporation. Is it possible that there's some guy writing E-mail that says, 'Oh, Squiggle is going to put us out of business'? Are you saying I shouldn't have tried to give precise answers? Is that what you're thinking? The issue is to give truthful answers. I gave totally, absolutely truthful answers. You're saying that 'Oh, it didn't look good.' O.K., fine. That's not what a deposition is about." What really bugged him, he continued, was "some notion that somebody says I don't have a good memory about things, that I showed a poor memory about things. That is an unbelievable lie! There is no part of that deposition where in any way, in any time, I show anything but the most excellent memory."

Boies, who earned credibility with reporters because he is so candid, concedes that he is stereotyping Gates. "What goes on in the courtroom is only a slice of what is relevant about him," he told me. "This is not a trial about Bill Gates. It is only in a limited way a trial about Microsoft. This is a trial about certain aspects of Microsoft's conduct. And it may not be the most important aspects of Microsoft. To get a sense of Gates as a person, you have to look far beyond what we're talking about in this trial."

VI—WHO IS BILL GATES?

GATES does not exactly look like a leader of men. Crowds do not part when he enters a room. His voice, though it has a high-pitched trill, does not command attention. There is no poetry in his speeches, no swagger in his gait. He is partial to wisecracks and to words like "cool," "neat," and "super." He sits slumped on a stage, looking less like a mogul than like a boy ordered to wear a suit. But while Gates may not fit familiar molds, he is a leader nonetheless. Rick Rashid has described the "awe" he and other scientists at Microsoft feel when they meet with Gates and he has read their technical briefing papers. One moment Gates is jotting equations on a white board or arguing passionately with the mathematicians about incipient infinite clusters—"I only roughly understand it," Rashid said—and the next he is arguing with economic specialists about monetary trading. Gates's breadth of knowledge continually astonishes Rashid.

At his birth, on October 28, 1955, William Henry Gates was given the same name as his father, grandfather, and great-grandfather, and he was nicknamed Trey. His mother, Mary, who died of breast cancer in 1994, devoted her considerable energies to myriad charitable and civic activities, most notably serving as chair of United Way International and president of the University of Washington's Board of Regents. His father, a powerful physical presence, at six feet six inches, and a dominant partner in his law firm, was himself the son of an entrepreneur who established a well-known furniture store in the Seattle suburbs. The family had a box at University of Washington football games, and counted the governor and members of Congress as friends.

"My mom was naturally social in a way that was incredibly great, reaching out to people," Gates told me, and he added that she "immediately made a stranger feel her warmth." His father always rigorously analyzed issues. Their son, whose birth came between that of two daughters, did not display much charm. As a teen-ager, he had a slight build and big feet; he wore his pants hiked high over his waist, buttoned the top button on his shirt, forgot to comb his hair and sometimes to bathe, and, unless his mother intervened, never put things away. Above all, he immersed himself in books and, later, computers.

Over a lobster salad in the unremarkable suburban house in which Bill Gates grew up (a nearby road is now called Mary Gates Memorial Drive), his father, who is seventy-three, told me, "We knew he was a smart kid. That was pretty evident. More than smart, he was so curious about everything. He did not possess the innate social skills that a lot of other kids come up with. He was shy, and didn't have a lot of self-confidence."

What was perceived as odd behavior—the rocking, the volatile outbursts, the jumping, the brilliance, and the shyness—has provoked cruel whispers that maybe Bill Gates is borderline autistic. Gates's father recalled that Bill's "rationality" stood out—his insistence on asking questions, on engaging in logical argument. At the private Lakeside School, where he enrolled when he was twelve, Bill and a schoolmate, Paul Allen, discovered computers. They wrote software programs, and started a business analyzing the traffic patterns of various communities. They used a Lakeside computer and won a contract from a major corporation to analyze the electrical-power needs of the Northwest and Canada. Because his family had ties to Congressman Brock Adams, Bill landed a job as a congressional page, in 1972, when he was sixteen. Because Gates loved politics, it's a mystery why his own government relations have proved to be so inept. Perhaps the answer may be found in something he told me this spring: "You don't have to have a lot of political protection to be allowed to innovate."

The roots of Gates's competitiveness may undoubtedly be found in a child-hood spent in a household where sport was transformed into Olympian con-tests. He traces his business talent to having been exposed to commerce by his father at the dinner table and to his own curiosity. A good friend of his, the in-vestor Warren Buffett, has a simple explanation for people like Gates: "They're wired in such a way that when they see business questions or problems or ac-tivities they tend to get the picture very quickly. They don't get tangled up in prejudices or biases they may have. They just tend to get the right answers. It's sort of like 'Why was Ted Williams a great hitter?' It's about seventy-five per-cent DNA."

AT Harvard, Gates rarely ventured outside his own circle, except when a dorm-mate and fellow math whiz, Steve Ballmer, persuaded him to attend par-ties. By his own admission, Gates was depressed in Cambridge and wondered what he would do with his life—at least, until Paul Allen, who had left college to work at Honeywell, outside Boston, visited him one weekend and showed him a copy of *Popular Electronics.* It contained a cover story on the M.I.T.S. Al-tair 8800, one of the first P.C.s, which was being sold as a kit for just three hun-dred and sixty dollars. A New Mexico company marketed the primitive machine, and in early 1975 Bill and Paul wrote to the president of M.I.T.S., telling him that he needed software to make the machine come alive. That win-ter, the two of them holed up in Gates's dormitory and madly wrote code. Allen then flew to Albuquerque to demonstrate how their software made the ma-chine talk. For three thousand dollars and a slice of royalties, Gates and Allen, at the ages of nineteen and twenty-one, had decided what to do with their lives. In the spring of 1975, Allen signed up as M.I.T.S.'s software director, and in June Gates took a leave from Harvard to join him. By July 1st, they were ship-ping their version of basic 2.0, as it was called. That November, the Gates-Allen partnership was christened Micro-soft.

Early photographs of Gates, Allen, and their handful of employees show a group of kids wearing open-necked shirts, scruffy beards, and determined smiles. Gates was a skinny, baby-faced young man with doelike eyes and oversized, octangular, clear-framed eyeglasses; Allen wore identical glasses and a Karl Marx beard. By the end of its first full year of operation, Microsoft (now hyphenless) had seven employees and twenty-two thousand dollars in revenue.

In 1979, Microsoft moved to Seattle. It now had twenty-eight employees and nearly two and a half million dollars in revenue, and its basic software was fast becoming the lingua franca of a new computer industry. Among the fateful choices that Gates and Microsoft would make, or have the good luck to have made for them, was I.B.M.'s decision to do business with the company. I.B.M. had contracted with Intel to produce computer-processing chips, or brains, for the first sixteen-bit machines; now it needed an operating system. Instead of understanding that software, not hardware, was the oil of the Information Age, I.B.M. chose to license from Microsoft the MS-DOS (Microsoft disk operating system) and other software programs. Years later, Dell, Compaq, and Gateway would sell what came to be known as Wintel—Windows plus Intel—machines. Microsoft became more dominant in software than Saudi Arabia is in the production of oil.

Another decision of considerable importance was the hiring, in 1980, of Gates's Harvard friend Steve Ballmer, who had become a Procter & Gamble marketing executive and had then gone to business school at Stanford. Ballmer helped professionalize both the marketing and the management at Microsoft; he was also a cheerleader—an unabashed enthusiast for Team Microsoft. Three years after Ballmer arrived, Paul Allen left. Allen and Gates were partners, but Gates claimed sixty-four percent of the stock to Allen's thirty-six percent; Gates was chairman, and Allen was the executive vice-president. ("I dropped out of school to run Microsoft without being paid while Paul had his M.I.T.S. job," Gates told me.) Allen had tired of his boyhood friend's propensity for yelling and his tendency to ignore him, which was what Gates did in offering not only a job but an ownership stake to Ballmer. Allen was also suffering from Hodgkin's disease, and although he recovered, he chose not to rejoin Microsoft. He sits on the board and is the company's second-largest shareholder, but his relationship with Gates endured a long frost—one that did not thaw until the mid-nineties.

In 1983, Microsoft announced the birth of Windows—a bet by Gates that users would prefer the friendlier point-and-click graphics pioneered by Xerox and then adopted by Macintosh. Microsoft had produced a product that captured consumer support. In 1984, Microsoft's sales almost doubled, to just under a hundred million dollars—a geometric growth that would be replicated again and again in subsequent years. This was a propitious moment to take Microsoft public, and after Bill Neukom signed off on the legal documents, on March 13, 1986, Microsoft stock went on sale for twenty-one dollars per share. The stock has since split eight times: someone who had invested ten thousand dollars in 1986 would have seen his stock value soar to just under six million dollars.

And yet Gates, fearing that companies, like athletes, lose their edge, was afraid that Microsoft was one minute away from extinction. Microsoft, therefore, to retain its lead, did what many companies do: leveraged strength to shore up weakness. It incorporated new software into Windows, including such features as simple word processing, a calculator, a calendar, new graphics, fax programs, and games. Then, more recently, it added a browser, enticing customers to buy upgrades on schedule and not to stray to a competing product. Microsoft brazenly used discounts and market dominance to keep computer manufacturers bound to it, and devised contracts that placed rival software companies at a disadvantage—a practice that the trial would highlight.

AS a chief executive, Gates can be brusque—ignoring social niceties and bluntly challenging fellow-executives to defend themselves after telling them, "That's the stupidest thing I've ever heard!" As a businessman, one Wall Street figure who knows him well observed, he is mature beyond his years, and yet in "emotional areas he's younger than his age." Gates has, after all, never had a boss, never been reprimanded or fired, and rarely confronted business adversity. At an Allen & Company retreat in Sun Valley, Idaho, several years ago, many witnessed a moment when Gates rushed up to John Malone, then C.E.O. of the nation's largest cable company, Tele-Communications, Inc., and yelled, "Why are you trying to screw me?" On the telephone, Malone recalled, Gates would often exclaim, "How could you do this to me? I thought we were friends!" I asked Malone, who admires Gates's strategic grasp, if he could think of another C.E.O. who had such outbursts. "I've known guys who have done that, but I always regarded it as manipulation," he told me. "Psychologically, he needs to win. 'You're with me or you're against me' kind of thing."

Gates can be extraordinarily considerate. When Russell Siegelman was a senior executive at Microsoft, he blacked out one day in 1993 and had to have emergency brain surgery. Siegelman, who later became a partner in the Silicon Valley venture-capital firm of Kleiner Perkins Caufield & Byers, remembers the note he received from Gates: "It was so Billish. It said, 'We're with you. Don't rush. It's your job when you come back.' He's not this guy who just thinks of business." Ann Winblad, a co-founder of Hummer Winblad Venture Partners, who dated Gates in the mid-eighties and has since been a close friend, says, "He sends hand-done birthday cards to friends." And at parties he loves "to lead sing-alongs," she added. "Bill knows the complete words to Broadway shows—the whole libretto." Each spring, Gates and Winblad spend a long weekend alone, usually at her North Carolina beach cottage, where they play golf, take walks on the beach, read, and ponder big and small questions. To those who question the idea of a married man vacationing alone with a female friend, Winblad answers, "People wouldn't ask if Bill went with a male friend."

According to most accounts, Gates has mellowed since marrying Melinda French on New Year's Day, 1994. She had joined Microsoft in 1987, and rose to an executive position before she started dating the boss. "It's hard to separate her influence from the stage of his life he's in," said Patty Stonesifer, who was Melinda's supervisor at Microsoft and is now the head of the Gates Learning Foundation. For an engagement party, in September, 1993, Gates, inspired by one of his favorite novels, dressed as Jay Gatsby; Melinda came as Daisy Buchanan.

The Gateses' version of East Egg, however, is beyond F. Scott Fitzgerald's imaginings. Bill and Melinda moved into a forty-thousand-square-foot compound that Gates built on Lake Washington at an estimated cost of seventy-five million dollars. The house features an underground garage for a hundred cars and a huge indoor trampoline. Why someone who is unconcerned with appearances should choose to live so ostentatiously is a mystery. "I had a couple of things in mind when I planned it," Gates told me in an E-mail. "One was to make it a showcase for technology, the other was that I wanted to make it big enough so I could have up to a hundred people over for charity events or to celebrate company successes. Having a great library or the incredible screens has been a lot of fun but I still can't enjoy these things without feeling a little guilty about it." Not too guilty, however. Around the base of a library dome is this inscription from *The Great Gatsby*: "He had come a long way to this blue lawn and his dream must have seemed so close he could hardly fail to grasp it."

VII–THE CHARM OFFENSIVE

IN Washington, D.C., the first wave of government witnesses seemed to tip the case toward the government. Microsoft was also being judged by public opinion, and that judgment was not going well. The company's public-relations department wanted Neukom and the other lawyers to be more accessible to reporters. They worried that even though polls showed that Microsoft was widely admired, in the long run the company would be hurt by the bad press.

"We have the wrong lawyers," a senior Microsoft executive said. "These are antitrust lawyers," he explained. "In most antitrust cases, there are no witnesses. It's all transcripts, briefs." His disdain for Sullivan & Cromwell was matched by his disdain for Neukom's approach to the trial: "He likes to think of himself as a lawyer's lawyer. . . . He's as much a legal nerd as we're computer nerds." This man equated David Boies with "the Johnnie Cochran school of law, swaying people with emotion," and went on to say, "Normally, you wouldn't hire Gerry Spence or F. Lee Bailey for an antitrust case, but here we should have." Neukom, on the other hand, insisted that colleagues focus on the law; he feared that a public-relations offensive would offend Judge Jackson and might telegraph Microsoft's trial strategy.

The debate became so intense in December that Gates himself got involved. He became convinced, he told me in an E-mail exchange, that the government had turned the case "into a show trial with the primary goal of embarrassing us every day, rather than focusing on the facts of their damaged case. In some ways, when we started this trial, we were a little old fashioned—we believed the real trial was in the courtroom." He told Neukom that Microsoft should be more proactive, and that he should be more accessible to reporters. Yet neither side in this internal battle wished to acknowledge that the person who probably most harmed Microsoft's credibility was Bill Gates. While polls showed that the public respected Gates, the audience that counted in this trial was one person: Thomas Penfield Jackson. A few days before the trial recessed for Thanksgiving, Microsoft's lawyers had received an ominous warning of what Judge Jackson thought about the Gates deposition. Warden had argued that Boies should cease playing the Gates tape in short, excruciating snippets, and just show it all at once. Jackson stared at Warden, rejected his request, and chilled him with these words: "If anything, I think your problem is with your witness."

Perhaps the best news that Microsoft received during the first months of the trial had come from outside the courtroom. Ostensibly, it was bad news. On November 24th, A.O.L. announced that, in exchange for $4.2 billion of its stock, it was acquiring Netscape and joining with Sun Microsystems to build an Internet service company that could rival Microsoft and I.B.M. The partnerships would bring three Microsoft competitors together into a single potential colossus. Neukom appeared on the front steps of the courthouse and declared, "This proposed deal pulls the rug out from under the government. It proves indisputably that no company can control the supply of technology." A month later, on the afternoon before the Christmas break, Judge Jackson startled the courtroom by announcing that this new alliance "might be a very significant change in the playing field." A sense grew that maybe the trial was dealing with yesterday, while the industry it concerned was being transformed tomorrow, and that maybe Microsoft was as vulnerable outside the courtroom as inside.

Gates suddenly began to show a warmer side. In December of 1998, he appeared, wearing a gray sweater, on *The Rosie O'Donnell Show*, and made it clear that he was there to talk not about the trial or about competitors but about his two-and-a-half-year-old daughter—what she liked to have read to her and how she liked to play. He allowed Rosie to break the news that Melinda Gates was again pregnant. He talked about his large house, and he showed off Arthur, a Microsoft talking toy.

In January, he appeared on Martha Stewart's TV program, where he talked about his daughter again and also about Stewart's mother, who, she said, was now on E-mail. "That's fantastic," Gates purred.

Later that month, he travelled again to the World Economic Forum, in Switzerland, and before he made his annual luncheon speech to journalists his handlers instructed the conference spokeswoman, Barbara Erskine, to announce, "Mr. Gates is not prepared to comment on the Department of Justice trial." Before he could hear a groan, Gates stepped forward and declared, "I'll take one or two questions on it, but at some point I'll get tired of it." He didn't tire of it. Although one of his close friends had told me that morning that Gates was depressed and angry about the antitrust suit, Gates himself told a different tale. He was asked if the trial made him angry at the Justice Department. With his left hand on his hip, he said, "No. I don't think bringing an emotional approach to an issue like that is very constructive."

Gates's charitable activities also became more visible. At a dinner given by

Rosie O'Donnell last December in New York, he and Melinda were honored—along with Jane and Michael Eisner, of Disney—by the For All Kids Foundation. The next day, the Gateses held a press conference to announce that the William H. Gates Foundation was making a hundred-million-dollar gift to speed the distribution of vaccines in the Third World. The Gates Foundation and the Gates Learning Foundation had made many generous gifts in the past, but this was presented in a far more public way. Gates is now poised to become America's foremost living philanthropist.

A FEW months earlier, Microsoft had retained Mark Penn, a pollster for Bill Clinton and Al Gore, to explore how Gates and Microsoft could be better perceived as good corporate citizens. An internal Microsoft E-mail exchange suggests that the company had gone to extraordinary lengths not to miss what it called "a public relations opportunity." On February 22nd, David Kaefer, the marketing research manager, sent an E-mail to Barbara Dingfield, the director of community affairs, who reports to Bill Neukom, and to nine other staffers. "This mail is intended to recommend and spur discussion concerning which five or six image attributes we should use to access the effectiveness of our branded philanthropic communication efforts," Kaefer wrote. He then listed "image attributes we have used in past research": approachable, arrogant, caring, greedy, good corporate citizen, only looking out for itself, etc. Kaefer said that a senior executive, Ann Redmond, had asked him to consult experts to "help us arrive at a preferred set of attributes," among which were these contenders:

· Microsoft cares about making a difference in my community
· Microsoft is a leader in good corporate citizenship
· Microsoft's charitable giving improves the lives of many people
· Microsoft is honest
· Microsoft is a company I trust
· Microsoft is a generous and supportive corporate citizen

When the trial resumed, for its tenth week, on January 4th of this year, Bill Neukom seemed like a different person: he mingled with reporters, shaking their hands, and chatting with them about holiday vacations. From then on, Neukom appeared almost daily on the front steps to field questions.

THE government's last witness, who appeared shortly after the trial resumed, was Franklin M. Fisher, an economics professor at M.I.T., who was known to be David Boies's favorite economist; Boies had first relied on him in 1970, for the I.B.M. case, in which Fisher argued that the computer giant was not a monopoly. Fisher was good-natured but professorial, ostensibly humble but brimming with certitude about economics, intellectually acute but abstruse. He was paid five hundred dollars an hour for testifying in court and also for every hour he had spent in preparation.

Fisher asserted that Microsoft was a monopoly engaged in unlawful practices, because it dominated P.C.s and because it had the power to raise prices at will and because there were barriers on competitors who wished to enter its market. "Computer manufacturers," he testified, "do not believe they have any alternative to the acquisition and installation" of Windows. By bundling and giving away its browser, Fisher added, Microsoft was guilty of classic "predatory" behavior.

Under questioning from the Sullivan & Cromwell attorney Michael Lacovara, Fisher made a startling admission. He was asked if consumers were being victimized by Microsoft, and, after hesitating, he declared, "On balance, I would think the answer was no, up to this point." Neukom smiled. David Boies stoically stared straight ahead, as did Joel Klein. William Kovacic, of the George Washington University Law School, who had been reading the daily transcripts of the trial, later told me that Fisher's admission was "the single greatest testimonial blunder for the government" in the entire trial, ranking with the harm done to Microsoft by Bill Gates's videotaped failure "to tell their story." The real harm to consumers, Fisher hurried to assert, would appear in the future, as Microsoft blocked innovation and raised prices—an assertion easier to make than to prove.

VIII–TRICK QUESTIONS

IT was now Microsoft's turn to call twelve witnesses, many of whom radiated hubris: they would turn the case around for Microsoft; they would educate the Judge; they would prove that David Boies was a computer illiterate; they would prove that they were smarter; they would take a bow. And indeed, some Microsoft witnesses would score.

Microsoft, however, was not always helped by its first witness, Richard L. Schmalensee, the dean of M.I.T.'s Sloan School of Management. He released an eye-glazing three hundred and sixty-four pages of written testimony, much of it contradicting his former mentor, Franklin Fisher. Pay no heed to the "small mountain of E-mails," to the "speculation" over who might be harmed, he said, for what counted was whether consumers were harmed. They were not, he said; nor was Microsoft capable of exerting monopoly power. Schmalensee, like Fisher, reminded those in the courtroom that economics is not always an exact science. The two "scientists" drew from the same pool of "facts," yet reached opposite conclusions.

With Schmalensee, as with others, Boies demonstrated a basic courtroom technique. "During a cross-examination, David takes a friendly walk down the hall with you while he's quietly closing doors," observed Jeffrey Blattner, who served as Joel Klein's de-facto chief of staff and was in court each day. "They get to the end of the hall and David turns on you and there's no place to go. He's closed all the doors." After allowing Schmalensee to express himself, Boies started closing doors. He approached the lectern, blowing his nose into a paper towel, which he then folded to fit into his back pocket. (He had forgotten a handkerchief.) How long had Schmalensee been "retained" by Microsoft? There was no formal retainer, though he had done work for the company since 1992. (He was paid eight hundred dollars an hour.) Was it accurate, Boies inquired, to refer to him as Microsoft's "house economic expert"? Was it true that Microsoft held a monopoly over operating systems for Intel-based personal computers? The expert witness said that he did not consider this a "relevant" question. After declaring that rival operating systems and such devices as the Palm Pilot posed a "significant" threat to Windows, Boies demanded to know whether the Palm Pilot was a "significant" threat today. Schmalensee retreated, saying, "As it stands, it is not a significant competitor. It is a germ of a potential competitor." Judge Jackson helped keep the witness on the defensive by asking whether the viable operating-system competitors he cited had made any money. Schmalensee responded, "I would be stunned if they were making a lot of money." Boies's strategy was obvious: if Schmalensee appeared to be contradicting himself, to be splitting hairs, his credibility would be tarnished.

MICROSOFT'S worst moment may have come in the testimony of its executive in charge of Windows, James Allchin. In court, after Allchin piously repeated what he had said in his deposition—that Microsoft combined the products to serve its customers better—Boies produced a December, 1996, E-mail from Allchin to his boss, Paul Maritz, which Boies said he considered one of the most incriminating pieces of evidence among the more than three million pages that the government had collected. As Allchin ruminated about "concerns for our future," the very first of eight concerns that he cited was how Internet Explorer was losing to Netscape Navigator. His solution—which Boies sees as proof that Microsoft was guilty of classic predatory behavior—was wickedly simple:

> I don't understand how IE is going to win. The current path is simply to copy everything that Netscape does packaging and product wise. Let's [suppose] IE is as good as Navigator/Communicator. Who wins? The one with 80% market share. Maybe being free helps us, but once people are used to a product it is hard to change them. . . . My conclusion is that we must leverage Windows more. Treating IE as just an add-on to Windows which is cross-platform [loses] our biggest advantage—Windows market share. . . . We should think first about an integrated solution—that is our strength.

In a more publicly devastating move, Boies attacked a Microsoft video that purported to show that a program written by a government computer expert to remove Microsoft's browser caused significant "performance degradation." Boies's technical advisers had noticed that the line at the top of the open window did not say "Windows 98," as it would have if the program had run, which meant that the video did not show what it claimed. Boies stunned Allchin by pointing this out. The witness still had days of testimony left, but Boies had already won the psychological war game between lawyer and witness.

Humiliated, and obviously furious at this mistake, Allchin left the courthouse on February 2nd, his arm shielding his face from cameras. The next day, he endured still another humiliation, when Boies showed that Microsoft's taped demonstration did not rely on a single P.C., as had been implied, but, rather, spliced together footage of at least two different machines. Boies was so psyched for his questioning of Allchin that day that this creature of habit, who usually skips lunch during a trial, asked his wife to bring him a bag of cinnamon-raisin bagels. He wolfed down seven of them while he studied documents in the witness room during the lunch break. At about 4 P.M., when Judge Jackson turned to face the witness and declared, "It's very troubling, Mr. Allchin," Boies knew he had achieved a Perry Mason moment. With Joel Klein and the entire Justice Department team beaming from the spectator seats, Boies abruptly announced that he was finished with the witness. Microsoft's lawyers hurriedly asked for a bench conference with Judge Jackson to request that he allow Allchin to prepare a new video overnight, which he would personally supervise and narrate.

The government got the headlines, but Allchin's testimony was not as bad as it seemed. Of the many claims made by Allchin in his hundred-and-thirty-nine-page deposition, Boies attacked relatively few, and, the next day, in court, Allchin did finally show that the government had wrongly asserted that it could decouple the browser from Windows: it had hidden the browser icon, but could not entirely remove the browser. Allchin had proved his point, but at what cost? Bill Neukom stood outside, cautioning the press not to mistake theatrics for substance. With his hands clasped, he tried to defuse the prosecutorial zeal of reporters, and he spoke lightly of the mishaps: "We make very good software. We did not make a good tape." Nevertheless, the headlines carried one message: Arrogant Microsoft.

Boies was shaky when he questioned William Poole, who had supervised Microsoft's relationships with Internet content providers, such as Intuit. Boies may have been paying for his insistence on personally conducting the cross-examination of eleven of the Microsoft witnesses. It was clear that his back was hurting him, for he walked more slowly than usual, and shuffled his feet. Things went better when he began questioning Cameron Myhrvold, the brother of Nathan Myhrvold, who was the chief technology officer; Cameron was a vice-president of Microsoft, and he supervised the division that worked with Internet service providers. He quickly corrected some of Boies's questions, as if he were helping the lawyer better understand exactly what he meant to ask.

Boies then slyly undercut his witness, saying, "Most of my questions are not trick questions. Some are."

"Would you tell me which ones?" Myhrvold asked.

"If I'm going to ask a trick question, I'll raise my hand," said Boies, and both Judge Jackson and Bill Neukom joined in the laughter.

Boies then lobbed a softball. Would Myhrvold agree that Internet service providers like A.O.L. and computer manufacturers were the most important distributors of browsers?

"I've certainly heard that," but it wasn't necessarily true, said the witness.

"Have you heard yourself say that?" asked Boies, provoking laughter as he ostentatiously raised his hand. And at that he asked the witness to look at page 43 of his written deposition, where he asserted a contrary view. Myhrvold then acknowledged that he had been mistaken.

Around this time, one sensed that Bill Neukom's nerves were frayed. When court adjourned on February 9th, as reporters and lawyers mingled, I was off to the side on the courthouse steps, chatting with Blattner. I was taking notes, and I noticed a pair of polished brown shoes attached to long legs suddenly stationed in front of us. It was Neukom, his hands clasped in front of his double-breasted suit, his purple polka-dot bow tie brighter than the tight smile on his face. He just stood there, listening. Blattner was stunned, because Neukom had studiously avoided speaking to him or catching his eye for months. Blattner looked at him, as if to say "What?"

For a moment, they glared silently at each other—Blattner puzzled and Neukom determined. Blattner's sunglasses, thick mustache, and dark hair that falls to his collar no doubt reinforced Microsoft's sinister stereotype of him. Ever since Blattner joined Justice, in March of 1998, Microsoft believed that he had orchestrated leaks to various reporters, and particularly to those at the *Wall Street Journal*, a claim Blattner denies. Microsoft knew that Blattner, as chief counsel to Senator Edward Kennedy's staff on the Judiciary Committee, had played a pivotal role in the sometimes vicious battle to deny Robert Bork a seat on the Supreme Court. Bill Gates spits out the name "Blattner" as if it were a curse, and on the court steps that day, after staring at Blattner for a long, silent moment, Neukom declared, "This is a public space." He would not move, so we did. On being asked weeks later about this encounter, Neukom said, unconvincingly, that he was not trying to make a statement. "I was interested in knowing what he was talking about," he said. "I may have misjudged his reaction. I didn't mean to make him feel uncomfortable."

Of the twelve Microsoft witnesses who took the stand between January 13th and February 26th, among the least effective was John Rose, then a senior vice-president and group general manager of the Enterprise Computing group at Compaq Computer. A weakness of the government's case, which Justice officials privately acknowledged, was that its lawyers had failed to recruit a P.C. manufacturer to testify against Microsoft. If Microsoft could demonstrate that it had not bullied manufacturers, the government's accusation that it had mo-

nopolized distribution would topple. Unfortunately, Rose looked like a cross between Jimmy Hoffa and John Gotti, in a black suit and white, cufflinked shirt,
with short black hair combed straight back, accentuating a receding hairline.
He shook the hands of reporters on the way in, looking cocky, as if he were accepting congratulations. When he got on the stand, he had a disconcerting
habit of smiling at the press section, and when he smiled his eyebrows curled
up and his white teeth glistened. Rose insisted that Compaq enjoyed a "front-
line partnership" with Microsoft, distinguishing this from the mere "partnership" it had with most other companies. Boies quickly portrayed Rose as a
puppy and Compaq as a company that jumped when Microsoft barked.

IX–COULD THEY SETTLE THIS?

OVER a late dinner in a Georgetown restaurant in mid-February, Bill
Neukom took off his tie and tried to relax. The witness phase of the trial was almost over, and he was still certain that the government had not proved its
claims and that Microsoft would triumph. Why, then, I asked, was there such
a disparity between what he saw and what the press reported?

"It's a combination of things," he said thoughtfully. "First, the technology at
the heart of this case is so complex and changing so rapidly that even the top
players in the industry can't predict for certain where it will go next. So it has
been a challenge to put the government's accusations into a proper industry
context for reporters. Second, a civil trial in federal court is not a completely intuitive, spectator-friendly theatre. It's not designed to be engaging to the
gallery. It's pretty dry stuff, frankly. Third, the Sherman Act is a very short couple of paragraphs interpreted by federal courts, and it's much misunderstood.
Some people want to believe that the Sherman Act is a sort of competitor-
protection act. . . . That's not what the law is. The Sherman Act recognizes
some competitors inherently have advantages over others, and it encourages
rough-and-tumble competition so consumers get the best product at the lowest
price. When you couple that with an intellectual-property business like ours,
you have a fourth level of complexity."

He continued talking: "Add to this deadline pressures. Our defense by its very
nature was complicated and extremely dense with facts and economic analysis.
We think the government's case has been short on facts but long on theatre. The
press has worked very hard . . . but given the deadline pressures, it's no surprise
that the theatre often won out over the dry substance in the daily coverage."

Nor has Microsoft been deft in its dealings with reporters. Nearly every Microsoft executive who sits for an interview, either in D.C. or on the Redmond
campus, is accompanied by someone from public relations. "My shadow is
joining us for dinner," a Microsoft official announced one evening. At dozens of
interviews on the Microsoft campus, someone from the public-relations office
was always present, scribbling furiously, and sometimes interrupting to sug-

gest that a question was out of bounds. The P.R. staff, in its best, no-surprises mode, prepared dossiers on reporters: a multipage memo would be sent to those about to be interviewed, offering glimpses of the journalist's bio, his or her alleged biases, beliefs, conflicts, friendships, and the questions that the reporter had asked in prior interviews. Before one of my visits to Redmond, John Pinette, a former Catholic priest, who would be my pleasant but omnipresent shadow, internally E-mailed a three-page, single-spaced document, much like a raw F.B.I. report, to people I would be interviewing. The memo asserted, for instance, that "David Boies and his wife are very close with Auletta." I had never met Mary Boies before Justice filed this case, and I knew Boies himself only superficially. Some excerpts:

> Our objectives in having you meet with him are to portray the company as still faithful to its fundamental vision—and working hard for customers. . . . Ken wants to know if we are demoralized, and we want to show people who are excited about the contributions they're making. If they're paranoid about anything, it's not the trial, but the competitor's latest development that could make their product obsolete. This is the human side of Redmond. Good people (genuine, positive, forthright) with good motivations (wanting to make a contribution vs. greed or anti-competitiveness).
> Your approach to this interview . . .
> If he thinks you're just stating the party line, you will lose credibility in his eyes. Be sincere. It's okay to acknowledge that we can always do better as a company.

At the end of one of several visits to the Microsoft campus, I asked Pinette why he took such voluminous notes and what he did with them. He evasively said they provided a record of what each interviewer said, so that when the reporter's piece appeared in print Microsoft could rebut any inaccuracies. Months later, after I had seen Pinette's E-mail, I asked him, "Why are you folks so controlling?" He replied, "Indeed, it is a very aggressive approach to preparing people for interviews." I asked where he'd heard that I was "very close" to the Boieses. "I saw it in another document written by someone else in P.R.," he said.

ON February 26th, after Microsoft's final witness completed his testimony, Judge Jackson recessed the trial, for what turned out to be thirteen weeks. During that period, pressures on Microsoft to settle intensified. Intel, on the eve of a March hearing, had suddenly reached an agreement with the Federal Trade Commission. Although the charges against Intel were narrower than those lodged against Microsoft, the two sets of charges were alike in that other companies in the industry needed access to the architecture of both the dominant chip maker and the dominant software company in order to design products that meshed.

In early February, Judge Jackson had held an unpublicized closed-door meeting with the parties. He told both sides that it might be better for all concerned if they settled the case instead of waiting for an imposed settlement. Then, in a status conference in his chambers on March 31st, Jackson told the lawyers that he had a new trial schedule: each side would be permitted three rebuttal witnesses, after which the court would recess for thirty days while Microsoft and the government prepared briefs setting out what they believed to be the incontrovertible facts of the case. Then would come final oral arguments, followed by a findings-of-fact ruling by the Judge. During another recess, each side would prepare a brief on how antitrust law applied to this case. Then would come more oral arguments, and after them a conclusions-of-law ruling. By splitting the facts from the law, which both Boies and Warden said was innovative, Jackson would inevitably prolong the trial. The less obvious consequence was that this schedule put pressure on both sides to settle, since the Judge was now going to begin showing his cards.

During the recess, a subtle but important shift took place in Microsoft's attitude regarding a negotiated settlement. Throughout the trial, a Microsoft insider admitted, Microsoft had thought that it would lose some and win some in this courtroom and win everything on appeal. By splitting the findings of fact from the findings of law, however, Jackson had altered this core assumption; now it feared that its chances of winning everything on appeal were more tenuous. Microsoft was now prepared, the insider said, to cut its losses. In secret meetings with Joel Klein, on February 24th, March 30th, and in the first week of June, Bill Neukom submitted discussion drafts that indicated more flexibility. Microsoft had submitted three different draft versions of a proposed settlement, but the Justice Department had rejected such a settlement as unsatisfactory. "We're running out of runway here," a Microsoft executive said then.

When the trial resumed, on June 1st, neither side would succeed in altering the trial's dynamics. When the last rebuttal witness had finished, on June 24th, Judge Jackson called another recess. Before doing so, he announced that he was directing each side to prepare by August 10th a brief specifying what they believed to be the incontrovertible facts of this case. "All right, gentlemen," Jackson said with a smile. "It has been almost all pure pleasure up to this point. Let's keep it that way."

X–IN SEARCH OF BILL GATES

DURING the spring recess, I went back to Microsoft to see Bill Gates. Among the forty-five buildings on the Microsoft campus, Gates's office, in Building 8, is unusual: its floors are carpeted and, compared with other offices, it is vast. At any other Fortune 500 company, it might house someone of the rank of, say, vice-president for community relations. Gates's office has few personal flourishes: the desk is a slab of plain oak, and the only pictures on a wall are two framed covers from *The Economist* given to him by his sister Libby—a diagram of an Intel chip and a chart describing the bandwidth of various radio frequencies. The P.C. was a Toshiba laptop with a docking station and two oversized monitors (one screen is separated into four quadrants, which stream information from selected Web sites all day). There is a gray couch and four chrome-based green-and-blue wool-covered Breuer-style chairs around a square maple coffee table. On a credenza rest several family pictures.

On the day we talked, in late May, Gates wore a handsome, royal-blue open-necked dress shirt buttoned at the sleeves, and with "WHG" embroidered on the chest, navy slacks, unpolished black loafers, and clear-framed oval eyeglasses. His skin was the color of eggshells, as if he had spent too many hours indoors. His hair was unwashed, the bangs chopped near the roots, as if by shears. The previous afternoon, Melinda Gates had given birth to their second child, a son, and Gates had spent part of the day at the hospital. That afternoon, Microsoft would announce the birth, yet Gates said not a word about it to me. Upon greeting me, he plopped onto a chrome-based chair, folded his arms across his thighs, and began rocking rapidly back and forth, slapping the carpet with the soles of his loafers as he came forward and creating the impression that his body was a metronome.

Gates has often been compared with another great business figure who ran afoul of the government, John D. Rockefeller. Both enjoyed a market share of more than eighty percent, made huge investments in R. & D., were generous philanthropists, were messianic in their belief that their business served the public weal, were not concerned with yachts or creature comforts, although they did enjoy extravagant homes. Each understood the underlying value of his business. Rockefeller knew that more money was to be made in processing oil than in drilling for it; Gates knew that more was to be made in creating software than in building hardware. And each endured a costly trial against the government that might have been averted had he been more flexible. The differences between the two men were also great, however. Rockefeller was scorned by the public, whereas Gates remains an icon of innovation for a majority of Americans. Rockefeller's Standard Oil dominated a scarce resource and the means of distributing it, whereas the intellectual property that Gates owns is not scarce, and a distribution system like the Internet can hardly be controlled.

The official line at Microsoft is that the trial in Washington, D.C., is "white noise"; everyone in Redmond, it is said, is focussing on business. But Gates is as agitated today about what he sees as the ludicrousness of the government's case as he was a year ago. "If you have talented people doing the right thing, the shares—the position of the product—can be changed," he said. "That's why we invest so much more in R. & D. every year. . . . Even with all the great people we have, we face probably more intense competition now than ever before. Only in a courtroom can somebody say, 'Hey, Linux is a serious competitor,' and the press laughs in a way that makes the judge think, O.K., that must be a false statement, that must be posturing."

In discussing with Gates what he sees as the great gap between the world of Washington and the business world he inhabits, I asked him if he felt another sort of disconnection when the Justice Department told him that he and Microsoft had done bad things and when he felt that he had done good ones. Did he sometimes feel, as a friend had said, like Joseph K.? "I don't know Joseph K., sorry," he said. On being told that Joseph K. was the main character in Franz Kafka's *The Trial*, Gates said, "He sounds like my kind of guy!"

Turning to the charges presented against his company, Gates said, "Let's look at what actually happened. They went in saying that the consent decree banned us supporting the Internet, putting the browser capability into the operating system. They said, black and white, 'Hey, all you have to do is delete these files and this pie here will be eliminated. So issue an order telling them to delete these files. It's that simple.' Well, it wasn't." He continued, "Our guy goes in, testifies under oath, 'Hey, if you delete those files that thing does not boot right.' " Nevertheless, Judge Jackson, in December of 1997, had ordered that the browser and the operating system be untied. "Where did that all end up? The appeals court was very clear: the consent decree does not touch on this, what's gone on here, in any way." He cited as equally satisfying the appeals court's admonition that government should not attempt to design software products.

Yes, there have been discussions with people at the Justice Department about a possible settlement, Gates said, but talking with them is frustrating. He explained, "We keep trying to get them to articulate what features under this new law they're trying to create—what features we are allowed to add and what features we are not allowed to add. And we say . . . in any discussion we have with them, 'What is your principle here? How should we have known that you would think supporting the Internet is a bad thing?' And we say to ourselves, 'It's the most defensible feature that we've ever added in.' . . . Didn't we create the product that won all the reviews? Didn't we create the product that people didn't have to pay extra for? . . . Somebody who was paying attention, they would know to laugh!" In the real world, he continued, Netscape is bought for billions of dollars. Yet in a Washington courtroom the government cries that Netscape has been foreclosed and Microsoft has killed Netscape by offering a free browser. "What the heck logic is there behind this?"

I asked if he regretted not having settled in May of 1998. "I wish we could have settled," he said. "I wished that at the time. I wish that now. Look, I'm not in this thing to prove some principle. Thank goodness, there are some principles and some laws in this country about how things are done. We've always wanted to settle this thing." The stumbling block, he said, was that he couldn't go back to the government for permission each time he wanted to add a new

feature, just because a competitor like Netscape whined about the added feature. "You have to have a business left when you settle," he said. At that moment, he saw no way out.

I asked Gates how he assessed the job that his legal team was doing. He
rocked back and forth in his chair several times before answering, then talked
about the five-year legal battle with Apple: "We went through a lot on that
one," including a bad press before the victory.

He hadn't answered the question, so I asked it again.

"Well, there's a lot of things about this that they don't control," he said.
"They don't control the leaking of the government." Then he said, "I haven't
been back there at all," and only "meet with the lawyers from time to time."
Then he trailed off.

"Do you think they've done a good job in the law?"

Again, there was a long pause before he replied. Then he said, "Well, as far
as this case goes they've certainly proved that Netscape was not foreclosed.
And they've certainly proved that there are immense benefits to developers
and users of our putting these Internet features as well as other features into
the product. They've done a very good job establishing those things. And those
are the issues at hand."

I then asked what he admired about Bill Neukom. There was a pause of
about ten seconds before he answered. Then he said, "He's a very good lawyer
himself and he also brings in, both into his department and through outside relationships, people with a lot of expertise." He paused, thoughtfully, then continued, "I myself am not a lawyer."

Gates was unhappy about the broad brush applied to him and to his company, and he pressed me to take one fact—one incident from Intuit, Intel,
I.B.M., from "all this mud that's been slung"—and find out whether it really
demonstrated bad behavior by Microsoft.

What about coercion, I asked—the charge that Microsoft muscled Intel to
stay out of the software business?

"I don't know what muscle means," he said.

What if his daughter came to him some years hence, I suggested, and asked,
Dad, how do you explain some of these E-mails and things like the threat to cut
off Netscape's air supply?

Gates was composed, but he answered in a shrill voice. "A great lie! A great
lie!" he cried out. "An unbelievable lie!" It was secondhand hearsay, he said.
His voice rising, yet better controlled, he went on, "Did anyone utter those
words? Our E-mail, every piece of it has been searched. I wish we *had* found
somebody who had said it. Then we could take him out, and we could hang the
guy, then we'd say, 'O.K., mea culpa. We found him—the guy who said, "I'll
cut off your oxygen." ' First of all, there's no law against saying that. Second of
all, I never heard anybody say it. Third of all—hey, if there's any company that
would know damn well whether it was said or not, this is the company. Every

piece of E-mail I have ever sent for the last ten years has been read and read, and if there is any way that people can misconstrue any statement that I've ever made it has been done. You look at any E-mail sent by me or received by me, and tell me what is it you think is at all inappropriate?"

What about his offering a million-dollar "favor" to Intuit if it chose his browser over Netscape's?

"The fact that I was willing to put a million dollars into joint marketing, a million dollars into helping them do the engineering, just shows I was desirous of getting them to exploit our technology," he answered. "And what's wrong with that? This is the kind of thing that blows the mind! Yes, I was so anxious to have them show off" the new features of the I.E. browser, which Netscape's browser did not have. "How can that be characterized as something inappropriate? If I hadn't offered that million dollars, you'd have to say to me, 'Bill, are you doing your job?' " Besides, he lamented, it's all a moot point: "no such thing ever happened," since Intuit declined.

When I asked Gates about the ethical dimensions of Microsoft's hardball tactics, he replied, "There is nothing I want more than to find something to do a mea culpa on. The fact that we're so successful, people really do want to know that we're behaving responsibly, in terms of how we work with partners, how we work with customers, how we think about things in long-term ways, and I believe Microsoft has been exemplary in those things. Go ask the analysts how Microsoft behaves with them in terms of the integrity of the information. Go ask some of our customers. You take our relationship with Apple. This is a company where, during the time they sue us to try and put us out of business, who was developing more software for the Macintosh than anybody else? They're not letting us get the [Mac Operating System] information. They're discriminating against us. They're doing joint marketing with all of our competitors. Just mistreating us every single step of the way. We're always trying to figure out some way to help them, to work with them. The notion that somebody could misconstrue those negotiations with Apple! We did something incredibly valuable to them. We invested in the company where people had lost faith in Apple. We renewed our commitment to do all these new versions of software at a time when that was very important to them." What people misunderstand, he continued, is that Microsoft's belated discovery of the Internet was really what drove it to bundle the browser and to focus more on Netscape. "We were slow. We hadn't recognized the importance of it. And this trial, in a sense, comes out of that."

BY early August, there had been no further contact between Microsoft and the Justice Department, and both sides privately agreed that if settlement talks were ever to get serious this would probably not happen until the fall, around the time of Judge Jackson's first ruling on the findings of fact. Microsoft received good news in July, when a Connecticut jury found in its favor in an antitrust suit brought by Bristol Technology which raised some of the same arguments as the Department of Justice. No matter how Jackson rules, though, Microsoft may lose even if it wins in court. Some people suspect that the case will rob the company of the drive and the passion that have contributed to its extraordinary success, as the I.B.M. case did. The shift within Microsoft could be seen in April, when Steve Ballmer said at a conference that the company might consider opening the source code to Windows 2000. "That could be significant—if they meant it," Boies told me during the recess. "It might change the remedy." He meant that if Microsoft lost in court the government might be less inclined to seek a "structural" remedy—like breaking up Microsoft—provided that Microsoft adopted a "behavioral" remedy.

Still, the government will always dog Microsoft, as will the more than three million documents that the Justice Department collected for the trial. As Gates saw it, "No matter what the outcome the lawsuit is a bad thing. The costs to the company and the taxpayers have been huge. The last thing any company wants is to be sued by the government." One reason for this is that any finding against Microsoft which is upheld on appeal might be used against the company in future lawsuits. Greg Maffei, the senior vice-president who is the chief dealmaker for Microsoft, said, "There's not a deal we were stopped from doing. Maybe subconsciously we shied away from things." What they now seek to avoid, he admits, are deals that the government can delay. Inevitably, Microsoft may come to second-guess itself. "I worry that it will make the whole industry more defensive," said Charles Simonyl, the chief architect at Microsoft Research, who fled Communist Hungary in 1966 and became a leading figure in the computing revolution. "I grew up in a society where people are afraid of talking. Now you worry about your E-mail. People say, 'Delete your E-mail.' "

Because of this trial, competitors and also former allies will more freely challenge Microsoft. While Jim Allchin remains, in his words, "super hard core" in his belief that Microsoft is fighting to innovate and thus serve the public good, he acknowledged that "the negative P.R. we've endured" may "embolden competitors." Rob Glaser, of RealNetworks, said, "We've sort of reached glasnost at this point, regardless of the outcome of the trial. In the past, a lot of companies did things because of an aura of fear or an environment of intimidation, whether or not there was actual intimidation by Microsoft. That's forever changed."

Perhaps all of this could have been avoided, but Microsoft, despite its rhetoric, was not truly hard core when it came to the antitrust battle. If Bill Gates and his company had been as ruthlessly practical as they insisted they were, they would have settled the case before it went to trial. But to Gates settling would also have meant settling for something unacceptable: a surrender of control over his company's intellectual property. As it turned out, Microsoft made a strong case that it had not harmed consumers, but Boies persuasively argued that the company had mugged its competitors. In the end, Microsoft mugged itself.

Now the company is taking its political problems far more seriously. Gates, who once told me that you don't need "a lot of political protection to be allowed to innovate," has hired top Washington lobbyists and substantially increased campaign contributions to both major parties. Around the time that the trial adjourned, he appeared before the Senate's Joint Economic Committee to talk about the future of the Information Age. A year earlier, after testifying matter-of-factly before the Judiciary Committee, he had rushed from the hearing room. This time, with hair neatly parted, he replied graciously to even the dimmest questions. "You've raised an interesting issue," he said repeatedly, and then he worked the room, bestowing "Hi, nice to see ya" handshakes on senators. It was as if Gates now understood that Microsoft, like the software that had made him rich, needed an upgrade.

AUGUST 16, 1999

THE

WEB

THE GILDER EFFECT

T O say that George Gilder is an optimist is to realize what a dowdy, cautious word "optimist" is. An optimist anticipates the better outcome; Gilder believes that each new day the world will bring forth boons so unexpected and wonderful that they couldn't be imagined the day before. He believes that now is incomparably the best time to be living on earth, and that in the future things will get even better. Ronald Reagan's first budget director, David Stockman, said of Reagan that if he walked into a room filled with shit he would look for a pony. Gilder is an optimist like that. It is no accident that Gilder—scourge of feminists, unrepentant supply-sider, and now, at sixty, a technology prophet—was the living author Reagan most often quoted.

On a cosmic level, Gilder is an optimist because he has faith in God, but in terrestrial matters he is optimistic because he believes that it is impossible to predict the future based on the past. "Any time in human history that people have projected existing trends, they have predicted catastrophe," he says. "If you imagine that the only resources you will ever have are the resources you have now, then inevitably you will predict their exhaustion. Malthus did it. Ricardo did it. In the nineteen-seventies, an international group of scientists, gathered under the auspices of the Club of Rome, declared that within a century there would be famine everywhere, energy resources exhausted, pollution risen to impossibly toxic levels, and, I believe, a new Ice Age on the way. What the doomsayers don't understand is that the reason humans prevail is creativity, and creativity always comes as a surprise."

Gilder's faith in providence is reflected in his personal life. He is famously a mess. He has often shown up for business meetings in socks of different colors, or wearing sneakers with a suit because he neglected to pack shoes. Tales of

Gilder's absent-mindedness are legion. There was the time he was having lunch with Mrs. Rockefeller and, his interest piqued by a remark on china patterns, he turned his soup bowl over to investigate its provenance, not noticing that the bowl was full. Gilder's practical disabilities seem to stem from a faith that the world is his friend, and if there comes a time when he really needs socks, somehow the world will supply them.

Fortunately for Gilder, he has lived through three moments during which optimism of his ecstatic variety has been rewarded: the Kennedy moment, the Reagan moment, and now the Internet moment. He flubbed the first one. Even though he admired Kennedy, he felt obliged, as a Republican, to balance his contempt for Goldwater with a skeptical attitude toward Democrats. He did his best to engage the spirit of the times; for instance, he tried (and failed) to organize a Republican Freedom Bus. The second moment he caught perfectly: in 1981, he published a book, *Wealth and Poverty*, that exalted capitalism as the fulfillment of the Christian mission on earth. The book was enormously influential in igniting the supply-side passions of the early eighties; it was a favorite of Reagan's and became a best-seller around the world, making Gilder rich for the first time in his life. But it is the third moment, the Internet moment—one that Gilder has been waiting for, longing for, praying for, ever since the late seventies, when he fell in love with the semiconductor industry—in which he has most spectacularly come into his own.

In the past year or so, the market in high-technology stocks has found itself periodically swayed by a phenomenon known as the "Gilder effect." Each month, Gilder publishes a newsletter, the *Gilder Technology Report*, in which he elaborates on what he calls his paradigm: his vision of the future of technology, in terms both sweeping (bandwidth will become virtually free) and specific (CDMA phone systems like Qualcomm's will displace TDMA systems like those of A.T.&T. Wireless). On the last page of his report, Gilder publishes a list of the thirty-odd companies whose products exemplify his paradigm. The list isn't supposed to be a list of investment bargains—Gilder has no interest in a company's financial history, and he doesn't analyze how well a stock is currently valued—but it has been taken as such by many of his readers. Once a month, at the appointed hour, these readers—who pay two hundred and ninety-five dollars a year for a subscription—rush on-line, scan his report for any new company, and then hurry to buy that company's stock. Since there are now approximately sixty-five thousand subscribers, this produces quite a startling effect. In last month's report, for instance, Gilder added Avanex, a fibre-optical-components company, to his list. His report came out on April 24th, when the market in technology stocks was floundering, but, within minutes of the report's publication, Avanex's stock price rose from fifty-five dollars to eighty. By the end of the week, it had passed a hundred and forty. TeraBeam, another company that Gilder recently wrote about, found that its value increased something like fortyfold in the weeks following his recommendation. Paradoxically, the Gilder effect has begun to erode Gilder's reputation as a prophet. Now that many thousands of people buy whatever stock he recommends, his judgments have become self-fulfilling. He no longer predicts markets; he steers them.

But Gilder is not, in the end, so very interested in markets, or E-commerce, or anything that might be described as "content." He is gripped, rather, by the poetics of communications technology itself: by the magical intricacies of its circuits and fibres, and, even more, by the way in which, in its most enchanted, wireless moments, it seems to evade materiality altogether. Gilder was one of the first writers to foresee the potential of the Internet: as early as 1990, in his book *Life After Television,* he wrote about "a crystalline web of glass and light," and "telecomputers in every home attached to a global fiber network." Perhaps one of the reasons his writing about technology has found such a wide audience is that, to him, technology's appeal is ultimately spiritual. In his forthcoming book, *Telecosm,* Gilder writes, "Futurists falter because they belittle the power of religious paradigms, deeming them either too literal or too fantastic. Yet futures are apprehended only in the prophetic mode of the inspired historian. The ability to communicate—readily, at great distances, in robes of light—is so crucial and coveted that in the Bible it is embodied only in angels."

THE week before he published his April report, Gilder was in San Francisco on business. That morning, he had gone running (he runs nearly every day); in the evening, Merrill Lynch was paying him to give a speech in Orinda—a suburb in Contra Costa County, which, owing to the large number of Silicon Valley executives who live there, is one of the wealthiest counties in North America. Merrill Lynch had rented a movie theatre for the occasion, and Gilder arrived early, as a man was affixing to the marquee the words "Merrill Lynch Presents George Gilder," underneath the title of the movie that was currently showing, *Erin Brockovich.* The main street of Orinda has the feel of a nineteen-fifties small town reconstructed for the set of a movie. Across the street from the theatre is a store called Yogurt Bear, and down the street from Yogurt Bear is a little fountain surrounded by flowers. Gilder had an hour to spare, so he decided to walk to a small café around the corner to fortify himself with a prespeech fruit smoothie. He selected a table outside, underneath an umbrella, and sat down, a little out of place in his black suit.

Gilder looks like a character from a nineteenth-century novel about an English village: the boyish church organist, perhaps, or the local priest on a bicycle. He is tall, pale, and spindly. He has blue eyes, thin lips, and a pointy chin. He wears metal-rimmed glasses. All his running has made him so wiry and springy that his limbs appear to be made of some resilient, lightweight wood or metal instead of flesh. Gilder sipped his smoothie and thought about his speech. It was going to be a slightly awkward business, this speech. The audience would expect to hear his newest opinions on companies, but he considered it his duty to his subscribers not to reveal such information to anyone before releasing it to them. All he could think about that afternoon was Avanex—he had spent the previous evening, over dinner in San Francisco, in a long and, for him, at least, impassioned discussion with Avanex's head of research and development—but somehow he was going to have to avoid so much as mentioning the company's name. Gilder is not naturally reticent. At a quarter to seven, he made his way back to the theatre. His knees and elbows and the wing bones of his back poked into the thin fabric of his black suit as he walked, like the metal spokes of an umbrella.

When the audience had settled, Gilder mounted the stage. To his right and to his left, in twin Deco murals painted on the sides of the proscenium, an enormous naked girl was suspended in joyous flight through a starry sky. Compared to the naked girls, Gilder looked even thinner and more umbrellalike than usual. He peered out at the audience through his glasses. He began in a rambling fashion to talk about his paradigm. The computer era—what he calls the "microcosm"—is over, he said. Now we are entering the age of the telecosm: an age of communications and networks. Every age of industrial development is characterized by a particular abundance and a particular scarcity, and those technologies succeed which conserve the scarce resource and waste the abundant one. Before the industrial revolution, land was abundant and power was scarce. Later, power became abundant and land relatively scarce. In the age of the telecosm, bandwidth will become virtually free. Gilder moved his hands up and down a great deal as he spoke, with flattened palms outward, in the manner of one directing airplanes on a runway. His gestures, though, bore no discernible relation to the substance of his sentences, so it appeared that his arms were being controlled by someone backstage who was unable to hear him speak and was forced to rely on guesswork. His voice sounded strained and whiny, as though he were struggling to be heard without a microphone. Gilder is not a natural public speaker. He used to roll his tie up and down, like a window shade, while he spoke, but he has, for the most part, overcome this habit. The real scarcity in the age of the telecosm, Gilder continued, is time: the ultimate impediment to a network's efficiency is the speed of light, which restricts the speed of information flow around the world. The answer is to bring information physically closer, by caching popular Web sites in many international locations so that they no longer have to be sent thousands of miles from their country of origin. This is why companies developing new storage technologies, such as Novell, Sun Microsystems, and Mirror Image, will become increasingly important.

After Gilder finished speaking, many people wanted to ask him questions, but nobody, it seemed, was interested in pursuing the intellectual implications of his paradigm. Nearly every question consisted simply of the name of a company whose market potential the questioner wanted Gilder to evaluate. This is usually the case when Gilder speaks, and it disappoints him, not just because he would much rather get into a discussion about technology than speculate about the stock market; it disappoints him because it demonstrates how widespread what he considers to be a wrong-headed conception of capitalism has become. Capitalism, to Gilder, is not about making money—at least, not in the grasping, individualist sense. It has been a source of great irritation to him over the years that the right has been almost as hard on the capitalist as the left: the two sides may differ on the merits of capitalism as a system, but they tend to agree that the individual capitalist is a figure of, at best, ambiguous morality, driven by greed or, to put it gently, rational self-interest. To Gilder, this is not only offensive but inaccurate. Rational self-interest, he argues, leads to caution, of a sort that might keep an existing enterprise in business but will never generate the kind of radical innovation that leads to new companies and large fortunes. The true entrepreneur has no time to stop and perform calculations. Instead, in love with the beauty of his idea, he rushes imprudently forth, gambling all he has on the chance to create something new. Rationality and prudence are for socialists, who believe that the future may be calculated based on the past; capitalists, who know that the future depends on human acts of creation and is thus incalculable, leap blindly into the unknown.

When *Wealth and Poverty* was first published, Gilder's depiction of the irrational entrepreneur was considered quite eccentric, but in the intervening twenty years it has become conventional wisdom. It is likely that both the extraordinary popular success of the book and the suspicion with which it was initially greeted by many economists were due in part to Gilder's fervent prose. The book is as much sermon as analysis, and its ideology of faith and anti-rationalism allows for a revelatory extravagance that could never accommodate a liberal program of improvement. Gilder is in the business of exhorting ardor for the future more than analyzing the world as it is, and his vocabulary suits this mission. Even his darker warnings are couched in language so grandiose and Biblical that they seem fables rather than admonitions against real possibility. In *Wealth and Poverty*, for instance, he writes, "The rates of taxation climb and the levels of capital decline, until the only remaining wealth beyond the reach of the regime is the very protein of human flesh, and that too is finally taxed, bound, and gagged, and brought to the colossal temple of the state—a final sacrifice of carnal revenue to feed the declining élite." In his celebration of the entrepreneurial leap, Gilder can sound like Ayn Rand, but there is an important difference between them: religion. Rand believed in the glory of selfishness; Gilder believes that capitalism properly understood is altruistic and dependent upon faith in God. (Rand was so disgusted by what she took to be Gilder's perverted sentimentality on this point that she devoted the last public speech of her life to denouncing him.) Gilder's explanation for his thesis is that, because an entrepreneur can never be sure of a return on his investment, starting up a business is like offering a gift to the world, in the hope, but never the certainty, that the gift will be reciprocated.

ONE Monday afternoon, about a month after he returned from San Francisco, Gilder got into his car and drove from his home in the Berkshires to Manhattan. He had several appointments in the city over the next few days before he had to fly to Madison, Wisconsin, to address the state investment board. There was, for instance, a do at the United Nations: an international evening devoted to figuring out how to narrow the gap between rich and poor. Gilder was to be a featured speaker at a table devoted to the impact of E-commerce. He arrived at the U.N. somewhat harried, tie askew, wheeling a suitcase and carrying a tote bag stuffed with papers. He was looking forward to skirmishes. This was, after all, the quintessential bleeding-heart event: he expected to be, as he had been in years past, the most conservative and the most optimistic person present. The dinner was not a situation in which Gilder would have found himself in the normal course of things; he was there because of his connection to its organizer, Peggy Dulany, née Rockefeller, whose father, David Rockefeller, had been a sort of substitute father for Gilder when he was growing up. Among the Rockefeller children of Gilder's generation are some notorious liberals: Peggy is a friend of Castro's; Abby has devoted years to ridding the world of flush toilets, for environmental reasons; Eileen is a proponent of alternative medicine. In this group, Gilder was the only one to turn out conservative—an eccentricity that is tolerated in his adoptive family with varying degrees of resignation. Gilder's real father died at twenty-eight, when Gilder was three, flying an Air Forces plane on the way to serve in the Second World War. Before Richard Gilder went into the Air Forces, he made a deal with Rockefeller, who had been his college roommate, that if he were to die in the war Rockefeller would take care of his son. By dying young, Richard Gilder, as his son puts it, "attained immortality and erected a standard of manhood which would forever prove unattainable." After his father died, his mother married his father's cousin, Gilder Palmer, and the two of them ran a marginally profitable dairy farm in Tyringham, Massachusetts.

Gilder comes from an old—though no longer, in his parents' generation, wealthy—East Coast family. One of his great-grandfathers was Louis Comfort Tiffany, the glassmaker; another was Richard Watson Gilder, the editor of the magazine *Century* and a friend of Grover Cleveland and Walt Whitman. Family legend has it that a handwritten manuscript of *Leaves of Grass* exists somewhere in one of the Gilder farmhouses, misplaced by a forgetful relative. The Gilders were painted by Cecilia Beaux and sculpted by Augustus Saint-Gaudens. A onetime fiancée of Gilder's, the novelist and playwright Jane Stanton Hitchcock, remembers attending a dinner at the house of Gilder's aunt in Washington Square sometime in the seventies, at which conversation turned to the way the war had torn the family apart. She realized only gradually that it was the Civil War they were talking about. But the family is not overly concerned with preserving past grandeur. When Gilder was fifteen and his family's barn, in which they kept cows and antique Tiffany glass, burned to the ground, they saved the cows.

Gilder went to the Hamilton School, Exeter, and Harvard. Hamilton was a progressive school in New York City: its students were taught how to launch protests, they practiced being unionists, and their sex instruction took the form of pretending to be salmon. Gilder was frequently disruptive, and he became known there for stealing books from the library. In all three schools, Gilder was a dreadful student. ("He has become disciplined in a way that one might not have expected when he was young," Rockefeller observes delicately, when asked about Gilder's career.) He was expelled from Harvard after his freshman year for failing courses, and, wanting to do the manliest, toughest thing he could think of, he joined the Marines. After six months, though, he reapplied to Harvard, was taken back, and eventually graduated, in 1962.

Gilder had attended enough Rockefeller dinners at the U.N. to know that if he didn't go on the attack his tablemates would agree with one another, and they'd all fall asleep—especially with an insipid topic like closing the gap between rich and poor. So when it came his turn to introduce himself, he said, "My name is George Gilder, and I'm an advocate of gaps." There was a silence. "Why?" someone asked. Gilder explained that entrepreneurship was the essence of capitalism, and, since some people were more entrepreneurial than others, gaps were inevitable. "So will the rich get richer and the poor poorer?" asked a concerned person at the table, who worked at a hedge fund. "No," Gilder told him impatiently. "There will be more and more rich people."

That evening, Gilder had been set up against Robert Hormats—the vice-chairman of Goldman Sachs International, who served as Deputy U.S. Trade Representative under Jimmy Carter and Assistant Secretary of State under Reagan. Gilder considered Hormats, whom he'd met a few times before, smart but hopelessly lefty, and was looking forward to sparring with him. Politics was not the only difference between them. Hormats is the sort of man who radiates success, good health, and contentment. He is the same age as Gilder but looks fifteen years younger; he is blond and broad-chested, and carries himself with an air of unimpeachable geniality, as though it had been his experience in life that people either agreed with him right away or rapidly succumbed, without animus, to his charisma and capacious intelligence. Gilder, on the other hand, darts into an argument with the aggressive glee of an underdog who sets out to shock, and feels he has failed if no one is offended. Although he is often treated as a guru, Gilder does not have a guru personality. It is not in his nature to cultivate an aura of gravitas and infallibility; instead, he dances twitchily about, fists flailing, glancing warily around him, clinging to his own anxiety as a sign that he is vital—that he has not yet surrendered to smug venerability. This sense of constructive malaise is a character trait, but it is also, for Gilder, a long-standing moral commitment. One of his favorite books in college, José Ortega y Gasset's *The Revolt of the Masses*, an exaltation of spiritual aristocracy, warns against the dangers of contentment. Ortega writes, "There are centuries which die of self-satisfaction through not knowing how to renew their desires, just as the happy drone dies after the nuptial flight."

As the evening proceeded, however, Gilder discovered, to his dismay, that he and Hormats agreed on most issues. Afterward, in an effort to explain this puzzling development, he mused that the Internet had tended to bring liberals and conservatives together: the freewheeling pluralism of Internet culture had inclined many liberals against government regulation, and because E-commerce seemed to lower the barriers to entry in many businesses it tended to make both liberals and conservatives more sanguine about the long-term prospects of the free market. "The heat of the herd," Gilder fretted to himself. He tends to feel that if people agree with him it is a sign that he is failing to think far enough ahead. Perhaps it was time to move on.

GILDER was not always so conservative. As a young man—in college, and for the first few years after graduation—he thought of himself as a progressive Republican, on the basis of his scorn for Goldwater and the John Birch Society and his support for the civil-rights movement. He worked at *The New Leader*, a magazine known primarily as an organ of the anti-Communist left. He cultivated a liberal aesthetic in his life style. He moved to New York and lived in the East Village, on Twelfth Street. He slept during the day, and in the evening he walked over to Slugs, a jazz club on East Third Street that was open almost all night. At Slugs, he would listen to Pharoah Sanders and Sun Ra and write love letters to Joan Didion, whom he knew slightly, through her boyfriend. When he wasn't writing letters to Joan Didion at Slugs, though, he was writing speeches for Nixon. (Later, he wrote speeches for Senator Bob Dole as well, though his relationship with Dole was rocky: once, his college roommate, Bruce Chapman, recalls, Dole took a speech of Gilder's, scattered it around the floor of his hotel room, and, pointing to the pages one by one, reproached Gilder—"Bad! Bad! Bad!"—as if he were a dog who had made a mess indoors.)

Gilder's sixties aesthetic lingers in his writing style, with its Beat-inflected run-on sentences. Pondering his twenty-seven-year-old self in a mordant E-mail, Gilder writes, "I am disgusted. This is a typical 20th century blade, a secular, liberal, priapic, poseur poetic, guilt ridden Wasp, infatuated with blacks in jazz and 'soul' and blues, sweating to suck up their swashbuckling manhood, sure that the world's greatest writers were Norman Mailer and Joan Didion and Robert Lowell (it would take him about a decade of heavy lifting to figure out that contemporary poetry is junk and most of his writer heroes nihilist fools or Marxoid fantasists), quite admiring of Castro and Ho Chi Minh as agrarian patriots, beating a bed in a weekly stint of Wilhelm Reichian Orgone therapy at a shrink's on East End Avenue, and disdainful of businessmen and technologists who were deemed to lack 'soul.' In general, a typical intellectual parasite on the noble body of Capitalism." Eventually, though, he moved to the right. He got to know William F. Buckley, Jr., who, some years before, had founded *National Review*. The publication of the Moynihan report on the black family, in 1965, spurred him into a lifelong campaign against welfare, and Theodore Draper's denunciations of Castro for *The New Leader* extinguished what sparks of leftist sentimentality he had once possessed. Back then, Gilder was obsessed with women. He picked up women everywhere: by the side of the road in the Berkshires, in hotel bars, on Greyhound buses, in diners, in museums and movie theatres, in the park. "He 'loved' them all, so he said," Gilder continues in the E-mail, "but he was in general, with women, as the best ones often detected, a jerk and a creep." He asked at least three women to marry him before one said yes.

Despite his relentless pursuits, Gilder never really attracted the sort of female attention he craved until the early seventies, when he discovered his vocation as an anti-feminist. In those days, he was living in Cambridge, editing the *Ripon Forum*, a magazine put out by the progressive-Republican Ripon Society, when he wrote and published a defense of Nixon's veto of the Mondale-Javits day-care bill, on the ground that, now that welfare had driven away inner-city fathers by rendering them superfluous, day care would deprive poor children of their mothers as well. The female members of the Ripon Society were outraged, and he was fired from his position almost immediately. It was Gilder's first taste of controversy, and he discovered that he liked it. It was fun being the object of attack. After one debate, on PBS, he remembers that "what seemed like hundreds" of women rushed forward onto the stage to argue with him. Since he had spent most of his youth looking for ways to arouse female passion, he reckoned he had found his calling. The aftermath of the day-care brouhaha, though, was not so exciting. Expelled from the Ripon Society, Gilder left Cambridge and moved to New Orleans to work for Ben C. Toledano, a friend of his who had recently decided to run for the Senate. The following few months were, Gilder now feels, the lowest point of his life. "I had no money," he says. "My love life was in a shambles, left behind in Cambridge. At one point, I decided to write *Sexual Suicide*. I'd work for Ben in the morning, and then I'd write all night long at the Café du Monde, on Jackson Square. I was lonely. I was a little creep down in the library writing my screeds and wandering the streets at night with four dollars and sixty-five cents in my pocket. But I did get through the book."

If the day-care controversy had made him something of a feminist target, *Sexual Suicide* was the book that elevated him, in the eyes of the women's movement, to a veritable Satan. The book now reads like a peculiar relic of the seventies, a kind of political camp, but at the time it caused a tremendous row, and in its wake Gilder was awarded the title of Male Chauvinist Pig of the Year by both *Time* and the National Organization for Women (a title he still refers to with some pride, noting that the previous year's recipient was Norman Mailer). The book argued that, without the taming and ego-bolstering influence of a wife and family to support, men were barbarous savages, liable to dash about raping and pillaging and generally wreaking havoc with their predatory lusts and destructively short-term attention spans. "Men lust, but they know not what for," Gilder wrote, with the lyricism of the damned. "They fight and compete, but they forget the prize; they spread seed, but spurn the seasons of growth; they chase power and glory, but miss the meaning of life." Gilder concluded that heterosexual marriage was the key to civilization, and that homosexuality, welfare (which, by making men financially superfluous to a family, led to emasculation and illegitimacy), and feminism (ditto) were its downfall.

His writings on the women's movement are the closest Gilder gets to pessimism. "Will the scientists and women's liberationists be able to unleash on the world a generation of kinless children to serve as the Red Guards of a totalitarian state?" he demanded in the apocalyptic conclusion of *Sexual Suicide.* "Will we try to reproduce the Nazi experiment, when illegitimacy was promoted by the provision of lavish nursing homes and the state usurped the provider male?"

GILDER now lives with his wife, Nini, and their four children, in the red farmhouse he grew up in, in Tyringham (population approximately three hundred and fifty). Nini comes from the nearby town of Lenox, and is, according to Midge Decter, who edited two of Gilder's books, "quality people." Gilder's mother, who is a professional pianist, lives half a mile away, and helps to home-school the Gilder children. (Each child has spent at least one school year at home, in part to inoculate him against noxious secular influences.) Gilder has set up his office in an old mill building in Housatonic, a neighboring village, just a few minutes away from the Norman Rockwell Museum. The setting couldn't be more tranquil: outside Gilder's window, the Housatonic River rushes over rocks; the only audible sounds are splashing water, wind blowing through trees, and someone typing next door. Nonetheless, some time after his return from San Francisco Gilder found himself preoccupied with an accident.

The day before giving his speech in Orinda, he had been driving his rental car somewhere in Oakland and had rammed hard into the Ford Ranger in front of him. Nobody was hurt, but he was startled and disturbed all the same, because he was sure he'd been driving slowly and carefully. He was convinced that the accident was a warning of some kind, but about what? Was he becoming sloppy? Complacent? Giddy with his own success? He couldn't stop thinking about it. Looking backward to change lanes and missing the big thing right in front of his nose that could have left him dead—the incident seemed fraught with meaning. Gilder does not, in any case, believe in accidents. Many years ago, in the mid-seventies, he retreated to a small Caribbean island to write his third book, *Naked Nomads.* The book described the plight of the single man: how without a woman to tame him he was more likely to commit suicide, more likely to commit a crime, and more likely to indulge in reckless behavior. One afternoon, taking a break from writing, Gilder stood for a moment at the edge of a small cliff, before climbing down to the beach to sunbathe.

Next thing he knew, he had inexplicably pitched forward and fallen face first onto the rocks below. That time, too, he had felt himself in the grip of significance. Lying in the hospital with a broken nose, he remembered that only the day before he had been writing about the fact that single men are six times as likely as married ones to die from "accidental falls." He, Gilder, was a single man, and there he was, falling.

The single man's tendency to get into accidents Gilder attributes to psychology, but in general his sense that even trivial events hold meaning is a religious one. He has become much more religious as he has grown older. He describes himself on his *Technology Report* Web site as "an active churchman." Satan now makes occasional but striking appearances in his work. He talks a lot about entrepreneurial creativity and human freedom, but it is not a radical, existential type of freedom he is referring to; it is, rather, freedom within a world that is already filled with ideas and meaning—put there by God, and waiting to be discovered through a mysterious combination of analytic brilliance and intuition. Gilder is, in fact, sufficiently committed to the idea that divine intelligence permeates all earthly occasions that he has turned away from Darwin and has begun reading writers such as Michael Denton and Michael Behe. Denton and Behe are not creationists as that term is usually understood—they don't reject the idea of evolution per se; they don't believe the world was created all at once, six thousand years ago—but they reject the idea that evolution is a purely mechanical process with no inherent purpose. They argue that the complex workings of molecular biology and the precise fitness of the cosmos for human life compel the conclusion that the universe—evolution and all—was designed by a benevolent deity for the purpose of producing mankind.

To Gilder's mind, most of what secularism gets wrong about the world can be summed up in the phrase "the Materialist Superstition." By this, he means the idea that the world is composed of physical matter, and whatever else may arise—love, religious feeling—is a product of matter and reducible to it. Included in this mistake, according to Gilder, is any sort of economics that imagines industrial development to have a momentum of its own apart from the genius of individual entrepreneurs; any psychology that conceives of consciousness as a side product of the brain; and, of course, any biology that understands evolution as a purely bodily process spurred by carnal need and random mutation. Gilder believes that quantum physics has confirmed his view: to him, the discovery that matter is, at base, composed not of inert, solid particles but of waves, fields, and probabilities means that matter is, at base, intelligence or spirit.

More than anything, Gilder is a romantic. Not only does he despise materialism; he also disdains rationality and calculation. Genius, to him, is to be found in intuitive, irrational leaps; in flashes of insight whose origins cannot be traced; in risks so bold that their outcomes cannot possibly be predicted. Human creativity, he believes, will flourish as long as minds remain open to chance, intuition, and mystery; it will wither when people imagine that they must proceed by empirical and logical means alone. This is why he holds that socialism is the work of the Devil. "The most dire and fatal hubris for any leader is to cut off his people from providence, from the miraculous prodigality of chance, by substituting a closed system of human planning," he wrote in *Wealth and Poverty*. But this creed is not just a fancy way of extolling the imagination; Gilder believes, rather, that evading reason allows a person to glimpse mysteries whose existence he otherwise would never suspect. "The mind has access to a higher consciousness, sometimes anomalously, after Jung, called a *collective unconscious*, sometimes defined as God," he wrote, in the same chapter. "As a person's mind merges with the living consciousness that is the ulterior stuff of the cosmos, he reaches new truths, glimpses the new ideas—the projections of light into the unknown future—by which intellectual progress occurs." This is no mere supposition on Gilder's part: he believes he has experienced that living consciousness directly, through ESP.

Back in the early seventies, when Gilder was working in Cambridge, he came home late one night to the house he shared in Watertown with a group of friends to find that a man with long black hair and "a demonic gleam in his eye" named Billy Delmore had turned up for a visit. Delmore was sitting by himself in the living room, performing what appeared to be magic tricks: finding a particular card in a pack and retrieving objects in the apartment that had been lost. Delmore told Gilder that he, too, could do this, and Gilder found that he could— almost immediately. For about six months, he became preoccupied with ESP, pondering what it was that made it work. It wasn't telepathy, since he wasn't reading anyone's mind: rather, he appeared to be gaining access to knowledge that nobody had, such as where the ace of spades could be found in a newly shuffled pack of cards. It was then that Gilder began to suspect that some sort of knowledge existed outside normal human consciousness—indeed, outside humans altogether—that was attainable if one could temporarily disable the everyday faculties of reason and sensory perception which prevented one from apprehending it. He hypothesized that the type of insight required to gain access to this knowledge was a vestigial faculty from a time in human history before language emerged—usable still if you knew how to make it work.

BEFORE he left New York, Gilder decided to drop in on a group of his subscribers who were meeting for dinner at the Palm, a restaurant on West Fiftieth Street. Subscribers had recently taken to organizing such events in a number of cities around the country, and Gilder sometimes showed up, though he never promised to in advance, for fear of unmanageable crowds. He was spotted right away as he walked in, and the group burst into applause. He shifted awkwardly through the room, acknowledging the clapping on either side of him with quick grins, looking about for a place to sit. Although surrounded by some of his most loyal followers that night, Gilder was a little nervous. The fact was that in the past few weeks many of his subscribers had lost a lot of money. In the case of a number of his recommendations (Northeast Optic Network, Novell, Motorola), the Gilder effect had evaporated almost immediately. Some angry investors had called him a "pump-and-dump artist"; others had threatened to call the S.E.C. And then there had been the Mirror Image fiasco.

A couple of months before, at a conference in Scottsdale, Arizona, Gilder had met a Norwegian named Alexander Vik. Vik was the chairman of a company called Mirror Image, and in the course of a conversation Gilder realized, to his great excitement, that Mirror Image fit his new information-caching paradigm perfectly. Even though he knew very little about the company, he took a risk and, mostly on the basis of that conversation with Vik, in his February letter he wrote a glowing report. The effect was immediate. Not only did Gilder's subscribers, as usual, rush to buy his recommendation, but so many others did as well that, in the next four or five days, the market capitalization of Xcelera, the parent of Mirror Image, increased by at least three billion dollars. Then disaster struck. The Washington *Post* and the New York *Observer* both published scathing stories about Mirror Image. Vik was interviewed on CNBC and came off as louche and arrogant; when asked about his failure to file quarterly financial reports, he breezily informed the interviewer that, since his company was headquartered in the Cayman Islands, he didn't have to. Rumors started circulating to the effect that Vik and his partners had sold most of their shares and were getting ready to jump.

It was scary. For a couple of weeks, Gilder thought he might have been taken for a ride, and he braced himself for a dramatic humiliation. Thankfully, he was saved. Ellen Hancock, who is the C.E.O. of Exodus Communications, the world's leading Web-hosting company, read Gilder's letter and sent her technical people to evaluate the company. On the basis of their recommendation, she decided to invest six hundred and thirty-eight million dollars in Mirror Image's technology. Gilder, with enormous relief, perceived that he had been vindicated—intellectually, if not financially. (Mirror Image's stock remained much lower than its Gilder-effect peak.) Still, he was shaken. He had always believed that taking risks in the absence of good information was what capitalism was all about, and if he wasn't willing to go out on a limb for technologies he believed in, who would? But the affair had made him wonder whether, now that he had such an influence on the allocation of capital, he could still responsibly hold to his report's operating assumption that ideas were all that mattered.

The dinner went better than Gilder had hoped. The subscribers could hardly have been more effusive in their expressions of allegiance: one compared him to Copernicus, another to the Holy Grail. One woman, an accountant, told Gilder that she remembered perfectly the day she had first read *Wealth and Poverty*, back in 1981: she had begun it in the morning, read it on the train to work, read it all through the day, and finished it late that night. Gilder, gratified to find someone who had discovered him as a writer first and a stock-picker second, lunged toward the woman across the table in order to shake her hand, but he knocked over a glass and retreated in confusion.

It was close to twelve before the subscribers let Gilder leave the restaurant. He emerged into the humid spring night and hailed a taxi to take him back to his hotel. He was pleased by the way things had turned out. In this group, at least, it seemed to him that he had succeeded not only in spreading the word about optics and wireless but in infecting people with his optimism as well. It was all very encouraging. Maybe it didn't even truly matter if he were to be taken for a ride by someone like Alexander Vik. After all, in the long run, he felt sure, the right technology would prevail, because in the long run good will prevail. Keynes may have talked a few people into believing that in the long run we'll all be dead, but that was typical pessimistic secularism speaking. Gilder bumped along in his taxi toward Central Park South and felt renewed hope for the future. Those few subscribers who had lost faith in his report after short-term losses had never really understood his project anyway, he thought. His eyes were adjusted for distance.

MAY 29, 2000

CLICKS AND MORTAR

AT the turn of this century, a Missouri farmer named D. Ward King invented a device that came to be known, in his honor, as the King Road Drag. It consisted of two wooden rails that lay side by side about three feet apart, attached by a series of wooden braces. If you pulled the King Drag along a muddy road, it had the almost magical effect of smoothing out the ruts and molding the dirt into a slight crown, so that the next time it rained the water would drain off to the sides. In 1906, when King demonstrated his device to a group of farmers in Wellsville, Kansas, the locals went out and built a hundred King Drags of their own within the week, which makes sense, because if you had asked a farmer at the turn of the century what single invention could make his life easier he would probably have wanted something that improved the roads. They were, in the late nineteenth century, a disaster: of the country's two million miles of roads, fewer than a hundred and fifty thousand had been upgraded with gravel or oil. The rest were dirt. They turned into rivers of mud when it was raining, and hardened into an impassable sea of ruts when it was not. A trip to church or to go shopping was an exhausting ordeal for many farmers. At one point in the early part of this century, economists estimated that it cost more to haul a bushel of wheat along ten miles of American dirt road than it did to ship it across the ocean from New York to Liverpool.

The King Road Drag was a simple invention that had the effect of reducing the isolation of the American farmer, and soon that simple invention led to all kinds of dramatic changes. Ever since the Post Office was established, for example, farmers had to make the difficult trek into town to pick up their mail. In the eighteen-nineties, Congress pledged that mail would be delivered free to every farmer's home, but only so long as rural communities could demonstrate that their roads were good enough for a mailman to pass by every day—which was a Catch-22 neatly resolved by the King Road Drag. And once you had rural free delivery and good roads, something like parcel post became inevitable. Through the beginning of the century, all packages that weighed more than four pounds were carried by private-express services, which were unreliable and expensive and would, outside big cities, deliver only to a set of depots. But if the mail was being delivered every day to rural dwellers, why not have the mailman deliver packages, too? In 1912, Congress agreed, and with that the age of the mail-order house began: now a farmer could look through a catalogue that contained many thousands of products and have them delivered right to his door. Smaller companies, with limited resources, had a way to bypass the middleman and reach customers all over the country. You no longer needed to sell to the consumer through actual stores made of bricks and mortar. You could build a virtual store!

In the first fifteen years of this century, in other words, America underwent something of a revolution. Before rural free delivery, if you didn't live in a town—and most Americans didn't—it wasn't really practical to get a daily newspaper. It was only after daily delivery that the country became "wired," in the sense that if something happened in Washington or France or the Congo one evening, everyone would know about it by the next morning. In 1898, mailmen were delivering about eighteen thousand pieces of mail per rural route. Within five years, that number had more than doubled, and by 1929 it had topped a hundred thousand.

Here was the dawn of the modern consumer economy—an economy in which information moved freely around the country, in which retailers and consumers, buyers and sellers became truly connected for the first time. "You may go to an average store, spend valuable time and select from a limited stock at retail prices," the fall 1915 Sears, Roebuck catalogue boasted, "or have our Big Store of World Wide Stocks at Economy Prices COME to you in this catalog— the Modern Way." By the turn of the century, the Sears catalogue had run to over a thousand pages, listing tens of thousands of items in twenty-four departments: music, buggies, stoves, carriage hardware, drugs, vehicles, shoes, notions, sewing machines, cloaks, sporting goods, dry goods, hardware, groceries, furniture and baby carriages, jewelry, optical goods, books, stereopticons, men's clothing, men's furnishings, bicycles, gramophones, and harnesses. Each page was a distinct site, offering a reader in-depth explanations and descriptions well beyond what he would expect if he went to a store, talked to a sales clerk, and personally examined a product. To find all those products, the company employed scores of human search engines—"missionaries" who, the historians Boris Emmet and John Jeuck write, were "said to travel constantly, inspecting the stocks of virtually all retail establishments in the country, conversing with the public at large to discover their needs and desires, and buying goods 'of all kinds and descriptions' " in order to post them on the World Wide Stock.

The catalogue, as economists have argued, represented a radical transformation in the marketing and distribution of consumer goods. But, of course, that transformation would not have been possible unless you had parcel post, and you couldn't have had parcel post unless you had rural free delivery, and you could not have had rural free delivery without good roads, and you would not have had good roads without D. Ward King. So what was the genuine revolution? Was it the World Wide Stock or was it the King Road Drag?

WE are now, it is said, in the midst of another business revolution. "This new economy represents a tectonic upheaval in our commonwealth, a far more turbulent reordering than mere digital hardware has produced," Kevin Kelly, a former executive editor of *Wired*, writes in his book *New Rules for the New Economy*. In *Cyber Rules*, the software entrepreneurs Thomas M. Siebel and Pat House compare the advent of the Internet to the invention of writing, the appearance of a metal currency in the eastern Mediterranean several thousand years ago, and the adoption of the Arabic zero. "Business," Bill Gates states flatly in the opening sentence of *Business @ the Speed of Thought*, "is going to change more in the next ten years than it has in the last fifty."

The revolution of today, however, turns out to be as difficult to define as the revolution of a hundred years ago. Kelly, for example, writes that because of the Internet "the new economy is about *communication*, deep and wide." Communication, he maintains, "is not just a sector of the economy. Communication *is* the economy." But which is really key—how we communicate, or *what* we communicate? Gates, meanwhile, is preoccupied with the speed of interaction in the new economy. Going digital, he writes, will "shatter the old way of doing business" because it will permit almost instant communication. Yet why is the critical factor how quickly I communicate some decision or message to you—as opposed to how long it takes me to make that decision, or how long it takes you to act on it? Gates called his book *Business @ the Speed of Thought*, but thought is a slow and messy thing. Computers do nothing to speed up our thought process; they only make it a lot faster to communicate our thoughts once we've had them. Gates should have called his book *Business @ the Speed of Typing*. In *Growing Up Digital*, Don Tapscott even goes so far as to claim that the rise of the Internet has created an entirely new personality among the young. Net-Geners, as Tapscott dubs the generation,

> have a different set of assumptions about work than their parents have. They thrive on collaboration, and many find the notion of a boss somewhat bizarre. . . . They are driven to innovate and have a mindset of immediacy requiring fast results. They love hard work because working, learning, and playing are the same thing to them. They are creative in ways their parents could only imagine. . . . Corporations who hire them should be prepared to have their windows and walls shaken.

Let's leave aside the fact that the qualities Tapscott ascribes to the Net Generation—energy, a "mindset of immediacy," creativity, a resistance to authority, and (of all things) sharp differences in outlook from their parents—could safely have been ascribed to every upcoming generation in history. What's interesting here is the blithe assumption, which runs through so much of the thinking and talking about the Internet, that this new way of exchanging information must be at the root of all changes now sweeping through our economy and culture. In these last few weeks before Christmas, as the country's magazines and airways become crowded with advertisements for the fledgling class of dot coms, we may be tempted to concur. But is it possible that, once again, we've been dazzled by the catalogues and forgotten the roads?

THE world's largest on-line apparel retailer is Lands' End, in Wisconsin. Lands' End began in 1963 as a traditional mail-order company. It mailed you its catalogue, and you mailed back your order along with a check. Then, in the mid-nineteen-eighties, Lands' End, like the rest of the industry, reinvented itself. It mailed you its catalogue, and you telephoned an 800 number with your order and paid with a credit card. Now Lands' End has moved on line. In the first half of this year, E-commerce sales accounted for ten per cent of Lands' End's total business, up two hundred and fifty per cent from last year. What has this move to the Web meant?

Lands' End has its headquarters in the tiny farming town of Dodgeville, about an hour's drive west of Madison, through the rolling Midwestern countryside. The main Lands' End campus is composed of half a dozen modern, low-slung buildings, clustered around a giant parking lot. In one of those buildings, there is a huge open room filled with hundreds of people sitting in front of computer terminals and wearing headsets. These are the people who take your orders. Since the bulk of Lands' End's business is still driven by the catalogue and the 800 number, most of those people are simply talking on the phone to telephone customers. But a growing percentage of the reps are now part of the company's Internet team, serving people who use the Lands' End Live feature on the company's Web site. Lands' End Live allows customers, with the click of a mouse, to start a live chat with a Lands' End representative or get a rep to call them at home, immediately.

On a recent fall day, a Lands' End Live user—let's call her Betty—was talking to one of the company's customer-service reps, a tall, red-haired woman named Darcia. Betty was on the Lands' End Web site to buy a pair of sweatpants for her young daughter, and had phoned to ask a few questions.

"What size did I order last year?" Betty asked. "I think I need one size bigger." Darcia looked up the record of Betty's purchase. Last year, she told Betty, she bought the same pants in big-kid's small.

"I'm thinking medium or large," Betty said. She couldn't decide.

"The medium is a ten or a twelve, really closer to a twelve," Darcia told her. "I'm thinking if you go to a large, it will throw you up to a sixteen, which is really big."

Betty agreed. She wanted the medium. But now she had a question about delivery. It was Thursday morning, and she needed the pants by Tuesday. Darcia told her that the order would go out on Friday morning, and with U.P.S. second-day air she would almost certainly get it by Tuesday. They briefly discussed spending an extra six dollars for the premium, next-day service, but Darcia talked Betty out of it. It was only an eighteen-dollar order, after all.

Betty hung up, her decision made, and completed her order on the Internet. Darcia started an on-line chat with a woman from the East Coast. Let's call her Carol. Carol wanted to buy the forty-nine-dollar attaché case but couldn't decide on a color. Darcia was partial to the dark olive, which she said was "a professional alternative to black." Carol seemed convinced, but she wanted the case monogrammed and there were eleven monogramming styles on the Web-site page.

"Can I have a personal suggestion?" she wrote.

"Sure," Darcia typed back. "Who is the case for?"

"A conservative psychiatrist," Carol replied.

Darcia suggested block initials, in black. Carol agreed, and sent the order in herself on the Internet. "All right," Darcia said, as she ended the chat. "She feels better." The exchange had taken twenty-three minutes.

Notice that in each case the customer filled out the actual order herself and sent it in to the Lands' End computer electronically—which is, of course, the great promise of E-commerce. But that didn't make some human element irrelevant. The customers still needed Darcia for advice on colors, and styles, or for reassurance that their daughter was a medium and not a large. In each case, the sale was closed because that human interaction allayed the last-minute anxieties and doubts that so many of us have at the point of purchase. It's a mistake, in other words, to think that E-commerce will entirely automate the retail process. It just turns reps from order-takers into sales advisers.

"One of the big fallacies when the Internet came along was that you could get these huge savings by eliminating customer-service costs," Bill Bass, the head of E-commerce for Lands' End, says. "People thought the Internet was self-service, like a gas station. But there are some things that you cannot program a computer to provide. People will still have questions, and what you get are much higher-level questions. Like, 'Can you help me come up with a gift?' And they take longer."

Meanwhile, it turns out, Internet customers at Lands' End aren't much different from 800-number customers. Both groups average around a hundred dollars an order, and they have the same rate of returns. Call volume on the 800 numbers is highest on Mondays and Tuesdays, from ten in the morning until one in the afternoon. So is E-commerce volume. In the long term, of course, the hope is that the Web site will reduce dependence on the catalogue, and that would be a huge efficiency. Given that last year the company mailed two hundred and fifty million catalogues, costing about a dollar each, the potential savings could be enormous. And yet customers' orders on the Internet spike just after a new catalogue arrives at people's homes in exactly the same way that the 800-number business spikes just after the catalogue arrives. E-commerce users, it seems, need the same kind of visual, tangible prompting to use Lands' End as traditional customers. If Lands' End did all its business over the Internet, it would still have to send out something in the mail—a postcard or a bunch of fabric swatches or a slimmed-down catalogue. "We thought going into E-commerce it would be a different business," Tracy Schmit, an Internet analyst at the company, says. "But it's the same business, the same patterns, the same contacts. It's an extension of what we already do."

NOW consider what happens on what retailers call the "back end"—the customer-fulfillment side—of Lands' End's operations. Say you go to the company's Web site one afternoon and order a blue 32-16 oxford-cloth button-down shirt and a pair of size-9 Top-Siders. At midnight, the computer at Lands' End combines your order with all the other orders for the day: it lumps your shirt order with the hundred other orders, say, that came in for 32-16 blue oxford-cloth button-downs, and lumps your shoe order with the fifty other size-9 Top-Sider orders of the day. It then prints bar codes for every item, so each of those hundred shirts is assigned a sticker listing the location of blue oxford 32-16 shirts in the warehouse, the order that it belongs to, shipping information, and instructions for things like monogramming.

The next morning, someone known as a "picker" finds the hundred oxford-cloth shirts in that size, yours among them, and puts a sticker on each one, as does another picker in the shoe area with the fifty size-9 Top Siders. Each piece of merchandise is placed on a yellow plastic tray along an extensive conveyor belt, and as the belt passes underneath a bar-code scanner the computer reads the label and assembles your order. The tray with your shirt on it circles the room until it is directly above a bin that has been temporarily assigned to you, and then tilts, sending the package sliding downward. Later, when your shoes come gliding along on the belt, the computer reads the bar code on the box and sends the shoe box tumbling into the same bin. Then the merchandise is packed and placed on another conveyor belt, and a bar-code scanner sorts the packages once again, sending the New York–bound packages to the New York–bound U.P.S. truck, the Detroit packages to the Detroit truck, and so on.

It's an extraordinary operation. When you stand in the middle of the Lands' End warehouse—while shirts and pants and sweaters and ties roll by at a rate that, at Christmas, can reach twenty-five thousand items an hour—you feel as if you're in Willy Wonka's chocolate factory. The warehouses are enormous buildings—as big, in all, as sixteen football fields—and the conveyor belts hang from the ceiling like giant pieces of industrial sculpture. Every so often, a belt lurches to a halt, and a little black scanner box reads the bar code and sends the package off again, directing it left or right or up or down, onto any number of separate sidings and overpasses. In the middle of one of the buildings, there is another huge room where thousands of pants, dangling from a jumbo-sized railing like a dry cleaner's rack, are sorted by color (so sewers don't have to change thread as often) and by style, then hemmed, pressed, bagged, and returned to the order-fulfillment chain—all within a day.

This system isn't unique to Lands' End. If you went to L. L. Bean or J. Crew or, for that matter, a housewares-catalogue company like Pottery Barn, you'd find the same kind of system. It's what all modern, automated warehouses look like, and it is as much a part of E-commerce as a Web site. In fact, it is the more difficult part of E-commerce. Consider the problem of the Christmas rush. Lands' End records something like thirty per cent of its sales during November and December. A well-supported Web site can easily handle those extra hits, but for the rest of the operation that surge in business represents a considerable strain. Lands' End, for example, aims to respond to every phone call or Lands' End Live query within twenty seconds, and to ship out every order within twenty-four hours of its receipt. In August, those goals are easily met. But, to maintain that level of service in November and December, Lands' End must hire an extra twenty-six hundred people, increasing its normal payroll by more than fifty per cent. Since unemployment in the Madison area is hovering around one per cent, this requires elaborate planning: the company charters buses to bring in students from a nearby college, and has made a deal in the past with a local cheese factory to borrow its workforce for the rush. Employees from other parts of the company are conscripted to help out as pickers, while others act as "runners" in the customer-service department, walking up and down the aisles and jumping into any seat made vacant by someone taking a break. Even the structure of the warehouse is driven, in large part, by the demands of the holiday season. Before the popularization of the bar code, in the early nineteen-eighties, Lands' End used what is called an "order picking" method. That meant that the picker got your ticket, then went to the shirt room and got your shirt, and the shoe room and got your shoes, then put your order together. If another shoe-and-shirt order came over next, she would have to go back to the shirts and back to the shoes all over again. A good picker under the old system could pick between a hundred and fifty and a hundred and seventy-five pieces an hour. The new technique, known as "batch picking," is so much more efficient that a good picker can now retrieve between six hundred and seven hundred pieces an hour. Without bar codes, if you placed an order in mid-December, you'd be hard pressed to get it by Christmas.

None of this is to minimize the significance of the Internet. Lands' End has a feature on its Web site which allows you to try clothes on a virtual image of yourself—a feature that is obviously not possible with a catalogue. The Web site can list all the company's merchandise, whereas a catalogue has space to list only a portion of the inventory. But how big a role does the Internet ultimately play in E-commerce? It doesn't much affect the cost of running a customer-service department. It reduces catalogue costs, but it doesn't eliminate traditional marketing, because you still have to remind people of your Web site. You still need to master batch picking. You still need the Willy Wonka warehouse. You still need dozens of sewers in the inseaming department, and deals with the local cheese factory, and buses to ship in students every November and December. The head of operations for Lands' End is a genial man in his fifties named Phil Schaecher, who works out of a panelled office decorated with paintings of ducks which overlooks the warehouse floor. When asked what he would do if he had to choose between the two great innovations of the past twenty years—the bar code, which has transformed the back end of his business, and the Internet, which is transforming the front end—Schaecher paused, for what seemed a long time. "I'd take the Internet," he said finally, toeing the line that all retailers follow these days. Then he smiled. "But of course if we lost bar codes I'd retire the next day."

ON a recent fall morning, a young woman named Charlene got a call from a shipping agent at a firm in Oak Creek, Wisconsin. Charlene is a dispatcher with a trucking company in Akron, Ohio, called Roberts Express. She sits in front of a computer with a telephone headset on, in a large crowded room filled with people in front of computers wearing headsets, not unlike the large crowded room at Lands' End. The shipping agent told Charlene that she had to get seven drums of paint to Muskegon, Michigan, as soon as possible. It was 11:25 A.M. Charlene told the agent she would call her back, and immediately typed those details into her computer, which relayed the message to the two-way-communications satellite that serves as the backbone for the Roberts transportation network. The Roberts satellite, in turn, "pinged" the fifteen hundred independent truckers that Roberts works with, and calculated how far each available vehicle was from the customer in Oak Creek. Those data were then analyzed by proprietary software, which sorted out the cost of the job and the distance between Muskegon and Oak Creek, and sifted through more than fifteen variables governing the optimal distribution of the fleet.

This much—the satellite relay and the probability calculation—took a matter of seconds. The trip, Charlene's screen told her, was two hundred and seventy-four miles and would cost seven hundred and twenty-six dollars. The computer also gave her twenty-three candidates for the run, ranked in order of preference. The first, Charlene realized, was ineligible, because federal regulations limit the number of hours drivers can spend on the road. The second, she found out, was being held for another job. The third, according to the satellite, was fifty miles away, which was too far. But the fourth, a husband-and-wife team named Jerry and Ann Love, seemed ideal. They were just nineteen miles from Oak Creek. "I've worked with them before," Charlene said. "They're really nice people." At eleven-twenty-seven, Charlene sent the Loves an E-mail message, via satellite, that would show up instantly on the computer screens Roberts installs in the cabs of all its contractors. According to Roberts' rules, they had ten minutes to respond. "I'm going to give them a minute or two," Charlene said. There was no answer, so she called the Loves on their cell phone. Ann Love answered. "We'll do that," she said. Charlene chatted with her for a moment and then, as an afterthought, E-mailed the Loves again: "Thank you!" It was eleven-thirty.

Trucking companies didn't work this way twenty years ago. But Roberts uses its state-of-the-art communications and computer deployment to give the shipping business a new level of precision. If your pickup location is within twenty-five miles of one of the company's express centers—and Roberts has express centers in most major North American cities—Roberts will pick up a package of almost any size within ninety minutes, and it will do so twenty-four hours a day, seven days a week. If the cargo is located between twenty-six and fifty miles of an express center, it will be picked up within two hours. More than half of those deliveries will be made by midnight of the same day. Another twenty-five per cent will be made by eight o'clock the next morning. Ninety-six per cent of all Roberts deliveries are made within fifteen minutes of the delivery time promised when the order is placed. Because of its satellite system, the company knows precisely, within yards, where your order is at all times. The minute the computer tells her your truck is running fifteen minutes behind, Charlene or one of her colleagues will call you to work out some kind of solution. Roberts has been known to charter planes or send in Huey helicopters to rescue time-sensitive cargo stranded in traffic or in a truck that has broken down. The result is a truck-based system so efficient that Roberts estimates it can outperform air freight at distances of up to seven hundred or eight hundred miles.

Roberts, of course, isn't the only company to reinvent the delivery business over the past twenty years. In the same period, Federal Express has put together, from scratch, a network of six hundred and forty-three planes, forty-three thousand five hundred vehicles, fourteen hundred service centers, thirty-four thousand drop boxes, and a hundred and forty-eight thousand employees—all coordinated by satellite links and organized around a series of huge, automated, bar-code-driven Willy Wonka warehouses. Federal Express was even a pioneer in the development of aircraft antifog navigational equipment: if it absolutely, positively has to get there overnight, the weather can't be allowed to get in the way.

E-commerce would be impossible without this extraordinary infrastructure. Would you care that you could order a new wardrobe with a few clicks of a mouse if the package took a couple of weeks to get to you? Lands' End has undergone three major changes over the past couple of decades. The first was the introduction of an 800 number, in 1978; the second was express delivery, in 1994; and the third was the introduction of a Web site, in 1995. The first two innovations cut the average transaction time—the time between the moment of ordering and the moment the goods are received—from three weeks to four days. The third innovation has cut the transaction time from four days to, well, four days.

It isn't just that E-commerce depends on express mail; there's a sense in which E-commerce *is* express mail. Right now, billions of dollars are being spent around the country on so-called "last-mile delivery systems." Companies such as Webvan, in San Francisco, or Kozmo.com, in New York, are putting together networks of trucks and delivery personnel which can reach almost any home in their area within an hour. What if Webvan or Kozmo were somehow integrated into a huge, national, Roberts-style network of connected trucks? And what if that network were in turn integrated into the operations of a direct merchant like Lands' End? There may soon come a time when a customer from Northampton could order some shirts on LandsEnd.com at the height of the Christmas rush, knowing that the retailer's computer could survey its stock, assess its warehouse capabilities, "ping" a network of thousands of trucks it has at its disposal, look up how many other orders are going to his neck of the woods, check in with his local Kozmo or Webvan, and tell him, right then and there, precisely what time it could deliver those shirts to him that evening or the next morning. It's not hard to imagine, under such a system, that Lands' End's sales would soar; the gap between the instant gratification of a real store and the delayed gratification of a virtual store would narrow even further. It would be a revolution of sorts, a revolution of satellites, probability models, people in headsets, cell phones, truckers, logistics experts, bar codes, deals with the local cheese factory, and—oh yes, the Internet.

The interesting question, of course, is why we persist in identifying the E-commerce boom as an Internet revolution. Part of the reason, perhaps, is simply the convenience of the word "Internet" as a shorthand for all the technological wizardry of the last few decades. But surely whom and what we choose to celebrate in any period of radical change says something about the things we value. This fall, for example, the Goodyear Tire & Rubber Company—a firm with sales of more than thirteen billion dollars—was dropped from the Dow Jones industrial average. After all, Goodyear runs factories, not Web sites. It is based in Akron, not in Silicon Valley. It is part of the highway highway, not the information highway. The manufacturing economy of the early twentieth century, from which Goodyear emerged, belonged to trade unions and blue-collar men. But ours is the first economic revolution in history that the educated classes have sought to claim as wholly their own, a revolution of Kevin Kelly's "communication" and Bill Gates's "thought"—the two activities for which the Net-Geners believe themselves to be uniquely qualified. Today's talkers and thinkers value the conception of ideas, not their fulfillment. They give credit to the catalogue, but not to the postman who delivered it, or to the road he travelled on. The new economy was supposed to erase all hierarchies. Instead, it has devised another one. On the front end, there are visionaries. On the back end, there are drones.

ONE of the very first packages ever delivered by parcel post, in 1913, was an eight-pound crate of apples sent from New Jersey to President Wilson at the White House. The symbolism of that early delivery was deliberate. When the parcel post was established, the assumption was that it would be used by farmers as a way of sending their goods cheaply and directly to customers in the city. "Let us imagine that the Gotham family," one journalist wrote at the time,

> immured in the city by the demands of Father Gotham's business, knew that twice a week during the summer they could get from Farmer Ruralis, forty miles out in the country, a hamper of fresh-killed poultry, green peas, string beans, asparagus, strawberries, lettuce, cherries, summer squash, and what not; that the "sass" would be only a day from garden to table; that prices would be lower than market prices; that the cost of transportation would be only thirty-five cents in and, say, eleven cents for the empty hamper back again. Would the Gotham family be interested?

The Post Office told rural mailmen to gather the names and addresses of all those farmers along their routes who wanted to sell their produce by mail. Those lists were given to city mailmen, who delivered them along their routes, so interested customers could get in contact with interested farmers directly. Because customers wanted to know what kind of produce each farmer had to sell, local postmasters began including merchandise information on their lists, essentially creating a farm-produce mail-order catalogue. A California merchant named David Lubin proposed a scheme whereby a farmer would pick up colored cards from the post office—white for eggs, pink for chickens, yellow for butter—mark each card with his prices, and mail the cards back. If he had three chickens that week for a dollar each, he would mail three pink cards to the post office. There they would be put in a pigeonhole with all the other pink cards. Customers could come by and comparison shop, pick out the cards they liked, write their address on these cards, and have the postal clerk mail them back to the farmer. It was a pre-digital eBay. The scheme was adopted in and around Sacramento, and Congress appropriated ten thousand dollars to try a similar version of it on a large scale.

At about the same time, an assistant Postmaster General, James Blakslee, had the bright idea of putting together a fleet of parcel-post trucks, which would pick up farm produce from designated spots along the main roads and ship it directly to town. Blakslee laid out four thousand miles of produce routes around the country, to be covered by fifteen hundred parcel-post trucks. In 1918, in the system's inaugural run, four thousand day-old chicks, two hundred pounds of honey, five hundred pounds of smoked sausage, five hundred pounds of butter, and eighteen thousand eggs were carried from Lancaster, Pennsylvania, to New York City, all for $31.60 in postage. New York's Secretary of State called it "an epoch in the history of the United States and the world."

Only, it wasn't. The Post Office had devised a wonderful way of communicating between farmer and customer. But there is more to a revolution than communication, and within a few years the farm-to-table movement, which started out with such high hopes, was dead. The problem was that Blakslee's trucks began to break down, which meant that the food on board spoiled. Eggs proved hard to package, and so they often arrived damaged. Butter went rancid. In the winter of 1919–20, Blakslee collected a huge number of orders for potatoes, but, as Wayne Fuller writes in his wonderful history of the era, *RFD: The Changing Face of Rural America*, the potatoes that year

> were scarce, and good ones even scarcer, and when Blakslee's men were able to buy them and attempted delivery, nothing but trouble followed. Some of the potatoes were spoiled to begin with; some froze in transit; prices varied, deliveries went astray, and customers complained loudly enough for Congress to hear. One harried official wrote Blakslee that he could "fill the mails with complaints from people who have ordered potatoes from October to December." . . . Some people had been waiting over four months, either to have the potatoes delivered or their money refunded.

Parcel post, in the end, turned out to be something entirely different from what was originally envisioned—a means not to move farm goods from country to town but to move consumer goods from town to country. That is the first lesson from the revolution of a hundred years ago, and it's one that should give pause to all those eager to pronounce on the significance of the Internet age: the nature of revolutions is such that you never really know what they mean until they are over. The other lesson, of course, is that coming up with a new way of connecting buyers and sellers is a very fine thing, but what we care about most of all is getting our potatoes.

DECEMBER 6, 1999

THE A-LIST E-LIST

I SPEND my days trying to contribute to a more just, caring, and environmentally sensitive society, but, like most Americans, I'm always on the lookout for subtle ways to make myself seem socially superior. So I was thrilled recently to learn about E-name dropping, a new and extremely petty form of one-upmanship made possible by recent strides in information technology.

I first became aware of this new status ploy when a colleague sent out a mass message. "Dear friends," his E-mail began. But before I could go on to the text my eye was drawn up to the list of other people it had been sent to. My friend had apparently sent this message—it was a request for help on an article—to his entire E-mail address book. There were three hundred and four names, listed alphabetically, along with their E-mail addresses. It was like a roster of young media meritocrats. There were newsweek.coms, wsj.coms, nytimes.coms, as well as your assorted berkeley.edus, stanford.edus, microsoft.coms, and even a UN.org.

I realized that I had stumbled across the *Social Register* of the information age. We all carry our own select social clubs on our hard drives, and when we send out a mass mailing we can flaunt our splendiferous connections to arouse the envy of friend and foe alike. It's as if you were walking down the street with your Rolodex taped to your lapel—only better, since having an E-mail friendship with someone suggests that you are trading chatty badinage, not just exchanging stiff missives under a formal letterhead.

So in theory a strategic striver could structure his E-mail address list to reveal the entire trajectory of his career ascent. He could include a few of his early thesis advisers—groton.org, yale.edu, oxford.ac.uk—then a few internship-era mentors—imf.org, whitehouse.gov—and, finally, a few social/professional contacts—say, davosconference.com or trilat.org. When he inflicts this list on his friends' in-boxes, they will be compelled, like unwilling list archeologists, to retrace his perfect life, triumph by triumph.

My friend with the three-hundred-and-four-name list hadn't exploited the full potentialities of the genre, so I cast about for other lists and began to analyze them. I learned a lot from these lists. For example, my view of *The Nation*'s columnist Eric Alterman has been transformed by the knowledge that he has just stopped using "Tomseaver" as part of his E-mail address. But, frankly, reading through the address lists of my friends, I found that there were longueurs. Entire passages were filled with names of insignificant people, such as family members I'd never heard of. I came to realize, as Capability Brown must have, that in the making of any beautiful vista pruning is key.

If Aristotle were alive, he would note that there are four types of E-mail lists. There are lists that remind you that the sender went to a better college than you did. There are lists that remind you that he has a better job than you do. There are those that remind you that he has more sex than you do. And, finally, there are those that remind you that he is better than you in every respect: spiritually, professionally, and socially.

I have begun fantasizing about assembling the mother of all E-mail lists, the sort that would be accumulated by a modern Renaissance man. Such a list would be studded with jewels (HisHoliness@vatican.com, QEII@windsor.org). But, more than that, it would suggest a series of high achievements across the full range of human endeavor. It would include whopping hints about mysterious other lives (coupboy@theagency.gov, Ahmed@mujahedin.com). It would reveal intimate connections with the great but socially selective (JDSal@aol.com, Solzhenits@archi.org). Of course, I wouldn't want only celebrities on my list; that would be vulgar. I would leave room for talk-show bookers, upper-bracket realtors, Sherpas, airline presidents, night-club publicists, rain-forest tour guides, underprivileged kids, members of the Gotti family, and a rotating contingent of the people I actually know, for whose edification the whole list has been constructed in the first place.

To take advantage of this list, I would need excuses to send out mass mailings as frequently as possible. I would have to change my address a lot ("From now on you can reach me at genius24@MacArthurgrant.com . . ."). I would send out a lot of general queries ("Does anybody know who is handling Ike Berlin's estate? I'm trying to find a first edition of the complete works of Hérzen . . ."). And I'd send out a few accidental mass mailings by hitting the Reply All button by "mistake" ("Your Holiness, it turns out I can't make it to Rome Tuesday. Maybe somebody else can bring the beer and soda . . .").

No longer would I be the ninety-eight-pound cyberweakling that I am now. Alec Baldwin would start sending me dirty jokes in hopes of making it onto my E-mail list. People would actually begin replying to my messages. The fact is, in the new information age, we can now be snobs on a scale never dreamed of by our ancestors. Is this a great time to be alive, or what?

SEPTEMBER 13, 1999

NICHOLAS LEMANN

THE KIDS IN THE CONFERENCE ROOM

T HE University of Virginia, Thomas Jefferson wrote in 1818, "should consist of distinct houses or pavilions, arranged at proper distance on each side of a lawn of a proper breadth." The Lawn, stately and renowned, is still the centerpiece of the university, but some years ago the university was having a hard time getting students to live in the dormitories, in accordance with Jefferson's plans, because the rooms were small and didn't have bathrooms.

Then somebody came up with a brilliant solution: make it an honor to live on the Lawn. The university set up an elaborate process to select the fifty-four most outstanding seniors, and gave them the dormitory rooms on the Lawn as a prize. Sure enough, since then rooms on the Lawn have been the object of an intense competition.

As soon as you move into your room on the Lawn, you may well get a letter from McKinsey & Company, the big management-consulting firm, inviting you to come to a meeting where you will be encouraged to apply for an important-sounding though undefined job called "business analyst." Even if you've never heard of McKinsey, you'll very likely go, partly out of curiosity, partly because it's a free meal and it's flattering to be wooed, but mostly because you have a keen sense that a job at McKinsey after graduation is somehow the functional equivalent of a room on the Lawn. It's the next prestigious thing to get, and desirable simply because it is that.

This process occurs not just in Charlottesville but across the top tier of the most highly selective colleges in the country—at perhaps two dozen schools, including all the Ivy League ones. Management consulting in general and the McKinsey business-analyst program in particular have been the plum post-college jobs of the nineties. McKinsey's looming presence permeates the atmosphere of the last couple of years of undergraduate life, and the first couple of years of postgraduate. If you're not thinking about McKinsey, your friends are.

It is only a small and select subculture of America's youth who are caught up in the world of management consulting. We are not talking here about Goths. We are not talking about residents of hip-hop nation. We are not talking about people who do things in Internet chat rooms that would disturb us deeply, if we knew what they were. We are talking, instead, about the kind of people who, at the moment of birth, scored a perfect ten on their Apgar test (non-parents: a healthiness grade that obstetricians give newborns); and then went on to ace every other organized competition that youth offers, up through college admission; and then continued overachieving to the point that they are outstanding even within their own heavily weeded-out cohort. These are the people whom the management-consulting business wants, and within their world the rise of consulting as a first career move has been dramatic.

The essence of the phenomenon isn't so much the number of graduates who actually become consultants as the size of the psychic space that consulting occupies at Ivy League schools. The general feeling is that in all the big wide world there are only two default fields of endeavor, as far as postgraduate employment is concerned: investment banking (ever so slightly fading) and management consulting (on the rise). The leading companies in these two industries make themselves ubiquitous on campuses every fall—people I talked with used words like "blitz," "deluge," and "onslaught" to describe their tactics. They send students letters. They put up posters and take out ads in the student newspapers, which grow fat with recruiting ads. They have outreach programs for minority and gay and lesbian students.

Every élite college's undergraduate career-placement office has become, to a large extent, a clearing house for the recruiting process, operating an elaborate system for getting multiple copies of seniors' résumés out to lists of companies they designate. After that, there is a round of interviewing, during which students sell themselves to the consultants, and then a round of expenses-paid visits to the consultants' offices, and then a round during which the companies sell themselves to the students to whom they've made offers. And then the whole process is repeated. Everyone—students, placement officers, and the staffs of consulting firms—puts an enormous amount of time and effort into this. McKinsey has full-time administrative employees whose job is to manage recruitment between the firm and just one university. Probably an absolute majority of all Ivy League seniors now participate in the recruiting ritual. It dominates senior-year conversation; students find themselves wondering whether there's something wrong with them if they're not interested in consulting and investment banking. Two new companies, WetFeet and Vault, have gone into the business of publishing expensive advisory materials for students going through the interviewing-with-consulting-firms routine. At Harvard, more than a quarter of every senior class—that's four hundred and fifty people—applies for about ten entry-level jobs at McKinsey's archrival, the Boston Consulting Group, a company that surely almost none of the seniors knew existed four years earlier, when they were writing their application essays suffused with intellectual and reformist yearning. Yale recently set up a committee to review the function of its career-placement office, partly in order to assure itself that the seniors were being made aware that there are options in life other than consulting and investment banking; its new director assured me they are aware, offering as proof the statistic that only seventeen per cent of the class of '98 went right into those fields.

The spectacle of career vogues sweeping across the élite young is not new. Being a business analyst at McKinsey, which means that you're a junior-grade gatherer and digester of great draughts of information for use in consulting studies, is the present-day equivalent of working for the C.I.A. in the nineteen-fifties, or the Peace Corps in the sixties, or Ralph Nader in the seventies, or First Boston in the eighties—the job that encapsulates the Zeitgeist of the moment. Its appeal arises partly from business's having become, in the eyes of college seniors, more exciting, central, and valorous than anybody in the university world could have imagined a generation ago. Before that happened, what you were if you wanted to stay on track but didn't have a specific goal was premed or pre-law. But doctors and lawyers have come to seem less glamorous (managed-care wage slaves and "i"-dotters, respectively) as businesspeople have come to seem more so.

The consulting vogue won't last forever. While it's here, though, it has a couple of features worth noting. The Ivy League schools were not national institutions flooded with applicants until the nineteen-sixties; before then, their students were drawn from a narrow slice of society, so it didn't seem remarkable that their career choices should be narrow, too. (Yale's recently reëxamined undergraduate-placement office didn't even exist until the late sixties.) Now these schools, in the personnel sense, work like a funnel: the students, chosen with fanatical attention to the principles of meritocracy and diversity, come from every possible background and location, only to be sluiced into an amazingly small career channel. This particular career vogue is also remarkable for how much of the propulsive force behind it is the employers' recruiting efforts, rather than impulses arising from within the students themselves. The consulting firms have figured out how to win over the hearts and minds of perfect twenty-one-year-olds, and how to use a big, ambitiously conceived, heavily government-supported national university system as a hiring hall for themselves.

MCKINSEY & COMPANY was not the first consulting firm (that was Arthur D. Little, founded in 1886, sixty years before McKinsey), and it is not the biggest (that is Arthur Andersen, with seventy thousand employees, compared with ten thousand at McKinsey), but, as a consultant might put it, it has the best brand. A focus group of consulting-firm interviewees to whom the name McKinsey was tossed out for instant associative response might say "network of famous alumni," thinking of Louis Gerstner, of I.B.M.; Harvey Golub, of American Express; Jim Manzi, formerly of Lotus; John Malone, the cable-television czar; Tom Peters, the business guru; or one of the seven governors of the Federal Reserve Board. Or they might say "blue-chip clients" (A.T.&T., Time Warner, General Electric, Oxford University, the Vatican). Or "buttoned-up style." Or "direct access to top management." Or "air of possibly deserved superiority." But probably, being campus interviewees, they'd say "credential-loving."

The man who built McKinsey, Marvin Bower, now in his nineties, was so focused on hiring graduates of Harvard Business School that McKinsey endowed a Marvin Bower Fellowship program there. Because Bower himself was a graduate of Harvard Law School, he also hired from there. Over the years, McKinsey also began hiring from Ph.D. programs, even in the humanities, and from résumé-enhancing fellowship programs. ("We are the largest employers of Rhodes scholars and Marshall scholars on the planet, outside of the United States government," one McKinsey partner told me.) The hiring through a highly discriminating institutional filter but without reference to exactly what you know makes a good fit with what consulting firms present themselves as doing: they're supposed to provide not so much a skill specific to the work of the client, like the best recipe for roof shingles, as sheer superior brainpower and breadth of vision. That's what makes their services valuable. Why not, then, hire just on the basis of how smart someone is, as long as his smartness has the public, easily communicated validation of a prestigious university's name attached to it? Better the top tier of undergraduates, God knows, than the second tier of business students—this is McKinsey, after all.

Business Analyst Zero was probably a student who, in 1973, was admitted to Harvard Business School and persuaded McKinsey to let him work there for a couple of years beforehand. Over the years, a few more business analysts wandered in, and in 1985 McKinsey set up a program for hiring and training them. Meanwhile, business-analyst programs at other consulting firms—B.C.G., Bain & Company, A.T. Kearney, Andersen, Booz-Allen, Monitor, Marakon Associates, Mercer, and Gemini—were beginning, too. In the nineties, because of inter-firm competition and an over-all boom in the consulting business (McKinsey's revenues are increasing by fifteen per cent a year), the business-analyst programs took off. Before long, the sum of all these companies recruiting like mad at the same few colleges made for quite a stampede.

Here's the rational dimension of the sales pitch that consulting firms make to college seniors: They pay, immediately on graduation from college, with no special training required, between fifty and sixty thousand dollars a year (and often significantly more in the second year). Usually, the programs last two years, after which, if you've done well, the consulting firm will lend you the money to go to business school—and then, if you return to the firm afterward and stay for two more years, the loan will be forgiven. For people who finish college heavily in debt, going to work for a consulting firm is a way to climb out of the hole quickly; and for the colleges, whose high cost is what created the debt, it would seem graceless not to help steer seniors toward financial peace. Consultants don't make quite as much money as investment bankers, but a lot of investment bankers' pay comes in the form of a bonus that may not materialize if the firm has a bad year. You're supposed to have more of a life (though not all that much more) if you go to work for a consulting firm than if you go to work for an investment bank—you're at work until eight or nine or ten every night, instead of eleven or twelve or one, and you get to meet clients, instead of spending all your time locked up in a cubicle running Excel spreadsheets.

Here's the unstated, psychological dimension of the sales pitch: For someone who is intensely ambitious but hasn't yet formed an ambition to do any one particular thing, a consulting job makes an ideal placeholder. It encapsulates that odd upper-meritocratic combination of love of competition, herd mentality, and aversion to risk. "They're very clever about marketing themselves as being for the top people," says Patricia Rose, the director of career services at the University of Pennsylvania. "They talk about the gruelling pace of the work. It's a kind of challenge—'I, too, can pull these all-nighters. I'm tough enough.' There's a little boot camp, a little macho. Do you have what it takes?" To get a business-analyst job at McKinsey is to add another glittering credential to your string, since you've beaten out so many people to get the job, and working there offers the comfort of knowing you'll be among your own kind (applicants have to submit their S.A.T. scores). The world's infinite possibilities haven't been reduced by a whit, only enhanced.

MCKINSEY set up interviews for me with a few business analysts, and then I met with some former ones on my own. They were obviously of a type. They were intelligent, idealistic, polite, direct, and nice, brimming as much with evidence of past effort by them and their parents and legions of teachers and instructors as they were with future promise. They looked me in the eye. They projected trustworthiness. They spoke in a sincere and slightly stilted patois. One young man described his choice to go to McKinsey in this way: "Law school was the intended destination immediately following college. When McKinsey came along, it was a very exciting opportunity to defer law school for two years—a two-year departure from the intended path of practicing law." A young woman I interviewed said, "You're always striving to make sure that as many doors are open to you as possible. You strive to do as well as possible so as many possibilities as possible are open to you. And then you repeat the cycle. This is a very nice springboard for whatever you want to do in the future."

The question about McKinsey analysts is whether they were already the McKinsey type before they got there, or were made into the type by McKinsey.

It's hard to answer, because if you're a business analyst the McKinsey culture, perhaps by design or perhaps by accident, exactly replicates your run of experiences up to that point. The first thing that happens when you get to McKinsey is that you go to yet another in your life's progression of élite schools—a short-term training program where they sand off whatever rough edges are remaining in your self-presentation while you network with the rest of your business-analyst class. You get videotaped role-playing with mock clients, and then you watch yourself while a coach gives you tips: Keep your hands on the tabletop. Make and maintain eye contact. Don't be confrontational. Don't raise your voice. Keep to the point. Get yourself unobtrusively in control of the rhythm of the encounter.

Then you go to the McKinsey office where you'll be working. McKinsey makes a big point of not having a headquarters; it is supposed to be a global association of equal partners, not a top-down corporation—there are eighty offices in thirty-eight cities, and more staff abroad than in the United States. The biggest office, though, is in New York City, taking up a good portion of a silver mirrored-glass skyscraper on East Fifty-second Street, in midtown Manhattan. In the reception area there are leather-bound copies of McKinsey publications and flattering articles about the company. It feels solid, substantial, almost scholarly. There is an impressively large library called the R. & I. department (that's for research and information). You meet your colleagues, you're installed in a small office, you buy some suits (but don't wear them when you work with Silicon Valley clients!), and, suddenly, you've become a hybrid of grad student and executive—in a modern skyscraper.

Life at McKinsey revolves around "engagements," which is what consulting jobs for clients are called. You are assigned to an engagement team of four or five or six people, and then, typically, you go out on the road. The routine is: Get on a plane with the rest of the team on Monday morning, fly out to Pittsburgh or Wilmington or Charlotte or wherever the client's headquarters is, check into a hotel, and set up a "team room" at the client's office.

Even though you've figured out that you must always maintain the cool, unperturbed McKinsey style, underneath it there is an inner swagger that is the secret psychological contentment of life on an engagement. Where are your college friends right now? Are they flying around the country, staying in hotels, taking meetings? Probably not. Are they practically living with incredibly brilliant and seasoned senior people who impart their hard-won wisdom all through the workday? Sharing every meal, going to the health club together, maybe sneaking out to the batting cages once in a while just for fun, or celebrating the end of the week with a dinner at the nice restaurant in town? Do they, in other words, belong to a SWAT team of business philosopher-kings, instead of just being scruffy twenty-two-year-old kids? Don't think so.

During recruiting season back on campus, when things got down to the competitive nub, the people from the investment banks used to tell you that if you went to work for a consulting firm you'd be spending your time on such grisly exercises as compiling lists of people who will lose their jobs in downsizing programs, or cutting pension benefits, or counting the cars in competitors' parking lots. But it's not like that! (Not that often, anyway.) The clients are people who live a different life, who have a different education—who, frankly, are of a slightly different class from the members of a McKinsey engagement team. They've always worked at the client and they go home to their families at five o'clock. They're, you know, great people, but they're not absolutely up on the latest financial-control systems and strategic thinking and marketing data. They are deeply rooted in the day-to-day of operating their division, but you—you have the ability to fly in, design a system, and then fly somewhere else and design another one. That's why the C.E.O. brought you in.

THE usual McKinsey engagement is advising a company on whether to enter a new business or a new territory. Should Big West Bancorporation begin to offer on-line accounts? Should it buy out LittleWest Savings in the neighboring state? Most of the people at the client's headquarters may not know exactly why you're there—they merely know that half a dozen people from the famously arrogant McKinsey have taken over the fourth-floor conference room and are working in there with the door closed. You know what they're thinking: that it's a cost-cutting engagement. And, if it is, you never get past the original suspicion.

The first time that you go into the offices of the client's people and interview them about the reputation of LittleWest Savings, or ask them for reports on their competitors' on-line banking programs, or (especially!) ask them what they do all day, you get resentment. In training, they told you to expect that, and how to deal with it. You say, respectfully but firmly, "Look, I may not personally have experience in banking, but I know how to analyze problems in a business context. I would hope you would have the consideration to help me out with it." In the short run, they don't have much choice but to crumple, in a dignity-retaining way. And over time you think you notice them developing a grudging respect for you. They can see that you're already in your team room when they get to work, and that you're still there when they go home. They must have some idea of what kind of pressure you have to perform under. They seem genuinely grateful for what you tell them in the regular progress reviews. Every once in a while, as the three months of a typical engagement wear on, one of them might even invite you over to dinner.

On Thursday night, you fly home—it's McKinsey policy that all employees return to the office on Fridays, which gives a final, tightening squeeze to the acculturative bond that was building up all week on the road. Whew! You answer your mail. You go to a company lunch where there might be a presentation by a partner, you run numbers, you dig up research, you work late (since all your friends are business analysts at one company or another, if you left work early there would be nobody to see anyway). Even though you are no longer physically at the client's, you are still, in your head, deep within the engagement—still business analyzing.

In truth, a lot of what you do isn't all that complicated—it's phoning around in search of basic market or industry or demographic information, conducting what-if exercises with numbers on a computer (. . . and if Brazil raises interest rates by two points what does that do to profitability?), and trying to learn a bit about the activities of the client's competitors. You are a twenty-two-year-old business analyst, after all, not a neurosurgeon. Still, you have the distinct feeling that, just as the recruiters promised, you are learning something at McKinsey that most people don't know, and that is somehow the key to understanding the world.

What is it? It's not exactly the method of intellectual inquiry you were taught in college, where you have the luxury of operating slowly and thoroughly—but it is a method and it does feel intellectual. Clients want McKinsey to help them make complicated decisions quickly. You learn how to "structure the problem": build a "logic tree" containing all of what you need to know in sequential order, figure out what information is missing, parcel out the getting of it to members of the engagement team. Consulting is full of "80-20 rules"— you try to get eighty per cent of the way to the decision based on twenty per cent of the information, or you get eighty per cent of the information in twenty per cent of the time it would take to get all of it. Either way, the point is to save time. So you make hypotheses and test them, rather than just doing research at leisure.

All the endless hours of work on an engagement, all the research, all the applied intelligence, will go into a "deck," a stack of bullet-pointed presentation sheets that you prepare on your computer, using the PowerPoint program. The aim of an engagement is not to give the client reading material, it's to reduce the issue to its pulsing essence. The client team comes into the room, you distribute the deck, and, crisply, calmly, rationally, brilliantly, you make your "clunk points," marching through them inexorably to the one unerring strategic conclusion. The client will try to flip through the deck—it's human nature. But McKinsey people are trained to deal with this problem. You keep the client locked into eye contact, and you work little guiding phrases into the presentation: "In a minute we'll examine, on page 4, the competitive situation in the Brazilian market, but right now I'd like to direct your attention to the third point on page 2." "Do you need to go back to page 1? I'd be happy to review it." The moment of pure gold comes when you, the business analyst, are called upon, briefly, to present a page or two of the deck.

All of life, it turns out, is unbelievably reducible to the McKinsey treatment: the structure, the logic tree, the bullet points, the deck. One former business analyst told me he reads the paper every morning and finds himself thinking, Hmm, Russia's falling apart; let's pretend it's an engagement. . . . Why not? The McKinsey method isn't merely about business, it's about making the chaos of the world yield itself to the intelligent and disciplined mind. You've been trained and selected over and over for all your life, and this is the payoff: at last, you can do something, you have an omni-applicable power to figure stuff out and explain it to people. In truth, it is more a simulacrum of intellectual mastery than intellectual mastery itself, but what's more important is how it feels. It feels as if you'd been given a key that opens up everything.

Several times in my interviews with business analysts, I spotted the person peeking at a legal pad on which were written a series of bullet points, and then he'd try to find an opening in the interview to launch into the three (or four, or five) reasons that he had chosen to come to McKinsey—"the training" always ranking high, the pay never mentioned. If I tried to take the conversation in a different direction while being presented to, it would be politely suggested to me that perhaps it would be more useful if we went through all the reasons first and then discussed them. A former business analyst, whom I interviewed in a hotel where she was staying, told me that when she'd checked in she hadn't been given the room she wanted, so, thanks to McKinsey, she asked to see the manager and gave him a little talk about how doing things like this would inevitably erode the hotel's brand. *Bingo,* new room.

As if the company you keep, the round of activities, and the method weren't enough to maintain the meritocratic vibe at McKinsey at full pitch, you also, as a business analyst, get incessantly assessed and graded in a way that recapitulates the essential psychological experience of your life thus far. After the completion of every engagement, you get an E.P.R., or "engagement progress report"—it's a McKinsey report card. The E.P.R. is divided into five sections: Problem Solving, Managing, Communications, Teamwork, and Client Relations. Then each section is divided into subsections, such as (in the case of Problem Solving) Issue Identification, Problem Structuring, Analytical Skills, and Developing Recommendations. In every category, you are graded on a zero-to-three scale. Then you go over the report with your E.M. (engagement manager) and your E.D. (engagement director) and sign the E.P.R., whereupon it is sent to your D.G.L. (development group leader), who supervises a small group of business analysts and gives periodic written evaluations. And, if you should choose to enter a long-term career with McKinsey, there will be a series of similar evaluations followed by promotion—or denial of promotion, in which case you leave—up the ladder from associate to partner to, finally, for one of every ten entering associates, senior partner.

THAT élite universities are now preparing people to go directly into business is not just the trend of the moment, though it certainly is that, but also a departure from a long historical tradition (if they had a function beyond pure scholarship, it was to train statesmen, and maybe ministers, doctors, and lawyers as well). One reason law school was until the eighties the leading placeholder thing to do after graduation is that it represented business at a remove, business as scholarship, not business itself. It is remarkable how rapidly the ancient prejudice of educated élites against business has disappeared, not just in the United States but all over the world, including places where it was much more deeply ingrained than here. Rajat Gupta, the head of McKinsey, a man whose air of intense calm, quiet, and unobtrusiveness is almost unsettling because it counterposes so dramatically with what a big shot he is, told me that McKinsey now can get the top graduates of the top universities in every country to come to work for it. "It took a long time in Japan to crack the meritocratic élite," he said. "A long time in France. We used to be voted the best employer in every country where we operate—in business. That was way back when. But now we're by far the most attractive employer, period, for the meritocratic élite."

If you're over a certain age, it is inescapably jarring to hear bright young Ivy Leaguers talk about business as cool—Of course! How could anyone have ever thought otherwise?—in a way that lacks the old familiar note of cynical-ironic detachment. These are idealistic people, too. Several of them spoke with obvious sincerity about wanting to use their McKinsey training to launch careers in charitable organizations, since they need strategies as much as corporations do. It was the idea of public life as the most exciting, central, vital place to be, the place where you can, as they say in application essays, "make a difference," that just didn't seem to have crossed their minds. I got a blank look when I brought it up. One business analyst, when I put the question to her, said, "Everybody wants to change the world. Everybody wants to leave their mark. The question is on what scale. We believe McKinsey is a way to change the world. I think it's less political action than interpersonal action that changes things."

But if the old disrepute of business in élite universities is now suddenly gone, then why shouldn't young graduates just go all the way, and work in actual companies instead of consulting firms and investment banks? Not just any companies, of course—companies with a hothouse aura of prestige, super-smartness, and cultural centrality, which is to say, right now, new Internet companies. You can't pick up a magazine and not come upon a picture of a crowd of young hot shots in polo shirts, projecting attitude in a way that McKinsey consultants aren't allowed to, standing in the office of their con-verted warehouse space waiting for their I.P.O. money to roll in. At McKinsey, because it is a partnership with no publicly owned stock, you can never make millions of dollars overnight.

Already there are signs that Internet startups have begun to pull in some of the talent that would have gone to McKinsey a year or two ago. Jeff Bezos, of Amazon.com, is himself a former junior employee at an investment bank, D. E. Shaw & Company, which is famous for its McKinsey-like hiring policies. Bet he's glad he made the switch! Rajat Gupta told me that McKinsey's annual turnover rate has gone up from seventeen per cent to twenty per cent in the last five years, partly because of personnel raiding by technology companies. So this may be the slightly-past-ripe moment of the consulting vogue.

Or maybe not. When the period of every Internet startup looking like a home run ends, technology will begin to look, to Ivy League seniors, risky—really risky, not just acknowledged-as-a-grace-note risky. These people have excelled in structured environments and have worked their way into a position in which, even though they're just at the outset of life, they can have a pretty well-assured future as long as they do one of a few select things. Maybe the leap from graduate school to McKinsey will turn out to be culturally a lot easier than the leap into beginning adulthood with a roll of the dice. A former business analyst who believes this theory said, "Don't underestimate how conservative these people are. These are the people who stayed home and did their homework. They went to the Ivy League because it's the brand name. They want to assure their future for decades. One guy described it to me as 'the blue-chip path.' Harvard, McKinsey, Harvard Business School. Nothing's gonna go wrong if you take that path."

In any event, something important will have happened. Let me just summarize it for you:

· The United States will have decided, in effect, to devote its top academic talent to the project of streamlining the operations of big business. This is a new development in the history of Western culture.
· We will have created a direct hiring track from élite colleges into a particular sector of the economy. This will only intensify the already considerable hysteria over college admissions, by giving it a hard rational basis for the first time: if you don't get into the right college, you still have another shot at graduate school, but you'll never be a business analyst.
· McKinsey and the other management consultants will have got a great deal. They stand at the end of a huge system that sends tens of millions of people to American public schools every year, administers the S.A.T. to two million people, and processes more than a hundred thousand applicants to the Ivy League colleges—all of this done either directly by government or by non-profit organizations subsidized by government—and then they pluck its very ripest fruit. Have I made that clear? I'd be happy to review it.

OCTOBER 18, 1999

THE WOMAN IN THE BUBBLE

T HE night before Good Friday, Mary Meeker, a thirty-nine-year-old investment banker with a pinkish round face, straight brown hair, and lively blue
eyes, boarded an airplane in San Francisco, stretched out in a first-class seat, and
did something she hadn't done in ages. She relaxed. She was going to spend
Easter with a friend who lives in Hong Kong and she was looking forward to it.
But what she was anticipating most eagerly was the prospect of two long flights
across the Pacific (fifteen hours there, thirteen hours back) during which she
would be cut off from the endless torrent of meetings, telephone calls, conferences, E-mail dialogues, and more meetings that constitutes her daily existence.

Meeker, who works for the investment firm Morgan Stanley Dean Witter, is
the top-ranked Internet analyst on Wall Street—the "Queen of the 'Net," as
Barron's has put it. Her main responsibility is recommending technology
stocks to investors, but she also works closely with Morgan's corporate-finance
department, which specializes in underwriting initial public offerings, or
I.P.O.s, of stock by Internet companies to investors, for a hefty commission.
Two days before her departure for Asia, Priceline.com, a Connecticut-based
firm that sells cheap airline tickets and hotel rooms to on-line customers, had
issued ten million shares—seven per cent of its total shares—through Morgan.
After consultation between Meeker and her colleagues in Morgan's capital-
markets department, the offering price was set at sixteen dollars; if the stock
found buyers, Priceline.com would become the most highly valued Internet
I.P.O. yet, with a total value of almost two and a half billion dollars. As it turned
out, the offering was far more than merely successful. Within seconds of its
début, Priceline.com's price rose to eighty-five dollars—five times the I.P.O.
valuation. The price subsequently fell slightly, but by the following evening,
when Wall Street closed early for the Easter weekend, it was at $80.50.

In other words, Meeker had just helped a company that had been operating for less than a year, and had lost a hundred and fourteen million dollars in 1998 on revenues of just thirty-five million, achieve a stock valuation of more than eleven billion dollars—almost as much as American Airlines. American, of course, owns valuable route franchises and reservation systems, to say nothing of airplanes. Priceline.com owns some high-powered computers and an easy-to-remember Internet address, and that's about it. Even Meeker, who had helped Priceline.com's management explain its business plan to Wall Street investors, was taken aback. "The Internet I.P.O. frenzy is unbelievable," she told me as she was preparing for her departure. "There are so many new companies coming out of the woodwork, and the level of demand from investors is so high. It's mind-boggling."

Every week, dozens of entrepreneurs try to get in touch with Meeker. Each one of them dreams of becoming the next Jay Walker, the founder of Priceline.com, who is now worth more than four billion dollars, at least on paper; securing the backing of the best-known analyst in the industry is a big step toward billionairedom. For this reason and others, the recent acceleration of the Internet boom has placed Meeker in a predicament. On the one hand, it has enhanced her reputation as a financial seer—her list of recommended Internet stocks is up by about a hundred and fifty per cent already this year—and has made her firm a lot of money. On the other hand, it has challenged her view of herself as an objective analyst and filled her with trepidation. Although many people view her as the ultimate Internet bull, which in some ways she is, her greatest fear is of being portrayed as the poster girl for Internet stocks in general, which she certainly isn't. "As the pace accelerates, and the values get higher and higher, it gets more and more dangerous," she said. She then compared the Internet frenzy to the infamous tulip-bulb mania that struck Holland in the early seventeenth century. "There is the same supply and demand imbalance," she said. "The difference is that tulip bulbs didn't fundamentally change the way companies do business. The Internet does. But, when all is said and done, there will be many stocks that in hindsight look like tulip-bulb stories."

Meeker has an immense capacity for work, but the frantic pace of activity in the Internet sector is starting to get to her. On the morning of the day she was due to leave for Hong Kong, she realized that she had forgotten her passport. After an urgent call to New York, a courier was dispatched to fly it out to the San Francisco airport. Fortunately, the courier reached the Cathay Pacific check-in desk before she did. Before she caught the plane, she told me, "I think we will have a big correction in Internet stocks sometime this year. I think a big correction would be very healthy. I personally would welcome it." With that, she climbed aboard and slept for thirteen hours.

IF the stock tables that appear in the daily newspapers are to be believed, we have just witnessed the most dramatic and concentrated period of wealth creation ever. During the last four years, about a hundred Internet companies have issued stock on Wall Street, and together they are now worth more than two hundred and fifty billion dollars. (It took John D. Rockefeller more than forty years to create Standard Oil, and Bill Gates more than twenty to build Microsoft.) The pace of paper wealth creation is still increasing. Just since the beginning of March, more than a dozen Internet companies have gone public, and about thirty others have filed for permission to sell stock in the near future.

The forces driving the Internet stock phenomenon remain somewhat mysterious, but Mary Meeker has undoubtedly played a crucial role. "It is a very small world," David Beirne, a general partner in Benchmark Capital, in Silicon Valley, told me. "The higher up you go, the smaller it gets. Everybody is connected, and she is at the center." Back in 1995, Meeker and a research associate wrote a three-hundred-page research paper, "The Internet Report," which hailed the nascent technology as a revolutionary medium. At that time, fewer than ten million people were on-line, and many people, Bill Gates among them, were skeptical about the on-line world's commercial possibilities. Meeker brushed aside this skepticism, and predicted correctly that the number of Internet users would grow to a hundred and fifty million by the turn of the century. She followed up that coup by writing "The Internet Advertising Report" and, with a colleague, "The Internet Retailing Report," both of which appeared in the first half of 1997. According to Morgan Stanley, roughly a hundred and fifty thousand copies of those reports are in circulation. "She has been the thought leader," I was told by Roger McNamee, who is a partner in Integral Capital Partners, a Silicon Valley investment firm. "Mary has provided an intellectual framework for understanding the Internet."

Respect for Meeker's work isn't confined to investors. Not surprisingly, she is also extremely well liked by Internet executives, many of whom have made fortunes by owning stock in the companies she touts. Tim Koogle, the chief executive at Yahoo, and Meg Whitman, the boss at eBay, the fast-growing auction site, are effusive in their praise of her, as is Jim Barksdale, Netscape's former chief executive. John Doerr, the leading venture capitalist in Silicon Valley, has called her "an awesome diviner of opportunity." Honeyed phrases like this aren't wholly mercenary. The people who developed the Internet see Meeker as one of themselves—not a buttoned-down East Coast investment banker but an iconoclast who intuitively relates to the infinite possibilities of the wired world. "Mary is, like, twenty at heart," according to Bo Peabody, the twenty-seven-year-old chief executive and founder of Tripod, which operates an on-line community of Web sites. "She is *so* into things that are new and adventurous."

I FIRST visited Meeker's office, which overlooks Broadway and Forty-seventh Street, about a month and a half ago, on the day the Dow first closed above 9,900. I found her to be just as her friends had described her: a plain-spoken, unpretentious Midwesterner. Of medium height, she was wearing a gray tweed jacket, black slacks, and no makeup. She had slight bags under her eyes, and she was in something of a frazzle. While she was away over the weekend, Morgan's E-mail system had broken down, and she had been unable to get her messages. "It was, like, totally retro," she told me, her voice conveying a mixture of anguish and disgust. "I had to call someone to come into the office on Saturday night to fax me my E-mails." She sat down behind her desk, grabbed an iced tea, apologized for her tendency to talk a mile a minute—"I tend to rattle on," she said—and started to talk a mile a minute.

Meeker was born in a small farming town in northeastern Indiana called Portland. The biggest local employer was Portland Forge, and Meeker's father was the No. 2 man there. In 1968, when the factory was taken over by a larger company, he made some money and started investing it. He talked about his investments with his daughter, and she became interested in the stock market. At DePauw University, in Greencastle, Indiana, she took a double major in business and psychology, and began subscribing to the *Wall Street Journal*. After graduating, she joined Merrill Lynch, also in Chicago, and spent two years there before getting an M.B.A. at Cornell. Then, in 1986, she joined Salomon Brothers, in New York. By the time she left, for Cowen & Company, another Wall Street firm, three and a half years later, she was a junior research analyst covering the personal-computer industry. In early 1991, she was hired from Cowen by Morgan Stanley, which was trying to build up its presence in the personal-computer sector.

Meeker's experience covering companies like Dell, Compaq, and, especially, Microsoft helped shape her views of the on-line world as it began to emerge in the early nineties. "If you looked at Microsoft and believed Bill Gates when he said, 'A personal computer on every desktop. A personal computer in every home,' it was easy to extrapolate, and see that Microsoft was going to be a big company someday," she told me. "The lesson I learned was to apply the same reasoning to America Online. Simple as it sounds, I believed in 1993 that everyone would use E-mail someday."

Meeker recognized early that using on-line communication was much cheaper and more efficient than relying on wood pulp and mailmen, and that as the Internet grew, and more and more people joined the network, its usefulness would increase exponentially. The latter point has been formalized in Metcalfe's Law, which was set down some years ago by Robert Metcalfe, the founder of 3Com. It states that the value of any network increases in proportion to the square of the number of people using it, so a network with five hundred people attached to it is a hundred times as useful as one with only fifty people attached. Once this elemental but fundamental fact was assimilated, it became easy to believe, along with the futurists Nicholas Negroponte and George Gilder, that the arrival of the Internet amounted to an industrial and social revolution.

AMERICA ONLINE was the first online service to be aimed at non-geeks. In December of 1993, Morgan Stanley managed a stock offering for it, and Meeker recommended its stock to investors—a move she now refers to as "a defining event in my career." At the time, America Online was losing money, its accounting was dubious, and many people on Wall Street were doubtful about its future. America Online's shares, adjusting for subsequent stock splits, were selling for about ninety-five cents each. Last week, they were changing hands for about a hundred and sixty dollars each. Meeker followed up her inspired America Online call with numerous others. She has recommended ten "ten-baggers," or stocks that subsequently increased more than tenfold—@Home, Amazon.com, America Online, CNET, Compaq, Dell, eBay, Intuit, Netscape, and Microsoft—and she takes justifiable pride in her stock-picking record.

Showing off one of her favorites (and illustrating Metcalfe's Law), she called up for me the home page of eBay, the Internet auction site, and asked me to name an item. I chose golf clubs. There were hundreds of golf-club auctions in progress, including one that offered an ancient set of hickory-shafted irons (latest bid: $234), and one for a set of vintage Patty Bergs, similar to clubs that Meeker had used in high school. "You want a set of golf clubs, and you're looking for a bargain, so where else in the world would you go?" she asked. All told, there were about two million items for sale that day on the eBay site—almost double the number there had been three months earlier. Meeker went on to say, "We've never seen companies grow this rapidly. eBay is the fastest-growing retailer in the history of the universe."

In the fall of 1994, Meeker came across a story in the *Times*, by John Markoff, about a new venture called Mosaic Communications, which had developed an easy-to-use device for navigating the World Wide Web. "I read the article, and a light bulb went on," Meeker told me. She visited Mosaic's offices, in Mountain View, California, and in April of 1995 Morgan rounded up a group of old-line media firms—they included Times Mirror, Knight Ridder, and Hearst—to invest in the new venture, which had changed its name to Netscape. Four months later, amid widespread publicity, Netscape, which even then was less than a year and a half old, sold a hundred and forty million dollars' worth of stock to the public, with Morgan leading the issue. Meeker refers to the date of the issue, August 9, 1995, as the start of Year One in the on-line era. "With the Netscape I.P.O., we really helped create a new business model," she told me. "We helped create a new way of financing companies."

Even the most unreconstructed stock-market bear wouldn't contest that statement. One of the great strengths of contemporary American capitalism, which relies on decentralized decision-making by hundreds of millions of individuals, is the ability to channel large amounts of money into promising new industries, and the growth of the Internet industry is an excellent example of this process at work. More centralized forms of capitalism, such as those found in Germany and Japan, have so far, at least, proved less well suited to developing the knowledge-based industries of the future. The only question—and it is one that Meeker herself is asking—is whether we are now seeing too much of a good thing. "I remember that in 1995, when I would speak with Marc Andreessen"—the co-founder of Netscape—"and we would try to count up how many people understood this stuff," she said, "we thought it was about four hundred."

PRICELINE.COM was started in July of 1997, by Jay Walker, a Connecticut entrepreneur who thought that he could make money by using the Internet to help airlines and hotels fill their excess capacity. Walker persuaded some venture capitalists to back his idea, and in April of last year he started a Web site on which customers can list the amount they are willing to pay for, say, a flight from Boston to Miami, or a hotel room in Dallas, on a given date. Priceline.com's proprietary database then searches for airlines and hotels that are willing to meet the posted offer. If one is available, the order is filled.

Last summer, Walker's financial backers got in touch with Meeker, and she passed the tip on to Andre de Baubigny, a younger colleague who acts as her gatekeeper, emissary, and sounding board. De Baubigny drove up to Stamford, where Priceline.com is based, and liked what he saw. He called Meeker from the car phone and urged her to visit the firm as soon as possible. Upon following his advice, she decided that Priceline.com satisfied the three major criteria she uses for screening I.P.O. candidates: it had a large potential market; it was using some clever technology; and it had recruited an experienced management team—its chief executive, Richard Braddock, was a former president of Citicorp. The downside was that the firm was losing huge amounts of money, but that isn't unusual in the Internet world, and Meeker pays less attention to past results than to potential. Moreover, some of Priceline.com's losses last year arose from an expensive marketing campaign, featuring William Shatner, that helped make it one of the most recognizable brands on the Internet. Meeker believes that brands will be just as important on the Internet as they are in tobacco and soap flakes. "This is a time to be rationally reckless," she told me. "It's a time to build a brand. It is really a land-grab time." The number of airline tickets sold on Priceline.com's Web site this year is now running at quadruple last year's rates, and the firm has recently started selling mortgages on-line. That is the sort of growth investors look for when they are deciding whether to buy Internet stocks.

Meeker and Morgan decided to compete for the Priceline.com I.P.O. business. Late last year, the firm organized a two-day "bake-off," at which several Wall Street firms made formal presentations. Morgan Stanley and Goldman, Sachs were two of the main candidates, and Morgan won out, thanks largely to Meeker. "We just think Mary is the best—that was the distinguishing reason we chose Morgan," Richard Braddock told me. "She has the credibility."

By no means does every fledgling company satisfy Meeker's criteria. Since the Netscape I.P.O., Morgan has underwritten more than a dozen I.P.O.s—among them @Home, CNET, and Broadcast.com—but it has also turned down a large number of opportunities, some of which involved quite well-known outfits. Two recent examples are iVillage and TheStreet.com. The first, which operates a net-

work of Web sites aimed at women, was founded by two high-profile media executives, Candice Carpenter and Nancy Evans. TheStreet.com, a financial Web
site that caters primarily to on-line traders, was founded by two men, James J.
Cramer, a writer and investor, and Martin Peretz, the owner of *The New Republic*.
A person familiar with what happened told me that Meeker and her colleagues
had become worried about the management team at iVillage, and that they believed TheStreet.com's market was too narrow to support rapid growth.
Whether these were the right decisions remains to be seen, as the businesses develop over the next few years. From a short-term perspective, Morgan's reticence
isn't looking too smart. Last month, Goldman, Sachs managed an initial offering
for iVillage, and the stock tripled on the first day of trading. The I.P.O. for
TheStreet.com, whose lead underwriter is also Goldman, is expected soon, and it
will probably take off as well, since the issuing firm has ".com" in its name.

Morgan could have made more money by being less selective, but Meeker
and her colleagues say that big-money investors tend to rely on the firm's seal
of approval. "If Morgan Stanley has its name on it, investors assume it's better
than Schlock Incorporated," Joe Perella, the head of Morgan's corporate-
finance department, mused. "When we have a market break"—a significant
downturn—"then we will see who the winners and the losers are." Perella,
who was a co-founder of the investment firm Wasserstein Perella, and who
played a big role in the takeover frenzy of the late nineteen-eighties, is a tall and
slick Wall Street veteran. He rarely speaks to the press, but when I visited his office recently he seemed happy to chat about Meeker and her role in the latest
mania striking the financial markets. "Mary is the right person in the right
place at the right time," he told me. "The energy level and the workaholism are
things that give her an advantage, because in the industry she covers there is
an unlimited amount of things to focus on." Perella also pointed out that
Meeker's influence stems, at least in part, from the peculiar nature of Internet
companies; namely, that nearly all of them lose money, and therefore need regular infusions of cash from investors. "It's not like Ford or Microsoft sitting
there with twenty billion dollars in its bank account," he said. "Mary can make
or break them with her pen."

I asked Perella how he would relate the Internet phenomenon to other speculative episodes he has witnessed, but he said that there was little to compare.
"This is more profound than somebody trying to take over a company with
junk bonds in the nineteen-eighties, or Charlie Bluhdorn using paper money to
build up Gulf & Western in the nineteen-sixties," he said. "It is the only thing
I've seen, in twenty-seven years, that seems to be affecting every industry
group. If you are covering retail, you need to know about the Internet. If you
are covering financial services, you need to know about the Internet. If you are
covering heavy industry, the same thing applies. I read this morning that Allied Signal is going to do a lot of its business on the Internet. The Internet is per-
vading every aspect of business, and of life."

• • •

A COUPLE of weeks after our first conversation, I returned to Meeker's office and asked her what was going to happen next in the Internet story. As she described her vision of the on-line world's future, she relied heavily on a phrase I hadn't heard before: "digital Darwinism." The phrase is based on the economics of increasing returns and on what are called "network effects." It ties in with the conceit, common among Internet cognoscenti like Meeker, that we are seeing the emergence of an entirely new commercial ecosystem.

The economics of digital Darwinism are pretty simple. During the last few years, economists have come to recognize that high-technology markets tend to be dominated by one or two firms, which enjoy high profit margins, and that companies establishing such an early lead are difficult to displace. The recent history of computer-industry I.P.O.s provides a good example. Between 1980 and 1998, about eighty-six per cent of the stock-market wealth created by new technology companies was generated by five per cent of the companies, and many firms that were well known a decade ago but didn't establish a leadership position have now vanished. Meeker thinks that history will repeat itself in the Internet sector. "There's no doubt in my mind that the aggregate market value for the Internet sector will be a lot higher in three years than it is today," she told me. "It is just a question of which companies succeed and which companies fail. I think there will be only a couple of handfuls of companies that really succeed." She advises investors to put their money in firms with names that have a chance of becoming what she calls on-line "super-companies"— America Online, Amazon.com, eBay, Yahoo, and @Home—and to avoid firms trying to compete with these market leaders. Many of the small firms, she says, will meet the same fate that corner stores do when Wal-Mart opens up nearby. "The Internet is a kind of small town," she says. "Everybody will go to www.something," and they won't go anywhere else, at least not often.

If Meeker is correct, the leading players may be able to reap monopoly profits, but that is by no means certain. A frequent criticism of Internet businesses is that there is no "barrier to entry"; that is, Web sites are so cheap to put on line that almost no capital is required, and anybody can steal a good idea and make it better. Meeker disagrees. "It's easy to say there are no barriers to entry," she says, "but in reality there's a new kind of barrier to entry. Yahoo has nearly fifty million registered users, and these are people who have devoted time to the system. There are more than twenty million stock portfolios on A.O.L. People are going to re-key them to another site? They don't want to do it. It's too much of a hassle."

Meeker advises Internet businesses to build up their customer base at all costs, even if that means giving away products, as Netscape did with its Navigator Web browser, or spending heavily on customer service, as America Online and Amazon.com do. "With A.O.L., my view was that if it got enough customers, and it built a sticky-enough environment, it would eventually be able to generate revenues and profits from those customers," she told me. "The question I always asked Steve Case"—A.O.L.'s chairman and chief executive— "was 'When do you reach critical mass?' It was one million customers. It was five million. At eight million, he said, 'Mary, shut up. Lots. Many.' A.O.L. finally became profitable at ten million." Amazon.com, on the other hand, still hasn't made a dime, but Meeker is relatively unconcerned. "My view of Amazon is that it's not just books, it's bits," she said. "If two years from now it has fifteen or twenty million customers, and it has their credit-card numbers, and they are happy, then it can make money. Books will be seen as the Trojan horse that got them all the customers—just like all those disks given away by A.O.L."

In the light of her bigger-is-better argument, Meeker usually advises a small on-line firm to find a bigger partner. Bo Peabody, at Tripod, remembers walking into Meeker's office about three years ago. "It was the first time that *PC Meter* had published its top twenty Web sites," he said. "She threw the article on the table and said, 'Game over.' What she was saying was that, now that we know who the top twenty sites are, this is going to be a very short game. These twenty sites will consolidate into ten, and that will be the end of it." Peabody followed Meeker's logic, selling Tripod to Lycos, a much larger Internet company, and he wasn't the only small company to sell to a larger one. The consolidation that Meeker foresaw is now affecting the Internet's biggest firms. Since January of this year, America Online has acquired Netscape; @Home has agreed to buy Excite; Lycos has agreed to merge with USA Networks; and Yahoo has agreed to buy GeoCities and Broadcast.com. The only big Internet player that hasn't been involved in substantial merger activity is Microsoft, and Meeker puts that down to the fact that it's currently hamstrung by its legal battle with the Department of Justice. Microsoft has been on her buy list since 1989, and the firm is now worth a stunning four hundred and seventy billion dollars, but she believes that its dominant market share will eventually be undermined by the Internet. "It's highly likely that sometime in the next ten years someone will make a great call, downgrading Microsoft's stock," Meeker told me. "But figuring out when to do it is going to be very, very tricky. Things can crack, but it can take years for the crack to become apparent."

Outside the Internet sector, the biggest losers in the Darwinian struggle, Meeker believes, will be retailers, travel agents, and other businesses that compete directly with on-line firms. In the last quarter of 1998, she pointed out to me, both Barnes & Noble and Borders reported slower rates of sales growth in their stores. Mattel, which mostly makes toys and games out of wood, metal, and plastic instead of computer chips, had a disappointing Christmas. Yet Meeker isn't a zealot. "Things rarely happen as quickly as one thinks, so there's rarely displacement as quickly as one thinks," she told me. "Television didn't kill radio. The Internet is not going to kill television, radio, or publishing." Nonetheless, she is critical of the big media companies for missing a historic opportunity. "Disney should have been Yahoo, A.T.&T. should have been A.O.L.,

Time Warner should have been Excite," she said. "Why didn't it happen? It was a series of judgment errors."

DURING the last few months, Morgan Stanley Dean Witter's telephone operators have taken more calls for Meeker than for anybody else at the firm. On a typical day, she receives about fifty voice-mail messages, roughly twice as many E-mails, and as many as a dozen requests for press interviews or public appearances. To deal with this deluge, she relies on de Baubigny, two secretaries, and three research assistants. All of them are expected to match her punishing schedule. Russ Grandinetti, who used to work for Meeker and is now the head of investor relations at Amazon.com, remembers flying to San Francisco with her on the first day of his job. On arriving, they worked through the day and most of the night, got up early the next morning, spent all day in meetings, then caught the red-eye back to New York, so they could be at their desks the following morning. "As we were getting on the plane, the steward said, 'Hello, Miss Meeker, it's nice to see you again,' " Grandinetti recalled. "I knew then that the next two years were going to be particularly intense ones."

Meeker's colleagues have learned to ignore an occasional blowup. "She's still the same Mary—one minute, she's screaming, throwing a tantrum, the next minute everything's great," Chuck Phillips, another research analyst at Morgan, whose office is just down the hall from Meeker's, told me, with a smile. "People get used to it." When I arrived at Meeker's office one day, I found her issuing a tongue-lashing to one of her assistants, who was late with a report she had requested. She let him have it in public, in front of an elevator, her eyes blazing. At the end of the dressing down, the unfortunate young man crept away like a scolded puppy, and Meeker came over to me and cheerfully said hello.

She can be just as harsh on Internet companies. In January, she issued a research note to Morgan's clients saying that she "would like these stocks to sell off to release some pressure from the system." Many Internet issues, including Amazon.com and Yahoo, immediately fell, as investors appeared to heed Meeker's words, but in the ensuing weeks they recovered strongly, and in many cases surpassed their previous highs. The market capitalization of eBay, for instance, is now more than twenty billion dollars, which is more than two hundred and fifty times its total revenues last year. (Microsoft, the world's most valuable company, sells at twenty-three times its revenues, and *that* figure used to be considered excessive.) America Online is worth about a hundred and fifty billion dollars—almost as much as General Motors, Ford, and Boeing combined. Despite these distortions, Meeker has not repeated her plea in print, largely because there wouldn't be any point to doing so. "It would be easy for me to say, 'Hey, based on traditional valuation methodologies, stocks are overvalued,' " she told me. "They'd go down for two weeks, and then go back up again, because the money flows will continue to drive the sector."

In trying to decipher what is happening to stocks like eBay and Priceline.com, Meeker falls back on the laws of supply and demand. On the demand side, she argues, there are two sets of big buyers: professional investors, who are determined not to make the same mistake they made last year, when they avoided Internet stocks and underperformed the market; and small traders, who have made so much money in the last few years that they now feel they are playing with the house's money. On the supply side, only a limited number of Internet shares are available. eBay has a hundred and twenty million shares outstanding, but only ten million of them are trading on Wall Street. The rest are owned by the company's founders and its original investors. Priceline.com has a hundred and forty-two million shares outstanding, but only ten million are publicly traded. With demand growing rapidly, and supply artificially restricted, there is only one way for prices to move. "A stock can go up and down based on money flows at a much more rapid clip than it can based on fundamentals," Meeker noted dryly.

The fact that most of the shares in companies like Yahoo and Amazon.com are not publicly traded also means that the enormous market capitalizations attributed to them are misleading. A firm's market capitalization is obtained by multiplying its share price by the total number of shares issued, a calculation that assumes that the stock price is a fair indication of the firm's value. For I.B.M. or General Electric, this is a reasonable assumption, since all the firm's shares are available for investors to buy or sell, but for Priceline.com or eBay it surely isn't, since the stock price reflects an artificial scarcity. If Priceline and eBay were to make all their non-traded shares available for purchase tomorrow, their stock prices would, almost certainly, plummet, and their multibillion-dollar market capitalizations would plummet with them.

WITH the Priceline.com I.P.O. out of the way, Meeker and her colleagues are busy looking for their next big money spinner. One night after work, Meeker, de Baubigny, and Ruth Porat, a senior executive in Morgan's corporate-finance department, went out to dinner together to run through some I.P.O. possibilities that were on the horizon. After the waiter took their orders, Porat opened a thick black folder that contained information on approximately two hundred privately owned Internet companies. "Let's talk about tier-one candidates first," said Porat, a slim, elegant thirty-nine-year-old mother of three. The first name on her list was a Colorado-based company that provides financial services online. "It's got revenues going from twenty-nine to eighty," Porat explained, meaning in millions of dollars. "I said it was still too early," she added.

Meeker nodded. A California company that makes Internet software was much closer to the starting line, Porat explained. It would be holding a bake-off, at which rival investment banks would compete for the lucrative business of taking it public, the following week.

"We all have to be there, right?" Meeker asked.

"Yes," said de Baubigny.

Porat grimaced. "I have to bring my kids," she said. "It's the first day of my vacation."

The conversation continued, with Porat methodically checking off her list, and Meeker and de Baubigny offering their views. At one point, Porat mentioned a firm that was also talking to Goldman, Sachs. De Baubigny said he still had some doubts about the company. Meeker, bristling at the mention of Goldman, disagreed. "When we first saw it a year ago, it didn't have a real story at all," she said, referring to the firm. "Now its story is good, the business is developing, and the numbers are better. Let's agree to make a pitch in a couple of weeks."

When the three of them had completed their decisions and finished their dinner, I asked Meeker if she had any regrets about the last few years. She mentioned that Morgan had missed the opportunity to do I.P.O.s for Yahoo, eBay, and Amazon.com, and she went on to say that the first case had been a "brain-dead mistake" (Meeker hadn't thought that Yahoo was ready to go public), and that the second had been a "screw-up" (Meeker and her colleagues had performed poorly at eBay's bake-off). Amazon.com was a different story. Meeker recognized the company's potential, and she knew its founder, Jeff Bezos, but she was overruled by the senior management at Morgan, because the bank had a long-standing relationship with Barnes & Noble, which was Amazon.com's main rival. Leonard Riggio, Barnes & Noble's chairman, asked Morgan not to raise money for a competitor, and Morgan agreed. The decision upset Meeker so much that she seriously considered quitting. Instead, she remained a vocal supporter of Amazon.com, and her support paid off last year, when it asked Morgan to sell five hundred million dollars' worth of junk bonds to help finance its rapid expansion. This time, Meeker's superiors ignored Riggio's objections.

THESE days, there is hardly a prominent firm in the Internet industry that doesn't do business with Morgan, but Meeker still worries about the future. "The feel of speculative excess and making too much money too fast reminds one that greed can be bad," she wrote in a January research circular, and it wasn't a throw-away line. When she wrote it, she had just visited a couple of private Internet companies that wanted to go public. "They were unbelievably arrogant about how successful they were going to be, and they were unbelievably arrogant about the valuations they wanted to achieve on their I.P.O.," she told me. "I was just pissed. I was, like, 'Come on, guys!' " According to Meeker, a second generation of Internet entrepreneurs is emerging, and it often suffers from what she calls "market-cap envy" of people like Andreessen and Bezos. "The first generation was, like, 'Hey, isn't this great! I'm a billionaire! Well, that's kind of embarrassing. What am I going to do with all this stuff?' " she said. "The next generation is saying, 'Well, if *he's* a billionaire, then *I've* gotta be a billionaire.' With every I.P.O., the envelope is pushed a little further. At some point, you have to scream uncle."

Meeker won't talk about how much money she herself makes, but it is safe to assume that she took home several million dollars last year. That is a lot of cash by most people's standards, but it is a pittance compared with the amounts being raked in by successful Internet entrepreneurs, many of whom are starting to spend their wealth on lavish estates. Meeker lives in an unremarkable apartment on the West Side, and though she has a summer house, in Amagansett, it is nearer to the train station than to the ocean. "It isn't all about money," she said. "I'm having fun, and I think I'm doing what I do best." In recent weeks, rumors have emerged on Wall Street that she may be leaving Morgan for a hedge fund, where she would be paid a lot more, but she has dismissed the rumors as tittle-tattle put about by her competitors. "I plan to be here," she told me.

Far from seeking a demanding new job, Meeker says she is hoping to spend more time on things other than work in the next few years. On the rare occasions when she does escape from the office, she skis, cycles, roller-blades, and wind-surfs. Eventually, she would like to get married and have children, as her colleague and coeval Ruth Porat has done. "I think human beings have a capacity to go twenty-four/seven for a certain amount of time when things are moving in a fast and exciting way," she said. "Then there's a time when you say, 'Wait a minute!' I think the whole industry is coming to that point." Perhaps, but some of Meeker's colleagues are skeptical about her resolve to ease up a little. "She's completely neurotic," one of them told me. "Can you imagine her doing anything at a slow speed? I just don't believe it."

Ultimately, Meeker's future depends on the fate of the industry she covers. Much as she might like to avoid it, her reputation and her life style are inextricably linked to the fate of stocks like Amazon.com, Yahoo, and eBay. Most of her arguments about how these stocks are behaving are correct as far as they go, but, to my mind, at least, they don't go far enough. Yes, the Internet is a revolutionary technology, but the entire sector is now in a condition classically defined as a speculative bubble. People are buying Internet stocks simply because they are already going up, not because they think the companies that issue the stocks are going to generate large profits in the future. At some point, the speculative bubble is going to burst, just as all such bubbles burst, from Amsterdam in 1637 to Tokyo in 1989. When this happens, the vast majority of Internet stocks, even the market leaders, will collapse and stay collapsed, and Meeker may have a lot more time on her hands.

Not surprisingly, perhaps, she isn't quite willing to make that logical leap. "I think many of these valuations are built on air, but I don't think *all* of them are," she told me during one of our conversations. "Some of these companies have extraordinarily powerful business models, and they are just at the point of figuring out how to monetize them." Yahoo, for example, has pre-tax profit margins of more than thirty per cent. eBay, despite its rapid growth, faces a payroll of just a hundred and forty employees. At the same time, however, Meeker didn't sound as though she wanted to give much reassurance to holders of Internet stocks. "Many of them are going to get blown up," she said. "I have no doubt about that."

APRIL 26, 1999

THE

AGE

MARISA AND JEFF

MARISA Baridis, a control-group analyst at Smith Barney, was part of what Wall Street people call the Chinese wall. The wall is an administrative structure that a large securities firm erects to keep its trading operation shut off from the activities of its investment bankers, who routinely acquire a lot of inside information that would be illegal to use in buying and selling stocks. Since the first step in detecting leakage of inside information is to find out what information the firm has, Marisa Baridis and her colleagues talked constantly to investment bankers and noted on a confidential "watch list" exactly where each deal stood and when an announcement that could affect the stock of any of the companies involved was expected. Then, as she once summed it up, they would "look for trading that was in line with what we knew was going to happen." On Wall Street, a Chinese wall is festooned with security precautions—paper shredders, separate computer servers, segregated trash pickup—because another way to think of the watch list is as the mother lode of inside information.

When Marisa Baridis joined Smith Barney, in 1993, she was in her mid-twenties. A business-administration graduate of Boston University, she also had a law degree from Touro Law School, on Long Island, although she had never taken the bar examination. She wouldn't have struck someone on first meeting as part of an enforcement operation. A petite young woman with pale skin and jet-black hair, she gave the impression of a certain fragility. Although the nineties bull market was gathering steam when she joined Smith Barney, control-group analysts were not among those young Wall Street types who were beginning to indulge their tastes for high-performance sports cars and staggeringly expensive co-op apartments.

Marisa Baridis's starting salary at Smith Barney was about forty-five thousand dollars a year. Still, she was hardly poor. Although she had often quarrelled with her father, a Greek immigrant who was a bridge-painting contractor in Philadelphia, he took care of the rent on her apartment, on the Upper East Side, as he had taken care of whatever she needed in college and law school. He also pressured her to take the bar exam. At one point, in order to make him think she'd taken it and failed, she sent him a doctored-up rejection letter received by someone else from the New York State Board of Law Examiners.

Even without the burden of rent, Marisa Baridis had no trouble getting rid of her salary. In fact, a couple of times she was feeling so pressed she told the credit-card company that an item she'd actually purchased had appeared on her monthly bill in error. She led the sort of singles life in Manhattan that included regular appearances at late-night clubs and memberships in fitness centers and shares in summer rentals in the Hamptons. In conversation, she sounded like a lot of other young people who worked in, say, the financial industry or the real-estate industry and lived in high-rise boxes on the East Side and worried a lot about their social lives—so that she could summarize a relationship that didn't work out by saying, "I'm like, 'Weren't you supposed to call me?' He's like, 'Yeah.' " She spent a lot of time E-mailing—not just questions to investment bankers about where a prospective merger stood but also the jokes that get passed around Wall Street electronically and messages like "Virginia just called. She said Michael and all those guys are going to dinner and then to some bar that Howard Stern is having a party at."

At Smith Barney, her performance appraisals occasionally mentioned problems like absenteeism and lack of focus. She seemed proud of holding such a responsible job in such a prestigious firm, but she wasn't getting along with her supervisor, and she sometimes found the work a strain. From the time she started with Smith Barney, she had been on Valium, prescribed by a psychiatrist. In the psychiatrist's view, Marisa Baridis had problems that went beyond a stressful job. Her parents had split when she was an infant, and she spent most of her childhood living with her mother, who was apparently physically ill much of that time and depressed to the point of inertia. After her mother died of breast cancer, when Marisa was fifteen, Marisa moved in with her father and his second family, but she hadn't felt truly welcome, despite the material objects her father gave her. Marisa Baridis's psychiatrist had concluded that she was suffering from low self-esteem, even self-hatred. Although she was an attractive young woman and had some good female friends, she tended to have miserable relationships with men. Her life, the psychiatrist said at one point, was an all too successful search for men who would abuse and betray her.

● ● ●

MARISA Baridis had heard of Jeffrey Streich before she met him. This was in the summer of 1996. For a couple of years, she'd taken a share in a Hamptons summer house run by a former girlfriend of Streich's named Tina Eichenholz, who told stories of her old beau's extravagance: on the third date, as Baridis remembered one story, Streich had given Eichenholz a five-thousand-dollar diamond bracelet. A stocky, dark-haired young man from Commack, Long Island, who had gone to community college and the State University of New York at Brockport, Streich was also involved with the securities business, but in an aspect of it that wouldn't have been familiar to the Ivy League investment bankers Marisa Baridis spoke to every day about mergers and acquisitions. He had begun his Wall Street career in what people in the trade call a bucket shop—a type of operation that Streich himself once summed up succinctly as "the bottom-of-the-barrel stock firm." A bucket shop generally pushes one or two stocks at a time—stocks that tend to be distinguished by how much the bucket shop itself owns of them and how little there is of substance to the companies that have floated them. Through high-pressure selling and some reporting gimmicks and such devices as parking blocks of stock in the accounts of customers without authorization, the bucket shop keeps the house stock at an artificially inflated price. At some point, the house has its money and its customers are stuck with a stock that in the conventional market is virtually impossible to sell.

"Before I was a broker, I was a normal human being making an honest living," Jeff Streich once said. "The only thing illegal I did, I think—when I was young I used to steal Pop Rocks." After he was a broker, he went a good deal beyond Pop Rocks. His first boss, Brett Hirsch—this was at a bucket shop called D. H. Blair—is Streich's contemporary, but he has been described as a sort of Fagin figure who trained young men in a variety of securities scams. The thirty or so brokers and cold-callers clustered around Brett Hirsch wanted what he had—a flashy car, a flashy girlfriend, the wherewithal to toss thousand-dollar chips on the table in Las Vegas—and they worked hard to please him. On his team, they led a sleazeball version of the high life—regular visits to a strip club in the East Sixties called Scores, a ready supply of cocaine, bachelor parties in Las Vegas, a trip to Rio for New Year's. Streich began as a cold-caller, making three or four hundred calls a day off microfiche lists of prospects bought from people who'd stolen them from more respectable firms. Among members of the Hirsch group, Streich was known as Heckel, a summer-camp nickname. The most inept cold-caller in the crowd was known as Schmeckel. Another broker was called Murray the Crook—although calling someone Murray the Crook in the Hirsch group was more or less like calling someone on an N.B.A. team Joe the Tall Guy.

The Hirsch group, in fact, could be described as too crooked—or at least too blatant—for the bucket shops. More than once, the daytime activities of the merry band included being escorted out onto the sidewalk en masse by company security guards. Jeff Streich, a smooth talker who seemed unburdened by compunctions, could be described as too crooked—or at least too blatant—for the Hirsch group. When the group moved from D. H. Blair to a firm called A. R. Baron, he was told that the multiplicity of complaints lodged against him by the National Association of Securities Dealers had made him too much of a liability to keep on board. Baron was hardly a pillar of rectitude itself. One of its officers at that time sticks in the mind of some law-enforcement people as a man who sometimes managed to spend twenty thousand dollars in a particularly festive evening at Scores.

Being left out of Baron didn't mean Streich had run out of moves on Wall Street. First, he joined A. S. Goldmen, where he was fired after four months for unauthorized trading; then he was briefly at a firm called Gruntal, where he was fired for telling customers that they wouldn't be held responsible for losses if the initial public offerings he was pitching went down instead of up; and then he went to Beacon, where he was fired after an N.A.S.D. complaint over his handling of the account of a semi-retired man from Chicago named Shy Glass. When Streich took over the account, Glass, who was in his seventies, had a four-hundred-and-forty-thousand-dollar portfolio dominated by Amgen, an early biotech company whose stock was solid and, as it happened, about to become even more valuable. Through unauthorized trading and forging a margin-account application, Streich transformed the portfolio into house stocks that had the advantage of paying him a cash kickback but the accompanying disadvantage of quickly becoming worthless. When it was all over, Shy Glass's portfolio amounted to thirty thousand three hundred and sixty dollars.

After Beacon, Streich put together his own "private placement"—the sale of a stock issue to a limited number of buyers, without a public offering. The company Streich had for sale, LJS Holdings, was what he described as a "laundromat-slash-café," although not the sort of laundromat-slash-café that had, say, a business plan or employees. The money Streich raised for LJS—two hundred thousand dollars or so—went straight into his pocket and out again in a matter of months, spent on drugs and expensive presents for women and gambling on sporting events. By the summer of 1996, Streich was by way of being a private investor, although not one with any money to invest. He was working out of an office maintained by a young man named Vincent Napolitano, in an apartment on East Sixty-fourth Street, helping Napolitano invest in initial public offerings. Brokers ordinarily ration out I.P.O.s among their best customers, so Napolitano had opened eighteen accounts under the names of various individuals and dummy corporations with tony titles like Synergy Plus, Inc.

Streich was living in a series of apartments on the Upper East Side, sometimes a step or two ahead of an eviction notice; his policy on rent seems to have been that it was the first month's that counted. That summer of 1996 he was running a group house in the Hamptons, which can be a business for somebody who isn't squeamish about how many people he assigns to each bedroom. He carried a lot of cash. In a group, he was the sort of person who wouldn't allow single young women to pay their share of a check. To them, he seemed protective, expansive—almost like a particularly generous big brother. "You get used to these cheap guys who want to go Dutch or worry that you ordered too many appetizers," a friend of Marisa Baridis has said. "Jeff was more like 'Let's get champagne!' " Marisa Baridis later described Jeff Streich this way: "He's the kind of guy that, you know, if you, like, asked for a pack of cigarettes he would, like, give you fifty dollars and tell you to keep the change." She meant it as a compliment.

Jeffrey Streich did have a drinking problem and a cocaine problem and a gambling problem and, of course, a lying problem. Marisa Baridis met him at drinks with a group of people at a casual Westhampton spot on the water called Dockers, in a summer-house atmosphere that made no great distinction between the Wall Street of Smith Barney and the Wall Street of fly-by-night bucket shops. He was in a wetsuit, apparently having come over by Jet Ski from the house he was running. This was early in the summer—before he was ejected from the house because the agent discovered that the new tenants were not two couples but forty groupers, before the marine-supply store sued because the check for the Jet Ski bounced. "She liked his style—she found him exciting," a friend has said. To friends, Marisa expressed surprise that somebody as sophisticated as Jeff Streich was interested in her.

JEFF Streich was not the first person to have suggested to Marisa Baridis—in that joking way which leaves open the option of being taken seriously—that she and a careful partner could trade profitably on her access to the Smith Barney watch list, although he was the first to describe the potential enrichment in terms of matching Mercedeses. Four or five other people, including the husband of her best friend from college, had brought up the subject, and she had dismissed it. But as she and Streich saw each other over the summer—always as part of a group—she began to consider his offer more seriously.

Although Marisa and Jeff were supposedly just pals, two people in a jolly crowd sharing an order of chicken fingers on the weathered deck of a bar in the Hamptons, or downing shots of Jägermeister during happy hour at a bar on the East Side of Manhattan, her friends sensed from the start that she had a crush on him. (They also sensed that he remained enamored of Tina Eichenholz.) Marisa had always had a weakness for big spenders and extravagant flatterers. "He knew exactly how to play her personality," one of her friends has said. "He'd tell her she was in a different category from everyone else. I think a lot of people would be like 'Give me a break,' but she believed him." When Marisa Baridis herself was later asked why, after spurning other opportunities, she began thinking about giving inside information to Streich, she said, "I don't know if I thought that was the way I could get him or power over him, have a

relationship with him. It was probably the only way. If I didn't have my position, I don't think Jeff and I would have had a relationship." In August, Marisa
and Jeff went out to dinner alone in New York for the first time. Before the meal
was over, she'd told him that Square Industries was going to be sold in a couple of weeks and could go up twenty percent.

Eventually, they agreed that she would leak him information and he would
do the investing, observing some safeguards to avoid drawing attention—tell
no one, trade moderately, stay away from options trading. They would split the
profits. Matching Mercedeses were not immediately forthcoming. Sometimes,
even after the entry on the watch list said the deal was going through, some accounting or legal problem held it up. Sometimes the deal didn't have the effect
on the stock that might have been expected. Then, a few days before Thanksgiving, Marisa went to a phone booth outside the offices of Smith Barney and
called Jeff to say that Owen Healthcare, the nation's largest manager of hospital pharmacies, was about to be taken over by Cardinal Health. A few days
later, that was precisely what happened, and the stock jumped from fifteen to
twenty-five. The various accounts controlled by Vincent Napolitano made a
hundred and seventy thousand dollars. Streich made thirty-five thousand dollars in his own accounts, partly by free-riding—buying and selling without
putting up any funds—with brokers he knew from bucket-shop days or from
Hamptons shares. Something had presumably gone wrong with the safeguards, though: in the day or two before the sale, the volume of Owen stock
being traded had jumped four hundred percent.

That is the sort of activity that tends to draw the attention of the market-
surveillance division of the New York Stock Exchange. The exchange has computers that can illuminate clusters of traders in the same Zip Codes or traders
with particularly large buys or traders who have multiple accounts and a sudden interest in the hospital-pharmacy industry. A report was sent to the Securities and Exchange Commission, and an attorney in the S.E.C. enforcement
division put in a call to Vincent Napolitano. Eventually, Napolitano provided
some trading records and appeared for a deposition. In the deposition, he said
what most people accused of insider trading say—that he'd made his trades
on the basis of his own research and what he'd heard around town. The investigation didn't go any further. Napolitano had mentioned Jeffrey Streich to
the S.E.C. attorney only in passing, when asked to name people who often
came to the office on East Sixty-fourth Street. Marisa Baridis's name had never
come up.

AN inside trader who uses a partner to do the investing has a built-in problem:
keeping track of the partner is virtually impossible. There is no way to know
whether the partner is tipping others. There is no way to know how much
money the partner has made by trading on the inside information. The problem

is exacerbated, of course, if the partner is someone like Jeffrey Streich. Streich was essentially using Marisa Baridis's inside information as currency. He traded tips to brokers in return for allowing him to free-ride. He met with Brett Hirsch to see about trading tips for I.P.O. lists. He gave tips to brokers for a share in their profits.

Streich was constantly being warned by Marisa that widening the network, and thus the volume of trading, could only bring suspicion, and he was constantly assuring her that he'd been keeping the information to himself. In fact, there were at least a dozen people getting inside information from Streich, some of them so routinely that when a tip hadn't come along for a while they'd phone and say, "Any pickles coming?" A pickle was information from the Smith Barney watch list. Streich assumed that Napolitano was also passing along Baridis information to other people. For that matter, so was Marisa Baridis. In January of 1997, about six months after her first tip to Streich, she had started tipping the husband of her best friend from college.

She suspected that Streich was cheating her on the split, and she was right. Streich lied about how much he'd bought. He lied about what the price was when he'd bought it. At one point, he convinced two brokers that they ought to chip in for a payment to the source of the inside information—he collected eighteen thousand dollars from them—and then he kept the money himself. For Marisa, getting any money at all from Jeff required constant badgering. At times, she threatened to quit providing information, but in April of 1997, when she moved from Smith Barney to a nearly identical job at Morgan Stanley— she was now making about seventy thousand dollars a year, working for the one old-line, white-shoe firm that had emerged from the changes of recent decades as a power on Wall Street—her arrangement with Streich remained unchanged. At around that time, she had dinner with Tina Eichenholz, who told her that Streich was playing her for a fool—that he and his friends were making an enormous amount of money and cheating her. Jeff denied it. "Did I believe Jeff that other people, his friends, his best friends, weren't involved in the trading?" Marisa said later. "I don't know if I believed him a hundred percent, but I decided to ignore what Tina had told me."

For a year or so after that first tip about Square Industries, the two of them had been involved in an intense but platonic relationship; they were, at least in Marisa's view, best friends. During most of that period, she had a more or less steady boyfriend, someone who had a lot of problems of his own, and their relationship was stormy. She once estimated that she and her boyfriend had broken up thirty or forty times—one time with so much gusto that the police had been summoned.

Then, in September of 1997, Jeff and Marisa went to the Mirage Hotel, in Las Vegas, with Marisa's college friend and her husband—a party of four that included two people who, unbeknownst to each other, were receiving inside tips from a third. At the Mirage, Jeff and Marisa became more than best friends.

That didn't mean that they walked off into a life together while the theme music played. For one thing, he'd stuck her with the hotel bill. She went straight from Las Vegas to Hong Kong for a three-week stint in Morgan Stanley's office there, and when she returned to New York, in October, she E-mailed a friend about Jeff: "He didn't pay the bill from the hotel in Vegas. It's two thousand dollars. He has been ignoring my phone calls and when I saw him out Friday night he completely ignored me. He keeps making derogatory comments when we speak. I have to borrow money to pay the Vegas bill. I fucking hate him."

But they seemed friendly enough when they finally met for dinner one evening in late October. This was at C. S. Barrington's, on Fifty-fourth and Second. Barrington's was a place that had one of those all-glass arcades built out onto the sidewalk, so that some diners—Marisa Baridis and Jeffrey Streich among them that night—seemed almost to be eating in a show window. Over a meal of chicken fingers and fried clam strips and spicy French fries and Southwest potato skins and something called Buffalo calamari, they talked about her love life and his housing problems and her tax problems and his tax problems (both of them were dealing with I.R.S. liens) and her fears that they would get caught at insider trading. Jeff mentioned the prospect he was about to see in his new job as a broker for waterproofing contracts ("I think I'm just going to take him to Scores, make sure the girls give him a nice little time"). Marisa shared some of her impressions of Hong Kong ("It's like Madison Avenue—Armani, Versace, Moschino. The price isn't that different. . . . It's not like you're in Italy, where you're getting Prada for cheaper"). They exchanged views on whether a club called Envy was hot and a club called Opera was good on Tuesdays and a club called Two Rooms was over. They talked about the relative merits of Belvedere vodka and Ketel One vodka—a subject of some immediate interest to Streich, since in the time they were together he had six Martinis.

Eventually, they talked about her split of the profits and about her suspicions that he was holding out on her. When Streich wanted to underline his sincerity, he'd say, "I swear on my mother's ashes." When Marisa Baridis wanted to do the same, she said, "I swear on Heather's life." Heather was her Yorkshire terrier. "Why wouldn't you trust me?" Streich said at one point. "I never gave you a reason not to." (By then, Streich and Napolitano had each made about a quarter of a million dollars on Marisa Baridis's tips, and the other people they tipped had made hundreds of thousands of dollars more; Marisa Baridis's even split had come to about twenty thousand dollars.) Finally, he handed her twenty-five hundred-dollar bills—a down payment on thirty-six thousand dollars he assured her she would soon get. In a van parked just outside C. S. Barrington's, Investigator Walter Alexander, of the Manhattan District Attorney's office, trained a video camera on their table through the floor-to-ceiling glass and recorded the entire conversation through a concealed microphone.

• • •

IN the mid-nineties, the Manhattan District Attorney's office had gone after the bucket shops. An attorney with expertise in the subject, David Gourevitch, was hired from the S.E.C. to lead a team that began with A. R. Baron, whose principals were indicted for running a criminal enterprise. During a lull in the Baron case, the team decided to prosecute a bucket-shop crime that had the look of a short and sweet conviction—the looting of the account of Shy Glass. After winning an N.A.S.D. arbitration, Glass's attorney, Kenneth David Burrows, had been aggressive about trying to collect what his client was owed. (Burrows did eventually recover a good deal of money from the company that had acted as Beacon's clearing broker.) He also pressed law-enforcement agencies. He got in touch with both the United States Attorney's office and the Manhattan District Attorney's office. Unauthorized-trading cases are often difficult to prosecute— the broker's defense tends to be that the client did authorize the transaction in one of their many telephone conversations—but Streich had made this one easy by his forgery. The D.A.'s office called in Jeff Streich and demonstrated to him and his lawyer that it had enough evidence to put him in prison for fraud.

Whatever differences may exist between people who work in Wall Street's most prestigious securities firms and people who work in bucket shops, they are as one when it comes to their response to being caught in an offense that could mean jail time: they look for someone else to turn in. Faced with serious charges in the Glass case, Streich offered information on Beacon and said that he'd been involved in an insider-trading ring whose participants he could name. He was willing to wear a wire to a meeting with the central figure herself—Marisa Baridis. A few days after Marisa Baridis had dinner with Jeff Streich at C. S. Barrington's, she was summoned to the chief counsel's office at Morgan Stanley. Two detectives were there, and they took her to the District Attorney's office for questioning. Within a few hours, the head of the Morgan Stanley compliance department was flying home from Hong Kong to oversee a damage-control operation that included hiring a law firm, a public-relations firm, a private-investigation firm, and a team of trauma specialists to minister to the remaining members of the control group. "It was a very painful time for the firm," the leader of the compliance department said later. The press had been predictably unkind. The phrase in the newspapers which stuck in his mind was Manhattan District Attorney Robert Morgenthau's comment that at Morgan Stanley, the fox had been put in charge of guarding the henhouse.

It was a painful time for Marisa Baridis, too. She spent that first night in jail. Then her father came up from Philadelphia and made bail. Her initial denial of wrongdoing hadn't lasted long. The videotape was devastating. She was actually seen accepting marked hundred-dollar bills, twenty-three of which were later found by the D.A.'s people in her apartment. On the tape, she had described the Chinese wall and said that for someone in her position to leak inside information was the most illegal thing you could do. When her lawyer, Paul

Schechtman, saw the tape some days later, he told her, "There are two phases of a criminal case—the guilt-determining phase and the sentencing phase. I think we should focus on the sentencing phase."

Marisa Baridis had turned the conversation so relentlessly to every element of the crime that one senior assistant district attorney who watched the tape thought at first that she might have been wired herself by some other law-enforcement agency. The agency he would have had in mind was the U.S. Attorney's office, which up to then had handled insider-trading cases. In fact, the federals were so irritated at what they considered poaching that they, in effect, stole Marisa Baridis as a defendant. Even after two senior assistant district attorneys rose in protest from the spectator seats in a federal courtroom, like a couple of strangers at a wedding taking the minister up on his invitation to speak now or forever hold their peace, she was allowed to plead guilty to federal charges, which carried some tactical legal advantages and made it impossible for the state to prosecute her. Among the conditions, of course, was that she reveal absolutely everything she knew about the insider-trading scheme and its participants. In other words, she had to give up somebody, too. All she had to offer was her best friend's husband.

IN a court of law, someone who receives inside information is called a tippee. Of the dozen people identified as tippees by Jeff Streich only Vincent Napolitano elected to go to trial. The rest of them showed up at a cramped and well-worn courthouse on Centre Street, in lower Manhattan, to plead guilty before New York Supreme Court Judge Edward McLaughlin and to swear, in most cases, that they were both remorseful and nearly broke. Although only one of the tippees received a sentence that included jail time, Judge McLaughlin did not attempt to hide his contempt for how easily they had yielded to temptation and how dissolute their lives had been. "I just wonder whether there are people who actually when they get access to inside information say, 'I'm going to turn down the chance to make thirty or forty thousand,' " he said at one sentencing. "The thirty or forty thousand becomes a hundred thousand or so. . . . It goes up the nose, down the toilet, and out the window."

Streich and Marisa Baridis couldn't be sentenced until they made good on their agreements to testify for the prosecution at Napolitano's trial, and, for one reason or another, that trial didn't take place until last fall, nearly two years after the videotaped dinner at C. S. Barrington's. At one point during the wait, Streich wrote to literary agents about the possibility of marketing his story as a book—a project that didn't go even as far as his laundromat-slash-café. "It's a story of greed, backstabbing, double-crossing, manipulation, and love, set in the high stakes, high pressure world of finance," he wrote. "This is a strong character-driven morality tale that plays out like Sleepers, Wall St., and Goodfellows, that is full of lovable losers."

Nobody who was involved in the aftermath of the insider-trading scheme had actually found Jeffrey Streich lovable, but the impression of Marisa Baridis was more complicated. "I submit to you that Marisa Baridis is one of the strangest people any of us will ever encounter," Adam Reeves, an assistant district attorney, told the jury during the trial of Vincent Napolitano, who was ultimately convicted. Baridis was, of course, a witness rather than the defendant in that trial—a witness who sometimes seemed bewildered by the questions she was asked, and answered so quietly that she was regularly asked by the lawyers to raise her voice—but she was sufficiently central to the narrative of the case to require some sort of explanation. Both lawyers seemed to take it for granted that, to some extent, she'd been a victim of Streich's manipulation, if not exactly an innocent victim. She wanted her cut, after all, and being bedazzled by a smooth-talking scoundrel did not seem to explain the inside tips to her best friend's husband. "To suggest that Marisa Baridis is shallow and superficial I don't think is a stretch," Napolitano's lawyer, Joseph Corozzo, Jr., said to the jury, although he also said, "I submit she is smart and she is devious." Some of the law-enforcement people who worked on the insider-trading case saw Marisa Baridis as a spoiled kid looking for thrills—someone whose daddy was still paying for her apartment when she was making seventy thousand dollars a year, someone who had said in the Barrington's transcript that carrying on the insider-trading scheme was fun. But even people who felt that way did not seem completely without sympathy for her. It was not easy to put aside that breathtaking betrayal at C. S. Barrington's.

"I FIND in my own thinking that I come back to one word constantly," Assistant District Attorney Adam Reeves said when Jeffrey Streich appeared before Judge McLaughlin to be sentenced for his crimes against Shy Glass and his role in the insider-trading ring. "It's the word 'betrayal' and . . . it ramifies in many different ways throughout this case." Streich had undoubtedly betrayed the trust of Shy Glass, Reeves said, and there was what some saw as "a very ugly form of betrayal" at Barrington's—although that had been at the behest of the authorities. The District Attorney's office itself had been betrayed by Streich, who was at one point declared in violation of his coöperation agreement after authorities discovered that he had not been forthcoming about the participation of two people—Tina Eichenholz and Vincent Napolitano. Streich, Reeves said, even betrayed the court, in a manner of speaking, since it was apparent that he had not always testified fully and accurately in the Napolitano case.

The previous day, Reeves had asked the Judge to impose a stiff prison sentence on Vincent Napolitano—charging, as the prosecution had charged from the start when the jury was out of earshot, that he was a loan shark and a bookie who had threatened Streich and others by claiming a connection to organized crime. (Judge McLaughlin gave Napolitano two-to-six.) But Streich's case, Reeves said, was much more complicated. Acknowledging that the crime against Shy Glass had been monstrous, Reeves argued that such monstrousness had to be weighed against coöperation that had been instrumental in the successful conclusion of two major investigations. Giving Streich a sentence that was as severe as the one given Napolitano, Reeves said, could have a chilling effect on the inclination of criminals to come forward with information on crimes that would otherwise go unprosecuted. "The dignity of our criminal-justice system is dependent on offering fair outcomes to people who do many unfair things," Reeves said.

There really wasn't much left for the defense lawyer to add. Reeves had even reported detecting remorse in Streich, and had not drawn attention to the fact that the principal criminal scheme Streich's coöperation had brought down would not have existed if he himself hadn't concocted it. "I have radically changed my life," Streich said. "I am no longer involved with drugs and gambling. I no longer take shortcuts that have plagued my whole life." Judge McLaughlin noted that Streich's "active, potentially dangerous coöperation" had produced convictions, but he also said, "There is no rational system that absolves entirely the conduct that you did." To use financial terms, Judge McLaughlin said, the sentence was deeply discounted—one and a third years to four years in state prison.

MARISA Baridis's friends are less likely than the district attorney to find any mitigating factors about Streich's betrayal that night. He had used her, as well as her inside information. Rather than do it in a way that spared her as much pain as possible, he had seemed to lead her gratuitously into a discussion of embarrassing personal matters while Investigator Alexander dutifully recorded the conversation from his van. In fact, Marisa's friends say they're astonished at how little anger she seemed to feel after she realized what he had done—almost as if his behavior were just a particularly extreme example of how relationships often end.

By the time Jeff was sentenced, Marisa had already appeared before Federal District Judge John Keenan for sentencing. A dozen people had shown up to be with the defendant. Her father was there. So was her new fiancé—someone she had met at the real-estate firm she now works for, and someone her friends judge to be a welcome break from the sort of men she'd been attracted to in the past. Four of her girlfriends were there, dressed so much alike, in black pants suits, that they appeared to be members of some sort of team. Her lawyer, Paul Shechtman, said the case had "destroyed her human capital"—her closest friendship, her career in the financial industry. Describing his client as someone whose psychological vulnerabilities made her an easy mark for Streich, Shechtman said, "We wouldn't be here today if Ms. Baridis hadn't met Jeffrey Streich in the summer of 1996."

In the interpretation of the case which Shechtman favors, money was not a serious motivation for what his client did—unless it was making money for Jeffrey Streich so that he could buy bracelets for her instead of for Tina Eichenholz. Even the leaks to her best friend's husband could be interpreted as a way of making Jeff jealous that she could deal with somebody else, although she'd waited nine or ten months to tell Streich that there was another tippee. She did say to Streich at Barrington's that she had tipped someone else, and that the unnamed other person paid her "with no ifs, ands, or buts." As it turned out, she was mistaken: her best friend's husband had also been cheating her on the split.

There was no sign of anger when Marisa Baridis made her statement to Judge Keenan, in a barely audible voice. "My friends blame Jeffrey Streich for what has occurred," she said. "I see it differently. He was no friend but I only blame myself. I have tried to understand why I acted the way I did and to deal with the pieces of my life that are left." The probation report had recommended that she not be sent to prison, and the federal prosecutor did not quarrel with that recommendation. Judge Keenan gave Marisa Baridis two years' probation. The general counsel of Morgan Stanley had sent a letter urging the opposite—a particularly stiff sentence. Morgan Stanley, of course, had also been betrayed, and, in an indication that old-fashioned manners are still valued somewhere on Wall Street, its general counsel pointed out, among other things, that Marisa Baridis had never apologized to the firm.

JEFFREY STREICH is now in prison. Although he's pleased Marisa Baridis got off without jail time, he said during a recent conversation in the prison visiting room, the notion that her insider trading was driven by an infatuation with him is nonsense—simply a convenient way to present her as a victim. In his version of what happened, insider trading had the same attraction for her as for anyone else—the power that comes from being the source of information and the money that could help support a style of living he summed up as "Prada and two dogs." He said that Marisa was simply a friend, and that he'd done nothing to woo her. He described their interlude in Las Vegas—an occasion for her to send elated E-mails back to friends in New York—as nothing more than two people who'd had too much to drink going to bed together.

Streich expressed regret for betraying his friends in the insider-trading scheme but much more regret for betraying the customers who trusted him as a broker. Although he is certain that his bucket-shop days are behind him forever—he intends to make his living in the construction business—he still seems proud of how good he was at selling stock over the phone. When other brokers had difficulty closing, he said, they'd often ask him to come on the line. In the entire time he was a broker, of course, he didn't sell one share of legitimate stock, but it occurred to him that he might have been good at that, too, if he had learned the business somewhere other than in the Hirsch group. Musing on that as he sat in the visiting room, he said, "If I had started at Lehman Brothers, I would have been all right. Maybe."

JULY 10, 2000

NO MAN'S TOWN

I HAD a little trouble finding Willard Rouse's office in Philadelphia, because it is in a negatively denoted location—across the street from a giant hole in the ground. In an old town house, a business suite has materialized for the purpose of overseeing the construction of a monumental performing-arts center, Philadelphia's answer to Lincoln Center. Rouse, a nephew of James Rouse, the man who figured out how to turn down-at-the-heels urban waterfronts into "festival marketplaces," and so set off the reinvention of the American city as a recreational site, chairs the project. He swept into what must have once been the living room of the town house, now given over to a conference table, and assured me that I hadn't kept him waiting.

"I was raising bloody hell!" he said cheerfully. He grabbed my notebook and drew, on a blank page, a rough cross-sectional plan of the overhanging balcony in the main concert hall. Hidden inside the overhang was a heating-and-air-conditioning duct. The problem was how to get to the duct to repair it after the building was finished. The architect and the contractor, Rouse said, wanted elegant, old-fashioned plaster on the wall outside the duct, and a series of metal plates at regular points to give repairmen access to it. Having finished his sketch, he gave me a look to communicate that this was idiocy of the most obvious sort.

"Who fixes ducts?" Rouse asked me. "Plumbers! I said to these people, 'Have you ever seen a plumber's hands? Plumbers have dirty hands! They're gonna put their dirty hands all over the plaster when they screw off the plate, and you can't wash dirt off of plaster, and pretty soon it's gonna look like dog shit! You can't do it that way.' They said, 'O.K., then we're gonna have to move the duct.' I said, 'No, you're gonna have to move me! Find. Another. Fucking. Way.' "

Rouse is a big, restless man with a gravelly, cigarette-cured voice and flyaway hair. He was wearing a dark suit without the jacket, a button-down shirt, a fancy tie, and tortoiseshell glasses, but this came across as a Clark Kent getup that might at any moment pop off in an explosion of ungovernable developer energy. Behind him hung a wall-size banner listing contributors to the performing-arts center. An extremely tall crane, nested in the soft subterranean dirt of the construction site, loomed just outside the window. The story about the duct was clearly meant to communicate not anger but joy—to get me to see him as a colorful, larger-than-life guy at the top of his game. And he is.

The national economic boom, after all these years, has come even to dear old Philadelphia. In the aftermath of the triumphant eight-year mayoral term of Ed Rendell, the city government has gone from quasi-receivership to solvency. Beginning in 1997, the city—not the metropolitan area but Philadelphia it-self—began showing a net annual gain in jobs, reversing the trend of decades. Philadelphia won the competition to be the site of this year's Republican National Convention. Real-estate prices are rising. Private schools are oversub-scribed. Small technology companies are springing up. The section of the city where we were, off Broad Street just south of City Hall, formerly a conveniently symbolic boulevard of broken dreams, because of the presence of enormous empty buildings like the old Bellevue-Stratford Hotel, has been rechristened the Avenue of the Arts. Just across Broad Street from the town house where Rouse and I were talking, Tom Stoppard's most recent play, *The Invention of Love*, which New Yorkers haven't been able to see yet, was playing to full houses. New restaurants had sprouted up and down the street. And these were just the preliminaries, because the performing-arts center, which is meant to be the an-chor of the neighborhood, isn't scheduled to open until December of next year.

Rouse himself nearly went broke in the early nineties, at the same time as the municipal government. Now he's back. He has just built a new office tower in Center City Philadelphia, the first one in years, but he has staged most of his comeback out in the suburbs, in a seven-hundred-acre office-park complex, which he developed, with the unconvincingly rustic name of Great Valley. The surrounding area, along Route 202, in the farmland beyond the old commuter towns, is Philadelphia's Silicon Valley.

The performing-arts center was started when the board of the Philadelphia Orchestra, prodded by the conductor, Riccardo Muti, began raising money for a new building. But that plan had stalled, in part because the traditionalists on the board wanted the symphony to stay in the lovely old Academy of Music building. Meanwhile, Mayor Rendell had been raising money for a new arts building of his own, but that effort had stalled, too. Rouse was part of a group assembled by Rendell that merged the two projects into one: a much bigger, more expensive, and flashier project than either side had imagined, containing two big performance spaces encased in a shimmering arch of glass. "People have to understand—P. T. Barnum has to be part of the game," Rouse told me.

"It's not culture for culture's sake. You know, 'Build it and they will come'? That's bullshit! Build it and sell the hell out of it, and they will come!"

PHILADELPHIA reached its peak in importance in the late eighteenth century, when it was the largest city in North America. It has never dropped out of the top five American cities, and you can get a sense walking around it today of a long period of equipoise situated somewhere between Colonial times and now. Philadelphia had a garment industry, an oil industry (oil was developed commercially first in Pennsylvania, later in Texas), and a publishing and advertising industry. It was a manufacturing center. Stetson hats and Botany 500 suits and Philco appliances and Breyers ice cream were made there. *The Saturday Evening Post* and *Ladies' Home Journal* were published from a stately brick building overlooking Independence Hall. Philadelphia was a sports town (it once had two baseball teams) and a political-machine town and a union town. It was an African-American town: W. E. B. DuBois's *The Philadelphia Negro* was the first case study of a black community in the United States. It was home to the Pennsylvania Railroad—to buffs, the most glorious of the lines in the glory days of railroads—and the famous "traction" (streetcar) companies owned by the Widener and Elkins families.

Sitting atop this peaceable kingdom was a group that one of its members, the sociologist E. Digby Baltzell (best known for popularizing the term "Wasp"), called Proper Philadelphians. In *Philadelphia Gentlemen: The Making of a National Upper Class*, published in 1958, Baltzell gave us a city that was tightly under the control of a defined coterie whose members blended social and economic prestige with a ruthless efficiency that enabled them to engage in "the exercise of power over other men in making the decisions which shape the ends of a predominantly business-oriented social structure." In other words, Baltzell's people didn't just go to a lot of débutante parties; they also ran the place.

These people lived in town at Rittenhouse Square, or at the outer reaches of the city in Chestnut Hill, or in the beautiful Main Line suburbs spread out along the railroad line. One thinks of their houses as having been hewed from blocks of stone, because they looked so solid and permanent. They rowed at the Vesper and played golf at the Merion Cricket Club and foxhunted at the Whitemarsh Valley Hunt Club early on weekday mornings, arriving at work ruddy and a little late. They kept their money at the Girard Trust or the Provident Trust, invested at Janney Montgomery Scott or Butcher & Singer, and took out business loans at the Philadelphia National Bank or the First Pennsylvania—all institutions run by men who had been born or carefully assimilated into the group. They served on the boards of the symphony and the art museum and the University of Pennsylvania and the hospitals. It was their city.

In this way, Philadelphia, with its powerful local establishment, was like most American metropolises. And, like most American metropolises, it isn't this way anymore. We are living in an age in which, as Manuel Castells, a Spanish-born sociologist-planner who teaches at Berkeley, puts it, "the space of places" has been superseded by "the space of flows." Money and information ricochet freely and instantaneously around the world—and with particularly intense force and velocity in boom times. One associates the toppling of establishments with busts, as in the case of the Great Depression and the group that Jay Gatsby was yearning to join. But today it is the boom that is toppling them, by buying and trading the institutions they formerly controlled. Philadelphia is for sale, which means that, as a place, it will become at once more prosperous and less autonomous—less in control of itself. As Castells puts it, "A growing social schizophrenia has resulted between, on the one hand, regional societies and local institutions and, on the other hand, the rules and operations of the economic system at the international level." If you understand the national boom mainly in terms of what's happening in Silicon Valley and on Wall Street, and perhaps also in terms of people left far behind in the ghettos and factory towns, you're missing how much it is altering the way American life is organized.

There are a few cities, like Seattle and Austin, where the new economy is producing a coherent neo-Baltzellian group, except with hiking boots and stubble. Not so in Philadelphia and most other places. Philadelphia's rising companies, situated on or around Route 202, can't perform the same function as the old ones for all sorts of reasons. The employees don't interact with each other, as in urban settings, because the area where they work (and other areas like it around the country) is laid out in the form of office campuses accessible only by car. Two of the most prominent and rapidly growing Philadelphia companies, for example, are Vanguard, the mutual-fund empire, and QVC, the home-shopping television network. Both serve national markets from isolated locations in the suburbs. The same goes for suburban Internet businesses like VerticalNet.com and Safeguard Scientifics. Brian Roberts, the head of QVC's parent company, Comcast, has recently taken on a major civic role, as the co-chair of the organization that brought Philadelphia the Republican Convention—along with the new performing-arts center, the most obvious symbol of Philadelphia's comeback. (The other co-chair, David Cohen, a lawyer who was Ed Rendell's right-hand man in City Hall, says that "he agreed to do it only because it was national.") The idea of what an American city should be has changed completely from the days of *Philadelphia Gentlemen*—conforming now, in effect, to the ideas of James Rouse, who built HarborPlace in Baltimore and preached a gospel of the city as "a garden for people to grow in" rather than a center of commerce, finance, manufacturing, and transportation.

SO where did the Philadelphia business aristocracy go? I put this question to Martin and Margy Meyerson—he a member of the pioneer generation of academic experts on cities, who became the president of the University of Pennsylvania, she a city planner and a veteran of many civic activities. The Meyersons were not born into Digby Baltzell's Philadelphia élite, but they came to town when it held sway, and they made a point of winning a dual life peerage. Both of them, in their late seventies, are fully vested Proper Philadelphians, but now they find themselves in a situation where the members of the club are standing with their noses pressed to the window, looking at the world outside, because that's where the deal goes down, rather than vice versa.

The Meyersons invited me to come as their guest to one of the regular monthly meetings of the Sunday Breakfast Club, a venerable organization that, for some funny old Philadelphia reason, meets not for breakfast on Sundays but for dinner on Wednesdays, at the Union League of Philadelphia, a club on Broad Street. Before the dinner, I went over to their house and talked for a while. They live a couple of blocks west of Rittenhouse Square—on the same street where I met Willard Rouse—in a large Victorian brownstone. Inside, there were spacious rooms with high ceilings, filled with books and art objects from all over the world, the bounty of a long upper-academic life. We sat down on low couches in the living room. There was a grand piano in the corner. A copy of Noel Annan's *The Dons* and a vase of fresh flowers sat on the coffee table.

Martin Meyerson, a small, almost elfin man, formally dressed, with a formal manner, had done some thinking in advance. "We have a President who is justly proud of the performance of the economy," he said, by way of starting the conversation, "but we have to explore what the patterns mean for the places that are not New York or Los Angeles or San Francisco. What goes on in Philadelphia, once a grand city? How is it doing? What are its successes and its difficulties?"

We got onto the subject of the Philadelphia institutions of the period when the Meyersons first arrived, more than fifty years ago. Martin Meyerson began ticking them off. "Drexel & Company was the great merchant bank, an affiliate of J. P. Morgan," he said. "It was run by the head of one of the great aristocratic families."

Over the years, the Philadelphia companies began to disappear. For example, there was Scott Paper, whose board of directors Martin Meyerson served on for many years. "A first-rate company," he said. "A little stuffy, but a first-rate company. It was run for a generation by Thomas McCabe, an important figure. A trustee of Swarthmore College."

"A good solid Republican," Margy Meyerson said.

"Yes, but one would say a Republican with a sense of the commonweal. Was he chairman of the Fed?"

"Yes."

"He was chairman of the Fed. Do you know Digby Baltzell's book?" He meant not *Philadelphia Gentlemen* but the more locally controversial *Puritan Boston and Quaker Philadelphia*, published in 1979. It's an exercise in invidious comparison which presents Philadelphia's élite as inferior to Boston's, and puts the blame on Philadelphia's Quaker heritage. "I take some issue with it, but I'm flattered to be one of the people it's dedicated to. Well, Scott Paper became a great international company. Then Mr. Dunlap came in"—that's Chainsaw Al Dunlap, the king of the corporate downsizers. "His aim was to get the quickest return on the company—to turn it into a salable firm. You might say this is what capitalism is all about. But the prevailing view was that a local firm should not be treated with such abandon, although many of the stockholders came out rather well. And then he didn't like Philadelphia, so he wanted to move the company."

"Was it Clearwater? Bradenton?" Margy Meyerson said.

"No, Boca Raton. He moved it to Boca Raton."

"Slash and burn," Margy Meyerson said. "It was sold to Kimberly-Clark. The stock went up a lot. But it didn't do the city any good."

We moved on to the local banks. "You could argue that now there is no major Philadelphia bank," Martin Meyerson declared.

"There was Philadelphia National," his wife said.

"Yes. It was not quite as important as the banks in New York or Chicago or California. But nonetheless it was important."

"One certainly knew the old banks."

"They weren't all necessarily run by old Philadelphia families."

"It's very sad to see your banks change," Margy Meyerson said, "because they have a visible presence, architecturally, showing solidity and presence in the community."

We went out into the spring evening, hailed a taxi, and rode the short distance to the Union League, which, as it happens, is right next door to the former downtown headquarters of Drexel & Company—now a Bally health club, where slender people in leotards can be seen through the windows of the former banking floor cheerfully bobbing up and down. Inside, we put on nametags and walked up a broad stone flight of stairs to a cocktail reception, where the Meyersons introduced me to many of their friends. Thacher Longstreth, the world's most aptly named person, was there—a towering seventy-nine-year-old Republican city councilman with a shock of white hair. I met Charles Dickey, who had run Scott Paper after Thomas McCabe, and G. Morris Dorrance, who had run the biggest bank in town for many years and is related to the Dorrances who founded Campbell's Soup. The current heads of these companies were not present. Somebody rang a bell, and we went in to dinner, where we heard Anita Summers, a retired professor of public policy at the University of Pennsylvania and the mother of our nation's Treasury Secretary, discuss education reform. I'm not allowed to tell you what she said, because the speeches delivered at the Sunday Breakfast Club are off the record. I sat across from a delightful man named Charles Grace—think of Dickie Greenleaf in *The Talented Mr. Ripley* if he had in fact been persuaded to return home and then a few decades had passed—who told me that he works in a "family office," having formerly been employed by Drexel & Company.

SOME of what became of the old Philadelphia is the result simply of a familiar development—the decline, or the relocation, of manufacturing. That explains the disappearance of Stetson and Philco and most of the local garment industry. The more recent part of the story, though, has to do with the advent of a vast international-asset souk in which practically everything is constantly being traded.

Just in the past ten years, wonderful years for Philadelphia, a large part of the Philadelphia Navy Yard was sold to an Anglo-Norwegian concern that plans to leave the shipbuilding business, so it will probably be closing down. SmithKline, the Philadelphia pharmaceutical company, merged with a British company called Beecham; in January, the new company, SmithKline Beecham, announced plans to merge with the British company Glaxo Wellcome. Of the two big local oil companies, Atlantic Richfield has long since moved to Los Angeles, and, more recently, Sun sold its exploration division to an Italian multinational.

The local phone company, Bell of Pennsylvania, became part of Bell Atlantic, which then merged with NYNEX, forming a new company with headquarters in New York. The Philadelphia Electric Company is about to become part of Commonwealth Edison, out of Chicago. CIGNA, one of the leading local insurance companies, recently sold off its property-and-casualty division to a Bermuda-based concern known as the Ace group. The two flagship Philadelphia department stores, Wanamaker's and Strawbridge & Clothier, were both sold to the May Department Stores Company, of St. Louis. One of the four big health-care systems in town, Allegheny, went bankrupt and was bought by a for-profit Santa Barbara company called Tenet. Breyers was bought by Unilever and left town. The commission for the new performing-arts center went not to Philadelphia's greatest architect, Robert Venturi, but to an Argentine named Rafael Viñoly.

Meanwhile, the conductor whose idea the new center was, Riccardo Muti, was acquired, so to speak, by La Scala, in Milan, and he has left town. The most prominent black leader in Philadelphia, William Gray, the minister and former congressman, has become the head of the United Negro College Fund and now spends most of his time in Fairfax, Virginia. (The new mayor, John Street, is trying to assume Gray's mantle.)

Drexel & Company wound up as part of the eighties junk-bond firm Drexel Burnham Lambert, which was forced into bankruptcy by federal prosecutors. All the other old Philadelphia investment houses—W. H. Newbold, Butcher & Singer, Janney Montgomery Scott—long ago ceased to be independent entities. And perhaps the rudest of the shocks of the boom years has been the sudden disappearance of all the major local banks. The Philadelphia Saving Fund Society, once the biggest thrift institution in the country and for many years the owner of Philadelphia's tallest commercial building, which used to hand out little savings envelopes to children in the Philadelphia public-school system, went under in the savings-and-loan crisis. Now the Mellon bank, of Pittsburgh, owns it, and the building is being made over into a hotel. Mellon also bought the Girard Trust, whose domed headquarters on Broad Street is going to become a hotel, too—both hotels affiliated with national chains, of course. The Provident National Bank was sold to another Pittsburgh banking company, P.N.C.

In the eighties, the biggest bank in Philadelphia, Philadelphia National, turned itself into a regional bank called CoreStates. At the end of 1997, a regional banking company from Charlotte, North Carolina, First Union, announced that it had purchased CoreStates, so the leading banking company in Philadelphia was now gone.

If you saw the movie *Trading Places*, you may remember a scene set inside the magnificent, soaring main room of a Philadelphia bank, with a second-story colonnade punctuated by Roman busts and a stained-glass window depicting the founding of the American republic—that's now First Union's downtown branch office. The old, august, possibly too powerful board of directors has been downgraded to a "regional advisory board." This is an especially ironic outcome, since in the early nineteenth century both the First and the Second Bank of the United States were headquartered in Philadelphia. The abolition of the Second Bank, by Andrew Jackson, ushered in a century and a half of elaborate government-mandated dispersion of power in the banking industry, so that Philadelphians wouldn't control money and credit in every other city. Over the past few years, these banking laws have been steadily dismantled in the name of economic efficiency, and the result is that now Philadelphia's money is controlled by people in Pittsburgh and Charlotte.

The takeover of CoreStates by First Union was probably the rockiest of Philadelphia's many mergers during the boom times. First Union has laid off about half the people on the CoreStates payroll—nine thousand people—and closed or sold half of the five hundred CoreStates branches. Four hundred thousand local customers have taken their business elsewhere. The stock is way down. Now many Philadelphians believe that they will wake up one morning and read that First Union itself has been acquired, or has sold off the former CoreStates to an even bigger national banking company.

IN *Philadelphia Gentlemen*, Digby Baltzell said that the function of the Philadelphia Club, which he called "the oldest of the well-known metropolitan men's clubs in America" (founded in 1834 and housed in the same building, on Walnut Street, since 1850, and therefore older even than many of the men's clubs in London), is "to maintain a continuity of control over important positions in the business world." It sure didn't look that way, though, on the afternoon I went there to interview Fred Heldring, the retired chairman of the old Philadelphia National Bank. Aside from the doorman, he and I seemed to be the only people in the building. There was an empty reading room downstairs, and a row of empty guest dining rooms upstairs. We met in a small library with a heavy oak table and oil portraits hanging on the walls in the spaces between bookshelves. Heldring is a man with big, clear, unblinking blue eyes, a blocky head, white hair, and dark bushy eyebrows, who speaks emphatically—in italics.

Heldring, who was born to a banking family in the Netherlands, came to Philadelphia to study at the Wharton School of Business, and got a summer job in the transit department at the Philadelphia National Bank. The company's house organ published a story about him, because an immigrant employee was so exotic. After it appeared, he was summoned by Graydon Upton, the head of the foreign department, who said that he had known of the Heldring family in Holland and that Fred should please come see him about a job when he finished at Wharton. Heldring remembered the day quite precisely: "I was sitting waiting for him on the banking floor. There were no offices in those days—the officers sat behind desks out in the open. It was *such* a slow tempo. The head of the foreign department was asleep at his desk. People walked *so* slowly."

He went on, "When I started in banking, you were *totally* secure of your position. You would have to *steal* to be fired. They didn't let anyone go, even in the Depression. There was no pressure on earnings *at all.* There was pressure to be the first to reach a billion in assets. There was no great pressure to perform. The board was made up of gentlemen. *Gentlemen!* Mostly native Philadelphians. Today, it's earnings, earnings, earnings, earnings."

There is a Web site for former employees of CoreStates which is full of sentimental postings about the vanished days of Philadelphia banking. The chief complaint in the postings is that all decisions are made in Charlotte, often according to computer programs that determine which loans to approve and which branches to open and which services to offer at what price. The secondary complaint is that First Union and the other new outside companies don't care about the civic life of Philadelphia. People told me that you can't fill a nonprofit board of directors in Philadelphia these days. An organization called Greater Philadelphia First, founded in the early eighties to be a benign civic oligarchy of chief executives, such as many American cities have, today has only four of the original twenty-three member companies represented on its board.

One ought to be wary of the idea that locally controlled banks and businesses are best suited to look out for the interests of ordinary people in their communities. Philadelphia's poor neighborhoods were hurting just as much before it became a branch-office city as after. Whether you have access to a loan officer matters less because now there are direct-mail, credit-card, and small-business-loan companies. When the local banks and companies go, the real effect is on the local grandees—people who, because of the boom, matter much less than they used to. Texas no longer has a big locally controlled bank. Los Angeles doesn't, either—or a morning newspaper. In the last decade, Boston has lost many of its big banks and its leading daily paper to out-of-town owners. The people who used to control these institutions are not suffering economically: they own stocks and real estate that are soaring in value. They have gone from being Baltzell's "business aristocrats" to being *rentiers.*

In their previous incarnation, they might be thought of as a little bit of sand in the gears of American capitalism—an ironic position, because they ran and profited from capitalism locally, and believed in it. Yet they also represented the introduction into business life of minor inefficiencies, such as the diffusion of economic power into regional structures, and of not strictly business consider-ations, like social lineage and the promotion of civic projects. Losing control of their institutions will, oddly, make them more purely capitalistic, not less. Their connection to the economy is now a much simpler and clearer one: the search for the highest possible return on investment.

During the twentieth century, there was quite a lot of sand in the gears of the economy. Powerful labor unions were sand in the gears. So was entrenched corporate management that didn't pursue stockholders' interests with ab-solute ruthlessness. Heavy government regulation, which forced airlines to serve small markets and utility companies to be local and banks to limit them-selves on the basis of geography and the services they could offer, was sand in the gears. Now we've cleared the sand out of the gears, and economic change will be able to make itself felt quickly and without impediment.

In most cities, the tableau will be something quite similar to the one Philadelphia presents: General prosperity. Downtown transformed into an en-tertainment site operated by national leisure-time companies. Business growth, also of national firms, in the distant suburbs. The late-middle-aged and the uneducated made superfluous. The poor neighborhoods depopulating, and getting poorer. More people with money. Fewer people with power.

Thus far in American history, rapid economic change and concentration of power have provoked strong, unpredictable reactions. People feel left out and try to use politics and government to slow down the pace of change and to build in intermediate structures that will protect them. Just beyond all those wonderful macroeconomic statistics and vast new fortunes, the boom, by so profoundly streamlining America's operations, is creating propitious condi-tions for a powerful counterreaction—with the goal of putting some sand back in the gears. The counterreaction could just as easily come from the right as from the left. But don't be surprised when it happens.

JUNE 5, 2000

SIX DEGREES OF LOIS WEISBERG

E VERYONE who knows Lois Weisberg has a story about meeting Lois
Weisberg, and although she has done thousands of things in her life and
met thousands of people, all the stories are pretty much the same. Lois (everyone calls her Lois) is invariably smoking a cigarette and drinking one of her
dozen or so daily cups of coffee. She will have been up until two or three the previous morning, and up again at seven or seven-thirty, because she hardly
seems to sleep. In some accounts—particularly if the meeting took place in the
winter—she'll be wearing her white, fur-topped Dr. Zhivago boots with gold
tights; but she may have on her platform tennis shoes, or the leather jacket
with the little studs on it, or maybe an outrageous piece of costume jewelry,
and, always, those huge, rhinestone-studded glasses that make her big eyes
look positively enormous. "I have no idea why I asked you to come here, I have
no job for you," Lois told Wendy Willrich when Willrich went to Lois's office in
downtown Chicago a few years ago for an interview. But by the end of the interview Lois did have a job for her, because for Lois meeting someone is never
just about meeting someone. If she likes you, she wants to recruit you into one
of her grand schemes—to sweep you up into her world. A while back, Lois
called up Helen Doria, who was then working for someone on Chicago's city
council, and said, "I don't have a job for you. Well, I might have a little job. I
need someone to come over and help me clean up my office." By this, she
meant that she had a big job for Helen but just didn't know what it was yet.
Helen came, and, sure enough, Lois got her a big job.

Cindy Mitchell first met Lois twenty-three years ago, when she bundled up
her baby and ran outside into one of those frigid Chicago winter mornings because some people from the Chicago Park District were about to cart away a

beautiful sculpture of Carl von Linné from the park across the street. Lois happened to be driving by at the time, and, seeing all the commotion, she slammed on her brakes, charged out of her car—all five feet of her—and began asking Cindy questions, rat-a-tat-tat: "Who are you? What's going on here? Why do you care?" By the next morning, Lois had persuaded two Chicago *Tribune* reporters to interview Cindy and turn the whole incident into a cause célèbre, and she had recruited Cindy to join an organization she'd just started called Friends of the Parks, and then, when she found out that Cindy was a young mother at home who was too new in town to have many friends, she told her, "I've found a friend for you. Her name is Helen, and she has a little boy your kid's age, and you will meet her next week and the two of you will be best friends." That's exactly what happened, and, what's more, Cindy went on to spend ten years as president of Friends of the Park. "Almost everything that I do today and eighty to ninety per cent of my friends came about because of her, because of that one little chance meeting," Cindy says. "That's a scary thing. Try to imagine what would have happened if she had come by five minutes earlier."

It could be argued, of course, that even if Cindy hadn't met Lois on the street twenty-three years ago she would have met her somewhere else, maybe a year later or two years later or ten years later, or, at least, she would have met someone who knew Lois or would have met someone who knew someone who knew Lois, since Lois Weisberg is connected, by a very short chain, to nearly everyone. Weisberg is now the Commissioner of Cultural Affairs for the City of Chicago. But in the course of her seventy-three years she has hung out with actors and musicians and doctors and lawyers and politicians and activists and environmentalists, and once, on a whim, she opened a secondhand-jewelry store named for her granddaughter Becky Fyffe, and every step of the way Lois has made friends and recruited people, and a great many of those people have stayed with her to this day. "When we were doing the jazz festival, it turned out—surprise, surprise—that she was buddies with Dizzy Gillespie," one of her friends recalls. "This is a woman who cannot carry a tune. She has no sense of rhythm. One night Tony Bennett was in town, and so we hang out with Tony Bennett, hearing about the old days with him and Lois."

Once, in the mid-fifties, on a whim, Lois took the train to New York to attend the World Science Fiction Convention and there she met a young writer by the name of Arthur C. Clarke. Clarke took a shine to Lois, and next time he was in Chicago he called her up. "He was at a pay phone," Lois recalls. "He said, 'Is there anyone in Chicago I should meet?' I told him to come over to my house." Lois has a throaty voice, baked hard by half a century of nicotine, and she pauses between sentences to give herself the opportunity for a quick puff. Even when she's not smoking, she pauses anyway, as if to keep in practice. "I called Bob Hughes, one of the people who wrote for my paper." Pause. "I said, 'Do you know anyone in Chicago interested in talking to Arthur Clarke?' He said, 'Yeah, Isaac Asimov is in town. And this guy Robert, Robert . . . Robert Heinlein.' So they all came over and sat in my study." Pause. "Then they called over to me and they said, 'Lois'—I can't remember the word they used. They had some word for me. It was something about how I was the kind of person who brings people together."

This is in some ways the archetypal Lois Weisberg story. First, she reaches out to somebody—somebody outside her world. (At the time, she was running a drama troupe, whereas Arthur C. Clarke wrote science fiction.) Equally important, that person responds to her. Then there's the fact that when Arthur Clarke came to Chicago and wanted to meet someone Lois came up with Isaac Asimov. She says it was a fluke that Asimov was in town. But if it hadn't been Asimov it would have been someone else. Lois ran a salon out of her house on the North Side in the late nineteen-fifties, and one of the things that people remember about it is that it was always, effortlessly, integrated. Without that salon, blacks would still have socialized with whites on the North Side— though it was rare back then, it happened. But it didn't happen by accident: it happened because a certain kind of person made it happen. That's what Asimov and Clarke meant when they said that Lois has this thing—whatever it is—that brings people together.

LOIS is a type—a particularly rare and extraordinary type, but a type nonetheless. She's the type of person who seems to know everybody, and this type can be found in every walk of life. Someone I met at a wedding (actually, the wedding of the daughter of Lois's neighbors, the Newbergers) told me that if I ever went to Massapequa I should look up a woman named Marsha, because Marsha was the type of person who knew everybody. In Cambridge, Massachusetts, the word is that a tailor named Charlie Davidson knows everybody. In Houston, I'm told, there is an attorney named Harry Reasoner who knows everybody. There are probably Lois Weisbergs in Akron and Tucson and Paris and in some little town in the Yukon Territory, up by the Arctic Circle. We've all met someone like Lois Weisberg. Yet, although we all know a Lois Weisberg type, we don't know much *about* the Lois Weisberg type. Why is it, for example, that these few, select people seem to know everyone and the rest of us don't? And how important are the people who know everyone? This second question is critical, because once you begin even a cursory examination of the life of someone like Lois Weisberg you start to suspect that he or she may be far more important than we would ever have imagined—that the people who know everyone, in some oblique way, may actually run the world. I don't mean that they are the sort who head up the Fed or General Motors or Microsoft, but that, in a very down-to-earth, day-to-day way, they make the world work. They spread ideas and information. They connect varied and isolated parts of society. Helen Doria says someone high up in the Chicago government told her that Lois is "the epicenter of the city administration," which is the right way to put it. Lois is far from being the most important or the most powerful person in Chicago. But if you connect all the dots that constitute the vast apparatus of government and influence and interest groups in the city of Chicago you'll end up coming back to Lois again and again. Lois is a connector.

Lois, it must be said, did not set out to know everyone. "She doesn't network for the sake of networking," says Gary Johnson, who was Lois's boss years ago, when she was executive director of the Chicago Council of Lawyers. "I just think she has the confidence that all the people in the world, whether she's met them or not, are in her Rolodex already, and that all she has to do is figure out how to reach them and she'll be able to connect with them."

Nor is Lois charismatic—at least, not in the way that we think of extroverts and public figures as being charismatic. She doesn't fill a room; eyes don't swivel toward her as she makes her entrance. Lois has frizzy blond hair, and when she's thinking—between her coffee and her cigarette—she kneads the hair on the top of her head, so that by the end of a particularly difficult meeting it will be standing almost straight up. "She's not like the image of the Washington society doyenne," Gary Johnson says. "You know, one of those people who identify you, take you to lunch, give you the treatment. Her social life is very different. When I bump into her and she says, 'Oh, we should catch up,' what she means is that someday I should go with her to her office, and we'd go down to the snack bar and buy a muffin and then sit in her office while she answered the phone. For a real treat, when I worked with her at the Council of Lawyers she would take me to the dining room in the Wieboldt's department store." Johnson is an old-school Chicago intellectual who works at a fancy law firm and has a corner office with one of those Midwestern views in which, if you look hard enough, you can almost see Nebraska, and the memory of those lunches at Wieboldt's seems to fill him with delight. "Now, you've got to understand that the Wieboldt's department store—which doesn't exist anymore—was a notch below Field's, where the suburban society ladies have their lunch, and it's also a notch below Carson's," he says. "There was a kind of room there where people who bring their own string bags to go shopping would have a quick lunch. This was her idea of a lunch out. We're not talking Pamela Harriman here."

In the mid-eighties, Lois quit a job she'd had for four years, as director of special events in the administration of Harold Washington, and somehow hooked up with a group of itinerant peddlers who ran the city's flea markets. "There was this lady who sold jewelry," Lois said. "She was a person out of Dickens. She was bedraggled. She had a houseful of cats. But she knew how to buy jewelry, and I wanted her to teach me. I met her whole circle of friends, all these old gay men who had antique stores. Once a week, we would go to the Salvation Army." Lois was arguably the most important civic activist in the city. Her husband was a judge. She lived in a huge house in one of Chicago's nicest neighborhoods. Yet somehow she managed to be plausible as a flea-market peddler to a bunch of flea-market peddlers, the same way she managed to be plausible as a music lover to a musician like Tony Bennett. It doesn't matter who she's with or what she's doing; she always manages to be in the thick of things. "There was a woman I knew—Sandra—who had a kid in school with my son Joseph," Lois told me. Lois has a habit of telling stories that appear to be tangential and digressive but, on reflection, turn out to be parables of a sort. "She helped all these Asians living uptown. One day, she came over here and said there was this young Chinese man who wanted to meet an American family and learn to speak English better and was willing to cook for his room and board. Well, I'm always eager to have a cook, and especially a Chinese cook, because my family loves Chinese food. They could eat it seven days a week. So Sandra brought this man over here. His name was Shi Young. He was a graduate student at the Art Institute of Chicago." Shi Young lived with Lois and her family for two years, and during that time Chicago was in the midst of political turmoil. Harold Washington, who would later become the first black mayor of the city, was attempting to unseat the remains of the Daley political machine, and Lois's house, naturally, was the site of late-night, top-secret strategy sessions for the pro-Washington reformers of Chicago's North Side. "We'd have all these important people here, and Shi Young would come down and listen," Lois recalls. "I didn't think anything of it." But Shi Young, as it turns out, was going back up to his room and writing up what he heard for the *China Youth Daily*, a newspaper with a circulation in the tens of millions. Somehow, in the improbable way that the world works, a portal was opened up, connecting Chicago's North Side reform politics and the readers of the *China Youth Daily*, and that link was Lois's living room. You could argue that this was just a fluke—just as it was a fluke that Isaac Asimov was in town and that Lois happened to be driving by when Cindy Mitchell came running out of her apartment. But sooner or later all those flukes begin to form a pattern.

IN the late nineteen-sixties, a Harvard social psychologist named Stanley Milgram conducted an experiment in an effort to find an answer to what is known as the small-world problem, though it could also be called the Lois Weisberg problem. It is this: How are human beings connected? Do we belong to separate worlds, operating simultaneously but autonomously, so that the links between any two people, anywhere in the world, are few and distant? Or are we all bound up together in a grand, interlocking web? Milgram's idea was to test this question with a chain letter. For one experiment, he got the names of a hundred and sixty people, at random, who lived in Omaha, Nebraska, and he mailed each of them a packet. In the packet was the name and address of a stockbroker who worked in Boston and lived in Sharon, Massachusetts. Each person was instructed to write his name on a roster in the packet and send it on to a friend or acquaintance who he thought would get it closer to the stockbroker. The idea was that when the letters finally arrived at the stockbroker's house Milgram could look at the roster of names and establish how closely connected someone chosen at random from one part of the country was to another person chosen at random in another part. Milgram found that most of the letters reached the stockbroker in five or six steps. It is from this experiment that we got the concept of six degrees of separation.

That phrase is now so familiar that it is easy to lose sight of how surprising Milgram's finding was. Most of us don't have particularly diverse groups of friends. In one well-known study, two psychologists asked people living in the Dyckman public-housing project, in uptown Manhattan, about their closest friend in the project; almost ninety per cent of the friends lived in the same building, and half lived on the same floor. In general, people chose friends of similar age and race. But if the friend lived down the hall, both age and race became a lot less important. Proximity overpowered similarity. Another study, involving students at the University of Utah, found that if you ask someone why he is friendly with someone else he'll say that it is because they share similar attitudes. But if you actually quiz the pairs of students on their attitudes you'll find out that this is an illusion, and that what friends really tend to have in common are activities. We're friends with the people we do things with, not necessarily with the people we resemble. We don't seek out friends; we simply associate with the people who occupy the same physical places that we do: People in Omaha are not, as a rule, friends with people who live in Sharon, Massachusetts. So how did the packets get halfway across the country in just five steps? "When I asked an intelligent friend of mine how many steps he thought it would take, he estimated that it would require 100 intermediate persons or more to move from Nebraska to Sharon," Milgram wrote. "Many people make somewhat similar estimates, and are surprised to learn that only five intermediaries will—on the average—suffice. Somehow it does not accord with intuition."

The explanation is that in the six degrees of separation not all degrees are equal. When Milgram analyzed his experiments, for example, he found that many of the chains reaching to Sharon followed the same asymmetrical pattern. Twenty-four packets reached the stockbroker at his home, in Sharon, and sixteen of those were given to him by the same person, a clothing merchant whom Milgram calls Mr. Jacobs. The rest of the packets were sent to the stockbroker at his office, and of those the majority came through just two men, whom Milgram calls Mr. Brown and Mr. Jones. In all, half of the responses that got to the stockbroker were delivered to him by these three people. Think of it. Dozens of people, chosen at random from a large Midwestern city, sent out packets independently. Some went through college acquaintances. Some sent their packets to relatives. Some sent them to old workmates. Yet in the end, when all those idiosyncratic chains were completed, half of the packets passed through the hands of Jacobs, Jones, and Brown. Six degrees of separation doesn't simply mean that everyone is linked to everyone else in just six steps. It means that a very small number of people are linked to everyone else in a few steps, and the rest of us are linked to the world through those few.

There's an easy way to explore this idea. Suppose that you made a list of forty people whom you would call your circle of friends (not including family members or co-workers), and you worked backward from each person until you could identify who was ultimately responsible for setting in motion the series of connections which led to that friendship. I met my oldest friend, Bruce, for example, in first grade, so I'm the responsible party. That's easy. I met my college friend Nigel because he lived down the hall in the dormitory from Tom, whom I had met because in my freshman year he invited me to play touch football. Tom, then, is responsible for Nigel. Once you've made all the connections, you will find the same names coming up again and again. I met my friend Amy when she and her friend Katie came to a restaurant where I was having dinner. I know Katie because she is best friends with my friend Larissa, whom I know because I was told to look her up by a mutual friend, Mike A., whom I know because he went to school with another friend of mine, Mike H., who used to work at a political weekly with my friend Jacob. No Jacob, no Amy. Similarly, I met my friend Sarah S. at a birthday party a year ago because she was there with a writer named David, who was there at the invitation of his agent, Tina, whom I met through my friend Leslie, whom I know because her sister Nina is best friends with my friend Ann, whom I met through my old roommate Maura, who was my roommate because she had worked with a writer named Sarah L., who was a college friend of my friend Jacob. No Jacob, no Sarah S. In fact, when I go down my list of forty friends, thirty of them, in one way or another, lead back to Jacob. My social circle is really not a circle but an inverted pyramid. And the capstone of the pyramid is a single person, Jacob, who is responsible for an overwhelming majority of my relationships. Jacob's full name, incidentally, is Jacob Weisberg. He is Lois Weisberg's son.

This isn't to say, though, that Jacob is just like Lois. Jacob may be the capstone of my pyramid, but Lois is the capstone of lots and lots of people's pyramids, and that makes her social role different. In Milgram's experiment, Mr. Jacobs the clothing merchant was the person to go through to get to the stockbroker. Lois is the kind of person you would use to get to the stockbrokers of Sharon and also the cabaret singers of Sharon and the barkeeps of Sharon and the guy who gave up a thriving career in orthodontics to open a small vegetarian falafel hut.

THERE is another way to look at this question, and that's through the popular parlor game Six Degrees of Kevin Bacon. The idea behind the game is to try to link in fewer than six steps any actor or actress, through the movies they've been in, to the actor Kevin Bacon. For example, O.J. Simpson was in *Naked Gun* with Priscilla Presley, who was in *The Adventures of Ford Fairlane* with Gilbert Gottfried, who was in *Beverly Hills Cop II* with Paul Reiser, who was in *Diner* with Kevin Bacon. That's four steps. Mary Pickford was in *Screen Snapshots* with Clark Gable, who was in *Combat America* with

Tony Romano, who, thirty-five years later, was in *Starting Over* with Bacon. That's three steps. What's funny about the game is that Bacon, although he is a fairly young actor, has already been in so many movies with so many people that there is almost no one to whom he can't be easily connected. Recently, a computer scientist at the University of Virginia by the name of Brett Tjaden actually sat down and figured out what the average degree of connectedness is for the quarter million or so actors and actresses listed in the Internet Movie Database: he came up with 2.8312 steps. That sounds impressive, except that Tjaden then went back and performed an even more heroic calculation, figuring out what the average degree of connectedness was for *everyone* in the database. Bacon, it turns out, ranks only six hundred and sixty-eighth. Martin Sheen, by contrast, can be connected, on average, to every other actor, in 2.63681 steps, which puts him almost six hundred and fifty places higher than Bacon. Elliott Gould can be connected even more quickly, in 2.63601. Among the top fifteen are people like Robert Mitchum, Gene Hackman, Donald Sutherland, Rod Steiger, Shelley Winters, and Burgess Meredith.

Why is Kevin Bacon so far behind these actors? Recently, in the journal *Nature*, the mathematicians Duncan Watts and Steven Strogatz published a dazzling theoretical explanation of connectedness, but a simpler way to understand this question is to look at who Bacon is. Obviously, he is a lot younger than the people at the top of the list are and has made fewer movies. But that accounts for only some of the difference. A top-twenty person, like Burgess Meredith, made a hundred and fourteen movies in the course of his career. Gary Cooper, though, starred in about the same number of films and ranks only eight hundred and seventy-eighth, with a 2.85075 score. John Wayne made a hundred and eighty-three movies in his fifty-year career and still ranks only a hundred and sixteenth, at 2.7173. What sets someone like Meredith apart is his range. More than half of John Wayne's movies were Westerns, and that means he made the same kind of movie with the same kind of actors over and over again. Burgess Meredith, by contrast, was in great movies, like the Oscar-winning *Of Mice and Men* (1939), and in dreadful movies, like *Beware! The Blob* (1972). He was nominated for an Oscar for his role in *The Day of the Locust* and also made TV commercials for Skippy peanut butter. He was in four "Rocky" movies, and also played Don Learo in Godard's *King Lear*. He was in schlocky made-for-TV movies, in B movies that pretty much went straight to video, and in pictures considered modern classics. He was in forty-two dramas, twenty-two comedies, eight adventure films, seven action films, five sci-fi films, five horror flicks, five Westerns, five documentaries, four crime movies, four thrillers, three war movies, three films noir, two children's films, two romances, two mysteries, one musical, and one animated film. Burgess Meredith was the kind of actor who was connected to everyone because he managed to move up and down and back and forth among all the different worlds and subcultures that the acting profession has to offer. When we say, then, that Lois Weisberg is the kind of person who "knows everyone," we mean it in precisely this way. It is not merely that she knows lots of people. It is that she belongs to lots of different worlds.

In the nineteen-fifties, Lois started her drama troupe in Chicago. The daughter of a prominent attorney, she was then in her twenties, living in one of the suburbs north of the city with two small children. In 1956, she decided to stage a festival to mark the centenary of George Bernard Shaw's birth. She hit up the reclusive billionaire John D. MacArthur for money. ("I go to the Pump Room for lunch. Booth One. There is a man, lurking around a pillar, with a cowboy hat and dirty, dusty boots. It's him.") She invited William Saroyan and Norman Thomas to speak on Shaw's legacy; she put on Shaw plays in theatres around the city; and she got written up in *Life.* She then began putting out a newspaper devoted to Shaw, which mutated into an underground alternative weekly called the *Paper.* By then, Lois was living in a big house on Chicago's near North Side, and on Friday nights people from the *Paper* gathered there for editorial meetings. William Friedkin, who went on to direct *The French Connection* and *The Exorcist,* was a regular, and so were the attorney Elmer Gertz (who won parole for Nathan Leopold) and some of the editors from *Playboy,* which was just up the street. People like Art Farmer and Thelonious Monk and Dizzy Gillespie and Lenny Bruce would stop by when they were in town. Bruce actually lived in Lois's house for a while. "My mother was hysterical about it, especially one day when she rang the doorbell and he answered in a bath towel," Lois told me. "We had a window on the porch, and he didn't have a key, so the window was always left open for him. There were a lot of rooms in that house, and a lot of people stayed there and I didn't know they were there." Pause. Puff. "I never could stand his jokes. I didn't really like his act. I couldn't stand all the words he was using."

Lois's first marriage—to a drugstore owner named Leonard Solomon—was breaking up around this time, so she took a job doing public relations for an injury-rehabilitation institute. From there, she went to work for a public-interest law firm called B.P.I., and while she was at B.P.I. she became concerned about the fact that Chicago's parks were neglected and crumbling, so she gathered together a motley collection of nature lovers, historians, civic activists, and housewives, and founded the lobbying group Friends of the Parks. Then she became alarmed on discovering that a commuter railroad that ran along the south shore of Lake Michigan—from South Bend to Chicago—was about to shut down, so she gathered together a motley collection of railroad enthusiasts and environmentalists and commuters, and founded South Shore Recreation, thereby saving the railroad. Lois loved the railroad buffs. "They were all good friends of mine," she says. "They all wrote to me. They came from California. They came from everywhere. We had meetings. They were really interesting. I came this close"—and here she held her index finger half an inch above her thumb—"to becoming one of them." Instead, though, she became the executive director of the Chicago Council of Lawyers, a progressive bar association. Then she ran Congressman Sidney Yates's reëlection campaign. Then her sister June introduced her to someone who got her the job with Mayor Washington. Then she had her flea-market period. Finally, she went to work for Mayor Daley as Chicago's Commissioner of Cultural Affairs.

If you go through that history and keep count, the number of worlds that Lois has belonged to comes to eight: the actors, the writers, the doctors, the lawyers, the park lovers, the politicians, the railroad buffs, and the flea-market aficionados. When I asked Lois to make her own list, she added musicians and the visual artists and architects and hospitality-industry people whom she works with in her current job. But if you looked harder at Lois's life you could probably subdivide her experiences into fifteen or twenty worlds. She has the same ability to move among different subcultures and niches that the busiest actors do. Lois is to Chicago what Burgess Meredith is to the movies.

Lois was, in fact, a friend of Burgess Meredith. I learned this by accident, which is the way I learned about most of the strange celebrity details of Lois's life, since she doesn't tend to drop names. It was when I was with her at her house one night, a big, rambling affair just off the lakeshore, with room after room filled with odds and ends and old photographs and dusty furniture and weird bric-a-brac, such as a collection of four hundred antique egg cups. She was wearing bluejeans and a flowery-print top and she was smoking Carlton Menthol 100s and cooking pasta and holding forth to her son Joe on the subject of George Bernard Shaw, when she started talking about Burgess Meredith. "He was in Chicago in a play called *Teahouse of the August Moon,* in 1956," she said, "and he came to see my production of *Back to Methuselah,* and after the play he came up to me and said he was teaching acting classes, and asked would I come and talk to his class about Shaw. Well, I couldn't say no." Meredith liked Lois, and when she was running her alternative newspaper he would write letters and send in little doodles, and later she helped him raise money for a play he was doing called *Kicks and Company.* It starred a woman named Nichelle Nichols, who lived at Lois's house for a while. "Nichelle was a marvellous singer and dancer," Lois said. "She was the lead. She was also the lady on the first . . ." Lois was doing so many things at once—chopping and stirring and smoking and eating and talking—that she couldn't remember the name of the show that made Nichols a star. "What's that space thing?" She looked toward Joe for help. He started laughing. "Star something," she said. " *Star . . . Star Trek!* Nichelle was Lieutenant Uhura!"

ON a sunny morning not long ago, Lois went to a little café just off the Magnificent Mile, in downtown Chicago, to have breakfast with Mayor Daley. Lois drove there in a big black Mercury, a city car. Lois always drives big cars, and, because she is so short and the cars are so big, all that you can see when she drives by is the top of her frizzy blond head and the lighted ember of her cigarette. She was wearing a short skirt and a white vest and was carrying a white cloth shopping bag. Just what was in the bag was unclear, since Lois doesn't have a traditional relationship to the trappings of bureaucracy. Her office, for example, does not have a desk in it, only a sofa and chairs and a coffee table. At meetings, she sits at the head of a conference table in the adjoining room, and, as often as not, has nothing in front of her except a lighter, a pack of Carltons, a cup of coffee, and an octagonal orange ceramic ashtray, which she moves a few inches forward or a few inches back when she's making an important point, or moves a few inches to the side when she is laughing at something really funny and feels the need to put her head down on the table.

Breakfast was at one of the city's tourist centers. The Mayor was there in a blue suit, and he had two city officials by his side and a very serious and thoughtful expression on his face. Next to him was a Chicago developer named Al Friedman, a tall and slender and very handsome man who is the chairman of the Commission on Chicago Landmarks. Lois sat across from them, and they all drank coffee and ate muffins and batted ideas back and forth in the way that people do when they know each other very well. It was a "power breakfast," although if you went around the table you'd find that the word "power" meant something very different to everyone there. Al Friedman is a rich developer. The Mayor, of course, is the administrative leader of one of the largest cities in the country. When we talk about power, this is usually what we're talking about: money and authority. But there is a third kind of power as well—the kind Lois has—which is a little less straightforward. It's social power.

At the end of the nineteen-eighties, for example, the City of Chicago razed an entire block in the heart of downtown and then sold it to a developer. But before he could build on it the real-estate market crashed. The lot was an eyesore. The Mayor asked for ideas about what to do with it. Lois suggested that they cover the block with tents. Then she heard that Keith Haring had come to Chicago in 1989 and worked with Chicago high-school students to create a giant five-hundred-foot-long mural. Lois loved the mural. She began to think. She'd long had a problem with the federal money that Chicago got every year to pay for summer jobs for disadvantaged kids. She didn't think it helped any kid to be put to work picking up garbage. So why not pay the kids to do arts projects like the Haring mural, and put the whole program in the tents? She called the program Gallery 37, after the number of the block. She enlisted the help of the Mayor's wife, Maggie Daley, whose energy and clout were essential in order to make the program a success. Lois hired artists to teach the kids. She realized, though, that the federal money was available only for poor kids, and, Lois says, "I don't believe poor kids can advance in any way by being lumped together with other poor kids." So Lois raised money privately to bring in middle-income kids, to mix with the poor kids and be put in the tents with the artists. She started small, with two hundred and sixty "apprentices" the first year, 1990. This year, there were more than three thousand. The kids study sculpture, painting, drawing, poetry, theatre, graphic design, dance, textile design, jewelry-making, and music. Lois opened a store downtown, where students' works of art are sold. She has since bought two buildings to house the project full time. She got the Parks Department to run Gallery 37 in neighborhoods around the city, and the Board of Education to let them run it as an after-school program in public high schools. It has been copied all around the world. Last year, it was given the Innovations in American Government Award by the Ford Foundation and the Harvard school of government.

Gallery 37 is at once a jobs program, an arts program, a real-estate fix, a schools program, and a parks program. It involves federal money and city money and private money, stores and buildings and tents, Maggie Daley and Keith Haring, poor kids and middle-class kids. It is everything, all at once—a jumble of ideas and people and places which Lois somehow managed to make sense of. The ability to assemble all these disparate parts is, as should be obvious, a completely different kind of power from the sort held by the Mayor and Al Friedman. The Mayor has key allies on the city council or in the statehouse. Al Friedman can do what he does because, no doubt, he has a banker who believes in him, or maybe a lawyer whom he trusts to negotiate the twists and turns of the zoning process. Their influence is based on close relationships. But when Lois calls someone to help her put together one of her projects, chances are she's not calling someone she knows particularly well. Her influence suggests something a little surprising—that there is also power in relationships that are not close at all.

THE sociologist Mark Granovetter examined this question in his classic 1974 book *Getting a Job*. Granovetter interviewed several hundred professional and technical workers from the Boston suburb of Newton, asking them in detail about their employment history. He found that almost fifty-six per cent of those he talked to had found their jobs through a personal connection, about twenty per cent had used formal means (advertisements, headhunters), and another twenty per cent had applied directly. This much is not surprising: the best way to get in the door is through a personal contact. But the majority of those personal connections, Granovetter found, did not involve close friends. They were what he called "weak ties." Of those who used a contact to find a job, for example, only 16.7 per cent saw that contact "often," as they would have if the contact had been a good friend; 55.6 per cent saw their contact only "occasionally"; and 27.8 per cent saw the contact "rarely." People were getting their jobs not through their friends but through acquaintances.

Granovetter argues that when it comes to finding out about new jobs—or, for that matter, gaining new information, or looking for new ideas—weak ties tend to be more important than strong ties. Your friends, after all, occupy the same world that you do. They work with you, or live near you, and go to the same churches, schools, or parties. How much, then, do they know that you don't know? Mere acquaintances, on the other hand, are much more likely to know something that you don't. To capture this apparent paradox, Granovetter coined a marvellous phrase: "the strength of weak ties." The most important people in your life are, in certain critical realms, the people who aren't closest to you, and the more people you know who aren't close to you the stronger your position becomes.

Granovetter then looked at what he called "chain lengths"—that is, the number of people who had to pass along the news about your job before it got to you. A chain length of zero means that you learned about your job from the person offering it. A chain length of one means that you heard about the job from someone who had heard about the job from the employer. The people who got their jobs from a zero chain were the most satisfied, made the most money, and were unemployed for the shortest amount of time between jobs. People with a chain of one stood second in the amount of money they made, in their satisfaction with their jobs, and in the speed with which they got their jobs. People with a chain of two stood third in all three categories, and so on. If you know someone who knows someone who knows someone who has lots of acquaintances, in other words, you have a leg up. If you know someone who knows someone who has lots of acquaintances, your chances are that much better. But if you know someone who has lots of acquaintances—if you know someone like Lois—you are still more fortunate, because suddenly you are just one step away from musicians and actors and doctors and lawyers and park lovers and politicians and railroad buffs and flea-market aficionados and all the other weak ties that make Lois so strong.

This sounds like a reformulation of the old saw that it's not what you know, it's who you know. It's much more radical than that, though. The old idea was that people got ahead by being friends with rich and powerful people—which is true, in a limited way, but as a practical lesson in how the world works is all but useless. You can expect that Bill Gates's godson is going to get into Harvard and have a fabulous job waiting for him when he gets out. And, of course, if you play poker with the Mayor and Al Friedman it is going to be a little easier to get ahead in Chicago. But how many godsons can Bill Gates have? And how many people can fit around a poker table? This is why affirmative action seems pointless to so many people: It appears to promise something—entry to the old-boy network—that it can't possibly deliver. The old-boy network is always going to be just for the old boys.

Granovetter, by contrast, argues that what matters in getting ahead is not the quality of your relationships but the quantity—not how close you are to those you know but, paradoxically, how many people you know whom you aren't particularly close to. What he's saying is that the key person at that breakfast in downtown Chicago is not the Mayor or Al Friedman but Lois Weisberg, because Lois is the kind of person who it really is possible for most of us to know. If you think about the world in this way, the whole project of affirmative action suddenly starts to make a lot more sense. Minority-admissions pro-grams work not because they give black students access to the same superior educational resources as white students, or access to the same rich cultural en-vironment as white students, or any other formal or grandiose vision of engi-neered equality. They work by giving black students access to the same white students as white students—by allowing them to make acquaintances outside their own social world and so shortening the chain lengths between them and the best jobs.

This idea should also change the way we think about helping the poor. When we're faced with an eighteen-year-old high-school dropout whose only career option is making five dollars and fifty cents an hour in front of the deep fryer at Burger King, we usually talk about the importance of rebuilding inner-city communities, attracting new jobs to depressed areas, and reinvesting in neglected neighborhoods. We want to give that kid the option of another, better-paying job, right down the street. But does that really solve his problem? Surely what that eighteen-year-old really needs is not another marginal in-ducement to stay in his neighborhood but a way to get out of his neighborhood altogether. He needs a school system that provides him with the skills to com-pete for jobs with middle-class kids. He needs a mass-transit system to take him to the suburbs, where the real employment opportunities are. And, most of all, he needs to know someone who knows someone who knows where all those good jobs are. If the world really is held together by people like Lois Weisberg, in other words, how poor you are can be defined quite simply as how far you have to go to get to someone like her. Wendy Willrich and Helen Doria and all the countless other people in Lois's circle needed to make only one phone call. They are well-off. The dropout wouldn't even know where to start. That's why he's poor. Poverty is not deprivation. It is isolation.

I ONCE met a man named Roger Horchow. If you ever go to Dallas and ask around about who is the kind of person who might know everyone, chances are you will be given his name. Roger is slender and composed. He talks slowly, with a slight Texas drawl. He has a kind of wry, ironic charm that is utterly winning. If you sat next to him on a plane ride across the Atlantic, he would start talking as the plane taxied to the runway, you would be laughing by the time the seat-belt sign was turned off, and when you landed at the other end you'd wonder where the time had gone.

I met Roger through his daughter Sally, whose sister Lizzie went to high school in Dallas with my friend Sara M., whom I know because she used to work with Jacob Weisberg. (No Jacob, no Roger.) Roger spent at least part of his childhood in Ohio, which is where Lois's second husband, Bernie Weisberg, grew up, so I asked Roger if he knew Bernie. It would have been a little too apt if he did—that would have made it all something out of *The X-Files*—but in-stead of just answering, "Sorry, I don't," which is what most of us would have done, he paused for a long time, as if to flip through the "W"s in his head, and then said, "No, but I'm sure if I made two phone calls . . ."

Roger has a very good memory for names. One time, he says, someone was trying to talk him into investing his money in a business venture in Spain, and when he asked the names of the other investors he recognized one of them as the same man with whom one of his ex-girlfriends had had a fling during her junior year abroad, fifty years before. Roger sends people cards on their birthdays: he has a computerized Rolodex with sixteen hundred names on it. When I met him, I became convinced that these techniques were central to the fact that he knew everyone—that knowing everyone was a kind of skill. Horchow is the founder of the Horchow Collection, the first high-end mail-order catalogue, and I kept asking him how all the connections in his life had helped him in the business world, because I thought that this particular skill had to have been cultivated for a reason. But the question seemed to puzzle him. He didn't think of his people collection as a business strategy, or even as something deliberate. He just thought of it as something he did—as who he was. One time, Horchow said, a close friend from childhood suddenly resurfaced. "He saw my catalogue and knew it had to be me, and when he was out here he showed up on my doorstep. I hadn't seen him since I was seven. We had zero in common. It was *wonderful*." The juxtaposition of those last two sentences was not ironic; he meant it.

In the book *The Language Instinct*, the psychologist Steven Pinker argues against the idea that language is a cultural artifact—something that we learn "the way we learn to tell time." Rather, he says, it is innate. Language develops "spontaneously," he writes, "without conscious effort or formal instruction," and "is deployed without awareness of its underlying logic. . . . People know how to talk in more or less the sense that spiders know how to spin webs." The secret to Roger Horchow and Lois Weisberg is, I think, that they have a kind of social equivalent of that instinct—an innate and spontaneous and entirely involuntary affinity for people. They know everyone because—in some deep and less than conscious way—they can't help it.

ONCE, in the very early nineteen-sixties, after Lois had broken up with her first husband, she went to a party for Ralph Ellison, who was then teaching at the University of Chicago. There she spotted a young lawyer from the South Side named Bernie Weisberg. Lois liked him. He didn't notice her, though, so she decided to write a profile of him for the Hyde Park *Herald*. It ran with a huge headline. Bernie still didn't call. "I had to figure out how I was going to get to meet him again, so I remembered that he was standing in line at the reception with Ralph Ellison," Lois says. "So I called up Ralph Ellison"—whom she had never met—"and said, 'It's so wonderful that you are in Chicago. You really should meet some people on the North Side. Would it be O.K. if I have a party for you?' " He said yes, and Lois sent out a hundred invitations, including one to Bernie. He came. He saw Dizzy Gillespie in the kitchen and Ralph Ellison in the living room. He was impressed. He asked Lois to go with him to see Lenny Bruce. Lois was mortified; she didn't want this nice Jewish lawyer from the South Side to know that she knew Lenny Bruce, who was, after all, a drug addict. "I couldn't get out of it," she said. "They sat us down at a table right at the front, and Lenny keeps coming over to the edge of the stage and saying"—here Lois dropped her voice down very low—" 'Hello, Lois.' I was sitting there like this." Lois put her hands on either side of her face. "Finally I said to Bernie, 'There are some things I should tell you about. Lenny Bruce is a friend of mine. He's staying at my house. The second thing is I'm defending a murderer.' " (But that's another story.) Lois and Bernie were married a year later.

The lesson of this story isn't obvious until you diagram it culturally: Lois got to Bernie through her connections with Ralph Ellison and Lenny Bruce, one of whom she didn't know (although later, naturally, they became great friends) and one of whom she was afraid to say that she knew, and neither of whom, it is safe to speculate, had ever really been connected with each other before. It seems like an absurdly roundabout way to meet someone. Here was a thirtyish liberal Jewish intellectual from the North Side of Chicago trying to meet a thirtyish liberal Jewish intellectual from the South Side of Chicago, and to get there she charted a cross-cultural social course through a black literary lion and an avant-garde standup comic. Yet that's a roundabout journey only if you perceive the worlds of Lenny Bruce and Ralph Ellison and Bernie Weisberg to be impossibly isolated. If you don't—if, like Lois, you see them all as three points of an equilateral triangle—then it makes perfect sense. The social instinct makes everyone seem like part of a whole, and there is something very appealing about this, because it means that people like Lois aren't bound by the same categories and partitions that defeat the rest of us. This is what the power of the people who know everyone comes down to in the end. It is not—as much as we would like to believe otherwise—something rich and complex, some potent mixture of ambition and energy and smarts and vision and insecurity. It's much simpler than that. It's the same lesson they teach in Sunday school. Lois knows lots of people because she likes lots of people. And all those people Lois knows and likes invariably like her, too, because there is nothing more irresistible to a human being than to be unqualifiedly liked by another.

Not long ago, Lois took me to a reception at the Museum of Contemporary Art, in Chicago—a brand-new, Bauhaus-inspired building just north of the Loop. The gallery space was impossibly beautiful—cool, airy, high-ceilinged. The artist on display was Chuck Close. The crowd was sleek and well groomed. Black-clad young waiters carried pesto canapés and glasses of white wine. Lois seemed a bit lost. She can be a little shy sometimes, and at first she stayed on the fringes of the room, standing back, observing. Someone important came over to talk to her. She glanced up uncomfortably. I walked away for a moment to look at the show, and when I came back her little corner had become a crowd. There was her friend from the state legislature. A friend in the Chicago Park District. A friend from her neighborhood. A friend in the consulting business. A friend from Gallery 37. A friend from the local business-development group. And on and on. They were of all ages and all colors, talking and laughing, swirling and turning in a loose circle, and in the middle, nearly hidden by the commotion, was Lois, clutching her white bag, tiny and large-eyed, at that moment the happiest person in the room.

JANUARY 11, 1999

DAVID DENBY

THE QUARTER OF
LIVING DANGEROUSLY

1/1/00 Nasdaq +85.6% for 1999

TODAY, while speaking to a friend on the telephone, I suddenly notice that I am jabbering—racing ahead and jumping over verbal fences, mashing participles, dropping qualifiers. I find that I have trouble saying one thing at a time; I have to say two things, or three, tucking statistics into my words as I go, joining pieces of information by association rather than by cause and effect. As I hang up, a little worn out by myself, I wonder, Who is this speed freak, this *nut,* gathering and expelling information in charged clumps, like a spasmodic Web site spilling bytes? This blurting activity on my part is new. I talk myself breathless, and sometimes make other people feel pressured, even bullied. What's causing the rush?

At fifty-six, I am no crazier than I was twenty years ago. But my habits have changed. Among other things, I spend a lot of time watching CNBC, one of the cable financial networks. The boys and girls of financial reporting, the Stalwarts, my new friends, go on the air every trading day at five in the morning and continue all through the day, mopping up after the market closes, at four, with recaps, surveys, and predictions. I can sit there for hours following the jags, up and down, of the three market indexes and listening to the Stalwarts interview strategists, analysts, and savants of various sorts, who spread their blankets and display their urns and gourds and give their opinions of shifting currents in the bazaar. Not all these people practice speed-talking—Joe Kernen, CNBC's stocks editor and a former broker, caresses the underside of a new I.P.O. like a gent taking his time. Yet many of them race like corsairs. They are driven by the tempo of the market, the pulsing, darting flow of money around the globe, its progression intensified, as the Stalwarts break for a commercial, by that rhythmic clickety-clack of electronic noise needled by a snare drum: *dig-a-dig-a-dig-a-dig-a-DIG-a-dig-a* . . .

Only eight or nine years ago, eager to escape the media noise and hustle, I was trying to slow down. I longed for the unfolding power of *duration*—the slow-moving images in Antonioni's mournfully beautiful movies, the magnificent weighted tread of a Bruckner symphony, the Rolling Stones songs that seemed to go on forever. I hate my new acceleration, though I know perfectly well what has caused it. In this boom period, you have the illusion that if you can just grab hold of the flying coattails of the New Economy investments you have the chance of getting rich very quickly. My new urgency is driven by greed: I am talking in Internet time. Wealth, much more than ever, seems a function of quickness. The market is a kind of crass metaphysical whip that hastens the annihilation of the passing moment: there is only the next instant, and the next, rushing toward you, and in the Internet age an ideally informed person would never sleep at all but would trade the markets and chase news and rumors through the links twenty-four hours a day.

I have decided that I want—I need—to make a million dollars in the stock market this year. For a wealthy man or woman, this no longer seems like a great deal of money. For a journalist on a salary, it is a great deal indeed, and the wish for it as a year's gain would have seemed ridiculous no more than a few years ago. For the record, I do not want to buy a yacht or a house in the country or a five-thousand-dollar gas grill (what would you do with it—barbecue gold-leafed weenies?). No, I don't want to buy anything in particular. I want the money so I can hold on to something very important to me.

I am amazed at myself—amazed that a writer with no business experience would place in jeopardy his substance and his peace and would risk falling among the rotting railroad ties and worthless certificates of a dozen schemes gone bust. But, like many Americans, I have begun to wonder if risk is now something I can afford to avoid, and if the usual grim historical lesson—the cautionary tale of euphoria, panic, and collapse—has any necessary power over me. The New Economy seems to be producing a New Man who, in imitation of the economy itself, is going through wrenching changes in the way he lives, works, buys, and interacts with other people. All of which makes me anxious, at times unbearably so, and finding myself in an odd predicament—greedy, obsessed, and ignorant—I have been looking around for companions and gurus to guide me in my steps. I must meet some people in the Internet and investment scenes in New York; I will read some economic history and literature—that is, the literature of greed—as I shift the pieces of my little pile from one place to another.

1/4/00 Nas −229.46, Dow −359.58

A BIG sell-off right at the beginning of the year. Are we at the end of the bull, the beginning of a panic? If we're at the end, then maybe historical precedent does have something to teach us. The displays of folly in London at the end of the South Sea Bubble of 1720 reached a carnival atmosphere of giddiness and gross absurdity—crazily extravagant parties, jewel-embroidered dresses, excited mobs roaming the streets. Excessive expenditure and social turmoil may be signs of too much capital sloshing around the edges of a speculative boom. Well, there has never been a period of wealth in New York like the one we are enjoying right now, though the new fortunes have not yet burst forth in comparable displays of conspicuous consumption. The California roots of the Internet craze, with its puritanical-utopian communitarian longings, have had a softening, even frowning, effect on mere display. The big-swinging-dick flamboyance of eighties Wall Street has been replaced by the earnestly hip Silicon Valley entrepreneur in black clothes. It's the investment culture itself that's been wild and perhaps frivolous: the millions flung by venture-capital firms at questionable ideas for startup companies; the increase in the price of technology and biotech stocks by multiples of twelve, twenty, or even forty within a six-month period; the obsession everywhere with the market. People trade tips at the newsstand; a man exultantly shouts out the name of a Scandinavian telecommunications company ("Ericsson!") as he passes me on the street. At my local hardware store, day traders compare notes at market close ("I bailed on Qualcomm early and got killed"; "I held it till three and made eight and a quarter"), and I myself have conducted strategy sessions with strangers during intermission at Carnegie Hall.

The current period of speculative energy has a unique character of high-mindedness and hope. The usual desire to get rich quick has merged with the sunrise ardor of creating a new way of buying, communicating, and doing business. Clutching copies of *The Red Herring* and *The Industry Standard,* we information-technology investors mutter the mantras to ourselves: The use of the Internet doubles every hundred days; the computer box is dead, but wireless is taking off like a rocket; total business-to-business transactions on the Internet will go from a hundred and forty-five billion dollars in 1999 to perhaps two trillion in 2004. But are these expectations realistic? Or do they function as a kind of pornography of hope? In such an overstimulated climate, there is a measure of relief in just buying something. Right or wrong, at least it's an act, a move. This is known as "buyer's panic"—the fear of being left out, or hosed, as some stock goes up by a multiple of six.

Over and over, I brood about my story, my *blunder.* It is a primal scene, the kind of wound that everyone carries around during a speculative period. My story takes place in our neighborhood Japanese restaurant, Bon 75, on Broadway, where my wife and I had lunch with our broker in 1986—early March, 1986, just before Microsoft went public.

"There's this stock," I said, holding a piece of sushi between chopsticks. "Microsoft. It makes the operating system for I.B.M. and all the clones."

"Never heard of it," our broker said, dipping his vegetable tempura in sauce.

If his right hand had been free, he might have written down the name of the company. But it wasn't, and the moment passed; I ate my salmon roe and failed to insist that he follow up, even though, at some level, I *knew*. The ten thousand or so dollars that we could have afforded to invest in 1986 would now be worth almost eight million. At the height of the South Sea Bubble, Alexander Pope wrote his broker, "'Tis Ignominious (in this Age of Hope and Golden Mountains) not to Venture."

Thinking about my story makes me sick. But then why do I also feel sick when I invest in some New Economy stock or fund? Success produces its own kind of hell: you might lose your gains. Pope made money in the South Sea speculation, but some months after that letter to his broker, at a time when everything had gone bust and thousands were ruined, he announced that "God has punish'd the avaritious as he often punishes sinners, in their own way, in the very sin itself: the thirst for gain was their crime, and that thirst continued became their punishment and ruin."

1/10/00 A.O.L. announces purchase of Time Warner for $165 billion

NASDAQ, recovering from the sell-off, goes up 167.05, the Dow to a record 11,572.20. A feeling of boundless possibilities excites investors everywhere. To hell with Pope's divine wrath. Whatever happens to A.O.L. and Time Warner, enormous new wealth is being created, and Alan Greenspan, like the Holy Ghost brooding with sweet wings over the earth, will protect us, measuring out the milk of liquidity, harmonizing our virtues and vices into an orderly progression toward salvation.

Feeling calm for a day, I have lunch with an old friend—I shall call him Craig Rumford—who is always calm. He is an investment banker, a mergers-and-acquisitions specialist, comfortably stationed at one of the most distinguished banks in the city. His corner-office windows take in a generous swath of the East River and Brooklyn Heights. He is a father of four, a fine-looking man with a high, intellectual forehead, a reader of serious books. I admire him greatly and want to understand what he does in his work, and this produces a certain comic element in our friendship. Whenever we meet, Craig wants to talk about books, music, and movies, and I want to talk about money. I suppose each of us envies the other his profession. But, despite Craig's calm, I have noticed, over the last few years, a certain regret creeping into his tone. During the eighties, he was in the middle of the leveraged-buyout frenzy, a player in several big mergers. Now, as we repair to a company dining room looking out over Staten Island and the Statue of Liberty (the rich are different from us: they have views), he sighs a few times, as if the action had passed him by. He is not that icon of the moment, an entrepreneur. He would like to leap into venture capital, but, with four children, he can't, really, and his frustration passes across the table to me.

1/15/00 Times pans investors

THE *Times* published a front-page article today saying that too many people are selling stocks after a few months or less, paying short-term rather than long-term capital-gains taxes, and making less money than they should. It's as if the feverish mentality of the day trader, who holds stocks for five minutes or half a day, had infected millions of people.

History, like a dark, ranting prophet, calls us fools. The *tulpenwoerde,* or tulip mania, in Holland, in the sixteen-thirties, is the paradigm of greed and speculation. It's always evoked in a boom period, and in the midst of the current bull market one is irked to hear of it—irked by the perfection of the historical didacticism, the superb equipoise of the banking and shipping power collapsing into near-chaos, and over what? Over flowers! The Turks had introduced tulips into Europe in the sixteenth century, and what adorned the gardens of courtiers, scholars, and bankers in Antwerp and Brussels passed, by the next century, to the Netherlands, where a trace of brilliant color, especially in the more exotic varieties, livened up the drab landscape. Botanists and aristocrats owned the tulips first, but a given strain could be reproduced through the splitting of outgrowths, so a rarefied taste became a marketable commodity in more ordinary bulbs, and in the winter of every year a kind of "futures" mania developed. People met in "colleges" (i.e., taverns) and traded contracts for the bulbs that would sprout in the spring. Sometimes they offered paper attesting to their credit, sometimes real assets, like oxen or furniture or tools, or even farms.

A significant part of the sanest, cleanest, most orderly society the world has ever known got caught up in *windhandel,* or "airy trade." Players traded their paper upward until the whole thing collapsed, in early February, 1637, when actual delivery of the spring tulips was looming and no further speculation that year was possible. Late buyers and people trading on credit got ruined.

Charles Kindleberger, in his menacing 1989 book, *Manias, Panics, and Crashes,* has traced a deep structure common to speculative periods. At first, there is a "displacement," perhaps in the form of a new species of investment. This is followed by "positive feedback," as inexperienced investors throw money into the market, followed by euphoria, as prices rise and common sense disintegrates. In this late period, the speculation spreads to different kinds of goods. New companies spring up and are floated in the market, and investors leverage their rising assets. You can guess the rest: overextended credit, swindles and frauds, and eventual collapse of the market.

How much of this describes our current moment? A fibre-optic cable, I tell myself, has a longer season than a tulip, but obviously the many technology stocks selling at a hundred and fifty or two hundred times earnings (if they even have earnings) can't all be winners in the future. Alan Greenspan is worried that more and more people are buying stocks on margin, and the newspapers claim that white-collar crime is rising. And yet, and yet . . . my own portfolio is going up rapidly, and, if this be *windhandel,* thank heaven for the wind.

1/19/00 YHOO +22$^{13}/_{26}$

IN a minor act of defiance, I liquidate, with my wife's approval, our holdings in two bond funds and cancel a life-insurance policy. In recent years, I have come to hate the idea of insurance so much that I unconsciously rebelled and "forgot" to pay the premiums. The policy has built up some dividends, which I can invest, and that's part of the attraction of cancelling. Trust the market to build a sufficient nest egg. Trust the market!

I can't say that I was ever a particularly bold or successful investor in the past. Before the nineties, I had no extra money to invest, and I balanced money in my 401(k) plan between stocks and bonds. I figured, like millions of others, that I didn't know enough to take chances; and I was unwilling to devote any time to learning more. John Maynard Keynes wrote that investment is "intolerably boring and over-exacting to any one who is entirely exempt from the gambling instinct," and for years I was exempt from that instinct. My job was to build a career, build a family. I was a middle-class professional, an Upper West Sider—the equivalent of a Dutch burgher—living among brown and gray buildings. As my wife and I earned, from jobs and freelance work and book royalties, we saved and, when we could, bought bonds through a broker or invested in safe-sounding mutual funds. But I didn't study. I barely checked the results.

My mother died in 1991, leaving me a little money, and I remember being vaguely annoyed by the responsibility of it. With a heavy heart, I began reading the *Wall Street Journal.* To my surprise, the paper's formality—pin-striped-chic single-column heads and long blocks of type—gave me a distinct tingle of pleasure. This, clearly, was grownup stuff. The *Journal* possessed the silencing dignity of money, and from its pages I learned the commonplace gospel of diversification and asset allocation. As I worked through the gathering bull in 1995, I tried to add more aggressive-sounding funds to our group. I didn't make much money, but it was fun holding the tiller, occasionally catching the wind, and turning the prow this way and that.

2/10/00 Dow −55.53, Nas +122.39

THE Dow Industrial average, it turns out, had its worst January in years. But the economy is booming, and tech stocks are doing fine. Better than fine, in fact—the interest-rate hike that Alan Greenspan imposed last week hasn't hurt the New Economy stocks, which raise their capital from the market itself or from venture capitalists. But the whole thing is dizzying, and a little remote, and I need to see some of the people who are driving this thing forward. I need to see what they look and sound like.

Rising at the extraordinary hour of 6:45 A.M. (film critics usually rise at ten or later, and more slowly than the Sun King), I make my way to a conference center on Desbrosses Street, in Tribeca. I leave the heavy brown nineteenth-century streets, noisy with trucks thudding over cobblestones, and enter what looks like an old loft building. On an upper floor, the landing opens into a large conference space with a glass roof and brilliant light. It is like walking into a shabby old soundstage on the Paramount lot in Hollywood and finding an enormous movie set. There is a long table set with bottles of Poland Spring water, freshly squeezed orange juice, pastries, and bagels. The attendees, about four hundred of them, have shown up for the monthly meeting of a group called New York InfoTech Forum, one of many such groups in Silicon Alley, where conferences seem to take place every day.

I enter a dense crowd in which the over-all mood is one of bounding, thriving conviviality. People introduce themselves without hesitation and whip out business cards—the cards flap back and forth like pictures of Sammy Sosa on the rear seat of a school bus. An eager young man tells me of a site devoted to grandparents. It will go after "mature demographics," addressing such issues as how to establish a "dynasty trust," and it will even set up discussion groups on such subjects as what to say to your kids if they are getting a divorce or adopting a child. (*But couldn't the mature demographics figure out these last two things on their own?*) It sounds a little dicey, though I could be wrong—with some heat the young man tells me that there are seventy *million* grandparents. (*Yeah, but how many of them surf the Web?*) I mutter my doubts to myself. Another guy has started up a site to facilitate general trade across the border from Mexico. (*But wouldn't this trade go along specialized channels that already exist?*) A young woman has a site to sell designer clothes to women. (*Why would a woman spend a thousand dollars or more for a dress that she can't try on?*)

Whatever my doubts, the eagerness is intoxicating. Certainly the haughty big-business style of yesteryear is dead. New Economy manners are "transparent," direct, unpretentious, pleasant, shameless. Circumspection is a mere irrelevance to these men and women, most of whom, at a glance, I judge to be in their thirties. They talk fast, so fast that I can't keep up with them. Some are lawyers, accountants, bankers, or venture capitalists of one sort or another, trying to expand their operation in Silicon Alley. Many of the Internet types themselves appear to be escapees from journalism, broadcasting, and advertising—the old-media professions are draining out fast. Such people are in a high state of transition, electrified and jubilant. They will link up buyers and suppliers; they will "tie in" with a company's internal applications; they will provide a "space" to auction off the toenail clippings of Madonna's masseur. They fix me with their eyes, waiting for a sign that I get it, that I feel it, that I realize the idea has . . . *scalability.*

We settle down for a speech from Mark L. Walsh, the C.E.O. of VerticalNet, one of the hot new business-to-business (B2B) Internet companies. Tall, fortyfiveish, with wire-frame glasses and a full head of curly gray hair, Walsh, who has a background in cable broadcasting, issues a torrent of claims, boasts, and visions. VerticalNet establishes separate Web sites, or vertical portals—Walsh calls them "vortals"—for unglamorous industries like poultry processing and waste management. He has fifty-six of these sites, gathered in twelve business sectors, or silos, and each site provides storefronts for manufacturers and brings together buyers and suppliers. The site is an exchange, a marketplace, a general store with a stove to warm the backs of the waste-management heavies as they schmooze—among other things, he wants to eliminate the executives' date on the golf course and the three-day Vegas trade show. His Web sites will offer a perpetual trade show; in order to hear about new products and meet people, you won't have to leave your duck farm in East Moriches, Long Island. As Walsh talks I sense that he might be more than a little contemptuous of the businesses themselves—that is, he appears amused by the contrast between the homely nature of poultry-processing firms and the amazingly clever, odorless thing he is going to do for them.

He tells us that stock in his company, which went public roughly a year ago, at sixteen dollars a share, has climbed to a split-adjusted price of four hundred and ninety dollars a share. He insists that even though VerticalNet has "a history of losses," the company, with nine billion dollars in market capitalization, is undervalued. The whole point is market share, not profits—not now, at any rate. "If you knew in 1979 what you know now about the development of cable," he says, reaching the clincher, "wouldn't you have borrowed every dollar you could, mortgaged your house, maxed your credit cards in order to get into cable?"

So there it is—the lure, the dazzling prospect. Someday we will look back on *this* moment as the instant in which enormous wealth was generated by Mark Walsh. But is his vision a triumphant actuality or an instance of *tulpenwoerde?* He is seductive, provocative, expansive, soaring—"Bulgaria leaped to digital without copper wire," he tells us, and assures us that golf doesn't stand a chance in the Third World, which will jump into B2B platforms without the intermediate step of developing a time-wasting culture of business sociability. Yes, but what if the leaping Bulgarians prefer links to links? If sociability can be supplanted by a "vortal," then why are we all gathered together on Desbrosses Street? I have a moment of furious doubt. I realize that all entrepreneurs have to do what Walsh is doing—keep their own people fired up, sustain the stock price. His speech is standard heroic-entrepreneur stuff. But his panache is a little unnerving: How many such projections are as unverifiable as his?

2/14/00 IMCL +3³/₄

THE *Journal* rather airily classes Walsh's company as a "concept stock." This does not have a good sound. But I am aroused by his talk, by the deep appeal it makes to ambition and hope. Over the past six months, my wife and I have increased the percentage of our holdings in equities. We have mainly invested in funds, but we have also bought some individual information-technology stocks, all market leaders. Goodbye, diversification. The 401(k) money, all of it, is now invested in a fund that draws heavily on large-cap Nasdaq stocks; we have sold some of our bonds, liquidated life insurance, dropped value funds that are going nowhere, taken a home-equity loan, and built up our "exposure" to aggressive growth, technology, and biotech stocks. *Exposure?* We are naked. I have become that journalistic cliché the momentum investor, who piles onto a hot market sector, and on paper, at least, we are making serious money. We even have a runaway biotech stock, ImClone, which sat in our portfolio for years and suddenly took off last fall. But I tremble, for almost ninety per cent of our money is in stocks, and perhaps seventy-five per cent of that money is invested in the New Economy, and this is living dangerously indeed.

What is this thing called greed? Is it a withering, soul-destroying force, a canker eating away at one's innards and shredding one's relationships? This is what religious, political, and economic moralists have always said, particularly after the end of a boom or the collapse of a speculative bubble. But doesn't it make more sense to speak of greed as a silent, stealthy, unappeasable longing? The Internet changes everything, boosters say, and it may be changing the coloration of avarice. At the moment, greed is not just a desire for personal wealth but an eagerness to be part of a social organism growing at enormous speed. You are not just tapping a tree in order to catch the milky substance in a cup. You are taking part in a social transformation akin to that wrought by the printing press, the telephone, and the automobile. Cupidity, at the moment, is fired by hope and seared by risk. And, whatever its savagery, it partakes as well of the softer virtues. It is, after all, an exaggeration of a most respectable passion, the desire to expand, and the degradation of a lovely emotion, the pleasurable warmth of orderly increase—increase of children, land, goods, flocks, houses, even furniture. In the Old Testament, God rewards the righteous with many sheep, many blankets in the tent.

But any unappeasable longing can be turned to vanity and lies. That is certainly what Anthony Trollope was getting at in his great 1875 novel, *The Way We Live Now*, which catches British society at a time when the big money made in the financial markets was changing the way people dealt with one another. At the center of *The Way We Live Now* is a nonexistent enterprise—the South Central Pacific and Mexican railway, which is supposed to run from Salt Lake City to Veracruz, two points between which it is hard to imagine many people wanting to travel.

Behind the scheme to float stock for this undertaking is one Augustus Melmotte, a shady financier, perhaps of French origin, around whom virtually all the other characters revolve. In order to give the scheme respectability, Melmotte enlists a variety of hard-up aristocrats to sit on a sham board. The great

railway, thus solidified with Quality, is sold to the public, and the public gratefully bids up the shares, much to Melmotte's profit. Not a single piece of track is
laid, but this doesn't prevent Melmotte from becoming the center of London society: around him, the spirit of merely claimed value is catching. In a mock version of the railroad swindle, the penniless swells on Melmotte's "board" take
turns issuing worthless I.O.U.s to one another after all-night card games. People live on credit, on promises, or by committing frauds of one sort or another.
They are forever propitiating, temporizing, cadging, forging, betraying. Trollope, I believe, was getting at a new kind of personality produced by the rapid
shifts in capital—the man or woman who is morally promiscuous, whose
character has the liquid properties of cash. Even sexual desire becomes speculative: a man may love a woman for a while, bid up her hopes, and then change
her for another. Greed, the book suggests, inevitably dissolves social honor.

2/17/00 Greenspan addresses House Banking Committee

I WATCH Alan Greenspan make his semi-annual report on the state of the
economy to the House Banking Committee. As he begins, I gaze at the little TV
screen in my kitchen with adoration. I'm in love with Alan Greenspan—a
partly bald, seventy-four-year-old Republican banker. He has been so effective,
this man, so *good*, flooding the market with liquidity at just the right time,
tightening at the right time. I admire his gravity, his civility, his realism, his
springing step when he crosses the street in Washington, a slender briefcase
held firmly under his left arm. So briskly he walks, his head down, brushing
past the cameras—no way is he going to tip off the press to what he's thinking,
not even with a glance. The economy, he says, is good; it's very good. Yet he is
troubled. And he explicitly says that higher rates of productivity, of all things,
are threatening to bring on inflation. He thinks people will expect greater corporate profits and will continue to invest, further heating up the market.

Such a worrier! Why does he have to make up a theory that almost no one
believes in? Suddenly, I am furious, and I shout at the TV. He is aiming his remarks directly at my portfolio, making up reasons to bring it down. And yet I
know his caution is morally beautiful; I know that in this hedonistic and frivolous republic it's as close to a tragic sense of life as anyone is likely to arrive at.
Human felicity has its limits; there is always a reckoning, always a price. Oh, I
fear his sorrow; I fear the burden of his pessimism. The bull, which was making
me prosperous, had to be brought to its knees. My hero was going to slay me.

2/20/00 Market closed

SUNDAY afternoon, and I'm sitting in the living room. Steam rises through
the pipes, which issue dolorous groans and knocks. The cat wakes up and
thwaps her tail, in syncopated rhythm with the pipes. Clang-*thwap* . . . clang-

thwap. From my older son's room, silence. Is he taking a nap? I'm too zonked to check on him. All New York apartments can be judged by the hums they give off when they are still, and now that the radiator has calmed down I enjoy the hum of this apartment—a steady surf noise of traffic from West End Avenue, brightened by the sound of someone practicing the violin somewhere, a good Upper West Side duet. But the day passes slowly, very slowly. I leaf listlessly through the *Times* and watch the political shows without serious interest. It is life at low ebb. When I'm not working or talking to the kids, I can hardly wait for Monday.

On a given weekday morning, I will take up my station in front of the kitchen TV, at least for an hour or two, sometimes more, and watch the action unfold on CNBC. I have opened an on-line brokerage account at DLJdirect, and I gather research from such sites as Silicon Investor and TheStreet.com. The sites can be feverish and brilliant, a composite of knowledge, gossip, and rant. On The Underground Trader, a site for day traders, the slap-happy investors flick words at one another like pilots screaming in the middle of a dogfight. "Can you believe this?" "Die, baby, die!" "Next stop, 100. Crash and burn, baby!" The investment sites have become the nation's true unconscious, the locus of what it *wants.* The porno sites, by contrast, are square and boring— just pictures of people posing or doing whatever it is they are doing, over and over. After the first excitement fades, one longs for the thrill of an initial public offering. Freudians associate greed with the infant's unwillingness to give up the breast, followed by the savage memory of the breast's withdrawal. But, greedy as I am, I do not hesitate to withdraw breasts from my screen. The true turn-on is elsewhere.

Like all addictions, investment mania produces self-disgust and counter-obsessions (cooking? fitness? travel?) whose purpose, never fulfilled, is to free the prisoner from his cell. At the moment, the key is nowhere to be found, and as I sit and worry I have noticed, if I'm not mistaken, that my breath has got a little shorter, my gut a little heavier, and my sleep a little lighter. I go to the gym, get on the treadmill, and watch . . . CNBC.

2/28/00 Dow −12.99% for the year

I'VE been thinking about mad Nyquist, the day trader—that's John Nyquist, a former chemical engineer, and just the kind of guy who gives Alan Greenspan nightmares. As the *Journal* tells it, Nyquist chucked his job a few years ago and moved from Chicago with his wife, Kate, to a house on the edge of a golf course in South Carolina. He spent his mornings day-trading and his afternoons play-ing golf while Kate looked after her mother, who was dying. He told Kate that everything was fine, but one day last April, early in the morning, he lured her to the balcony of their bedroom to look at some birds—egrets and herons, he said—and when she leaned out he threw her from the balcony and then rushed down to finish her off. But at the last minute, with his hands around her throat, he fell back and blurted out, "I lost all our money." He had blown seven hundred and eighty thousand dollars in assets, including his wife's retirement account, which he raided by forging her signature. It is said that he wanted to collect on her life insurance to pay off his debts. But he couldn't go through with it, and he's in prison now, sentenced to five years on charges of assault and battery with intent to kill. Kate Nyquist recovered, and is trying to get on with her life.

This is a horror story. But it is also funny in its way, since Nyquist's mania is a rushed, farcical-tragical version of what so many of us are doing. Nyquist is our fool, our scapegoat, and when I read his story, at breakfast one morning, I laughed out loud. All that dread, all that dread that his act releases!

The component of his madness which strikes me the hardest is that he lied: he lied to his wife, who might have saved him, telling her that everything was O.K. even as he was squandering her funds. With Nyquist in mind, I fall on my knees before my ambition and make the obvious vows: I will not invest in derivatives or anything else I don't understand. I will not buy stocks on margin. I will not short-sell declining stocks, since that operation would take full-time vigilance. I will not become a day trader. I will not lie to anyone about what's going on. I will not lose myself.

I wonder how many of these promises I will have kept by the end of the year.

3/10/00 Henry Blodget speaks

PEOPLE are eager to hear what Henry Blodget has to say, but he listens well, too, and over lunch at the Judson Grill, on a very hot day for the market, he leans across the table as I ask a question and stares at me intently, drawing his mouth down into a small, concentrated circle. Blodget analyzes the value of Internet stocks for Merrill Lynch, and he's good at what he does. His most renowned call came in December, 1998, when Amazon's stock was selling at two hundred and forty dollars a share, and he predicted, in the face of much skepticism, that it would go to four hundred dollars within a year, at which point the stock (adjusting for stock splits) shot to five hundred and fifty within a month. Though Blodget's been doing this kind of analysis as long as anyone else (since 1995, when Netscape became the first Internet stock to go public), he's only thirty-four, and blond, with high cheekbones and a long, handsome face.

I first met him nine days ago at an Internet conference, where he gave a keynote speech. Talk about Internet speed! Blodget took off like a shot and never came down to earth. His voice was dry but strong and clear, and he talked in bursts, which were outlined, in a PowerPoint presentation, on big screens to the left and the right of him.

There are now three hundred or so publicly traded Internet companies, and he told us right away that at least seventy-five per cent of them will disappear and never make money. Still, he said, "We believe the Internet stock phenomenon thus far is mostly rational." It's not a land boom, it's not the biotech bubble of 1991. Amazon's mere existence renders the entire Borders chain worthless. A "transfer of value" is going on, and prices are so high not because investors are irrational but because lots of capital is chasing a relatively small amount of shares. "The leading stocks are proxies for the growth of the Internet." If you don't invest in it, he said, moving his hands in parallel in front of his body, "you're not hedged against its impact on the rest of the economy." Each Internet stock may be overvalued, "but the Internet itself is undervalued." At some point, there will be a "rebalancing of supply and demand," and Internet stock values will move more in line with historical norms.

As Blodget leans over the table and talks to me at lunch, I decide that he is attempting to work as a stabilizing force in the midst of the maelstrom—a navigator who harnesses the wind without neglecting the tear in the mainsail or the spar swinging close to his head. It's been an amazing time for his sector— and for my investments, too. Yesterday, Thursday, March 9th, the Nasdaq index closed at 5,046.86. It has gone from 4,000 to 5,000 in just forty-eight trading days. In ten weeks, our portfolio as a whole has gone up twenty-five per cent; I am on track to meet my goal, though everything would have to continue to go right for the rest of the year for this to happen. Yet, despite high returns, I am more nervous than ever. On CNBC, the Stalwarts are talking to various gurus who warn of doom; rumors are hitting the press of startup Internet firms running out of cash. "Look," Blodget says, "you have to develop calluses. Some of these stocks are going to drop twenty or thirty per cent in a day." For safety, he recommends establishing a core holding of the market leaders—say, a hundred shares of Yahoo or A.O.L.—and buying more shares on the dips, and then selling a comparable number of shares as the price rises.

I have to ask: "Do you ever feel like a man riding a stallion to the edge of a cliff?"

"I feel like a man riding a stallion across an endless plain, and someday the horse will begin to slow," he says.

3/15/00 Nas −124.01

ALL day, there has been a rising pressure in my esophagus, as if a Spalding were being driven up a garden hose. I have to calm myself. This quarter, the Nasdaq has been swinging up and down by a hundred or more points a day, and I'm following it too closely and banging my head on the kitchen counter. Now and then, in a fit of despair, I throw myself at a book of poetry or a long essay or a classic novel, but apart from the Trollope and a new enthusiasm, *The Financier,* by Theodore Dreiser, whose capitalist hero Frank Cowperwood possesses all the qualities of coolness that I lack, I can't stay focussed on anything. My concentration breaks, and I start calculating multiples in my head. It is the investor's disease. If I now have eighty-seven cents invested in fund X, how much will I have at the end of the year if it continues to grow at the same rate? I'm making myself rich in fantasy by doing fourth-grade math exercises.

There is no way out of this; one can only go *through* it. At the end is success or trouble. The thing that I want to hold on to by making a million dollars is my apartment—the apartment that offers a nice distillation of Upper West Side hum. My marriage is breaking up—it has been for more than a year—and I don't want to leave my home. There's nothing special about the apartment, but I'm used to it. Since my wife and I are amicably dividing everything down the middle, I must give her financial assets equal to the market value of the apartment if I am to hold on to it. That's a lot of money: the boom has *windhandeled* up the value of my neighborhood. Selling the place (it's a co-op), splitting the take, and buying two smaller apartments would make infinitely more sense, but, as the man said, I would prefer not to. I know the price of my preference. What started out for me as a practical and emotional need has transformed itself into greed, pure and simple.

3/31/00 Nas +12.3% for the quarter

A VICIOUS, frightening final week in the quarter. Earlier in the year, the Nasdaq dipped and came back three times, and this week another correction got under way—a nauseating drop of seven hundred points in a few days, then a partial recovery, starting around three o'clock yesterday, Thursday, March 30th, and continuing today. Still, the index was off 7.9 per cent for the week, and some of the drops were extreme. For instance, VerticalNet's share price dropped fifteen dollars today alone.

I am exhausted, drained, disappointed. For the quarter, our portfolio went up about seventeen per cent, which would be a fine return at any time, though the gains have fallen considerably from the high point on March 10th, when I had lunch with Henry Blodget. I will have to be awfully lucky to come even within sight of the goalpost.

As the Nasdaq collapsed this week, and the second- and third-tier New Economy stocks plunged, the scolds and moralizers came out of their corners hurling dead tulips. Their message: The speculative boom is over. Investors will buy only those New Economy companies that show solid profit. Well, maybe. The gross domestic product increased for the last quarter of 1999 by a fantastic 7.3 per cent. Trying to slow the economy down, Alan Greenspan will raise interest rates again in May, but the American people are flush, and Greenspan can't stop them from investing.

Still, something has snapped. My friend Craig Rumford, the investment banker, says that the inevitable period of shakeout that Henry Blodget spoke of is already upon us. Craig has jumped the fence after all. He still specializes in mergers and acquisitions, but he has left his distinguished firm and joined an on-line investment bank. I visit him at his new digs. For him, it is a good moment: many of the small New Economy companies will join together or swallow one another up. In *The Financier,* the ten-year-old Frank Cowperwood decides to go into banking after watching a lobster devour a squid in a fish market. "Things lived on each other—that was it," he concludes. The New Economy has spawned plenty of lobsters and even more squid, and Rumford the consolidator is happy, back in the game again, though his clothes are all wrong: "Can't use any of the shirts with French cuffs. All the suits are going to the far end of my son's closet." In line with New Economy manners, the sartorial style at his new firm tends toward a polo shirt and slacks—with a Brioni jacket. We may remember the Brioni jacket as the flourish of a historical juncture: the time of the Great Consolidation.

4/7/00 Nas +9.27% for the year

IN the wake of the Microsoft anti-trust decision, a plunge in the Nasdaq index, a shudder, another enormous plunge, followed, the same day, by an enormous recovery. On Tuesday, April 4th, I was talking to a friend on the telephone at around one-fifteen and the index was down 575 points. "It's a crash," we agreed solemnly. What else could you call it? I hung up, went to a doctor's appointment, returned a little more than an hour later, and stood in the kitchen blinking at the screen. The Nasdaq had come back about 400 points. Still, three-quarters of our gains for the year were wiped out. On paper—or, if you like, onscreen—we had lost around two hundred thousand dollars in the past two weeks, but after the first shock I didn't feel a thing; that is, the initial chagrin gave way to a weirdly disembodied sensation, as if this were happening to someone else. A few hours after that, this feeling, which I interpret as helplessness—we're all fools, no one can control or predict the market, etc.—gave way to scorn. Why the panic selling? I repeat the mantras: The means are in place to transform this society through new technology. Nothing has changed. I have not sold, will not sell, and will wait for the recovery—which begins, as it happens, by the end of the week. On the telephone, Henry Blodget says, "That dip was a violent reminder that the stock market is not a savings account that just happens to be earning forty-per-cent interest a year." Yet he also predicts that in three to five years New Economy stocks, which are now worth about a trillion dollars, or five per cent of the American capital markets, will go to two or three trillion dollars, or ten to fifteen per cent. Earnings will continue to lag, but this does not sound like a bad place to invest.

Yet there is no safety for me or for anyone else. With my welfare in mind, a friend tells a curiously self-punishing story. His clever older brother called him in the early fall and tipped him off to a pharmaceutical stock called LeukoSite. The price was seven dollars. My friend bought the stock, and, after a few months, when he noticed that the stock had more than tripled, he sold it and made a nice profit. Several weeks ago, his brother called again. "You haven't sold LeukoSite, have you?" My friend allowed that he had. A dead silence followed. LeukoSite had been taken over by Millennium Pharmaceuticals, and the stock was then worth three hundred dollars a share. If my friend had held on and sold at the peak, he would have made about a million dollars. There it is: the million, not *my* million, but, still, a million, and it's unreachable.

My friend showed neither weakness nor poor judgment by selling when he did. Regret over his loss would be absurd at any time except at this incredible moment, in which multiples of forty, in a period of seven months, do occur now and then. So he did feel regret, even chagrin, though his sorrow over the lost money was mixed with something else—relief that his whole life was not tied up in investment. He had a good job; he had friends, people who depended on him. He had a life. What he meant to convey, I think by telling me *his* primal story, was that an obsession with money is disfiguring. The game is good; it's never been better, anywhere. But, still, my friend was telling me that one has to breathe. Greed is not in itself a shameful feeling—there are those tents in the Old Testament lands, and the patriarchs taking satisfaction in the large flocks of sheep gathered outside—but one has to live apart from greed. And even I have to breathe, one minute after another, one day after another. I have to slow down and breathe.

4/10/00 WEBM 189

I GO to the annual literary gala thrown by the PEN American Center in support of writers who are political prisoners. Listening to the speakers, I am relieved to be there, relieved not to think of the market, for the Nasdaq is again collapsing. The market will create me; the market will also betray me.

But there is a man at my table. A reporter, he says. He covers the tech sector. I have to ask. "WebMethods," he says. It provides infrastructure software to help companies connect to one another over the Internet. It's down from its highs, but it's solid. Or so he says. As the speeches go on, I borrow a pen and jot its stock ticker symbol—WEBM—on the back of my program. Before long, today or maybe tomorrow, I will check it out.

APRIL 24, 2000

ADRIAN NICOLE LEBLANC

LANDING FROM THE SKY

I N 1987, when Jessica was nineteen and already had three children, she returned home to her mother's fifth-floor tenement apartment, on Tremont
Avenue. She had been staying with her boyfriend, and when they broke up she
had nowhere else to go. Living with her mother, Lourdes, wasn't easy. (Some
names have been changed.) Lourdes, who was thirty-six, hadn't had a job in
years. Money was tight, visitors were frequent, emotions ran high. Jessica no
longer had a room of her own; she now slept on a velveteen couch in the *sala*,
or living room.

Like her mother, Jessica slept late—through the sounds of working people
picking their way around the previous night's detritus, the sibilant noise of old
wooden brooms slapping against cement, the tinkle of smashed glass as it
dropped into the gutter, the whoosh of water buckets clearing away vomit and
cigarette butts and pork-rind bags. Jessica's three-year-old daughter, Serena,
shared a room with Lourdes. Jessica's twin girls had a crib next to the couch.
Even though Jessica was living with her kids, she wasn't really looking after
them: she might bathe them, or style their hair, but Lourdes had more or less
been raising Serena, and Jessica's friend Rosa, who loved children, often took
care of the twins. Jessica's first loyalty was to the street.

Jessica and her mother argued constantly about Jessica's irresponsibility,
but Lourdes's pronouncements carried little weight: she, too, loved to party
and, in recent years, had sometimes been a reluctant mother to her own kids.
Jessica had always wanted to be taken care of; Lourdes, who had had to raise
her own siblings, wanted to be taken care of, too.

Tremont marks the north end of the South Bronx; Lourdes's apartment was
just off the Grand Concourse. The neighborhood drug trade was booming, and
although cellular phones hadn't hit the street level of the business yet, there

were plenty of beepers—on boys riding skateboards, on boys buying Pampers for their babies or heading for the stores on Fordham Road and Burnside to steal. But the boys who caught Jessica's eye were the ones walking out of the bodega with cash and attitude. They pushed open the smudged doors plastered with Budweiser posters as if they were stepping into a party instead of onto a littered sidewalk beside a potholed street. It was similar to the way Jessica stepped onto the pavement whenever she left the three girls with her mother and descended the four flights of stairs, to emerge, expectant, from the paint-chipped vestibule. Outside, anything could happen.

The block was hectic, but her appearance usually caused a stir. Jessica created an aura of intimacy wherever she went. You could be talking to her in the middle of Tremont and feel as if a confidence were being exchanged beneath a tent of sheets. Guys in cars offered rides. Grown men got stupid. Women got worried or jealous. Boys made promises they didn't keep.

Although Jessica wanted to be somebody's girlfriend, she was usually the other girl, the mistress; boys called up to her window after they'd dropped off their main girls. Her oldest daughter, Serena, whom she had had when she was sixteen, belonged to a boy named Kuri. Jessica had met Kuri at a toga party on Crotona Avenue, when she should have been in school. He was a break dancer, a member of the Rock Steady Crew. One thing led to another, and they ended up in a bedroom on a pile of coats.

Kuri, who had a steady girlfriend, refused to admit that Serena was his child. When Lourdes asked Jessica who the father was, she lied and told her it was a neighborhood boy she'd dated. Then one day she came home with a video of the movie *Beat Street,* in which Kuri had a small part. Lourdes had heard enough about Kuri to be on the alert as they settled down with their dog, Sparky, to watch the film. In it, a boy who looked a lot like Serena did a break dance and challenged a rival crew to a battle at the Roxy.

"Hold that pause," Lourdes shouted. "That's Serena's father! I will cut my pussy off and give it to that dog if that ain't Serena's father!"

After Serena's birth, Jessica dropped out of school. She became increasingly depressed, and even attempted suicide by swallowing pills. When she was in the hospital getting her stomach pumped, she learned that she was pregnant with twins, by Kuri's brother. He acknowledged the children, but he cheated on her, and now she was home again.

At Lourdes's, the life of the apartment moved in lockstep with the life of the street. The beginning of the month, when the welfare check came in, was a good time—a time to buy things, a time to go out dancing. Lourdes packed the shelves with food. She sent Jessica to the dollar store to get King Pine and cocoa butter and shampoo. Outside, the drug dealers enjoyed the surge in business. By late afternoon, Lourdes was up—blasting Spanish music, clanking around the kitchen, cooking rice and *gandules* and pork chops. Evelyn, her younger daughter, was coming home from working at C-Town; Phil, her older son, was back from his classes at Hunter College, holed up in his room. Jessica's baby brother, Joey, rolled in and out with his posse. Boyfriends and neighbors were dropping by. Lourdes was an excellent cook: she fed them all.

Everything changed at the end of the month, when the money ran out. Lourdes would take to her bed. Meals were sometimes reduced to white rice and ketchup. Jessica gave the girls sugar water before bed to fill them up. Joey stole fruit from a nearby Korean market and bread from a grocery store across the street. Jessica might try to cajole the girls' fathers to provide Pampers, but they didn't always come through.

Phil and Evelyn were trying to stay out of trouble, but Joey and Jessica were playing the odds. Joey was drifting into crime; Jessica still counted on being rescued. "Jessica was a dreamer," Lourdes recalled recently. "She always wanted to have a king with a maid. I always told her, 'That's only in books. Face reality.' Her dream was more upper than herself." Lourdes would caution her beautiful daughter as she disappeared down the dreary stairwell: "God ain't gonna have a pillow waiting for your ass when you fall landing from the sky."

Jessica did take a fall. The decade that followed brought high times and hard times, and the hard times usually came from Jessica's thralldom to her chosen saviors. Her life would change utterly, and then change again. In some ways, though, Jessica was lucky. Not everyone survives being rescued.

BLIND DATE

ON January 23, 1988, Jessica met George—Boy George, he was called—on a blind date arranged by Evelyn's boyfriend. It would be a double date, and she agreed to it on one condition: "If he's ugly, bring me home at ten."

The night of the date, Lourdes and her daughters waited by the window, looking down onto Tremont. "George pulled up in a car that was like the ocean," Lourdes says. It was a graphite Mercedes-Benz, and he saluted Lourdes through the sunroof. As soon as Jessica saw him, she adjusted her curfew. He was so handsome in his leather trenchcoat—with dark hair, a goatee, smooth skin, dark-brown eyes—that she was willing to surrender the next day or two. Suddenly, Lourdes "remembered" that she couldn't babysit.

Boy George understood the cue: he recalls giving Lourdes some high-quality cocaine and a thousand dollars in cash. Lourdes was not the first difficult mother he'd encountered, nor was it the first time he'd heard a response like hers: *Baby, you can keep my daughter out all night.* Jessica admired his savvy, although the implications of the transaction embarrassed her.

"She'd just sold her to me for a thousand dollars," Boy George says. "I could have been a serial killer and sliced her up." Actually, a thousand dollars was nothing to Boy George. At the time he and Jessica met, he was running the largest heroin operation in the borough, bringing in a quarter of a million dollars a week.

The young couples went to the movies and dinner, and then Boy George suggested they go to a club. Jessica had dressed conservatively, and she asked to stop by Lourdes's apartment so she could change. Contact lenses replaced her eyeglasses. Her hair, which had been stretched into a tight bun, now fell around her neck in a soft, loose mane. The long skirt, blazer, and plain pumps were exchanged for spandex tights and knee-high boots. Then, there was the makeup. Jessica called this "dressing *puta.*" When she returned to the car, Boy George asked, "You sure you the same girl?"

He and Jessica ended the night in a five-hundred-dollar suite at the Loews Glenpoint Hotel, in Teaneck, New Jersey. Boy George asked her about her dreams and fears and actually listened to her answers. She told him what she had never told Lourdes: that one of her mother's boyfriends had sexually abused her for years. Boy George held her all night. Jessica was overwhelmed: despite all he'd paid for, he didn't expect her to have sex with him. He ordered room service and fed Jessica strawberries in the king-size bed. "I felt like a princess," she says. "I felt loved." As it turned out, not having sex with a girl on a first date was one of Boy George's most successful strategies.

The following morning, Jessica encountered her first brunch—sliced fruit fanned out on silver trays, cold cuts rolled into cylinders, bread baked in animal shapes. All this was arranged on a large cloth-covered table beneath an ice sculpture of two swans in a melting embrace.

THE FIFTY-DOLLAR RULE

NOT long after their first date, Jessica paged Boy George from a pay phone on the Grand Concourse. Snow was falling. Jessica didn't have a winter coat. Her penny loafers were soaked.

Boy George was at Grand Billiards, playing pool. He didn't want to interrupt his game, so he dispatched one of his workers. "I'm calling for Boy George," the worker said.

"Oh, hello." Jessica remembers that she used her softest voice, just loud enough to be heard above the traffic. "I was wondering if you could do me a favor." Jessica opened many conversations exactly like this. She was beginning a request for money, which would be followed by an explanation that would continue as long as necessary, like falling dominoes. She needed a ride. She didn't have money for a cab. She needed a ride to a friend's house to collect twenty dollars. The girl owed her the money. She needed the money to buy milk for her hungry daughters.

"Hold on a minute," the worker said. Boy George took the receiver.

His voice was calm but sharp. "Listen, if you are calling me just for money, don't call. Don't you call me for money."

"Mmnnn," Jessica said.

"Where you at?" Boy George asked.

"A Hundred and Seventy-sixth and the Concourse."

"Stay there. Someone will be by to pick you up."

The worker drove her to Grand Billiards. They waited in the car. Boy George joined them with three friends. Jessica asked him for money a second time.

"I only like to say things once. If you calling me for money, don't call."

"Fuck you," Jessica snapped.

In retrospect, Boy George thinks he should have "served her" with a proper beating. Instead, he ordered the driver to go to Lourdes's building, dragged Jessica out of the car, and frog-marched her up the stairs. At some point, he noticed that she was wearing a pair of jeans he had seen on Lourdes.

"Whose jeans is those?" he asked.

"They mine."

"Why your mother have them on then?"

"It's not like what's mine is mine. We the same size. We—"

"Shit," he said. He inspected the cabinets and the refrigerator. "There was nothing," he recalls. "There was nothing in that subway station."

Within a few hours, his employees returned to the apartment laden with grocery bags. Joey rushed to his window and looked down over Tremont. Two Jeeps were parked outside, still stuffed with groceries.

"There was so much food that the bags didn't fit in the kitchen," Joey says. "There was food in my room under the bed." Meat—chicken, pork chops, steak—filled the refrigerator and the freezer. Lourdes sobbed as each grocery bag was carried beneath the lucky horseshoe stuck above her door.

"He got everything," Jessica says. "Everything." She was sure, because she and Lourdes tried to figure out items he had forgotten or overlooked. He had even bought a flea collar and dog food for Sparky.

The next day, Boy George brought Jessica bags of clothes. From now on, Jessica had to *represent*. He and Jessica sat on the couch in the crowded living room. He asked Jessica where she slept.

"You sitting on my bed right now."

It wasn't a fold-out bed. It was a couch. Boy George recalls saying to himself, "What the fuck is going on here?"

BOY George gave Jessica a job packing heroin at one of his mills, near Aqueduct Avenue, though she worked there only briefly, because the smell of the heroin made her ill. He also gave her money for her daughters, but he didn't much want them around. Once, Jessica left Lourdes's apartment to run an errand and didn't come home for a week. "I just dropped my kids for him," Jessica says. "At night, he would say, 'Don't leave and go back to them.' I just did what my mother did to me." Soon, Jessica moved out completely.

Boy George had a number of apartments—one on Henwood, one on Morris, two in a Manhattan building called Normandie Court—and he would move Jessica from one to another. "He'd bring home a whole lot of videos, and I would just watch TV. I didn't have to get a job. I was to cook and clean and take care of the things, and I would get my allowance at the end of the week."

In the early days, Jessica's allowance was generous—a thousand dollars a week or more. George also surprised her with vacations and jewelry. He didn't want her gold to be thin and bendable. It had to be thick. If Jessica liked a necklace—a heart of sapphires, say—he would tell his jeweller, "We'll take that, but make it different." He got her a diamond Rolex and added her birthstone to it. He gave her a belt buckle with her name spelled out in emeralds. To George, looking good meant looking unique. He wanted Jessica customized, like his cars.

"He matched me up," Jessica says. No stained clothes, nothing borrowed, no jeans with a yellow sheen from the cheap soap at the laundromat. He took Jessica shopping in Greenwich Village and introduced her to the fifty-dollar rule. Nothing under fifty dollars was to be taken off the rack. No ten-dollar stores, no V.I.M., no Payless.

Jessica enjoyed going shopping. She added to a growing collection of leather coats—full-length and waist-length, in rainbow colors. She gave some of Boy George's sweatsuits to Joey, supplied Pampers for the children, and bought sneakers for everyone. She gave Lourdes cash and paid her rent and her electric bills.

At first, Boy George discouraged Jessica from spending time at Lourdes's, and soon he forbade it. He considered Jessica's mother a bad influence. Occasionally, he allowed the twins, who were living with Rosa by then, to be brought over to whatever apartment he and Jessica were living in. Serena remained with Lourdes. Weeks might pass without a visit from Jessica. Lourdes says, "I didn't even know where my daughter lived."

SNOW IN THE POCONOS

SOON after Jessica met George, her brother Joey got together with a girl named Marisol. Marisol was a sportier, sweeter version of the girl Jessica had been. Joey and Marisol met outside a bodega when Joey was hanging out at the western end of Tremont, robbing people. That day, she had her hair pulled up severely, with two lollipops stuck in the topknot of her bun. At four feet nine, Marisol was chunky and proud of it. She preferred tight pants, and shirts that exposed her midriff. The spandex pants that were in style were called bubble gums. Marisol had a pair in every color—blue, red, green, yellow, black, pink, and turquoise. "I used to rock those, they used to cling to my butt, I used to love it," Marisol says. That day, she was wearing the turquoise pair. She swished into the store and out again. Joey stood before her in a red leather hooded jacket, the hood trimmed with what looked like rabbit fur. He was holding a pack of Mike & Ike candy in his hand. He grinned. "We began to conversate," Marisol recalls. Soon Joey brought her home to meet his family.

Jessica was the most beautiful girl Marisol had ever seen: light-skinned, with "dead" hair—straight and shiny, like a white girl's. She had sleepy eyes, a big butt, large breasts, manicured nails, and a wide smile crowded with white, even teeth. She smelled like a rich girl—not of the sharp scents you got at the dollar store but of a name-brand perfume. And she was friendly, which surprised Marisol, because a girl with all that could have been a snob.

IN early 1989, Boy George told Jessica that they were going to the Poconos, and he invited Joey and Marisol to come along. They all drove off in a white stretch limousine. Marisol remembers wishing the chauffeur would loop around her block so she could show the car off to her friends. After the limousine crossed the George Washington Bridge, Boy George opened the cooler and pulled out a bottle of Moët. He was in an expansive mood and wanted everyone to drink. He himself would not drink, because he was training as an amateur boxer. Marisol didn't want to drink, either, because alcohol made her queasy, and Jessica wasn't feeling in a partying mood just yet. "Whoever doesn't drink has to walk—I'm leaving you on the side of the road," Boy George told them. Marisol remembers that she began to smile, thinking it was a joke. "He means it," Jessica whispered. "Listen to him, 'cause he'll leave you, and he will—he did it to me." Marisol and Joey drank. Jessica had to drink until the champagne ran out. Then she got sick, and Boy George told the chauffeur to pull into the breakdown lane. With her head jutting out the window, Jessica vomited, clasping her hair and her gold chains at the nape of her neck.

A few hours later, the Mount Airy Lodge appeared, like a palace tucked in the snow. Boy George paid for their rooms in cash, and handed Joey a set of keys. The rooms George rented were called Crystal Palace Suites, and each one was big enough for an entire family. Everything was color-coördinated in gold and powder-blue. There was a TV, a stereo, a fireplace with a log that never stopped burning. There was a red heart-shaped Jacuzzi in the huge bathroom. The bed was round, and there were mirrors on the walls and on the ceiling. The living room opened onto a heated swimming pool. The room was so interesting, Marisol thought, you would never need the street. When Boy George and Joey headed off to ski, Jessica was grateful for Marisol's company. George could sometimes stay away for days, and she hated being left alone.

Around midnight, she and Marisol were still sitting beside the swimming pool. Suddenly, the lights went out, leaving the girls in darkness, except for the underwater spotlights of the pool. A croaky voice broke the silence. It was George pretending to be Jason, from the movie *Friday the 13th*. "We were so scared," Jessica says. "That was when there were things that could scare me." Boy George tossed Jessica in the water, fully clothed.

Back in their own Crystal Palace Suite, Marisol and Joey pretended they were on their honeymoon. They made love on the round bed and ordered food and watched TV and made love again in the heart-shaped Jacuzzi. From their bed, they watched the sunrise. "We broke night," Marisol says. Over the next six years, Marisol and Joey had two children, but this was their only honeymoon. They were both fourteen.

DO NOT PASS GO

BOY George didn't keep his other girlfriends a secret, and he expected Jessica to take his telephone messages. "I'd get hit if I got mad when the other girls called," she said. Sometimes, Jessica took the liberty of calling the girls back. "Don't beep my man," she'd say, or, "Don't you be calling my husband." When Boy George came home, he would berate her. "What are you doing beeping my girls back? You're not allowed to beep my girls back."

Jessica could tell when he was going on a date, because he wore slacks instead of jeans. "Why don't you just wear your jeans if you going out with the boys?" she would ask.

"Why don't you fucking shut the fuck up?" he'd reply.

More and more, Jessica saw George late at night if she saw him at all. Sometimes, he locked her in the apartment. He no longer gave her a regular allowance, and he was gone for weeks at a time. During the spring of 1989, she borrowed money from her girlfriends; she didn't dare touch the stacks of cash he left lying around the apartment. Materially, in fact, her life was no longer very different from her life with Lourdes, except that the apartment was "hooked up," and she had a telephone. (She didn't know it at the time, but federal investigators had installed a wiretap.)

By then, Boy George was beating Jessica more frequently. She knew she'd received a particularly bad one if she came to at his mother's. (Once, he left her there after hitting her with a two-by-four.) Some beatings, such as the one that cracked her skull, were handled by a private physician.

ON the morning of May 1, 1989, Boy George got a call from a lieutenant of his, who told him to "do a Jimmy James Brown"—make a run for it. When Boy George stepped outside, he was arrested by agents from the Drug Enforcement Agency and local police officers, who had been following his organization for almost two years. Twenty-two of his employees had already been brought in.

It was fourteen months before Boy George's case went to trial, and for most of that time he was housed at the Metropolitan Correctional Center, in lower Manhattan, better known as the M.C.C. At first, Jessica went to see him almost every day. Eventually, she managed to bypass the usual procedure—which involved guards and forms and stamps and metal detectors—by using a paralegal's pass that one of Boy George's private investigators procured for her. Ostensibly, Jessica was conducting research for Boy George's case. In fact, she ran errands for him all over the city, buying him sneakers and sweatsuits, checking on his mother, bringing him homemade food, yachting magazines, and pornography. They shadowboxed for hours in the attorneys' room. Finally, he had time for her.

Jessica relished the attention she was now getting. One day, Boy George even gave Jessica his favorite charm for safekeeping—two tiny gold boxing gloves, which symbolized the Golden Gloves competition he still hoped to win. She wore the gloves on a slender gold chain around her neck. "Because I'm his champ," she said proudly. At the same time, Jessica never underestimated his reach. Boy George had a hit man. He was fond of saying, "If I can trust you, I can kill you."

To prove her devotion, Jessica agreed to get a tattoo. "If you love me, you'll do it," Boy George told her. He decided on the words "Jessica loves George," over her heart; she had it done in a tattoo parlor on Avenue C. For the next one, though, George wanted something fancier. He read through the trade magazines until he discovered a tattoo artist in Elizabeth, New Jersey, who had been rated one of the nation's best; George's driver took Jessica there.

The second tattoo, high on her right thigh, was elegant: a heart with a rose and "George" written beneath it, in script. The day after she got it, Jessica wore a skirt with a slit, so she could show him. When he saw the tattoo, he pronounced with appreciative incredulity, "You stupid bitch!"

Altogether, she got six tattoos in his honor, including a poem, written on a scroll, just above her left shoulder blade:

> George
> No matter where I am
> or what I'm doing
> You're always there
> always on my mind
> and in my heart . . .

As Boy George prepared for his trial, Jessica settled into her new freedom. She moved back in with Lourdes and Serena, but there were some weeks when she went out dancing every night. Serena often tried to block the door to keep her mother home. "I used to always break her stockings, so that she would have to come back in," Serena recalls. "But she never came back in—she would fight me to get to that door."

"The twins had each other; Serena had nobody," Jessica's older brother, Phil, recalls. "Serena suffered a whole lot more than Jessica did." Evelyn had taught her niece to open and heat a can of Spaghettios when she was hungry, and never to open the apartment door when she was alone. Serena watched cartoons all morning and afternoon while everyone slept. She would try to shush her baby sisters when they made noise. She was five. People often said of her, "That child is too grown!"

Joey was serving time in a juvenile facility for attempted murder, but Marisol still came by the house regularly. She and Serena kept each other company. She styled Serena's hair. They poured baby powder on the floor in the dining room and pretended to be ice skating.

To celebrate the birthday of a friend of Jessica's, Boy George told her to take a thousand dollars from his stash. He booked a limousine to deliver her and her girlfriends to Victor's Café, on Fifty-second Street, in Manhattan, where they ate a seemingly endless meal. He even called the restaurant on the pay phone to send his love. The *plátano* had candles. Handsome waiters sang.

IN August of 1990, Boy George and five co-defendants went on trial. In November, George was convicted of conspiring to run a continuing criminal enterprise and of tax evasion, and the following April was given a life sentence with no option for parole. The judge told him that he was the most violent person ever to have set foot in her courtroom.

After the sentencing, Boy George phoned Jessica: "He told me, 'They have your name down on papers already, they gonna arrest you,' and he wrote to my mother to say that I was going to suffer like a dog."

Two weeks later, Jessica heard the cop-call. The cop-call was a neighborly warning sounded by anyone who spotted the police, for anyone who might like to know. Jessica walked to the kitchen window to see what was happening. The street had been blocked off. Cruisers were parked and others were pulling up. Then someone pounded on the door, and she heard, "Police! Open up! *Policía!*"

Jessica called Marisol, who ran all the way from her mother's. Jessica was handcuffed and brought down to the M.C.C. The timing of the arrest warrant, she later learned, arose from the need to protect her: the D.E.A. had intercepted information that Boy George, presumably fearing she would turn state's evidence, had put out a contract on her life. But investigators also had information about her brief employment packing heroin. In December, she pleaded guilty to conspiring to distribute heroin and was sentenced to ten years in a federal penitentiary.

SOMEWHERE FAR AWAY

BY 1994, Jessica's friend Rosa had added Serena to her growing brood of other people's children; at Lourdes's, the child had missed most of first grade. Jessica had been concerned: "The hanging out, the people coming in and out, my daughter didn't have no privacy." From prison, she had warned her mother, "The friends you're hanging out with are going to lead you to me. Believe me, there is a bunk waiting for you."

Rosa was stocky and strong; she always had a toddler in the crook of her arm. Young mothers would go to their jobs, or out dancing, or they'd need time to work out problems with their men, and they'd leave their kids with her. A strict and practical woman, she could always be trusted. But Jessica's children were a priority. "They were happy, they weren't going from house to house," Rosa recalls. "They used to go to school every single day." She worried most about Serena, who, in turn, constantly fretted over her younger sisters. "I told her, 'Serena, I'm the one who is supposed to take care of you. You do what I tell you to do, and I'll take care of the girls.' "

But it was hard to take care of the girls in the Bronx, and it would only get harder as they got older. Serena didn't sleep well, because of all the street noise and the gunfire, and she would cry out for Lourdes in the middle of the night. Junkies shot up in the stairwells and had sex on the roof. The only play area for the children was a concrete space between two buildings. Rosa's older brother had recently joined a growing number of Bronx friends and neighbors who had moved upstate, and the news that drifted back to Rosa was all good. Apartments were spacious. Children could play outdoors safely. There were factory jobs. The schools were strict about classwork and attendance. Rosa's family would help her take care of the children, so that she could go back to work.

In the spring of that year, when Serena was eight, Rosa moved upstate with Jessica's girls to a housing project in Troy. The same month, Jessica was transferred, at her own request, to a medium-security women's facility in Danbury, Connecticut, and she would spend most of her sentence there. She wanted to be closer to her children.

The prison was situated on a hilltop that was also home to a flock of geese. It looked like a high school with barbed wire around it. Inside, spotless floors shone against beige cinder-block walls. The women in Jessica's unit lived in gray cubicles, or "cubes." Each cube had bunk beds and two squat lockers, one on top of the other. The bathrooms were down the hall.

That summer, Jessica took a particular interest in a correction officer named Ernesto Díaz. Díaz supervised the compound's power plant, where Jessica had been trained as a lagger—someone who wraps pipes with insulation. She worked the night shift. Most of the time, there wasn't much work to do, especially since Díaz didn't believe in what he called "bright work," or busy work—mopping floors that were already clean, polishing already shining brass railings, painting over paint.

When he could, Díaz says, he left the women alone. "Don't make my shift rough, and I'll treat you like a human being" was his philosophy. The inmates often sat and talked, or wrote letters, or listened to the radio, or napped. Díaz occasionally shared treasures of free-world food, like Kentucky Fried Chicken, cranberry juice, or doughnuts. Mr. Doughnut became his nickname.

Díaz was accustomed to the flirting; it was a chronic condition of an officer's life at a women's prison. At the plant, he says, women would dance around his desk, sometimes touching themselves and making suggestive remarks. Jessica danced everywhere—in the supply room, in the office. "There were other ones that did it," Díaz recalls, "but she was very good at it." Soon they found themselves having long conversations. He told her about his wife and children. Jessica told him about her daughters, especially Serena, and about her own unhappy childhood and her turbulent relationship with Lourdes. He gave her an article about child abuse. Several inmates noticed the increasing amount of time Jessica and Díaz spent alone.

At first, Jessica considered Díaz merely a challenge, but as time went on she found herself moved by his concern for her. She appealed to Queenie, an inmate who practiced Santeria, and one night they performed a ritual to help matters along. Queenie instructed Jessica to obtain an apple. They removed the core, wrote Díaz's name on a piece of paper, rolled it up and stuck it inside the apple, and then topped it off with honey. It was tucked away in Díaz's locker.

Jessica and Díaz grew closer. He prepared linguine with clam sauce for her, let her listen to his house-music tapes, brought her a bottle of her favorite perfume. She showed him gifts she had been preparing for her daughters for Family Day, in August.

Family Day was one of the facility's biggest events: there were hamburgers and hot dogs and Sno-cones for the children; there were performances and games. Jessica hadn't seen Serena in more than a year; she hadn't seen the twins since her arrest. "It was all she talked about for several weeks," Díaz says. Jessica had sent Lourdes all the requisite forms well beforehand. She had even included a free voucher for the forty-five-minute bus ride, and the bus left directly from the Bronx. But when Family Day finally arrived no one showed up.

Jessica was devastated. Díaz brought her a rose and a sympathy card. He offered to mail the gifts to the children, and even included a *Jurassic Park* videotape for the twins and a bottle of perfume for Serena. "That was when she really started to get interested in me," he says. Díaz also volunteered to visit Jessica's children in Troy, which meant a great deal to her. He and Jessica fantasized about a future together. Before long, they arranged to have sex in the back of a storage room, but the circumstances made physical intimacy difficult; mostly, they talked through the night. Díaz was struck by Jessica's longing for contact with her mother.

In the fall, Jessica discovered she was once again pregnant with twins. She told the prison authorities that she'd been raped, by a guard she couldn't identify, but the internal investigation led to Díaz—plenty of snitches volunteered their suspicions about Jessica and Mr. Doughnut. In the meantime, Jessica was transferred to "the camp," a minimum-security facility up the road.

Minimum-security status meant fewer restrictions than before, but Jessica had little interest in her new freedoms. One of her roommates remembers that she rarely left her bed. Her pregnancy had gained her a certain amount of institutional notoriety, however, and her friends tried to cheer her up. They made a special jailhouse dish, which involved mashing together everything sweet you could lay your hands on and spreading it over a layer of crushed cookies. They made hooch by mixing fruit with bread from the cafeteria and stowing it above a ceiling panel until it fermented. They painted Jessica's toenails.

The authorities wanted to run a DNA test on the fetuses, but Jessica refused, in order to protect Díaz. She was still corresponding with him through the mother of a prison friend. She read and reread his letters before she had to toss them down the toilet. She prayed for an early release and daydreamed about what she'd do when she got out. She wrote Serena that she wouldn't be returning to the Bronx: instead, they'd all go somewhere happy, somewhere far away. Rosa chastised Jessica for filling the head of a nine-year-old with such notions. She knew where Jessica's dreams had led, and she was determined to keep Serena's head out of the clouds.

THE CHILDREN'S ROOM

SEVERAL months later, in the spring of 1995, Evelyn and Marisol brought Serena and the twins for a visit. The visiting room was light and airy. At one end was a play area, which greeted guests with a detailed list of rules. A large sign said, "Welcome Back!" Since some children believed that they were visiting their mothers at work or in the hospital, visitors were not supposed to use the words "prison" and "jail" to describe the place.

Jessica appeared carrying a clear plastic bag full of crocheting. She wore a teal cotton sweatsuit over an ironed white T-shirt. She had colored her hair red with jailhouse dye, but it had grown out, revealing brown-black roots. She wore almost no makeup, and her face looked full and vulnerable. Serena and the twins ran to her and hugged her. Then the twins drifted toward the play area. Serena hovered near Jessica, who tried to defuse the awkwardness by showing her what she'd made: sweaters for the unborn twins and a peach-and-yellow coverlet for Serena.

Jessica then showed her daughter a copy of her most recent sonogram. "See, Baby A, that's his head, his eyes, the ears." Jessica outlined the bodies with her fingernail. "There's Baby B. His eyes there, his ears? You can't really see him on that one, but there's his head. They real big, right? That's what the doctor said, they got big heads."

With fluid movements, Jessica untied Serena's ponytail and combed out the knots with her fingers, then made a perfect topknot on the crown of her daughter's head. Rosa had little time to fuss over the girls' appearance, but Jessica had always enjoyed making her daughters pretty. Serena loved to be touched. She bit her lip and leaned into Jessica's side. Jessica rested a hand on her large belly. Serena lifted it and placed her own hand beneath.

"Mommy," Serena whispered, and reminded Jessica of what they had done when Boy George's mother brought her to visit two years before. Jessica helped Serena count the change, and then they walked over to buy a bagel from a vending machine. Serena slipped the coins in the slot and pressed the button; inmates weren't allowed to touch money.

Soon it was time for pictures. The inmate photographer suggested that they take the photographs outdoors. Ordinarily, Jessica loved having her picture taken. When George was in the M.C.C., he would say, "Baby, take a roll of thirty-six." He sent her magazine pictures of poses for her to copy. Now she seemed self-conscious and tentative. Instead of turning to the side to show off her profile, as most girls did when they were pregnant, she faced the camera. She removed her prison-issue glasses and positioned herself beside a bush. Serena looked as though she wanted to slip behind the thick, scratchy branches, but Jessica hugged her in.

"Come on," Jessica said quietly. She took Serena's hand. Serena placed her other hand on her hip and tried to smile.

AFTER the twins were born, Jessica returned to prison in a dark mood. Her feelings for Díaz had cooled. "Whatever I felt for him, it all turned dead when he didn't turn up in the hospital," she said. She was glad that she'd decided to carry the pregnancy to term, but she hardly saw her sons before Evelyn came to collect them. One of the officers who was assigned to Jessica's hospital room even confiscated the babies' footprints. Close friends knew to leave her alone. She slept a lot and refused to eat. She brooded for days at a time.

Evelyn and Lourdes had planned to raise the twins, but this arrangement soon fell apart, and the boys followed their older siblings to Rosa. But this was only Jessica's latest disappointment with her mother. Lourdes rarely visited or wrote, and she almost never sent money. When she appeared at Danbury, the summer after the boys were born, her daughter was initially less than welcoming.

"She finally getting tits," Jessica said, gazing at her mother. "Ma, you fat. You aren't just chubby, you are fat. So tell me, what, are you pregnant or is it a tumor or what?"

"I don't *know*," Lourdes said beseechingly. She pouted into her double chin. "I have to go to the doctor's. That's why I can't stay. I have to see a social worker."

"You don't need to see no social worker. You can talk to me."

"Do my hair?" Lourdes's hair was long, and when she lifted it off her neck Jessica noticed that she was wearing the gold chain with the two tiny gold boxing gloves. Jessica touched them tenderly. "He'd be surprised that I still have that," Jessica said. "Probably thinks I sold it." Then she asked Lourdes the questions she always asked. It was a litany of lost objects, as if Jessica could never accept her mother's failure to safeguard what she was holding for her. What became of the purple shearling coat? The leathers? The gold chains? The rings?

Lourdes recited her lines: "I don't know," and "I told you." She let the implication of the pauses do the work. Jessica bent forward. "Give me your earrings," she whispered. She sat back and said casually, "Let me try your earrings on."

"Be careful," Lourdes warned, glancing at the guard on duty.

"One hand washes the other," Jessica said, explaining that the guard was "a friend."

"Sometimes the right hand doesn't know what the left hand is doing," Lourdes said.

After the visit, Lourdes stood outside waiting for Jessica to be searched, so she could appear in a window for a final wave goodbye.

Lourdes retrieved a charm bracelet from her pocket and slipped it on. It was a gift from a new boyfriend, whom Jessica didn't approve of, because she'd heard he was violent. The letters spelled out "LOVE." "Good thing she didn't take this," Lourdes said. "I'd have to get another one new! See how she took my earrings like that?"

Jessica appeared. Lourdes waved. She waved with every step down the hill until she couldn't see her daughter anymore.

LITTLE JESSICA

THE longer Jessica was in prison, the more strongly she identified with her ten-year-old daughter. Although they had very little contact, she felt she could imagine what Serena was going through. In 1996, Queenie offered to tell Jessica's fortune for her birthday. She told Jessica that Serena was going to run away. "You're never gonna see her again," she warned. Jessica couldn't get Queenie's prophecy out of her head. Her mind filled with memories of herself as a teen-ager, when she had sometimes cut herself to relieve the anguish. Would things be as bad for her daughter? "Serena reminds me of me," Jessica often said.

But it was Rosa and Marisol who oversaw the girl's coming of age. In 1996, Serena learned that her favorite aunt was moving to Troy. By then, Joey was back in prison, and he had married another woman. Marisol and her children would be just four doors down from Rosa's. Serena was thrilled. On the brick wall below the white siding next to the front door, Serena chalked, in screwball script, the words "Marisol's House."

Marisol's door was always open to Jessica's kids. Marisol let Serena and her friends roller-blade around the kitchen and living room, and she would abandon her housework "like the quickness" to join the girls in double-dutch. While Marisol cooked, Serena would sit on the counter, keeping her company. They watched talk shows and traded advice. Serena complained to Marisol about Rosa's rules. Rosa's discipline seemed onerous: when Serena started developing, Rosa wouldn't allow her to wear anything tight or revealing. Marisol defended Serena: "She look beautiful. She all into her body."

"She a child, Marisol," Rosa said. "It ain't right."

By 1997, Rosa was working full-time. She needed Serena to help with her younger siblings, and Serena, now twelve, chafed at the responsibility. She was already looking eternally bored—languishing in doorways, leaning against parked cars, scuffing the dirt around the neighborhood's embattled trees. After school, whenever she could, she brought her little brothers to Marisol's house.

Marisol noted that she had inherited her mother's voluptuous body, and privately referred to her as "a little Jessica." She also served as a mail drop, relaying messages from Jessica to Serena, and providing Serena with stationery and stamps to write her mother back. More and more, the subject of boys appeared in Serena's letters, after updates on her twin sisters and brothers, and on her progress in school. In March of 1998, Serena wrote:

> I went to the store with Mommy Rosa and they'es boys was outside and kept on looking at me. So I didn't want M. Rosa to leave me by myself in the store but the baby's had to use the bathroom so she went around the corner to take them + ask me to pay for the stuff so I did, but when I came out the boys started kicking it to me you know trying to talk to me. One boy was like what's up cutie and was like hi, he was like, don't you live on 11th street, I was like no, he was like yeah you don't remember me I was riding my bike I was like no, then he ask me for the 7 digits (my #) I told him no because I am already taken. This boy was so cute. I only said that I was taken because I am not allowed to have no boyfriends. . . . This other boy try to kick it to me in front of my mother and just ignored him cause he was butt ugly. Well mommy, I gotta go I love you so very mush and of course miss you more then N-Ething.

Marisol and Rosa had the same hopes for Serena—that she not get pregnant, that she finish school, maybe even go to college—but their strategies were different. Rosa's approach was to repress all signs of womanhood, whereas Marisol thought it wiser to tell Serena the truths as she knew them. Still, Marisol found it hard to be optimistic: one of Serena's friends already had a baby, and another was expecting. "She'll come out pregnant when she's young," Marisol predicted dolefully.

WHEN Lourdes and the girls visited Jessica in the spring of 1998, eight months before her release date, she was in a sombre mood. She had been in a residential-therapy unit, and her abandonment of Serena increasingly haunted her. She worried less about the twins; they really belonged to Rosa, who had raised them since they were babies. But Serena was old enough to have memories of the early days. Jessica wondered what Serena remembered of Boy George, or of her father, Kuri, who had been shot dead around the time Jessica went to prison.

After Jessica greeted the girls, they sat together in a corner of the visiting room, and Jessica started her usual primping and grooming. She styled the twins' hair, using her fingers as a comb, and picked lint from their clothes. She noticed a plastic price-tag thread on Serena's shoe and bit it off. She braided Serena's hair and started to talk to her about the kind of night life they would share when she came home. "They gonna think we sisters. We gonna dye our hair blond. We don't have to ask anybody. I be like, 'C'mon, Serena, get dressed! We going to a club!' "

"*Ay,*" Lourdes said, but the exasperation felt fraudulent.

"You just jealous," Jessica said. When she was a teen-ager, she took her mother dancing. She made Lourdes pretend they were sisters, but the ruse wouldn't work anymore. Lourdes had aged visibly over the past several years. She lumbered instead of scurrying—circulatory problems made it hard for her to walk. Smock dresses had replaced the Lycra leggings. Hush Puppies had replaced the stiletto heels.

Serena flapped her knees distractedly. "Your legs! Keep your legs closed!" Lourdes said sharply. Serena rolled her eyes.

Jessica noticed the young son of another inmate. He stood beside another boy in front of the vending machines. "Serena, come on. Look how cute that boy is!"

"You so bad," Serena said.

"Come on! Come on! You so pretty! Look how cute he is!" Jessica pulled Serena's hand and positioned her in line. Serena bought some candy. She leaned into Jessica, shyly.

"You so bad, you so bad," Serena repeated. Jessica smiled.

STEPPING OUT

AT eight-fifty in the morning on December 17, 1998, exactly seven years after she entered prison, Jessica left the Danbury Correctional Facility. She took a bus to Port Authority and then a subway to the Bronx. She had a streak of gray in her hair and twenty-five extra pounds. She was thirty years old.

Boy George, in a maximum-security prison cell in Beaumont, Texas, said that he was happy about Jessica's freedom. "Not envious at all," he said. "I was praying for her the other day." The only thing that worried him, he said, was Jessica's susceptibility to the influence of others. "She's got to say, 'Am I gonna be a free-for-all? Or am I gonna be a person who has limits here?' Is it all about sex, Calvin Klein, is she gonna parlay with that? Or is she gonna say, 'I got five children. Now, that's a lot of children.' " He paused. "If she doesn't find the right man, she did all that time for nothing. She did that time for shit."

He said that he'd like to hear from Jessica, whom he affectionately calls "the troubled child," or "the crazy one." Boy George has written letters to Jessica in care of Lourdes, but he hasn't heard from her.

AFTER her release from prison, Jessica spent December and the early part of January, 1999, in a halfway house just north of Fordham Road, in the Bronx. The halfway house was on a block with a brisk drug trade. Jessica got a job in Yonkers at a company that raises funds for churches and schools. Toward the end of January, she was allowed to move in with her sister, Evelyn. Five months later, she got her own place, a basement apartment in the north Bronx.

Jessica met her current boyfriend, Gabriel, when she went dancing one night at Jimmy's Bronx Café. A student at John Jay College of Criminal Justice, in Manhattan, he is thirty-two, and wants to pursue a career in law enforcement. There are always going to be criminals, he says, and there will always be a need for people to catch them. Gabriel lifts weights six times a week, and his body is muscular and well defined. He works as a recreation specialist at a state park and, to supplement his income, sometimes performs as a stripper. He is polite but reserved. "He sounds Italian," Jessica says, happily. Jessica has dated other men since getting out of prison, but this is different.

Within days of their meeting, she brought Lourdes to meet him. Lourdes promptly warned him to treat Jessica properly, because "my daughter's been abused enough." She then crowned him as her son-in-law. On the ride home, when Jessica told her that Gabriel attended John Jay College, Lourdes nearly yelped. "Not everybody gets to go to that college," she shouted, as though a victory had been won. She ordered Jessica not to play head games with him.

Jessica hopes that Gabriel is the one. He calls her back when she pages him. He lets her know of his whereabouts, especially when he goes out with his friends. He writes her love notes, leaves tender messages on her answering machine, offers little gifts—a Beanie Baby, vanilla shower gel. She wants to lose the weight she gained in prison, and he has promised to help her, although he tells her that he likes her body just the way it is.

SINCE September of last year, Serena has had a boyfriend, Manuel, a slender boy with liquid eyes and a Roman nose. To Rosa's way of thinking, a nineteen-year-old with earrings and a tattoo is only interested in one thing. As soon as she found out about him, she forbade Serena to date him. "All she was doing was caring, but caring for me in the wrong way," Serena says. She and Manuel met on the sly. Serena says, "I grew to love him, I had to see him. I'd call him when she was in the bathroom, tell him, 'Meet me at Video World.' " She'd run through the housing project, taking the dirt path that led behind the dollar store, and jump into his idling Sunbird. He took her to McDonald's and treated her to her favorite Value Meal. "He always made sure I had, regardless," Serena says.

Jessica has supported the relationship between Serena and Manuel. During Christmas vacation, she arranged for a rendezvous between them in the Bronx; shortly afterward, though, Rosa learned that Serena had failed all her classes, and grounded her. Jessica and Serena commiserated on the telephone, sometimes three times a day. Friction increased between Rosa and Jessica. Marisol worries about Serena's being torn between the two, but now she has a fifth child and a full-time job, and she has little time to spare for her own children, let alone her niece.

FULL CUSTODY

IN February, Jessica filed for full custody of Serena. Rosa has not contested the application; she believes that Serena will be safe with Jessica, and Serena wants to move back to the Bronx. Last month, Jessica and Lourdes went up to Troy for the custody hearing. That morning, after Serena had put her four-year-old brothers on their school bus, she, her mother, and her grandmother watched the movie *Gremlins* in the *sala*, surrounded by mementos from birthday parties and baby showers and christenings. Serena and Jessica cuddled on the sofa. Serena had pulled her hair back loosely in a bun. She wore a black cotton peasant dress with bright embroidery trim, which Lourdes had given her. She looked the way Jessica does in a photograph taken at her baby shower, just before Serena was born.

"You didn't even notice my new tattoo," Jessica prompted Serena coyly. She lifted her chin to the light. She had a beauty mark inked above her lip, on the left, just like Marilyn Monroe.

"I told you already," Serena said, brushing her away good-naturedly.

Jessica explained that the friend who gave her the mole had promised to alter her six Boy George tattoos for free. She traced her body with her manicured fingernail, showing how she planned to cover the poem on her shoulder with a butterfly, to blacken the George from the heart on her right thigh. She wanted to get a new tattoo around her ankle: the two masks of drama, with the inscription "Cry now, laugh later," the inversion meant to celebrate her new life.

"What are you gonna be, a newspaper?" Lourdes asked.

"That's art," Jessica said.

"That's fucking disgusting," Lourdes said. "When a man kisses you—"

"If a man can't handle it, that's his problem," Jessica said.

" 'Property of George' across your ass?" Lourdes went on. She kept her eyes on the TV.

Serena and Jessica went upstairs to dress. Serena's bedroom walls were covered with magazine cutouts of Puff Daddy, Whitney Houston, Ginuwine, and Lauryn Hill. Beside them she'd hung photographs of Jessica, Evelyn, and Marisol with her children, and several drawings that Jessica sent her from prison. In one, a melancholy angel drops a handful of hearts down to earth from a cloud. On the old entertainment center that she uses as a bureau is a favor from a cousin's Sweet Sixteen: a girl in a fancy dress afloat in a champagne glass, purple and white ribbons spilling from the rim. Although Serena is only fourteen, she and Jessica have already started to plan for her party, so that they'll have time to save. Serena wants to pass out flyers the way night clubs do, and trail a banner behind a Goodyear blimp. Anything's possible, Jessica told her.

Jessica popped in a house tape she'd brought, a gift from Gabriel. Music blasted from the speakers.

"Jessica! Serena! Turn down the music!" Lourdes yelled. Then she came upstairs to join them.

Serena outfitted her grandmother in a pair of sweats, and loaned her a pair of sneakers, a gift from Manuel. He also gave Serena a necklace that reads "I Love My Baby," for Valentine's Day. Serena likes jewelry, but she has forbidden her mother to wear the necklace with the gold boxing-glove charm; she has heard about how Boy George used to mistreat Jessica, and doesn't like what it represents.

At the custody hearing, everyone agreed that Serena should finish the school year in Troy and stay on for the summer, in order to complete an internship at an educational and employment-training program for public-housing kids that Rosa steered her toward.

LOURDES was evicted from her apartment recently, and is currently camped out on a futon sofa at Jessica's, where she feels in the way. Just before Lourdes's arrival, Jessica quit her job; she says that her boss was disrespectful to her. Moreover, the hours had not been ideal. Jessica wants her next job to be strictly nine-to-five, so that it won't intrude upon her responsibilities. "When five o'clock comes," she says, "and I have to go home and cook and take care of my daughter, that's exactly what I'm going to do." Jessica says that her main concern is her family: her reunion with Serena, her relationships with Gabriel and with her other children, her mother's precarious health.

Lourdes is unsure of Jessica's future. She marvels at her daughter's ability to sustain such open faith in love: "A broken rib, that mends. A broken heart, that never mends." She is more confident about her granddaughter's prospects. If she were to tell it straight to Serena, she would say this: "Honey, the boys that are growing up now, it's only for your pussy. A girl has to be smart now. Study. Be somebody." If you're ignorant, Lourdes believes, you have to use your looks to survive, but with an education you can support yourself, men or no men. "They respect you, because they know they could lose you right there and then."

Four days a week, Serena takes the bus to her program, in downtown Troy. She drops her book bag and plunks herself down in front of a state-of-the-art computer. She spins around on the office chair as she waits for the modem to connect. Self-portraits of public-housing kids surround her, alongside African proverbs and quotations from Olive Schreiner. A poster reads, "Keep It Afloat."

Serena loves computers. Her current project involves developing her own Web site. On it, she has posted her autobiography: "My name is Serena. I am 14 years old. I am Puerto Rican, 100%. . . . My favorite subjects are English and Math. Lunch is my favorite time of the school day because I get to talk to my friends. . . .

"My birth mother was put in prison when I was five years old. . . . I decided to move with my twin sisters' godmother because they were living with her. She took me in with no problem. None of us are her real kids, but she still took all of us . . . kids in and raised us as her own. My birth mother is now out of jail, and I am moving with her in the summer to catch up on our relationship. . . .

"In the future, I would like to be a teacher. I would first like to finish high school and go on to college. When I'm done with school, I would like to work on getting a nice house and getting a good job. Then I would like to get married and have two kids, a boy and a girl. Then I just want to raise my kids. When they are all grown up, I want to travel the world.

"I want to teach kindergarten class because they are easier than older kids. I would like to go to Fordham University. It is in Bronx, NY, where I used to live."

APRIL 24, 2000

MOBY DICK IN MANHATTAN

W HEN James Wilcox is working at the St. Francis Xavier Welcome Table, as the church's Sixteenth Street soup kitchen is called, on the first and second Sunday of every month, it's hard to tell he's an acclaimed novelist. It took some of his fellow-volunteers years to figure it out. None of them had read *Modern Baptists,* his first novel, published in 1983, which was hailed in a *Times Book Review* front-page piece by Anne Tyler as "startlingly alive, exuberantly overcrowded." Nor were they familiar with its five siblings, three of them set in the fictional Tula Springs, Louisiana, which has been compared by more than one critic to William Faulkner's Yoknapatawpha County.

Wilcox himself was much too shy to tell them about any of this. He looks younger than his age, which is forty-five, and has a slightly ruddy complexion, medium build, and sandy hair. Though he's nice-looking, he agonizes over his author photographs and didn't want one on his last book. Yale-educated, he speaks with no trace of a regional accent. His Southern roots are evident only in the elaborate courtesy with which he waits on the soup kitchen's "guests," as he unfailingly calls them when he is dispensing juice and coffee. He betrays little reaction even when something really grabs his attention, like the saga of a woman who was plagued by the stench from a neighbor who kept twenty-two cats in her Murray Hill one-bedroom apartment.

"For years, I never knew what Jim did," I was told by George Deshensky, a lawyer who is one of the directors of the soup kitchen. "Then, one day, someone said, 'He's a published author.' So we'd introduce him that way. We didn't know what he published or where." Deshensky began relying on Wilcox as a "calming influence" when altercations threatened to break out in the line—something that happened with some regularity. Since then, during the eight years that Wilcox has been working at the soup kitchen, he and Deshensky have become close friends and Deshensky has read his books. Still, Deshensky was surprised when, after he complimented Wilcox on the empathy he shows for the soup kitchen's impoverished patrons, Wilcox replied, "I'm only a check or two from being in the line myself."

There have always been struggling novelists, of course, as well as a handful of best-selling, highly publicized multimillionaires. But in the past twelve years James Wilcox has published six novels to rave reviews. While his books are classified as "literary fiction" by the publishing industry, they aren't inaccessible or highbrow. He has been described as a "comic genius" (*Vogue*), "a master" (*Kirkus Reviews*), "a natural. . . . One of the most promising fiction writers on the national scene" (*Los Angeles Times*), "among the classic American humorists" (*Newsday*), and "Dickensian in [his] wealth of eccentric characters" (*New York Times*). He has a high-powered agent, Amanda (Binky) Urban, of International Creative Management, who has consistently got him advances that were larger than could be justified strictly on the basis of the number of his books sold. In other words, among novelists Wilcox counts himself one of the lucky ones. Even so, the current state of publishing has consigned him to a life of near-poverty.

At my insistence, Wilcox, who is single and lives alone, showed me his tax returns for the past ten years. His best year was 1988, when he had a gross income of $48,600 before agent commissions (of ten per cent) and expenses. He now remembers that year as an aberration—a time when he could eat out occasionally, and even take a cab. And since that time, as the market for trade-paperback fiction has shrunk and authors' advances have declined, his income has dropped accordingly. In 1992, he earned twenty-five thousand dollars. Last year, it was fourteen thousand dollars. The advance for his current novel was ten thousand dollars; in a concession, his publisher gave him two-thirds up front, rather than the customary half. When I visited him recently, he had just finished the last of three meals he'd extracted from eighteen pieces of chicken he bought at Key Food for three dollars and forty cents.

Nor is Wilcox's plight confined to making ends meet. HarperCollins, which published his last five books, didn't exercise its option for his current project. Only Hyperion, the Disney publishing subsidiary, showed any interest in the manuscript, and then mostly because Rick Kot, the editor who championed Wilcox at Harper, had recently moved to Hyperion. Hyperion is a smaller house, less able than HarperCollins to indulge a distinguished but unprofitable author. In Wilcox, commerce and art are now at a standoff, with Wilcox's future as a novelist at stake. At a time when some unpublished first novelists are igniting bidding wars and hauling down advances of half a million dollars, "we were lucky to get ten thousand dollars," Urban says of Wilcox's current contract. "This book is absolutely critical. Something has to happen."

• • •

LIKE Deshensky, I'm a friend of Jim's, who, before I began this story, had no idea of his dire financial plight. I met him a little more than a year ago, at a dinner party given by Urban to celebrate his latest novel, *Guest of a Sinner.* Urban is my agent, too, but I hadn't realized that she represented Jim until I spotted a copy of *Sort of Rich,* his fourth book, one day on her bookshelf and, because I was already a Wilcox fan, asked her to introduce me.

Sort of Rich is one of my favorite books. I bought it after reading a *Times* review, found something to think about on almost every page ("The twenty-four chicks Mrs. Dambar had purchased last week had dwindled to three as a result of an unpleasant disease and six or so getting lost on a walk she had taken them on to strengthen their leg muscles"), and returned to the bookstore a week later to buy another copy, as a gift. It was no longer in stock and wasn't being reordered—a situation that may help explain why it ultimately sold just forty-seven hundred copies in hardcover. Jim himself, I must confess, made less of an impression on me at Urban's dinner. Besides being overshadowed that night by last year's playoff between the Knicks and the Bulls, he was characteristically shy. We barely spoke. Afterward, though, he phoned and reminded me that we had actually met at a party five years before. He even remembered what we had discussed—piano playing.

Since then, we've met from time to time to play piano duets. Jim could have been a professional musician, and almost was, on both the cello and the piano. In our duets, he generally plays the more difficult "primo" parts, and, although he always maintains that he doesn't want to perform, we've given three small recitals this year. We've even joked about taking our act to the American Booksellers Association annual meeting: anything to ingratiate ourselves with—or, at least, make an impression on—booksellers. In the course of our practice sessions, I began to suspect that Jim wasn't exactly flush. He mentioned that he couldn't afford to have his piano tuned, and that, in any event, it was on loan to a friend, since he couldn't fit it into his studio apartment. Otherwise, I didn't think much about his finances; and, given Jim's nature, they are not a topic he'd ever mention. We'd sometimes eat out after our sessions, usually in modest restaurants, but once at a place that must have run forty dollars a person. Only now do I realize how that must have shattered his budget, or that he would often walk the sixty-six blocks between his apartment and mine to save the fare.

WILCOX'S first break as a writer came at Yale, when he submitted a short story to Robert Penn Warren, then on the Yale faculty, and was one of twelve students admitted to his fiction seminar. Like Warren, Wilcox hails from the South. He grew up in Hammond, Louisiana, a town of fifteen thousand, not far from Baton Rouge, where his father, James H. Wilcox, plays the French horn and headed the Music Department of Southeastern Louisiana University before he retired. At Yale, Wilcox had dabbled in theatre, at one point dancing in the aisle clad only in a fur loincloth, in an avant-garde production of Ionesco's *Rhinoceros.* But Warren's book *Understanding Fiction* has been an enduring influence on Wilcox's work. He wrote several short stories for Warren's seminar and a novel as a senior thesis. Though he was awarded honors for his effort, he was disappointed that Warren showed none of his work to his agent. But Warren did recommend Wilcox to Albert Erskine, a legendary editor at Random House, who was looking for a new assistant.

Wilcox arrived for his job interview neatly dressed and well groomed—an anomaly in 1971, when shoulder-length hair and T-shirts were the norm at Yale. Erskine, a Southerner, who had also lived in Baton Rouge, later told Wilcox he had got the job because he was the only applicant with the manners to remain standing until he was invited to sit. Erskine had worked with William Faulkner and John O'Hara. He was credited with discovering Malcolm Lowry and Eudora Welty. He edited James Michener. "It made me tremble that he'd known Faulkner," Wilcox says. He was hired, at a yearly salary of seventy-five hundred dollars.

Wilcox was plunged into the world of high-end trade publishing, writing flap copy and doing line editing, and he was gradually allowed to offer more substantive criticism. James Michener, after receiving editorial comments from Wilcox on the manuscript of his best-selling novel *Centennial,* sent Wilcox a letter telling him to call his travel agent. He invited Wilcox to go anywhere in Europe at Michener's expense; Wilcox chose Paris, and spent ten days there in 1974. At the other end of the publishing-income scale, Wilcox worked on novels by Cormac McCarthy, which sold only modestly. Even Erskine, Wilcox learned, could be taken to task for literary fiction that didn't sell. But Erskine stubbornly backed writers he believed in, and his stature enabled him to get away with it.

The job gave Wilcox plenty of insight into what worked and what didn't, in both the literary and the commercial sense. Much of his effort, like his editing of *The Save Your Life Diet,* which became a best-seller, was hardly destined for literary seminars. He advanced from editorial assistant to associate editor at Random House, and in 1977 he moved to Doubleday as an associate editor. That meant being caught up in the swirl of agent lunches, book parties, and deal-making, and also meant rising at five-thirty to read manuscripts. "It was incredibly demanding. I had no time to write," he says. His life was at least superficially glamorous. Through Random House, he had become friends with the dashing photographer, author, and Africa enthusiast Peter Beard and was invited for a pair of weekends at Beard's house in Montauk, where he and Beard discussed Conrad and Faulkner, and he found himself mingling with celebrities. He met Catherine Deneuve, Terry Southern, Margaux Hemingway; he had dinner at Mick Jagger's; he came to know Andy Warhol, and Warhol's agent, Roz Cole, agreed to represent Wilcox.

In 1978, at the age of twenty-nine, Wilcox felt that time was running out. At Random House, Toni Morrison had had the office across the hall. She'd already written two novels, and she'd encouraged Wilcox to write. At Doubleday, he was further bolstered by Jacqueline Kennedy Onassis, who also encouraged him to try writing. Though he was now making eighteen thousand dollars a year, he had no savings. He had published none of his own writing. But he knew he had to devote himself to writing full time; his efforts during nights and weekends had been both draining and unsuccessful. It took him a year to muster the courage to leave Doubleday. The first time he approached the office of the editor-in-chief, he was too nervous to go in. He circled in the hallway, mustered his courage one more time, and came back. "I couldn't go through life wondering if I could write something," he says.

In the disciplined and methodical way that is characteristic of him, Wilcox addressed himself to reducing his living expenses. He had found a twelve-by-twenty-foot studio apartment on East Twenty-fourth Street for a hundred and ninety dollars a month. It was a fourth-floor walkup and was lighted only with a bare fluorescent fixture, but the building was clean and comparatively quiet. Just then, too, he was lucky enough to sell a treatment for a screenplay he'd collaborated on with a friend from Yale. That brought in ten thousand dollars, less commissions, when it was optioned by Columbia Pictures. (It was never produced.) The money sustained him for a year.

Wilcox wrote one short story after another. He sent his manuscripts to *The New Yorker, Harper's, The Atlantic, Redbook,* and they were rejected everywhere. He began submitting them to smaller, less well-known outlets. "All I got was rejections," he says. When one story had made the rounds and come back, he sent off another. His money was running out. In 1980, he started typing address labels for a lawyer. He'd spread them out on his apartment floor, then organize them by Zip Code. He could tell that that upset his mother—the thought of her Yale-educated son on hands and knees fiddling with address labels.

He sent seven stories to *The New Yorker,* and all of them were rejected, but he was heartened by correspondence with one of its editors. His first letter from the editor, which accompanied the first rejection, was "an encouraging rejection," Wilcox says. "It was a thrill to get a real, typewritten letter from *The New Yorker.*" In response to the second story, the editor wrote at greater length, offering criticism of the work. He also commented on each of the five ensuing submissions. Finally, after a year, the editor called Wilcox to say he was accepting a story, and the magazine would pay twenty-two hundred dollars. It seemed a fortune to Wilcox.

"Mr. Ray" appeared in the January 26, 1981, issue. "The old woman had worked hard on the 'No Smoking' sign, embellishing the stark black letters with ivy and birds and a dog she forgot to put the tail on," it began. Being published in *The New Yorker* was a milestone for Wilcox—an affirmation, of sorts—

and he happily sent a copy of the magazine home to his parents. But the piece didn't exactly cause a stir in Hammond, Louisiana. "Jimmy sure has good punctuation" was one neighbor's only comment. Another, pointing to an unrelated cartoon on one page, asked, "Where did Jimmy learn to draw like that?"

"Mr. Ray" is set in the fictional town of Tula Springs, Louisiana, and that aspect of the story had drawn approving comment from the editor. After the story was accepted, but before it was published, Wilcox began a novel set in Tula Springs. He wrote the first half in six months, while living on the money from "Mr. Ray." Since Cole was no longer representing him, he offered the unfinished manuscript to another agent; after reading it, the agent said he couldn't sell it. Wilcox was discouraged, but a little later a friend read it and said it was funny. Wilcox persevered for another year, and in June of 1982 he finished the book, which he had entitled *Modern Baptists*. He offered it to two more agents, and both rejected it as unsalable. Then Harriet Wasserman, an independent agent, agreed to handle it. Knopf, Simon & Schuster, and Viking all turned it down.

Rick Kot, then a young editor at the Dial Press, heard about *Modern Baptists* from another editor, who said he had read it and had hated to turn it down, but it was a comic first novel—a tough sell. Kot called Wasserman and asked for the manuscript. Though he liked it, he was cautious about publishing it. "It's always a gamble publishing a first novel," Kot says. "With a comic novel, it's an even bigger gamble. It's a marketing truism that the sense of humor is very subjective. Comedy is a very tough category. *Modern Baptists* fitted the convention of Southern humor, but it was more serious, more ambitious." The *New Yorker* story offered confirmation that Wilcox had talent. Though Kot had concentrated on nonfiction, he offered sixty-five hundred dollars for the book, and, not surprisingly, since that was the only offer, it was accepted.

The main characters in *Modern Baptists* are Bobby Pickens (always known as Mr. Pickens), a forty-one-year-old bachelor who works at the Sonny Boy Bargain Store, and F.X., his improbably handsome half brother, who has just been released from Angola State Penitentiary after serving time for dealing cocaine at a nearby dinner-theatre-in-the-round.

At one point, Mr. Pickens, who has fallen in love with a young employee at the Bargain Store named Toinette Quaid, aspires to the cloth:

> Mr. Pickens knew that once he got his preaching diploma, he would open a church for modern Baptists, Baptists who were sick to death of hell and sin being stuffed down their gullets every Sunday. There wasn't going to be any of that old-fashioned ranting and raving in Mr. Pickens's church. *His* Baptist church would be guided by reason and logic. Everyone could drink in moderation. Everyone could dance and pet as long as they were fifteen—well, maybe sixteen or seventeen. At thirty, if you still weren't married, you could sleep

with someone and it wouldn't be a sin—that is, as long as you loved that person. If you hit forty and were still single, you'd be eligible for adultery not being a sin, as long as no children's feelings got hurt and it was kept very discreet. But you still had to love and respect the person; you couldn't just do it for sex.

However, upon being spurned by Toinette Mr. Pickens finds himself alone with Toinette's chunky friend Burma LaSteele:

He stood before her in his new orange bikini briefs and his matching orange undershirt. His belly button was plainly visible; the underwear was two sizes too small.

"Why pretend?" Mr. Pickens said, pulling the T-shirt over his head. His white hairless chest swelled out into a sizable belly, from which Burma averted her eyes. . . .

"Mr. Pickens," Burma said, turning away. "Please, get dressed. You're drunk."

"This is your chance, Burma. Why blow it? You're getting old—there's gray in your hair, gray in mine. We're going to die, all of us, we're going to die miserable, unloved. I can't stand it anymore. At least one of us can be happy. You, Burma. You be happy. You deserve it more than any of us. You're good, Burma. You're a good, good woman. I can see your heart. It's pure and unselfish and good." Tears ran down his cheeks and his nose began to run. "Take it. Grab life before it passes you by." He stepped out of the briefs, and she beheld him stark naked, except for his left sock, the one with the hole in it, which he had forgotten to take off.

Kot says that *Modern Baptists* needed little editing—given Wilcox's own editing background, his manuscripts are meticulously written—but he insisted that Wilcox rewrite the ending. "He had Mr. Pickens die in a train wreck, which violates every convention of comedy," he explains. So Mr. Pickens' car runs out of gas as he tries to commit suicide by crashing into a telephone pole.

Shortly after Kot finished the editing, early in 1983, he was fired—not for signing up books like *Modern Baptists* but as part of a sweeping cost-cutting campaign that accompanied the consolidation of Dial into its owner, Doubleday. Fortunately, a surviving editor at Dial, Allen Peacock, liked *Modern Baptists* and kept it alive. The publicist for Dial was also enthusiastic about the book, and she had a good track record with reviewers. Positive blurbs were rounded up from prominent writers, including Robert Penn Warren and Brendan Gill. The book soon developed the momentum of a modest hit. In its Forecasts section, *Publishers Weekly*, the trade bible, gave *Modern Baptists* a "boxed" review—one that not only was favorable but put booksellers on notice that *Modern Baptists* could be a hit. The book was published in June, 1983.

Then, in mid-July, rumor had it that Anne Tyler, a "hot" novelist on the heels of the huge success of *Dinner at the Homesick Restaurant*, was reviewing the book for the *Times*. Many books are review-proof, and their publishers can afford to be indifferent to the *Times*, but literary fiction like Wilcox's lives or dies on the strength of its Sunday *Times* review.

On July 31st, on the *Book Review*'s front page—the most coveted position in the book industry, one that Kot says many writers would "give their right arm for"—Tyler wrote, "Every reviewer, no doubt, has methods for marking choice passages in a book. Mine is a system of colored paper clips; yellow means funny. *Modern Baptists* should be thick with yellow paper clips on every page, but it does even better than that. While I was reading it, I laughed so hard I kept forgetting my paper clips. Mr. Wilcox has real comic genius. He is a writer to make us all feel hopeful."

The review was a godsend, triggering a wave of favorable reviews, from nearly every major paper. Wilcox had a brush with celebrity when a producer for Barbara Feldon (Agent 99 of *Get Smart*) called to say that Ms. Feldon might be interested in having Wilcox as a guest on her cable-TV talk show. Hollywood was said to be interested in the screen rights. It was, of course, dizzying to be the subject of so much acclaim so soon—especially for someone as modest as Wilcox. "He was thrilled, or what passes for thrilled with Jim," Kot says. "He said something like 'Oh, gosh.' " Wilcox never inquired about the size of the first printing ("I didn't want to know; I assume it was low," he says), which was five thousand copies. The book went back to press four times, and ultimately sold eleven thousand copies in hardcover. The Literary Guild optioned it. Penguin bought the paperback rights, for ten thousand dollars. It was published in the United Kingdom. For his next novel, Wasserman was able to negotiate an advance of $27,500. Dial bid on it, but Harper & Row, which had meanwhile hired Kot as an editor, outbid Dial. Wilcox dared to believe that his future as a novelist was secure. He stopped writing short stories.

Having read the first hundred pages of the new manuscript, Kot had high hopes for it. "It was a coup to get him," he says. "I saw a writer with a promising career, someone we wanted to develop. I loved his work and liked him personally. Harper wanted to do more literary fiction." As it happened, literary fiction was driving what was then the hottest category in publishing—trade paperbacks. The runaway success of Jay McInerney's *Bright Lights, Big City*, which was originally published in trade paperback rather than hardback, had publishers scrambling to develop their own lists of hot novels in that large-type, softcover format, which typically sold at about half the hardcover price, rather than the one-fifth to one-fourth charged for mass-market paperbacks. In the past, trade publishers had typically auctioned reprint rights to paperback publishers and split the ensuing royalties with the author; that was what had been done with *Modern Baptists*. But because costs for trade paperbacks were only slightly higher than those for mass-market paperbacks, they could be profitable with even relatively modest sales. The Harper deal for Wilcox's new book included both hardcover and softcover royalties, a so-called hard-soft deal, which has now become commonplace.

Wilcox's second novel, *North Gladiola*, was published in 1985. Its heroine, Ethyl Mae Coco, is the prime suspect in the murder of Tee-Tee, a chihuahua belonging to the Tula Springs beauty college—and Mrs. Coco had, in fact, once thrown a pan of lukewarm bacon grease on Tee-Tee. Kot's main concern was to build on Wilcox's audience for *Modern Baptists* and avoid the notorious "sophomore slump" that has felled numerous promising first novelists. He was quickly reassured. The novelist Bobbie Ann Mason hailed *North Gladiola* as "a scream." Reviews were again enthusiastic, though the *Times Book Review* didn't again give it the front page. There were no author tours, however, and no bookstore readings. Not every review was positive. After Harper's publicity department sent Wilcox a copy of a negative review, he asked that only positive reviews be sent him. Harper complied, but one negative review slipped through, leaving Wilcox much upset.

Ominously, sales of *North Gladiola* fell well below those for *Modern Baptists*. It never came close to "earning out" the advance, as the publishers' phrase has it. Wilcox could barely bring himself to look at the royalty statement. "I'd open it and sort of squint at it," he says. "All I saw was a minus. Then I filed it away." He was concerned. "The momentum of *Modern Baptists* was being rapidly lost," he says. Like many authors, he began to wonder if his agent—Wasserman—was the best agent for him. "A movie deal fizzled out, even though there seemed to be a lot of interest," he says. "I like and respect Harriet, but I wanted more to happen." Though it was painful, Wilcox severed his ties to Wasserman. Then he called Urban, who had been recommended by colleagues, and who had had great success with literary fiction, representing, among others, Jay McInerney and Bret Easton Ellis. Urban loved *Modern Baptists* and *North Gladiola*, and agreed to represent him.

Despite the weak sales of "North Gladiola," Urban negotiated Wilcox's best deal yet—a two-book contract for seventy thousand dollars. That advance largely accounts for Wilcox's peak earnings of $48,600 in 1988. In 1987, when the first of the two manuscripts came in, *Miss Undine's Living Room*, in which Olive Mackie runs for superintendent of Tula Springs' Department of Streets, Parks, and Garbage, Kot had the first serious problems he'd encountered in Wilcox's work. An ensemble of characters, none of them particularly sympathetic, flew in the face of literary convention. Kot invited Wilcox to dinner to discuss possible solutions.

"With *Miss Undine*, Rick was very clear," Wilcox says. "After I turn in a manuscript, Rick takes me out to a nice dinner. We've been to Union Square Café, Bouley. It's a shame, really—the only time I get to go to these places, I'm too nervous to eat. He didn't like any of the *Miss Undine* characters. He said there was no center."

Wilcox considered Kot's criticism. But his mild demeanor conceals a strong will. "Maybe I've read too many positive novels with wonderful characters," Wilcox says. "I've read genre fiction. I read Judith Krantz when I was at Doubleday. The main characters are always rugged and handsome if they're men and gorgeous and buxom if they're women. They have a drive to succeed, and they do succeed. They forge ahead in life. Why can't I write about more heroic characters?" He answers his own question. "I'm not a positive thinker. Southerners tend not to be. Faulkner, Welty, O'Connor—they're in the tradition of Hawthorne or Melville. There is depravity. We're not good people unless we really try. Popular fiction is Emersonian. He transcends the dark side of human nature. Self-reliance. We can become better people. I don't subscribe to this. The sense of reconciliation readers want is not that easily won. Unearned idealism usually does more harm than good. I absorbed this from Robert Penn Warren. He wrote a poem about a night flight to New York in which he thought about Emerson at thirty-eight thousand feet, the point being that at that distance from life you can indulge in Emerson's view of human perfectibility. I don't see Olive as positive or negative. We're all pretty mixed bags. Our faults are very much tied in to our virtues. Most of our lives are not weddings, funerals, and crises. We're not in a plane that's about to crash, and we're not about to launch a new line of high-fashion clothing. We mostly have routine days. We can't see where we're going. I've heard the most interesting things standing in the checkout line at Wal-Mart." Wilcox declined to make any significant changes in *Miss Undine*.

Wilcox's world view may have been reinforced one evening soon after he put the finishing touches on that book. At a dinner party he attended, he bit into a piece of chicken and broke off a crown from a tooth. As he was walking home, castigating himself for having gone to a cut-rate dental clinic (his "dentist," actually a student, had received a failing grade for the crown installation), an attractive couple, walking arm in arm, approached him. They told him they had a weapon, then mugged him. In addition to his cash and credit cards, they stole his crown, which he'd carefully kept in his pocket. The new crown set him back eight hundred dollars.

Then he received a letter from the Internal Revenue Service announcing that he was being audited for his 1985 income, of $11,800. In addition to examining all of Wilcox's banking records, the auditor, obviously suspecting that Wilcox was hiding income, insisted on visiting his apartment. Wilcox deducted a third of his annual rent, because he had divided his small studio space into three areas—a sleeping area, a sitting area, and a work space. The auditor examined the table where Wilcox worked—which, given the size of the apartment, was close to the refrigerator—and accused Wilcox of eating there. Wilcox said he didn't ("It's much too depressing to eat next to the typewriter"), but the auditor argued that he *could* eat there, so the area wouldn't count as an office. It also lacked a solid wall, which would have cut off his view of both windows. The auditor found no undeclared income, but did disallow Wilcox's home-office deduction, which came to four hundred dollars. "He seemed very respectful," Wilcox says of the auditor, who had admitted that this audit was his first assignment for the I.R.S. "He didn't make me feel creepy, like a tax cheat, which I guess he could have."

Miss Undine was published three weeks later. (A dental college figures prominently in the plot.) Some readers and reviewers have said it's their favorite among his works. The reviews were almost uniformly positive. But the influential Michiko Kakutani, in the daily *Times*, sided with Kot, noting the lack of positive characters. Sales slipped to five thousand copies.

Sort of Rich, Wilcox's next novel, which came out in 1989, brought a New Yorker, the newly married Gretchen Dambar, to Tula Springs, which somehow reminded her of both Baroness Blixen's African farm and Parsippany, New Jersey. Kot thought it Wilcox's best work—"a close to perfect novel." In an effort to boost sales, Wilcox attended the American Booksellers Association annual meeting, in Washington, D.C., and he was featured at a Harper luncheon for literary novelists. He was also sent to bookstores for readings and did a brief tour of the South. He got a television booking on a 6 A.M. show in New Orleans. A painfully small crowd showed up for autographs in Jackson, Mississippi. The reviews were very positive. But sales slipped again.

By now, Wilcox couldn't bring himself even to open his royalty statements. "They're very depressing," he says. None of the advances had earned out since *Modern Baptists.* "I'd really been hoping to earn out with *Sort of Rich,*" he says. "I knew that the publishers were paying out more than they were making. I was doing the best I could. This isn't a good situation. I'd love them to see some benefit from all they'd done for me. This was hard on me. I felt they were all hoping something would happen."

Kot and Urban talked, and agreed that something had to change in order for Wilcox to "break out" from sales of fewer than five thousand hardcover copies. On the strength of the manuscript for *Sort of Rich,* Urban had negotiated a new, forty-five-thousand-dollar, one-book deal. But Wilcox had now done four novels set in Tula Springs. No momentum was building. No one told Wilcox this in so many words, but when he himself suggested a change of pace from Tula Springs both Kot and Urban were enthusiastic. He decided to bring some of his characters to New York.

"I hate to be so marketing-driven," Kot says. "But we had to get a handle for Jim. The big-selling novelists, like McInerney, were tapping very specific markets. Young. Urban. David Leavitt had the first gay short story in *The New Yorker.* They were generating extra-book publicity. What could we put Jim forward as?"

Without such publicity, the once promising market for literary fiction was faltering. Nan A. Talese, who publishes literary fiction as the president of her own imprint at Doubleday, says, "There are four thousand serious book buyers in this country that you can count on for literary fiction. That's your basic number, including libraries, if there isn't a bell or a whistle, like having a very beautiful author do a tour across the country without any clothes on. That's how we're selling books these days." At the same time, the trade-paperback fiction market had become saturated. Even as hardcover sales were fading, so was the Wilcox backlist. As computers proliferated in bookstores, the Harper sales force was growing more discouraged about Wilcox's prospects. "They'd look on their computers and see that his last book only sold three, so they'd say, 'We'll only take two this time,' " Kot says. "The sales force was grumbling mildly, saying it was getting harder and harder to get his books out in stores."

Kot was enthusiastic about the new book. It had a great title, something much more contemporary—*Polite Sex*. F.X., the handsome miscreant from *Modern Baptists*, made a reappearance. Kot pitched the book to the sales force as "Wilcox comes to New York." For the book, he hoped for a bigger urban sale. He commissioned distinctive new cover art, which won an award for graphic design. Harper managed to get seventy-five hundred copies into stores. *Time* asked for a photograph of Wilcox in anticipation of a major review.

But publication day came and went, and no major review appeared. The "news" that Wilcox had moved his setting to New York made no waves. Not only did *Polite Sex* fail to attract the urban readers Kot and Urban had hoped for but it seemed to alienate his core group of Southerners. Despite consistently favorable reviews, Wilcox's fifth book sold worse than any of the previous ones.

Kot called Urban. "I said, 'Binky, we only sold three thousand. I can't afford to pay any more. We have to be realistic." He reminded her that Harper (now HarperCollins, as a result of a merger) had kept all Wilcox's books in print, even buying backlist rights to *Modern Baptists*. Kot offered twenty thousand dollars for Wilcox's next book—half his prior advance. Urban knew she couldn't sell Wilcox on the open market after the numbers on *Polite Sex*, and, besides, she was not thrilled with the new book, which Wilcox was already writing. She worried—even as she remained convinced that Wilcox had the potential to produce a huge success—that his writing was becoming too serious, too inward, increasingly esoteric. Wilcox took the twenty thousand dollars, happy to be able to keep writing.

There was a quiet sense of dread about Wilcox's sixth novel, *Guest of a Sinner*, which was published last year. Inspired in part by the woman with twenty-two cats he'd heard about at the soup kitchen, it is darker, more complex, than the earlier books. "After his father had swerved into a tree to avoid hitting a squirrel," one passage goes, "Eric had never once, in the fifteen years since, questioned if the squirrel's life was worth his mother's. Not out loud, at least. Mrs. Thorsen had been killed, while Lamar, properly buckled up, had survived without a scratch. Eric's mother always refused on principle to wear a seat belt, mainly because she thought it was the liberals who made its use a law, but also because it wrinkled her clothes." Kot was concerned because Eric, the main character, is less likable at the end of the story than at the beginning. And, though nothing seems forced or didactic, the book does have weighty themes of religion and faith. Worse, it proved impossible to describe the plot to the sales force, let alone give the book a marketing "handle."

Guest sold four thousand copies. For his latest book, Kot has offered Wilcox ten thousand dollars. "What was I going to do?" Kot asks. "I'd given it our best shot. We had to get a lower advance."

THE economics of literary fiction are stark. Consider the cost to HarperCollins of publishing *Guest*. While specific numbers are closely guarded, several people with access to HarperCollins' results provided this summary. Every book has a fixed "plant cost," which covers copy editing, setting type, proofs and proofreading—about ten thousand dollars for *Guest*. Added to that is the "PPB" (printing, paper, and binding), a variable cost, depending on the number printed; a press run of six thousand for *Guest* added about nine thousand dollars. Marketing expenses, which in the case of *Guest* included advertising (a one-fifth-page ad in the *Times Book Review* cost five thousand dollars), author touring, and posters, came to just over ten thousand dollars. The advance added twenty thousand dollars. And before any of these costs are covered, twenty-five per cent of gross sales goes to general overhead. Six thousand copies of *Guest*, retailing at twenty dollars, would yield $57,600 in gross sales to HarperCollins (retailers and middlemen keep just over half the cover price), so a charge for general overhead would be $14,400. Thus, total costs were approximately $63,000. *Guest* yielded no subsidiary-rights revenues. (In a hard-soft deal, the paperback edition is accounted for separately.) At four thousand hardcover copies sold, *Guest* produced about $38,000 in revenue to HarperCollins, leaving a deficit of $25,000. HarperCollins aims for a fifteen-per-cent return on investment, which means that *Guest* would have had to sell more than seven thousand copies to generate the roughly $73,000 necessary to meet that standard.

Given the way that the publishing industry allocates costs—particularly the practice of assigning an arbitrary percentage of gross sales to cover general overhead—it's easy to see the appeal of the blockbuster. A novel that sells a hundred thousand copies may never pay back its advance yet can be solidly profitable. Those are the books that generate the large revenues for general overhead, which includes, among other things, the editors' salaries.

But what about the speculative first novels that, with no author track record whatsoever, can command astronomical advances? Lately, people in the publishing industry have been buzzing about *The Day After Tomorrow*, a first novel by Allan Folsom published this spring by Little, Brown, which brought a two-million-dollar advance. That money could more than sustain Wilcox for the rest of his natural life. Nan Talese explains, "The first novel that is sexy or

promotable, or has just been sold to the movies, can get a huge advance, because it's something new," and she points out that *The Day After Tomorrow*,
the work of a Hollywood scriptwriter, had been pre-sold to the movies. "You
know how Americans are about 'new.' There's no track record for the bookstores to pull up and say, 'That author only sold five thousand copies.' They see
that the publisher has a lot at stake and is really going to get behind this, touring the writer, making special galleys, and so on. That's the plan." This strategy has been fuelled by the success of novels like *Damage*, by Josephine Hart,
and *The Secret History*, by Donna Tartt, both sexy first novels with attractive
authors which were enormously profitable despite large advances. "It's a very
odd atmosphere," Talese says. "Publishers are willing to gamble lots of money
on something that might hit big, but more hesitant to invest smaller sums and
stay with an author as he or she builds an audience."

Who knows whether *The Day After Tomorrow* will change that thinking.
A *Times* critic dismissed it, noting that "the author has a great deal to learn."
The book's jacket copy claims that it "reinvents the thriller." It does not say
what the book is actually about: an international conspiracy to clone Hitler
from his frozen head. Although ads have touted it as a "No. 1 National Best-
Seller," the book recently dropped off the *Times* best-seller list after eight weeks,
never having reached the top spot.

Brand-name fiction writers remain the safest commercial bets, even though
they, too, can command huge advances. Bill Shinker, who until recently was
the publisher of HarperCollins, says, "You know that on a Sidney Sheldon or a
Barbara Taylor Bradford there's no way in hell the advance will ever pay out.
You can still make money. Those authors will sell at such a predictably high
level that it will cover a lot of overhead. Wilcox is a labor of love. He's never
going to pay your overhead."

But even a labor of love—and Shinker says he loves Wilcox's fiction—can't
go on indefinitely. "After one or two books, we saw a pattern emerging. He
wasn't alone in this. Trade paperbacks that once sold in multiples of what the
book sold in hardcover were now selling half the hardcover sales. A very sad
development, but we were up against it."

Even though Kot moved to Hyperion in 1993, HarperCollins did make a bid
under its contract option for Wilcox's next work. It was low—seventy-five
hundred dollars. "We felt we'd got into a rut with Jim," Shinker says. "I had no
explanation for why the books weren't performing. He had fabulous reviews
but never the sales to live up to them. The kind of fiction he was writing, there
might have been a time in the sixties or seventies when he would have sold in
mass-market paperback. But taste has changed. Today, multicultural, black,
Hispanic, Japanese—that's the trend. The books that Jim did, as good as they
are, fell through the cracks."

Shinker felt that HarperCollins had to make a bid that stood a chance of
earning out. "God bless him if he goes someplace else" is what Shinker says he

felt. "Maybe they'll bring a fresh eye and can do something. It's frustrating when you like somebody's work and you can't make it happen for them."

WILCOX has struggled with his current novel, in part because of the mounting pressure he feels from his publisher and his agent. After *Guest*, Urban took him to lunch for a serious talk. (He can't bring himself to discuss money with Kot.) She said he had to consider his audience. "A problem with selling his books is who will buy them," she says. "That's what a bookseller asks. Literary fiction is not selling well. You need a target market. Women buy books, but his aren't women's books. It's pathetic. Why can't you just write good books? But there's too much competition for people's attention. I told him, 'We have to have something.' "

Urban's message got through. Wilcox is a great fan of the English novelist Barbara Pym, a brilliant writer of small-scale social comedy, and he is haunted by the knowledge that Pym wrote six published novels and the seventh was turned down. She spent the next sixteen years writing unpublished novels, and was rediscovered only at the end of her life, when the London *Times Literary Supplement* hailed her as one of the most underappreciated novelists of the twentieth century. Wilcox's first instinct was to go back to *Modern Baptists*; after all, it had sold reasonably well. He thought he might do a more comic, slapstick story of a New Yorker who returns to his Southern roots. He tried a short story in that vein, written in the first person, and sent it to *The New Yorker*. It was rejected. He tried about sixty pages of a novel, and sent them to Urban and Kot. He could tell they were cool. Urban told him it seemed forced; it wasn't funny. "I've never worked so hard starting a book," he says. "My advance was going down. It was a difficult time for me. I was very aware of the need for an audience. I don't want to be like Barbara Pym—I want to sell this to someone."

Then something new came to him. In *Guest of a Sinner*, a minor character had come to terms with being gay and had begun having an affair with a garbageman. Wilcox found himself pondering the possibility of a relationship between a gay man and a straight man—not a sexual affair but a coming together on common ground of two people who didn't share the same sexuality. He mentioned this idea to Kot, who remembers Wilcox describing it as "a comic *Death in Venice*."

Kot was excited. "I could play this, run with this," he says. "It sounded like fun." A comic *Death in Venice* might not exactly fly off shelves, but the phrase was *something*—it was a "handle" for the sales force. Mann's classic novella had a beautiful young male character that might appeal to a gay audience, yet the novella as a whole appealed to mainstream readers and it inspired both a movie and an opera. With the Pulitzer Prize–winning *A Thousand Acres*, the novelist Jane Smiley had just scored with a *King Lear* in Iowa.

Was a comic *Death in Venice* any less probable? Hyperion's publicity people loved it. Urban, too, liked the idea. Kot could sell his new publisher, Hyperion, a fresh approach to Wilcox. It gave him the ammunition to outbid Harper-Collins and continue editing Wilcox. Even without a finished manuscript or an outline, Hyperion committed itself to publishing it, albeit with a small advance and little money at risk. The initial contract explicitly referred to the work as "a comic updating of *Death in Venice.*" The marketing idea was to graft a gay audience onto Wilcox's existing readers.

No one knows how large the gay book-buying audience is. Kot says that a successful nonfiction book on a gay theme can sell twenty-five thousand copies; Randy Shilts sold many more. "It's well defined," Urban says. "Publishers can market, sell, advertise to this audience. This is an audience that could support Jim's books. It has developed in the last few years. It's strong. We have to have *something.*"

But Wilcox's shrinking advance has, somewhat perversely, diminished rather than heightened his commercial sensibility. "It's so little money that I'm going to write this exactly the way I want," he says now of his new book. "I feel a burden has been lifted. When I was getting the pages together, I was worried. Can Binky sell this? Now I know it's never going to be a big commercial book. In a way, I'm much happier."

The first sign that Wilcox might not play along with the new "gay" marketing scenario came when he crossed out the reference to "a comic updating of *Death in Venice* before signing his new contract. "This thing just got out of hand," he says. "I never said it was a comic *Death in Venice.* I said it was a comic *reversal* of *Death in Venice,* and even that's inappropriate. All Hollywood wants is high concept. That means you can describe it in one sentence. *Twins* is what you get. That whole mentality has become a part of publishing. It's sold before you write it. Reviewers review the concept, not the book. That's why first novelists are getting five hundred thousand dollars. I worry about these marketing categories, trying to define things. Can't people just be people? I don't want it marketed as a gay novel. People hear 'gay' and they think 'sex.' If this were commercial, there'd be Big Sex. Well, there's no sex. None. The gay man is unattractive, a little overweight. He can't get a date. He's a Catholic." Worse, from a commercial perspective, the beautiful young man, the Tadzio of *Death in Venice,* has vanished. The main characters are now aged seventy and forty-one. "Tell the sales force it's going to be *Moby Dick* in Manhattan," he says of his new novel. "Maybe they can sell that."

WILCOX now adheres as strictly as he can to a hundred-dollar-a-week budget. He almost never buys clothes. He owns one suit, which is five years old. His blue denim shirt he bought on the sidewalk for five-ninety-nine. A blue chambray shirt was bought at a bargain store on Third Avenue. ("It's amazing the bargains you can find in Manhattan," he says.) For a while, he had a queen-sized bed, but he tired of having to turn sideways to get into the bathroom. Now he sleeps on a worn brown velour sofa bed, a friend's castoff. He has just bought a used air-conditioner. He does his own laundry (a dollar-fifty a load) and ironing. He tries not to eat out, and he never takes cabs. When he's working on early drafts of his novels at his electric typewriter, he uses non-self-correcting ribbons; he switches to the more expensive self-correcting ribbons only for the final draft. Despite all these efforts, though, he has lately had to borrow money from his parents to pay his rent, now four hundred dollars a month—something he hates to do. He has lost all confidence that his future as a novelist is secure.

The most recent advance has left Wilcox no choice but to supplement his income. Last semester, he taught a fiction-writing seminar at the Camden campus of Rutgers University. That brought in $5,700. Unfortunately, the train fare to and from Philadelphia caused him to run up fourteen hundred dollars in not yet reimbursed charges on his Visa card, which contributed to a recent cash crisis. He appeared as an extra in a Macy's television commercial for a hundred dollars. He has just completed a piece for *Allure* on the difficulties of being a handsome man. He sees it as research for a character in his new novel, and he's grateful for the assignment. The piece, if it runs, will bring in four thousand dollars, nearly half his last book advance.

There is no bitterness in Wilcox, no sense that life or the publishing industry has treated him unfairly. On the contrary, in many ways Wilcox seems to be living the life he always wanted—that of the artist. He grew up in a musical family, steeped in the lore of Mozart, the archetype of the struggling genius. "He is essentially romantic," the writer Gene Stone, a friend of Wilcox's, told me. "This is how a serious novelist is supposed to live. He may be the last of his kind in America." Yet nearly all his closest friends say they have now detected in him a worrisome level of anxiety about his financial plight. "There are days when he's frustrated and nearly in tears," Stone said, and Polly King, another friend, observed, "He lives in his own private hell of worry."

Wilcox concedes as much, yet brushes aside such concerns. "Publishing is filled with ups and downs," he says. "I know that. I feel, frankly, very fortunate to be able to write, to have the time and the means. It's almost beyond my wildest dreams. Writing a novel was the be-all and end-all for me. When I thought I could live on advances, after the Anne Tyler review, I was thrilled. Now it's going downhill, but I still feel lucky to be under contract. I'll do whatever I have to do to make money and keep writing."

Ultimately, he says, he's sustained by his readers, however small a group they may be. "Comedy is very mysterious. I'm thankful some people find what I'm doing amusing." He gets a small but steady stream of fan mail, from such improbable places as Montana and Indiana. He showed me one letter, from a reader in Canada, dated June 28, 1989:

Dear James,

It has been a day. And now I can't sleep. I am dying for a glass of lemonade but of course I have no lemons or fake stuff, even, to make it with. Instead I have a cup of iced tea which is probably unhealthy to drink at this time of night. . . .

I was lying in bed trying to sleep—my husband's asleep, my coming little baby in my stomach (I'm five months pregnant) is asleep, my three cats are asleep, my old daddy, who lives in the apartment upstairs since my mom died four years ago, had another heart attack tonight—his second in two months, this one is worse, they say—and so I'm worried and thirsty and tired.

Which does bring me to why I'm telling you this. . . . I'm clutching to the things that I love. And I love your books. Tonight when I couldn't sleep I thought I would read a book—so I went to my bookshelves and started scanning titles—I came to your three books which I've read at least twice each (though I don't usually do that). Anyway—please write another novel fast because I can't sleep (and even if I could I wouldn't if I had one of your books to read afresh). Is that a lot to ask? I'd do the same for you. Is it very hot where you are? My air conditioner's coming Thursday.

Yours sincerely . . .

JUNE 27, 1994

BILL BUFORD

SWEAT IS GOOD

A THURSDAY morning in March, just before six. The city unseasonably balmy, T-shirt weather, a breeze coming off the Hudson. I'm standing on the corner of Ninth Avenue and Thirty-ninth Street, near the Port Authority bus terminal. This is the industrial heart of the Garment District, a metaphorical ribbon that stretches halfway across the middle of Manhattan. On one side is Bryant Park, now the site of the spring and autumn fashion shows, when the park fills up with billowing white tents—the sexiest, weirdest free show in town, if you're a journalist or in the business. To the west, around Seventh, you find the fashion houses themselves, track lighting and blond wood partially in view from the street. One block more, Eighth Avenue, and it's clamor, not glamour—the factories that make the clothes. For all the upheaval in the garment industry, it's remarkable that in this part of the city so little has changed in the hundred years since the first boom of immigrants—four million Germans, Italians, Eastern Europeans—made it the largest concentration of clothing manufacturers in the world. It makes sense that the essential labor would be the same; no one has yet figured out how to replace the sewing machine. But so, too, is the way it's paid for—by the piece. In the nineteenth century, completed garments were delivered down the middle of the street by "push boys"; today they're called "floor guys." And, perhaps most surprising, the number employed in the nineteen-nineties is roughly the same as it was in the eighteen-nineties—about eighty-five thousand, although today those eighty-five thousand are scattered around the five boroughs, each, it seems, with its own ethnic constituency and its own expertise: evening dresses in the Garment District, say; trousers ("bottoms") in Chinatown; T-shirts, sweatshirts, and, for that matter, just about anything else in Brooklyn's Sunset Park.

On the corner where I'm standing, a Mexican man and his daughter are removing heavy paper sacks from the back of a battered station wagon. The
sacks are steaming with roasted corn. Behind them is a familiar immigrant
business: "*Envíos de Dinero*," the display says (money transfers)—"México,
Ecuador, El Salvador, República Dominica." In the windows are help-wanted
ads. "*Aviso necesitamos operarias para cover stitches con Singer machines.*" Machine operators needed. "*Se necesita un planchador con experiencia.*" An experienced presser.

I'm here to meet Marlon Persaud, a man who runs a cutting factory. Six in
the morning was the only time when he said he might be free, and in fact, of the
many "contractors" I've approached, Marlon is the only one prepared to see
me so far. The garment business has become the enterprise that everyone loves
to hate, and its members, adopting a practice of talking to no one but their own
kind, have actively retreated from view. From where I'm standing, the business
looks like an easy one to dislike. The buildings nearby have all the charm of
rusting fishing trawlers. They are monstrosities of fifteen, twenty floors; the
windows are painted black or blocked out by plywood. What, you find yourself
thinking, is there to hide? The few windows not blocked out are caked with filth
and reveal little: stacks of fabric, or boxes and boxes of something—buttons,
perhaps, or plastic zippers. Bits of plumbing and precarious electrical wiring
wander across the outside like some kind of mechanical spider's web, a mish-
mash mess broken up by an occasional ventilation fan (a *very* occasional ventilation fan). You look at these buildings and wonder why, in modern
Manhattan, they are still standing. But, here at 6 A.M., I see that they are very
much in use.

Across from me, people are appearing in clusters, slipping past a door protected by a husky man to keep out unwanted intruders. Inside, they will be expected to work at the concentrated fury that's a feature of piecework. In fact,
their labor is a factory owner's only real expense—these are not high-capital
enterprises—and one of the frustrations of the Department of Labor is that any
business caught violating the employment laws can close overnight and re-
open down the street with a different name. There is always space, and the
sewing machines and cutting tables are all easily available for purchase secondhand, as any tour of these streets reveals. And of course everyone knows
everyone else. Many garment factories are run by the people who found their
first employment in them. Illegal immigrants become legal immigrants become
entrepreneurs. Or, put another way, the exploited become the exploiters. One
block from where I'm standing, a factory will lock up its doors later today, its
principal creditor being its employees: they are owed a hundred thousand dollars. The irony is that the owner—a Korean woman, now hiding in her home,
refusing to answer the phone—was running a legal factory: she paid a minimum wage, kept time cards, paid overtime. She just didn't have enough to pay
what she was paying.

Sweatshops, a perennial feature of the immigrants' story in the early twentieth century, became a news story again in the early eighties, when the garment industry had a renaissance of sorts. The United States had relaxed its immigration policy, and New York became newly crowded with unskilled, non-English-speaking people prepared to do—well, anything. This was around the time when Marlon, an Indian immigrant from Guyana, entered the business, as a floor sweeper, then a spreader, a grader, a marker, a patternmaker, and, finally, a cutter, taking home more than eighty thousand dollars in one year, enough to buy his first house. He started his own enterprise four years ago. Today, he has a factory of sixty-five hundred square feet, on two floors of one of these Thirty-ninth Street monstrosities. In the style of the district, the windows are blocked out; fluorescent strip lighting runs the length of the cutting tables. As we talk, people start to appear, a dozen, maybe more, a mix of men and women, mainly Hispanic.

Marlon is a couture cutter, at the high end of the first step in the manufacture of clothes: someone from Seventh Avenue phones with an order, sends over a pattern by messenger, arranges for the delivery of bundles of fabric. This morning, Marlon is preparing an evening dress—lots of silk and chiffon bits—an order he received the night before and which he is expected to complete by the end of the day. Once he figures out how to lay out the pattern, he will ask one of his workers to spread a stack of fabric, a hundred and fifty layers; stretch it tight; then cut it with a lathelike tool. Marlon is a success. Manhattan will always need high-fashion expertise. But even he can feel the pinch of a business that has more people in it than work to sustain them. In the last three years, his "table minimum" (what he charges to get out of bed) has dropped by half. Now, in the early spring—that interregnum between the fashion seasons, when sewing-machine operators tend to sit at home by the phone waiting for a call—Marlon does his shopping. This is when many of his neighbors go belly up. "In April," he says, "I'll be able to get anything I might need cheap. Tables, spreaders, cutters. Maybe even a better factory space." Marlon is proud of what he pays his staff; the average weekly salary is about three hundred and fifty dollars, which, though considerably more than the minimum wage, isn't a lot for Manhattan. But the average weekly salary in a Vladivostok garment factory is fifteen dollars.

WHAT is a sweatshop? My understanding was fashioned twenty-five years ago. In 1974, I was a student at the University of California at Berkeley and— determined to pay my own way, looking for a job—found myself below San Pablo Avenue, near the bay, in a factory that had all the design flair of an aircraft hangar: aluminum walls, no windows, floor fans, rows and rows of fluorescent lighting, and an overwhelming sense that the entire operation could be packed up and shipped off overnight. A new clothing manufacturer, Snow

Lion, was looking for cutters. In that Sierra Club–friendly town, Snow Lion made outdoor clothes, sleeping bags, and camping jackets, the fat-man kind that, in winter, used to render so many California college students into identical-looking Michelin Men of indeterminate sex and girth. Snow Lion made such bubble clothes, but bubble clothes of a new type, made of a lightweight, quick-drying fabric that was meant to be as warm as goose down—the thing that prefigured the thing that came before Gore-Tex.

There were three whites in the company: the founder, William Simon, with whom I would have one conversation, two years later, when he confessed that his real ambition wasn't to be a millionaire running a factory of immigrant labor but to write a novel about the revolution ("'68 and all that"); the floor manager, a roly-poly figure with a bulldog face and the easy manner of a neighborhood cop; and Steve, the sandy-haired supervisor of the cutters. And now there was a fourth: me. Most of the people in the factory were Chinese, but there were, unusually for the time, a large number of Hindi-speaking Indians.

One was Vikram Singh. (His name and some details about his background have been changed.) He and I were hired at the same time. Vikram was in his early twenties, although I always thought of him as much older, for no other reason than that our situations were so different. When my work was done, I rejoined a houseful of Berkeley undergraduates. Vikram, a recent immigrant self-consciously embarking on a new life, crossed the bay to the far side of San Francisco, where he lived in one of the subsidized housing projects. He had recently married—I would meet his wife later, a pretty, petite woman, always dressed in a sari, with a shy manner and deep brown eyes—and by his third month on the job she was pregnant. He made the announcement in a manner which suggested he'd be making the same one every year or so for many years to come. Vikram had a lean, mature face, thin feminine arms, a wiry build, and, initially at least, an immigrant's deferential manner. He always wore the same thing: a white cotton shirt and a pair of lightweight dark-brown wool trousers, a uniform attractively at odds both with the informal style of bluejean Berkeley and with what I assumed had been the hot-weather fashion of where he was from. Vikram was from Trinidad, a country I didn't know and pictured only in caricature: a cartoon Caribbean of calypso and rum. I knew nothing about the Indian population there, or the sad history of indentured labor, or what it meant to be a member of a self-contained, self-preserving culture that had been imported across the globe because it was prepared to work cheap.

The term "sweatshop" is American and originates from the end of the nineteenth century—Webster's dates its first use to 1892—and was meant to describe "sweated labor," work that a big clothing manufacturer contracts out to a smaller firm. The manufacturer would determine the design of an article of clothing, buy the fabric, and then get smaller sewing shops, the contractors, to do the work. The labor was "sweated" because of the conditions of the factories—cramped, crowded, and full of damp heat from the steam-driven pressers—and because of the furious, perspiring frenzy of piecework. Today, the term seems to mean many things, all of them bad. According to Jay Mazur, who is the president of UNITE, the garment workers' union, a sweatshop is any factory that doesn't allow its members to organize. According to the government, a sweatshop is a factory violating more than one of the fundamental labor laws, which include paying a minimum wage (currently $5.15 an hour) and keeping a time card, paying overtime, paying for training, and paying on time. In the beginning, Snow Lion did not pay for training (you didn't earn much until you got up to speed), didn't keep time cards, and didn't pay overtime. It was a sweatshop. But, in the popular mind, just about any factory that pays by the piece is a sweatshop. This is the sullying, uncharismatic feature of the garment business. Piecework seems pre-industrial, pre–assembly line. Didn't Henry Ford put an end to this kind of thing? You go to the bathroom, you don't get paid. You get a phone call—from your daughter, say, who has had an accident at school—and you don't get paid. You get ill yourself and you don't get paid. In piecework, a human effort is assigned a specific cost, like a unit of electricity or a weight of raw material.

And yet the people doing piecework are under no illusions; they know the deal. When I worked in a sweatshop, I wasn't alone in recognizing that there were other kinds of jobs. I liked this one, because, provided I could put in the extra effort, or the extra hours, I'd always have the chance to get some extra money. It was, I now see, a good time for the garment trade and would continue to be for the next decade or so, when the likes of Marlon could enter the business and work hard enough to buy a house at the end of a year's labor. Budding revolutionary-novelist proprietors had not yet seen how to have the same thing made in Siberia for a lot less. I was—I would learn later—in sweatshop heaven.

My job consisted of a simple, relentlessly repeated routine. I began by clamping down my synthetic mountain fabric at one end of my long cutter's table, rolling it out taut, and clamping it down at the other end. I went back to the beginning of the table and marked out patterns on the fabric with chalk—two pieces for a sleeping bag, five pieces for a jacket. Then I returned once again and cut out the pieces with an electric rotary-blade cutter. Finally, I returned to bundle each item up, tucking a perforated tally sheet inside. This sheet was the basis of my paycheck: I'd tear off one perforated tab for each garment I cut—forty cents for a sleeping bag, sixty-five cents for a jacket—and hand over my tabs when my shift was completed. Other tasks in the assembly—trimming, sewing, finishing—also had perforated tabs to be torn off. At first, I couldn't cut more than twenty jackets a shift, fewer than three meticulously, tediously carved parcels an hour.

When I began, I believed that mindless work would actually allow for an active mind: that with nothing to think about, it would be possible to think. In fact, small repetitive tasks, done under pressure, remove any chance of thought, except possibly one or two small thoughts, irritatingly small thoughts, which, like the work itself, are also endlessly repeated. I would often arrive prepared, with a specific subject I wanted to think about—an essay I was meant to write, say—but in the course of my work some small thought would present itself and, locked in by the routine of everything else, would become fixed and never leave. It might be something trivial, the lyrics of a song, invariably a terrible song, and never all of its lyrics ("You're just too good to be true, can't take my eyes off of you . . ."). Or it might be something someone had said or done. I remember repeating: *Why did she have to kiss him?* A girlfriend problem. Clamp it down (look at my watch—twenty seconds gone). Run back. Pick up the patterns (ten seconds). Mark them out with chalk (ninety seconds). *And on the lips, too.* Toss the patterns to one side. Run back. Turn on the rotary blade. Buzz, buzz, buzz (two minutes, five seconds). *Couldn't she have kissed him on the cheek?* Run back. Bundle the first one. *Or maybe a little peck?* Bundle the second one (twenty-five seconds gone, running late). *Especially such a wet kiss!* Bundle the third. Run back, start again. (Shit, twenty seconds behind my target.) *What else did she do?* And that, for eight hours, would be the sum of my mind's activity.

I got faster. My three jackets an hour had long been increased to fifteen when I tried to see just how many I could do. Finally I got to twenty, although I could never sustain the pace. If I had, that would have been an earning of thirteen dollars an hour, a good wage in 1974—not bad now. Vikram Singh was also fast, and we had competitions. When I hit twenty, he got twenty-one. He had such a lithe, effeminate build—how did he do it? When I matched him, he beat me again. And then one night, on my own, having already worked an eleven-hour day, needing the money, late on rent, no one else in the factory, I sliced off the tip of my finger, all of it happening, in the way of these things, in an eerie slow motion: my hand always moving just ahead of the cutter, fingers spread, holding down the fabric while I was carving out the curve of a sleeve, when—zip!—for some reason the blade went left by two inches, making a shortcut diagonal, ruining the sleeve, and slicing through the top of my finger. It fell onto the fabric, the fingernail intact. I put it into my pocket, which was already filled with chalk—a souvenir to display to my roommates at breakfast—the rump of my finger now a gushing red spout. When I got to the hospital, I discovered that a doctor could sew the tip back on. ("The cut-off bit? Yes, it's here in my pocket somewhere—hold on a second.")

I seemed to have passed through some kind of initiation rite. The roly-poly manager now smiled when he saw me. Vikram, my fellow-cutter (who still had his fingers), actively befriended me. We'd meet on a dock on breezy San Francisco Sunday afternoons, our time off, and he'd have brought fish heads (twenty-five cents a bag), which he'd put into a net and lower off the side. We'd drink a bottle of beer, and then pull up the net, which, miraculously, had filled with crabs. We returned to his home, a Monopoly board of tower-block apartments, where his wife made a crab curry, along with a number of other Indian dishes, more than I could count, which we'd have, sitting on the floor, one dish after another, until I moaned with pain, astonished at how much they'd persuaded me to eat.

MANHATTAN above the retail line is a different city, an older city, more anarchic, more like the New York of the movies: modernity in a state of constant disrepair. On the street level, you see new Manhattan. It's like so many fast things breaking a sound barrier: the stock-market *boom*, the real-estate *boom*, the banking *boom*, the restaurant *boom*. But mystery begins when you go upstairs. Upstairs you find your sole proprietors—Cuban travel agents, Bombay psychics, and some guy in a bad suit trying to sell socks to the Egyptian Army. Upstairs are zigzaggy fire escapes, open windows, and a sense that anything's possible. Especially in Chinatown. In Chinatown, the gambling is upstairs. You can find sex upstairs. And sweatshops.

Now that I know what to look for, I see them everywhere. The telltale sign is the extractor pipe—for expelling the steam from the pressers. I see them on Hester Street, their windows characteristically boarded up, but with bolts of colorful fabric stacked out on a fire escape. They're tucked away on Allen: an artist friend takes me upstairs to a loft above his studio, packed high with rolls of something pink and synthetic, where women in their twenties are making bikinis, a radio blasting Chinese pop. We walk in, smile, poke around, with no one looking up for longer than a moment. The more I look, the more I see. I start to think of sweatshops as spores carried by the warm night air, looking for a habitation where they can settle and spread. There are forty-two hundred registered garment factories in New York. Half of them, according to Louis Vanegas, an investigator for the Department of Labor, are probably trading illegally in some way. Another five hundred have owners who haven't quite got around to informing the authorities that they exist (which is also illegal). There are sweatshops on Orchard Street, just down from the Lower East Side Tenement Museum, where great-grandchildren of the museum's original residents gather to marvel at the conditions of nineteenth-century immigrants, unaware or else just uninterested that, two blocks away, there are contemporary equivalents with no entrance fee.

I am standing on Mott Street, one of the busiest places in Chinatown, surprised that, on earlier visits, I missed what now seems so obvious: just above the fish stalls, with their bright iced displays of squid and oysters and red snapper, crowding already crowded sidewalks, are sweatshops, several floors of them, each with telltale steam pouring out of boarded-up windows. Except that they are not sweatshops; they are garment factories, a distinction insisted upon by the people who run them. I'm here at the invitation of Wing Ma. He is around forty—coyly, he won't tell me his exact age—a short man, even by Chinese standards, but with a big man's grin, a gigantic happy grin that makes him a very easy person to like. For the last thirteen years, he and his wife have been running a garment factory that, in its heyday, employed a hundred and fifty people. Now they have less than half that. Even before I enter their factory—the third floor above Seafood International—I can see that it's of a different order from other places. There is an elevator, a man who operates it, a buzzer to let you in, and a big sign, prominently displayed, which says "No Homework"—work employees take home to be completed on their own sewing machines. Homework is popular with young mothers and factory owners hard pressed to meet a deadline. It is also illegal, because it's unsupervised (with no way of measuring overtime or insuring that the work isn't being done by children). The sign says "This shop obeys the labor laws!" to the people who matter: the inspectors from the Department of Labor.

Wing Ma has a union shop, not, you sense, because he thinks a union is a good or a bad thing but because it's what a man of his station is expected to have. It's a feature of being a member of this particular club, the heart of the heart of Chinatown, and Wing Ma is very much a member. He is a vibrant illustration of gung ho. He's a regular visitor to the Garment Industry Development Corporation, a clean and bright place on Centre Street with on-the-job classes for garment workers wanting to get ahead; it's a public service, a testimony to the industry as a happy thing, even though, Wing Ma admits, it serves little practical purpose, except, possibly, in the instructions it offers in how to become American—how not to hawk in public or blow your nose with your finger, and other things that Wing Ma is too embarrassed to admit. "You see," he says in his gung-ho way, "I am American already! I forget these things already! I am no longer Chinese!" He is a board member of other Chinatown ventures, and is one of a handful of factory owners who sit down with the union every three or four years to negotiate a new contract. The current one pays workers no less than $6.40 an hour—around twenty-five per cent more than the minimum wage—and provides health care and other benefits, which, according to Wing Ma, adds another thirty per cent to the cost of producing a garment. (In Sunset Park, he says, menacingly, they don't pay health care—how are we meant to compete with that?)

Wing Ma takes a call.

"Two thousand. O.K., O.K. And by when? Tuesday? And the pockets, normal pockets? O.K. And a plastic zipper? No zipper! How can you have pants with no zipper? Elastic. No problem. Very easy. By Tuesday. Noon. Fine."

It's Thursday, and a fellow factory owner is starting to panic that he won't meet his deadline. A missed deadline is a feared thing. Because there is a shortage of work, no factory wants to be seen as not being able to deliver. There are also penalties: Many manufacturers deduct a great whack from the bill when an order is late. Some refuse to pay: Two thousand trousers by Tuesday, you delivered them on Thursday, you broke the deal, no money. So, when it's looking too tight, a factory will subcontract to another one to get a job done. That factory, in turn, might subcontract to a third—the whole fragile paper chain held together by everyone's ironclad determination to deliver on time.

This paper chain was at work in the scandal involving Seo Fashion, a Thirty-eighth Street factory producing blouses with the Kathie Lee label. Her deal was with Wal-Mart, which had licensed a company in New York to make the blouse. When it started selling well, more were needed—a lot more: fifty thousand, now, now, now. The New York company went back to the manufacturer that first made the garment, an outfit called Bonewco. Bonewco took the order but couldn't fill it in time and so subcontracted a manufacturer in Alabama. The manufacturer in Alabama took the order: it couldn't fill it, either. It sub-subcontracted the work to a company in New Jersey. But even that company couldn't complete the order, and it sub-sub-subcontracted it to Seo Fashion, in midtown. In the end, Wal-Mart got its order, and each firm in the paper chain was able to say that delivery had been made on time. But it doesn't take an accountant to know that the invoice trail was a rocky and slow one to follow and that it was going to be a long time before the workers of Seo Fashion saw any money. And in fact, before then, that money's non-arrival had become a splashy front-page story in the *News*. Kathie Lee broke down on television, and Frank Gifford appeared on Thirty-eighth Street, handing out crisp hundred-dollar bills to the unpaid workers, who were grateful, I'm sure, although a larger problem remained unaddressed.

This morning, Wing Ma's panic order comes from a place run by his friend David Chan. I had met Chan and Wing Ma together, during an earlier visit to Chinatown. Chan and Wing Ma are probably about the same age, but Chan has the manner of a much more senior figure: rounder, slightly bloated, with a bored, unflappable, I've-seen-it-all look—as cynical and unsurprised as Wing Ma is gung ho. He arrived here from Hong Kong in 1969, aged twelve, and by the time he had his own factory, only a few years later, business was booming. "I was like Hong Kong boss," he said, remembering glory days. "Show up at noon. Manufacturers begging for work. They sent me turkeys at Thanksgiving, gift baskets at Christmas, and trips to Florida in the winter."

What changed was that big orders began going abroad. When Chan started, no more than a third of manufacturing was done outside the United States. Today, it's as much as ninety per cent. I asked a simple question: How did this come about? I was surprised by the reply. Both men started quoting pieces of trade legislation. "806!" they said. They mentioned 807, NAFTA, and C.B.I. The two men were referring to agreements that have facilitated making clothes abroad. It was their conviction that the government has systematically sought to destroy the garment industry here.

"Nobody likes us," Chan explained. "We know that. We're the ugly bit of manufacturing. Let other people make American clothes."

The first blow was the Caribbean Basin Initiative. At least, it was the most obvious. At a time of revolutionary insurgencies—Nicaragua, El Salvador, Grenada—the Reagan Administration took steps to reduce the appeal of left-wing governments in America's back yard. The idea was to supplant ideology with jobs and come up with ways of encouraging American companies to open plants in the region. (The clothing manufacturers would need little encouragement.) And thus was born a complex piece of legislation that not only made it easier for big clothing companies like Wal-Mart and the Gap to go to Caribbean countries for labor, with fewer problems of tariffs and quotas, but even subsidized the effort. For a number of years, a United States government agency put up millions of dollars to help erect factories that, today, are filled with workers earning as little as twenty-five cents an hour making American clothes.

Wing Ma takes another call.

"Of course," he says, immediately deferential. "No problem! Yes, I wondered about that, too. How many again? Six hundred. Of course. I'll pick it up. No, no, no, it's my pleasure."

When he hangs up, his face crunches into a scowl. "Manufacturers," he says. "They're so rude." The call concerns an order which he filled last week. The pattern called for sewing a flap onto the back of a jacket. "It was unusual," Wing Ma says, "but it seemed to work." Evidently, it was a mistake: the flap wasn't meant to be sewn on. But, even though the mistake was made by the manufacturer, Wing Ma will incur the expense of correcting it.

The manufacturer has all the power, Wing Ma says, because he's always ready to go to someone else who can do it for less. He tells me about his last big K-mart order, two years ago. It was to make a pair of women's trousers, fashionably designed, gathered at the waist, but of a very cheap polyester. The trousers were to sell for $12.99; he figured that, if the order was large enough, he could make them for about two dollars each. In the end, the order was very large; K mart asked for two hundred thousand, but kept reordering until 1.3 million pairs had been made. According to Wing Ma, when K mart came up with another design, he was told that he would have to knock fifty cents off the unit cost or else K mart would go abroad. So K mart went abroad. It became a regular thing: there'd be a nice order, an unrealistic price, and the business would end up going abroad.

Wing Ma believes that something else was going on as well. The garment industry was, by then, the enterprise that everyone loved to hate. Better to move your work out of the country, especially out of ugly old Chinatown. So when he learned, last year, that K mart's president, Floyd Hall, was coming to New York, Wing Ma organized a protest and asked the union to join in. He shows me a placard: "K MART TELLS NEW YORK CITY GARMENT WORKERS DROP DEAD!"

What happened? I ask.

The union told us not to do it.

The union? I ask, perplexed.

The union, for its part, says that it spoke to K-mart management and was told that it had no intention of abandoning Chinatown. (K mart tells the same story.) It's possible that the union just didn't know what to do. "*We* lead these things," the local's manager told me. "We don't let the employers lead them." The union seems to have found itself in the unfamiliar situation of having both owners and workers on the same side, with both sides in danger of losing what they had. After all, there is now a global workforce; there is no global union.

According to David Chan, American factory owners are now a desperate lot. They've become disaster watchers. A hurricane in the Caribbean: Great! A volcano in Central America: Wonderful! Floods, pestilence, riots. Yes, yes, yes! Catastrophes abroad are good for business at home. What insurers call acts of God have become the industry's biggest ally. I ask Wing Ma an obvious question: Shouldn't he be getting out?

"I can't," he says. "I've put half a million dollars into this business."

Before I leave, I ask for a tour. It's a big place, around twelve thousand square feet, and it has the distinction of having real windows. They're open. There is a breeze. I ask Wing Ma about the people who work here. He answers me, in a fashion. I learn, for instance, that some workers have been with him since 1985. Some of the newer ones tend to be Fujian immigrants. Many of the Fujianese don't speak Mandarin, and there is a language problem. They live nearby, he says, waving his hands dismissively, or in Sunset Park. Their husbands are in construction or in the restaurant trade.

It becomes evident that he doesn't know what many of them do—there is little socializing between boss and workers—and when I mention that I'd like to meet some he snaps, "Why would you want to do that?" His lips pucker up as if he's eaten something bad.

That night, I visit the kind of place where some of Wing Ma's workers might live, a fourth-floor walkup above a produce stand near the corner of Bowery and Canal, a perfectly normal dwelling for a family, a trendy small loft, say, except in this essential respect: there are a hundred people in it, most of them from Fujian. Actually, on the night I visit I am told there aren't a hundred in residence, only about sixty. I don't know how you can tell. There are two aisles separating three corridors of accommodations. On the floor level is a closet with a bunk bed inside; above it is an additional half room with another bed. Triple stacking. Someone has had to think hard and imaginatively to get so many people in one place. And then, of course, there is the smell, which is distinctive—a powerful punch, sure, but an oddly familiar one as well. It is, I realize, not unlike what comes off an old person's skin, someone too ancient to bathe: a crushed smell of dirt and urine and grease and feces, something you suspect no soap will ever reach. That's when I think I'm about to get sick. So this, it occurs to me, is how I will show my gratitude. These people, immigrants, unable to speak English, vulnerable in all kinds of ways, welcome a stranger into their home, who, in return, gawks at them like creatures in a zoo, and then vomits.

I'm with a friend, a Chinese speaker, and when we finally get outside I find my mind entertaining a cornucopia of bourgeois pleasures—a soapy hot bath, crisp cotton sheets. We don't move for a while, refilling our lungs with the now clean-seeming air of the Bowery. High up in a nearby building I spot rows of the familiar fluorescent lights. It's nearly eleven at night. Even now, even at this hour: a sweatshop on a deadline.

SNOW LION moved to bigger premises toward the end of my first year. I was spared the task of the move itself (which took most of the workweek, and for which the principal complaint was that everyone was paid an hourly wage), because during the academic term I had a weekend schedule. The Friday before, the floor manager had waited for me so that he could give me the new address, and the news that my friend Vikram Singh had become a supervisor. He also had a piece of information that he knew I'd enjoy learning: in the new place, the tables were going to be longer.

Because of the kind of cutting we did—one layer at a time—the length of the table was meaningful. Rolling out the fabric and then having to run back used up more time than any other segment in the cutting process; with a longer table, a cutter could get in two extra units before having to rush back. The company would make more money; I'd make more money, too. The equation is a feature of piecework when it's functioning equitably, and it's one that people outside the business don't always understand. The popular notion of sweatshop workers is that they are ignorant, desperate people exploited by a factory owner getting rich on their slavelike labors, but as I made my way around New York I found myself naturally sympathizing with workers *and* owners, if only because the plights of both parties are so bound together. Translated, the floor manager that evening was saying this: "Great news. I've figured out how you can do even more work for me!" And my reply was "Hip, hip, hurray!"

The new place had two unusual features: big windows and, just as important, a parking lot. When I started, most of the sewers were dropped off in the morning by their husbands. Once we'd settled into the new place, they started arriving in their own vehicles. A car had become an expression of achievement, and the parking lot was its display. And, appropriately enough, the biggest, most conspicuous car—something square and flamboyantly impractical—was driven by the fastest sewer, a fleshy, round-faced Chinese woman in her early thirties who, at full speed, was a blurry marvel to witness. She was the factory miracle, known to complete twice as many jackets as anyone else, and the reason my weekend schedule was tolerated, even required: I gave her something to do on Monday mornings.

The new place had another novelty: time cards, and we were told that we had to use them—told insistently, because at first no one bothered. Why time cards when you're being paid by the piece? I now suspect that the factory must have had a visit and a warning from labor inspectors. Today, they rarely issue warnings. Their position is that a worker has been cheated of wages, and that money must be paid back or else the clothing will be seized as "hot goods"—goods made illegally—and held until somebody in the chain (contractor, manufacturer, or retailer) comes up with the cash. You can sometimes spot an inspector, sitting outside a factory, drinking coffee from a paper cup, clocking when people enter and leave, in order to compare the results with the time cards inside: provided there are time cards inside. Factory owners like Wing Ma and David Chan attribute this new, highly moral, highly inflexible approach of the Department of Labor to what they call the Kathie Lee factor: there's public approval to be had in harassing the garment factories. Meanwhile, if the factories themselves can't make a go of it, they say, then far more people will be out of pocket.

When Vikram was made supervisor, I felt a reflected pride on his behalf. He hadn't been working that long; he hadn't been in America that long. But the promotion seemed to change him. He seemed to smile less, and he held himself in a new way, more upright, straighter, and with his chin—just so. Almost preening. And there was an impatience in his manner which I hadn't seen before. The promotion had created an awkwardness between us.

With the new vigilance about overtime, I worked with only one or two other cutters, sometimes on my own. Working alone was the preference: no distractions, no shoptalk, no cigarettes out back with a friend, only the night, dead quiet late on a Friday, except for the long San Francisco moan of a foghorn when the weather came in. The fact was you didn't want to socialize. You were there to make money. There was an honesty about the task, a bluntness. This is not a task that's meant to pass from one generation to the next. People are there because they have a job that's going to help them get to the next place.

Then things went genuinely wrong between Vikram and me—little stuff at first, persnickety things, which came to a head one Friday when I arrived and discovered that I had been accused of cheating. At issue were the perforated tabs, your credits for the pieces you do. More tabs had been turned in than there were garments to match. A lot more, evidently. It had been the crisis of the week. By the time I arrived, Vikram had let the suspicion fall on me. I was taken aside by the manager. Had I cheated, I was asked. No, I said, and that was the end of it. But I remember the icy stare that passed between Vikram and me.

Vikram had already become someone I was no longer comfortable with. He had become obsessed with sex—he used to phone to tell me about women he'd persuaded to go off with him, prostitutes from University Avenue, Berkeley hitchhikers. Then the floor manager told me about an incident from earlier in the week. One day, at the end of a shift, Vikram locked a woman in the factory and threatened to beat her with a pipe. The incident was hushed up, but I found myself thinking compulsively about the details. A strong man in a fury. A young woman. A locked garment-factory door. When I asked Vikram about it, he dismissed it as a family matter: the woman was a relative, who was threatening to tell his wife about his sexual escapades. I understand the matter differently now. Sexual abuse is a feature of a business in which lots of women are accountable to what is often one man. And there is the image of the locked door. In the Triangle Shirtwaist Factory fire, in 1911—three floors incinerated in minutes, a hundred and forty-six dead—many of the casualties resulted from women being trapped inside, pressed against locked doors, unable to get out.

The next month, I quit.

I WANTED to see the sweatshops in Sunset Park but didn't know how I'd be able to get inside. An idea presented itself: I would just walk in.

The idea was proposed by a P.R. person from UNITE. The union has an outpost in the heart of the district, at Seventh and Sixtieth, a "workers' justice center," and the P.R. person had also been curious to see firsthand what the conditions were like. I suggested we might go together. It's one thing, I felt, to walk in off the street on your own: "Hi, I know you run a horrible sweatshop and I'd just like to have a look around." It's a bit easier when you can do it with company.

We visited a dozen plants, maybe more, enough to get a picture. Laws were being broken. Time cards were not being kept. People were working overtime and not getting paid for it. And we suspected that the wages were close to the legal minimum, if not below it—and that they were being paid in cash. These were not foursquare, on-the-up-and-up, apple-pie, American-flag businesses (even though we found several American-flag labels there—J.C. Penney, Bradlee, Diane von Furstenberg). But they weren't all that bad, either. The bathrooms, which I had been warned would be disgusting, were clean. The fire exits were marked, and the aisles were clear. There were windows and light. And there was plenty of space, not a feature of Manhattan garment factories. And while we did spot one child—I had been told to expect underage laborers—it was a small boy, hiding shyly beneath the table of his mother while she sewed (an illegal practice, but scarcely a heinous one).

Silant Chung runs the Sunset Park justice center—she had given us our list of sweatshops—and when we returned I reported that the places had looked, well, not so bad. This was not the impression she had assumed the visit would make. Earlier, she had arranged an interview with a garment worker, and that, too, hadn't quite left the impression she was hoping for. He had invited me to call him Xie Zhin, fearing that if he used his real name it might get him in trouble with the local factory owners. Zhin was forty-three, a sewer on a Merrow machine, the most elementary kind of machine, a labor not normally undertaken by men. His wife was a sewer as well, and they lived in a two-bedroom Brooklyn apartment with two children, paying five hundred and fifty a month—not cheap, in the circumstances. They were from the countryside ("peasants"), about twenty-five miles from Fuzhou, and had come here, illegally, five years ago, and then contrived to secure political asylum. I asked Zhin about the conditions of the factories (reasonable), his workday (often twelve hours long, during busy periods), and his pay, which averaged out to something a little less than minimum wage but on which he paid no tax: his take-home, then, wasn't all that different from what some union workers get. This fly-by-night, stuff-it-in-the-mattress existence sounded about right; this was life in Sunset Park.

I asked him what he would like to see changed. In fact, what I said was: "Of all the possible conditions, what would you like to see improved?" I was expecting a union answer: health care, a minimum wage, overtime pay. Or an attack on profiteering owners.

"We want more work!" he said, with Silant Chung translating. "We want more business. The factories don't have the business they once did. Because of that, we are all under pressure. I am here because I want people to know about our plight. We'll do anything. But the work is not coming our way."

This was not a union answer.

The irony is that the work Zhin wants might be going to the country that he left, at great expense (thirty thousand dollars) and danger (a three-month trip in the hold of a cargo ship). China is another country where manufacturers are now finding people happy to be paid many times less than what an American factory worker can live on.

The whole business is now characterized by ironies: A government that has one branch prosecuting American sweatshops while another one encourages establishing them abroad. An industry that contributes to a watchdog institution to insure that there are no sweatshops in America while contracting agencies which specialize in setting up huge factories in the poorest countries for the cheapest possible price, no questions asked. William Simon, the founder of Snow Lion, never got around to writing that novel about the revolution, but he did set up a new company, Odyssey International, which *Forbes* describes as having been built on Simon's conviction that camping and outerwear companies should "move their production to cheap-labor countries in Asia." And, finally, there's a union that's still repeating the rhetoric of an earlier era ("Remember the Triangle Shirtwaist fire!") while rarely recognizing how much an American garment worker's life has changed.

The union's commemoration of the Triangle Shirtwaist Factory disaster—held on the 25th of March, just outside the building, on Greene Street, off Washington Square—was itself an illustration of many of these ironies. There were speeches and displays: a roll call of the dead; a fire-engine ladder extended no higher than the sixth floor, its maximum reach eighty-eight years ago, as the fire burned two floors above; an invocation of the conditions ("Thirteen cents an hour! Seven days a week!") of sweatshops in China. And then Charles Kernaghan stepped up to the platform. Kernaghan is the Ralph Nader of overseas garment factories. He was the one who held up an article of Kathie Lee clothing during a 1996 House hearing on international human rights and described the conditions in the Honduras factory where it was made. He is a popular speaker on university campuses and something of a rent-a-rant (Washington Square on Thursday, Workmen's Circle on Sunday, and coming soon to a protest near you): he always brings along a visual prop (a Teletubby today), and has a feel for the evocative detail ("She, along with the other sixty thousand workers in El Salvador, needs a ticket to go to the bathroom"). It's stirring stuff, but what, realistically, is the objective?

The Honduran workers making Kathie Lee clothing were, as Kernaghan established, paid only seventy-five dollars a month, and, by our reckoning, seventy-five dollars a month sounds exploitative. Even so, it's twenty-five per cent more than the country's average wage. How much should they be paid instead? Three times the national average—a hundred and eighty dollars? What's actually being exploited isn't a body of workers in a factory in Honduras but the disparity between two economies. The result, here, is a showroom culture of happy shoppers. The result, also, is a domestic industry that has been rendered redundant. For a hundred years, the garment business has been built on immigrants prepared to do the work that no one else wanted to do, and they did it, with discipline and phenomenal displays of will, in order to change their station in life. Now that opportunity has been taken away from them, and the immigrants from China and Honduras and the Dominican Republic are discovering that the work is being done by the people they left behind.

On my last visit to Chinatown, I found myself standing in front of a machine shop that had been vacated. I peered through the window—a dusty arrangement of abandoned machine parts. Across the street was another kind of shop, filled with secondhand sewing machines—so many that they cluttered up the sidewalk in front. One street over, there were more machines. I was surrounded by evidence of an industry packing up and getting out of town. It was a sultry afternoon, thunderstorm weather, and my gaze wandered up to an open window on the second floor. I caught the eye of a Chinese presser, perspiring, wearing an old-fashioned sleeveless undershirt, his bony shoulders exposed. It was a picture from another time. It could have been 1940 or 1910 or 1890. The presser was probably about fifty-five, and he stared at me in the bored way of a man stuck in a routine who had just found a momentary visual diversion. In a year's time, I thought, he won't be here.

APRIL 26, 1999

JOHN UPDIKE

A SENSE OF CHANGE

WAS shocked when, a few years ago, my stepson, still a college lad of modest means, handed me the stray change on his bureau top—perhaps two dollars' worth—because he did not like to have it jangling in his pocket. Gratefully, even greedily, I accepted the handful of pennies, nickels, dimes, and quarters. To me, once, these coins were huge in value, if not as huge as the fabled "cartwheels"—silver dollars—that now and then rolled as far east from the Western states as Pennsylvania. One of the advantages of having been a child in the Depression is that it takes very little money to gladden the heart. The Lincoln pennies we used to collect in piggy banks and glass ashtrays were not negligible: five would buy a Hershey bar, six a Tastykake, one a licorice stick, eleven (including a war-time tax) a child's ticket to the movies. Two hundred of them, dutifully accumulated over months and packaged in four paper wrappers holding fifty each, could be exchanged at the Whitner's Department Store book counter for an album of cartoons from *Collier's* or an agreeably lightweight novel by Thorne Smith or P. G. Wodehouse. The wrappers were solemnly broken open and each penny respectfully counted by the saleswoman. Now spare pennies sit like a puddle of sludge in a dish on the counter of the post office or the convenience store, and sometimes a salesclerk, rather than bother counting out four cents in change, blithely hands you a nickel.

Copper Lincoln cents—pale zinc-coated steel for a year of the war—figure in my earliest impressions of money, although an old Indian Head, discontinued in 1909, would still turn up in the thirties. Lincoln pennies are being minted ninety years later, the longest-lived of American coins and the first non-commemorative ones to bear a President's image. The other coins of my childhood have slowly ebbed from circulation: the Buffalo nickel (1913–38), crowded to the rim, obverse and reverse, with its heroic representations of Manifest Destiny's two victims, the defeated Indian and his all but exterminated pet prey; the Mercury dime (1916–45), so called because Miss Liberty wears an anomalous winged headdress atop her icy female profile, a profile that originally belonged, we children of Berks County did not realize, to Elsie Kachel Moll, from Reading, who had married another local, the poet Wallace Stevens, and during their seven years in Manhattan had posed for not only the iconic head on the dime but the full-length Miss Liberty on the fifty-cent piece; and the Standing Liberty quarter (1916–30), whose figure (not Elsie Stevens's) was criticized for showing too much naked flesh and was more heavily draped in the second year of its issue. This coin, as it yielded to the Washington quarter, first minted in 1932, was treasured by small boys because, if it was turned upside down and partly covered with a knowing thumb, the wings and head of the flying eagle on the reverse became striding legs and a penis. By the time the Walking Liberty half-dollar (1916–47), with its full-length sashaying lady about to put her foot on a rising sun, gave way to Ben Franklin and the Liberty Bell, I, at the age of fifteen, had ceased to hold coinage so close to my face and to count on it for erotic insight. Half-dollars were less rare then than now— men accustomed to carrying pocket watches and pocket knives did not shun big coins—but a child seldom gained possession of one, unless it was to mark a holiday or a birthday. Fifty cents was a lot of money.

These metallic tokens projected a potent magic. My best friend, a lawyer's son, had a little tin box of money that, when I visited his home, he used to show me with an avid, ceremonial secrecy. My own, more meagre hoards resided in relatively frivolous piggy banks, most important a grinning, red-tongued Mickey Mouse guarding a slotted treasure chest whose bottom could be opened with a key. I had won the bank in a third-grade spelling bee—the clinching word, I think, was "lonely"—and this quaint repository's disappearance, somewhere in the second half of the century, constitutes one of the inconsolable losses of my life.

Money, which is now so preponderantly a matter of electronic notation, or else a breezy riffle of twenty-dollar bills cast down by an A.T.M., was in those hard-up times an earthy out-growth, like the sparkling diamonds that the dwarfs pile up in Disney's *Snow White*. My family—my possibly incomplete impression was—deposited my father's salary, received in cash in a small tan envelope, in a red-and-white "Recipe" box that sat on top of the icebox. To dip into it, I had to get a kitchen chair to stand on, and my withdrawals were supervised; indeed, everyone's withdrawals from it were announced, like the stations on a train journey. When the box was empty, we were out of money.

My father, as a schoolteacher in charge of basketball admissions, used to bring home the cash receipts, and I often watched him count them—the various denominations of coins mounting in slick stacks that, when they reached a certain height, were deftly slipped into a paper cylinder, which was then smartly tamped at both ends. When I tried it, the coins ran away, over the edge of the table onto the carpet and even beyond, a coin often ending upright on its edge in a floor crack way over in a corner. This willful, kinetic quality of metal money I notice now at the poker table, where a quarter tossed into the pot will unaccountably wobble to its feet, as it were, and travel clear across the table as if seeking another master.

THE sensuous pleasure of handling money carries into the very thought of it. "Pennies from Heaven" was a song, and "We're in the Money" another. American millionaires—Ford and Rockefeller and, upholding Pennsylvania's honor, Andrew Carnegie and Andrew Mellon—were folk heroes, Paul Bunyans of cash. The millions who for a coin or two went to the movies did not seem to begrudge the tuxedoed personas of Louis Calhearn and Eugene Pallette and Guy Kibbee their pillared estates, their lawns and swimming pools, their buffed and chauffeured English limousines, their beautiful giddy daughters in chiffon and pearls. To see such well-endowed lives projected in black-and-white on a big silver screen was itself pleasurable, like feeling coins swim through your fingers or imagining—as in many a crime movie—a suitcase full of bundled bills. The American masses of the Depression had not quite lost the feudal ability to identify with an overlord's riches, alleviating their own poverty with vicarious enjoyment of an aristocracy's assets. The men and women who drudged their lives away in the local factories—most prominently, Wyomissing's Berkshire Knitting Mills, fondly known as the Berkie— shared in the pith of a great enterprise, though their share, Marxists would point out, was insufficient. American society's refusal to crack beneath the dire load of the Depression owed something to an imaginative wealth that, via the movies, solaced the masses with debonair images of luxury. Images were in a way superior to the real thing, if we believed those Hollywood comedies in which the rich were often foolish and not infrequently miserable: they suffered from ulcers, financial reversals, and the discontents of excessive propriety; they were hostages to their fortunes, and prey to complications from which ordinary men were exempt. Our hearts went out to them, and their happy endings became ours. Movies, mediating between Myrna Loy and the twelve-dollar-a-week shopgirl, spun a web of trust, of sympathetic connection, like the bonds of patriotism and brand-name loyalty.

A coin, too, bespeaks trust, passing from hand to hand as an abstract signifier of value. Coins were once worth their weight in silver or gold; opportunists clipped their edges and passed them on for the face amount. Then the underpinning of real metallic worth was removed, and the value inhered in nothing more than a general consent. A "pretend" level of wealth was invented, less substantial but also less perishable and cumbersome than food or clothing or jewelry. This lightly worn immutability accounts for some of the fascination that money holds. Like that of words and feelings, money's value is impalpable. Yet money lasts, it doesn't flit by. Nor does it ask anything of its possessor. It melts, like ice cream, but very slowly, in the warmth of inflation. It has endurance and extension. These little disks and shallow sculptures enlist us in a conspiracy of users; a penny from a child's hand is worth just what it is from a grownup's. Getting and spending confer an instant dignity.

In that penny-proud world of my childhood, paper and cardboard play money carried the pretense to an even airier level. Whole afternoons went by in the counterfeit transactions of Monopoly. The war brought food tokens—little hard cardboard disks, red and blue—and stamps, and War Bonds, urged upon the public by movie stars and heroes and President Roosevelt himself, as immutable as the profile on a coin. Before the Depression, my grandfather had invested in stocks and bonds and lost most of his money; now all of us, children included, were hustled by the wartime emergency back into an economy of credit and certificates, a giant trusting of the government to see us through and pay back its debt. My adulthood's slow divorce from hard cash was under way.

To one who acquired his sense of money in the Depression, any payment, however modest—fifty-five dollars, say, for a poem, or a hundred for a reprint permission—seems impressive. My allowance was thirty-five cents a week, my father's salary was twelve hundred dollars a year. Measured by these sustenance sums, nineties remunerations appear huge; I often must resist the impulse to send back checks to editors and lecture agencies on the ground that I am being grossly overpaid. On the other hand, nineties expenses are a constant outrage. Four hundred and fifty dollars for one night in a hotel! Seventy-five dollars for a theatre ticket! Two million dollars for a condo on an airshaft! Thirty-three cents for a three-cent stamp! Eighty cents—can you believe it?—for a nickel candy bar! It is like going to Italy, except that these are not lire but almighty American dollars. "The almighty dollar," "sound as a dollar," "another day, another dollar"—even the sayings from my childhood have been devalued by inflation. I simply cannot afford to live, it daily seems to me as I size up 1999 prices in the dollars of 1939. No, not the dollars; a Lilliputian in Brobdingnag, I still think in terms of 1939 quarters, dimes, nickels, and pennies. Or am I, hoisting up onto the counter a nickel that feels as hefty as a millstone, the Brobdingnagian?

APRIL 26, 1999

METAMONEY

THE New Money, like the New Testament, or the New Coke, would like to be seen as the fulfillment of the fine old thing that came before. Same good green-and-black color scheme, same noble statesmen, same cryptic serial numbers, same signature from the entirely unknown Treasurer of the entire country, Mary Ellen—"Withrow," is it? (In Student Council votes in junior high, wasn't it always the girl who had just moved to town, the girl no one knew, who got the treasurer's job?) Same great seal, same government buildings, though we do see the other side of the White House. Even the same piece of hidden American poetry on its face: "This Note Is Legal Tender for All Debts, Public and Private." "Tender for all debts," the motto on the American heart: every debt, public or private, forgiven, dismissed, and treated, well, tenderly.

It ought to work. But, as happened with the New Coke, nobody is buying it. The new twenties, following the fifties and hundreds, have been appearing in cash machines and wallets, and they have got anything but what you would call money notices. Everybody hates them. Edward Rothstein in the *Times* has come out against them, and there's even on-line rebellion against the New Money, including a heated discussion group on A.O.L.

Everybody who sees the New Money says that it doesn't look like money. Everybody says that it looks like coupons, like play money, like funny money, like fake money, or, most often, like "Monopoly money." This is an odd objection, since the New Money doesn't look anything like Monopoly money. "I don't know why they say that, because, if you've ever noticed, Monopoly money is quite small in size, it comes in different colors, and it doesn't feature portraits of famous Americans on the front," a Treasury official has said plaintively, and accurately. So what *do* people mean when they say it?

The trouble started with the whole idea of making the New Money by fid-dling around with the Old Money. The New Money, if you haven't seen it yet, keeps the main graphic elements of the Old Money, and wiggles them a little. The medallion around the head of each President who appears on it—the same guy as before—is twice as big, and has become a simple oval; the Presidents' faces are more detailed and three-dimensional; most of the fancy cartouche and tobacco-leaf framing elements are gone, and a brutally simple, Cubist sans-serif number is inserted on the back.

It would be easy to say that the enlarged, oversized Presidents look more like celebrities for a celebrity age. You could do it, but, as a great, undollared Presi-dent said, it would be wrong. They don't look famous. Old Hickory, who used to just stare out defiantly, below that white shock of hair, on the twenty, looks pensive and worried, while Franklin, on the C note, looks oddly like Hannah Arendt, anxious and modern. They share the quality first discovered in Richard Avedon's portraits of politicians and then passed on to Chuck Close's portraits of artists: anybody just looking straight ahead, if made big enough, looks *guilty*, of something or other. Most troubling of all, there's a lot of blank space on the New Money. The back of the fifty, for instance, is completely bor-derless, white from the edges in. The old complicated framing devices, all those egg-and-dart patterns, have been sucked right off. The elements are the same, but the whole thing is a lot sparer. The New Money just looks—well, the New Money looks cheaper than the Old Money.

When money changes, it doesn't usually change like this. In France, for in-stance, the money has just changed, too. But in France the old paladins—Delacroix on the hundred-franc note, Montesquieu on the two-hundred—have been dismissed outright, like government ministers, and been told to take their style, their pale, imitation-watercolor palette, with them. Even Delacroix's Lib-erty, who kept him company with her gallant bare nipple, has been retired. The new heroes on French money bring along their own distinct emblems: on the two-hundred, there's Eiffel (with his half-completed tower); on the hundred, there's Cézanne (with his cardplayers); and on the fifty-franc note—the French ten-dollar bill, the one you really use—there's Saint-Exupéry, with his Little Prince. And not just the Little Prince but also that sheep he wanted the aviator to draw—"If you please, draw me a sheep!"—looking wistful. When you pay a bad-tempered taxi-driver in Paris today, you hand over Cézanne and his anxi-ety, and the driver hands you back the Prince and the Sheep and their contempt for the grownups' money-obsessed ways. Even the British have changed their money several times recently. The Queen has been aging on it. She has been growing old—slowly, discreetly, but unmistakably. An odd, Dorian Gray–like conception: money with liver spots and lines.

Our money, though, has stayed the same for so much longer than anyone else's that it has become fixed—evergreen. (Not even the Presidents aged, since they were all dead anyway.) It would be nice to say that our money stayed the same for so long because it was so well designed, but really its having stayed the same for so long was just a reproach to the idea that good design matters much in the first place. Like Häagen-Dazs ice cream in its pristine period, when all the flavors came in the same carton, the Old Money showed that people are remarkably insensitive to packaging when they like the product. That our tens and twenties and fifties and hundreds looked, at a glance, just about the same never seemed to bother anybody. The pretense of a mixup—"Hey, wasn't that a twenty I gave you?"—was a con man's line. When it comes to kinds of money and kinds of ice cream, in a country that is made of both, you can always manage to tell the flavors apart.

What the Old Money had wasn't good design but a terrific period feeling. The *Times* calls the look Belle Époque, but it was more American than that. The Old Money looked like the old Gilded Age. Though it got standardized in the nineteen-twenties, its design and its iconography date from the period right after the Civil War: the just finished Capitol, proudly shown off; the tobacco-leaf motif; President Grant as a hero. How beautifully the Old Money managed to evoke the spittoon-and-Sunday-oratory world of the post–Civil War! It was there in the way that the heraldic ribbon above Andrew Jackson put the "The" of "The United States of America" right above his head, like a hinge. It was there in the solid, shadowy lettering of "Twenty Dollars"—the kind you still see inscribed on the forgotten statues of the 1876 centennial exposition in Fairmount Park, in Philadelphia. Even the leftover eighteenth-century Masonic symbols—that pyramid! that eye!—felt reassuring. (You see, we can assimilate *any* cult, it said. Check out our Mormons, well groomed and orderly in Utah.) The Old Money presided over calm avenues, and it was melancholy, too, in the stately way of Gilded Age sadness. Is there a sweeter American image than that single motorcar chuffing along outside the Treasury Building on the back of the old ten? It has stayed there right up through the era of the Santa Monica freeway and drive-by killings, still asking the same forlorn question: *Will the horseless carriage ever catch on?*

The Old Money was the old us. French money says, We have more culture than we know what the hell to do with, we might as well put it here. English money says, We have the Queen and a funny system of change, that's us, take it or leave it. (And the touching, absurd systems of the Mediterranean countries, counted out boastfully in tiny increments—*thousands* of pesetas, *millions* of drachmas, *billions* of lire—say everything you need to know about the insecurity of little states.) Our money said that America was basically a big green country inhabited by politicians and weirdos. The fixed, cigar-store Indian stillness of the American dollar—its essential sobriety—seemed the right counterpoint to our perpetually adolescent free market, with its rush and its frenzies and its absolute lack of memory. Money, after all, is the thing that makes a free market possible, but it is possible only as a product of an unchallenged state that sets rules and tolerates no competition. Money is exactly the kind of government program that liberals always want to throw money at.

Our money was so stable, so unchanged over such a long time, in fact, that it produced a companion genre—funny money, play money, fictional money, Monopoly money. It doesn't exist in anything like the same abundance in other countries (when you go to buy funny money for a kid in France, you get the American kind), because it depends on there being something so familiar and unchanged that it can be evoked by a few rudimentary tokens: the face in the oval, the black on the front and the green on the back. American money was so familiar that a few coarse indications—even, as in Monopoly, a handful of typographic gestures—were enough to let you know what it was supposed to be.

That is where the problem lies for the New Money. All the clues that the New Money sends out, its little spray of signifiers—the oversized President's head, like but not quite like the familiar smaller one, the Gilded Age complexity indicated but not quite present—announce it as a familiar genre, parody money, one of those inventions that look enough like money to stand for money without actually being money. Had the French done the same thing—kept Delacroix and made Liberty's nipple and breast bigger—the new francs would not have been new money, either; they would have been burlesque money.

The New Money isn't newly minted money. It's metamoney. We are disturbed by the New Money because it uses the traditional satiric devices of exaggeration, displacement, and oversimplification, and therefore seems to be offering some kind of comment on the Old Money. It seems to be getting at us in some obscure way. It does have an *X-Files* side. Wherever the New Money seems perfectly blank, it can be made to reveal a whole microworld of symbolism and eerie stuff, such as watermarks, embedded "security threads," and hidden signs. There is a little line toward the bottom of the portrait of Jackson that says, in microscopically small type, "The United States of America." (Apparently, even the best color Xerox would render it as a broken, wavering line.) Hold the hundred-dollar bill casually up to the light and you see, to your shock, a smaller mimic portrait of Franklin with a significantly different expression; he looks sly and vaguely self-satisfied—Bad, rather than Gentle, Ben—while the smaller "ghost" of Grant on the new fifty looks angry. Presumably, the terrorists in their Bekáa Valley lair, who by their counterfeiting skills helped bring on this whole business, are holding the New Money up to the light with tears in their eyes. How do we do *this,* in the name of Allah? Faking one President was hard enough, faking him and his evil twin . . . So the money has arrived at a contemporary insight: scrutinize a President long enough, and what you find is not reassuring but weird.

THE New Money, created by the forces acting on all of us now—fear of terrorism high among them—is an expression of a New Gilded Age as surely as the

Old Money was the expression of the past one. The Old Money had too much going on, right there on the surface. It had more whorls and whirligigs and details and slogans and mottoes and signatures than you knew what to do with. That excess of symbolism was part of a general overspill at the time. Henry James, arriving home almost a hundred years ago, at the climax of the last Gilded Age, was overwhelmed, above all, by the excess of decoration in the hotel lobbies, like that of the old Waldorf-Astoria, on Thirty-fourth Street. The magazine stands with bronze-incised floors! The flower shops spilling over with roses! The marble basins in the barbershops and the hall of mirrors in Peacock Alley! A hundred small details of overcharged luxury. He thought that it was vulgar and overdone, of course, but he saw that at least this deliberate overcharge overflowed—that in America commercial calculation and generosity had, for a moment, become the same thing. Where the Gilded Age was gold, the gold was solid.

The New Money looks like our Gilded Age. In its combination of overkill and emptiness, the New Money evokes the new midtown hotels, with their black-and-white "Deco" marble lobbies, wedged into tiny lots, and then the cold sealed rooms immediately above—the luxury falling off as soon as you've checked in. It calls to mind the new generation of "luxury" multiplex movie theatres, where you're drawn in by a little Egyptian décor and buttered popcorn, and then, ticket bought, find yourself with nothing but a sticky floor and a tiny screen. The comforting come-on and then the sudden abrupt blankness—*that's* the look of the New Gilded Age, and the New Money has it. The New Money cuts off the flow of meaning as soon as you've, so to speak, "bought it." It's Camden Yards money—see, just as good as the old place, sonny, with all the old-fashioned charm you're used to. Have another hot dog. And underneath—the part of the stadium shown only to Rupert Murdoch—in the security control center, the cables run out to the surveillance cameras that keep a secret eye on the crowd, just as the electronic doodads in the money that let you get in wink at you beneath their reassuring nineteenth-century façade. Faux-retro reassurance and security-strip paranoia now share the same bedroom, or dollar bill.

The New Money comes to us at a time when money, the kind you put in your pocket, no longer makes the world go round. Cash is now the closest thing we have to contraband. When you see a lot of it in a movie, you know that something crooked is up. Rich men now have neither moneybags with dollar signs on them nor bulging wallets but discreet, thin credit cards and a blinking line of electronic numbers. Only those among us who are still deceived go to the cash machines, thinking, Hey, we're in the money! The government is even minting pennies at a several-million-dollar loss—losing money by making it. So the New Money may not be funny money, but it isn't filthy lucre, either. It's just an honest greenback, doing the day's little jobs—like placating a maître d' or paying a babysitter—that no one else wants to do. No wonder the Presidents look tight-lipped. They've been demoted, and they know it. The real economy winks and blinks electronically, secretly, all night long, from Shanghai to Seattle: encoded secure site whispering to encoded secure site. Ben and Abe and Andy must realize this. It's why they now look so anxious. They're working for tips, just like the rest of us.

NOVEMBER 9, 1998

DISPLAY CASES

W E make our lives within the cycles of capitalism, and they shape our existence as inexorably as the cycle of seasons and weather and plenty and famine shaped the lives of our peasant ancestors. For the most part, we feel that we understand what makes the money come, and where it goes, not a whole lot better than our rural fathers understood what made the rains come and the crops grow. Like them, we are left to brood, pray, and occasionally sacrifice a fisher-king (like poor George Bush) when the plains seem too brown. Or we can read the political economists—the worldly philosophers, in Robert Heilbroner's fine and famous term—and try to find out from them exactly what is going on. Mostly, though, their models seem as baffling to us as the crystal spheres and epicycles of Ptolemaic astronomy must have seemed to the medieval peasant. "You see, it's complicated," they tell us. "Now, go home, yeoman, and roister." A few of the worldly philosophers are, by reputation, supposed to offer something more, and first among them is Thorstein Veblen, the eccentric American economist who, exactly a hundred years ago, began a new train of thought about the money economy with a short, bizarre, brilliant book, *The Theory of the Leisure Class.*

We go to Veblen because he promises to explain what we want to understand, which is why, if free and efficient markets are as free and efficient as they tell us they are, the world they make is as queer as it looks. Veblen wanted to explain not just who wins and who loses in business but why the winners, who have won so much, seem to enjoy themselves so little—why they crowd anxiously into the same twenty-square-block neighborhood and the same four beach hamlets, spend thousands of dollars to be schlepped by Sherpas to their deaths on the tops of distant mountains, pay big wads of money to put fat in their mouths, and even bigger wads to have it sucked back out through their thighs. Where an economist might attempt to explain how one exporting country can make money by selling its coffee beans cheaper than the next, Veblen attempts to explain why, when you offer two identical cappuccinos for sale on opposite sides of the same street, one for six dollars and the other for two, you will see people knock each other down as they flock to pay the six. (There is no better place in New York to read Veblen than the window of the E.A.T. café, at Eightieth and Madison, where, with the coöperation of the Three Guys coffee shop down the street, this experiment in Veblenian consumption has been running for about two decades now.)

Veblen, in his centenary, is having a revival because he appeals, oddly, to two current fashions in intellectual life: the fashion for cultural studies and the fashion for evolutionary psychology. The contributors to a new book, *Thorstein Veblen in the Twenty-first Century*, edited by Douglas M. Brown, make the case that, in effect, Veblen did more than anyone to turn the study of capitalism from production, power, and prediction to consciousness, consumerism, and culture. Veblen, his admirers say, was the first to claim that capitalism's real purpose is consumption, that it works insidiously through the spread of consciousness, and that the job of the social critic is to describe the cultural field that transmits it. The evolutionary psychologists, for their part, argue that what Veblen saw in Baltimore or Chicago a hundred years ago is pretty much what the biologist sees between competing male peacocks as they spread their tails in the lek—fighting for females by showing how much they have to waste. "We are creatures of waste, evolved to burn off our time, our energy, our very lives to show that we can do so better than our sexual competitors," the biologist Geoffrey Miller has written in a long essay about conspicuous consumption, "Waste Is Good," in the British magazine *Prospect*. Veblen can be considered the man who saw how shopping deformed human nature, and also the man who showed how shopping reflected it.

Thorstein Veblen was a largely unknown forty-two-year-old instructor in economics at the University of Chicago when *The Theory of the Leisure Class* was published. He came from a Norwegian farm family and grew up in Minnesota, and though his first biographer probably overemphasized just how isolated and "Scandinavian" his background was, a little Norwegian goes a long way toward making you reluctant to put on any kind of display. (Look at Walter Mondale.) And Veblen seems to have inherited a genuine, gut-level distaste for show. It's both odd and apt that the three most eloquent satirists of American display in the first half of the twentieth century—Veblen, Fitzgerald, and Lewis—were all Minnesota boys abroad.

Veblen was a likable, difficult, undisciplined, deeply lazy man—an intellectual drifter, who went from Minnesota to Johns Hopkins and on to Yale, where he got a Ph.D. in philosophy. He then couldn't get a job for the next seven years; his first was at Chicago, and, on leaving there, he was kicked off the faculty at one school after another, supposedly for seducing his students and other men's wives. He seems to have been a womanizer of the sleepy, they-keep-throwing-themselves-at-me sort—certainly no other writer of his time was as resolutely feminist—and he was a comically, lovably indifferent lecturer.

It was his discovery of the anthropologist Franz Boas that woke Veblen from his dogmatic slumbers. Boas had studied the plenty-societies of the Northwest Coast Kwakiutl Indians, and had discovered and recorded their now famous ritual of the potlatch, the competitive feast of gift-giving at which men who once fought by hand now fought with property. Inspired in part by Boas's insight that anthropology could explain economics, Veblen began *The Theory of the Leisure Class* with a myth. Like his contemporary Freud, imagining that human neurosis could be traced to the murder of the father-chief in prehistory, Veblen imagined that the money trouble had begun way back, with the transfer from a state of "peaceable savagery" to one of "predatory barbarism." The peaceable savage was a creature of material appetites who was satisfied when he was satiated. This natural state was superseded by the coming of the predatory barbarian, a category that for Veblen includes the Kwakiutl warrior, the medieval feudalist, and, in America, the businessman—anyone who lived off the labor of others. The distinguishing characteristic of predatory-barbarian society is a ruling class that doesn't do physical labor—a leisure class. (Even a banker who goes to the office every day is, in Veblen's scheme, a member of the leisure class.)

Veblen's sociology is a hash of Social Darwinism, race-conscious anthropology, and William James pragmatist psychology, but his picture has a purpose. In tribal and feudal societies, he argues, the leisure class had certain occupations—making war, exploiting vast tracts of land, running slave plantations—that gave it prowess and status: its members could fight, and actually owned other people. With the growth of modern industrial society, only the outward show remained, and it became a powerful symbol. In Veblen's scheme, the Ralph Lauren effect is universal: even when membership in the leisure class no longer depends on being able to ride horses and own land, it is still symbolized by polo and ranches. "Manners are symbolical and conventionalised survivals representing former acts of dominance," he writes. "In large part they are an expression of the relation of status—a symbolic pantomime of mastery on the one hand and of subservience on the other." The rules of this "symbolic pantomime" became Veblen's subject.

It was founded on the practice of "invidious comparison." For pre-industrial predatory barbarians, it was pretty clear who stood where: you just counted slaves and acres. For industrial society, though, there is no obvious way to rate predatory barbarians except to see where they shop and what they buy. Since you can't count the slaves or acres of the stranger on Madison Avenue, the only way to know where he stands is to see how much he pays for his cappuccino.

Veblen called this urge to show off your status by spending your money "conspicuous consumption." He was thinking of the kinds of overkill that were going on around him in the eighteen-nineties. (The hosts of one famous New York party, at the Waldorf-Astoria in 1897, were proud to announce that it had cost them three hundred and seventy thousand dollars; August Belmont came to the party in a ten-thousand-dollar suit of gold-inlaid armor.) And yet he saw that, even among the very rich, conspicuous consumption was usually more complicated than that, involving a tension between the need to display money and the need to be seen to display old money. "Archaic simplicity" had to be evoked in order to demonstrate the age and solidity of your "industrial exemption"—your freedom from the necessity of working with your hands. Conspicuous consumption had to combine "a studious exhibition of expensiveness with a make-believe of simplicity."

Veblen understood that the whole society had to be implicated, however insidiously, in leisure-class showing off. The leisure class, for instance, likes to borrow the styles of display of the lower classes: the only people at the horse races are tycoons and touts, and in Veblen's day the only people to carry sticks were millionaires and muggers. The rich imitate the poor, Veblen explained, because the underclass is the only other group in the society that has an industrial exemption, even if it doesn't much want it, and the leisure class can "pantomime" the exemption without having to suffer the consequences of exclusion. (So today rich white boys can wear black-and-silver Starter jackets knowing that they're not ever going to be treated like gangstas.)

Veblen also understood that some members of the middle classes had to be drafted into the leisure class, too, on an honorary basis. That way, they could instruct other, less favored middle-class people on exactly how to be impressed. In America, this advisory, status-creating but not quite status-sharing class would be called "college professors." (They had come to share the tastes without having the income, Veblen said, so that "there is no class of the community that spends a larger proportion of its substance in conspicuous waste than these." Even today, the only people you see making gastronomic tours of France are German millionaires and American college professors on sabbatical.)

FOR Veblen, what distinguished "pecuniary" or capitalist civilization in its American Gilded Age form was that the symbolic pageant of invidious comparison replaced nearly every other kind of human relation. It was reflected in the dogs we buy: Veblen hated dogs, and maintained that the only reason people liked Pekinese and purebred terriers was that they were expensive. The dog, he wrote, has "a servile, fawning attitude towards his master, and a readiness to inflict damage and discomfort on all else." (He exempted the cat from invidiousness because "she lives with man on terms of equality.") It was there in the lawns we grow, which pathetically mimic aristocratic pastures, and in the lower-middle-class man's decision to overwork so that his wife could become the bearer of "vicarious leisure." It was sports and schools and shaving. It was all there was.

In Veblen's world, invidious comparison went right down to the skin. The corset was a perfect symbol of ridiculously conspicuous consumption. Acutely uncomfortable and impeding, the garment was designed, he argued, to make it plain that the woman who wore it was unfit for labor while being very well fit for sex. It made her a drone and a trophy. (In one of the bright little master-strokes that fill his book, he points out that the only other people who dress like rich women are liveried servants: both wear a uniform that announces their function while preventing them from performing it.)

The explicit rationale that the corset enforcer gave the corset wearer, though, was its naturalness—wearing it made her more feminine, made her feel like a natural woman. Fashion was always driven forward, he declared, by this double-stroke engine of an invidious reason and a natural rationale until it was overwhelmed by what he called "aesthetic nausea":

> The ostensible usefulness of the fashionable details of dress, however, is al-ways so transparent a make-believe, and their substantial futility presently forces itself so baldly upon our attention as to become unbearable, and then we take refuge in a new style. But the new style must conform to the require-ment of reputable wastefulness and futility. Its futility presently becomes as odious as that of its predecessor; and the only remedy which the law of waste allows us is to seek relief in some new construction, equally futile and equally untenable. Hence the essential ugliness and the unceasing change of fashion-able attire.

Veblen is insistent—far more than Marx—on reducing aesthetics to eco-nomics: "The superior gratification derived from the use and contemplation of costly and supposedly beautiful products is . . . a gratification of our sense of costliness masquerading under the name of beauty." Take the case of two spoons, he proposes, one handwrought silver, the other machine-made. The handwrought spoon costs twenty dollars and the machine-made one ten cents. Yet the predatory barbarian will always find a reason for preferring the handwrought spoon—he will call it "better made," "simpler," or "richer," de-pending on the need—because the predatory barbarian's whole aesthetic (which is to say, yours and mine) is unconsciously derived from his knowledge of price and relative status. A yuppie couple may have an elaborate rationale to explain why they buy linen tablecloths and copper pots, but really it's because they don't want to be known as Sta-Prest and Silverstone folks. (Already, in 1899, Veblen pointed out that the fashion for candlelight dinners was pure in-vidiousness; nobody thought candles were romantic until they were archaic.)

And why have servants? Because we are too busy to do the housework, of course. But what are we busy doing—except all the other activities that the pageant of status demands? "Under the requirement of conspicuous consumption of goods, the apparatus of living has grown so elaborate and cumbrous, in the way of dwellings, furniture, bric-a-brac, wardrobe and meals, that the consumers of these things cannot make way with them in the required manner without help." A peaceable savage, seeing that he couldn't live his life without the help of an expensive staff of retainers, would change his life. The law of conspicuous consumption makes the sensible choice impossible. For Veblen, the law of conspicuous consumption made the economic apples fall up. It was not enough to build a better mousetrap in order to see the world beat a path to your door. In the real world, it was better to build a worse kind of mousetrap, if you could promise that it would attract a better class of mouse.

THERE have been five distinct styles of Veblenian display in the American century. The five styles correspond, with beautiful and unsuspicious neatness, to twenty-year periods. Each one happened as, in Veblen's terms, "a fresh increase of wealth" gave rise to "a new standard of sufficiency." We can see the expression of the five styles if we look in order at five museum buildings. (The museum has become, as Veblen suspected it would, the temple of devout observance in the pecuniary culture—the institution that, like the churches of his day, seems to be outside the system but is an integral part of it.)

The century began with pure display, or ridiculously conspicuous consumption. This was the style that Veblen himself described, and it remained in place until around 1929. The Metropolitan Museum, built between 1880 and 1926, is a temple devoted to conspicuous consumption of the past. It is as loud a building as you could want, declaring its "industrial exemption" and announcing that its makers have gone out and captured the European past. (The lingerie form of pure display was the corset, its fashion the Worth gown, its favorite New York restaurant Delmonico's.)

Veblen himself glimpsed that the excesses of pure display would soon look vulgar. "Considered as objects of beauty," he wrote presciently, "the dead walls of the sides and back of [a luxury apartment building], left untouched by the hands of the artist, are commonly the best feature of the building." Counter-display, or conspicuously inconspicuous consumption, which ran from around 1930 to the end of the Second World War, propelled the first Museum of Modern Art. Built in 1939, it was the temple of the simplified style that the Rockefellers, as Veblen saw, had begun to introduce to the American leisure class at the turn of the century. Counter-display is conspicuously inconspicuous, unmistakably so—it's chastened, but chastened on Fifth Avenue. (Its fashion style was the chemise, its lingerie the shift, and its restaurant the sequence of "serious" French restaurants that began with The Colony.)

The problem with counter-display was that it induced aesthetic nausea even more quickly than styles of display usually do—you can go on not being that other thing only for so long, until people forget what that other thing was that you're not. *Counter*-counter display, or inconspicuously conspicuous consumption, reigned roughly from 1950 to 1965. Though it was one of the most appealing moments in the history of American display, it's easy to overlook, because it got assimilated to what came next. It was the style of a moneyed class that had come to feel aesthetic nausea at the constraints of counter-display but was too confident for self-parody. It was opposed to the puritanical constraints of Bauhaus modernism but was attached to a romantic rhetoric of truth, indigenous culture, organic form, and so on. Frank Lloyd Wright's Guggenheim is the perfect monument of this style. It puts on a show, twisting and turning, but the show is an advertisement for "natural" values. (Counter-counter display's dress, meanwhile, was summed up in the rich but unornamented style of pillbox hats and knee-length high-waisted sheaths. Its restaurant was La Côte Basque. Its lingerie was the bra, made most famous by the still eerily erotic "I dreamed I went to work in my Maidenform Bra" ads—an extension of the practicality of the chemise but given an extra twist, like the Guggenheim.)

IT was John Brooks, for many years the business correspondent of this magazine, who in his terrific 1979 updating of Veblen, *Showing Off in America*, coined the term "parody display" for what came next. Conspicuously ridiculous consumption dominated from 1965 to 1985. Parody display was pure irony; it depended on putting everything in quotes and announcing that there was nothing in the world but styles and their recyclings. It included, as Brooks pointed out, luxury styles like high-tech décor—which stood Veblen's "industrial exemption" for the rich on its head (and reinforced it in spoof form)—and designer jeans, on which Gloria Vanderbilt and Levi Strauss collaborated to make the last first. It rested, above all, on the idea that anything could gain status by being made ironic. You could buy the cheaper cappuccino in order to spoof the more expensive one. The basis for invidious comparison wasn't what you owned but the spirit in which you owned it.

The monument to parody display remains Michael Graves's unbuilt project for an extension to the Whitney Museum. Graves would have placed a quasi-Chippendale cabinet next to Marcel Breuer's classic reformed-modernist museum, with a kind of ghastly incised smile above to join them. His museum had to be understood as an in-joke, the new museum metaphorically digging the solemn old museum in the ribs and telling it to get with it. (If parody display proposed any voyage, it was to Miami Beach, where one could mock the tastes of one's grandparents and enjoy them at the same time. Brooks insisted that the parody form of lingerie was the silicone implant, which offered breasts that could be both ogled and laughed at.)

Parody dining might have seemed harder to pull off, but it was achieved in the unexpected evolution of the Four Seasons restaurant in the Seagram Building. Made as a monument to fifties counter-counter display, a lovely repository of modernism plus luxury, it came a little too late to work on its own terms; it became successful only when it evolved into the prime site of the parody business lunch, where you went to be conspicuously seen not eating the food or looking at the décor. At the height of its popularity as a site of parody dining, every day at lunch a chocolate bombe would be wheeled out for the single and express purpose of not being eaten by women editors—who would recoil in horror at its presence and order black coffee.

FOR the most part, our picture of conspicuous consumption in America has remained fixed there: a half century of fool's gold followed by an age of wrought irony. Yet in the eighties an odd thing happened. Once everything becomes ironic—even Saturday-morning cartoons—then soon nothing is ironic, and what stands out is no longer the ironic but the eccentrically earnest. In a world where everything is taken as parody, the people who get attention, and then status, are the few who really mean it. George Trow once wrote an elegiac lament for the impossibility of an American man, post-1965, wearing his hat in any manner except ironically. At last, in this decade, a man came along who could wear his hat unironically, and that man was Matt Drudge.

Still, the new sincerity had absorbed the crucial lesson of parody display, which is that everything—even *really meaning it*—can be reduced to style. The Frank Gehry–Thomas Krens Guggenheim, in Bilbao, considered strictly as a symbol, is a perfect embodiment of the new devout observance. Where in the last Gilded Age the Metropolitan announced that America had claimed the Old World and brought it home as booty, the new Guggenheim is the symbol of our art and style taking over the Old World. The museum is less famous for the pictures it contains than for its romantic exterior, the subject of photographs, music videos, magazine spreads, fashion layouts. It is in no way a joke, an ironic gesture, a spoof, or an in-joke. Yet, unlike the first Guggenheim, which follows the rule of Veblen's corset, the new Guggenheim makes no claim to be natural. It is a sincere extravagant gesture made to the glory of extravagant gestures.

This kind of post–parody display—call it consumingly ridiculous conspicuousness—has been the dominant mode of showing off in America for about fifteen years. (Post–parody display has a lot in common with pure display: the thong, with its uncomfortable body definition, is a kind of corset in stenographic form.) The rhetoric of post–parody display is romantic, but its style is retrospective: things are audacious, dangerous, courageous, even when the prized activity—making violent genre films, say—involves no risk at all or a risk so highly stylized and fixed in advance that it is simply a ritual reënactment of old risks. Compare Malcolm Forbes's ballooning expeditions, a high point of parody display—expeditions with an element of self-spoof in them, meant as a campy joke—to Richard Branson's dead-serious balloon expeditions. The ultimate leisure-class expression of post–parody display is the canned Mt. Everest expedition, something that is elaborate, dangerous, hugely expensive, and undertaken as an exercise in conspicuousness. Edmund Hillary went to the top of Mt. Everest because it was there. Sandy Pittman went to the top of Mt. Everest because, if she did, she would be, too.

PLAYING the Veblenian game is a lot of fun, but how seriously should we take it? Among mainstream economists, the response to the Veblen account of conspicuous consumption has always been, basically, so what? What looks wasteful to some is sensible to others: Veblen takes his prejudices and calls them natural, and takes other people's taste and calls it "waste." The bearded Veblen, for one example, thought that shaving was conspicuous consumption. (Well, says the man with the three-blade razor in his hand, maybe so.) It's true that the things other people want may be weird, or surprising, or not to our liking, but, given that they want them, the working out of the market for those things and the economic laws that govern them are the same in Newport or East Hampton as they are anywhere else. Veblen had to claim that the desires of the peaceable savage—a creature nobody has ever met—are "natural," while those of the predatory barbarian are not. Only if you believe that you know what people ought to want can you believe that there is anything strange about the fact that often they want things that you don't.

Anything in human existence not immediately necessary to keep you alive can be explained away as Veblenian display—including all art, architecture, design, and ideas. The three-blade razor is an example of invidious display, and so are New York's Deco skyscrapers, each one rising higher than the next in a classic case of competitive conspicuousness. The run of pure display, counter-display, etc., may have given us American museums—but, in doing so, it gave us the American museum.

In the end, the amateur reader, encountering Veblen, is likely to want to reclaim him for the comic-obsessive strain in American literature. One of the curious things about Veblen's career is that, once he had his theory out there, he didn't really build on it. Although he wrote some good and some successful books afterward—particularly one on the university, and one pleading for rule by "technocracy"—they lack the deadpan, pseudo-anthropological, Gulliver-like humor of the *Theory*. In 1918, Veblen came to New York to be an editor of the *Dial*, then, in 1920, took an academic appointment at the New School for Social Research. But he was out of there after three sloppy years, and he went to live in a cabin he had bought years before in Northern California, which was, after all, the right place for an inspired oddball to end up.

His admirers still like to tap-dance around the weirdness of his theory—besides the fierce attacks on small dogs and clean-shaven men, there are frequent references to the "dolicho-blond type of European man"—but the crankiness is what gives savor to the writing, reminding us at times of the older Oliver Wendell Holmes, the Autocrat of the Breakfast Table. Veblen and Thoreau, in fact, remain the wellsprings of most first-rate American journalism, Thoreau leading direct to E. B. White and the Shy Guys, and Veblen to the Wise Guys and Tom Wolfe.

What the too avid Veblenian can miss is that good stuff emerges not in spite of but because of the system of invidious comparison. If the predatory barbarian can't see the difference between the painting and its price tag, the Veblenian can't always see the difference between Michael Jordan and his sneakers. "Reason not the need," King Lear says, when Goneril asks him why he needs all those retainers, all that waste and display. "Our basest beggars are in the poorest thing superfluous." "Reason not the need" is the hidden motto on the American dollar. There is nothing reasonable about needs, which isn't to say that needs can't be reasoned about, or at least argued over. ("Well, Father, but do you *need* a fool?") The arguing over it is what we call life. There is nothing to do with a day except to live it, a great American poet once said, and there is nothing to do with a dress, a great American shopper added, with a sigh, except try it on. Beyond that, it's all just the pursuit of happiness, and nobody ever promised that its path was going to be self-evident.

APRIL 26, 1999

AFTER SEATTLE

FOR Juliette Beck, it began with the story of the Ittu Oromo, Ethiopian nomads whose lives were destroyed, in vast numbers, by a dam—a hydroelectric project sponsored by the World Bank. Beck was a sophomore at Berkeley, taking a class in international rural development. The daughter of an orthopedic surgeon, she had gone to college planning to do premed, but environmental science caught her interest, and the story of the Ittu Oromo precipitated a change of major. Beck was a brilliant student—"One of these new Renaissance people, so smart they could be almost anything," a former professor of hers recalls. She was intellectually insatiable, and her eagerness to understand the dynamics of economic development propelled her into several academic fields, notably the dry, dizzying politics of international finance and trade. By her junior year, she was teaching a class on the North American Free Trade Agreement. "It was one of the most popular student-led classes we've had," her professor says. "I understand it's been cloned on other campuses."

Beck had found her strange grand passion—international trade rules—at an auspicious time. Besides the popularity of her class, there were the events last November in Seattle, where fifty thousand demonstrators shut down a major meeting of the World Trade Organization. Beck, who is twenty-seven, was a key organizer of the Seattle protests.

"The Spirit of Seattle," she says, crinkling her eyes and grinning blissfully. "Your body just tingled with hope, to be around so many people so committed to making a better world." Beck says things like "tingled with hope" and "making a better world" with no hint of self-consciousness, and in the next breath will launch into a critique of the Multilateral Agreement on Investment, a set of international trade rules that she and other activists have fought against for the last several years. (The M.A.I. would limit the rights of national governments to regulate currency speculation or set policies regarding investment.) This odd fusion of hardheaded policy analysis and utopian idealism has an exhilarating edge, which may account for some of Beck's habitual high spirits.

Almost six feet tall, she retains, to a striking degree, both the coltishness of adolescence and the open-faced, all-American social style of the Girl Scout and high-school athlete (volleyball, tennis, basketball) she was. Zooming around the scruffy, loft-style offices of Global Exchange, the human-rights organization in San Francisco where she works, she seems conspicuously lacking the self-décor of the other young activists around the place—piercings, tattoos, dreadlocks. It may be that she's simply been too busy to get herself properly tatted up. While we were talking in her office on a recent evening, she tried to deal simultaneously with me and with a significant fraction of the seven hundred E-mail messages that had piled up in her in-box—reading, forwarding, filing, trashing, replying, sighing, grumbling, erupting in laughter. She was determined, she said, to have an empty in-box before she left, in a few days' time, for Washington, D.C., even if it meant pulling consecutive all-nighters.

"Where I grew up, in suburban San Diego, it was so strange," she said. "Politics didn't exist. The only political gesture I ever saw there was during the Gulf War. People drove around waving American flags from the backs of pickups. That was it. When we were teen-agers, the consumerism was overwhelming. If you didn't wear Guess jeans, you didn't exist. When I got to Berkeley, I was just like a *sponge.* At one point, I realized that, in my entire education, having gone through good public schools, advanced-placement programs, and all that, I had never learned anything about the American labor movement. Nothing. I don't think I ever heard the term 'collective bargaining' inside a classroom. No wonder we were all so apolitical!"

After college, Beck went to work as an environmental engineer for a small Bay Area firm. The pay was good, and the work was interesting, but she found herself spending most of her time competing with other firms for contracts. "It made me realize I didn't want to be doing work that was all about money." So she made the downward financial leap into the non-profit sector (and was recently forced to move from chic, expensive San Francisco to cheaper, inconvenient Oakland, where she lives in a group house with no living room). It's a step she says she's never regretted. "I think a lot of people in my generation—not a majority, maybe, but a lot—feel this void," she told me. "We feel like capitalism and buying things are just not fulfilling. Period." She became an organizer for Public Citizen, Ralph Nader's consumer group, which was campaigning, along with labor unions and other allies, to stop the Clinton Administration's effort to get renewed "fast track" authority to negotiate trade agreements with limited congressional oversight. (The problem with such authority, according to its opponents, is its bias, in practice, in favor of industry.) The campaign was successful—the first major defeat in Congress for trade advocates in sixty years. "That was a great victory," Beck said happily. "We defeated some of the most powerful forces on the planet."

Those powerful forces, once they had recovered from the shock, responded with a public-relations offensive. William Daley, the Secretary of Commerce, embarked on a National Trade Education Tour, meant to persuade the American people of the wisdom of free trade. Daley was met by protesters at every stop. In Los Angeles, Beck helped coördinate his unofficial reception. "We just *dogged* him." Longshoremen refused to coöperate with the Secretary, she said, for what she called "a photo op at the docks." She went on, "They said, 'No way, come down to our headquarters and we'll have an honest discussion on trade.' He said no. These fat cats only want to talk on their terms. Even the kids at a high school in Long Beach where Daley spoke asked him tough questions. We really caused that tour to flop. Daley had a bus full of C.E.O.s and flacks from the Business Roundtable, but a lot of bigwigs flaked when they saw how hokey the whole thing was." Six corporate leaders, including the chairmen of Boeing and A.T.&T., had in fact appeared with Daley at the tour's kickoff, then made themselves scarce when it began to smell of disaster.

Beck's delight in such disasters is wicked and shameless. I recalled a news story she had circulated by E-mail a few weeks before. The story was about Michel Camdessus, the managing director of the International Monetary Fund, getting hit in the face by a fruit-and-cream pie just before he gave a farewell speech to mark his retirement. Beck's cover note exulted, "The head of I.M.F. got his just desserts this weekend—a parting pie shot!"

Beck likes to call the I.M.F., the W.T.O., and the World Bank "the iron triangle of corporate rule." In her view, these institutions—their leaders, clients, political allies, and, above all, true bosses, multinational corporations—are frog-marching humanity, along with the rest of the planet, into a toxic, money-maddened, repressive future. And she intends to persuade the rest of us not to go quietly.

In her office at Global Exchange, still crashing through the underbrush of her in-box, she suddenly pulled up short. "Oh, check this out," she said, and pointed to her computer screen. "Have you seen this?"

I had. It was a report prepared by Burson-Marsteller, the Washington publicity firm, which had been leaked and was making the electronic rounds. It was titled "Guide to the Seattle Meltdown: A Compendium of Activists at the W.T.O. Ministerial." Burson-Marsteller's cover letter began, "Dear [Corporate Client]," and characterized the report "not so much as a retrospective on the past, but as an alarming window on the future." The report offered profiles of dozens of groups that had participated in the Seattle protests—from the Anarchist Action Collective to Consumers International to the A.F.L.-C.I.O.—naming leaders, giving Web-site addresses, and including brief descriptions, usually lifted from the literature of the groups themselves. The cover letter mentioned possible "significant short-term ramifications for the business community" because of the "perceived success of these groups in disrupting Seattle" and, more portentously, warned of "the potential ability of the emerging coalition of these groups to seriously impact broader, longer-term corporate interests."

Burson-Marsteller was at least trying to reckon with what had been revealed in Seattle. The press, the Seattle authorities, the Clinton Administration, the W.T.O., and many other interested parties had largely been ignorant of the popular movement being built around them. Suddenly challenged, everyone had scrambled to respond, some (the police) attacking the protesters, others (Bill Clinton) rhetorically embracing them (while his negotiators continued to pursue in private the controversial policies he was renouncing in public), but all basically hoping that the problem—this nightmare of an aroused, mysteriously well-organized citizenry—would just go away. Burson-Marsteller knew better. Its "compendium" had even picked up on demonstrations being planned for April against the World Bank and the I.M.F. during meetings in Washington, D.C. This was before anything about those demonstrations had appeared in what movement activists insist on calling the corporate press.

I say "movement activists" because nobody has yet figured out what to call them. Sympathetic observers refer to them as "the Seattle coalition," but this title reflects little of the movement's international scope. In the United States, the movement is dramatically—even, one could say, deliberately—lacking in national leaders. It is largely coördinated on-line. I picked Juliette Beck almost at random as a bright thread to follow through this roiling fabric of rising, mostly youthful American resistance to corporate-led globalization.

GLOBAL free trade promotes global economic growth. It creates jobs, makes companies more competitive, and lowers prices for consumers. It also provides poor countries, through infusions of foreign capital and technology, with the chance to develop economically and, by spreading prosperity, creates the conditions in which democracy and respect for human rights may flourish.

This is the animating vision of the Clinton Administration, and it is a view widely shared by political leaders, economic decision-makers, and opinion-makers throughout the West. It is also accepted, at least in its outlines, by many important figures in business and government in Third World countries, where it is known as "the Washington consensus."

Critics of this consensus dispute most, if not all, of its claims. Growth, they argue, can be wasteful, destructive, unjust. The jobs created by globalization are often less sustaining and secure than the livelihoods abolished by it. Weak economies abruptly integrated into the global system do not become stronger, or develop a sustainable base; they just become more dependent, more vulnerable to the ructions of ultravolatile, deregulated international capital. In many countries, the benefits of economic growth are so unequally distributed that they intensify social and political tensions, leading to increased repression rather than to greater democracy. To the hoary trope that a rising tide lifts all boats, critics of corporate-led globalization retort that in this case it lifts only yachts.

Nearly everyone, though, on both sides of the globalization debate, accepts that the process creates winners and losers. And it is globalization's losers and potential losers—and all those with doubts about the wisdom of unchecked, unequal growth—who propel the backlash that found such vivid expression in Seattle. One odd aspect of that backlash is the ideological opposites it contains. American right-wing isolationists of the Patrick Buchanan variety are as hostile to the international bodies that promote economic globalization as they are to the United Nations. In Britain, unreconstructed Tories continue to loathe and oppose the European Union, a prime mover of globalization. Meanwhile, young British anarchists also hate the E.U., and the bulk of the Seattle coalition is being drawn from the American liberal and radical Left.

The booming popularity of the movement on college campuses is another odd aspect of its makeup, since American college graduates are unlikely to find themselves, even in the short term, on the losing side of the great globalization ledger. And yet students, whether fired up by their coursework, like Beck, or simply sensing that this is where the subcultural action is now, have been turning out in surprising numbers for mass "teach-ins" on the W.T.O., the I.M.F., and the World Bank—even eagerly swallowing solid doses of the economic history and international financial arcana that come unavoidably with these topics.

Kevin Danaher, a co-founder of Global Exchange, sees nothing incongruous about young people getting excited about the dismal science. "Economics and politics have been kept falsely separate, traditionally," he says. "We're just trying to drag capital-investment decision-making out into the public realm. That's the terrain of struggle now. The anti-apartheid divestment campaign set the precedent."

Danaher, who in a doctoral dissertation examined the political economy of United States policy toward South Africa, was one of the leaders of the American divestment campaign. Since that campaign's contribution to ending apartheid and bringing democracy to South Africa can scarcely be overstated, his bullishness about the prospects for democratizing the rules of the new global economy may be understandable. He talks, somewhat messianically, about replacing the "money cycle" with the "life cycle," but then puts his ideas to the test by running a bustling non-profit business. Global Exchange, besides its human-rights research and activism—it has mounted corporate-accountability campaigns, targeting Nike, the Gap, and, starting this month, Starbucks for their international labor practices—operates two stores in the Bay Area, plus an on-line store, selling crafts and coffee and other goods bought directly, on demonstrably fair terms, from small producers in poor countries; it also offers "reality tours" of such countries as Cuba, Haiti, and Iran to high-disposable-income travellers not yet ready for cruise ships.

Addressing young audiences, Danaher—who is forty-nine, has a shaved head and a white goatee, and retains enough of the speech patterns of a working-class New Jersey youth to carry off the most populist harangue—makes a cross-generational pitch. He acknowledges the difficulty of understanding what it is that an institution like the World Bank even does, but then urges people to educate themselves and, in recent speeches, to come to Washington in April. "It's going to be Woodstock times ten," he told one college class, pulling out the stops. "I was at Woodstock, I was at Seattle, and Seattle changed *my* butt."

THE World Bank lends money to the governments of poor countries. It was founded, along with the International Monetary Fund, after the Second World War to help finance the reconstruction of Europe. When the Marshall Plan usurped its original purpose, the Bank had to reinvent itself, shifting its focus to Asia, Africa, and Latin America, where the elimination of poverty became its declared mission. This was the first in a long series of institutional costume changes. Today, the Bank, which is headquartered in Washington, D.C., has more than ten thousand employees, a hundred and eighty member states, and offices in sixty-seven of those countries, and lends nearly thirty billion dollars a year. It ventures into fields far beyond its original mandate, including conflict resolution—demobilizing troops in Uganda, clearing land mines in Bosnia. The I.M.F., whose founding purpose was to make short-term loans to stabilize currencies, has similarly had to shape-shift with the times. Also headquartered in Washington, it now makes long-term loans as well and tries to manage the economies of many of its poorer member states.

Both institutions have always been dominated by the world's rich countries, particularly the United States. During the Cold War, this meant that loans were often granted on a crudely political basis. Indeed, the World Bank's first loan—two hundred and fifty million dollars to France, in 1947—was withheld until the French government purged its Cabinet of Communists. In the Third World, friendly dictators were propped up by loans. Robert McNamara, after presiding over the Vietnam War, became president of the World Bank in 1968, and he expanded its operations aggressively, pushing poor countries to transform their economies by promoting industrialized agriculture and export production. There were fundamental problems with this development model. By the time McNamara retired, in 1981, his legacy consisted largely of failed megaprojects, populations no longer able to feed themselves, devastated forests and watersheds, and a sea of hopeless debt.

Bank officials have consistently vowed to improve this record, to start funding projects that benefit not only big business and Third World élites but also the world's poor. Accordingly, projects with non-governmental organizations and other "civil society" groups, along with efforts to promote access to health care and education, have increased. But Bank contracts are worth millions, and multinational corporations have remained major beneficiaries. In 1995, Lawrence Summers, then an under-secretary at the Treasury Department—he is now its Secretary—told Congress that for each dollar the American government contributed to the World Bank, American corporations received $1.35 in procurement contracts. One of the Bank's major proposals at the moment is for the development of oilfields in Chad, in central Africa, and the construction of an oil pipeline running more than six hundred miles to the coast at Cameroon. The environmental impact of this pipeline is predicted by many to be dire, the benefits to the people in the area minimal. The big winners will, in all likelihood, be the Bank's major partners in the project—Exxon Mobil and Chevron.

More onerous than ill-advised projects, however, for the people of the global South has been the crushing accumulation of debt by their governments. This debt now totals more than two trillion dollars, and servicing it— simply paying the interest—has become the single largest budget item for scores of poor countries. About twenty years ago, the World Bank and the I.M.F. began attaching stricter conditions to the loans they made to debtor countries to help them avoid outright default. More than ninety countries have now been subjected to I.M.F.-imposed austerity schemes, also known as structural-adjustment programs. Typically, these force a nation to cut spending in health, education, and welfare programs; reduce or eliminate food, energy, and transport subsidies; devalue its local currency; raise interest rates to attract foreign capital; privatize state property; and lower barriers to foreign ownership of local industries, land, and assets.

This is where the World Trade Organization comes in—or, rather, where its agenda dovetails with the work of the Bank and the I.M.F. All three institutions have always sought to increase world trade. (The W.T.O. is the successor to the General Agreement on Tariffs and Trade, which began in 1947 and was folded into the W.T.O. in 1995.) But the W.T.O. is the spearhead of the present surge toward economic globalization. It is a huge bureaucracy that makes binding rules intended to remove obstacles to the expansion of commercial activity among the hundred and thirty-five countries that constitute its membership. This means, in practice, an incremental transfer of power from local and national governments (the bodies likely to erect such obstacles) to the W.T.O., which acts as a trade court, hearing, behind closed doors, disputes among members accusing one another of creating barriers to trade. These "barriers" may be health, safety, or environmental laws, and a W.T.O. ruling takes precedence over all other international agreements. A country found to be impeding trade must change the offending law or suffer harsh sanctions. The effect is to deregulate international commerce, freeing the largest corporations—which, measured as economic entities, already dwarf most of the world's countries— to enter any market, extract any resource, without constraint by citizenries. Speaking anonymously, a former W.T.O. official recently told the *Financial*

Times, "This is the place where governments collude in private against their domestic pressure groups."

There is, in other words, little mystery about why the W.T.O. and its partners in free-trade promotion, the World Bank and the I.M.F., have become the protest targets of choice for environmentalists, labor unions, economic nationalists, small farmers and small-business people, and their allies. Trade rules among countries are obviously needed. The question is whom those rules will benefit, whose rights they will protect.

The fifty thousand people who took to the streets of Seattle chanting "No new round—turn around!" had clearly decided that the W.T.O. was not on their side when it came to steering the direction of global trade. But even that might be too broad a statement—for the coalition that gathered there was wildly diverse, its collective critique nothing if not eclectic. Many of its members would probably not agree, for instance, that trade rules are "obviously" needed. That's my view, but the movement against corporate-led globalization contains many people who accept fewer rules of the capitalist game than I do.

THE Direct Action Network (DAN) probably belongs in the deeply anti-capitalist category. But the group is less than a year old and extremely loosely structured, so its ideology isn't easy to get a fix on. What does seem certain is that the shutdown (or "meltdown," as Burson-Marsteller has it) of the Seattle Ministerial would never have happened without the emergence and furious efforts of the Direct Action Network.

Juliette Beck was present at DAN's creation. Late last spring, a young organizer named David Solnit, who was well known in the movement for his dedication and ingenuity, and for his giant homemade puppets—Solnit's allegorical figures have appeared in demonstrations from coast to coast—approached Beck with a plan to shut down the Seattle meeting. Dozens of groups, including the A.F.L.-C.I.O. and Global Trade Watch, a leading branch of Nader's Public Citizen, were already planning for Seattle. But no one was talking shutdown. Solnit thought it could be done, and he figured that Global Exchange could help. Beck and Kevin Danaher called in the Rainforest Action Network and a Berkeley-based group called the Ruckus Society, which specializes in nonviolent guerrilla action, and DAN was hatched.

Solnit was the dynamo but not the leader. "DAN is lots of lieutenants, no generals," Danaher says. The word went out, largely over the Internet, about DAN's plans, and dozens of groups and countless individuals expressed interest. The DAN coalition developed along with what is known as the "affinity-group model." Affinity groups are small, semi-independent units, pledged to coalition goals, tactics, and principles—including, in DAN's case, nonviolent action—but free to make their own plans. Members look out for one another during protests, and some have designated roles: medic, legal support (avoids arrest), "spoke" (confers with other affinity groups through affinity "clusters"), "action elf" (looks after food, water, and people's spirits). Thousands signed up for training, and for "camps" organized by the Ruckus Society, where they could learn not only the techniques of classic civil disobedience but specialized skills like urban rappelling (for hanging banners on buildings), forming human blockades, and how to "lock down" in groups (arms linked through specially constructed plastic tubes). Solnit coördinated a road show that toured the West in the months before the W.T.O. Ministerial, presenting music and speakers and street theatre, urging people to get involved and come to Seattle.

They came, of course, and the combination of strict civil-disobedience discipline (the only way that the lines around the hotels and meeting places and across key intersections could have held, preventing W.T.O. delegates from gathering) and polymorphous protest (dancers on vans, hundreds of children dressed as sea turtles and monarch butterflies, Korean priests in white robes playing flutes and drums to protest genetically modified food) could never have been centrally planned.

The affinity-group model proved extremely effective in dealing with police actions. Downtown Seattle had been divided by a DAN "spokescouncil" into thirteen sectors, with an affinity cluster responsible for each sector. There were also flying squads—mobile affinity groups that could quickly take the place of groups that had been arrested or beaten or gassed from the positions they were trying to hold. The structure was flexible, and tactically powerful, and the police, trying to clear the streets, resorted to increasingly brutal methods, firing concussion grenades, mashing pepper spray into the eyes of protesters, shooting rubber bullets into bodies at short range. By the afternoon of November 30th (the first day of the meeting), the police had run low on ammunition, and that evening the mayor of Seattle called out the National Guard.

There were hundreds of arrests. Beck, who was teargassed on a line blocking the entrance to the convention center, had credentials, through Global Exchange, to enter the theatre where the W.T.O. was supposed to be having its opening session. She went inside, found a few delegates milling, and an open microphone. She and Danaher and Medea Benjamin—another co-founder of Global Exchange—took the stage, uninvited, and suggested that delegates join them in a discussion. The interlopers were hustled off the stage. Beck elected not to go quietly. Marshals put her in a pain hold—her arm twisted behind her back—and dragged her through the theatre. A news camera recorded the event. "Then CNN kept showing it, over and over, them carrying me off, whenever they talked about the arrests," she says. "My claim to fame. Except I wasn't arrested! They just threw me out."

Ironically, the only protesters not following the nonviolence guidelines—a hundred or so "black bloc" anarchists, who started smashing shopwindows—were hardly bothered by the police. The black-bloc crews, whose graffiti and occasional "communiqués" run to nihilist slogans ("Civilization Is Collapsing—Let's Give It a Push!"), were masked, well organized, young and fleet of foot, and armed with crowbars and acid-filled eggs. The police in their heavy riot gear could not have caught them if they'd tried. The targeted shops belonged to big corporations: Nike, the Gap, Fidelity Investments, Starbucks, Levi's, Planet Hollywood. Still, other protesters chanted "Shame! Shame!" Some even tried to stop the attacks. There were scuffles, and suggestions that the black blocs contained police agents provocateurs—hence the masks. Medea Benjamin, who had helped produce the original exposé of Nike's sweatshops in Asia, found herself in the absurd position of siding with protesters who were defending a Niketown. And her fear (shared by many) that a few broken windows might snatch away the headlines in the national press proved justified.

The political spectrum represented in the protests was improbably wide, ranging from, on the right, James Hoffa's Teamsters and the A.F.L.-C.I.O. (who fielded tens of thousands of members for a march) to, on the left, a dozen or more anarchist factions (the black blocs were a rowdy minority within a generally less aggressive minority), including the ancient Industrial Workers of the World. All these groups had found, if not a common cause, at least a common foe. Some unlikely alliances were cemented. The United Steelworkers union and Earth First!, for example, had a common enemy in the Maxxam Corporation, which logs old-growth forests *and* owns steel mills, and the two groups are currently working together to end a bitter lockout at a Kaiser Aluminum plant in Tacoma.

Inside the besieged W.T.O. Ministerial, there was a rebellion among countries from the global South, which raised the possibility of another, truly formidable alliance with some of the forces out in the streets. The leaders of the poorer countries, though often depicted as pawns of the major powers, content to offer their countries' workers to the world market at the lowest possible wages—and to pollute their air and water and strip-mine their natural resources, in exchange for their own commissions on the innumerable deals that come with corporate globalization—in reality have to answer, in many cases, to complex constituencies at home, many of whom are alarmed about their own economic recolonization. In Seattle, delegations from Africa, Asia, the Caribbean, and Latin America—rattled by the total disruption of the Ministerial's schedule, and furious about being excluded from key meetings held privately by the rich countries—issued statements announcing their refusal to sign "agreements" produced at such meetings. In the end, no agreements were signed, no new round launched, and the Ministerial finished in disarray. This insurgency was often depicted in the American press as a refusal by the representatives of the poor countries to accept higher labor and environmental standards being imposed on them by the West, but that was not the gist of the revolt, which ran deeper and echoed the fundamental questions being asked outside in the streets about the mandate of the W.T.O.

"COALITION-building is hard," Juliette Beck said. "There's no doubt about it. But it's what we do." We were sitting in a deserted café in some sort of Latino community center one Sunday night in Berkeley, sipping beers. "At Global Exchange, we try to think of campaigns that will appeal to the average Joe on the street. We're really not interested in just organizing other leftists. Big corporations are a great target, because they do things that hurt virtually everybody. My dad, who's very right-wing, but libertarian, hates corporations. The H.M.O.s have practically ruined his medical practice, mainly because he insists on spending as much time with his patients as he thinks they need. After Seattle, he read a column by the economist Robert Kuttner, and suddenly, he said, he got what we're trying to do. Kuttner apparently explained that corporations just naturally grab all the power they can, and when they've grabbed too much there has to be a backlash. That's what led, a hundred years ago, to trust-busting and federal regulation after the robber barons did their thing, and that's what's causing this movement now. It was nice to hear my dad say that."

Across the street was a café/bookshop/community center, this one run by an anarchist collective (we were, remember, in Berkeley) called Long Haul Infoshop, which distributes a radical journal called *Slingshot*. In a special W.T.O. edition, *Slingshot* had derided Global Exchange and "other despicable examples of the corporate left"; another column slammed Medea Benjamin for her defense of Nike. I asked Beck about the attacks from the left. She sighed. "Yeah, there's been a lot of fallout. A lot of people believe property destruction isn't violence. But that wasn't really the issue in Seattle. The issue was what message, what images, we were sending out to the world. There's always going to be disagreement. When it comes to these institutions—the W.T.O., the I.M.F., the World Bank—we have reformists and abolitionists. If we're talking about the World Bank, I, for instance, am an abolitionist."

I asked Beck if she considered herself an anarchist.

She shrugged, as if the question were obtuse.

DAN seemed, at a glance, to be an anarchist organization, or at least organized on anarchist principles, I said.

"Sure," Beck said, still looking nonplussed. Finally, she said, "Well, I definitely respect anarchist ways of organizing. I guess I'm still learning what it means to be an anarchist. But the real question is: Can this anarchist model that's working so well now for organizing protests be applied on an international scale to create the democratic decision-making structures that we need to eliminate poverty?"

I took this opportunity to float a theory, somewhat grander and iffier than Kuttner's, about the historical forces that cause anarchism to flourish. Anarchism, I said, first arose in Europe as a response to the disruptions of peasant and artisanal life caused by industrialization and the rapid concentration of power among new business élites. After a good long fight, anarchism basically lost out to socialism as an organizing vision among workers—and lost again, after a heady late run, in Republican Spain, to Communism (which then lost to fascism). But anarchism was obviously enjoying some kind of small-time comeback, and, if today's Information Revolution was even half as significant as both its critics and its cheerleaders like to claim—the most important economic development since the Industrial Revolution, and so on—then perhaps the time was ripening, socialism having been disgraced as an alternative to capitalism, for another great wave of anarchist protest against this latest, alarmingly swift amassing of power in the hands of a few hundred billionaires. Did Beck know that the term "direct action" was used by anarcho-syndicalists in France at the turn of the last century?

She did. She also knew, it seemed, that anarchism has become wildly popular among Latin American students who are fed up with what they call *neoliberalismo* (their term for corporate-led globalization) but disenchanted, also, with the traditional left. And she knew that the students who went on strike and took over the National University in Mexico City for nine months recently were mostly anarchists. But did I know (I didn't) that it had been a structural-adjustment edict from the World Bank that led the Mexican government to raise student fees, which sparked the strike and the takeover?

Beck drained her beer. DAN, whatever its historical analogues, had been thriving since its triumph in Seattle, she said. The network was now directing most of its considerable energies toward the April action in Washington, D.C., which people were calling "A16," for April 16th, the day the I.M.F. planned to meet. She was going to Washington herself in a couple of days, and then joining a road show, which would start making its way up the East Coast, beating the drums for the big event.

"I AM Funkier Than You," the bumper sticker said, and it was almost certainly true. But the Mango Affinity Group, as the road-show crew had taken to calling themselves, had scored this big, extremely grubby van free from a woman in Virginia simply by asking for a vehicle on the A16 E-mail list serve, so they were not complaining. Liz Guy, an efficient DAN stalwart usually known as Sprout, had pulled together both the crew—eight or nine activists, aged nineteen to thirty-two, including Juliette Beck—and a tight, three-week, show-a-day itinerary that ran from Florida to Montreal before looping back to Washington. I found them in St. Petersburg, bivouacked under a shade tree on the campus of Eckerd College, working on a song.

Beck introduced me. They were a sweet-voiced, ragamuffin group, drawn from Connecticut, Atlanta, Seattle (Sprout), and the mountains of British Columbia. This afternoon was going to be their first performance together, and, judging from the situation as showtime approached and they began lugging their gear into a low-roofed, brutally air-conditioned hall, somebody had blown the publicity. There was virtually no one around except their hosts—two young DAN guys, Peter and Josh, who were hopefully laying out anarchist and vegan pamphlets and books on a table. Peter and Josh, embarrassed, said they had just returned from a Ruckus Society camp. Evidently, they had left arrangements in the wrong hands. "Let's do a skate-by, see where people are," one of them said, and both jumped on skateboards and shot off.

"Woodstock times ten," Kevin Danaher had said. Pure hooey, I now thought. In truth, A16 did not have going for it many of the things that had converged so resoundingly in Seattle. The planning for the protest was far more rushed. The W.T.O.'s Seattle Ministerial had been, moreover, a momentous gathering, meant to kick off a so-called Millennial Round, whereas the World Bank/I.M.F. spring meetings were strictly routine, and scheduled to be brief. Big labor, finally, had no special interest in the World Bank and the I.M.F., and the A.F.L.-C.I.O., while endorsing the A16 protest, had decided to concentrate its energies this political season on preventing the permanent normalization of United States trade relations with China. A demonstration by union members to press these issues was scheduled to take place in Washington on April 12th. And it wasn't the only event threatening to disperse attention from A16. There was a big protest planned for April 9th, also in Washington, organized by a movement called Jubilee 2000, to demand debt cancellation for the poorest countries.

The hope, of course, was that all these protests would produce some sort of anti-globalization synergy that might just culminate, on A16, in the type of massive turnout that would certainly be needed to have any chance of shutting down the World Bank and the I.M.F. meetings. On the Internet, as always, anything looked possible. Caravans were being organized all over the country, reconnaissance was being conducted on "targets" in Washington, anti-capitalist revolutionary blocs were breaking away from the DAN-centered action with furious objections to mealymouthed talk of "fair trade" and alleged "collaboration with the enemy at large"—to, that is, meetings being held by organizers with the D.C. police to try to prevent bloodshed. (In fact, the D.C. police had gone to Seattle to observe the demonstrations, and had spent a million dollars on new riot gear for A16.) Beck had told me, back in San Francisco, "I get so tired of the Internet and E-mail. We couldn't do this work without it, but, really, it's not organizing. There's nothing like face to face."

Now in Florida, Beck, perhaps getting desperate for some F2F, approached two young women who had wandered into the frigid hall, possibly just to get out of the afternoon heat, and started regaling them with a spiel about how the World Bank and the I.M.F. are "partners in crime." The young women, who wore tank tops and looked as if they belonged on a beach somewhere, nodded politely but said nothing. In the background, Damon, a tall, dark-skinned, curly-haired musician from British Columbia, strummed a guitar, and the rest of the Mango Affinity Group busied themselves making posters denouncing exploitation.

Blessedly, between the skate-by and Damon's guitar, people began to trickle into the hall. Soon there was an audience of thirty or so, and the show began.

Damon disappeared inside a towering, black-suited puppet with a huge papier-mâché head, sloping skull, and cigar stuck between his lips, Beck slapped a "World Bank/I.M.F." sign on his chest, and he began to roar, "You are all under my power!" The crowd laughed, and he roared, "It's not funny, it's true!" They laughed harder. A political skit followed, with a series of fresh-faced young women getting thrashed by an I.M.F. henchman for demanding health and safety standards, then put to work in a Gap sweatshop. "Right to Organize" also got pounded. Afterward, Beck led a teach-in called Globalization 101, with pop quizzes on the meaning of various trade and finance acronyms, and Hershey's Kisses tossed to those who got the answers right. One middle-aged trio—Eckerd faculty, from the look of them—seemed well versed on the topic. Then the Mango members introduced themselves individually—Leigh, from an "intentional community" in Atlanta, Ricardo, from a Canadian "solar-powered coöperative" where people grew much of their own food. Sprout took the opportunity to encourage people to form affinity groups, explaining what they were and how they worked.

I was struck by Sprout's poise. Talking to dozens of strangers, she somehow made her presentation seem like an intimate conversation, with pauses, eye contact, murmurs back and forth, little encouraging interjections ("Awesome!" "Cool!") when she felt she'd been understood. Twenty-five, physically small, and dressed with utter simplicity—loose shirt, cargo pants, no shoes—she achieved, with no theatricality, an effect of tremendous presence. It occurred to me that Sprout, with her neighborly voice and unerring choice of words, could easily be very successful in a completely different arena. On another sort of road show, for instance—the sort that dot-com startups mount, touring and performing for investors and analysts, before taking their companies public. The same was true for Beck. And both women came from cities (Seattle, San Francisco) that were crawling with rich dot-commers more or less their age. What was it that made them choose this raggedy, low-status, activist's path instead? While the rest of the country obsessed over its stock portfolio, these brainy young people were working killer hours for little, if any, pay—quixotically trying, as they sometimes put it, to globalize the world from below.

Next on the program was a rousing folk song, with Damon on guitar and Sage, his regular bandmate from B.C., on drums. Their vocal harmonies sounded fairly polished. Then Sprout produced a viola, slipping without fanfare into the tune, and began improvising fiddle breaks of steadily increasing warmth and precision. I caught Beck's eye. Who *was* this woman? Beck could not stop grinning. The Mango group then ruined the soaring mood, as far as I was concerned, by leading the crowd in some mortifyingly corny chants—"Ain't no power like the power of the people, cuz the power of the people don't stop!"

Beck asked for a show of hands. How many people thought they might go to

Washington for A16? Fifteen or twenty hands shot up, including those of the two women in tank tops. I was amazed that they had even stayed for the show. A signup sheet was circulated.

Next came nonviolence training, for which ten or twelve people stuck around. Leigh and Sprout led the training, which lasted into the evening and included a lot of "role-playing"—people pretending to be protesters, police, I.M.F. officials, workers trying to get to work. There were drills in quick decision-making among affinity groups: Shall we stay locked down or move when threatened with arrest and felony charges? Group dynamics were dissected after each scene. Sprout demonstrated unthreatening body language. Hand signals for swift, clear communication were suggested. Peter and Josh, the two local DAN guys, joined in the training, and it was soon obvious that they had a lot of experience. Peter, who was wiry, bushy-bearded, and soft-spoken, firmly refused to be bullied by some of the bigger, more aggressive men in the group. It became clear that effective nonviolent protest needed a cool head, and that bluster wasn't helpful. Toward the end of the evening, Leigh presented a list of things to bring to an action. Most were common-sense items like food, water, and herbal remedies for tear gas. The rationale for others was less self-evident. Maxi pads?

Leigh and Sprout glanced at one another. "If the cops start using chemical warfare, some women start bleeding very heavily," Leigh said. There was a brief, shocked silence. "They're good as bandages, too," she added.

What about gas masks?

"They can become targets," Josh said. "In Seattle, the cops tried to tear them off, and if they couldn't reach them they fired rubber bullets, or wooden bullets, or these wooden dowel rods they had, at the masks. Some people got a lot of glass in their faces. Masks can be dangerous."

The trainees stared.

"One thing that's good to have is big toenail clippers," Peter said cheerfully. "Put 'em in your pocket, and if you're arrested, and just left in a cell or a paddy wagon, somebody can fish them out of your pocket and cut off your cuffs with 'em. They use cheap plastic cuffs when they arrest a lot of people, and if they leave you sitting for ten or fifteen hours it's a lot more comfortable if your hands aren't tied behind you."

Ten or fifteen hours?

"It happens. It happened to me in Seattle."

It had happened to Sprout, too—seventeen hours in an unheated cell alone, doing jumping jacks to try to stay warm.

The tone of the gathering was entirely sober now. Somebody asked about carrying I.D. during an action.

"It depends whether you want to practice jail solidarity," Beck said. "That's something you need to decide with your affinity group."

None of the trainees knew what jail solidarity was.

"Noncoöperation with the system," they were told. It might be widely used in Washington—to clog the jails and courts and try to force mass dismissals of charges.

But the details of jail solidarity could wait for another session, Beck said. It was late. People were tired. DAN would be offering more nonviolence training locally in the weeks ahead, and everybody going to Washington for A16 should get as much training as possible.

WE stayed that night with Peter and Josh. They lived in a mobile home near a strip mall in Clearwater. People slept on couches and chairs and on the floor, in the van, on a back porch, and on a tiny plywood dock on a fetid canal behind the trailer. I tried to sleep on the dock, but mosquitoes kept me awake. There was a full moon, and low, cotton-puff clouds streaming across it at an unusual speed. The clouds were glowing a sort of radioactive mauve from all the strip-mall lights.

At some point, the mosquitoes woke Beck, who was also on the dock. Out of the darkness, a restless voice: "We need a name. For the movement as a whole. Anti-Corporate Globalization isn't good enough. What do you think of Global Citizen Movement?"

I thought it needed work.

Beck started talking about plans she had for disrupting the Democratic Party's national Convention this summer, in Los Angeles. She mentioned a Millennium Youth March.

"You're thinking big."

"That's my job."

I wanted to know what would happen in Washington on A16.

"Me, too," she said, and I thought I heard her sigh. "For now, crowd-building is the main thing. That's why I'm really glad I'm on this road show. I kind of feel like I should be in D.C., walking the site, doing messaging, doing logistics, but I'm going to stay with this as long as I can."

"Messaging" meant press releases, banners, slogans—even sound bites for protesters to give to reporters, should the opportunity arise. I had begun to think that for the American public effective messaging about the I.M.F. and the World Bank was a hopeless task. In Nigeria and Venezuela, yes, everybody knew and had strong opinions about structural adjustment and I.M.F. debt. That was never going to be true in this country. People might turn out in large numbers, for many different reasons, on A16, but it would basically be Americans expressing solidarity with people in poor countries who are on the receiving end of bad policies. That wasn't a formula for real political leverage. The plight of, say, the Ittu Oromo would never move more than a few faraway hearts. In the great shakeout of economic globalization, most Americans probably believe, not unreasonably, that they will be among the revolution's winners. As for the big goal—democratizing international decision-making, in order to eliminate poverty—it seemed to me impossibly abstract.

I was loath to tell Beck that. While she seemed quite dauntless, her identification with her work seemed, at the same time, perilously deep. She once told me that she thought it was significant that she had been born in 1973, the same year that Richard Nixon allowed the dollar to float—"and the I.M.F. should have been allowed to die!" On another occasion, she'd said, "I really feel lucky to be doing this work. When I started studying the World Bank in college, I couldn't believe how evil it was, even while it's supposedly all about fighting poverty. I thought, you know, it would really be an honor to dedicate my life to fighting this evil institution. And that's all we're asking people to do: help us drag these institutions out into the sunlight of public scrutiny, where they belong. They'll shrivel up like Dracula!"

While I tried to doze, Beck reminded me that the World Bank and I.M.F. had pressured Haiti to freeze its minimum wage, that NAFTA was a failure from beginning to end—details available if I needed them—and that the United States Supreme Court was hearing a crucial case, which I should watch closely when I got back to New York. It seemed that the federal government was trying to stop the Commonwealth of Massachusetts from boycotting companies that did business in Burma, which uses forced labor.

At dawn, finally agreeing that sleep was hopeless, Beck and I took a canoe that was tied to the dock and paddled off down the stinking canal, gliding past the battered, moldy back doors of mobile homes. It was a Sunday morning. Everybody in the trailers seemed to be asleep—probably dreaming about their stock portfolios. The mangroves on the banks slowly closed over our heads. We tried to push through. There seemed to be wider, brighter water ahead. Beck was happy to keep going, but I was in the bow, catching spider webs with my face. In the end, we turned back.

The Mango Affinity Group held a morning meeting on the little dock. While trying to decide who would be responsible for grocery shopping, they started goofing on the hand signals developed by DAN for anarchist consensus decision-making, cracking each other up. Beck was supposed to be guiding the discussion—facilitating, they called it—but she had the giggles, too. Group morale seemed high.

Bushy-bearded Peter came out of the trailer, yawning and stretching. He started filling a plastic bag with grapefruit from a low, gnarled dwarf of a tree. The fruit looked awful, with upper halves all blackened as if by grime falling from the sky, but Peter assured me they were fine. I cut one open. It was the best grapefruit I had ever tasted.

Inside the trailer, there was a small room devoted to Josh and Peter's book and periodical distribution business. They had a dense, nondoctrinaire selection, with sections on Organizing, Anarchism/Social Theory, Animal Liberation, Punk, Direct Action, Media, Globalization, Feminism/Sexuality, and

Youth Oppression/Radical Education. They had ten Noam Chomsky titles, lots of Emma Goldman, a guide to "understanding and attacking mainstream media," arguments against compulsory schooling, even a collection of Digger tracts (seventeenth-century free-love proto-anarchists). Josh and Peter's catalogue included an introduction that traced their own political development from 1996, when "we were straightedge as fuck," to more recent days, when "our distro grew greener and more anarchistic."

Elsewhere in the trailer, somebody had put on a Delta blues tape. Out in the living room, I found Josh sprawled on a couch. He was a quiet guy, in his early twenties, with sparse blond muttonchops and small blue eyes. He was wearing a baseball cap and talking to a glum-looking young woman with an elaborately pierced nose. I started asking Josh about himself. He wasn't a student, he said pleasantly. He had realized he could learn more outside school. He didn't have a job. "But I need to get one, just to make money. The problem is, I'm really too busy to work."

Through a window, I could see the Mango Affinity Group loading up the van. Beck and Sprout, the lanky, tireless trade wonk and the barefoot fiddler, had their heads bent together over a map. Today, the road show went to Gainesville. Tomorrow, Valdosta, Georgia.

APRIL 17, 2000

THEY LOVE ME!

I N mid-March, the veteran Mob attorney Oscar Goodman and about a hundred other prominent members of the Las Vegas community boarded a jet chartered by the Mirage casino and took off for Biloxi, Mississippi. Their host, a gambling impresario named Steve Wynn, had invited them to visit his newest spectacle: the Beau Rivage hotel and casino—its lobby perfumed by forty-foot magnolia trees, its Japanese restaurant encircled by more than four thousand stalks of bamboo, and its ten-million-dollar Brazilian-hardwood marina touted as the most expensive (per slip) in the world. Wynn, who got his start in Las Vegas in the sixties as a liquor distributor, is largely responsible for the Strip's renascence. In 1973, he took over the Golden Nugget casino, and in the past decade he has built the Mirage, Treasure Island, and the Bellagio, which has its own gallery of modern art ("Now appearing: Van Gogh, Monet, Renoir, and Cézanne"). Wynn seems himself to have undergone a transformation, in the public mind, paralleling that of Las Vegas; today, a newcomer in town rarely hears his name unattended by superlatives and the word "visionary," and he is thought by many to exert a kind of hegemony over whatever interests him in Nevada's political, business, and social life. In March, the political event of the moment was the Las Vegas mayor's race.

Ten days before the flight to Biloxi, Oscar Goodman had declared himself a candidate. The trip, therefore, would provide him an opportunity to work a moneyed, influential crowd, and also to importune Wynn for his support. Wynn thus far had been unwilling to commit himself to Goodman, with whom he had been friendly for decades. But *any* show of favor would help. Goodman's law partner, David Z. Chesnoff, told me, "When Steve, on this trip, referred to Goodman as 'Mr. Mayor' it boosted his credibility with those people."

Goodman's credibility certainly needed a boost. His candidacy had been greeted by many pundits in town with derision. Four days after he filed, the Las Vegas *Review-Journal,* Nevada's dominant newspaper, ran a lead editorial headed "ANYBODY BUT OSCAR," with the subhead "Mob Mouthpiece Wrong Guy for Mayor." The editorial declared, "As the most visible personification of the 'new' Las Vegas, he'd be a P.R. catastrophe." Goodman appeared undaunted by the attack. ("I learned a long time ago, as a criminal lawyer, that you can never show weakness," he says. "I used to come into court with the biggest losers, and I'd swagger around like, 'Are you kidding? You are *trying* my client?' ")

On this trip, Goodman, a man who, at sixty, is so animated and charming when he chooses to be that his odd looks—he has a hawk nose and beady eyes—become appealing, is said to have tried out a line that he would use repeatedly as his campaign progressed: "I'm running for mayor, I need your financial support. And if you don't give it to me"—he breaks into a squinty-eyed grin—"I'll have you *whacked!*"

Thus began a somewhat strange episode in American electoral politics. A man who had spent much of his professional life defending mobsters, who was viewed by some law-enforcement officials not merely as an independent defense lawyer but as a consigliere, and who had adopted Mob tenets as his own—reviling prosecutors and the F.B.I., excoriating "rats" as subhuman, and refusing to represent any client who was willing to coöperate with the government—was offering himself as a candidate for public service. Las Vegas, of course, is a singular place, one where there is a "comfort level" with the Mob, as a longtime resident explained to me; where the walls of a popular deli, Freddy G's, are lined with photographs of the town's luminaries, including criminals (and gold plaques are placed at the end of each banquette, for those who have, in one way or another, passed on); and where stigma attaches more popularly to the government (certainly to the F.B.I. and the I.R.S.) than to the outlaw. According to Goodman's campaign manager, Jim Ferrence, when one of Goodman's opponents ran a TV ad showing footage in which Goodman likened Feds to Nazis, it helped Goodman more than it hurt him. Even so—even here—Goodman was the darkest of dark horses. Before he decided to run, he says, "My friends would tell me, 'You couldn't win for dog catcher!' "

IN the course of the last fifteen years or so—while representing defendants like Philip Leonetti, the underboss in the Philadelphia crime family headed by Nicodemo Scarfo; Nick Civella, the boss of the Kansas syndicate; and, most famously, Tony (the Ant) Spilotro, who was the Chicago outfit's overseer in the Southwest—Goodman had been musing about running for office. He considered various posts—senator, lieutenant governor, mayor—and from time to time consulted political advisers. His preoccupation seemed far-fetched, but his impulse was a common one: to revisit, relatively late in life, a decisive fork in the road he had faced when he was young—and take the other fork. Goodman was raised in a middle-class Jewish family in Philadelphia. His mother is an artist and his father was a prosecutor for many years and, subsequently, a criminal-defense attorney; his father's great ambition was to become a federal district-court judge, but, according to Goodman, he was never named to the bench because he refused to make a required political contribution—a thwarting that Goodman refers to as "heartbreaking." Having majored in sociology at Haverford College, a school founded by Quakers, Goodman says that he lost interest in material things and became imbued with a desire to do good. He thought of becoming a rabbi, but a Bryn Mawr girl he'd fallen in love with, Carolyn Goldmark, dissuaded him, and he decided to go to law school instead.

After visiting Las Vegas on a junket in 1964, Goodman decided that it was a tantalizingly open field—"a clean, crisp beacon in the desert"—brimming with opportunity for an enterprising young lawyer, and he and Carolyn, whom he had married in 1962, moved there, as he likes to say, "with eighty-seven dollars between us." At that time, the casinos, already the economic lifeblood of the town, were openly run by the Mob. A friend of Goodman's, a longtime Las Vegas resident, expressed a nostalgia widespread among her peers: "Before the I.R.S. came in, in the seventies, it was a real Western town, where people took care of their own. Yes, there was skimming, and the government didn't get its full share. But if you worked in a casino and anyone in your family was sick, there was money to take care of that—it was all so personal, everyone knew everyone. Now the corporations have taken over the casinos, and ownership changes almost every year."

As federal prosecutions of Mob cases got under way in the late sixties and early seventies, Goodman won some cases against the government and became more and more sought after—even by someone as high in the organized-crime hierarchy as Meyer Lansky. Goodman's anti-materialism evidently faded—"There was never a day I didn't make money," he asserts—and his reputation as a rich, flamboyant, confrontational Mob lawyer was established. "He was only twenty-nine years old, and he used to drive around town in a white Rolls-Royce—it was like he was saying 'Up yours!' " a former government prosecutor recalled. Goodman became known for his zealousness: he called the Feds liars and crooks, and he regarded the representation of his clients as a moral crusade. He insisted, time and again, that there was no such thing as the Mafia—that it was a concoction of the federal government—and he developed a demeanor with prosecutors that was so threatening ("I'll have your job for this!" or "I'll bury you!") that he could have passed for one of his clients. As for those clients, he treated many of them more like family—"with a small 'f,' " as he would say.

When it came time for his daughter's bat mitzvah, Goodman didn't give a party at one of the casinos, as was commonly done. The reason he didn't was that many of his clients, listed in Nevada's so-called Black Book as members of organized crime, would be prohibited from attending. (Indeed, as Chesnoff told me, "Oscar and I, between us, have represented practically every person who's in the Black Book.") So Goodman threw the party in a lodge at the top of Mt. Charleston, and F.B.I. agents, parked at the bottom of the hill, took down each car's license-plate number. Some of those invited were discomfited by the presence of such fellow-guests as Tony Spilotro. "When Spilotro came in, I left," Brian Greenspun, the editor of the Las Vegas Sun, told me.

Goodman had many clients who were accused of unspeakable acts, but no client was considered more vicious by law-enforcement officials than Spilotro. A Chicago native who had become adept, early in his career, at collecting money due on high-interest Mob loans, Spilotro established himself in Las Vegas in the early seventies and eventually became Chicago's head of operations there. A man with flat eyes in a doughy face, who generally dressed in black, Spilotro had a reputation as an extraordinarily prolific executioner; the F.B.I. ultimately asserted that he had committed at least twenty-two murders, including one in which he placed the victim's head in a vise and popped his eyeballs out before slitting his throat. (That act was memorialized in the movie Casino, about Spilotro and another Goodman client, Frank Rosenthal, known as Lefty. Goodman played himself in the movie.) In 1981, Spilotro faced an indictment for racketeering. According to Frank Cullota, a boyhood friend who became Spilotro's chief lieutenant and, eventually, a government informant, Spilotro once planned to kill an informant and an entire grand jury by poisoning their catered food. Spilotro was facing two indictments—one for racketeering and burglary, one for murder—when, it is widely believed, a contract was put out on him by the Chicago Mob, in April of 1986. Two months later, he and his brother were found buried in an Indiana cornfield.

Spilotro had been a fixture of Goodman's practice and, in many ways, its star. For fourteen years, as Goodman has stated on numerous occasions, it was he who represented Spilotro in case after case, and did it so successfully that in all that time Spilotro spent only one week in jail. (On that occasion, Goodman happened to be in another state when Spilotro was arrested, and Spilotro chose to stay in jail rather than ask another lawyer to get him out.) Chesnoff, Goodman's longtime partner, who has also specialized in representing the Mob, told me, "Tony didn't do anything without consulting Oscar." He paused, considered, and then added, "I mean, in regard to his legal situation." Their relationship was obviously close; to some it seemed symbiotic. A former Organized Crime Strike Force attorney who developed cases against Spilotro once told me, "I think Oscar used Spilotro as much as Spilotro used him. Spilotro was like a national advertisement for him: 'If I can keep him out of jail . . .' "

Goodman has described Spilotro as "kind and sweet and gentle as a human being can be," and his law-firm associates, too, tend to speak warmly about how Spilotro was always "polite" and "respectful," and to demonize the F.B.I.

for its long attempt to see him incarcerated. (One colleague of Goodman's even told me he believed that F.B.I. agents, who trailed Spilotro constantly, must have been within view of that Indiana cornfield and watched as the Spilotro brothers were beaten to death and buried.) But another longtime client of Goodman's, Dean Shendal, an emotionally volatile man, with no mean reputation himself in the old Las Vegas—he was once a fighter, later a rodeo cowboy, and, in the sixties, part owner of Caesars Palace—declared, "Spilotro was scum." What did he think, then, about Goodman's having built his reputation, in considerable part, on keeping Spilotro free for fourteen years? "I think Oscar feels guilty about that," Shendal asserted, in a deep, gravelly voice. "In fact, I think that's part of why he wanted to run for office."

Shendal is so fond of Goodman that tears well up in his eyes as he describes his virtues (Goodman adopted four children, and has represented some clients for free), but the thing that probably solidified their friendship at the start was Goodman's attitude toward informants. Shendal went to jail for a couple of months in 1971 rather than testify about the interests of Meyer Lansky, Joseph (Doc) Stacher, and others in the Sands hotel. " 'Snitch' is the magic word for Oscar," Shendal told me. "Oscar will not represent anyone who is a snitch, like that guy Sammy (the Bull) Gravano"—a mobster who won his freedom by testifying against John Gotti. "He murdered nineteen people, and he's walking around!" Shendal said heatedly. "Believe me, he will not breathe for long. If I saw him, I'd kill him myself!"

Shendal acknowledged, though, that this shared credo was increasingly anachronistic. "Today, it's very different—they queue up to tell on one another," he said. How uphold *omertà* if none of your clients want to anymore? Moreover, most of the really big, high-profile mobsters are either dead or in jail. Goodman's last big Mob case went to trial in 1996. And although Americans have long been infatuated with the Mafia, there is not much romance in pornographers and drug dealers, both of whom are to be found among Goodman and Chesnoff's clients. According to one associate, Goodman said a couple of years ago that he was tired of it all.

ON March 4th, the day before the filing deadline for mayoral candidates, Goodman, who had been considering running since early December, was still undecided. His wife was in favor of it, but all his children were opposed. "They were afraid of what people would say about me, but I knew I'd been Caesar's wife," Goodman told me. "I thought a lot about what Tony Spilotro used to say: 'The only way they're gonna get me is the frame.' " Now Goodman and Chesnoff were still weighing his prospects, seated in Goodman's office—a setting worthy of *The Godfather*, with a green marble floor, a low-hanging crystal chandelier over a huge semicircular desk, a big green velvet desk chair, the walls showing photographs of Goodman with famous friends such

as Robert De Niro and Tommy Lasorda, and with clients, many of them holding champagne bottles at victory celebrations (among them Philip Leonetti,
Nicodemo Scarfo, Natale Richichi, Frank Rosenthal, Joey Cusumano, Allen
Glick, and Tony Spilotro), along with a drawing of Goodman bearing the notation "Se Habla Sicilian." A poll done by a friend of his had shown his negatives to be so high that Goodman was convinced he couldn't win. But Chesnoff
was still arguing that the poll had demonstrated a way for Goodman to overcome those negatives—"because," Chesnoff told me he'd said, "if you put it in
the context of defending the Constitution, not criminals, then people would
respond to that."

As they were debating, Chesnoff continued, a call came in for Goodman from
"a very prominent guy in town, a guy with money, who knows what the story
is, and I said, 'Oscar, ask him if he'd support you, and if he says yes it'll be an
omen.' " The man did say yes, and that afternoon Goodman announced that
he was running. Chesnoff instantly began making calls to raise money. In the
next three months, he and Goodman raised $1.4 million. When I asked Good-
man who the propitious caller was, he said he didn't want to identify him because "he owns a topless club."

Goodman insists that he believed from that moment that he would win—
even though the clear front-runner was Jay Bingham, a well-regarded former
county commissioner, who had been campaigning for months, had already
raised four hundred thousand dollars, and had been given the support of the
power blocs that mattered most: the casinos on the Strip (which technically lies
outside the city's municipal boundaries), the developers, the Chamber of Commerce, and the Mormon community. Three days after Goodman filed, however, Bingham withdrew, citing heart problems. "I filed, and he dropped
out—he said his doctor said it would be 'too stressful,' " Goodman said, with
heavy sarcasm. Was he saying that Bingham had withdrawn rather than face
him? "No, I'm not going to say that," Goodman parried. To this day, speculation persists about whether there were other reasons for Bingham's withdrawal. Some suggest that Goodman might have had damning information
about him, related to his tenure as county commissioner. One friend of Goodman's expressed another view. "Jay Bingham had been promised a cake-
walk—that there would be no real campaign and that it would be handed to
him," this person told me. "And I think he was scared. I think he believed the
myth—that Oscar's Mob soldiers would come after his family."

In the early weeks of the campaign, a city councilman, Arnie Adamsen,
picked up much of Bingham's support, and his own closest competitor was a
developer, Mark Fine. But Adamsen was a bland candidate who relied on his
knowledge of municipal issues and referred to himself as "Mr. Crossing Guard,"
and Fine bore the burden of his vocation. (Although polls indicated that "defending the Constitution" was an effective counter to "Mob lawyer," Ferrence,
Goodman's campaign manager, said, there *was* no counter to "developer.") In

any case, Goodman told me that in this contest, as in all his years as a trial lawyer, "I was competing against myself, a hundred per cent." Here that was especially true, though perhaps not in the way Goodman meant. Not only was he absorbed in the exercise of winning by setting his own standard of excellence but he had to compete against the person he had been. Erasing that image of the "Mob mouthpiece," as the Las Vegas *Review-Journal* had put it—the angry, often menacing persona that Goodman had cultivated for so long—was crucial to his campaign. Mark Fierro, the media consultant who was to create Goodman's TV spots, recalled having watched Goodman's first debate and come to realize how much "media training" this candidate needed. On the softball questions, Goodman was articulate, appealing, even inspiring, but then came a hostile question from one of his opponents' supporters, and Goodman snarled, "Get back to that microphone! I want to talk to you!" Fierro said, "And that was what the eleven-o'clock news showed. But he learned fast. I reminded him of what Jack Kennedy supposedly said when facing the camera: 'I think of all my nieces and nephews sitting on the other side of the camera, in their pajamas.' I said, 'Oscar, it has to be *Uncle* Oscar.' "

Almost immediately, local TV was dominated by Goodman ads. In one ad, the words "Oscar Goodman's top five accomplishments" appeared on the screen, followed by shots of each of his four children as toddlers and then as young adults, with their graduate degrees itemized. The fifth was an image of Oscar and Carolyn, with the caption "We never missed a soccer game." Saccharine, perhaps, if it were not intended as an antidote to other, lingering images of Goodman, such as his appearance on the Geraldo Rivera show, when he held up a rubber rat and then, twisting its neck, said, "We bite their heads off!" Another ad explicitly tackled the issue of Goodman's mobster affiliation. It featured representatives of law enforcement—a former Organized Crime Strike Force attorney, a former F.B.I. agent, and a former United States Attorney—all saying, in essence, that Goodman was aggressive but had never crossed the line, and would make a fine public servant.

Referring to these rather surprising testimonials from the institutions he had attacked for decades, Goodman told me enthusiastically, "The F.B.I., police—everyone—came forward, unsolicited!" Well, not exactly. Of the three, the endorsement by the former strike-force attorney, Richard P. Crane, Jr., was the most curious. Goodman had fought the strike force furiously throughout the seventies and the early eighties in Las Vegas; Crane had been an attorney on the force from 1970 to 1976 and had then gone into private practice in Los Angeles. "Calling Dick Crane was an idea I came up with," Chesnoff told me. "He's very connected to gaming people in town. He owns part of the Barbary Coast hotel and casino."

Crane's casino interest suggests that his world view—or, certainly, his milieu—has changed since the days when he was prosecuting many of those associated with casinos, which had meant battling Goodman. Crane, along with several partners, built the Barbary Coast in 1979, and now has an interest in its parent company, Coast Resorts, Inc. One of his partners in the hotel was Michael Gaughan, whose family initially had a stake in it; Michael's father, Jackie Gaughan, was once publicly called an informant by Goodman. Today, however, everyone in this small, highly incestuous world appears to have come to terms—Coast Resorts and an affiliate even made a campaign contribution of fifteen thousand dollars to Goodman, and Crane, after all, vouched for Goodman's integrity in a TV ad. Everyone except, oddly, Goodman himself. He was plainly glad to get Crane's endorsement, but when I told him that Crane had characterized him as someone whose temper and threats were a kind of shtick—something they had even laughed about together—Goodman's eyes narrowed. He said that Crane certainly had not responded that way at the time—indeed, he said, Crane had tried to have him indicted for threatening a federal officer. (Goodman believed—erroneously, it turns out—that it was Crane's family that manufactured the urinals found in many men's rooms: "Whenever I saw the name 'Crane,' " Goodman told me, "I would try to aim for it.")

The support for Goodman expressed by the law-enforcement representatives in his commercials was far from universal. Stanley Hunterton, a criminal-defense attorney and civil litigator in Las Vegas who had been special attorney on the strike force from 1978 to 1985, and had spent years on cases against Tony Spilotro, recalled, "A lot of the F.B.I. agents I worked with thought Oscar was consigliere—socializing with his clients, meeting them in their homes. Oscar did all those things. I didn't care. It was not a crime. But they called me during the campaign, so upset they could hardly form a sentence. They'd say, 'Fuck! Fuck! How can it be?' And I would say, 'It *is*. Get over it.' " Hunterton added that he'd borne no personal animus against Goodman; he'd become a trustee with Oscar and Carolyn of the area's élite private school, the Meadows (which Carolyn founded, and fashioned in part on Brearley, her alma mater). He also told me that on several occasions he had "extended an olive branch" to Oscar, but that Oscar "never would take it. He'd be kind of surly. He really *does* hate the government."

HAVING done all they could to inoculate Goodman against attacks on his relationship with his Mob clients, Goodman's campaign strategists continued to brace themselves for the worst. Britain's Channel 4 and Non Fiction Films had made a ninety-minute documentary about Goodman and his clients, entitled *Mob Law*, which was broadcast last year. Goodman, who had the opportunity in the film's extensive interviews to present himself fully, appears self-righteous, seething with hatred for law enforcement, alternately fatuous (when he is playing the provocateur) and threatening. In one scene, he has an unrehearsed confrontation with a former F.B.I. undercover agent who tried to set him up in an obstruction-of-justice case. The former agent gets the better of him in their shouting match, saying that Goodman turned the world upside down to suit his ends, making evil good and good evil. Goodman starts to leave and then, turning—with a look and a tone that bespeak the company he has kept for nearly thirty-five years—says, "Drive safely." In another scene, he pulls bundle after bundle of cash from clients out of his desk drawer, thrusting them toward the camera and saying, challengingly, "Nothing wrong with that! Or that! Or that!"

"I literally had dreams—nightmares, really, several times—of him with those piles of cash, in *Mob Law*," Ferrence said. "There was so much! . . . In a pinpointed attack, you could have taken him out in a week."

Goodman was such an easy political target that his opponents, underestimating him, ignored him. Adamsen finally did start attacking Goodman; he went after him particularly hard on Megan's Law, which Goodman had once publicly opposed—coming out with an inflammatory TV ad, and also a mail piece, about ten days before the May 4th primary. Adamsen limped into the general election, set for early June, but by that time it was too late. Now all the money was flowing to Goodman, and Adamsen's defeat seemed preordained; he mounted no more attacks.

Meanwhile, Goodman was having the time of his life. Campaigning called on him to perform an exercise that was no different from what he had always done, almost reflexively, in everyday life. "He has an incredible talent for controlling events, not just in a courtroom but in any forum he's in," Chesnoff commented. "He's *on* a lot, but it's not like some people, who are on for the sake of being on—with him, it's to win. He's very success-oriented—in a hundred ways, from morning to night." Now each person Goodman encountered really did represent an opportunity to win, and to win something tangible. Galvanized, Goodman worked sixteen-hour days—harder, several seasoned consultants said, than they had ever seen a candidate work. He walked nine precincts, getting out there even when he was suffering from gout. Ferrence estimated that he may have met as many as a quarter million people. Dreading the slightest illness, and phobic about germs, he was someone who had always tried not to have to shake hands. ("Ugh! To touch someone's skin!" Goodman said, grimacing, when I asked him about this recently.) But now he sought out every hand in sight. "I am a great believer in vitamin C," he told me. "I kissed ninety-three babies and never got sick! Two thousand milligrams a day," he added prescriptively.

In the beginning, Goodman didn't know many of the issues, and Adamsen, after his years on the City Council, tried to take advantage of that. But Goodman is a speed-reader and a quick study; he took home reams of material, and was soon, one adviser said, "a policy wonk." He vowed from the start that he was going to wage a positive campaign. If that was principled, it was also pragmatic. As Adamsen and Fine went after each other, Goodman took the high road, and his polling showed that the only effective counter to attacks on his vulnerabilities—the Mob, Megan's Law, and so forth—was to stay positive.

Goodman struck populist chords, presenting himself as an outsider, even though he is a multimillionaire and a member of Las Vegas's social élite. "I've always represented the underdog—I think you want Oscar Goodman negotiating for you!" he said in his speeches. He promised voters in the Asian, African-American, and Hispanic communities of Las Vegas, whom he courted assiduously, that once he was mayor he would surround himself with a "rainbow coalition." He wanted to bring redevelopment funds to Las Vegas's desperate West Side (an African-American community, which tourists never see). He wanted developers to have to pay impact fees for every new home built—why should they continue to have a free ride? He preached a kind of communal self-acceptance: Las Vegans should not feel embarrassed about their Mob heritage but should embrace it, since it fascinates the world. ("When they lift a rock here, they don't want to see Mickey Mouse—they want to see Bugsy Siegel!" he said.) He was unabashed about his love for Las Vegas, and he is not surprised that the city is now attracting about forty-five hundred new residents a month. (He once told me, without irony, "Move to Las Vegas and you never have to leave! You want New York, we have New York. You want Venice, we have Venice. You want Paris, in September we'll have Paris." He was referring to Las Vegas's best-known city-theme hotels.) Much of what Goodman said that he wanted to do was, of course, typical campaign rhetoric: attract new businesses, improve education, revitalize the downtown (creating an artistic corridor of bookstores, coffee shops, music clubs), bring a major-league team to Las Vegas. But he presented it all with much more verve than his opponents did. He was a celebrity, it turned out, and Adamsen and Fine were just candidates. When he went to Costco on the weekends, or to a baseball game at Cashman Field, he was surrounded by people who wanted to shake his hand and get his autograph.

Goodman had his share of enemies, too, of course—people who, in the words of one associate, want to "white-bread" the city. They included Sherman Frederick, the publisher of the *Review-Journal,* who said that Goodman's election would be his "worst nightmare"; residential developers like Mark Brown, then senior vice-president of the Howard Hughes Corporation, who said that Goodman's election "would set Las Vegas back a hundred years"; and a number of casino heads, like Terry Lanni, the C.E.O. and chairman of M-G-M Grand, who thinks Goodman is too emblematic of the "old" Las Vegas. (Lanni, a tightly wound person with a formal manner, is one of the most fervent apostles of the "new" Las Vegas. Describing a recently opened adjunct to the M-G-M Grand, called the Mansion, which was built in the style of a Tuscan villa at a cost of roughly six million dollars per unit, he said, "We tried to create an understated elegance—and a sense that you are not in Las Vegas.")

UNLIKE most of the Strip's leading players, who kept their distance from Goodman until after the primary, Steve Wynn appears to have edged closer and closer to him as Goodman gathered strength. Wynn had a unique ability to gauge that strength, inasmuch as he has his own sophisticated political apparatus. He began assembling it in 1991, upon realizing that he had no way of knowing whether the huge sums of money he was pouring into political races were being spent effectively. He set up his own computerized polling operation, with databases, phone banks, and constant outreach to the community, in particular the senior community, which is Las Vegas's largest and most active voting group. The data he collects can be shared with his favored candidates. Polls are carried out on whatever interests Wynn—gambling initiatives in states where he wants to build casinos, for example, and every other kind of political race. Wynn also conducts "voter registration" drives for some twenty-five thousand employees of his, and he issues a voter's guide, with his candidates starred.

Wynn is said to have been polling the mayor's race from the start and, as he watched Goodman gaining, to have extended an endorsement through informal channels: one Las Vegas resident told me that in the week or two before the primary "the word went down in the Wynn properties that Steve *really* liked Oscar." The day after the primary, this somewhat discreet liaison went public. Goodman told me that Punam Mather, who runs the Mirage polling operation, called him and said, "The Mirage and all of its power are backing you." Wynn then announced that he, too, was for Goodman. "When Steve came out publicly, it was a big deal, as it always is," Brian Greenspun said. "A lot of the gaming people, although they don't like to admit it, wait for his cue." Many casinos and other big-business interests, which had not contributed to Goodman before, now did so. (Lanni's M-G-M Grand, however, did not.)

On June 8th, Goodman won by a landslide, capturing sixty-four per cent of the vote. Two weeks later, as he prepared for his swearing-in and his first City Council meeting, and fell asleep each night over a copy of "Robert's Rules of Order," he was still euphoric, declaring, "I'm a wunderkind! Gore is calling me, Clinton's calling me! I'm the strongest Democrat in Nevada, with the possible exception of Harry Reid!"—Nevada's senior senator. As I set out with him on a round of his appointments, he told me, "You're going to see something you've never seen before." He had declined the city's offer of a driver—"I like to be by myself"—and was at the wheel of his Mercedes convertible, with an "OBG" license plate. Several people honked, waved, and gave him a thumbs-up. "People are happy I won!" he said. "It wasn't supposed to happen—they feel like *they* beat the system!"

In the corridor of a municipal building, a young woman approached and pumped his hand, saying, "I think you are wonderful. I'm your biggest fan!"

"Really?" Goodman responded, smiling, and peering at her intently. "Why do you say that?"

"I think you're the greatest person on this planet—in this universe!"

"Did you hear that?" Goodman asked, as we walked away. "That's how people respond to me. They *love* me."

One thing darkened his mood, however, and that was a host of new, false friends. During lunch with an executive of a county commission, who praised him for having run "a brilliant campaign—just like a trial," Goodman was warm and convivial, but as soon as the man was out of earshot he told me, glowering, "That guy is so full of it. Now these people are all saying they were for me. They weren't! That's O.K. All I care about now is being a great mayor. But I am keeping a list of those who were never for me, who spoke out against me as though I were the Antichrist. It's not a long list, but it's a list. And I don't care how long it takes, but I will get them."

I remarked that he sounded like some of his former clients.

"Well, why let your enemies survive?"

ON July 1st, three days after taking office, Goodman appeared with Steve Wynn for a press conference at the Bellagio. Wynn had been exploring the possibility of buying a National Basketball Association or National Hockey League team—one he would like to see playing in a downtown arena, the construction of which would be financed by the public. To this end, he had commissioned a survey by the Republican pollster Frank Luntz. At the press conference, Luntz delivered broad-brush findings: an overwhelming majority of Las Vegans want a sports arena, and a majority would support its construction even if local tax dollars were involved. Luntz declined to release the detailed results of his polling. Just how the arena would be financed was an open question, to be considered by a committee of government and business leaders—a committee that Wynn announced he would form. Goodman, who had said during the campaign that he would not support a sports facility if it involved raising taxes for Las Vegans, seemed to find Wynn's enthusiasm contagious. "I think this could be the beginning of transforming downtown into the city of the millennium," he declared.

Wynn and Goodman had been discussing this idea throughout the campaign, according to associates of Goodman's. If Las Vegas were to have its own major-league team, something that would help to further legitimatize this chimera in the desert as a real metropolis, there would be a great deal in it for each of them. For Goodman, it would be the most dramatic achievement he could hope for in his mayoralty; and if the N.B.A., say, were to accept Wynn as an owner, it would bring him the kind of respectability that, for all his success, and for all the homage paid him in Las Vegas, still eludes him. Moreover, siting the arena downtown would benefit both men. Presumably, it would help in the revitalization of downtown that Goodman has declared to be his highest priority. And Wynn's Golden Nugget—a thriving, if garish, property—happens to be downtown, in increasingly desolate surroundings.

The plan has elicited some negative public reaction. In mid-July, a Las Vegas weekly, *City Life,* published a critical piece with the cover line "Wynn's Pleasure Dome," in which Robert Parker, a sociology professor at the University of Nevada at Las Vegas, declared that Wynn's scheme "socializes the costs of construction and privatizes the profits." A local business official whom I interviewed about Wynn's project commented, dryly, that the committee formed to consider the project was "the Steve Wynn committee—formed not by the governor but by Steve." Other gambling powers on the Strip are opposed, this official continued, because the downtown site so favors Wynn, because two of the other casinos already have their own arenas, and because of the loss of gaming dollars. (Betting on N.B.A. teams would probably be banned if one were based in Las Vegas.) "Oscar can't afford to be only in Steve Wynn's corner," the official said. "But how do you buck Steve Wynn? I think he put Oscar in a difficult position."

The Goodman-Wynn pas de deux will be an interesting performance to watch in the coming months—one to rival the choreography in the water ballet "O" at Wynn's Bellagio. Goodman is not naïve about the uses of power: one associate of his told me that when Goodman returned from a meeting with Wynn at which they discussed the arena Goodman commented, rather uneasily, that Wynn had said he wanted Goodman "to have all the credit." Should the arena continue to evoke public disfavor, Goodman may be disinclined to be Wynn's spear-carrier. A person on friendly terms with both men commented to me that Goodman—who has a penchant for exacting retribution, after all—may well be nursing a quiet grudge against Wynn for withholding his support at the start of Goodman's campaign. (Recently, Goodman reiterated what he had said during the campaign about being opposed to any financing of an arena that would raise people's taxes—a statement that could not have pleased Wynn.) Moreover, if Goodman is thinking about a future elective office he has a particularly fine line to tread. He is said to have remarked to one friend that he would like to be on the Nevada Supreme Court— an even more wildly incongruous notion for the Mob mouthpiece than the mayoralty, one would think, but a position that might be especially gratifying in the light of his father's history. One of Goodman's advisers told me that he believes Goodman is considering challenging Governor Kenny Guinn in 2002. No one running for office in Nevada would want to alienate Wynn. On the other hand, Goodman knows that his strongest positive polling was as an "outsider" (he worried about hurting that image when Wynn announced for him), that his winning vehicle now is as the "people's" mouthpiece, and that his continuing proximity to Wynn is at once a blessing and a curse.

SEVERAL weeks into Goodman's mayoralty, when we met for a final interview, he eyed me warily. "What have you been doing?" he demanded. "Talking to my enemies?" The City Hall mayor's office seemed bare and antiseptic compared with his chandeliered den. In it were several pictures of his family, a bureaucrat's furniture, a pile of the day's press clippings (for years, he has filled scrapbooks with every article in which he is mentioned), and an Air Police Support cap, which was given to him when he went up in a police helicopter during the Las Vegas floods, in early July. Goodman, who was aware that the pundits were saying he would be bored by the job's tedium and would be frustrated by his lack of power (he has only one vote on the five-member City Council), wanted me to know that that was not the case. "I love every second of this job—every second! I swear, it has added twenty years to my life," he declared.

Certainly, any public perception that Goodman is weak would be insupportable to this man. And if there is tedium Goodman is intent on banishing it. He says he is in the office by 6:30 A.M. and works a fourteen-hour day, setting an example for the rest of City Hall, and that he has begun to shake up the bureaucracy, clearing out long-established fiefdoms. ("I've been doing in three weeks what it would take someone else a year to do," he boasted.) He even appears to enjoy City Council meetings. At one, he conducted a mini-trial to determine whether the revocation of an African-American family's restaurant license had been justifiable; the vote was 3–2 that it had not, going Goodman's way. (While this was a well-orchestrated demonstration of his siding with an African-American family against a municipal establishment, Goodman has made no meaningful move to bring into being the "rainbow coalition" that he trumpeted in his campaign; the arena study committee, which Wynn proposed and to which Goodman, its co-chair, has been making appointments, now has twenty-six members—"the best brains in Las Vegas," Goodman proclaimed—all but one of whom are white.)

Goodman says he has begun to feel that the office itself has a kind of gravity, representing something larger than his personality—a notion that had not dawned on him before. According to an associate, he was asked to go to the deathbed of a federal marshal. At first, he said he could not, but he was told that, as mayor, he really should. So, overcoming a lifelong dread of illness and hospitals, he went, and was surprised and moved by the family's gratitude. William Cassidy, who has known Goodman for twelve years, having often worked for him as a private investigator, and who is now his chief of staff at City Hall, believes that Goodman has been transformed. "He has shed his armor and exposed his heart," Cassidy told me. "I think his ability to define himself has been limited by the narrow confines of the world in which he operated. Now he can meet people, *shake their hands,* and address their misery."

Cassidy's observation had made me wonder whether the managed metamorphosis in Goodman's campaign could, to some degree, have been real, and, if so, how the new Goodman might regard—and perhaps annotate—the old. Hadn't it been just histrionics, for example, when he said that he would rather his daughter went out with Tony Spilotro than with an F.B.I. agent?

"Not even close!" Goodman shot back. "Tony Spilotro never lied to me. He always protected me. He never let me get involved in any questionable behavior. . . . It drove those F.B.I. guys nuts! They said he had committed twenty-two murders! He gave me the opportunity to become a good lawyer. I put my puss in the face of the government. I caught them in lie after lie. I got their search-and-seizure motions suppressed. When I made that statement about my daughter, I meant it. Tony was more honorable than the people who were trying to get him."

Dean Shendal was no fan of the F.B.I., I ventured, and yet he had told me that Spilotro was "scum."

Goodman, with a thin smile, replied, "Dean wouldn't say that if Tony were alive."

Couldn't Goodman's refusal to represent clients who coöperate with the government be seen as putting them at an unfair disadvantage? Don't clients often find themselves in a changed situation as a prosecution continues, and find that their best option is to coöperate?

"I would never represent a rat!" Goodman interrupted. "I object to it as a moral proposition. Did you know who can't be buried in a Jewish cemetery? People who deface their bodies, people who commit suicide, and people who inform."

People who inform? What about people who murder?

"They can be buried there. Better to murder than to be a rat." Seeing my skepticism—Jewish law is in fact more complicated than his description—Goodman picked up the phone and called a rabbi friend at Chabad, a Chassidic organization. The rabbi wasn't there, but the woman who answered the phone, hearing the identity of the caller, said excitedly, "Mr. Mayor, it's an honor!"

Goodman put down the receiver and declared, for what was surely the hundredth time, "I love this job. I love it." He glanced at me, measuring my reservations. Then he said, very deliberately, "You know who's the only person I ever heard of who said 'I love it' as much as I love this job?" He paused, delighting in what was coming, and smiled. "Nicodemo Scarfo, when he was pouring .22s into someone's head. This guy testified that as Scarfo did it he said, 'I love it! I *love* it!' "

AUGUST 16, 1999

THE

LIFE

MR. LUCKY

O N the day last November when John Falcon learned that he had won forty-five million dollars in the New York State lottery, he realized with trepidation that he was finally going to have to do something about his teeth. At the time, Falcon was a struggling performance artist—the creator, director, and star of a one-man autobiographical show entitled *A Short Puerto Rican Guy Sings Songs of Angst,* which he has performed at Off Off Broadway theatres over the past several years. In *Short Puerto Rican Guy,* Falcon tells the story of his life—his childhood in the Bronx, his coming of age as a gay man in New York in the seventies—through renditions of show tunes and favorite songs by contemporary Broadway composers. Falcon has a powerful tenor voice and an engaging stage presence. Although self-mockery is part of his act—"I have about eleven hours of material," he announces near the beginning of the show. "It's a Puerto Rican *Nicholas Nickleby*"—he prefers tragedy to comedy. The parts of the show that mean the most to him come when he stands with his legs planted apart and his arms flung wide and his eyes scrunched shut and belts out numbers about heartbreak, loss, loneliness, disappointment, and pain. In order to sing these songs, Falcon draws upon his own reservoirs of disappointment and pain, which are considerable, and which are responsible for the bitter suspicion that the reason he has so far been singing to a crowd of seventy friends at a tiny performance space in SoHo, rather than to large, admiring audiences on Broadway, has little to do with his talent and a lot to do with his teeth.

I met Falcon one afternoon in January, when I visited him at his brand-new apartment, on the twenty-fourth floor of a building in the East Fifties, just off Sutton Place. Falcon pays forty-five hundred dollars a month for it, which is thirty-eight hundred and seventy-five dollars more than he was paying for his last apartment, a rent-stabilized one-bedroom in a fourth-floor walkup on East Eighty-second Street. His new home was built in 1983, and has the distinct flavor of the decade. Its two and a half bathrooms are decorated with enough marble for a small mausoleum; in the living room there is one wall of copper-tinted mirrors and there are two walls of floor-to-ceiling windows. Falcon has an unobstructed view of midtown Manhattan, and, to the southeast, he can see River House and some of Queens. Moving into the apartment is one of the biggest changes Falcon has made since he came into his fortune, along with getting himself a private banker, finding someone to write his will, joining a gym, and starting on serious rehearsals for a revival of *Short Puerto Rican Guy*. He is also researching dentistry—a dominant theme of his new life.

Falcon speaks of "the teeth" the way another person might refer to "the in-laws," as wearying but inescapable facts of life. The teeth do have their limitations: they are craggy, with gaps and overlaps. Falcon, who is forty-three, also has long black hair, which he usually keeps pulled back in a ponytail but sometimes wears down in a stiff curtain, created with the help of a blow-dryer and a product called Spray It Straight. (One damp night, when Falcon and I were out walking, he caught sight of his shadow on the sidewalk. "Look at the hair!" he gasped. "It's frizzing. If I stay outside too long, I turn into Angela Bassett.") In addition, although he has brown eyes, he wears contact lenses that are tinted a pale-purple color, and give him the aspect of a surprised-looking alien. The hair and the eyes are style choices, but the teeth are an unsought burden. As we stood in his new kitchen, he told me about a producer who, after presenting his show once, failed to include him on subsequent cabaret bills. "She pushed everyone but me, and I think it is because of the way I look," he said. "Every blond-haired, blue-eyed, model-type person, she pushed." He shrugged, and added, "New York has plenty of blond sopranos, but how many short dumpy Puerto Rican guys who can sing like Ethel Merman are there?"

In the past couple of months, Falcon has been laying the groundwork for his personal transformation by interviewing dentists, who have told him that he needs a good year of work, with bridges and caps and implants, all of which will set him back at least a hundred thousand dollars. One day, I asked whether the doctors he'd consulted were proposing to match the color of the new teeth to the color of the old teeth. Falcon looked at me as if I were insane, which is something that he did whenever I asked a certain type of question, such as whether he'd figured out a monthly budget for himself, or whether he thought he'd ever work again. "I told them to forget about matching color," he said. "I want them all brilliant white. I want Matt Lauer teeth. I want to be able to read the news with these teeth."

Although becoming rich has diminished some of the angst in Falcon's life—he no longer has to choose between shoe shopping and paying his utility bills—it has given him a lot of new things to worry about. Among them is the need to figure out what effect being rich will have on his creative work, which until now has been based on his conception of himself as an underdog. One interesting consequence of winning the lottery is that he can no longer use an "I can't afford it" excuse to avoid doing something he'd rather not do, such as have his teeth fixed. Falcon's jackpot will also force him to find out whether fixing the teeth will actually make the difference that he hopes it will—whether money really can buy the happiness and success that he has so far been denied by a hurly-burly world.

AS the renewed celebrity of Regis Philbin illustrates, we have begun to live in a windfall society. This was always a country where, the story went, anyone could become wealthy through his own hard work; but the idea that you might luck into wealth, rather than earn it, has started to seem strangely plausible. If all you have to do to become a millionaire is work as an early grunt employee of Netscape, or make some fortuitous predictions about an obscure tech stock, then wealth and power aren't reserved for the wealthy and powerful anymore.

Falcon found out that he was worth forty-five million dollars on November 1st, at around five in the afternoon, when he was about to leave the offices of the publisher Harcourt Brace, where he had worked for the previous two years as a software formatter, making sure that blocks of text fit onto the page. Before shutting down his Mac for the night, he checked the Lotto results on the Internet, having bought a ticket a few days earlier. He had been playing the same numbers—his addresses over the years, strung together—every week for two and a half years, and when he saw the winning formula he recognized it instantly. "I just kind of sat down in my chair, and I called my boss, Laurie, and I said, 'Laurie, take a look at this.' Laurie knows that I am a bit of a hacker, so she said, 'How did you do that?' I said, 'No, this is real, this is Yahoo!' " Falcon had no idea what he was supposed to do next, so his boss suggested that he call the lottery office downtown. "I said, 'Hi, how do I redeem a ticket?' The guy told me to come down to the office, and they'd give me the money. I said, 'Well, I think I have won the forty-five-million-dollar Lotto.' He said there was a five-digit number on the side of the ticket, and I read him the number, and he said it was the winning ticket. I asked how many people had won, and he said, 'One.' It was like someone punched me in the stomach."

With Falcon's fortune has come a measure of celebrity, which he seems to enjoy, though he has kept the attention of certain media at bay, declining appearances on German television, Jerry Springer, and Montel Williams. Two weeks after he learned that he had won, the lottery agency held a press conference to announce his good fortune, and that landed him on the front page of both the *News* and the *Post*. Local television stations gave him good play, not just because of the size of his prize but because he was such a ham at the press conference. (When he was asked about the first thing he bought after winning, he adopted a puzzled expression and said, "Milk?") Falcon is recognized frequently when he is out and about in New York, and most of the attention is good-natured. One day, we were trying to hail a cab on First Avenue, near his building, and the driver of a beat-up, low-riding automobile rolled down his window and shouted, "Can't you afford a limousine?"

Falcon will receive his money in installments over the next twenty-five years. In 1999, he got a million one hundred and twenty-five thousand dollars, of which about seven hundred thousand was left after taxes. He has put most of that money into Treasury bills, although he plans to do some more thoughtful investing with the help of a financial adviser recommended by a friend. Falcon has hired another old friend to come to his apartment every couple of weeks to catalogue his receipts and pay his bills, and that's just as well, because Falcon's system—which is to throw every bit of paper relating to finances into a file box and then hide the box in a closet—is unlikely to satisfy the I.R.S. should its representatives ever audit him.

There are people who insist, after coming into an unexpected fortune, that their lives won't change dramatically, but John Falcon is not one of those people. After winning the lottery, he never returned to his office, and declined a week or two later to help out his boss, who was short-staffed, when she called to ask if he would cover for her. ("I said, 'Are you crazy! I'm never getting up that early again!' ") He travels on public transportation less frequently now, Sutton Place being shockingly ill-served by the M.T.A. He has an unlisted phone number, although at his old, listed number he still gets messages from cold-calling investment advisers and from young women who, cooing into his answering machine, say that he once gave them his phone number but that they never got around to calling until now. (For example: "If this is you, Mr. Lucky, I just want to congratulate you. I just want to talk to you. I don't need anything. I just think you are outrageous.")

Falcon has been devoting many of his waking hours to shopping. The first luxury item he bought was a half-pound of Danish Lurpak butter ($3.99), and that was soon followed by the order of a glass chair from the Pace Collection, for five thousand five hundred dollars. The glass chair, with its intimations of Cinderella, has been the focus of some consternation among Falcon's family and friends. When I talked about the chair with his mother, Rose, a forceful sixty-eight-year-old woman who was a schoolteacher in the South Bronx and now lives in Orlando, with Falcon's father, a retired metallurgist, she shrieked, "This monstrosity! I thought he was really traditional, all mahogany. When he calms down, he is going to be into the mahogany again."

Falcon has distinctive decorating tastes. In his old apartment, which was dark and cluttered, he went for a rococo look, with swag curtains over an airshaft window, gold-painted plaster cherubs on the walls, and homemade floral couch cushions edged with fringe. In the new apartment, however, Falcon says he is striving for an Art Deco, Gershwinesque aesthetic, and so far he has invested in a fair amount of glass and chrome. He bought a chrome dustpan and brush. He bought an enormous chrome salad spinner. He bought what he thought was a chrome kitchen clock from a shopping Web site, only to discover that it is made of chrome-colored plastic. He plans to rent a baby-grand piano for the living room, and when I went to the apartment one recent afternoon he had a borrowed cutout of the instrument laid on the floor, to demonstrate how much room it would take up. I stood where the piano stool would be, and remarked that he would have an amazing view over midtown while he played, but he gave me that "Are you insane?" look and said, "Oh, I can't play."

Although he can now afford to shop anywhere, Falcon has not entirely lost the habits of frugality. Even the glass chair was on sale, reduced from eleven thousand dollars. Friends have been encouraging him to think more like a millionaire—"I am hoping he has his hair blown out once a week now, instead of once a month," his friend Judy Karasik said to me—but Falcon resists such suggestions. "Most people want me to behave differently," he told me. "Most people want me to go out and buy a Ferrari. People push what they would do themselves onto me."

One morning in January, I went shopping in SoHo with Falcon and a friend of his, a woman named Thayer Hochberg, whom he met at a singing workshop almost ten years ago. Falcon said that he wanted Hochberg's opinion because she had good taste, but it seemed that what he really wanted was someone to disagree with. We started in Portico, where Falcon had his eye on a large overstuffed couch in a beige damask which cost just over four thousand dollars.

"I want something very gushy," he said.

Hochberg looked unconvinced. "It's eight feet long," she said, skeptically. "And it's beige. You don't like beige."

"I don't like *wearing* beige," Falcon corrected her. He threw himself on the cushions, and said, "I couldn't sit on this naked, though. It would chafe, and I would get rashes."

We left Portico empty-handed, and stopped off at Aero, a little farther along Spring Street, where Falcon flirted with the idea of buying a chrome-and-glass magazine rack that was priced at seven hundred and fifty dollars, but moved on when he offered five hundred dollars and was rejected. An Art Deco sign outside the Lin/Weinberg gallery, on Wooster Street, caught Falcon's eye, and we went in and found an Edward Wormley sofa from 1953, which had clean modern lines and was covered in pearl-gray wool. It cost twelve thousand five hundred dollars, and Hochberg loved it. It seemed to make Falcon uncomfortable.

"I was thinking of something much more tasselled," he said.

"Think dark-fuchsia cushions," she said.

"Think twelve thousand dollars," he said.

SHORTLY after Falcon and I met, we flew to London together for a three-day weekend. We went to see a new West End musical called *Spend Spend Spend,* based on the true story of Viv Nicholson, a factory worker from a poor mining village in Yorkshire, who, in 1961, won a hundred and fifty-two thousand pounds, the largest-ever fortune in the British equivalent of the lottery, only to squander it all within three years. (She told the newspapers at the time that she intended to "spend and spend and spend.") Falcon wanted to see the show, he said, "so that I can learn what not to do," but it was clear from the moment we started making travel plans that he didn't need any lessons from Viv Nicholson.

He decided that we would fly in the cheapest coach seats available. "Why should I spend another thousand dollars on a business-class ticket?" he said. "I could buy a glass magazine rack for that." We flew from Kennedy on a Thursday night, on Virgin Atlantic. The plane was full, and we were squeezed into a pair of seats at the back of a cabin, right next to the toilet. Falcon was delighted with a free translucent plastic backpack, which contained earplugs and an eye shield and a miniature toothbrush. He hoarded the cheese and crackers from his meal, "for the dark hours."

In London, I found myself assuming the role previously played by Falcon's friends: the travelling companion who can't believe the incredible cheapness of the millionaire at her side. Falcon had selected the Cranley Gardens Hotel, which he'd stayed in before, and which cost just seventy-nine pounds a night. It has a handsomely decorated lobby, with dark wood and high, elegant ceilings, but our rooms were tiny, and painted an institutional pink—"Am I here for an abortion?" Falcon said, throwing his bag onto the twin bed. Having checked in, we headed for the West End. Falcon wanted to see the new Andrew Lloyd Webber, and we went to the half-price ticket booth on Leicester Square. In Soho, we stopped off at a branch of an inexpensive chain store called Cecil G's. Falcon had spotted a rack of discounted leather jackets, down to ninety-nine pounds, from about three hundred. He tried one on, and it was a bad fit—too long in the sleeves, too tight around the hips. Even so, he stood in front of the mirror for a while, tempted. I asked how the leather felt, and he fixed me with his purple eyes and said, "Like a really good Naugahyde."

On one of our three days in England, we went to Stonehenge, at Falcon's suggestion, since he is a student of astrology. For our excursion, we joined a busload of Japanese tourists, mostly college-age women. En route, the bus drove through Belgravia, where the tour guide announced, "This land is all owned by the Duke of Westminster. He's a very rich man. In fact, he is a millionaire." At this, Falcon gazed out the window and smiled to himself.

When we got to Stonehenge, it looked, with its standing stones and its fallen stones and its fragmented stones, rather like a mouthful of teeth in need of dentistry, and, after wandering around for an hour or so, we and the Japanese went on to Bath, to visit the Roman ruins. We walked from what was once a swimming pool to what was once a cold plunging pool and on to what was once an exercise courtyard. "It's a bit like Crunch," Falcon said. Then we stopped off at the eighteenth-century Pump Room, and Falcon admired the décor, stroking a curtain and saying, "Do you have any idea how much this fringe would cost in New York City?"

On Saturday evening, we went to see *Spend Spend Spend*, at the Piccadilly Theatre. Falcon settled into his seat and flicked through the program, which told the story of how Viv Nicholson and her husband had won what today would be the equivalent of almost five million dollars. In the first scene, we saw the present-day Viv, working as a hairdresser in her home town and being berated by one of her customers—"You silly cow!"—for having squandered so much money. I thought I could feel Falcon flinch in the seat next to me. Then we flashed back to the nineteen-sixties, and saw the young Viv—sexy and cheeky and vivacious—buying champagne and a fur stole and a new house and dancing on the tables with joy. As the show progressed, however, things turned sour: Viv's friends and family tried to exploit her; she and her husband spent more and more time drinking and fighting; then her husband was killed in a car crash. Viv's heart was broken, and in quick succession she married three gold-digging men who beat her or bored her, or both. She went broke and eventually returned to the same meagre life she'd begun with.

As we left the theatre, I asked Falcon whether he'd experienced the same frenzy of excitement as Viv had when he discovered he'd won. "The first month was a blur," he said. "I literally didn't sleep for two weeks. When I thought about it, I got dizzy. I didn't tell anyone. I didn't tell my mother. It was too mind-boggling. It still is. I am still waiting for someone to knock on the door to my new apartment and say, 'You're going to have to go, because that check bounced.' Maybe that's why I am so afraid to spend it. When I was a kid, we moved from the South Bronx to Wilson Avenue, in the North Bronx, and I had dreams that I would have to leave there and go back to the South Bronx. This is almost like the same thing: I keep thinking they're going to tell me that I have to go back to my old apartment."

UNTIL last November, when the first check came from the Lotto people, Falcon did not have a checking account, or a bank account of any sort, and he conducted all his financial affairs with the help of a check-cashing joint at Tenth Avenue and Fifty-eighth Street. He owed money to so many creditors that he was afraid any account he opened would be garnished. Describing his pre-Lotto self, Falcon referred to an article that appeared in the *Village Voice* a few years back, called "The Privileged Poor." "They had great wardrobes, they managed to get into all the best restaurants, they went to the theatre, and they had no money," he explained to me one day. "Once you paid your phone bill and the cable, you had three months before you had to pay the rest. In the old apartment, I always thought they were going to turn off my electricity." There have been different reactions among Falcon's friends to his sudden change in status: one of his best friends has become cool and aloof, but another friend, an artist named Maria Yoon, who is even more impoverished than Falcon was, says that his winning the lottery is the best thing that ever happened to her because he said he'd give her his old computer.

Falcon's mother says that her son was "born to be a millionaire. He even looks like a millionaire. He walked like a millionaire, that kid. He was born into a poor family, but that was a mistake." In spite of such predestination, it was not clear, until last November, just how Falcon would come into his birthright, because above all he seemed to have a talent for being broke. He always had an artistic streak, and attended the High School of Art and Design, in Manhattan, where he studied fashion design. He demonstrated a leaning toward the performing arts by singing "People (Who Need People)" at Carnegie Hall on graduation day. He briefly attended F.I.T., and then embarked upon a twenty-odd-year career of short-term jobs. He quit most of them after fighting with a boss. Falcon appears to have worked at every department store in Manhattan, and also at every museum, and a catalogue of his experiences reads like Dilbert as revenge tragedy. He left MOMA: "I hated the people." He left the Whitney: "I wanted to go to London." He left the Met: "They asked me to vacuum. I said, 'I don't even vacuum my own house.' " At the Jewish Museum, he left after declining to apologize for telling one of his co-workers that she needed to go into therapy. Although his parents bailed him out numerous times, a couple of years ago his mother gave him an ultimatum, which prompted him to take the Harcourt Brace job. She told me, "I said, 'Hey, sucker, you have got to work. I'm not going to keep paying your rent.' " (As partial recompense, Falcon gave his mother a ten-thousand-dollar check for Christmas, and is sending her to a weight-loss spa for a month, at a cost of sixteen thousand dollars. He gave his father and his sister, Debbie Coll, who lives in Orlando, each ten thousand dollars, too, and has established college funds for a niece and nephew.)

Besides being somewhat feckless, Falcon has, over the years, suffered some very bad luck. In the middle and late eighties, he and his boyfriend ran a collectibles shop on the Upper East Side called the Book and Chotchka. The relationship ended unhappily in 1989, and as a consequence the business closed down and Falcon was left penniless. Not long afterward, he was the victim of a vicious gay-bashing attack, which he still has trouble discussing. "For that, we are going to need major, copious amounts of alcohol and a psychiatrist," he said when I raised the subject. He was set upon by a group of youths while walking in his neighborhood late at night, and ended up in Bellevue with a smashed jaw. His jaw is now augmented by two metal plates, and the messed-up teeth are a legacy of this period. After the attack, he says, "it took me a year to be able to walk out of the house without being afraid."

Falcon hasn't had a long-term relationship since that time, which seems to be just the way he wants it. "I am very happy where I am right now," he told me. "After my last relationship ended, and the attack, I had to learn to be by myself for the first time. I am very protective of that now, and I like being in charge of my destiny. I am not going to give that up without a fight. Any new person would have to convince me to give up closet space."

I pointed out that Falcon has a lot more closet space these days.

"It's true," he agreed. "It was a funnier line in the old apartment."

IN *A Short Puerto Rican Guy Sings Songs of Angst*, Falcon includes a jazzy comic song called "My Simple Wish." One day, he showed me a grainy video of his show, taped in September of 1998 at Here Performance Space, and the song brought the house down. That's partly because the lyrics, by David Friedman, are witty. The song begins with the words "I wanna be/Rich, famous and powerful/Step on all my enemies/and never do a thing/I wanna be/Rich, famous and powerful/so all I have to do at night/is sit around and sing," and concludes:

> If we were
> Rich, famous and powerful
> We could
> Take all those agents
> and casting directors
> tiny apartments
> and back tax collectors
> Critics and casting calls
> Chilly rehearsal halls
>> People who bore us
>> and jobs in the chorus
> and kiss them all
> good
> bye!

Falcon did a good job of personifying artistic petulance, strutting around the stage and tossing his hair. But the audience members, as they sat in the bare-bones theatre, were doubtless also laughing at the patent improbability of the wealth-and-celebrity scenario befalling Falcon. For every John Leguizamo and Claudia Shear, performers whose autobiographical shows break out because of some spark of conceptual originality, New York has thousands more whose chances of hitting it big are minimal. The odds that John Falcon would win forty-five million dollars in the lottery were a little more than eighteen million to one; but the odds of his becoming rich, famous, and powerful the other way were probably smaller still.

Now, of course, he can bankroll himself. Early next year, he intends to rent a theatre for a new production of *Short Puerto Rican Guy*; he'll hire a band to back him and will have a big advertising budget. He'd also like to record a CD.

Ultimately, he hopes to start a non-profit theatre company, and he also dreams of having his own room in which to perform, "like Bobby Short sings at the Carlyle for three months a year, and then he goes to France."

One afternoon, when Falcon and I were riding in a cab through his old neighborhood of tenements and dry cleaners, I remembered something that he had said about the time he was attacked: because the assault had come during a spate of bias crimes in the city, the local newspapers were interested in Falcon's story, and he was invited to appear on talk shows. He'd deflected most of the attention. "It wasn't going to be my fifteen minutes of fame," he had told me.

Now that Falcon has been granted another chance at notoriety, I wondered whether he regretted that once again his fame was due not to his talent but to his luck. Not at all, he said. "But back then I was a victim," he explained. "Now I am like a winner, or something. It's a bit more positive." But, I asked, wouldn't people be interested in him because of the peculiarity of his situation, rather than the singularity of his talent? "Yes, but that's fine," he said. "If they come to my show, and they like what they see, then *that* is my talent."

Paradoxically, winning the lottery has presented him with something of a creative stumbling block. Falcon's ambitions for *Short Puerto Rican Guy* are considerable. In it, he told me, he has tried to address sweeping themes of love and loss: "Here we are, together on earth, experiencing these emotions, let's share this," as he put it. He now has to integrate his new fortune into the show because it is a big part of his life story, and he's not sure how to go about it. "I think winning the Lotto is too phantasmagorical ever to be really personal," he said. "It is something that people want to have happen to them, but they really have no idea. You fall in love; you get jilted—everyone knows what that is like. But the Lotto thing—no one can relate to it, really. They all think they know, but they don't. And it's hard to find a song already written that applies."

So Falcon is in a curious predicament: the fortune that will enable him to devote himself full-time to his art also undermines his vision of the kind of artist that he wants to be. He's been dealt an extraordinary story line, when what he'd like is an ordinary one. Of course, as problems go, it's not a bad one to have; and just as soon as his teeth are fixed he'll be able to give it some serious thought.

APRIL 24, 2000

THE INN CROWD

TWO mountain ranges define the village of Washington, Virginia. In the middle distance, behind Main Street, looms the gentle eastern face of the Blue Ridge. Below, near the center of town, rises a weed-choked scarp known informally as Mt. Critzer.

One side of this man-made berm belongs to Steve Critzer, a road builder whose yard is a haphazard garden of heavy equipment, some of it half a century old. Much of the machinery is almost sculptural in its decay: a stooped and corroded crane, half a fire truck, a grader lost in honeysuckle, a backhoe bucket lying on the ground like an amputated limb, gangrenous with rust. "It looks like hell," says Critzer, who is bearded and bearlike, and who sells as scrap what he can't pillage for parts. "But that's what we do." Critzer and his family live amidst this metal retrospective in a worn clapboard house his great-great-grandfather built in 1851.

On the other side of the berm sits a house that once resembled the Critzers'. Now it is painted sea-foam green, with trim the color of Devonshire cream and windows swagged with Fortuny silk. An urn-shaped fountain tinkles on the patio. The gates are adorned with putti. Inside are trompe-l'œil paintings, a cocoa leather ceiling, and floors of Tinos marble.

The house belongs to Patrick O'Connell and Reinhardt Lynch, owners of the Inn at Little Washington, a world-renowned establishment that sits just across the road. The Inn's rooms, advertised as "charming jewels, each unique in mood and utterly decadent in detail," cost up to a thousand dollars a night during peak season. A party of six recently spent twenty-six thousand dollars on dinner at the Inn. That's twenty-two hundred dollars more than the annual per-capita income of Rappahannock County, of which Washington is the county seat. "The guest has that rare privilege of feeling just as he might if he'd stayed at a royal château," says O'Connell, the Inn's chef. Patrons include Barbra Streisand, Paul Newman, Andrew Lloyd Webber, Al Gore, and Alan Greenspan.

As the Inn's reputation has grown over the past twenty years, the owners have bought and buffed nearby properties. Other buildings around town have been renovated as quaint shops and guesthouses catering to Inn diners. As a consequence, this modest community, which hasn't grown much beyond the boundaries that George Washington surveyed in 1749, presents a sometimes dissonant mixture of mountain burg and period theme park. "We want guests to have a sense of the town, a somewhat controlled sense of the town," says O'Connell. "A different history is being created. Not necessarily a false one, but a new and different vision, one that we and our guests are charmed by."

But many residents are alarmed rather than enchanted by O'Connell's grandiose vision, and they have battled the Inn as intransigently as the "Deathless Dead" whose names are etched on the town's Confederate monument. The result has been an uncivil war marked by the kinds of smear tactics, lawsuits, and political scandals more commonly associated with that other Washington, sixty-two miles away. The fight, now in its third decade, also recalls the days when feuding mountain families burned barns and poisoned wells. "It's *Village of the Damned,*" says Donna Kevis, a bed-and-breakfast owner, referring to the horror film in which an idyllic town becomes possessed by demonic forces and tears itself apart. Kevis and her next-door neighbor are on opposite sides of the Inn controversy, and they no longer speak, even though he is godfather to her only child.

THE metamorphosis of Washington, Virginia, population 198 (including jail inmates), into an embattled outpost of gastronomy seems almost surreal to those who remember the town before the Inn opened, in 1978. At the time, Washington's social and commercial center was Merrill's, a gas station at the main crossroads, where men in duckbill caps and bib overalls liked to perch on the chairs and piles of tires out front. They rotated between Merrill's and the porch of the nearby Cash Store, which sold everything from bulk seed to a dark suit of such sturdy weave that the store owner boasted it could endure a lifetime of weddings, funerals, and church services.

On one flank of town lived mountain folk evicted by the government from log homes in the Shenandoah National Park in 1937 and resettled in block houses with chicken coops and outhouses. Descendants of local slaves lived across town, in "Blacksburg." A trickle of outsiders, known as "come-heres," had joined the mix, as had weekenders from Washington, D.C., who began buying mountain properties outside town. But Rappahannock County remained essentially what it had been for decades: a rocky, rural domain with stirring scenery and a sagging economy. Almost a third of its residents lived in poverty. Washington, the county's only incorporated town, retained its Colonial street grid and striking architectural skeleton—redbrick courthouse, mud-chinked log cabins, a few antebellum mansions—but many of the buildings were vacant and dilapidated.

"You knew everybody in town," the former mayor Newbill Miller recalls. "You knew everybody's dog in town." A sign over the gas pump at Merrill's captured this easygoing air: "If you can't stop, smile as you go by."

In the early seventies, two women from Washington, D.C., opened a crafts shop in a building across from Merrill's. They decided to add a restaurant, and approached O'Connell and Lynch, who had moved to the county a few years before and started a catering business popular among wealthy weekenders. The women were so charmed by the two men that they not only leased them half the building but also advanced them twenty-five thousand dollars for building improvements. Mayor Miller presided at the Inn's ribbon-cutting. Many locals welcomed fresh life at the center of town and enjoyed dining at the Inn, where an entrée of roast chicken with fresh tarragon cost just $4.95.

Two weeks later, a food critic anointed the Inn one of the best restaurants within driving distance of the capital. Overnight it was booked solid. The owners raised prices and undertook a lush redecoration by an English set designer: William Morris wallpaper, richly patterned carpets, a collage ceiling modelled on the Houses of Parliament. The Inn also added guest rooms appointed with rare orchids, antique fainting couches, canopied beds, and lavishments familiar to readers of *Architectural Digest,* such as Frette linens and Scalamandré silks. The Inn has become mainly a destination for sybaritic celebrations and romantic getaways, a reputation the Inn nurtures by indulging the guests' most extravagant requests: a pearl necklace planted in a plate of oysters, a spouse surprised with a closet full of minks. "It's an atmosphere that lends itself to fantasy, to people craving a little European-style escape," O'Connell explains.

I first met O'Connell and Lynch in the restaurant's terrace room, where we sat beneath a canopy of tasselled linen inspired by a Napoleonic campaign tent. Nibbling figs and Bordeaux tea cakes, the two men, now in their early fifties, present a complementary pair. O'Connell is tall and slender, with close-cropped ginger hair, an engaging smile, and a theatrical manner (he studied drama in Washington, D.C.). Lynch, who was raised in Indiana but left there after becoming a conscientious objector to the Vietnam War, is compact, boyish, and intense. He is the Inn's business manager and host; O'Connell runs the kitchen.

O'Connell, who began as a short-order cook and later became chef at a French restaurant near Washington, D.C., is famed for creating unexpected combinations of American and French flavors. Dinner at the Inn opens with an *amuse-gueule* such as potato cornets layered in salmon, caviar, and crème fraîche. This may be followed by a first course of black-eyed peas draped with country ham and foie gras and drizzled with pan juices. A palate-cleanser of sassafras granité precedes equally eclectic entrées, such as veal sweetbreads braised in port with mushrooms and huckleberries. The signature dessert reflects the Inn's self-conscious decadence: an opulent sampling of cakes, tarts, and puddings, it is called Seven Deadly Sins.

This cornucopia is matched by a fourteen-thousand-bottle wine cellar and theatrical service. "You come here for the total experience," said Crawford Malone, a wine broker and former sous-chef for Paul Prudhomme, who was dining with colleagues on a winter weekend. A team of tuxedoed waiters glided to his table bearing chargers hand-painted with 24k. gold, then set the plates before each guest with the stylish precision of synchronized swimmers. Malone admired not only the food and service but the cutlery, glassware, and flowers— all the finest available. "It's a level of art you don't often see in this country," he sighed.

In 1986, Craig Claiborne, of the *Times*, declared dinner at the Inn "the most fantastic meal in my life." The next year, the Inn joined the exclusive Relais & Châteaux group of small luxury hotels and restaurants. It has since won the James Beard Restaurant of the Year Award and the Mobil Travel Guide's first ever five-star prize for both food and lodging. But each uptick in this soaring reputation has brought a corresponding dip in relations with the town.

The first friction occurred when Mayor Miller asked the Inn to remove its new sign. Some locals felt that "Little" Washington was demeaning. O'Connell says mail addressed to the Inn at Little Washington was initially marked at the post office "Return to sender—no known address." Soon afterward, the Mayor charged that tree planters flanking the entrance to the Inn encroached on the public right-of-way. Miller says he was simply enforcing local rules. But his true motive, the innkeepers say, was to rein in two upstarts who didn't kowtow to a "feudal" power structure, headed by "landed gentry" such as Miller, a cattle breeder and seventh-generation local. "This is a foreign concept here, that change can be for the better," O'Connell says.

Another source of tension was the fact that the innkeepers lived together. At first, O'Connell says, "they thought we were brothers." But before long, local males began referring to the two men as "the queers." Some warned that AIDS might spread through the Inn's food or the town's drainage fields. The innkeepers initially got on better with the county's women, and hired many as waitresses and kitchen staff. But O'Connell relates that experience with a faux mountain accent and evident distaste. "A local woman would arrive with pink curlers, baby on hip, Coca-Cola in hand, another young 'un in back and another bringing up the rear, and Big Mama and other relations offering support," he says. "They'd greet you, 'Mistah, I need a job, I need it baaad.' "

After working at the Inn, O'Connell claims, some women found themselves "unable to marry a local. They'd seen a bit of the light." This edification included trips he led to Washington, D.C., for cooking classes at Williams-Sonoma and trying on clothes at Neiman Marcus. "I often think how wonderful if I'd grown up in a town like this," he says, "where the Vice-

President is coming, where Barbra Streisand is coming, where people from France are coming—such a wonderful contrast to going to the general store."

To many townsfolk, this condescending attitude is the root of most conflicts between the Inn and the town. One of the first big fights, however, occurred between the innkeepers and the two women from Washington, D.C., over the terms of their lease-to-buy contract. This led to a court injunction and an ugly legal dispute—until then rare events in this small town. But what really stunned the innkeepers' once adoring landladies was the vitriol that followed. "They told everyone in the county what creeps we were," recalls Louise Sagalyn, a painter, who, along with her business partner, has been purged from the oft-told tale of the Inn's meteoric rise. (In a typical instance, O'Connell recently wrote in a trade magazine that he and Lynch used only their meagre savings to open the Inn in a "rundown garage"—which the building hadn't been for twenty years.) "These two men are extraordinarily mean-spirited, and the town has picked up on that," Sagalyn says.

The innkeepers disavow any malice. But this early spat set the tone for many conflicts that followed. Soon after the Inn opened, once sleepy town meetings became angry set-tos over issues such as zoning variances—sometimes with court stenographers present, because either townspeople or the Inn had threatened a lawsuit. Many locals who had taken jobs at the Inn quit or were fired, often under hostile circumstances. In 1986, the Inn dismissed Kaye Kohler, a veteran waitress, then had her arrested for trespassing when she returned the following night. (She said she hadn't been fired and was reporting for work; the Inn said she was staging a protest.) The charge was later dropped; among other things, Kohler's lawyer argued that the magistrate issuing her arrest warrant had eaten for free at the Inn many times. Kohler then sued for defamation and unfair dismissal and won a modest out-of-court settlement.

The Inn's arrival also spawned new bureaucracy in a town that has traditionally loathed government and taxes. In the mid-eighties, Washington established a levy on food, lodging, and beverage—almost all of it collected from the Inn. An architectural-review board was set up to approve exterior changes in town, in part because the innkeepers tried to paint the restaurant salmon and ended up with "hot pink," O'Connell says. "It was a pulsating Miami Beach building." (The Inn's columned façade is now a more sedate lichen and putty.)

Conflict even found its way into the Episcopal church across the street from the Inn, when the Reverend Jennings Hobson III agreed, in 1982, to lease the church parking lot to the restaurant. "I love the car flesh," Hobson confesses, recalling some of his favorite sightings: a red Rolls, a Lamborghini, three Mercedes 300 SLs from the nineteen-fifties. But some congregants don't like to see the church serving Inn guests. "If it was a bunch of rusty Pintos, there wouldn't be so many complaints," says Hobson, who also enjoys dining at the Inn. "It's a class issue." For a time, teen-agers hung out at the parking lot and sometimes heckled Inn patrons, usually women, with wolf whistles and epithets like "rich bitch." Several arrests for public drunkenness ended the loitering.

In the late eighties, new shops and guesthouses sprang up to serve the Inn's patrons. Before, most diners had come and gone the same night (occasionally by helicopter, another irritant to early-rising locals). Now many visitors stay over and stroll conspicuously through town. (One couple was overheard discussing where to hang their new Chagall.) "It's amazing how these guys have succeeded in the middle of nowhere," Manja Blazer, an Inn guest from suburban Washington, told me on a recent winter morning. "It's like nothing, this town." She was dressed for a walk on Main Street in black leather pants and jacket, a silk scarf, and matching purple hat, gloves, handkerchief, and pumps. Some of the shops offer gold jewelry, pre-Columbian art, and Oriental rugs, at prices up to twelve thousand dollars. The Inn also runs its own gift shop, peddling items such as "our elegant and sinful pure silk signature tie."

Seated on a bench by the Country Café, where she works as a waitress, Lindsay Knight watches two women in full-length fur coats stroll by. "It's intimidating and a little annoying," she says of the Inn traffic. "They think the whole town has to stop for them. Limos will block the street and sheriffs will tell them to move, but they don't care." Some Inn guests visit the Country Café for breakfast or lunch. Knight finds them "very particular," and also cheap. "I get fifty cents or a dollar tip. Maybe that's all they have left after the Inn."

The Country Café, with fare such as wing dings and ham steak, is the rare business that still caters to locals. The Cash Store closed in 1990, leaving residents with no place within walking distance to buy staples. Most townsfolk haven't eaten at the Inn for years because of its prices—a hundred and twenty-eight dollars per person for the Saturday-night prix-fixe, before tip and wine (a 1945 bottle of Château d'Yquem was recently uncorked at a price of ten thousand dollars). To some in this frugal mountain culture, the fin-de-siècle excesses of Inn patrons seem offensive. "Just because the Lord gives you more money doesn't make you a damn bit better—you're just who you are," says Clabert Smoot, a retired custodian, who refers to Inn guests as "damn rogues." Older residents also lament the change in atmosphere since, as they put it, "the quaintness came to town." When Merrill's and the Cash Store closed, men lost their traditional spots in town to gossip and "loaf." By now, the Inn owns much of the town center—seventeen properties in all, including Merrill's and the post office.

BUILDING by building, Lynch and O'Connell are refurbishing Washington, guided by their vision of "what one wished the town history had been," O'Connell says. The Inn's garden, for instance, includes what O'Connell calls "an appendage of the great house," a folly that will be adorned with roses and a carillon to mimic an old ruin. "The idea is to create little vistas," he says. "A building speaks to you and demands of you what it wants. You're the conduit to make it happen. If you're a gifted person, you don't own the gift—you have a responsibility to exercise it."

But some in Washington fear that this form of exercise will ultimately transform the entire town into a period resort for the rich. These fears crystallized in 1990 when the Inn unveiled its plans for a baronial, block-long addition with turrets, an indoor pool, formal gardens, and parking for forty cars. "In the Hudson River or Loire Valley, it would have fit perfectly," says Donna Kevis, the B.&B. owner, who was then head of the architectural-review board. "It didn't belong here."

Faced with overwhelming opposition, the Inn was forced to withdraw its plans, but not before innkeeper Reinhardt Lynch made his first run for town council. During the campaign, he urged three Inn employees who weren't residents of town to register and vote. Lynch lost anyway, and was subsequently convicted of "voting fraud" and sentenced to a sixty-day jail stay (suspended), a thousand-dollar fine, and eighty hours of community service.

The 1990 showdown hardened the battle lines. When Lynch ran for town council again, in 1994, anonymous mailings were distributed containing news clips about his voting-fraud conviction, as well as tax documents embarrassing to Inn allies. (Lynch tied for last, but won a council seat on a coin flip.) Around the same time, townspeople thwarted the Inn's attempt to buy an antebellum church and began to pepper the Inn's frequent improvement projects with stop-work orders.

Lynch and O'Connell had to fight such an order when they bought and gutted the plain frame house beside the Inn which became their home. "We did a little new history on it," O'Connell says of the house, now a neoclassical structure. Because the new picture windows at the rear of the house looked out on what they call Steve Critzer's "junk yard," the innkeepers dispatched a landscaper to speak to the road builder about screening the view with decorative trees and shrubs.

This approach, by proxy, irked Critzer. "They think that someone working heavy equipment must just be an ignorant country person you wouldn't possibly want to know," he says. Critzer devised his own solution: when the town dug a new water system several years ago, he asked that the leftover dirt be dumped in his yard to form a three-hundred-foot berm between his yard and the innkeepers' cottage. The innkeepers then offered to pay for landscaping the berm, but Critzer turned them down to insure that "we could move the dirt later on without a Philadelphia lawyer showing up." So Mt. Critzer has been left to sprout pokeweed and locust. But at least it provides screening. "Now," says Critzer, "if I want to relieve myself while working in the yard, I don't have to step too far behind a truck."

IN the nineties, the Inn has come to completely dominate the local economy. "It's like one of those rare exotic plants that thrive in parched soil," says O'Connell. Its annual tax bill for food and lodging totals about a hundred and twenty thousand dollars—roughly two-thirds of the town's entire budget. The Inn has also attracted other commerce, created jobs, and boosted real-estate prices. Lynch and O'Connell give generously to local charities. All this has won the innkeepers a small but staunch band of allies. "Those guys put this town on the map," says Louise van Dort, an interior designer who works for the Inn and acts as its fiercest advocate. A chain-smoking, blunt-spoken Dutch native, she has a bumper sticker on her office wall that reads "For a Small Town This One Sure Has a Lot of Assholes." Van Dort is impatient with the notion that the Inn threatens the town. "Things grow, things change—I used to wear a size 10," she says. "Even if the Inn hadn't come, things would have changed." Inn supporters point out that the alternatives for the town might have been far worse: if not continued decay, then polluting industry or tacky strip malls.

Still, many residents complain that Washington is "almost like a company town," says Tanya Ritchie, an artist and gallery owner, who points to the Inn's treatment of Kaye Kohler, the fired waitress. Immediately after Kohler won her small out-of-court settlement, the Inn called the vineyard where Kohler then worked to cancel the Inn's wine orders. In the early nineties, Lynch loudly protested Kohler's hiring as the town's administrator. More recently, a B.&B. owner was warned that giving Kohler part-time work would jeopardize referrals from the Inn. "It's all about control," says Ritchie, the rare local merchant unafraid to speak publicly about the Inn.

Except for the occasional face-off at town-council meetings, which sometimes degenerate into jeering between the Inn's foes and its allies, the innkeepers now dwell in almost total isolation from town. Locals rarely work there anymore, except as dishwashers and maids. O'Connell says this reflects the ever higher standards of his guests. "People have a whole different set of expectations when they've flown from London for what they've been told is America's best meal," he says. "It's just not appropriate to say to guests, 'Howdy, how y'all doing, want to see a picture of my bumper crop of turnips?' " Most of the Inn's seventy-four-person staff is recruited from the Culinary Institute of America and other top schools, as well as from abroad.

The staff members tend to keep to themselves, as do Lynch and O'Connell. "I walk the dogs after midnight, when no one's on the street," Lynch says. O'Connell never strays far from the kitchen, which runs around the clock. "You operate in a different time zone than is operational around here, where there's a lot of 'porch-setting,' " he says, as members of the kitchen staff, wearing Dalmatian-print pants and Moroccan-style caps, strain soup, chop lobster, and pick filaments from sweetbread. "We're putting out a plate every thirty seconds."

The fact that Lynch and O'Connell now deal with locals largely through proxies, however, has meant that battles over the Inn are intensified by a store-house of personal slights and ancient grudges. For instance, van Dort, the innkeepers' advocate, admits that she recently terrorized her neighbors by spreading false rumors about the Inn's plans—payback, she says, for nasty gossip told about her by a rival designer.

This toxic intimacy makes it hard for even come-heres to remain neutral for long. "If you go down the middle, you get hit by both sides," says Tanya Ritchie. Town Councillor Charlie Tompkins discovered this as well when he tried to conduct shuttle diplomacy between the two camps. In a town so insular that people recognize each other's license plates, he couldn't visit anyone without the other side accusing him of plotting. "The suction from the factions is enormous," he says. "The malevolence here pretty much gets to everyone"—including Tompkins, who has joined the Inn camp and now passes on malicious tidbits about his neighbors.

MEANWHILE, the Inn's business continues to grow. Lynch and O'Connell recently finished a five-million-dollar remodelling of the kitchen and two adjoining rooms (which feature a gold-leaf-and-leather ceiling and a tapestry from a seventeenth-century French manor). The innkeepers have also just done a costly makeover of a cottage for V.I.P.s. And they may soon buy and renovate a tavern where George Washington is said to have danced the minuet. "We have more at stake" than townsfolk, O'Connell says. "They can move. We have twenty years' investment here."

However, locals, some with roots here going back two centuries, aren't about to abandon the fight. "It's a terrible thing to say, but it's one of those things that will perpetuate itself," Newbill Miller says.

O'Connell agrees, though characteristically he sees things in more theatrical terms. "This is a film. Think of the sets!" he exclaims. "I could play a bigot. I can do the accents. The end is one of those ambivalent finales—everyone will think they're right." He wishes it were otherwise. "The best revenge is to outlive them," he says. "However, they've produced a new generation."

One of the very few people who remain nonaligned is John McCarthy, a county zoning official. He believes both sides are guilty of pettiness and paranoia that obscure their common interests, such as protecting the area against exurban sprawl. But he, too, doubts that there's much impulse to make up and move on. Asked how the drama will end, McCarthy smiles wanly and recites a maxim that is strangely popular in Washington, Virginia: "Good friends will come and go, but a good enemy will last you a lifetime."

MARCH 29, 1999

MY MISSPENT YOUTH

A FEW months ago, I was walking down West End Avenue, in Manhattan, and I remembered with a sadness that nearly knocked me off my feet just why I'd come to New York seven years ago, and why I was now about to leave. Certain kinds of buildings seem almost too gorgeous to exist—in the United States, anyway—and I'm still amazed that massive, ornate residences like 838 West End Avenue, with its yellow façade and geometric terra-cotta panels, or 305 Riverside Drive, with its elegantly carved limestone cornices, receive mail and spill kids out of their front doors like pretty much any domicile anywhere. When I was growing up in northern New Jersey, just twenty-five miles from Manhattan, I had no idea that ordinary people could live in such places. Then, when I was seventeen, I walked into an apartment at West End Avenue and 104th Street and decided that I had to be one of those people.

It was the summer of 1987, and I was learning how to drive a stick shift. My father, who is a composer, had allowed me to drive him to Manhattan in our Plymouth Horizon to drop off some scores with a music copyist. There was nothing particularly striking about the copyist's apartment: it was a modest four-room prewar with moldings around the ceiling, and I have since mentally supplied it with faded Persian rugs, NPR playing on the radio, and porcelain hexagonal tiles that were coming loose in the bathroom. It's difficult to imagine a time when I didn't walk into someone's apartment and immediately start the income-to-rent-ratio calculations, and I would now guess that the apartment had been rent-controlled for decades, and that the copyist paid perhaps three hundred dollars a month. But on that summer night, looking out the living-room window toward the river that so famously and effectively keeps *here* safely away from *there*, money was the last thing on my mind; I just knew that this was where I wanted to live, and from that moment on every decision I made was based on that conviction.

I've always been somebody who exerts a great deal of energy to get my realities to match my fantasies. I'm also pretty good at "getting by"—especially if you apply the increasingly common definition of the term, which has more to do with keeping up appearances than with keeping things under control. So it wasn't until recently that I realized I wasn't having such a good time in New York anymore. Like a social smoker whose supposedly endearing desire to emulate Marlene Dietrich has landed her in a cancer ward, I have recently woken up to the frightening fallout of my own romantic notions of life in the big city: I'm twenty-nine years old, and I am completely over my head in debt. I have not made a life for myself; I have purchased a life for myself.

For the better part of the last year, the balance of my Visa card has hovered around seven thousand dollars. A significant chunk of that debt comes from medical expenses, particularly the bills for a series of dental procedures I needed. As a freelance writer, it would cost me three hundred dollars a month to buy health insurance in New York State. That's far more than I can afford, so I don't have any. Although I try to pay the three-hundred-and-thirty-nine-dollars-a-quarter charge to keep a hospitalization insurance policy that will cover me if some major disaster befalls, I am often late in paying, and it gets cancelled. But medical expenses represent only a fraction of my troubles. I also need to make an estimated quarterly tax payment of fifty-four hundred dollars this month, which is going to be tough, because I recently paid back three thousand dollars to my now ex-boyfriend, who lent me money to pay last year's taxes, and I still owe three hundred dollars to the accountant who prepared the return. My checking account is overdrawn by a thousand seven hundred and eighty-four dollars. I have no savings, no investments, no pension fund, and no inheritance on the horizon. I have student loans from graduate school amounting to sixty thousand dollars. I pay $448.83 per month on these loans, installments that barely cover the interest that's accruing.

It's tempting to go into a litany of all the things that I do not spend money on. I have no dependents, not even a cat or a fish. I do not have a car. I've worn the same four pairs of shoes for the past three years. Much of the clothing in my closet has been there since the early nineties, the rare additions usually taking the form of a sixteen-dollar shirt from Old Navy, a discounted dress from Loehmann's, or a Christmas sweater from my mother. I've lived without a roommate only for the last two years. My rent, a thousand and fifty-five dollars a month for a four-hundred-square-foot apartment, is, as we say in New York City when describing the Holy Grail, below market. I do not own expensive stereo equipment, and even though I have a television, I cannot bring myself to spend the thirty-five dollars a month on cable, which, curiously, I've deemed an indulgence. With the exception of a trip to Egypt to visit a friend, in 1998, I have not spent money on overseas travel. I've still never been to Europe.

Instead, I've confined my spending to certain ephemeral luxuries that have come to seem like necessities. I'll go to Starbucks in the morning, and then order sushi for lunch. I'll meet a friend for drinks and drop forty-five dollars on Merlot and chicken satay. I make long-distance phone calls almost daily, with no thought of peak calling hours or dime-a-minute rates. I have a compulsive need to keep fresh-cut flowers in my apartment at all times, and spend eight to ten dollars a week on tulips from the Korean market. But these extravagances are merely symptoms of a larger delusion. It's easier to feel guilt over spending sixty dollars on a blender, as I did last month, than to examine the more elaborate reasons that I've found it increasingly impossible to live within my means.

Once you're in this kind of debt—and by "kind" I'm talking less about numbers than about my particular brand of debt—all those bills start not to matter anymore. If I allowed them to matter, I would become so panicked that I wouldn't be able to work, which would only set me back further. I've also noticed that my kind of debt is surprisingly socially acceptable. After all, I went into debt for my education and my career—broad categories with room for copious rationalizations, and I make full use of them. I live in the most expensive city in the country because I have long believed that my career is dependent upon it. I spend money on Martinis and expensive dinners because, as is typical among my species of debtor, I tell myself that Martinis and expensive dinners are the entire point—the point of being young, the point of living in New York City, the point of living. In this frame of mind, the dollars spent, like the workings of a machine which no one bothers to understand, become an abstraction, a vehicle of taste.

AS I try to sort out the origins of my present financial situation, I always come back to the ineffable hankering I had as a teen-ager for some sort of earthier, more "intellectual" life style. I come from an affluent New Jersey suburb whose main draw is its good public-school system, but I wanted to live someplace that looked like Mia Farrow's apartment in *Hannah and Her Sisters*. (Little did I know that it *was* Mia Farrow's apartment.) To me, this kind of space connoted not wealth but urbanity. These were places where the paint was peeling and the rugs were frayed and the hallways were lined with books; places where smart people sat around drinking gin and tonics, having interesting conversations, and living, according to my logic, in an authentic way. As far as I was aware at seventeen, rich was something else entirely. Rich meant monstrous Tudor-style houses in the ritzy section of my town. Rich was driving a BMW to school. I had the distinct feeling that my orthodontist, who had a sprawling ranch house with front steps that were polished to look like ice, was rich. None of these particular trappings of wealth held my attention. In fact, nothing outside of the movies really held my attention until that night in 1987 when I saw the apartment on 104th Street.

I planned my escape from the suburbs through the standard channels: college selection. My logic, informed by a combination of college guidebooks and the alma maters of the brides featured in the *Times* wedding announcements, went something like this: Columbia rather than N.Y.U., Wisconsin rather than Texas, Yale rather than Harvard, Vassar rather than Smith. My ranking system had little to do with the academic merits of the schools. It was more a game of degrees of separation between me and an apartment full of houseplants on the Upper West Side. Somehow, Vassar emerged as the best contender for closing that gap. I wanted so badly to go to a particular kind of artsy college and mix with a particular kind of artsy crowd that I wasted an alarming amount of time during my senior year of high school throwing trash into various wastebaskets from across the room, saying, "If I make this shot, I get into Vassar."

As it turned out, I did go to Vassar, and although it would be five years until I entered my debting era, my time there did more than expand my intellect: it expanded my sense of entitlement so much that, by the end, I had no ability to distinguish myself from the many extremely wealthy people I encountered there. A sense of entitlement can certainly be an asset, but it has also played a supporting role in my financial demise—mostly because it made it hard to recognize where ambition and chutzpah end and potential bankruptcy begins.

WHEN I graduated, in 1992, I followed a herd of my classmates into Manhattan; many of them moved back in with their parents on Park Avenue. I got an entry-level job in publishing, and, along with a couple of friends, rented a five-room prewar apartment with chipping paint on 100th Street off Riverside Drive, a mere five blocks from the scene of my high-school epiphany. Such expert marksmanship! I was ecstatic. My job, as an editorial assistant at a glossy fashion magazine, paid eighteen thousand dollars a year. The woman who hired me, a fifties-era Vassar graduate, told me that she hoped I had an independent source of income, as I certainly wouldn't be able to support myself on my salary. But I did support myself. My roommates—an elementary-school teacher, who was making nineteen thousand dollars a year, and a film student, who worked part time at a non-profit arts organization—supported themselves, too. We each paid around five hundred and fifty dollars a month in rent and lived as recent graduates should, eating ramen noodles and ninety-nine-cent White Rose macaroni and cheese.

Looking back, I see those years as a cheap, happy time. It was a time during which a certain kind of poverty was appropriate. Unlike the West Seventies and Eighties, my neighborhood seemed like a place for people who knew the city, for people *from* the city. Though I was living hand to mouth, I loved it there, and looked forward to moving ahead in my career and one day being able to afford my own place in the neighborhood. Then, that seemed well within the realm of possibility. It was 1993, I was twenty-three, and I'd received a raise, so that I was earning twenty-one thousand dollars a year. I had no idea that this was the closest I'd be to financial solvency for at least the next decade.

I'd been told I was lucky to have got a job at a magazine—I had, after all, graduated into what was being called the worst job market in twenty years—and even though I had little interest in its subject matter, I didn't dare turn down the position. Within my first week on the job, I found myself immersed in a culture of money and celebrity. Socialites sat on the editorial board in order to report on trends among the rich and famous. Editorial assistants who earned eighteen thousand dollars managed to wear Prada, have regular facials, and rent time-shares in the Hamptons. Many of them lived in doorman buildings, for which their parents helped foot the bill.

This wasn't my scene. I felt as far away from my *Hannah and Her Sisters* fantasy as I had in the suburbs. After a year of office work, I decided that an M.F.A. in creative writing would provide the most direct route to literary legitimacy. I applied to Columbia, which, not coincidentally, happened to be within walking distance of my apartment. It also has one of the most expensive writing programs in the country, a fact that was easy to forget, because the students, for the most part, seemed so down to earth and modest. In their flannel shirts and roach-infested student housing, they seemed as earnest and poor as I was, and I figured that if they could take out twenty-thousand-dollar-a-year loans, so could I. In the three years that I spent at Columbia, borrowing more than sixty thousand dollars to get my degree, I was told repeatedly—by fellow-students, faculty, administrators, and professional writers whose careers I wished to emulate—not to think about the loans. Student loans, after all, were low-interest, long-term, and far more benign than credit-card debt. Not thinking about them was a skill that I quickly developed.

IF there is in this story a single moment when I crossed the boundary between debtlessness and total financial mayhem, it's the first dollar that I put toward my life as a writer in New York—despite the fact that I was hanging out at the Cuban coffee shop and traipsing through the windblown trash of upper Broadway. The year I entered graduate school was the year I stopped making decisions that were appropriate for my situation and began making a rich person's decisions. Entering this particular graduate program was a rich person's decision. Remaining there when it became clear that I was not going to get any scholarship money, and that the class schedule would prevent me from holding down a day job, was also a rich person's decision.

But it's hard to recognize that you're acting like a rich person when you're becoming increasingly poor. Besides, I was never without a job. I worked for an anthropology professor for nine dollars an hour. I read manuscripts at ten dollars a pop for an ersatz literary agent. I worked at a university press for ten dollars an hour. Sometimes I called in sick to these jobs and did temp work at midtown offices for seventeen dollars an hour. A couple of times, I took out cash advances on my credit cards to pay the rent. There was a period during a particularly miserable winter, in 1994, when I tried to make it through three weeks on thirty-four dollars, walking sixteen blocks to school in subzero temperatures and stealing my roommates' food, hoping they wouldn't notice. One day, I slipped on the ice three times, got in a cab, and decided to take out a private loan from Columbia for two thousand five hundred dollars. A thousand of it went to pay off part of a credit card. I used up the rest within a month.

There were a handful of us who were pulling stunts like this. One of my roommates had maxed out her credit cards in order to finance a student film. I knew several women, and even a few men, who were actively looking for rich marriage partners to bail them out. One aspiring novelist I know underwent a series of drug treatments and uncomfortable surgical procedures in order to sell her eggs for twenty-five hundred dollars. Whether or not one is paying twenty thousand dollars' tuition a year to try to make it as a writer, New York City in the nineties is a prohibitively expensive place to live for just about anyone. Although I devoted a lot of energy to being envious of Columbia classmates whose relatives were picking up the tab, it later became clear to me that the need for outside financial support is not limited to those in entry-level jobs or expensive graduate programs. These days, pursuing a career in the arts in New York is often contingent upon inheriting the means to do so.

As I was finishing at Columbia, however, I began to get some freelance work, so I continued to hedge my bets. I was publishing magazine articles regularly and, after a few months of temping at insurance companies and banks, scored some steady assignments that, to my delight, allowed me to work as a full-time freelance writer. After five years and eight different roommates in the 100th Street apartment, I was earning enough money to move into my own place. More important, I had found a two-year sublet in a rent-stabilized building, and the fact that I had done so through a Columbia connection seemed almost sufficient justification for the money I'd spent on grad school.

Things were going well. In 1997, I was twenty-seven, teaching a writing course at N.Y.U., publishing in a variety of magazines, and earning about fifty-five thousand dollars before taxes. (The teaching job paid only twenty-five hundred dollars for an entire semester, but I was too enamored of the idea of being a college instructor to wonder if I could afford to take it.) I had a decent-sized apartment with oak floors and porcelain hexagonal tiles that were coming loose in the bathroom. Like an honest New Yorker, I even had mice lurking in the kitchen. I bought rugs and a fax machine. I installed a second telephone line for the fax. Finally, I was leading the life I'd spent so long preparing for.

Then came the dental bills, which I was forced to charge to Visa. I tried not to think about that too much, until I ended up making a few doctor's visits that, because I was uninsured, I also charged to Visa. When April rolled around, I realized that my income was significantly higher that year than it had been in any previous year, and that I had woefully underestimated what I owed in taxes. Despite a profusion of the typical freelancer's writeoffs—movies, magazine subscriptions, an $89.99 sonic rodent-control device—I was hit with a bill of more than twenty thousand dollars. And although the I.R.S. apparently deemed sonic rodent-control devices an acceptable deduction, it seemed that I'd earned too much money to be eligible to write off the nearly seven thousand dollars (most of it interest) I'd paid to the student-loan agency or the three thousand dollars in dental bills. In the months it took me to assemble that twenty thousand dollars, I had to reduce my student-loan payments from the suggested eight hundred dollars to the aforementioned $448.83 a month. Most heartbreaking of all, my accountant determined that my sixty-dollar pledge to WNYC—my Upper West Side tableau couldn't possibly be complete without the National Public Radio coffee mug—was not entirely tax deductible.

It was around this time that I started having trouble thinking about anything other than how to make a payment on whatever bill was sitting on my desk, most likely weeks overdue, at any given time. I began getting final disconnection notices from the phone company, letters from the gas company asking "Have you forgotten us?," collection calls from Visa. A friend who had been a member of Debtors Anonymous urged me to put a note over my phone that read, "Owing money does not make me a bad person." I didn't do this, partly because it wouldn't have fit in with the décor of my apartment, and partly because I wasn't sure she was right. She did, however, persuade me to call Visa and put a hold on my account for six months, which would reduce my payments to a hundred and five dollars a month and freeze the interest. This required telling the customer-service representative at Visa that I was experiencing some financial "hardships." When she asked me to be more specific, I told her that I had medical expenses, and hung up the phone feeling as if I had a terminal illness.

I noticed that I was drinking more than I had in the past, often alone at home, where I would sip Sauvignon Blanc at my desk and pretend to write when in fact I'd be working out some kind of desperate math equation on the tool-bar calculator, making wild guesses as to when I'd receive some random eight-hundred-dollar check from some unreliable accounting department of some slow-paying publication, how long it would take the check to clear, what would be left after I set aside a third of it for taxes, and, finally, which lucky creditor would be the recipient of what remained. There's nothing like completing one of these calculations, realizing that you've drunk half a bottle of $7.99 wine, and feeling guiltier about having spent $7.99 than about being too tipsy to work. One night, I did a whole bunch of calculations and discovered that, despite having earned a gross income of seventy-eight thousand dollars in 1998, despite having not gone overboard on such classic debtor's paraphernalia as clothes and vacations and stereo equipment, despite having followed the urban striver's guide to success, I was more than seventy-five thousand dollars in the hole.

There are days when my debt seems to be at the center of my being, a cancer that must be treated with the morphine of excuses and rationales and promises to myself that I'm going to come up with the big score—book advance, screenplay deal, Publishers Clearinghouse prize—and save myself. There are other days when the debt feels like someone else's cancer, a tragedy outside myself, a condemned building next door that I try to avoid walking past. But the days when I can pretend that money is "only money" are growing farther and farther apart. I have friends who are getting rich off the stock market and buying million-dollar houses. I have other friends who are almost as badly off as I am, and who compulsively volunteer for relief work in Third World countries as a way of forgetting that they can't quite afford to live in the First World.

But New York City, which has a way of making you feel like you're in the Third World just seconds after you thought you'd conquered all of Western civilization, has never really belonged to the rest of the country. I suppose that part of the city's magical beastliness is the fact that you can show up with the best of intentions, do what's considered to be all the right things, achieve some measure of success, and still find yourself trapped in a financial emergency.

AS I write this, I have to be out of my sublet within months. Even if I try to assume control of the lease, the landlord will renovate the apartment and raise the rent to two thousand dollars. When I reported this calamity to a friend the other day, hoping she would gasp in sympathy, she instead replied, "That's cheaper than our place." A two-bedroom apartment down the street recently rented for forty-five hundred a month. A small studio on the Upper West Side will go for an average of twelve hundred and fifty dollars. West 104th Street is totally beyond my means. Worse, 104th Street is now beyond the means of most of the people who made me want to live here in the first place. The New York that changed my life on that summer night when I was seventeen no longer exists.

Several months ago, on a day when the debt anxiety had flared up even more than usual, I found myself fantasizing about moving to Lincoln, Nebraska. I'd been to Lincoln twice on a magazine assignment, met some nice people, and found myself liking it enough to entertain the notion of moving there. But both times I'd discarded the idea the minute the wheels hit the tarmac at LaGuardia. Surely I'd never be able to live without art-movie houses and twenty-four-hour takeout. During my last round of panic, however, I convinced myself that it was a good plan. I can rent an apartment there for three hundred dollars a month. I can rent an entire house, if I want one, for seven hundred dollars. Full-coverage health insurance will cost me seventy-five dollars a month. Apparently, people in Nebraska also listen to NPR, and there are even places to live in Lincoln that have oak floors. Had I known that before, I might have skipped out on this New York thing altogether and spared myself the financial and psychological ordeal. But I'm kind of glad I didn't know, because I've had a very, very good time here. I'm just leaving the party before the cops break it up.

OCTOBER 18, 1999

A HAZARD OF NO FORTUNE

APARTMENT-HUNTING is the permanent New York romance, and the broker and his couple the eternal triangle. A man and woman are looking for a place to live, and they call up a broker, and he shows them apartments that are for sale or rent, but the relationship between those three people is much more complicated than the relationship between someone who knows where homes can be found and two people who would like to find one. For one thing, the places are not really his to sell, not really theirs to buy. A tangle of clients and banks, bids and mortgages, co-op boards and co-op skeptics surrounds their relationship. *Hypothèque* is the French word for mortgage, and a hypothetical air attends every step you take: if you could . . . if they would . . . if the bank said . . . if the board allows.

Yet the broker, at the top of the triangle, is a happy man. First, he forms a liaison with the wife, which unites them against all the things that husbands have—doubt, penury, a stunted imagination. Together, the broker winks at the wife, they will scale the heights, find a poetic space, a wking brk frplce, something. But by late morning he has formed a second, darker, homoerotic alliance, with the husband. The two guys share musky common sense, and their eyes exchange glances—she's so *demanding*, pretty much impossible. Now, a couple of guys like us, we could be happy together, take what we can get, fix a place up. The skilled broker keeps the husband and wife in a perpetual state of uncertainty about whose desires will be satisfied.

Over lunch, it becomes plain that the broker has a past, as lovers will. He did something else before—he was a journalist, or a banker, or in advertising. He chose to be a broker because it gave him freedom, and then (he admits) in the nineties it began to give him money, more money than he ever thought possible. He looks sleek in his Italian suit, while his couple feel for the moment like out-of-towners, hicks in cloth coats and rubbers. As coffee arrives, the couple hear his cell phone buzzing, muffled somewhere near his heart. He finds the phone, mutters into it, then speaks up: "Hey, I'm in the middle of lunch." But the husband and wife are temporarily bound together: There is another—one he may love more than us.

The only time the broker loses his poise is when the Rival Broker is waiting for him in the lobby of the building where she has the "exclusive." Ethics and tradition insist that the two brokers show the apartment together, and suddenly the broker, so suave, so sexy, becomes an ex-husband, the two brokers like a couple after a bad divorce, polite only for the sake of the child—the apartment.

The billets-doux of the couple's relationship with the broker are the layouts, the small black-and-white schematic maps of apartments, with key descriptive points set off in bullets: "Triple mint" (meaning not actually falling down); "Room to roam" (a large, dark back room); "Paris rooftops" (a water tower looms in the window of the bedroom). A New York apartment layout is the only known instance of a blueprint that is more humanly appealing than the thing it represents.

One apartment succeeds another. There are the absurd apartments, nestled in towers among towering buildings four feet away, so that every sunless window shows another sunless window, and you could wake every morning to reach out and touch your pallid neighbor with your pallid hand. There are the half-shrunk apartments, with a reasonable living room and two more rooms carved out behind that you have to enter sideways. Then, there are the apartments that are genuinely unique to New York. A hugely expensive "duplex" in the West Seventies, for instance, turns out to be a basement and a sub-basement—the basement where you used to put up your sloppy cousin from Schenectady, the one who never took off his Rangers sweater, and the windowless sub-basement where the janitor was once found molesting children. The apartment's chief attraction is wistfully announced on its blueprint. It is "Near Restaurants."

WHEN you're in a tiny hotel room, apartments begin to crowd your imagination and haunt your nights. They turn into bright-eyed monsters, snaking through your dreams like subway cars. Last Christmas, having decided to try to bring my family home after five years abroad, I found myself walking in fact, and then in spirit, through all these apartments, again and again. As a distraction, I picked up a book I had packed for the journey, William Dean Howells's *A Hazard of New Fortunes*. A little more than a hundred years old, it's still the best book about middle-class life—or is it upper-middle? anyway, the lives of salaried professionals—in New York, a great American novel. Instead of fussing about hunting whales or riding rafts or fighting wars, or any of those other small-time subjects, it concerns something really epic: a guy in the magazine business looking for an apartment in Manhattan.

Howells is out of favor now. All literary reputation-making is unjust, but Howells is the victim of perhaps the single greatest injustice in American literary history. The period from 1880 to 1900, Henry Adams once said, was "our Howells-and-James epoch," and the two bearded grandees stood on terms as equal as the Smith Brothers on a cough-drop box. But then Howells got identified, unfairly, with a Bostonian "genteel" tradition, nice and dull. Now James gets Nicole Kidman and Helena Bonham Carter, even for his late, fuzzy-sweater novels, along with biography after biography and collection after collection, and Howells gets one brave, doomed defense every thirty years. Yet Howells, though an immeasurably less original sensibility than James, may be the better novelist, meaning that Howells on almost any subject strikes you as right, while James on almost any subject strikes you as James. Howells's description in *A Hazard* of New York, and of New York apartment-hunting, at the turn of the century comes from so deep a knowledge of what capitalism does to the middle classes, and how it does it to them, that it remains uncannily contemporary. We've spent billions of dollars to prevent our computers' mistaking 2000 for 1900; *A Hazard of New Fortunes* suggests that the error may have been a kind of truth.

In the novel, a diffident and ironic literary man, Basil March, sublets his house in Boston and comes to New York to edit a new magazine, a fortnightly to be called *Every Other Week*. It is to be the first "syndicate" magazine, with the contributors sharing in the profits. (These days, it would be an Internet launch.) Gradually, we learn that the money behind the magazine comes from a backwoods Pennsylvania Dutch natural-gas millionaire named Dryfoos, who, newly arrived in New York, has invested in the magazine as a worldly diversion for his unworldly son, Conrad, who dreams of becoming a priest. (Howells began writing *A Hazard* in the late eighties, when he moved to New York from Cambridge, after editing the *Atlantic Monthly* for ten years.)

Although the action of *A Hazard* eventually takes in the more "panoramic" material of strikes and riots, Howells's genius was to devote the first hundred or so pages of his book to the Marches' apartment-hunting. Isabel March, Basil's wife, who is an old Bostonian, joins him for the search, leaving the children behind in Beantown. They begin with the blithe certainty that it will take a couple of days. "I cut a lot of things out of the Herald as we came on," she tells her husband at their hotel on the first morning, taking "a long strip of paper out of her handbag with minute advertisements pinned transversely upon it, and forming the effect of some glittering nondescript vertebrate." She goes on, "We must not forget just what kind of flat we are going to look for":

> "The sine qua nons are an elevator and steam heat, not above the third floor, to begin with. Then we must each have a room, and you must have your study and I must have my parlor; and the two girls must each have a room. With the kitchen and dining room, how many does that make?"
>
> "Ten."

"I thought eight. Well, no matter. . . . And the rooms must all have outside light. And the rent must not be over eight hundred for the winter. We only get a thousand for our whole house, and we must save something out of that, so as to cover the expenses of moving. Now, do you think you can remember all of that?"

The modern reader waits for the shock to strike, and it does. They wander from one apartment building to another—all named, with unchanged real-estate developers' pretension, after classical writers. ("There is a vacant flat in the Herodotus for eighteen hundred a year, and one in the Thucydides for fifteen," she sees, lamenting, "What prices!") They visit six apartments in the afternoon, then four more that night. They are all too small, too expensive, too strange—too, well, New York.

One or two rooms might be at the front, the rest crooked and cornered backward through increasing and then decreasing darkness till they reached a light bedroom or kitchen at the rear. . . . If the flats were advertised as having "all light rooms" [the janitor] explained that any room with a window giving into the open air of a court or shaft was counted a light room.

Basil blames the brokers: "There seems to be something in the human habitation that corrupts the natures of those who deal in it, to buy or sell it, to hire or let it. You go to an agent and tell him what kind of a house you want. He has no such house, and he sends you to look at something altogether different upon the well-ascertained principle that if you can't get what you want, you will take what you can get." And yet the Marches become not repelled by apartment-seeking but addicted to it:

It went on all day and continued far into the night, until it was too late to go to the theater, too late to do anything but tumble into bed and simultaneously fall on sleep. They groaned over their reiterated disappointments, but they could not deny that the interest was unfailing.

The Marches become mesmerized by the ads, the layouts, the language. "Elegant large single and outside flats" were offered with "all improvements—bath, icebox, etc." Soon the search for an apartment becomes a consuming activity in itself, self-propelling, self-defining—a quest. "Now we are imprisoned in the present," Basil says of New York, "and we have to make the worst of it."

IMPRISONED in the present. It seems not to matter when or with how much money you look for an apartment in New York. I've done it officially three times: once as a grad student looking for one room for two, with thirty-five hundred dollars in my pocket to last the year; once as a "yuppie" (we were called that, de-risively, before the world was ours), looking for a loft or a one-bedroom; and now as a family guy with a couple of kids. The numbers and the figures change, but the experience remains the same, and feels different from the way it feels anywhere else, with a jag of raised hopes and dashed expectations.

The city is, it's true, shinier than it has ever been. It gleams. It is as if the "broad-band pipe," the philosophers' stone of our era, had already come into existence as a blast hose and washed off the grime. The newsstands that once seemed mainly to stock *Screw* now stock *InStyle* and *Business 2.0.* Even the smells have changed. The essential New York smell twenty years ago was still Italian and Wasp: tomato and olive oil and oregano, acid and pungent, min-gled with the indoor, Bloomingdale's smell of sweet, sprayed perfumes. Now, inside the giant boxes that have arrived from America, from the malls (the Gap and Banana Republic and Staples), there is a new, clean pharmacy smell, a dis-concerting absence of smells, the American non-smell.

The New Yorkers who arrived in the seventies, the post–*Annie Hall* wave of immigrants, are dismayed by the new shine. They liked the fear and dilapida-tion that they saw when they came, since it meant that living here required courage. Life in New York was a broken-field run, demanding, even in the "nice" neighborhoods, a continual knowing, sideways-glancing evaluation of everyone else on the street, and what kind of threat each person might repre-sent—white faces in dark shoes searching fearfully for dark faces in white shoes. Today, the rich stroll down the street as though the place belonged to them. (It always did, but now they show it.) A lot of New York existence is like a fantasy mordantly imagined in the nineteen-seventies: picture a city with po-lite taxi-drivers and children in strollers crowding the avenues, where every-one is addicted to strong, milky coffee.

The horizon seems so secure that places to live these days seem to be conju-gated in the future indefinite—some of the apartments one looks at are purely notional, like Priceline.com profits. Not only do the neighborhoods not quite exist yet—whole blocks are now annexed to Tribeca that five years ago were shabby streets fringing City Hall—but the apartments themselves don't exist. Amid the noise and dust of construction work, you enter a "welcome" shed, where you are shown eight-by-eight-inch samples of "finishes": brushed alu-minum for the kitchen appliances, maple for the floors, white pine for the kitchen cabinets, one blue tile that is meant to stand for the finished bathroom. The eight-by-eight samples are stapled to a sheet of masonite, like a science project done the night before the science fair.

You sign a paper promising not to sue if you are killed while examining the nonexistent apartments. This is fair; you are simply acknowledging that searching for an apartment in New York is potentially fatal, like scaling Ever-est. ("They got up to 3-C in plenty of time, but they dawdled in the kitchen, and didn't begin the descent back until it was already growing dark and the squalls were threatening in the service elevator.") You walk into a vast space, into the dust and crashing sounds of an entire world being emptied out, century-old plaster spilling down chutes. The broker leads you up a steep plank to a two-by-four square hole. You duck down and squeeze through—it is like the entrance that leads the Artful Dodger and Oliver into Fagin's den. Then you are in the remains of the wrecked warehouse, with a row of three windows down at one end and perhaps silver tape laid out on the floor: your home. The second broker leads you to the corner window. "I love this line," she sighs with pleasure. "Extrapolate from the finishes," someone orders.

But the Marches have been here, too; you see their Gilded Age forms, like ghosts on North Moore Street, and they are in the same bewildered state:

> Mrs. March had out the vertebrate, and was consulting one of its glittering ribs and glancing up from it at a house before which they stood. "Yes, it's the number—but do they call *this* being ready October 1st?"

Isabel boldly goes into the empty place and, "with the female instinct for domiciliation which never failed her," she begins to settle the family in the still unfinished house as the landlord "lent a hopeful fancy to the solution of all her questions." Isabel explains to her skeptical husband, "It's the only way I can realize whether it will do for us. I have to dramatize the whole thing."

DRAMATIZE the whole thing. You can take the Marches with you everywhere in New York. In their day, too, people were haunted by the sixties—the strife at home—which they had agreed to identify in retrospect as a time of true idealism, since mislaid. And then, one also begins to sense, their boom was like ours in its subtle articulation into two phases. In the first phase, having money became a way of entering an older, existing society; in the second, money created its own society. Howells's early novel *The Rise of Silas Lapham* described the plight of the typical millionaire-adventurer trying and failing to make his way in Boston society of the eighteen-seventies, "hemmed in and left out at every turn by ramifications that forbid him all hope of safe personality in his comments." By the time of *A Hazard*, money is the only ramification left.

Although our boom sometimes seems one continuous curve of money and manners that began around 1984, it, too, has had two phases. In the eighties, the familiar mechanisms that give new money the appearance of old—turning money into charity or culture—still operated, at times feverishly. Newly rich men in the eighties were driven by the same amalgam of guilt and gilt that drove the robber barons of the Gilded Age to have their portraits made by Sargent and buy Renaissance or even Impressionist pictures. To buy a risky picture in the nineteen-eighties—a Fischl, a Salle, a Koons—was to give commercial risk the patina of aesthetic risk. The circles of social life turned more or less the same elaborate machinery that they had turned a century earlier: the cogs in the greed wheel turn the money wheel, which turns the culture wheel, which turns the social wheel—until at last the aspirant gains a seat at the central wheel table, where the hostess is called "Mrs." (Mrs. Wrightsman, Mrs. Astor), and he has at last arrived.

By the nineties, new rules had begun to fall into place, just as they did in Howells's nineties. Everyone in *A Hazard,* rich or poor, is an immigrant: there are no native New Yorkers, no indigenous established society. There are just people with new money, or people dependent on it, having dinners for each other. The unwashed Dryfooses, Isabel discovers, to her shock, do not know that they are out of society, because they do not know there is a society to be in. (The Dryfoos daughters don't even take piano lessons; they play the banjo.) Dryfoos buys the magazine to occupy his son, not to achieve a social position; when he wants to have a dinner party to celebrate the new magazine, it turns into a glorified office party, the same old faces. In today's New York, too, the parties that people talk about seem to be glorified office parties, propelled not by hostesses but by verbs and gerunds: launches and startups and initial public offerings.

In a society in which money has gained its sovereign virtue, art—and the ascension it symbolizes—no longer matters in quite the same way. When George Bellows's 1910 painting *The Polo Crowd* was bought by an unnamed millionaire a few months ago, it violated essential Veblenian status-creating principles. The picture was being sold by the Museum of Modern Art because "it did not fit into its collection"; i.e., wasn't good enough. It went for three times the estimate. The guy who paid twenty-seven and a half million dollars for the painting didn't buy it because he wished to acquire status from it; its status had been officially denied by the status-granting institution. He bought it because he liked it. Society totters.

ISABEL has the apartment dream, too! "It was something about the children at first," she tells Basil, and then it was "of a hideous thing with two square eyes and a series of sections growing darker and then lighter, till the tail of the monstrous articulate was quite luminous again." March says, laughing, "Why, my dear, it was nothing but a harmless New York flat—seven rooms and a bath."

Haunted by that dream, Isabel returns to Boston, and Basil, in a fit of resignation, rents a horrible furnished apartment that she has seen and rejected. "He was aware more than ever of its absurdities, he knew that his wife would never cease to hate it," but he also "felt a comfort in committing himself and exchanging the burden of indecision for the burden of responsibility."

The magazine begins to prosper, and March tries to do good with Dryfoos's money by going downtown to offer work to a German-American socialist translator named Lindau, who taught him Heine back in the Midwest, when he was a boy. He finds Lindau living in Chinatown, on Mott Street. "But what *are* you living here for, Lindau?" he asks. Lindau explains that he has come here to see poverty. "How much money can a man honestly earn without wronging or oppressing some other man?" Lindau asks, and then answers his question: "It is the landlords and the merchant princes, the railroad kings and the coal barons . . . it is these that *make* the millions, but no man *earns* them. What artist, what physician, what scientist, what poet, was ever a millionaire?"

"THAT'S Tom and Nicole's, that's Barbra's, that's Bruce's, that's the one Bruce gave to Demi after the divorce, that's Madonna's," the broker goes, pointing upward at all the great turrets, the high crowning spires, of the classic apartment buildings of Central Park West. Apparently, they all belong, like feudal keeps, to the stars who have immigrated to New York, as Howells did, as the Marches did. Perhaps they wave at each other, tower to tower, in the morning, as neighbors should.

Isabel and Basil, you realize, were the first victims of a persistent American illusion: even the upper-middle classes in a plutocratic society, Howells believed, are always in precarious shape, and usually don't know it. In New York, they do. Outside New York, the bourgeoisie does tend to live in ways not entirely unlike the rich. The Marches' little house in Boston, though hardly grand, is a house, with a house's accoutrements and pleasures, as would be the case in Cambridge (or Philadelphia) today. New York tends to invite the middle classes to live alongside the rich, and then makes visible the true space between them, draws a line in outside light. Unlike London and Paris, the two other great capitals of bourgeois civilization, Manhattan has never really been symbolized by middle-class housing. The sweep of semidetached houses in Knightsbridge or Kensington, the long boulevards filled with bourgeoisie in the Sixteenth and Eighth Arrondissements of Paris sum up the image of those places. New York, on the other hand, is famous for William Randolph Hearst's penthouse and Sister Eileen's basement apartment, or, more recently, for the Trump Tower aerie and the Tribeca loft. A nuclear family living in a little house in Manhattan is a *sight.* The old enclaves of the true bourgeoisie, Riverside Drive and York Avenue, were on the margins of the island, and their high period was a short one. (My great-aunt, like everybody else's, moved into a fifteen-room apartment on Riverside Drive in the forties, and it had been broken up by the sixties, barely a generation's worth of extra closets. Each of its divided parts now costs more money than my great-uncle made in a lifetime.)

At one moment in *A Hazard,* Isabel and Basil pretend to be millionaires simply in order to see what lies beyond their means. "They looked at three-thousand- and four-thousand-dollar apartments and rejected them for one reason or another which had nothing to do with the rent; the higher the rent, the more critical they were." Inspired by them, we decided to do it, too.

What you find, though, when you search—well, not the spires (what, are you kidding?) but the spaces that hold up the spires—is not luxury, twisting staircases and panoramic windows, but the old American representations of normalcy and domestic comfort. What you find isn't Fred Astaire's apartment in *Daddy Long Legs* but Meg Ryan's apartment in a Nora Ephron movie, the apartment where Hannah lived in the Woody Allen film, the flat that Mr. Blandings is desperate to escape in order to build his dream house. There are kitchens that look like kitchens, living rooms like living rooms, bedrooms like bedrooms. A millionaire's life in New York is still what normal life looks like on a cereal box. And this is exactly what draws the people in the spires to live in the spires: the movie star who moves here announces that he likes New York because he can live like a normal person, because his kids can have normal lives, and, in a weird way, he means it.

FOR Howells, the inevitable result of plutocracy, exemplified by the apartment madness and Lindau's despair, is popular revolt and its repression. A trainmen's strike threatens to paralyze the city, and Basil, in a fit of reportorial responsibility, goes to "cover" the strike and sees Lindau struck down by a policeman—and then sees Dryfoos's saintly young son lose his life in an attempt to rescue the old socialist.

Howells himself became a Tolstoyan (i.e., mushy) socialist, and he wrote for Basil March a long concluding speech in which March realizes that the hazard of new fortunes is his, too. "What I object to is this economic chance world in which we live and which we men seem to have created," he tells Isabel. A working man should be guaranteed his livelihood and his repose, and it is insupportable that he is not:

> At my time of life—at every time of life—a man ought to feel that if he will keep on doing his duty he shall not suffer in himself or in those who are dear to him, except through natural causes. But no man can feel this as things are now, and so we go on. Pushing and pulling, climbing and crawling, thrusting aside and trampling underfoot, lying, cheating, stealing; and when we get to the end, covered with blood and dirt and sin and shame, and look back over the way we've come to a palace of our own, or the poorhouse, which is about the only possession we can claim in common with our brother men, I don't think the retrospect can be pleasing. . . . People are greedy and foolish and wish to have and to shine, because having and shining are held up to them by civilization as the chief good of life. . . . We can't help it. If one were less greedy or less foolish, someone else would have and would shine at his expense.

THIS economic chance world in which we live. A hundred years ago, the one thing that Howells—and Henry Adams and so many others—knew for sure was that a society with a tiny plutocratic class, a precarious middle class, and a large and immigration-fed proletariat simply could not go on.

Now, at the turn of another century, we find it is the only thing that has gone on, in nearly perfect duplicate. August Belmont celebrated the last fin de siècle in a suit of golden armor; everyone who celebrated this fin de siècle in costume with the Soroses came away, we're told, with a bronze medallion, embossed with the hosts' profiles. Three-star chefs are flown in from Paris for a night's diversion; ghost mining towns in Colorado are revived and fully peopled for two weeks each summer as "camps" where the rich can entertain their courtiers. Someone has just bought the International Center of Photography, a grand old mansion on Fifth Avenue, in order to turn it back into a private house, reversing the century-old process by which the mansions of the fin-de-siècle rich became institutions. The plutocracy has never been so plutocratic.

What makes it possible for the economic chance world to go on so peaceably now, with hardly a hint of the opposition that Howells took for granted? It is that a sense of Hazard has been replaced by Hope. It seemed to Howells that hazard and fortune were as right together as pride and lions, that risk and moneymaking were one. What's striking about this new Gilded Age isn't just that people are selling hope but that everyone is buying it. All the folk memories of busts and depressions past seem to have vanished; the rhetoric of hope has overcome even the romance of risk, the sinister glamour of greed.

The new tycoons are not in industry, like Howells's, or in asset stripping, like Tom Wolfe's. They don't look like old man Dryfoos, grasping and raw. They look, more often, like his son, Conrad, all quivering sensitivity and high-minded devotion to the future. The places of the new fortunes are not sweatshops or mines—not here, anyway—but ateliers reclaimed from the light-industrial Old New York the Marches knew. Six computers, a server, a wall of glass brick, a stamped-tin ceiling, a bright post-ironic attitude—these are the materials of a dot-com company, of the new fortunes. It is hope (and its Siamese twin, debt) that empties out the buildings on North Moore Street and calls on you to extrapolate from the samples, hope that keeps you looking, that gets you to dramatize the whole thing. If it is a bubble—and common sense tells you that it must be—it has a bubble's bright, single highlight, and it encloses Manhattan from Ninety-sixth Street to the harbor. Hope is what gives this age its odd and original gleam, a strange ingenuous glow different from that of the Marches' age, a century ago, when even the people who had the gold knew the age was merely gilded. "Having and shining, having and shining": we still believe it. But now we shine first, and assume that, if the glow is bright enough, we will all have later.

HOWELLS, like Basil, was radicalized by his experience in New York in the eighteen-nineties. "I abhor it," he wrote to Henry James of American capitalism, "and feel that it is coming out all wrong in the end, unless it bases itself anew on a real equality." But, like Isabel, he also learned that New York is a city of accommodations. This double movement gives his masterpiece its pathos and its enduring moral. Later, he wrote of himself and his wife, "We are theoretical socialists, and practical aristocrats. But it is a comfort to be right theoretically, and to be ashamed of one's self practically." "Practical aristocrats": a lovely calling, nice work if you can get it.

It is at least a relief to discover that at the end of *A Hazard of New Fortunes* the Marches find a place to live for good. If the explicit moral of the novel is radical, its dramatic point is Isabel's acceptance of New York domestic arrangements, and her education in the irony necessary to accept them. Dryfoos, after the death of his son, goes off to Paris, selling *Every Other Week* to Basil and his publisher for a song. There is a big empty space on the second floor of the building, right above the editorial offices, and Basil and Isabel decide to live there with the kids. It is a sign of Isabel's transformation that this idea—in Boston, she thinks, fit only for Irish laundresses—is now acceptable to her. She has become as diffident and ironic as her husband, as someone seeing life pass by from the El. She has become a New Yorker, and she will live above the store. "In New York," she reflects at last, "you may do anything."

FEBRUARY 21, 2000

I WANT THIS APARTMENT

JILL MEILUS is a New York City real-estate broker. Like Superman, she can see through walls. Walking down a Manhattan street with her is a paranormal experience. "Nice building," you might remark as you pass a handsome but unrevealing prewar façade, to which she might respond that the J-line apartment on the third floor has a new kitchen, that the guy in 8-A is being transferred to Florida and will entertain any offers of more than two hundred thousand dollars, that the super is a chain-smoker, that there is a one-bedroom for sale because the owners are having money troubles or are having twins or made a new fortune or are splitting up. New York is the big showoff of American cities, yet its residential life is almost invisible to the ordinary passerby. Even so, you cannot hide from a real-estate broker. The other day, Jill took one of her customers to view a SoHo loft—a nice, six-hundred-and-fifty-thousand-dollar sort of place, with a lot of windows and chintz upholstery and silver gizmos artfully scattered around. Jill's customer, a television actress, whom I will call Vivian, liked the loft, so she paced off the dimensions and counted the closets, and eventually came upon a locked door beside the kitchen. She told Jill that she wanted to see what was behind it; after all, the price of the loft could be calculated per square inch, let alone square foot, and behind the door were a few of those high-priced inches. Jill considered the request and then sighed. "Vivian, I wish I could show it to you, but I can't," she said. "The owners of the loft are sado-masochists, and that is their dungeon." "Oh," Vivian said. She looked disappointed. After a moment, Jill brightened. "I know that it'd be a great space for a second bathroom," she added, "and the owners do promise to remove the dungeon fixtures as a condition of sale."

The total value of all privately owned apartments in Manhattan is estimated to be $102.7 billion, and about seven per cent of those apartments turn over every year. In 1998, for instance, the combined sales of all coöperative and condominium units came to $7.9 billion. Many of those units are one-bedroom starter apartments, but some are larger, and a few are a lot larger. Last year, the company that Jill works for, the Corcoran Group, sold a pretty big place on Central Park West to Ian Schrager for nine million dollars, and recently another brokerage had almost closed a deal for a twenty-two-million-dollar apartment that occupies the top three floors of the Pierre Hotel, and is being purchased by a Wall Street analyst with a rather pessimistic view of the stock market. The Corcoran Group handles twenty per cent of the sales of New York residential real estate. There are about four hundred Corcoran Group brokers, making it the second-largest brokerage in the city—smaller than Douglas Elliman and bigger than the three other major brokerages, Brown Harris Stevens, Halstead Property, and Bellmarc Realty. These are good days to be a real-estate broker in New York. Because prices are so high and the volume of sales is so large, brokers in New York are making more than their counterparts in other big, expensive cities, like Houston and Los Angeles. The top broker in New York earned close to two million dollars last year, and a typical broker is making sixty thousand and has no trouble finding people who want to sell and people who want to buy.

When I first met Jill, she had just got a new exclusive, a

PREWAR 2BR FOR $279K. GV/PRIME Charming home just steps off Fifth Avenue on best blk. View of brownstones and lots of sun! Seller relocating!

It was actually a cheery but bantam two-bedroom co-op on West Eleventh Street, in Greenwich Village, which another Corcoran broker had sold to a young investment banker two years ago for a hundred and sixty thousand dollars. The banker was getting married and moving to Texas. As the apartment's exclusive agent, Jill was handling all the advertising and marketing. Although any broker from any company could show the apartment to customers, Jill had to be present at all showings, and she would split the commission with the eventual buyer's broker. In effect, she was the seller's representative. She would keep the entire commission if she happened to sell one of her exclusives to one of her own customers, because then she would be representing both the seller and the buyer. Everywhere else in the country, brokers typically share listings and can show a house at any time, by themselves, because keys are usually left in a lockbox outside the house which any broker can gain access to. The New York City system is very New York–like: complicated, arcane, and logistically nightmarish. Not only do brokers have to be available to show their exclusives to other brokers and their customers but they also have to be able to take customers to see apartments on the market which other brokers are handling, and this means they have to arrange with those other brokers to see their exclusives. At the moment, Jill had two apartments that were her exclusives, and about a dozen customers who were actively looking to buy, with price limits ranging from around a hundred and sixty thousand dollars to just under two million.

Jill is chestnut-haired, self-effacing, midsize, and fortyish. She specializes in downtown real estate and has a lot of artists and writers and architects as customers, which means she goes to work wearing big, hairy sweaters and stretch pants rather than an uptown broker's wardrobe of smart black trouser suits and moderate-height heels. She grew up in a suburb of New York and has lived in the city since she began college. She now lives in an insanely huge loft, for which she pays an insanely low rent—so low that she begged me not to print it, knowing how such a thing would make her the object of pure, embittered resentment. Not that having a great place to live wouldn't stir up envy anywhere in the world; it's just that in New York the span between crummy places and fantastic ones is wide. So is the span between the apartment that is an incredible bargain and the one that is wildly overpriced. Only in New York are you likely to find so many identical apartments with so many unidentical price tags. The fact of Jill's living circumstances came to light when I asked her whether selling real estate was like working in a chocolate factory—that is, whether you were tempted to consume the best merchandise yourself. "Most brokers have some kind of good deal," she said sheepishly. "I mean, we get to see everything and we usually end up with something kind of strange and great." Even so, there have to be times when brokers must feel unrequited. One afternoon, I went with Iva Spitzer, a broker with Douglas Elliman, to see a pre-war apartment on West Fifty-seventh Street that she was handling. It was quite nice: about fifty-five hundred square feet; eleven rooms or so; a terrace running around the entire apartment; north, south, east, and west views, including a dead-on view of Carnegie Hall; triple-height ceilings; a majestic living room, with cove lighting and a sky scene painted on the domed ceiling; a shuttered napping room; black-walnut flooring; a master bathroom bigger than an average bedroom, with the original sunken marble bath and a huge stall shower with sixteen brass shower spigots mounted on the walls and a dinner-plate-size brass showerhead with a few hundred pinpoint spray holes; and a yawningly large professional-quality kitchen with Sub-Zero everything and a stainless-steel fendered range. I could easily imagine living there, until Iva mentioned that it was a rental that happened to be priced at thirty-five thousand dollars a month. I asked if it frustrated her to handle such a place. "No, it's an incredible place, but I don't really see myself here," she said, sounding philosophical. "I see someone like Sean Penn here. Or Puff Daddy."

Real estate can be an aggravating profession. "It's a sort of manic-depressive business," Jill likes to say. "It's always either totally crazy or dead. Things fall through all the time. If you get devastated by stuff like that, you can't go on." Up until twenty years ago, residential real estate in New York City was usually handled by "social brokers"—older women who sold apartments now and then to their friends over afternoon tea or at the hairdresser's. In those years, very little property in Manhattan was actually bought or sold. What few hundred listings existed were handwritten on index cards, collated on knitting needles, and filed in leather binders. The coöperative and condominium conversions that began in the nineteen-seventies turned thousands of rental apartments into real estate that could be bought and sold. Suddenly, there was a lot more money to be made, and real-estate brokerages began attracting actresses and artists and teachers, people who liked the independence and mobility of the job and were used to a certain amount of unpredictability and rejection, and usually came to real estate after another career. Jill was a chef at a couple of popular New York restaurants before she got her broker's license, eleven years ago. She worked from home for a while after she had a baby, and had returned to her office, in the Flatiron district, a year before we met. Iva Spitzer had also been a chef—at a restaurant in Boston—before going into real estate. Barbara Corcoran, the owner and founder of the Corcoran Group, had held twenty-six short-term jobs before she started her business; her favorite was waitressing at a diner in New Jersey. She liked it because it was a people job.

EARLY one Tuesday morning last month, I went with Jill to the West Eleventh Street two-bedroom. It was the first day she was showing the apartment. She had advertised it in the *Times* over the weekend and had also posted a description of it on the Corcoran Group Web site, and already she had got a dozen queries. The apartment house was an elegant eight-story brick box built at the turn of the century, with a curlicued bannister running up the stairs and tiny Juliet balconies on each landing, but the interior had been gutted and rebuilt in the early eighties, and the apartments were now stripped-down and undetailed, with chalky-white drywall walls and hollow-core doors. The seven hundred square feet of the apartment were diced up into a galley kitchen, one full bath, a rectangular living room, one average-sized bedroom, and one dwarfish one. Most normal people living in normal cities would probably consider it far too small to live in for the price, but by New York standards it was a sunny, snug, well-located apartment, which would probably sell quickly. In New York, "quickly" means "quickly" and sometimes even "viciously." When the market in New York is heated up, war breaks out. Real estate gets most people agitated, but in New York it seems to provoke a special fervor. Brokers start accepting only sealed bids, and bids offering more than the asking price are taken for granted. So is offering all cash, proposing to forgo the mortgage-contingency clause in the contract, begging to sign a contract on the spot, and tendering press releases and family portraits to plead one's case. One of Jill's colleagues had a customer who bartered for an apartment with rare French movie posters, which he guaranteed would appreciate in value.

The owner of the apartment had already gone to work when we arrived, but she had obviously tidied up before she left. A few fresh magazines were fanned out on her coffee table like a deck of cards, and all the wastebaskets were empty. Her cat was on the sofa, chewing on a piece of wire and daydreaming. It was a chilly but brilliant day and the apartment was filled with light. Right after we settled in, a broker named Jackie called from the lobby, and a moment later she stepped through the door with her customer, a pale young man with a shaved head. The customer surveyed the little living room and then walked to the window and gazed out onto the street.

"Boy, it's really sunny," Jackie said.

"All day," Jill said.

"Such a pretty block," Jackie added.

"Quintessential Village," Jill said. She turned to the young man and told him, "By the way, none of the walls in here are structural, so you can move them all around if you want to."

The customer wandered out of the living room, into the bigger bedroom, and then into the bathroom. "I'm not in a rush to buy," he called over his shoulder. "I've only been looking for about a year." Jackie shot Jill a look.

After a minute, the customer said, "You know, I just realized that I forgot my glasses, so I'm going to have to come back and look another time." He wandered out the front door. Jackie trailed behind, mouthing "I'll call you" to Jill.

"She'll never call," Jill said, closing the door behind them.

A few minutes later, another broker—Bill from Douglas Elliman—appeared at the door, accompanied by another pale young man. This one was carrying a briefcase, which he dropped in the kitchen doorway. When he was out of earshot, his broker whispered to Jill, "Look! That's good! When people put their bags down, it means they plan to stay for a while."

The young man came back into earshot. "Wow, there's a lot of light in here," he said.

"None of the walls are structural, so you can move anything," Jill said. "I mean, if you want to."

"The light is really beautiful," the customer said.

"It's a historic block," his broker added.

"It's beautiful light," the customer said, "and I like the exposed brick." He took another turn around the living room and said, "I love this building! This feels so good!"

"You could take down the wall between the bedrooms," Jill said. "Or between the kitchen and the little bedroom."

The customer wasn't listening. "That's my deal, see. I need light. And this has light. It's awesome. Beautiful. I really like it."

A broker named Edna arrived, leading her customer, a poker-faced young woman who said she worked as a recipe tester for a gourmet magazine. Edna dawdled by the door while the woman scanned the apartment. Then they huddled in the living room and waited for the young man and the Douglas Elliman broker to leave. Once they had gone, Jill turned to Edna and her customer. "So?" she said.

"I love it," the young woman said. "I want it."

Jill raised her eyebrows.

"I really, really love it," the young woman went on. "By the way, are dogs O.K.?"

Jill lowered her eyebrows. "No dogs," she said. "Sorry."

Edna clutched at her throat and gasped. "Oh God. No dogs? No dogs? You have *got* to be kidding. Well, there goes my deal. She wants to buy the apartment right now. However, she has a dog."

The young woman started to tremble. "My dog is like . . . *adorable!* She looks like Benji! She's totally quiet! Look, I want this apartment! I really want it!"

Jill asked her if the dog was bigger than a cat. The young woman chewed on her lip for a minute and then said, "Well, I don't know how she would compare to a cat, but if you cut a wheaten terrier in half that's what she looks like. Her name is Hunni, and she licks everybody, and everybody loves her. I can pay all cash for the apartment. I'll pay the asking price. I mean, I really love this place."

"Let me think," Jill said, jiggling her foot. "O.K., maybe I should present it to the co-op board as . . . as a cat-like dog named Hunni. Why don't you write a letter to the board and describe her and talk about what she does during the day and what she does during vacations, and then we can present it from there." The young woman looked buoyed, said she would write the letter that day, and offered to bring Hunni over to meet people in the building.

"That might be premature," Jill said. "I'd go with the letter."

The next day, a letter supporting Hunni's residency application arrived by fax at the Corcoran Group offices. Jill passed it along to the co-op board president, who said that Hunni sounded very likable but the answer was still no.

BECAUSE of the idiosyncrasies of the market, New York brokers come to know more about their clients than brokers elsewhere ordinarily do. If you are buying a house in the suburbs, your broker might never know the exact details of your economic circumstances. In New York, most privately held apartments are part of either a co-op or a condominium association. Anybody with enough money can purchase a condominium, but a prospective buyer of a co-op must submit supporting material to the building's board of directors, including letters of reference, a complete statement of net worth, and, often, tax returns going back several years, and then must sit for an interview with the board's admissions committee. Even with a mortgage in hand, a buyer isn't guaranteed a deal until he or she gets the committee's approval. A good broker will help a buyer prepare the board package, which means that he or she will see your letters of reference, figures on your net worth, and your tax returns—details many people consider rather personal. Because New Yorkers move so much—more than other Americans do—they often work with a broker repeatedly. Several of Jill's customers were people who had bought or sold through her before. And, whether it's because prices are so high in the city or because New Yorkers are peculiarly indecisive, it seems to take some people a long, long time to buy a place to live, and they therefore spend a long, long time with their brokers. Two of Jill's active customers had been looking for two years, and a few more had been looking almost as long. In the meantime, their lives had changed, their jobs had evolved, they'd got more money, they'd had kids, they'd colored their hair, their marital status had wavered. Some had come to regard Jill as a friend. She worried over them and kept an eye on their psychic real estate as well as on their real real estate. A few of her customers have asked her to play matchmaker if she ever had a customer she thought they'd like.

Jill was fretting that day over Lucy, a customer of hers who worked in film production. Lucy had been looking for an apartment for two years. Jill wanted her to buy the Eleventh Street apartment but despaired that she couldn't commit. "Lucy really needs to get focused," she said, sighing. "She's backed out of a few deals already and she just puts herself through agony every time. We had a talk one day about whether we should keep working together, and whether our relationship was getting to be too much of a burden, but I think we worked it out." Bertram, an architect who'd been looking with Jill for a year, was "a perfectionist, and very apprehensive," Jill told me. "He thinks he wants to live downtown, but I think he should really be looking in Chelsea, considering what he can pay, so we're working on that." Bertram had an accepted offer on a place in Chelsea, but Jill knew him well enough not to consider it a done deal. While she was waiting for another broker to show up at West Eleventh, she checked her voice mail. There was a message from Bertram saying he'd decided to withdraw his offer on the Chelsea place, because he'd heard from a resident of the building that another apartment there had just sold for less than he was offering. "I knew it. He got stressed out," Jill said. "He was so nervous anyway." She also got a message from a customer telling her he'd decided he could spend more, so she could expand the price range as she searched for him; a message from a customer who was preparing his board package and had forgotten to get letters of reference and was in a panic; and a message from an art dealer who had read about Jill on the Corcoran Web site and was interested in the Eleventh Street place.

The Corcoran Group is now selling an apartment a day through its Web site. Barbara Corcoran believes that the Internet will eventually replace much of the work now being done by brokers. A typical person buying an apartment in New York City calls in response to a newspaper ad and then sees an average of fourteen apartments before buying; someone real-estate shopping on a computer sees floor plans, photographs, long descriptions, and a biography of the broker before making a call, and then seems to need to see only four apartments before buying. Instead of making brokers obsolete, Internet real-estate shopping will make the marketing part of their job more critical, and waste less of their time dragging customers around town. In the meantime, though, being a broker remains a full-time—even a day-and-nighttime—job. As the next broker was heading up to see West Eleventh Street, Jill mentioned that she'd had a terrible dream the night before. She dreamed that she had run into a friend whom she'd been showing apartments to—a real person, whom she really is showing apartments to—and the friend told her that she'd just bought an apartment from another broker. The apartment was in the West Fifties. "It was just awful!" Jill said. "I've been showing her apartments forever. I said, 'Lil! You told me you would never live in the West Fifties!' I couldn't believe it. I think that when I see her I'm going to feel really upset, even though it was just a dream."

THERE were two big stories in New York real estate that week. One was that a four-bedroom duplex loft that had been on the market for seven years—an unofficial record for longevity—and had been handled at one time or another by every broker in town (including Jill) had finally been sold. The other was that at a recent closing the attorney had threatened to withhold twenty-five thousand dollars of the broker's commission, so the broker grabbed the contract away from the attorney, which compelled the attorney to smash the broker's arm onto the table, bruising it severely and breaking her watch. A few brokers who had heard this tale suggested that in the future all closings be moderated by a therapist. Iva once remarked that she became the center of attention at any gathering as soon as she mentioned she was a broker; everyone had a horror story or a happy story to recount, and wanted to know whether the market was going up or down and whether a person had got a good deal or had been ripped off and whether she knew about Building X or Apartment Y. The experience, she said, was sort of like telling people at a dinner party that you're a doctor, and finding yourself besieged with moles to examine and surgery stories to hear.

"Shopping for apartments, I think, is horrible for most people," Jill said. "They get very emotional." We had taken a break from West Eleventh Street and were walking back to her office. The air was fresh and sweet and cold, and the sky was as blue as a swimming pool, and all the buildings on the block glowed a little in the afternoon sun. We passed a brownstone with wide stairs and a handkerchief-size garden. "Really nice inside," Jill said, nodding toward it. "I showed it to some people last year, and they almost bid on it, but they were thinking of starting a family, and it would have been too small." This made her think of Vivian, who is currently single but wants a two-bedroom. "She's so lovely," Jill said. "And I guess she's optimistic, even though she complains to me how impossible it is to meet men." That made her think of Greg, who is also single, and whose loft she had just got as an exclusive, because his next-door neighbor's daughter went to school with Jill's daughter. And that made her think of an apartment for sale on the Upper East Side that Greg might like to buy after she sold his loft. And that made her think of Lucy, for no particular reason except that she thought about her often, and decided she would take her back to see something at London Terrace, a large prewar complex in Chelsea, because, even though Lucy had bid and backed out on something there before, Jill thought she might have finally reached the point where she would just buy something halfway decent, so she could stop looking. Around every corner we turned was another building that Jill knew or had sold something in or had handled in some way. It was as if to her the city's buildings all quivered with change and movement: her view was like time-lapse photography that reveals commotion in something that otherwise, in quick glances, appears to be entirely still.

A few days later, Jill sent me a message saying that she'd sold the West Eleventh Street apartment to a couple—a film editor and a network-news employee—for two hundred and seventy thousand dollars; that Vivian had decided not to bid on the loft with the dungeon; that Lucy had agreed to look at London Terrace again; that the art dealer who came to her through the Web site hadn't bid on West Eleventh but wanted Jill to take her around. She had got a number of new customers who had answered the ad for West Eleventh, and would lose a few old ones, at least temporarily, once they'd found a place, bought it, and moved. It was business as usual.

FEBRUARY 22, 1999

HIGH-HEEL HEAVEN

T HE first thing I noticed when I entered the two-hundred-year-old town house in Bath that serves as Manolo Blahnik's weekend retreat was the alligator. About three and a half feet long, with olive-brown skin and black hatch marks flecking its body, it was sprawled imperiously across a Queen Anne table at the end of the foyer. The jaws were parted, and the teeth shimmered in the fading light.

It was a dismal, rainy afternoon, and we had just come from lunch—though Blahnik had been in no mood to eat. He has a bad back, and it was giving him so much trouble that day that he wore a brace. We rushed through the meal and then walked along the cobblestoned streets toward his house, which sits in the middle of one of those Georgian crescents that provided Jane Austen with just the right setting for *Persuasion*. He perked up the second we arrived. Opening the door, Blahnik swept into the hallway and cried out, "Honey, I'm home!" Then, with a manic swirl, he tossed his powder-blue cashmere sports jacket across a bust of the eighteenth-century actor David Garrick, raced toward his alligator, and embraced it. With the stuffed animal nestled in his arms, Blahnik turned, and, in a voice that somehow blends the diction of Winston Churchill with the accent of the Gabor sisters, said, "There is simply no creature on earth that compares to a Louisiana alligator. Not iguana or python or ostrich or anything else you might want to make into a shoe. I suppose saying that makes me an enemy of the people. I'm sorry. I say kill them humanely, with a shot or something. But give us the skins. I mean, can you imagine where I would be today without wonderful babies like this? Cahnn you i-*maah*-gine?"

Apart from its symbolic stature—as something forbidden, luxurious, and astonishingly expensive—alligator skin is no more essential to the shoes of

Manolo Blahnik than lesser leathers, or, for that matter, the dozens of other materials he relies on: satins, silks, brocade, crystal, silver lamé, sequins, rhinestones, buckles, bangles, beads, Velcro, pearls, neoprene, rubber, rawhide, chinchilla, lace, mesh, or (for the first time this year, but only for a few of his luckiest and wealthiest customers) diamonds, emeralds, and rubies. They are all just grace notes in the symphony of footwear Manolo Blahnik has composed over the past thirty years.

In most seasons, the product of another designer—a perilously high-heeled sandal by Jimmy Choo, for example, or a snakeskin sling-back by Christian Louboutin—will become the shoe of the moment. But Blahnik persists, and his creations have become an obsession for thousands of women (and not a few men). With their delicate straps and definitive spikes, Blahnik's shoes are objects of such fanatical devotion that one can easily imagine a fetish known as "the Manolo" retroactively airbrushed onto the pages of *Justine*. "Manolo Blahnik's shoes are as good as sex," Madonna has said. "And they last longer." Joan Rivers, who has been an adherent to the cult of Blahnik for many years, and who claims to exercise each day in a pair of his flats, put it more directly. "His shoes are slut pumps," she told me on the phone one day while she was on her treadmill. "You just put on your Manolos and you automatically find yourself saying 'Hi, sailor' to every man that walks by."

Shoes have always had meaning. The Chinese bound the feet of women, and the Victorians forced them into confining footwear; simple, comfortable shoes emerged during the French Revolution to go along with the idea of equality. Manolo Blahnik's shoes are about sex—bold, even slightly menacing sex. They are erotic and feminine and extravagant without ever quite becoming vulgar. They represent a kind of haughty independence. Joan Crawford would have worn them. So would Dorothy Parker. In the fulsome language of Hollywood trade papers, fuming starlets no longer walk out over the selection of the wrong leading man; they "put their Manolo down." When society women don't get what they want, they "wheel on their Blahniks" and flee, heels clicking. The aura of Blahnik hovers over the television series *Sex and the City*, where, as Carrie Bradshaw, Sarah Jessica Parker programs her answering machine to say simply, "It's Carrie. I'm shoe shopping." Parker was a Blahnik fan before she knew who he was. "You have to learn how to wear his shoes—it doesn't happen overnight," she told me. "But by now I could run a marathon in a pair of Manolo Blahnik heels. I can race out and hail a cab. I can run up Sixth Avenue at full speed. I've destroyed my feet completely, but I don't care. What do you really need your feet for, anyway?"

Blahnik's shoes often cost twice as much as those of his competitors, yet many models sell out overnight. They seem to weigh little more than a fistful of feathers and are always made by hand; dozens of people attend to each shoe before it is finished. Still, I wondered if Blahnik's workmanship was really so different from that of other designers. To the uninitiated eye it can be hard to tell.

So I called Cynthia Marcus, who is in charge of ladies' shoes at Neiman Marcus, which sells about thirty thousand pairs of Manolo Blahniks each year (at prices that start at about five hundred dollars), to ask where, exactly, he fits in. There was silence on the line while she took a deep breath to roll the question around in her head. "Honey," she said finally, "how important is Manolo Blahnik? I'll tell you. If he wanted me to change the name of the store to Neiman Blahnik, I'd do it in a heartbeat."

THE best shoes in the world are made in Italy, and Blahnik keeps four factories there working constantly. He sells nearly a hundred thousand pairs of shoes and boots in America every year and could easily double or triple that number, yet he has no desire to expand. You cannot buy Manolo Blahnik shoes in most European countries or in many American stores. Although he is a citizen of Spain, he makes only token efforts to sell shoes there. He has no stores in Italy, relies on a single outlet in France, and works out of the same cramped shop off the King's Road in London that he has used for twenty-seven years. Blahnik has turned away many offers to make him part of the new wave of conglomeration that has consumed the fashion industry. His sister, Evangelina, and his American partner, George D. Malkemus III, run the company. But as a designer Blahnik works alone. He has no deputies, assistants, entourage, or hangers-on. He draws every shoe himself, and in many cases he also stretches the leather, glues the soles in place, and whittles the last—the wooden form used to shape the shoe. When his shoes are ready to ship, he will sometimes stand on the factory loading platform with a lighter in his hand, singeing loose threads.

Blahnik calls his house in Bath "the shoe mausoleum," and he spends as much time there as possible, because he says it's the only place he can truly escape or relax. But Blahnik never escapes, and he never relaxes. He travels constantly between London, where he lives, and Milan, with trips to America and Asia. ("Those little Japanese women are simply mad for me," he said one day, as I watched him sketch shoes for Japanese *Vogue*. "Can you imagine?") Blahnik, who is fifty-seven, works incessantly, turning dozens of ideas into richly detailed and provocative drawings for the three hundred styles of shoe he will make each year. "If you don't come see what I have in Bath," he said one day when he invited me to visit, "you cannot possibly understand how strange I really am."

Blahnik has a daunting, almost imperial bearing; he was born to wear a cape. A friend once described him as Claus von Blahnik—as played, of course, by Jeremy Irons. He dresses crisply, in bespoke clothing. His silver hair is always gelled and his aquiline nose seems to hover in the air like a small bird. It is impossible not to notice him. The Four Seasons in Milan, which is the preferred billet for the nomadic fashion crowd, is often filled with the most jaded people on earth. Yet, once, as I was waiting in the lobby, I saw a dozen heads turn away from Naomi Campbell to a more distant figure: Manolo had entered the room. And, as soon as he did, Campbell's head turned, too.

Like many of his colleagues at the top of the fashion business, Blahnik is used to getting his way. He can be petulant and eccentric in several languages. In Milan, where he spends nearly three months a year, he *must* have Room 212 at the Four Seasons. At the St. Regis in New York, it's the tenth floor or nothing. Blahnik will travel to America only on what he calls "the quick plane"— the Concorde. At home, he eats little; on the road, when he can't dine in the hotel, he tries to eat at the same restaurant each night. Blahnik takes three baths a day. ("Are you kidding? When it's hot, I take six.") He calls his eighty-five-year-old mother, in the Canary Islands, almost as often as he bathes. He would never dream of travelling without his version of the nuclear football: a custom-made leather valise full of bone-handled hairbrushes, antique shaving utensils, fifty-year-old Italian linens, and an ample supply of silver mirrors, all of which would have been standard equipment for a gentleman's portmanteau two hundred years ago.

Manolo Blahnik has the attention span of a kitten. He rarely finishes a sentence. One minute he will be talking with passion about Nubian folk music, which he reveres. And the next he is launched on a critique of young designers, who he feels are far too reliant upon MTV and other artifacts of an instant society. ("These little kiddies today, they don't even know what a shoe is. To them design is what they see in magazines. It's not based on human life. They will suddenly scream, 'Oh my God! My collection is going to be so very Anna May Wong,' because they stayed up late one night and saw a movie. *Please.*") He reads widely in English and French, and fluently enough in Spanish and Italian. ("My life is a torrential river of books," he told me, and then went on to describe, in torrents, the plot of the latest novel by Guillermo Cabrera Infante, who is one of his favorite writers.)

Blahnik appears to have seen every movie, and he loves discussing casts, crews, and antecedents. Once, I asked whether he had seen the most recent film version of *Romeo and Juliet.* He answered, but it is never possible to discuss one film with Blahnik unless you are willing to talk about ten: "Do you mean the Baz Luhrmann *Romeo and Juliet*, with Claire Danes? I loved it. . . . I loved it. The best *Romeo and Juliet* in my memory was Renato Castellani in the fifties, early, with what's the name of that girl, I don't even know the name of that girl now, the English girl . . . and Laurence Harvey. Too old, both of them. But a *beeeautiful* movie. And then I loved also the other version with Zeffirelli. It was cute. The teen-age one. Don't push me to go on, I'll go mad. But I love that new one that was set in California. It was MTV nonstop. But that's all right. I'm not mad about that child, though. Leonardo. The boy."

For a man who inhabits a world ruled by ephemera, Blahnik despises change. He got so upset when the Spanish company that produced his favorite pomade went bankrupt that he considered trying to buy and revive it. (Not long ago, when we were together in Milan, he saw, in one of the city's most expensive pharmacies, a French hair gel, Tenax, his chosen substitute. After the clerk said that the store had sixty-one tubes in stock, he promptly bought them all.) So when Blahnik told me that I would have to travel to Bath and see his shoe archive to appreciate him in all his strangeness, I was pretty sure he was selling my imagination a bit short. I had no idea.

MANOLO Blahnik only has eyes for feet. He says that he simply cannot stand the thought of a naked body. When he stops by the Prado, the Louvre, or the British Museum, as he does often, he can talk about the sculptures with great sophistication and in precise detail as long as you ignore the torso. He can distinguish the work of Praxiteles from the Aphrodite of Doidalses with a glance at their chiselled toes. He will talk about the feet of fishermen for hours. (They are ideal, Blahnik says, because a life spent barefoot on the sand "rubs them to perfection.") He also has opinions about arches (the higher the better) and the proper alignment of a woman's toes (the second toe should be slightly longer than the big one). Slovenliness appalls him, and the words "clean" and "groomed," when applied to a human being, are the highest accolades he has to offer. ("Jennifer Aniston came into the store last year. She's a cute little girl, groomed to perfection, and, my God, is she *clean.*") Blahnik cannot abide bright shades of nail polish, or even the newer, more fashionable muddy dark shades; he finds them all vulgar. ("You should use crimson or a nude color," he says, sternly. "Or clear varnish. And that is all.") He can stare at heels all day, and then go home and draw them all night. "I'm simply mad for extremities," he said. "I always have been. The rest of the body seems so dull to me."

Thinking about shoes seems to give Blahnik the energy of a switched-on teen-ager. At lunch, he had been sour and in pain. By the time we arrived at his house, which is shrouded in wisteria, his mood had changed completely. Blahnik likes to work there; the ground floor has an airy study with a large drafting table and a mesmerizing picture of James Dean. "I don't like beautiful boys in general," he said when he saw me staring at the photo. "But he was so much the *most* beautiful boy." In his bedroom, Blahnik has a Horst photograph that his sister and her daughter gave him; it's of a pair of disembodied legs and feet. He told me that Horst, whom he admired greatly, died in November because "he couldn't bear to confront the new century." When Blahnik talks about artists whose aesthetic vision he admires, his voice soars an octave. And it soars often. "Manolo lives for beauty," André Leon Talley, an editor at *Vogue* and one of Blahnik's oldest American friends, told me. "He is the Proust of shoes. Ugliness makes him bleed." There are books lying everywhere in the house, essays mostly, and biographies, but also great piles of art books, on subjects ranging from medieval churches to nineteenth-century stonemasonry.

There are also dozens of videos—everything from *Alphaville* to *Pleasantville* to *Z*.

By the time we climbed the great stone staircase to the third floor—which is where the shoes begin—Blahnik was practically vibrating. He told me that the house, which offers sweeping views of the pale tiles and red rooftops of Bath, had once been occupied by the actress Helen Mirren. She should see it now. The drawing rooms were built for tea dances and whist. Now every room has cupboards that stretch from the floor to the ceiling, and each shelf is filled with shoes. Imelda Marcos wouldn't believe this place! Pumps! Sling-backs! Sandals! Mules! Shoes in the bathroom and the attic and the closets and the halls. Shoes stuffed into boxes and packed under beds. Shoes have taken over the guest rooms, the bedrooms, the studies. There is only one from each pair, but there are thousands, and they represent almost everything Manolo Blahnik has ever made. "Look at this place," he said with real pride as we reached the landing. "There are shoes here to make you vomit."

When Blahnik opened the first of the cupboard doors on the third floor, it was as if he had stumbled into a children's fable, something he had never seen before. He gasped. "Look. Look at these shoes. Look. This is what I love," he said, picking up a shoe that would seem, to most eyes, the antithesis of his style. It was flat, dark, heavily brocaded. A court shoe with almost no heel. "These are the things that people don't want from me. The people want high heels. They want sex. They want danger. That's the disease. I'm so incredibly bored with sex. I don't want to hear about it ever again."

Blahnik was whipping through his collection now. He grabbed a satin mule, the shoe he is perhaps most famous for—the decadent backless bedroom slipper that he reinvented as a bawdy street shoe. It is a style that has been copied by every other designer. "Here it is. The mule. It's horrible! What was I thinking? If a shoe fetishist saw this, he would go nuts." Then he grimaced. "I have one, you know . . . a shoe fetishist. He is in prison somewhere in America. He writes me letters. Sends them by express mail. He is a madman. He says"—and now he slipped into a perfect imitation of Hannibal Lecter—" 'The only thing that will get me through the day is seeing a pair of Manolo Blahnik heels.' Do you have any idea how much that freaks me out?"

This seemed a bit odd coming from the man who took stiletto heels from the world of prostitutes and introduced them into society. Didn't you create it all, I asked? What was the point of the Absolut Blahnik advertisement, for example, the one with the model drifting on a raft in the moat of the Vittskövle Castle, wearing only a bathing suit and a pair of Blahnik's shiny, spiked, black leather boots, which crept up above her knee—boots that would have sent Leopold von Sacher-Masoch into an uncontrollable frenzy? It's not as if the sexual power of the high heel were unknown. High heels change a woman's posture and her gait. They accentuate the length and contour of the ankle and leg while curving the foot, making it seem smaller. High heels are an erotic pedestal. They tilt the breasts forward, pull the stomach in, and push the rear out. And that's before you take a single teetering, contorted step. As William A. Rossi observed in his bizarre 1976 book, *The Sex Life of the Foot and Shoe*, "Women have always had an affinity for fragile foundations and willowy walking, and men have always responded erotically to the sight of it."

Blahnik knows this well. "I understand that some people associate high heels with sex," he conceded. "To me, there is so much more. I happen to love artifice in a woman. Without that, there is no mystery. High heels create artifice. It's the way you walk. You create a motion, a space, it's sinuous. You become a living sculpture. Even if it's not successful sometimes. It's so exciting. It's the transformation that I live for. The sexual part means nothing."

This kind of talk drives George Malkemus crazy. Malkemus, who has run the American end of the business for nearly twenty years, is a pleasant, compact fellow with a good head for numbers and an uncanny ability to endure Blahnik's tectonic shifts in mood. "I have heard it a thousand times," he told me. "All I can say is that when Manolo sees the shoe, just when he sees it, it's orgasmic. For him, that shoe isn't really about sex. The shoe *is* sex."

Obsessives stalk Blahnik. On the train from Bath to London one day, a woman recognized him and started talking about shoes. After a few minutes, he stood up and said, "Madam, I am sorry to say that I am visiting my niece, who lives in Swindon. I must now leave the train," and he fled. One terribly famous movie star used to wander frequently into his New York store and sit for hours, watching women try on shoes. Blahnik appears each year in America with his new collections for Neiman Marcus, and women swoon when he shows up. "When Manolo goes out to our Beverly Hills store, it's an absolute mania," Cynthia Marcus told me. "You cannot believe what happens. We will do two or three hundred thousand dollars' worth of business in a couple of days. In one store. The women fall all over him. They bring him bags full of shoes to sign. They are insane."

Blahnik autographs all the shoes, high on the arch, so his signature won't wear away. It is a peculiar fact about Blahnik that women feel they can tell him anything. Customers will describe the most intimate details of their sex lives— and the effect his shoes have had on them. There are times when their comments leave him gasping for air. "Sometimes I just have to say, 'Madam, please, I must ask you to refrain,' " he told me in Bath as we worked our way through his shoes. "Honestly, where were these people raised?"

IN June, a book about Blahnik and his work will appear in England, and, with the help of his twenty-six-year-old niece, an architect who recently graduated from Cambridge, he has spent a good deal of time cataloguing and organizing his shoes. The book is written by a British journalist, and Blahnik has no connection with the project, although he was granted the right to approve the pictures. He views the book mostly as a way to put his designs into some coherent order. But Blahnik wants me to see that, while he loves his work, he doesn't take it all that seriously. He pulled out a classic hiking boot made in Corinthian leather and a construction boot with a three-inch heel. ("Isn't this *faaab?*") "This is called the Prairies," he said of another. "Look, it's an Indian moccasin in high heels. And this is quite funny, and what about the L. L. Bean look over here. And look, look! There are work-boot high heels. Isn't that camp? And these are high-heeled gardening shoes. Very practical."

He means that, by the way. Blahnik says he loves it when women wear his shoes in the mud. He may be obsessed with cleanliness, but he likes his shoes to get a workout. "Best of all would be in stables," he told me. "I want them to be dirty." Blahnik remembers the genesis of every sandal or sling-back that lines the wall. "Look at this—isn't that sick?—it's for a wedding in Africa, where the girls have to walk in high-heeled boots." He held out an elaborate and beautifully made ankle boot, fashioned from pony skin, with open toes and lots of eyelets.

I asked what he meant about a wedding in Africa. "I don't know. I made it up. It's not normal. You wouldn't wear it in England. It has to be hot. In Africa you can wear this. Not here. In Africa." He raked through dozens of shoes at great speed. "This one is Kate Moss's favorite shoe. Absolutely. She has about a million pairs." Next, he grabbed a feathery mule that he said would have been perfect for Marilyn Monroe. He went on to cite her famous remark about not knowing who invented the high heel but that "all girls everywhere owe him a lot." He talked about her for a while, so I asked whether he had heard Elizabeth Hurley's recent comment that she would have to kill herself if she ever became as fat as Monroe. Blahnik froze. "Marilyn Monroe fat?" he shrieked. "How *daaarrre* the bitch? How dare she talk that way about Marilyn Monroe, the woman who marked the century?"

Blahnik claims that he wants his shoes to be comfortable. He noted that while Roger Vivier—who is often credited with inventing the stiletto heel— was a brilliant designer, "it must also be said that he nearly crippled an entire generation of women." A surprising number of Blahnik's customers did tell me that his shoes are relatively easy to wear. I heard from quite a few others, how- ever, including some of his fans, who said that they were among the most highly refined torture chambers ever invented. One friend bombarded me with E-mail calling him a misogynist and a psychopath. "There are lots of women who think high heels are an evil conspiracy to cripple women by men who didn't like their mothers," Valerie Steele told me. Steele is the chief curator of the museum at the Fashion Institute of Technology and the author of *Shoes: A Lexicon of Style.* "It's all really kind of silly." Still, walking around in three-inch heels can't be as pleasant as sinking your feet into a pair of anatomically cor- rect Birkenstocks (a word, by the way, that Blahnik can't bring himself to utter). I asked if he ever felt sorry for all those women teetering through their lives on the spikiest of high-heeled shoes.

"Oh, my God, they love it," he said. "How could I feel sorry for them? Sorry. Sorry for who?"

By now, we had made it to the fourth floor, and Blahnik's enthusiasm showed no sign of flagging. "Oh, this is Madonna's shoe from the *Evita* première. I love Madonna, you have to admire her. She hides her lack of talent so well."

On a wall nearby, there is a picture of Blahnik from 1971, when he lived in Notting Hill. A mop of hair is piled on top of his head. With bangs. He looks mod, swingerish, almost cool. He is much more distinguished-looking now.

"Some kind of bitter ones say the doctor orders them to stop wearing my shoes," he continued. "They say, 'I can't wear this and I can't wear that.' I say, 'Madam, buy flat shoes.' It is not my understanding that anybody anywhere makes a person buy an expensive high-heeled shoe. There are women who like the shoes I make. For other women, there are other shoes." Then, as an afterthought, he added, "My mother cannot even walk in flats. She doesn't know how."

We reached the final set of cabinets near the back of the house—his fantasy collection, full of pastels and flowers. "This is the Escher," Blahnik said, pulling out a psychotropic pump. "This was for Marianne Faithfull when she did drugs. Look at the lime-green sandal. It's the C. Z. Guest look. I did this one for Bianca. Look at the little foot. She has such tiny, tiny feet. Look. That was my first shoe. My very first shoe—1971. How embarrassing." It's a giant platform heel in turquoise and yellow. He hates platforms and never made another. "They are hideous. Simply hideous. Anything to do with the current rage makes me sick. Did you ever watch the fashion channel? If you look at it for ten minutes then you realize how horrible and stupid this business is. How shameful and pretentious."

There was just an attic left, and it could be reached only by a dangerous-looking ladder. I passed. "Nothing there but shoes," he cackled. "Shoes. Shoes. Shoes. It is so sick. Isn't this just the sickest thing you have ever seen in your life? Come on, be honest."

Before I could say a word, though, Blahnik let out a long, deep sigh. "Oh, God, I'm in Heaven."

MANOLO Blahnik was born in 1942, in the Canary Islands. He remembers it as a "paradise" of Renaissance buildings, colonial houses, and spare, empty churches. Blahnik's father, who died in 1986, was originally from Czechoslovakia, and his mother is Spanish. They ran a banana plantation there because, as Blahnik put it, "on the Canary Islands before the war there was nothing but bananas and me and my sister and my parents." His mother, who still lives in Santa Cruz de la Palma, was a soignée sophisticate who travelled to Paris and Monte Carlo and Madrid to shop. At home, she used to whittle clogs because she wasn't impressed with the workmanship of the town cobbler. "As a boy, I got attracted to peasant shoes," Blahnik told me. "My mother would make Catalan espadrilles with a black ribbon in the middle. I thought that they were so exciting. I still do."

It was often a lonely childhood, though Blahnik says he never minded. For fun, he would capture lizards and make shoes for them out of tinfoil that his mother saved from cartons of Camel cigarettes. Blahnik also made shoes—of ribbon or lace—for dogs, cats, birds, and anything else he could get his hands on. "I lived a complete fantasy as a child. There was nothing there but what came out of our brains." Even after the war ended, Blahnik said, the Canary Islands remained isolated. "We went years without publications from Europe or the Iberian Peninsula. We got everything by boat from Argentina. My mother had *Vogue*, of course, and *Bazaar*, and my father took *Time* and *Life*. We would wait every Friday for the boats to dock with all those packages of magazines. I can still see them wrapped up so neatly and tied in bundles. And that was my life. Can you imagine?"

By the time he was twelve, Blahnik and his sister, Evangelina, who is a year younger, were as inundated with culture as two children living on a remote Spanish island could be—piano lessons, ballet, instruction in several languages, even Swedish gymnastics. "We tried everything," he recalled. "We had this magical setting for our youth. I live there still in my memory." Blahnik remains close to his sister, who runs the European part of the business from their office in London. Evangelina has the same silver hair as Manolo and the same aristocratic bearing, yet she is as reserved as her brother is flamboyant.

Blahnik's father had hoped he would become a diplomat. ("Can you imagine? Me? Patiently dealing with the fate of nations?") After studying politics and law at the University of Geneva, he quickly moved into literature and architecture. From there, he went to Paris before settling in London at the end of the sixties. For a while, Blahnik thought he wanted to design stage sets. With a friend, the photographer Eric Boman, he travelled to New York in 1971, because "that was where you went to make it."

"When you are young, you don't have a clue," he told me. "You just think you can do it if you try." Paloma Picasso, who is a lifelong friend, arranged for Blahnik to show his drawings to Diana Vreeland, then the editor of *Vogue*. "My God, how I was terrified. I am still terrified thinking about it. She looked at my drawings," he went on, "and then she started to scream." At this point, Blahnik broke into what I can only imagine is a pretty fair Vreeland imitation: " 'How *amuuusing*. Amusing.' That is all she kept saying. 'Amusing.' She asked me how long I was in New York, and she said, 'You can do accessories very well. Why don't you do that? Go make shoes. Your shoes in these drawings are so amusing.' I did what she told me. It was like a commandment from God."

Blahnik went home and got to work. He started small, needed little money, and succeeded at once. But he didn't really know what he was doing. "It took many years to realize how to do shoes, learn how to make them lovely and arty and technically perfect." In fact, his first collection was infamous. "I forgot to put in heels that would support the shoe," he told me. "When it got hot, the heels started to wobble. It was like walking on quicksand." Blahnik remains in London for convenience. "It's like an airport to me," he said. "Though I do like certain things about the English. The madness, the eccentricity. London is like a multi-multi whatever. It's fusion. It's everything. But I sometimes wonder if I should have stayed in America. I worship the American women, after all. They are as tough as nails, and they have these incredible minds. They scare me. I love that."

I CAUGHT up with Blahnik and George Malkemus around Christmas, in Milan. Spending time with them when they are together is a bit like being thrust into the cast of *What Ever Happened to Baby Jane?* ("This is my idea, George, and they are my shoes. Can I talk?" Blahnik blurted out at dinner one night, when Malkemus was describing a plan to make limited editions of shoes that will cost as much as fifteen thousand dollars a pair. "I swear, George, if you interrupt one more time I will stab you.")

When Malkemus is in Milan, they spend most of their time at the factories, making sure that Blahnik's vision will translate into enough shoes—and the right shoes—to satisfy their customers. ("I could care less whether a shoe I make sells," Blahnik told me more than once. "That's what I have George for.") Malkemus agrees, sort of. When I visited him at Blahnik's boutique in Manhattan, he showed me a pair of sling-backs called the Carolyne, named for the New York socialite Carolyne Roehm. It is Blahnik's most successful shoe. "This is beauty and sex and what every woman wants to have on her foot," Malkemus said. "Now, look at this shoe"—he pointed to a sandal with fringed leather running in various directions down the foot. Malkemus squirmed when he touched it, as if it had fleas. "Manolo adores this. Will we have this shoe in the shop? Of course. Will we sell more than ten pairs? Never."

Blahnik's favorite factory is run by a family with whom he has worked for twenty-five years, but, on our way there, he asked me not to mention their names. "There are only a few things that can really get me going," he said. "Industrial espionage is one of them." Malkemus turned from the front of the Mercedes to tell Blahnik that, for the third time in as many weeks, a fairly well-known competitor had asked this factory to make his shoes.

"I can't take it anymore," Blahnik shouted as we pulled up to a tidy suburban building that looked more like a school than a factory. "It's not right. It's not ethical. I don't go to people's homes, to where they have been for twenty-five years, and steal from them. 'I want your shoes. I want your factory.' How demeaning. How vile. How can he even face himself?"

A handsome woman named Nadia walked us through the factory to the office. It is not unusual for other successful designers to fax their drawings to Italy and then to check in from time to time. Blahnik would make every pair of shoes himself if he could. I watched as he cut patterns—just as a dressmaker would—and shaped the fabric to fit the last. He then laid strips of masking tape across the shoe so that he could glue on pearls, sequins, or beads.

"So opulent. So modern. Madame Vreeland would have gone mad for these." Blahnik was looking at a new baby-blue-and-lavender crocodile shoe with jewels set into the heel. "I can hear her now," and he put his high-dame voice back on—" 'Give me opulence. Give me opulence. Nothing less will do' "—before slipping back into himself. "These could be for the Queen of Naples Ball. Maybe. Or for a tryst. Yes. A trysting shoe. But these shoes are so ridiculous. Who has the money to spend four thousand dollars on a crocodile shoe? What am I doing, George? Have I completely lost my mind?" I watched as he scraped an almost invisible drop of glue from the side of a thousand-dollar stiletto.

"What will happen to your brand when you stop?" I asked. The question surprised him. "Well, I'm not going to turn myself into McDonald's, if that's what you mean. They're just shoes. I'll make as many as I can, and when I die I suspect the world will survive."

Lunch had been spread out along the worktables, but when a secretary announced that the man who makes their finest lasts had arrived Blahnik was out of his seat in five seconds. He dove across his desk, narrowly missing a plate of mozzarella. He grabbed a dozen drawings. "My God, George, get the others. We must hide the drawings."

"What's going on?" I asked, when the sheaf of papers had been temporarily deposited in the trash basket.

Blahnik looked at me darkly. "That man is very talented," he told me. "There are not many like him left. But I don't trust him. He talks to Prada. I know it. He talks to Gucci, he talks to everyone."

AFTER returning from the factory, we decided to take advantage of the late shopping hours. The warm weather and Christmas season had conspired to fill the stores along the Via della Spiga with half the population of Milan. It was hard just to make our way down the old stone streets.

We passed a billboard that displayed a vintage 1960 ad for Moët & Chandon, which featured a picture of Cary Grant and Kim Novak. "Oh, Kimmy, Kimmy, Kimmy!" Blahnik shouted, loud enough to turn heads. Then he ran up to the ad and kissed the Plexiglas that covered her face. "I adore you. Just adore you. I always have." We looked at the Christmas decorations in a few windows, but soon it was time to make our way back to the hotel. Before we did, though, I asked Blahnik if there was a "right woman" to wear his shoes, a muse. "Not at all," he said. "They don't have to be glamorous. I don't care who wears them.

After I make them, the rest doesn't matter." Malkemus rolled his eyes and whispered, "Bullshit." Then he pointed to an elegant young Indian woman. She was dressed in a plain sari and a cashmere shawl. She moved as if there were a cushion of air between her and the ground. "Manolo," Malkemus said mischievously. "Look at that." Blahnik turned, but said nothing as she strode by. Then he let out a kind of yelp.

"Did you see that, George!" he shouted, completely beside himself. "She was wearing my clear heel. She was wearing it, George, and it looked perfect. It was made for her. My God, George, what a joy. Wasn't she beautiful? Wasn't she absolutely beautiful?"

MARCH 20, 2000

A PARTY FOR BROOKE

I T is March 17th, and my friend Brooke Astor has invited me to lunch at the Knickerbocker Club, on the corner of Sixty-second Street and Fifth Avenue. In choosing the date, neither of us recalled that it was St. Patrick's Day. The parade—all those bagpipers looking like brightly colored stuffed dolls, all those high-stepping drum majorettes—would be barrelling past the clubhouse, and thousands of people would be lining the curbs on both sides of Fifth Avenue. But no matter. Arriving at the Knick, I am confident that Brooke will have already found her way through the crowds, and so it turns out. She is waiting for me upstairs in the dark-panelled library, nattily dressed in a brown-and-cream tweed suit, with a high-crowned hat to match. Her eyes, which are an unusual shade of green, have a merry sparkle in them. On March 31st, she will be celebrating her ninety-fifth birthday; a party is to be given for her that evening at the Café Carlyle, by half a dozen friends who have elected to remain anonymous. Brooke is full of energy (in our youth, she and I would have called it "pep") as we exchange a kiss and take a table by one of the many-paned library windows overlooking the Avenue. We will have a drink there before we undertake a novel experience: that of jointly standing back and observing not my friend the private Brooke but the public personage who bears her name, that "grande dame" of New York society, which is the last thing she ever intended to be, and which she regards as a media invention.

Hitherto, our lunches have been happy-go-lucky affairs, but today we have an unwritten agenda to deal with. Brooke has announced that the philanthropic activities of the Vincent Astor Foundation, over which she has presided since 1960, will shortly be coming to an end. The trustees will start giving away whatever money remains in the foundation's till—some twenty-five million dollars—thus bringing the amount of money that it has dispensed to a total of a hundred and ninety-five million dollars. As a journalist, I am interested in learning why she and the trustees have decided to put an end to the foundation. Before getting down to business, however, we catch up on the latest news and gossip—gossip not of a particularly hair-raising nature but racy enough to make us feel that we are still actively in the midst of life. I am twelve years younger than Brooke, but this is a gap that has been continuously diminished by the passage of time: over the years, we have become contemporaries. We share a host of friends who have died and whom we welcome back into our lives by naming them. Our minds skip from one apparently unrelated person to another: when we order our drinks—a Campari for Brooke, a gin-and-tonic for me—the word "gin" leads me to quote Eliza Doolittle, in *My Fair Lady*, as saying, "Gin was mother's milk to her," to which Brooke responds that she knew Rex Harrison. The trail is a fairly straight one from Eliza Doolittle to Rex Harrison, after which it bends a little, by way of Portofino, where Harrison and Brooke and her second husband, Charles Marshall, spent many happy summers, to Max Beerbohm, whom Brooke often visited in nearby Rapallo; then it goes on to Ezra Pound ("A mean-hearted tennis player," Brooke says, "speaking such disagreeable language") and, finally, by an unexpected detour, to Henry Adams. As a student in Washington, D.C., Brooke met Adams, who gave up his regular afternoon nap to chat with her. I remark on her having known a close descendant of two of our earliest Presidents, both born in the eighteenth century, and Brooke claps her hands with delight at the thought of this formidable leap backward in history. "I do cover a lot of ground, don't I?"

Seated at the window, we are alone in the big, book-lined room; we suspect that most members have considered it prudent to avoid the club on a day when it resembles a besieged fortress. Characteristically, Brooke feels otherwise: the parade is a happy addition to our meeting. She leans into the embrasure of the window and begins to wave to the ranks of shamrock-bedecked men and women marching along the Avenue. Some of the marchers glance up and wave back, evidently grateful to have this trim little stranger urging them on. A young man dressed all in green and carrying four brass kettledrums at waist height makes a low bow to her and bangs his drums with extra zest. "What fun this is!" Brooke says. "We ought to be down there with them. I hope their feet aren't hurting."

The sight of the young people marching puts her in mind of her favorite topic of the moment, which is education. She tells me she is not yet ready to let anyone know the names of the institutions that will be receiving the last of the grants from the foundation, but she says that at least one of them will have something to do with improving the services provided by public-school librarians to schoolchildren throughout the city. She has made the acquaintance of Rudy Crew, the chancellor of the city's Board of Education, and has become one of his outspoken admirers. "He is on the right track, and I am all for him," she says. "I missed a lot by dropping out of school and getting married—married when I ought to have been learning Latin and Greek! My mother took me out of Miss Madeira's school, because she was afraid I would learn too much and become a bluestocking. Well, there was precious little danger of that! I love books, but I love life, too. Sometimes I wonder why, at my age, I like to go out every night, but I do." And then, as we discuss her love of parties, Brooke lets slip another of her financial intentions. "For a long time, I've been a member of the board of the Metropolitan Museum, and every year the foundation underwrites a holiday party for the whole staff—over two thousand people! And we are setting aside a million dollars to pay for that party in perpetuity, long after I'm gone."

BROOKE as a dropout? Brooke as a teen-age bride? It is hard to imagine, given the primness of her family background. Her father, John Henry Russell, Jr., was an officer in the Marines; her mother was of Southern stock—a flirtatious social butterfly. Brooke has always said that she liked being an only child. She also liked the fact that, thanks to her father's career, she passed her childhood in such distant places as Hawaii, Panama, Peking, and Santo Domingo. In Washington, the Russells owned a little house on the corner of De Sales and Seventeenth Street, and her mother's parents, George Henry Howard and Roberta Brooke McGill Howard, owned a house on N Street. Brooke had been named after her Grandmother Howard but—fortunately, in her view—was never called Roberta. Her grandfather, who was an attorney, may have been a source of her literary bent: in his spare time, he wrote unsuccessful novels and plays. Brooke, who has published two engaging memoirs—*Patchwork Child* and *Footprints*—as well as two novels, started composing poems and keeping diaries at the age of seven. A diary entry in January, 1913, begins:

> Saturday. Got up at 8. Wrote poems until 11, then skated till 1 o'clock. Gwladys came to tea, began my novel, Beauty Blackwell. Poem enclosed "Bleat, Bleat, Bleat." Skated with Johnny Malone, Rainwater and Shay and Gwladys. She came to tea and we wrote stories.

A few days later:

> Went to Gwladys to tea. Mrs. Williams scolded me. I came home and cried, and burnt my novel. Alas!

Brooke kept diaries faithfully throughout her adolescence. She has crushes on boys, decides that they are all pills, founds a secret society whose members communicate only by signs, begins to draw amusing pen-and-ink caricatures, and, a few days short of her sixteenth birthday, well chaperoned and claiming to be almost eighteen, attends a prom at Princeton. There she meets a recent graduate, John Dryden Kuser, who has bright-blue eyes, dances badly, and talks well: he asserts that he is one of the seven neorealists in the world. Brooke is much impressed. Within a year, the neorealist is to become her first husband. She is seventeen and utterly ignorant of sex. The honeymoon is a disaster, and so are the remaining eight years that she spends with him, living in the New Jersey countryside. The alcoholic son of a very rich family, he is given to physically abusing Brooke and to incessant womanizing. The only fortunate consequence of the marriage is a son, Tony, born when Brooke is twenty-four. Kuser seeks a divorce—he is eventually to marry five times—and Brooke, startled by this turn of events (in her family, divorce was not an option), goes off to Reno. Then, with the help of her financial settlement, she comes to New York and takes an apartment at 1 Gracie Square. She is in her middle twenties and is eager to make a place for herself in Scott Fitzgerald's Jazz Age—ideally, in a literary milieu. She enrolls in courses in short-story writing and playwriting at Columbia University, and, with the help of family connections, she swiftly makes friends with the drama critics John Mason Brown and George Jean Nathan, the playwrights Robert E. Sherwood and Noël Coward, the novelists Joseph Hergesheimer and Glenway Wescott, and the actresses Dorothy and Lillian Gish. Clare Boothe Brokaw, the editor of *Vanity Fair* (she was not yet married to Henry Luce), gets on splendidly with Brooke. (In *Footprints* Brooke writes, "The men who liked her never liked me; and the men I liked quite often did not like her. It worked out very well.") Brooke writes book reviews for *Vogue* and, in 1932, marries a stockbroker named Charles Henry Marshall (always known as Buddie), a Yale classmate and close friend of Cole Porter's. She thrives in the marriage (during which she works as an editor at *House & Garden*); she afterward describes Marshall as the great love of her life. Her son, Tony, seeks to emulate Marshall, and eventually takes his name. Brooke and Buddie have twenty years together before he dies in her arms, of a sudden heart attack, at their country place, in the Berkshires. She is desolated. Her life—her well-nigh perfect life—has apparently come to an end. But not so: to her astonishment, within a year she is married to Vincent Astor, and her career as a public personage begins.

WE have finished our drinks, and we make our way into the dining room, which looks out upon the comparative quiet of Sixty-second Street. The waitresses appear eager to serve us; Brooke has always been admired for her good manners, which are manifested by her showing equal attentiveness to all who cross her path. Once she has ascertained that our waitress and her family are enjoying good health, Brooke orders a sandwich and I order a salad, and I put an inevitable question: What was Vincent Astor really like? Brooke replies,

"Vulnerable, cranky, manly," but then she wishes to make me understand how different their backgrounds were, first in respect to her family's "comfortable" economic circumstances and his family's enormous wealth, and second in respect to their upbringings: her childhood was charged with family love, and his was largely empty of it. His father, John Jacob Astor, who went down with the *Titanic*, in 1912, was too busy building hotels to pay him much heed, and his mother, who later became the fashionable Lady Ribblesdale, appears not to have been much interested in him, either. Brooke, as Marshall's wife, and Vincent, who was married to the former Minnie Cushing, had been casual acquaintances until, at a dinner party designed expressly to lure Brooke out of her bereavement, Vincent fell instantly, importunately in love with her.

Vincent stood six feet four inches tall, and his broad face wore an inscrutable, often sour expression. He trusted only a few people outside the circle into which he had been born. (One such person was Franklin Delano Roosevelt, like him a Hudson River squire; in 1933, to the dismay of many of his fellow-Democrats, F.D.R. enjoyed a postelection celebratory cruise on Vincent's yacht, the *Nourmahal*—a costly plaything symbolic of those "malefactors of great wealth" whom he had been inveighing against throughout the campaign.) Vincent was in his early sixties and Brooke was in her early fifties when they met. Although at that moment she was certain that she would never marry again, she did remember having been told by a friend that people who have been happily married are the soonest to remarry, and so it befell her. Within a matter of hours, Vincent, with boyish ardor, was storming her by telephone and in letters—sometimes as many as five in a single day. He told her that his wife had been asking for a divorce, which he had been refusing to contemplate, but now . . . if only Brooke would consent to marry him! It was preposterous, it was unthinkable, there were a hundred reasons to keep at a wary distance from him, with his reputation for being truculent and often deliberately rude. Nevertheless, there were the letters, every word of which contradicted the accepted view of him.

They married, and were together for eight years. Vincent had suffered injuries to his lungs during the Second World War, and he smoked constantly, but his doctor assured him that there was no reason for him to stop. He had always disliked parties, so Brooke became for the first and last time in her life a homebody. Vincent was an interesting companion, and they established a routine of seasonal comings and goings—Maine in summer, the old Astor country place on the Hudson in spring and fall, Phoenix during part of the winter, and New York City during the rest of the year. Despite their contentment, Vincent's health failed steadily, and he spent more and more time fussing with his will. Brooke has written that it was almost a game with him—a social occasion on which, surrounded by lawyers and real-estate consultants, he felt in a cheerful mood. In 1948, he had created a foundation; now he looked forward to handing it on to Brooke. They decided that its purpose should be defined in the most universal terms possible—"the alleviation of human misery." Vincent would say to her, "Oh, Pookie, you're going to have such a hell of a lot of fun with the foundation when I am gone," meaning, perhaps, not so much fun as satisfaction.

When Vincent died, in 1959, he left approximately sixty-seven million dollars to Brooke and sixty-seven million dollars to the foundation. To the advisers who had hovered about him over the years, it was cause for alarm and dismay that he had placed so much trust in Brooke's ability. They were especially concerned to learn that she was ready to take an active role as president of the Vincent Astor Foundation. Certain of them had hoped that Brooke would go off on an extended cruise somewhere, in the usual way of rich widows, and leave "serious" matters in their hands. But Vincent had made other plans for her, and she was determined not to fail him. "They had forgotten, if they ever knew, that I had spent most of my life as a working woman," she says. "During all those years with Buddie, I was a magazine editor. I was keeping long hours and making decisions, just like any other executive. I acquired the discipline that everyone has to possess to succeed in New York. I was a woman, but not a fearful one. The first two directors of the foundation were men, and I had a good many differences of opinion with them. Finally, I decided to work with a woman director, Linda Gillies, and she and I have, as you might say, looked out of the same window. Women can be good at that."

Lunch is over, and we make our way down through the deserted building. Brooke is off to the foundation, whose offices consist of a cluster of small rooms at Park Avenue and Fifty-fourth Street; her chauffeur has succeeded in outwitting a maze of police barricades and has backed her car up to the front door of the Knick. In she scrambles, on her way to an afternoon of work.

MARCH 24TH. I arrive at Brooke's apartment on the dot of four, the hour that had been appointed for our next meeting. (Brooke and I have an old-fashioned high regard for punctuality.) The apartment, to which she moved after Vincent's death, is high up in one of those handsome redbrick Georgian buildings that line Park Avenue in the Seventies. It faces mostly east and south, with high ceilings and sunny terraces ("Ideal for dogs," Brooke says). A maid ushers me into the library—a sea of chintz-covered chairs and sofas, where afternoon sunlight floods in upon vases of flowers, silver-framed photographs, and books, which, in all Brooke's houses, find their way out of the shelves designed to contain them and usurp every available flat surface, including, in neatly stacked ziggurats, the floor. Over the mantel hangs a Childe Hassam "flag" painting—this one painted on the very day in 1917 when our entrance into the First World War was being celebrated. It depicts Fifth Avenue from Thirty-fourth Street northward, and all the buildings being hung with flags and bunting. An exhilarating picture it is, full of high hopes.

Brooke enters, this time dressed in red. The hour is a little early for tea and far too early for cocktails, so we settle for some ginger ale—"mine in a small glass," Brooke tells the maid. The early hour was chosen because later in the afternoon there is to be a meeting of the acquisitions committee of the Metropolitan Museum—an event that Brooke has no intention of missing. Briskly, we return to our discussion of the foundation. From the start, it has acted on the principle that, because most of the Astor fortune was acquired in New York, the foundation's money should be spent within the five boroughs of the city. A second principle is derived from advice given to Brooke by her friend John D. Rockefeller III, who told her, "The person who has control of the money should also be personally involved in the giving. It is a lot of work, but it is worth it." Brooke and Linda Gillies are constantly out and about, taking in with alert eyes and ears the essence of a proposed project, since it may or may not resemble the description that was offered in its application for a grant. "In recent years, composing applications for grants has become an accepted literary form," Brooke says. "Sometimes they are fact and sometimes fiction."

The foundation in its early days concerned itself with youth services and public housing. It contributed a large sum to the development of Bedford-Stuyvesant, and in respect to other housing projects it sought to solve the problem of their inhumanly large scale and bleak surroundings by providing them with well-designed parks and playgrounds. As the years passed, Brooke became more and more interested in historic preservation—a field beset by crises. Typical of her spirited response to such crises was her improvised rescue of a number of rare Federal-style houses in lower Manhattan, adjacent to Fraunces Tavern and Coenties Slip. In the late seventies, the houses were about to be bulldozed out of existence and a parking lot put in their place. A newly organized not-for-profit preservation group called the New York Landmarks Conservancy (of which I was one of the founders) had been negotiating in vain to buy the property; not only was the price beyond its means but an executive of the company that owned the site had become obsessed with tearing down the ancient buildings as symbolic of a New York City past that he despised.

One day the conservancy heard a rumor to the effect that the obsessed executive was plotting to demolish the houses over the coming weekend. Brooke had already visited the site and had indicated that the conservancy could expect assistance from the foundation when her board of trustees met in a few months' time. When the emergency arose, the conservancy telephoned Brooke in the country and asked if the Astor Foundation would provide sufficient money for the down payment. She replied that she thought the foundation would be willing, whereupon the conservancy made haste to sign a contract for the property, forestalling the bulldozer by a matter of hours.

Through a similar timely intervention, Brooke helped to save the north wing of the Villard Houses, on Madison Avenue just behind St. Patrick's Cathedral. The wing was then a near-ruin and is now the accurately restored headquarters of the Municipal Art Society, with an architectural bookshop and several good-sized exhibition galleries. (It was in the south wing of the Villard Houses, once owned by Mrs. Whitelaw Reid—and now occupied by a new version of Le Cirque, presided over by Brooke's friend Sirio Maccioni—that Brooke attended her first New York City party, in the nineteen-twenties.) All told, the foundation has provided grants to almost three thousand causes, the largest single grant being ten million to the New York Public Library, and one of the smaller being a grant to the Animal Medical Center to provide free care for pets of indigent old people. ("Old people tend to have old pets," Brooke says. "They need help.") She states candidly that what she calls the crown jewels of New York City—the Metropolitan Museum of Art, the New York Public Library, the Pierpont Morgan Library, the Wildlife Conservation Society (formerly known as the New York Zoological Society), and Rockefeller University—will receive the bulk of her personal fortune. The twenty-five million dollars remaining in the foundation will go to some fifty organizations that the foundation has looked upon with favor in the past. "No doubt there will be some unlooked-for exceptions, especially in the field of education," Brooke adds, jumping to her feet: it's time to set off for the Met. "I am always surprising myself at the last moment and I am not afraid of surprises."

MARCH 31ST. The invitation to the party stipulated eight o'clock and black tie, and I approach the Café Carlyle at precisely eight, wearing a purple bow tie that serves as my version of black. It began snowing earlier in the day, and now the wind is rising. On Madison Avenue, umbrellas are blowing inside out, and the snow, as it strikes the warm sidewalk, turns into slush. I had expected the party to start late because of the storm, but no. Although many of Brooke's friends are elderly, they have long since demonstrated their physical toughness; they are survivors, who believe (as Zelda Fitzgerald once wrote) that weather is for children. In they come, shaking the snow off their hats and coats, stamping their boots on the marble floor of the vestibule. Cocktails are being served in the oval interior space of the hotel, which is known as the Gallery. Within a few minutes, the space is as jam-packed as a subway car at rush hour, and evidently that is just the way everyone wishes it to be. There is much laughter amid exclamations of delight at recognizing old friends, and this is odd, because most of the guests encounter one another at parties at least once or twice a week and have been doing so for decades. Nevertheless, their delight appears to be authentic, and all the more intense because of the person whose birthday they are celebrating.

"Where's Brooke?" The recurrent question is answered with a gesture, indicating the point at which she was last seen. As usual, Brooke is making an effort to be everywhere at once, and, because she is small, she is nearly invisible as she threads her way through the crowd. She is wearing a long evening gown of dark-green velvet—"A fine dress to dance in; I can kick up my heels"—and around her throat is a necklace of large emeralds in a platinum setting. I am familiar with its history, which Brooke recounted in *Footprints*, describing an incident that took place after Vincent's death:

Mr. Bulgari, the Italian jeweler, sent over a colored transparency of the emerald necklace and earrings for which we had selected the stones in London in 1958. With the transparency there was an impatient note from Vincent asking how soon it was to be finished as he wanted it for my birthday. Now here it was, two years later. I certainly did not feel in the mood to buy such an expensive present, but I went to see my banker, who said, "Vincent ordered it for you and wanted you to have it. If you like it yourself, I think you should buy it." I *did* like it. Vincent loved jewelry and had very good taste. It is pretty and not ostentatious but very elegant, and so I bought it. Considering that it was really Vincent's last personal gift to me, I am very sentimental about it.

"I don't wear it very often," Brooke says now, tapping the necklace, "but it *was* to be a birthday present and this *is* my birthday and I think Vincent would be very pleased."

I suggest that the necklace gives her something of the appearance of a grande dame—the thing that she vehemently claims not to be. "Oh, fiddle-sticks!" Brooke says. "In the first place, it requires society with a capital 's' to provide an arena for grandes dames to perform in, and such a society doesn't exist anymore—at least, not here in New York. In the second place, I would never try to compete in such an arena. It's the way I have run the foundation, personally checking up on everything we do, that has made me a public figure, but it certainly hasn't made me a grande dame."

Over the babble of voices, I ask my final question: "Once upon a time, you wrote that you would never give up the foundation. What has led you to change your mind?"

"Something so simple," Brooke replies. "I'm determined to make a tidy ending—to leave everything just as I wish it to be, in my kind of apple-pie order. Sometimes I pretend to fear that in helping to save so many monuments I have myself become a sort of monument, but I am not immobile—I am still on the march. 'Don't die guessing,' my mother said, and I have hearkened to her words. Wonderful as the foundation has been as an experience, it has necessarily tied me down, kept me within bounds. Even now, I have so many local sites that remain to be visited. Next week, I will be going up to the Bronx to inspect the renovation work being carried out on an old hospital there; I will also be cutting a ribbon in Harlem soon, to celebrate the restoration of a row of houses built on land owned by Vincent's great-grandfather. These houses are a model for the reclamation of the whole of Harlem, which has the finest stock of buildings in the city and deserves to be reborn. But I am at a very advanced age, and there are still so many places in the world that I haven't seen, so much that I haven't done! Imagine—I've never been to Russia, I've never seen St. Petersburg!"

A wave of newly arrived friends encircles Brooke and, at the urging of the Carlyle staff, bears her away to the Café, where tables have been set up all around a small dance floor. This is the room in which the singer Bobby Short regularly performs, and, sure enough, Short is on hand to make Brooke welcome. Once everyone has been seated, the dinner begins—caviar, chicken hash, red and white wine, champagne—and it is followed by speeches, which are wisely brief and genuinely affectionate. Annette de la Renta conveys a salute from William Astor, of the English branch of the family, who has been unexpectedly grounded in Florida by the storm. She is followed by David Rockefeller, Elizabeth Rohatyn, Barbara Walters, Brian Bedford, and Tony Marshall, who, as Brooke's son, speaks touchingly of the happiness that he and his mother have shared for more than seventy years.

Brooke rises to respond. She always speaks at ease, without preparation, phrases springing to her lips with the unguardedness of someone who has long known exactly who she is. This evening, she offers the merest handful of words, but in their brevity they have a ring of the gnomic. She says, "I know that you are here because you like me, and I know that I am here because I like you. All of you are always in my heart." Bobby Short seats himself at the piano, saying, "Whenever Brooke comes here to the Café, I play a certain favorite song of hers." He launches bouncily into Cole Porter's "Just One of Those Things." I think of Cole and Linda Porter and Brooke and Buddie Marshall dining in Paris, in the Porters' suave house on the Rue Monsieur, a long time ago.

As Short segues into "Happy Birthday to You," everyone stands and awaits the arrival of the birthday cake. For a few moments (all birthday parties have this crisis in common), no cake is forthcoming, and Short urges upon us a second round of "Happy Birthday." At last the cake, ablaze with candles, is wheeled out onto the edge of the dance floor. Brooke readily blows out the candles. Tradition holds that, whatever her wish may have been, it is sure to be granted. The hour is late. Beyond the windows, snow is falling and is expected to continue falling throughout the night. Here in the Café, everything is safe against the storm. And Brooke is dancing.

APRIL 21, 1997

CONSCIENTIOUS CONSUMPTION

Y OU'RE a highly cultured person who has never cared all that much about money, but suddenly, thanks to the information-age economy, you find yourself making more dough than you ever expected. The problem is: How to spend all that income without looking like one of the vulgar yuppies you despise? Fortunately, a Code of Financial Correctness is emerging. It's a set of rules to guide your consumption patterns, to help you spend money in ways that are spiritually and culturally uplifting. If you follow these precepts, you'll be able to dispose of up to four or five million dollars annually in a manner that shows how little you care about material things.

Rule No. 1: Only vulgarians spend a lot of money on luxuries; restrict your lavish spending to necessities. When it comes to members of the cultivated class, the richer they get the more they emulate the Shakers. It's crass to spend sixty thousand dollars on a Porsche, but it's a sign of elevated consciousness to spend sixty-five thousand dollars on a boxy and practical Range Rover. It's decadent to spend ten thousand dollars on an outdoor Jacuzzi, but if you're not spending twenty-five thousand dollars turning a spare bedroom into a new master bath, with a freestanding copper tub in the middle of the floor and an oversized slate shower stall, it's a sign that you probably haven't learned to appreciate the simple rhythms of life.

An important corollary to Rule No. 1 is that you can never spend too much money on a room or a piece of equipment that in an earlier age would have been used primarily by the servants. It's vulgar to spend fifteen thousand dollars on a sound system and a wide-screen TV, but it's virtuous to spend fifty thousand dollars on a utilitarian room, like the kitchen. Only a bounder would buy a Louis Vuitton briefcase, but the owner of a German-made Miele White

Pearl vacuum cleaner, which retails for seven hundred and forty-nine dollars, clearly has his priorities straight.

Rule No. 2: It is perfectly acceptable to spend lots of money on anything that is "professional quality," even if it has nothing to do with your profession. For example, although you are not likely ever to climb Mt. Everest, an expedition-weight three-layer Gore-Tex Alpenglow-reinforced Marmot Thunderlight jacket is a completely reasonable purchase. You may not be planning to convert your home into a restaurant, but a triple-doored Sub-Zero refrigerator and a ten-thousand-dollar AGA cooker with a warming plate, a simmering plate, a baking oven, a roasting oven, and an infinite supply of burners is still a sensible acquisition.

Rule No. 3: You can never have too much texture. The high-achieving but grasping consumers of the nineteen-eighties surrounded themselves with smooth surfaces—matte black furniture, polished lacquer floors, and sleek faux-marbleized walls. To demonstrate your spiritual superiority to such people, you'll want to build an environment full of natural irregularities. Everything they made smooth you'll want to make rough. You'll hire squads of workmen with ball-peen hammers to pound some rustic authenticity into your broad floor planks. You'll import craftsmen from Umbria to create the look of crumbling frescoed plaster in your foyer. You'll want a fireplace built from craggy stones that look as if they could withstand a catapult assault. You'll want sideboards with peeling layers of paint, rough-hewn exposed beams, lichenous stone walls, weathered tiles, nubby upholstery fabrics. Remember, if your furniture is distressed your conscience needn't be.

The texture principle applies to comestibles, too. Everything you drink will leave sediment in the bottom of the glass: yeasty microbrews, unfiltered fruit juices, organic coffees. Your bread will be thick and grainy, the way wholesome peasants like it, not thin and airy, as shallow suburbanites prefer. Even your condiments will be admirably coarse; you'll know you're refined when you start using unrefined sugar.

Rule No. 4: You must practice one-downmanship. Cultivated people are repelled by the idea of keeping up with the Joneses. Thus, in order to raise your own status you must conspicuously reject status symbols. You will never display gilt French antiques or precious jewelry, but you will proudly dine on a two-hundred-year-old pine table that was once used for slaughtering chickens. Your closet doors will have been salvaged from an old sausage factory. Your living-room rugs will resemble the ponchos worn by Mexican paupers. The baby gates on the stairs will have been converted from nineteenth-century rabbit hutches. Eventually, every object in your house will look as if it had once been owned by someone much poorer than you.

You will never spend large sums on things associated with the rich, like yachts, caviar, or truffles. Instead, you will buy unpretentious items associated with the proletariat—except that you'll buy pretentious versions of these items, which actual members of the proletariat would find preposterous. For example, you'll go shopping for a basic food like potatoes, but you won't buy an Idaho spud. You'll select one of those miniature potatoes of distinction that grow only in certain soils of northern France. When you need lettuce, you will choose only from among those flimsy cognoscenti lettuces that taste so bad on sandwiches. (You will buy these items in boutique grocery stores whose inventory says "A Year in Provence" even as their prices say "Ten Years Out of Medical School.")

Accordingly, you will pay hugely inflated prices for all sorts of things that uncultivated people buy cheap: coffee at three seventy-five a cup, water at five dollars a bottle, a bar of soap for twelve dollars. Even your plain white T-shirt will run fifty dollars or more. The average person might be satisfied with a twenty-dollar shovel from Sears, but the sophisticated person will appreciate the heft and grip of the fifty-nine-dollar English-made Bull Dog brand garden spade that can be found at Smith & Hawken. When buying your necessities, you have to prove that you are serious enough to appreciate the best.

Rule No. 5: If you want to practice conscientious consumption, you'll want to be able to discourse knowledgeably about everything you buy. You'll favor catalogues that provide some helpful background reading on each item. You'll want your coffee shop and your bookstore to have maxims from Emerson and Arendt on the walls, because there is nothing more demeaning than shopping in a store that offers no teleological context for your purchases. You'll only patronize a butcher who hosts poetry readings. Remember, you are not merely a pawn in a mass consumer society; you are the curator of your purchases. You are able to elevate consumption above the material plane. You are able to turn your acquisitions into a set of morally informed signifiers that will win the approbation of your peers. You are able to create a life style that compensates for the fact that you abandoned your early interest in poetry and grew up to be a corporate lawyer. You care enough to spend the very most.

NOVEMBER 23, 1998

OUR MONEY, OURSELVES

HAVE never understood money. More than that, I was trained in the hazardous, complex art of not understanding money at an early age. This isn't to suggest that everything about my relatively privileged childhood was a pleasant pecuniary blur—that my desires as a girl weren't regularly deemed too expensive, or simply excessive, or that the rudiments of saving against a rainy day were not imparted to me. My favorite piggy bank was a chubby, cloudy-white glass milk bottle (labelled "Daphne," in big block letters, to distinguish it from my sisters' piggy banks, which were otherwise identical) with a slot in the middle of its round tin lid. I remember the satisfying noise, like the clink of good china, that the bottle made when it was weighty with change; I would pick it up and shake it, feeling well accounted for. But since my mother, a refugee from Hitler's Germany, didn't believe in giving allowances (she considered them to be one of many misguided Americanisms), I never accumulated enough money to buy anything ambitious, and there came a time when I realized that the piggy bank's value was more symbolic than actual. Indeed, one of those piggy banks still resides on a closet shelf in the room I shared with my sisters in my parents' apartment. The pennies and nickels and quarters in it are more than three decades old by now, and I find it odd that these elderly coins aren't worth more—having been around for so long and witnessed so much in the way of domestic dramas.

My parents were affluent, although the word "affluent" had not yet, in the sixties, replaced the simpler and more viscerally descriptive term "rich." We lived on Park Avenue, in a duplex with a curving staircase, and in the summers we lived in a house that was an hour outside the city, several blocks from the ocean. There was a chauffeur, a stern Dutchwoman who looked after the six of us, and a cook who presided over the kitchen. There was also Willie Mae, the laundress, who loudly cracked chewing gum as she ironed my father's underwear and custom-made Sulka shirts. For tailoring needs, there was Mrs. Karbe, a short square woman who was able to hold entire conversations with straight pins in her mouth.

And yet such was my family's inordinate, even pathological, discretion on the subject of its own wealth that I continued to believe my father sold chairs, rather than shares, well after I had outgrown other Gidget-like malapropisms. The larger meaning of money—its social potency—was kept deliberately veiled, as though it were a secret weapon, a force that could send things spiralling fatally out of control. There was so much hemming and hawing around the basic economic facts that I was surprised the first time—I was ten years old and at sleep-away camp—I heard my family knowingly referred to as "rich." Rich? I didn't feel remotely rich. For one thing, I shared a room with my two sisters; it was only from my friends who lived in smaller apartments, without staircases, that I learned it was desirable—virtually an upper-middle-class standard—to have a bedroom of your own. These same friends had more Danskin outfits than I did, in an enviable array of colors, and seemed far more casual about spending money. My mother may have ordered one or two expensive dresses apiece for us to wear to synagogue, when we were on display, but she was indifferent about what we wore to school, where no one whom she cared about saw us. She briefly campaigned for school uniforms, and ceaselessly inveighed against the clothes obsessions of adolescent girls. I can remember desperate arguments over the purchase of an extra pair of shoes: we were allowed one "good" pair, for *shabbos*, and one everyday pair, and any more than that was deemed frivolous. At dinnertime, my five siblings and I often argued over seconds, and our refrigerator never burst with fruit—inviting mounds of cherries, peaches, and plums—like the one in the Short Hills basement of Brenda Patimkin's parents, in *Goodbye, Columbus*. (Even if it had, we weren't allowed to range freely in the kitchen and open fridge doors at our whimsy.)

It was as though my mother were acting the part of being the wife of a rich man without really believing in the role. Or she believed in it schizophrenically, with one ledger kept for my father—for whom nothing was too good or too much—and another ledger kept for us children. This tendency was undoubtedly exacerbated by the differences in my parents' backgrounds, which were subtle but important: they were both German immigrants, united by their Orthodox Judaism, but my mother's father was a lawyer and a philosopher, a member of the Kant Society in Germany, while my paternal grandfather was a canny businessman, a fur merchant who would have preferred his grandsons to go into the *sechoira* (merchandise) business rather than what he called "the paper business" (Wall Street). Although I don't believe my mother ever balanced a checkbook, and I know that she was never confined to a weekly budget, I can still hear her saying "Cherries are expensive!" on a summer weekend, when one of us protested the meagre amount she had bought, as though somewhere someone were keeping close watch on such vainglorious expenditures. My mother scorned the randomly acquisitive habits of upper-middle-class Americans; she never threw leftovers away, and she loved to intone pennywise, pound-foolish phrases like "Enough is as good as a feast." (My father's peccadilloes, which included a tendency to warehouse electric shavers and eyeglasses, were lovingly exempted from these strictures.) She was so careful to convey the message that she was not entirely at ease with the life style she'd come into when she married my father—or, more to the point, that she in any way endorsed "marrying up"—that I came to believe, unlike the Bennet daughters in *Pride and Prejudice*, that there was something intrinsically admirable about men who didn't make money.

Another thing added to the confusion, and that was my father's prominence as a philanthropist. A generous dispenser of funds to charities large and small, he sat on the board of countless Jewish institutions—from rickety, fanatically religious yeshivas in the backwaters of Brooklyn to big-city hospitals with gleaming secular reputations—and endowed any number of scholarships and chairs in the family name, in both New York and Israel. Throughout my childhood, my parents attended an astonishing number of dinners on behalf of these institutions, where they frequently took a table that cost thousands of dollars and often had the honor of being seated on the dais. (Actually, in the segregated men's-club atmosphere of these functions, my father would sit on the dais with other honorees in starched shirt-fronts, while my mother had to make do at a more plebeian table below.) My father was also capable of throwing the odd donation to a political candidate, and of suddenly being pressed into service on behalf of some non-Jewish cultural organization. By the time I had reached my teens, it had become clear to me that my siblings and I were viewed by the world as having been born with silver spoons in our mouths, no matter that we had developed an intricate system of hiding food—especially sweets—from one another at home, in case there wouldn't be enough to go around. This faux reputation as an heiress has dogged me ever since; it took a firm hold when I was in my twenties and my father, as part of his ongoing commitment to a Jewish school of the arts, endowed Merkin Concert Hall, on the Upper West Side.

At the time, I was renting a dark subterranean apartment that had been robbed by my super, and by then I had all but given up on making the two parts of the picture fit together in my own mind, much less in other people's: the shame and contempt that attached to the subject of money within the family versus the public recognition and deference accorded my parents. Who, one might wonder, was I in all this? Someone looking in on a scene of plenty, my nose pressed wistfully to the window, or someone who was born to the scene, nestled in the silken folds of privilege? My mother went to great lengths to convince her children that money was not only intrinsically poisonous but not ours to claim on the grounds of blood ties. What were we to my father's money, and what was it to us? We were connected, she implied, only by sheer happenstance. None of us were ever offered a strand of pearls or a jazzy little sports car on reaching some signpost of maturity, like college graduation. (Once my father took me to buy a fur coat, but the only one who emerged from the showroom wearing fur was him.) It wasn't as though we weren't thrown the occasional perk, of a kind my parents deemed worthy—a trip to Israel, say. But no one compares downward. In the world of Jewish princes and princesses which I inhabited, I didn't look to friends who had less than I did; I looked to the ones who had more, who seemed to glide on a surface made shiny and smooth by parental largesse. At some point, I took to muttering darkly to my mother that charity began at home, but she would always fix me with a contemptuous look and ask, "And what exactly is it that you lack?" She managed to make me feel ungrateful and grabby at once, as though my bad character doomed me to be a scheming Goneril rather than a selfless Cordelia.

THIS ambivalence about money—its rightness and wrongness, when it was meant to be a visible facilitator and when it was supposed to hang back shyly— led inevitably to an atmosphere of self-consciousness and false restraint. Well before I had heard the term "conspicuous consumption," it seemed to me that being genuinely rich implied a certain compulsive delight in spending and accreting. As a girl, I was a devout reader of "Archie" comics, which featured Betty and her rival, the "gorgeously rich" Veronica Lodge, as well as the brilliantined, ever-scheming Reggie, who was also "lumpy with loot." The pages were filled with wisecracks about the allure of wealth and the importance of finding a rich boyfriend. ("Let's do something romantic!" one character says— "like counting money or watching armored cars unload.") Beneath the jokes, however, lay a serious mid-century appreciation of the mercantile ethos: "If it draws people and shows a profit," explains the perennially put-upon Mr. Lodge to his daughter, "that's good business." I also watched *The Beverly Hillbillies* on television—this was a decade and a half before money-lust came out into the open, with *Dynasty* and *Falcon Crest*—and noticed an insouciance about living high on the hog that was nowhere in evidence in my own family, despite our maids and our fancy address. (The glamour of a good address has been brought home to me many times since, of course. Once, when I was in my late twenties and having lunch with a well-known novelist, he asked me where I grew up. When I answered, hedging as I always did, "On Sixty-fifth and Park," he leaned across the table, his dark eyes blazing with curiosity, and asked, "On Sixty-fifth? Or on Park?")

Although my family's now-you-see-it, now-you-don't approach to money may have been particularly heated, I slowly came to realize that this private obfuscation was embedded within a larger cultural evasiveness. I noticed that other people were caught in a similarly ambivalent grip. No one was honest about the subject of money; worse yet, not many people seemed to recognize that they were being dishonest. People either deified money or demonized it, conducted themselves like Ayn Rand characters, as if the profit motive were the only thing that mattered, or pretended that they didn't give a fig for worldly wealth and that those who did were beneath consideration. The latter type tended to strut around the groves of academe, where a spirit of apology for being white and the beneficiary of the American system of free enterprise was standard among the Columbia University humanities faculty in my student days, and the one English professor who wore bespoke suits was rumored to be on the payroll of the P.L.O. Anyone who has been exposed to a basic humanistic education in the last fifty years has absorbed money's bad reputation. Rich people rarely came in for a kind word in the novels we read for our courses, although the preoccupation with the simple fact of money was so much in the forefront that, as Lionel Trilling observed, "the novel is born with the appearance of money as a social element." Most of us came of age with the sense that money is inherently impersonal, if not morally suspect; we were raised to believe that financial success can't compensate for loneliness, and may even be conducive to it.

Of course, this attitude underwent a shift in the late seventies and early eighties, when all vestiges of Depression-era thrift and upper-class noblesse oblige were replaced by ostentatious one-upmanship, and the adage "Never buy what you can't afford" gave way to "You can't afford not to buy it." This was the period when real estate, as one writer put it, became "the great conversation starter in the social life of the middle class." Everywhere you looked, someone was buying an apartment the size of a yacht or hiring out Blenheim Palace for parties, and even artists were expected to have ten-thousand-dollar-a-month lofts in SoHo. In what was one of many disquieting cultural shifts, the young children of the wealthy were no longer instilled with a becoming sense of modesty but were to be found at trendy Upper East Side tables, ordering costly plates of spaghetti that they barely nibbled at. How far this seemed from the unease, the feeling of unworthiness my siblings and I had felt, cowering in the back of the car when Jimmy, the chauffeur, dropped us off at school—a block away, for fear that someone might connect us to the Cadillac or the Lincoln and the capped driver behind the wheel. Or from Poorhouse, the make-believe game my sister and I played, in which we tied kerchiefs around our heads and imagined that we were the directors of a Dickensian-style orphanage, where the primary activities consisted of disciplining our dolls and eating deconstructed sandwich cookies. Still, I sometimes wonder whether our game didn't have within it the glimmerings of a social conscience—a sense of the precariousness of financial fate, and of how little it depended on one's innate human worth. This sort of counter-identification is hard to imagine today, when my daughter comes home from school talking excitedly about the "stretch limo" a friend of hers has boasted of riding in, and likes to pretend that she is "rich" and lives in a "mansion."

FOR all the loosening up that the eighties brought—the uncensored embrace of "champagne wishes and caviar dreams," in the greasy phrase of *Lifestyles of the Rich and Famous* host Robin Leach—money remains quite firmly in the closet. It, far more than sex, lingers as our deepest collective secret, our last taboo. Even now, you are more likely to get a woman to confess that she has committed incest with her father than to disclose what her father earns, or whether she's being subsidized by any of his money. A shrink I know tells the following joke: "A guy comes to a psychiatrist and tells him about his sexual perversions and fantasies down to the last sordid detail. Then, at the end of the session, the shrink asks him how much he makes a year. To which the fellow answers, 'Hey, I'm sorry, that's too personal.' " We may think we talk openly about money—and in daily discourse we do indeed chatter about mutual funds and book advances and the resale value of beach houses. But we don't really tell each other very much. To this day, I can't figure out how it is that many of the people I know are able to live in New York on their salaries, much less send their children to private schools. As far as I can see, most of my peers handle money with the same mixture of entitlement and panic that I do. There is, for instance, the friend—a therapist married to an editor—who mutters about making ends meet and talked to me about sending her only child to public school rather than to the private school that was clearly her destination, but indulges in regular jaunts to Paris and biweekly forays to Paradise Market, where the fruits and vegetables glisten like jewels, and are priced accordingly. Yet another friend, a writer, opts for cut-rate haircuts and takes her free reviewers' copies of books to Barnes & Noble in order to exchange them for birthday gifts, even as her parents furnish the apartment they bought for her with auction finds from Sotheby's and Christie's. More dramatically, there's the friend who has conspired to live—or, at least, to dress—way beyond her means. Both she and her husband are in "creative pursuits," and her weakness is "what I put on my back." She explains, "I spend it in dribs and drabs, and it all goes on credit cards with huge balances. I keep myself blind to exactly what I spend on clothes, the Armani jackets and the occasional thirteen-hundred-dollar black cashmere sweater. Every pair of Clergerie shoes I buy for three hundred and fifty or four hundred dollars really costs five hundred dollars, if you figure out the interest. My big terror is that I'll get killed in an accident and my father will find out that I was mired in credit-card debt."

The simple truth is that I haven't the vaguest idea what kind of money even my closest friends live on. Once in a while, something seeps out, when I happen to hear about a grandmother's stock that was "borrowed" to underwrite a new computer system, or an inherited piece of art work that was traded in to help purchase a larger apartment. (The clotheshorse concedes that her and her husband's earnings—even with their cramped "college dorm" apartment and credit-card stratagem—don't support their life style. Her father-in-law kicks in some of the children's tuition, and her divorced parents each give them money, ranging from birthday checks to more significant annual gifts.)

My friends, I might add, can't have a much better idea of how I make ends meet, working as a book critic and living in pleasant, if not grand, circumstances—a two-bedroom condo on a block listing toward the decrepit off upper Lexington. They must surmise about me as I do about them. Do they surmise that I don't live on what I earn? If so, they'd be right. I feel some discomfort about this, but it also allows me to circumvent the sense that money might have the ability to define me, might throw me into a context of second-rate aesthetic choices and chronic anxiety. The strangest thing about my situation is that I myself don't have full knowledge of it: I receive a certain amount of financial help from my family, without having any idea what my father, who recently died, at the age of ninety-one, was actually worth. (Less than I infer? Much less? Or more? Much more?) There has never been a discussion about this in the family, nor, since my father's death, has anyone mentioned his will or his estate. To try and get a purchase on the mystery, as I did some years ago, by making a visit to my father's white-shoe lawyers, is to come up against an impregnable code of silence. Money is not supposed to matter, much less be discussed, lest—lest what? Lest I think that it's mine to do what I like with? Lest I order a gold-plated dinner service for twenty-four? I received a tight-lipped welcome at our lawyers' office, where they had me confused with my sisters, and the only thing I actually found out was that my family's money was held in what even the firm's patrician senior partner admitted was the most illiquid state possible. I could conjecture that my inability to learn more had something to do with my being female—with the invested power of the patriarchy, with men trading crisp information in rooms high above the city—and that wouldn't be entirely inaccurate. Two of my three brothers work on Wall Street, and they've clearly been told more about the situation. (One of them manages the family accounts.) Still, we all seem to walk around hoping that the less we inquire the more there will be, in a sort of see-no-evil, hear-no-evil fog that will lift one day to reveal a green vista of cash.

Maybe this is why I keep most of the money I have personally earned in an insanely liquid state—in a checking account, to be exact. In the face of my family's clamped-down way of handling its resources, this is my version of keeping a wad of bills under the mattress: it's as if I never know when the knock on the door will come and I will have to flee, with just the shirt on my back, my family having ceased looking, in however ambiguous a fashion, after my interests.

WE all harbor fantasies of how we were meant to live; it's an image that we carry around in our heads, beckoning like a kitchen in *Architectural Digest* done up with the latest in appliances and finishes. I may not admire people who make money, but I envy whatever making money brings them—I want what they've got. Take the summer in New York, for example. Where is the beach house I dreamed of decorating unambitiously, with pleasant knockoffs from Crate & Barrel or Pier 1? I realize that this isn't a question to lose sleep over, but it throws me back on that old familial feeling of not understanding how much money there was and how it was to be used. "Surely," a man who knows my family says to me at a dinner party, "you have a place in the Hamptons." Ah, but surely I don't. Is there money buried somewhere in some account or trust which I could avail myself of in order to buy—or rent—such a place? I don't know the answer; I know only that I've been trained not to pose the question. Neither I nor any of my five siblings, with twenty children of our own between us, have ever rented a house in the summer, and it was only a few months ago that my oldest brother, a successful hedge-fund manager who owns a sprawling multimillion-dollar residence in the city, finally bought one. Even he spent more than a decade of summer weekends bringing his wife and four kids out to my parents' place—a functional brick house with a pool in a beach community frequented by Orthodox Jews who require a synagogue within walking distance. Now not only has he found something in the same town as my parents' house but he appears to have inherited the Merkin gene for excessive discretion: all of us, including my mother, heard about his purchase from someone outside the family.

What really puzzles me is that my brother and I—and, it seems, everyone else I meet in Manhattan—inevitably refer to ourselves as upper middle class. Can this category really be so elastic as to include people who shop endlessly in "the bubble," as my internist refers to the rarefied reaches of Madison Avenue in the Sixties and Seventies; people who sit in huge apartments on Central Park West when they're not in their upstate weekend homes; and the harried professional urban couples who live in Battery Park City, rent a cottage on the Cape for two weeks in the summer, and aren't the beneficiaries of invisible infusions of parental wealth? If everyone is upper middle class, where does rich begin? A European banker in his mid-forties explained the distinction to me over lunch in his bank's private dining room, offering up the assessment that "wealth" signifies ten million dollars in liquid assets, while "real money" means a hundred million dollars' net worth. "To be genuinely entrepreneurial," he added, "you need two hundred or three hundred million to play with."

ONE summer when I was in my early thirties, I was invited to spend a few days at the Canadian vacation home of my publisher, a brilliant maverick who had gone from being a textbook salesman to owning the company outright. I flew up by private jet; it was lushly appointed and smelled of fine leather. There was a staff of two, a pilot and a cabin steward who fussed over me, and I remember sitting there, sipping soda, and thinking that I could get used to this very quickly. (I suppose there are people who are unmoved by luxury, but I've never met any, and I'm not sure I'd trust them if I did.) I was standing and talking to my publisher in his heated swimming pool, behind the tennis courts and statuary and gardens, which yielded fresh raspberries. A man who was worth many self-made millions, he struck me as having a fairly unimpeded approach to matters of finance, so I was surprised when he asked me, apropos of nothing, what I thought was "behind" my father's philanthropy. I didn't want to explain—nor did I fully know—what moved my father so forcibly in this direction. In truth, I resented the question; it sounded unaccountably suspicious, even defensive (why, one might ask, didn't the publisher give more of *his* money away?), and it unnerved me that something I had been brought up to think of as admirable might be considered suspect. I was, of course, cynical enough to have formulated my own theories about the status-climbing that accompanied charitable enterprise. I also knew it was as good a way as any of leaving an imprint—of laying claim to a bit of immortality. But it had never occurred to me to impugn the impulse itself. The whole thing was awkward, and it made me wonder—not just about him but about the world view I had been raised in.

I believe his inquiry was made possible, at least somewhat, by the simple fact of my father's being Jewish. Jewish money is often fairly recently minted, and although my publisher's wealth was as new as could be, it's fair to speculate that he, a Gentile, mimicked the habits of the Wasp aristocracy when he made it: short of being Rockefellers or du Ponts, wealthy Wasps, I've been told, are less inclined to be charitable than wealthy Jews. They seem, rather, to be busy with horses and boats and what one Anglo-Saxon friend calls "the great Wasp affliction"—watching as their offspring fail to replenish the diminishing family fortune. I sensed a bit of reflexive anti-Semitism in my publisher's question—a suggestion of the vulgar parvenuism that Jews have inescapably been associated with. ("Their fortitude, such as it is," wrote the happily biased H. L. Mencken, "is wasted upon puerile objects, and their charity is mainly a form of display.")

But that was only part of it, the part that made me feel righteous and misunderstood on behalf of my tribe. The other part was more disturbing: the brute realism of my publisher's approach to his money (some of which he used to underwrite the lavish life styles of his children). My father's generosity undoubtedly did a lot of good, but it derived to some degree from the disdain he felt for the money-making business—from a need to be cleared of the taint of filthy lucre. My publisher seemed free of this, and I couldn't help thinking that had I been his daughter he would surely have bought me that place in the Hamptons instead of supporting every Jewish organization that came calling. Although I didn't see my father as someone who felt a need to atone for his money, his sense of self-worth clearly came from his philanthropy rather than from his financial success in itself. The encounter in the pool made me aware for the first time of the strangely hidebound approach to money that I had grown up with. For his part, my publisher wasn't afraid to admit that his money was his and would benefit his own; he didn't need to put distance between himself and his wealth—to reconfigure its baseness into something glittering and prideful, a diadem of sorts.

NOT many people are as unabashed as this baronial man was able to be. "Among the cultural élite, it's not yet proper to acknowledge that he who has the most money wins," a theatre producer told me recently. "It's a luxury of people who've inherited money—like my parents—to say that money doesn't matter." He believes that inherited wealth made his father "soft." "Inherited money is shameful," he declares matter-of-factly, adding that, as a result, "It's very important to me that I live off my paycheck."

Clearly, inherited money is more vexing to those who have it than earned money. A woman in her late thirties who is informed and competent in her professional life admits, "I don't know how much money my husband has, and we've been married five years. It's not like I haven't asked. He hems and haws and says it's always changing." She adds, "He has a small inheritance, and I guess it represents something he's uncomfortable about, something he's not sure he's earned." But how many of us look at people with money, inherited or otherwise, and really think it has been earned? Don't many of us think, Why them and not us? "Money," another friend suggests, "is sort of like morality. Everyone has their own private benchmarks. Not letting people know what you have protects you from judgment."

Naturally, our own irrational demands strike us as having the force of needs, while other people's needs strike us as capricious indulgences. Few of us are able to look calmly and cogently at the issue, caught up as we are in envy and comparison. "People see money as making them special—like genitalia," an analyst who has treated a lot of wealthy patients observes. "What possible difference could two inches make? But, also like genitalia, money is private—it's one of those things you're not supposed to show."

This can result in what a friend of mine describes as "the West Side ethos," where the whole point of dressing is to "muffle the impact of privilege." She explains, "The Upper West Side is the last bastion of moneyed liberalism. We have money, but we're slightly embarrassed about it." And another woman, an interior decorator who spends freely on herself, insists, "Anytime I've complimented a woman on what she's wearing, she says she bought it on sale. There's this anguish about spending—about openly spending on nice things." It's almost a relief to come across someone as down-to-earth as one woman I talked with, a widow in her seventies. "When I came to America, at age nineteen, I appraised myself," she said. " 'I'm pretty, I'm young, and I want to marry a man with money.' Not that I wanted that much, but I didn't want to struggle. I wanted a guy who could take me out beautifully, offer me an apartment and a nice life." The majority of us consider ourselves to be more enlightened; we like to think we're subscribers to Matthew Arnold's gently didactic view: "Life is not a having and a getting;/But a being and a becoming." And yet we continue in our entrancement. Woody Allen, at least the latter-day Woody Allen, has become our contemporary F. Scott Fitzgerald, filling the screen with the haunts and customs of the rich. He admits openly to what he calls "an enormous aesthetic fascination with wealth—with wealthy, rich kids, high prices." He adds, "To me, it's like staring into a fireplace—endlessly riveting."

"DIAMONDS are cold," my mother used to say, although I noticed that it didn't stop her from wearing the ones she owned, or from marrying a man who could afford to impress her with a chunk of an engagement ring. Money may not keep you warm, but it can take on the aspect of an embrace—indeed, it can be a stand-in for love, especially if the real thing is in short supply. "It's only money": sure, but do any of us really believe that? Freud conferred odious status on money. He thought it symbolized feces in the unconscious, but at the same time he was consciously obsessed with generating more of it. "My mood also depends very strongly on my earnings," he wrote to his confidant Wilhelm Fliess. "Money is laughing gas for me." And we know what he means; we all recognize the absolute power money has to inflate our spirits and dispel anxiety.

Nowhere is this charged dynamic more explosive than in the romantic sphere, from the first date, when a man offers to pay for dinner (or doesn't). All my relationships with men have teetered uneasily around the issue of who pays for what. In the first place, I am never sure whether I am to view myself as the hunted or the huntress: someone whom men are after "for" her money, as my mother frequently intimates (when, that is, she's not intimating that there's no money to go after me for), or someone who seeks to be saved from the pinched aura of her childhood, from its behold-the-kingdom-but-none-of-it-is-yours atmosphere, and find a truly giving, unambivalent provider.

This lack of clarity helped to undermine my marriage, beginning with the scene that took place in my father's study shortly after the birth of my daughter. As my husband and I perched on a sofa, ignorant as to why we'd been summoned, my father launched into one of his benevolent-patriarch speeches about futurity and procreation and responsibility. It sounded innocuous enough, until he pronounced that of course he was willing to help us buy a bigger apartment, as he had helped my siblings before me (I was the last to marry)—on the condition, that is, that we were willing to sign an agreement stating that we would be keeping kosher in our new place. I was stunned: even by the control-besotted standards of my family this was blackmail. I hadn't been religiously observant for years, though I was the only one of my parents' flock to go astray. I mumbled something about not compromising my independence and my nonexistent religious beliefs, to which my father roared, "I'm not interested in what you do or don't believe in!" After a tense moment or two, my husband and I picked ourselves up and left. I remember a brief, sweet discussion about living on our joint funds, which were fairly negligible. For a moment, I saw us as a version of the newlyweds in *Barefoot in the Park*, growing ever more amorous in our tenement digs while the water from the apartment above leaked through our ceiling and the radiators hissed to a standstill. It was a dream in which the absence of money was a boon, a way of purging the past—a release from the whole edifice of family and money and New York strivings.

In the end, we didn't sign and we got the apartment anyway, but the marriage unravelled a few years later. Since then, my doubts have grown: Am I loved for my yellow hair alone or for my real-estate potential? One unforgettable conversation on the subject occurred several years ago at a birthday dinner for the man I was then seeing. We had been invited out by his parents, and we somehow landed on the subject of apartments. My boyfriend, who had essentially moved in with me, had been telling me for months that the early-morning noise of the garbage trucks outside my building was depressing, and that I was too "big"—too large a presence, I hoped he meant—for the apartment I lived in. I owed it to my child, he said, to provide a better environment; my building faced a school that bused in underprivileged children with emotional problems, a circumstance that he found troubling. Under his scrutiny, my apartment began to look shabbier than it actually was, and I found myself scouring the real-estate section on a weekly basis. I don't know how much of this my boyfriend's mother knew, but the two of them were close, and she was probably kept abreast of all the rumblings. At any rate, she leaned forward over dessert and said, "I myself have always needed light." I understood what she meant, in the code of such exchanges: she required an apartment on Fifth or on Central Park West (which, in fact, she had), and who could require anything less? I was offering her son a room without a view; couldn't my parents do better for me? I answered that I liked light myself, and blushed—like a prospective bride offering an insufficient dowry—on behalf of my apartment.

And then there was the older man who came trailing rumors of inherited wealth of his own. For a while, it looked as though I had met someone who understood the unique form of deprivation that is felt by children of rich but withholding families. We had long talks about the limitations of money and the ways in which it could be used to subvert rather than create happiness. He pointed out to me that I had never escaped from my childish money confusions; I was looking for a kind of protection, a primary reassurance, that couldn't be bought—even I could see that. Still, I couldn't help noticing that he hadn't escaped from the shadow of his past, either. He vacillated between making expansive gestures and stingy counter-gestures—inviting me, when we began dating, on a weekend to Florence, and then asking me if I would pay for my own plane ticket, all the while making it clear that he had considerable resources to call upon should he care to. I was puzzled as to the reality of his situation: he seemed to be supporting his two grown daughters, but he made a big deal of contributing a twenty-dollar coffeemaker to my apartment, where he frequently ate both breakfast and dinner. Things were no doubt made worse by the fact that a close friend of his described him to me as "loaded," and yet another acquaintance told me that he had heard that my friend was the scion of a soft-drink fortune. As I know from my own fictitious fortune, nothing multiplies faster than the myth of personal wealth, which breeds ever more baroque fantasies in the eye of the beholder, even if there isn't much to back them up. I knew I shouldn't care either way about the state of his finances, but I didn't want to be tantalized only to be shut out of the kingdom once more. In the end, we were both too irrationally invested in what money meant. I yearned for a "what's mine is yours" embrace, for a plenitude of cherries; he had been divorced twice and feared being exploited—giving with no guarantee of return. One night, just when it seemed that we had settled into the rituals of domestic togetherness, he reminded me, as I was getting into bed, that I owed him money for a dry-cleaning bill. There it was again: It's only money. It's only everything. We broke up the next day.

APRIL 26, 1999

WHO SPEAKS FOR THE LAZY?

F OR a white American male, in good health and in possession of an advanced degree from an Ivy League school, I have, over the past twenty-five
years, made a ridiculously small amount of money. And when I say small I
mean *small*. Until five years ago, my best year netted me a little more than sixteen thousand dollars, and most years my annual income after taxes fluctu-
ated between eight and ten thousand. Really. Being a writer only partially
explains this woeful fiscal history. The real question is not so much how I've
managed to survive but why I have accepted living in humble circumstances
when my tastes are anything but. It's a question that friends, for whom my
way of life has often been a subject of rueful and hilarious conversation, have
speculated on. Here are some of the answers they've come up with: came of age
in the sixties; never came of age; has an aversion to authority; has a structural
anomaly of the brain; lost his mother when he was ten; was an only child; was
an only child of parents who survived the war in Europe; read too many books
at too early an age; found a really cheap, rent-stabilized apartment; is generally
a moody, shiftless, self-absorbed individual.

Not making a lot of money says something about a man in a society where
financial success is equated with acumen, resourcefulness, and social standing. Aside from those who enter professions in which money is not the main
consideration—teaching, say, or diplomacy, or documentary filmmaking—
the nonmoneyed are thought to lack the confidence or wherewithal to make
the big bucks. There is an assumption that a feeling of ineligibility keeps us
from realizing the earning potential both in ourselves and in the marketplace.
It is, of course, just this entrepreneurial inner child that self-help books mean
to awaken. True or not, success American-style is seen to be a matter of

gumption, of get-up-and-go: economic hardship isn't about race or class, it's about character. Want money? Follow the appropriate twelve-step program, demonstrate the requisite stick-to-itiveness, and—badda badda bing—you're rolling in it.

Although it would be nice to say that the absence of a portfolio in my case suggested a well-developed ego, an indifference to the world's approval, I'm afraid that emotional immaturity as well as financial shortsightedness are nearer the mark. When I was in my twenties, it didn't matter that other men my age earned eighty grand a year while I survived on eight. I was healthy, strong, O.K.-looking, with a good head of hair (never discount male vanity as consolation for practically anything). There'd be time, I thought, to remedy matters. And let's be clear: I did not disdain the dollar. I was no ascetic, and my spiritual itch was more than satisfied by reading Hermann Hesse. In truth, I was materialistic to the core: I loved money; I loved the idea of money; I even liked novels about the rich and movies about how the poor became rich. I liked everything about money except the prospect of buckling down and making it.

My father used to say that I became a writer so that I wouldn't have to work. Most writers will snort at this: what is writing *but* work? He had a point, though. The thought of being bound and defined by work that didn't interest me sent shivers down my spine. The solution was a string of part-time jobs that I could blow off whenever I wanted to—until I made it as a writer. Between 1971 and 1981, I drove a cab, hefted sacks of grain in an animal-feed ware-house, served time as a night watchman in a rundown hotel, lifted boxes on and off a conveyor belt, tutored philosophy, worked construction, loaded and unloaded trucks for U.P.S., and hauled freight along the Louisville-Cincinnati-Lexington triangle. None of these jobs paid more than four dollars an hour, and until 1992 I had no bank account: no checking, no savings. Also no car, no credit cards, no cashmere socks. Sometimes I moved from one city to another simply because I had a chance to house-sit or because a friend offered to put me up. I don't defend, and I most certainly don't recommend, this way of life. It may, in fact, no longer be feasible, given today's success-oriented ethos and the way prices have risen. In the mid-seventies, a quart of milk cost thirty cents in Boston; a carton of cigarettes, two dollars in South Carolina; filet mignon, four dollars a pound in Kentucky. One of the best Chambertins I ever drank set me back seventeen dollars in New Jersey.

Looking back, my peripatetic, hand-to-mouth existence puzzles more than it embarrasses me. Why did I settle for so little when I wanted so much more? And yet at the time it seemed like the life I should lead. Not because I wanted to be a writer (it wasn't as if the words to "Vissi d'arte" filled my head) but because I saw myself—and this is where it does get a little embarrassing—in the light of books I had read as a teen-ager. I was great for poets and poetry and for whatever seemed fantastic, romantic, and tragic in books. I didn't exactly iden-tify with Marlowe, Coleridge, Byron, Keats, Poe, Baudelaire, Rimbaud, and

Pushkin, but their examples did make me feel that hewing to the straight and narrow would somehow be disloyal to their own fervid imaginings.

One of the dangers of reading the right books at the wrong age is the tendency to confuse the creator with the creation. Since Des Esseintes, Pechorin, Stavrogin, Julien Sorel, Maldoror, and the Corsair could have been given shape only by men very much like themselves, I decided around the age of fourteen to become a blasé voluptuary, a weary adventurer who travelled the world over, conquering women and boredom. This foolishness didn't last long, but for a time words and expressions like "anomie," "ennui," "spleen," "melancholy," and "alienated consciousness" made it difficult for me to think practically about the future.

But to say that I avoided long-term employment merely out of some misguided application of literature to life (where Emma Bovary sought liaisons, I sought leisure) would be preposterous. I never wanted to work. Even as a kid, I thought working for money, whether I needed it or not, was a bad trade-off. In 1960, planted in front of an old R.C.A. console, I warmed to the ersatz beatnik Maynard G. Krebs, on *The Many Loves of Dobie Gillis,* who on hearing the word "work" would involuntarily yelp "Work!" as if an angry bee had suddenly dived into view. I didn't want to be Maynard G. Krebs, but then I didn't want to be much of anything. That annoying question kids have to contend with— "What do you want to be when you grow up?"—left me stupefied.

Not that I didn't have ambition. I had plans: I was going to write big, fat novels and make potloads of money. But what good is ambition without energy? It's nothing more than daydreaming. Novels demand drive and Trollope-like commitment. Naturally, I wasn't up to it, although I did manage to become a regular contributor to various publications. Yet even as a recognized member of a guild I was a spectacular non-go-getter. You would not have seen my shining face at conferences, panel discussions, readings, parties, or wherever else editors, agents, and publishers showed up. Networking and self-promotion, the hallmarks of literary aspirants, demand hustle, and hustling, among other things, means moving briskly. I stayed home. I wrote about books, literary trends, academic criticism. And though I occasionally took on an assignment to write about boxing or business (experience obviously not required), my earnings pretty much stayed on an even keel. I wrote book reviews for the *money.*

SOME men are born lazy, some acquire laziness, some have laziness thrust upon them. But, however gained, laziness remains ill-gotten. Because we make a virtue of what is necessary, the precept of work is like a commandment sans stone tablet. It's man's nature to work; without work, people tend to wilt. On the other hand, some people droop by design. Look at small children: not all are animated tykes scampering about the playground; there are always one or two likely to sit by themselves, ruminating on the fact that they have ten fingers and toes instead of nine or eleven. They are the suspect ones, the nascent lazy, and, left to their own devices, will probably not metamorphose into the movers and shakers of their generation.

Although laziness in its simplest terms is the disinclination to work, the condition is not reducible to a simple formula. For most of recorded history, laziness was thought to arise from the natural confluence of mind and body. The lazy suffered from melancholia, or an excess of black bile (carried by the blood to the brain), which in extreme cases kept them from finding solace in spiritual devotion. Those in whom the spirit failed to move or to be moved were afflicted with acedia—a condition that the early Church fathers felt deserved a measure of compassion, along with the usual tsk-tsking. But as the world grew older, and time got tangled up with the idea of progress, work, or busyness, rather than piety, took on antonymic meaning where laziness was concerned. By the late Middle Ages, acedia had come to include the notion of worldly sloth. And who was responsible for sloth? You were. Sloth didn't just slide into the world along with your squalling body; you had to seek it out and embrace it.

As a secular sin, laziness reached its apogee during the Industrial Revolution, when any sign of malingering was seen as a threat to the capitalist order. If you didn't work, you didn't produce, and if you didn't produce you were a parasite; you were, my friend, subversive. Don't get me wrong: I'm not defending the lazy. All I'm saying is that the subject makes people take extreme views. When Boswell suggested that "we grow weary when idle," the otherwise sensible Dr. Johnson remonstrated, "That is, sir, because others being busy, we want company; but if we were idle, there would be no growing weary; we should all entertain one another." Is he kidding? The man obviously never hung out with the deadbeat crowd I used to know, for whom prying the cap off a Schlitz was a good day's work. Most people disdain the lazy not only because they serve no useful purpose but because their own metabolisms and circadian rhythms seem to recognize those whose own systems are out of sync. The lazy are different from you and me. I mean, of course, just you.

MEDICALLY, however, I'm fine. Two blood tests, years apart, revealed no bacterial parasites or high concentrations of viral antibodies, or any other noxious agents that could account for my usual indolence. No toxins in the air, no food groups, no glowing chunks of kryptonite rob me of my powers. Nor, when I look around, can I lay the blame on the sixties, or on my being an only child, or on my retreating into books at a tender age, or, for that matter, on family history. Although the early death of a parent so constricts the heart that it can never regain its original shape, plenty of children suffer loss and sadness and go on to lead busy, productive lives.

Sometimes the only good explanation for the arc life takes is that a person has only so much spring in his step, that one is born to travel only so far. And, while most of us want to get to the top, not all of us are willing to make the climb. My father wasn't entirely mistaken in claiming that I turned to writing in order to avoid work. Let's face it, some boys and girls become writers because the only workplace they're willing to visit is the one inside their heads. And even then it's a tough commute, since the same urge that leads them to write may also keep them from doing their work. That general discontent with the world which is at the bottom of all writing tends to pull writers down, deplete them of initiative, and make them wonder if it's worth doing at all. This applies as well to writers who churn out prose at a ferocious clip as it does to those of us who, like Bartleby, prefer not to. The trick is to turn that urge to one's advantage. "I write of melancholy, by being busy to avoid melancholy," wrote the industrious Robert Burton.

Likewise, writers who know themselves to be lazy conscientiously and routinely meet their inertia head-on. Profound laziness is not so much about doing nothing as it is about the strain of doing practically *anything.* Lazy people can accomplish things, thank you very much. We have our paroxysms of activity, the occasional eruptions of busyness and bursts of productivity. Walter Benjamin, for instance, acknowledged that he had entered "the world under the sign of Saturn—the star of the slowest revolution, the planet of detours and delays," yet the man's formidable essays didn't, as they say, write themselves. Our first essayist, Montaigne, also professed to have a wide streak of laziness, and Cyril Connolly, whose journal *Horizon* helped keep English letters afloat during the Second World War, gloated, "Others merely live; I vegetate."

But vegetation among writers and thinkers takes peculiar forms. Someone who sits and conjures up names and explanations for characters or subatomic particles cannot be said to be doing nothing. A world of difference exists between a valetudinarian fused to his bed and Max Beerbohm, who never voluntarily went out for a walk, because "it stops the brain." Still, the standard, hackneyed conception of laziness prevails. "Doomed as I was to a life of perpetual idleness, I did absolutely nothing," says the landscape painter in Chekhov's story "The House with an Attic." "I spent hours looking out of the window at the sky, the birds, the avenues, read everything that was brought to me from the post, and slept. Sometimes I left the house and went for walks till late at night." Yes, yes, we've heard all this before. Don't be fooled: there's no uniformity about the lazy. Energetic people may all be alike, but the lazy cruise along at their own varying rates of speed. Some bite the bullet and go off to jobs; some stay home while their more energetic spouses tackle the workaday world; some really do watch the grass grow, or, its millennial equivalent, daytime television.

THERE is something preëmptive about laziness, something that smacks of a decision to refuse all offers even before they're put on the table. The lazy don't come to the table. And I think there is a philosophical component in this resistance. At bottom, laziness is negation, turning one's back on what others neutrally, cheerfully, or resignedly go to meet. The truly lazy—the ones who cannot bring themselves to greet and meet, to scheme and struggle, to interact on a daily basis with others—are, in effect, refusing to affix their signatures to the social contract. Given that success hinges on understanding, using, and occasionally subverting the social contract, the lazy don't stand a chance.

The secret to failure is far more elusive than the secret to success. Lagging behind when one could have advanced isn't just about laziness; it's about all the things that psychoanalysis takes a rather serious view of—the absence of love, coping with anger, rationalizing failure, the reluctance to supersede or replace one's father. Heavy stuff, and perhaps true, but the acknowledgment of which never put a dime in my pocket. Laziness just is. It's like being freckled or color-blind. Indeed, when the world was younger, intelligent people believed they had no choice in the matter of who was naughty or nice, passive or active. Hippocrates' theory of "temperament," which anchored Western medicine for two millennia, put some muscle behind varieties of human behavior. Well, not muscle exactly—more like four cardinal humors, whose relative proportion in the blood determined personality and moods. The Church fathers were on the right track; only the messenger and the manner of delivery were wrong. It's not black bile that causes Oblomov-like symptoms but a certain kind of electrochemical activity in the left frontal lobe of the brain, or whatever. The point is, everyone enters the world predisposed physiologically to think and feel in certain ways.

Happenstance also has its place; I don't deny that. But do any two people react identically to the same stimuli? The event that jump-starts one person's psyche does not necessarily have the same effect on another's. It's one thing to concede that certain tendencies can be reinforced or weakened by experience; it is quite another to think that some event during my formative years, which might have occurred but didn't, would have had me sharing a bucket of KFC with Bill Gates, or loping down a runway in Milan wearing a spiffy outfit by Valentino. In short, there's no contradiction in thinking that temperament defines you and thinking that you're still in charge of your life: temperament is the gas, but you've got a foot on the pedal.

Because of some elusive sequence of recombinant DNA and early experiences, I always knew I'd write things. I also knew I was an incurable lazybones. This accounts, in my case, for the odd tension between writing and laziness which Samuel Beckett describes to a T: "There is nothing to express, nothing with which to express, nothing from which to express, no power to express, no desire to express, together with the obligation to express." As a solid constituent of the couchant class, I can say that the obligation to express does not weigh heavily. Still, I have my moments—moments when I feel like addressing the fading shimmer of my own skin. I want answers. Or, more precisely, one big answer. In a sense, life is like an examination that has only one question—the one that asks why you're taking the exam in the first place. Having been instructed to "fill in the blank" (an aptly phrased command), you ponder, and then wonder if perhaps the truest answer is no answer at all. But in the end, because there is, after all, plenty of time to reflect and you do want to leave the room, you hunker down and fill in the blank. My own response is hardly profound or incisive: I'm taking the exam because I like writing sentences, and because—well, what else do I have to do?

As for the laziness that moves with me wherever I go, I have finally found a way to make it "work" for me. Lassitude, aloofness, low-grade depression, coupled with a healthy respect for money, have gradually steered me to the obvious vocation. Yes, dear reader, I have become a screenwriter.

APRIL 26, 1999

ACQUIRED TASTE

U P until this minute, I didn't even know that it was possible to have good taste in dustpans. But I am standing in front of one of the world's finest dustpans—admiring its capacious, open-mouth design, its sturdy metal construction, the elegant horsehair of the accompanying brush—and I can't tell you how much I yearn for it. If I owned this dustpan, I would be the sort of person I want to be. I'd take the time to appreciate the beauty of everyday objects. I'd inhabit a world of simple craftsmanship, not of mass-produced clutter. I'd be one of those rare souls who have so much cultivation to spare that they can be thoughtful even about their cleaning equipment.

I've come across this admirable dustpan in a store called Restoration Hardware. And on my way to the sales desk I look around and find there's so much else I want. I want the ribbed steel flashlights I remember from summer camp. I want the red casino dice. I want the soft leather chair that is an exact replica of the one Teddy Roosevelt took with him on long train trips. I want the old-fashioned kazoo, the mission-style magazine rack, the Moon Pies that I didn't even know were still made, the Biedermeier-urn table lamp, the glass-and-steel Pyrex beakers just like the ones my doctor used to keep the tongue depressors in.

I'm no novice when it comes to precious yuppie consumerism. I've done J. Peterman, Smith & Hawken, and Williams-Sonoma. But the selection at Restoration Hardware has aroused the curatorial greed even in a Stickley-hardened veteran like me, and I am not alone. Four years ago, Restoration had just five stores, in California. Now the company is thriving, with sixty-five outlets nationwide, including a massive new flagship store in Manhattan, at Broadway and Twenty-second Street. It plans to open thirty more stores in 1999, continuing a rate of expansion that could eventually make it the Starbucks of home furnishings. If you are a college-educated person between thirty-five and fifty-five, with a household income above seventy-five thousand dollars, you might as well just surrender your Visa card now, because sooner or later you're going to find yourself traipsing up to a Restoration cash register aglow at the prospect of owning a pair of mammoth black suède fireplace gloves.

Of course, the shopping malls are stuffed with sensibility-drenched stores catering to upscale professionals. They tend to have Louis Armstrong singing "What a Wonderful World" on the sound system, French-café posters on the walls, and deceptively rustic names. But, even compared with its competitors, like Pottery Barn and Crate & Barrel, Restoration Hardware is unusual. It isn't organized by product categories, with fifty lamps in one section and a variety of plates and glasses stacked up in another. Instead, it has gone further than just about any other store in organizing itself around a particular life style. If you happen to like the atmosphere of long-lost American craftsmanship which Restoration exudes, the store gives you the squeegee, the bathtub, the hand lotion, the doorknobs, the chocolate syrup, the ginger ale, and the hand-forged scissors that go with it. In fact, hardware accounts for only seventeen per cent of Restoration's sales; thirty per cent is furniture, and much of the rest is spread among hundreds of category-smashing items, like mint-flavored tennis balls that will freshen your dog's breath while he fetches. And wandering amid the whole array will be the customers—little groups of highly educated Java Jacket people in their alumni sweatshirts oohing and ahing over the unusual items and quirky juxtapositions.

Restoration Hardware customers aren't drawn from a wide demographic. There are few droopy-jeans contractors looking for power tools. (The store has no power tools.) This is hardware for the lords of the service sector. It's the basic PBS-NPR cohort: vineyard-touring doctors, novel-writing lawyers, tenured gardening buffs, unusually literary realtors, dangly-earringed foundation officials, and the rest of us information-age burghers. In fact, the company's success is testimony to the increasing size and cohesiveness of the educated class. Restoration's customer base correlates to education level even more closely than to income. And the chain has been able to expand into one upscale suburb after another without running out of graduate-degreed shoppers willing to be delighted by the J. Kerouac Moving Blanket, the plastic-ball-valve dripless fat baster, William Morris recliners, delicate wire-mesh French flyswatters, and endless quantities of Adirondack chairs.

Not surprisingly for a company this dense with Zeitgeist, Restoration Hardware is based in Marin County, California. It's somehow fitting that the same county that had half of America worshipping crystals in the seventies has us fetishizing kitchen fixtures in the nineties. Restoration's headquarters are in an office park in Corte Madera, just up Highway 101 from Sausalito. The work area there is furnished with standard-issue gray modular office furniture, along with just a few upholstered sofas from the stores. The staff is young and mostly female, and includes plenty of liberal-arts majors hired away from other educated-class retailers. During the job interviews, they're asked to describe their own home furnishings, to make sure they have appropriately informal but classic tastes. The dress code is brunch casual; the staff people joke that when they get together in one room it looks like a Gap catalogue come to life. "We're kind of loose," they insist over and over again when you phone to make an appointment: don't worry about being a little late, don't dress up. Some of the employees bring their dogs to work, so there are little condo dogs wandering from room to room.

I walked in one day, and the buyers were just bursting out of one of their merchandise meetings, giddy about the Aqua-Troll. This is an eighteen-inch-tall plastic troll with a sprinkler inside. When you attach a hose and turn on the water, his head pops up, and he douses your yard. Twice a week, the buyers bring favored items to these meetings, and try to show why they would fit in at Restoration. When it comes time to make a decision, everybody gets a vote, but, in keeping with the tenor of today's educated-class workplaces (which tend to be officially egalitarian, but are actually dominated by one charismatic leader), the decisive vote is cast by Restoration's founder, C.E.O., and visionary, Stephen Gordon.

Gordon wears his power and newfound wealth lightly. He's a casual, unaffected forty-seven-year-old, who, in fact, looks a little like the whimsical Aqua-Troll. He's achingly sincere about his products and mellow with his colleagues, who seem to revere him, praising him over and over for being "loose" and "real"—words that appear to be the supreme compliments at the headquarters. As a sort of Baby Boomer Everyman, he has no need for market research; his key to success is to fill his stores with the things he craves.

Gordon was born in 1951, in the upstate New York town of Plattsburgh, on Lake Champlain. It was a small industrial town, with a state college, an Air Force facility, and, as Gordon remembers it, a fairly rigid class structure. His father's income as a shoe-store owner put the Gordon family squarely in the middle class, but his mother's sophisticated cultural tastes encouraged them to aim higher. While Gordon was growing up, he was never allowed to work with his father in the shoe store. "I was supposed to do something better than be in retail," he says.

Protestant grandees used to build summer lodges in the Adirondacks near Plattsburgh; it was where an earlier generation of East Coast aristocrats would go to get simplified. And this world of "Wasp graciousness," as Gordon puts it, was what fired his ambitions. Even today, he says, he feels a kinship with what he knows of Ralph Lauren. They were two ambitious boys who longed for the world of slow, croquet-dabbled afternoons. But Gordon is younger than Ralph Lauren, and nobody who came of age in the late sixties can have uncomplicated feelings about the Protestant establishment. He went off to college at New Jersey's Drew University at the height of the Vietnam War and became an active, if internally divided, member of radical student groups. One day, a group he was with organized a protest rally in nearby Morristown, where they stood outside various office buildings and shouted "Pigs!" at the people trying to get to work. "I had such conflict," Gordon recalls. "Part of me had this in-credibly ambitious side that I was afraid of expressing. I really wanted to suc-ceed. I had this feeling of 'Gosh, can't you let me get squared away and make it before we trash the system?' "

A few years later, with a couple of degrees in psychology, Gordon became a counsellor near Eureka, California, which was then a funky Victorian seaport town between the redwoods and the ocean in Northern California. Succumb-ing to "entrepreneurial thoughts," as he recounts, he bought a Queen Anne house, and set out to turn it into a bed-and-breakfast. But he couldn't find a re-tail supplier for the fixtures he needed to restore the place, and in 1979, sens-ing a market niche, he began selling knobs and gadgets to the other urban refugees who were migrating to Eureka to realize their restoration fantasies.

Soon Gordon found, as all members of the educated class must, that this job wasn't merely a way to make a living—it was a means of self-expression. He began stocking quirky items that had nothing to do with hardware but simply appealed to him. To guide customers through the eclectic mixture of products, Gordon began writing little signs. His company has grown, but Restoration still has a little sign posted next to each item, and Gordon still writes all the texts himself—more than nine hundred descriptions, according to a staffer who bothered to count. Between about a hundred and four hundred words long, each sign describes the lineage of the item, or the memories and pensées it pro-vokes. "Traditional furniture stores never really took a stand," Gordon says. That's probably because they didn't realize they had to. Gordon's signs are inti-mate, self-revelatory, and grammatically erratic, like the "Staff's Favorites" tags one finds at independent bookstores. They evoke the earlier age of simple family traditions which is Restoration's paradise lost. "My mother always set our din-ner table with salt cellars on very special occassions [sic]," Gordon writes in a sign that accompanies a pair of cut-glass cellars with silver spoons which he sells for twelve dollars. "Growing up I didn't see many other families setting the table with these delightful little vessels yet I vividly remember (call me quirky) visiting my then girlfriend's home in upstate New York and her mother, Mar-jorie, had salt cellars. This was my senior year in college and I thought this per-haps yet another reason I should bond with the woman who is now my wife."

Gordon has ransacked his childhood tactile memories and turned them into nostalgic inventory. He sells a replica of the chair that his third-grade teacher sat on back at the Elm Street School in Plattsburgh. He sells the old classic Boston Ranger pencil sharpener, which you probably haven't seen in decades. He sells vintage gyroscopes, old crystal-radio kits like the ones he used to build, and the compartmentalized school-lunch trays we all used to slide along the cafeteria serving lines—at four dollars a tray, they are one of Restoration's fast movers. (People tend to buy them for their kids to eat on at home; a salesperson at one of the stores told me that parents buy fifteen or twenty at a time and use them at birthday parties.) He sells Quackenbush nut bowls like the ones his Aunt Shirley and Uncle Jim used to serve walnuts to their guests.

Nor does Gordon stint when it comes to evocations of his other youthful infatuation, rich Protestants. Beneath all the offbeat items that catch your eye at
first glance—the foot duvets, the dog-biscuit mix for people who bake their
own—there is also a line of furniture and furnishings that wouldn't be out of
place among the non-health-conscious grandees at the Knickerbocker Club.
There's the Morgan Leather Club Chair, the Cirque Lounge Ice Bucket, the Hotel
Royale Silver Plated Olive Picks to adorn your Martinis, and the 1936 Penguin
Cocktail Shakers. When Gordon can't find Wasp gentility, he creates it. Recently, he became enamored of fireplace matches. He found some eleven-inch
matches with charcoal-black heads which were so richly textured that they
looked like beautiful wool when they were bunched together. He packaged
them in a clean white box—not in a normal quantity of, say, fifty but in a boun-
teous collection of three hundred and sixty, which is probably more fireplace
matches than most families need in a decade. And then he made up a name for
them, Jenson-Baines Fireplace Matches, so they sound like a *Mayflower*-
descended Beacon Hill law firm. And as you cruise through the store you find
numerous other items that have been given suspiciously perfect Wasp names:
the Jameson Tray Top Coffee Table, the Connaught Pedestal Soap Dish, and
Jemson Pillar Plates. In the world that Restoration restores, upper-class tradi-
tionalism mixes effortlessly with proletarian authenticity. It's a classless utopia,
in which a workman's wrench can be displayed alongside a yachtsman's log.

THIS sensibility didn't emerge all at once, and it didn't take off immediately.
Gordon worked as a merchant at his store in Eureka for a full ten years, dreaming of expansion. Finally, in the early nineties, he opened three stores in the
Bay Area, and then, with the help of some outside investors, expanded into
Southern California, and into Phoenix and Portland. More outside capital
flowed in, allowing more expansion, and this past summer Restoration completed an initial public offering, raising just under seventy-five million dollars
for further growth. Some New Age entrepreneurs experience crises of conscience when their start-up boutiques go corporate. But Gordon, no small-is-
beautiful romantic, has had few apprehensions about running a big company.
His office is decorated with pictures taken inside a private jet he rented while he
was pitching Restoration to investment banks prior to the I.P.O.

The director of Restoration's catalogue division is a woman named Marta
Benson, who graduated with a degree in philosophy from Wesleyan College, in
Connecticut, in 1984. "I'm proud of being a merchant," she says. Restoration
people envelop the word "merchant" with spiritual resonance, the way some
people use the word "poet" or "sculptor." "I went to see *The English Patient* a
couple of years ago," Benson recalls, "and it was so moving and so beautiful,
and I thought, All I do is sell stuff. But I'm reconciled to it, because I'm selling
stuff that has meaning."

The Restoration buyers frequently call manufacturers and plead with them to revive classic lines they have abandoned—the sturdy old-fashioned metal fans they used to make instead of the flimsy modern plastic ones, the classic plaid thermoses instead of the flashy pink ones. While I was sitting in Marta Benson's small office one day, she leaped up from her chair to demonstrate what is wrong with American retailing. She bounded over to a shelf where she keeps items that are being considered for Restoration's catalogue, and held up a small wooden brush with white bristles, which was wrapped in a cardboard-and-plastic package and looked like any brush you might find at the local discount drugstore. "Look at that!" she exclaimed contemptuously, holding up the cheesy plastic bag and the gaudy pink-and-purple label stapled on top. "What were they thinking?" She ripped off the cardboard label and threw away the plastic. "Now look at this!" she said triumphantly, holding up the un-adorned brush. The clean shape of the brush was revealed, along with the noble grain of the wood.

Here was the theology of Restoration Hardware made manifest. The single urge that unites Restoration's diverse products is repentance. The store's theory is that we as a society have sinned. In the sixties, the seventies, and, especially, the eighties, we worshipped the Golden Calf. We indulged in a consumption binge, filling our homes with mass-produced junk, trendy fashions, and showy luxuries. Now it's time to relearn old values, rediscover timeless furnishings. A year ago, the company produced a video for potential investors which neatly captures the chain's social vision. The voice-over explains, "Lurking in our collective unconscious, among images of Ike, Donna Reed, and George Bailey, is the very clear sense that things were once better made, that they mattered a little more." Images of the forties and fifties fill the screen. "What happened? Slowly but surely we became a nation obsessed with production and, of course, consumption." At this point, we see images of huge suburban developments, large outlet stores. "This was pretty heady and pretty good. We got so proficient at making things, we had unlimited choices and an endless array of goods." The "plastics" scene from *The Graduate* comes along. "The retail environment came to reflect this mentality—more square footage, more, more, more. Then, one day, the generation used to having everything recoiled, and became the generation searching for something."

Restoration evokes the places we have thoughtlessly abandoned: the small communities that ambitious people leave; the downtowns that have been hollowed out by car-friendly shopping malls; the local industrial crafts that are being driven out of business by our global economy; the old-fashioned family traditions we have neglected in the rush to be modern and mobile. Restoration reminds us that it is not too late to avoid the spiritual trap set by our relentless upward mobility. We can rediscover the essential things, and, best of all, we can do so while shopping.

• • •

OF course, the real world offers complications. As I was browsing in the Restoration store on University Avenue in Palo Alto recently, I saw a young lady get arrested. She was a dishevelled blond woman in a Disney T-shirt who seemed to be off her medication. She was following elderly women around the store and taunting them with "Hey, you rich bitch!" and "Where'd you learn to walk like that—at your fancy social events?" The store staff gently tried to persuade her to leave, but she kept harassing customers. Finally, the police were called. Two officers came in, and after some discussion they handcuffed her. She sat quietly on Restoration's velvet Zoe Sofa waiting for a police car.

Obviously, for all that Restoration renounces luxury and opulence, it can still arouse class resentments. If the crazy lady had been coherent, she could have argued that Restoration's virtuous simplicity is more exclusive than the straightforward gaudiness of, say, the Gilded Age. Anybody can make money and buy a Newport mansion. But it takes a lifetime of cultural training to navigate the unspoken sumptuary codes that guide educated-class tastes. These educated élites, the crazy lady could have pointed out, keep talking about the soul, but their spirituality begins to look like a status item, since it tends to manifest itself in pricey cocktail shakers and forty-dollar coffee-table books. Here are these hypocrites, she could have continued, who benefit from the wealth surge of the information-age economy and then build little faux-authentic chapels for themselves in their two-story great rooms. To an outsider like her, Restoration probably looks like a restricted educated-class country club: No Sensibility, No Service.

But the populist critique isn't entirely fair. For if the success of Restoration and similar upscale retailers proves anything it is that today's educated élite is fundamentally different from past élites. It's more anxious about its own affluence, and so seeks to spend its money to prove (to itself) that it hasn't been corrupted by materialism. This isn't a cohort bravely marching forward to assert its stamp on the future. It's an élite that looks backward, and seems to spend less energy on revolution or innovation than on cultural restoration. It's almost touching the way we Restoration Hardware browsers fetishize the artifacts of days gone by, pining for the old wisdom that our ancestors apparently possessed but that we feel we lack.

In a characteristic moment, Nietzsche mocked modern man by saying, "He needs history because it is the storage closet where all the costumes are kept. He notices that none really fits him." Perhaps Nietzsche is right. None of the old costumes fit. But maybe the dustpans do. Maybe the little salt-cellars can bring back the old traditions and the old virtues. And, anyway, at only twelve dollars it's worth a shot.

JANUARY 25, 1999

ABOUT THE TYPE

This book was set in Photina, a typeface designed by José Mendoza in 1971. It is a very elegant design with high legibility, and its close character fit has made it a popular choice for use in quality magazines and art gallery publications.